T0390839

CRUCIBLES OF POWER

CRUCIBLES OF POWER

SMOLENSK UNDER STALINIST AND NAZI RULE

MICHAEL DAVID-FOX

 Harvard University Press

CAMBRIDGE, MASSACHUSETTS | LONDON, ENGLAND   2025

Copyright © 2025 by Michael David-Fox

All rights reserved

Printed in the United States of America

First printing

Library of Congress Cataloging-in-Publication Data

Names: David-Fox, Michael, 1965– author.

Title: Crucibles of power : Smolensk under Stalinist and Nazi rule / Michael David-Fox.

Description: Cambridge, Massachusetts ; London, England : Harvard University Press, 2025. | Includes bibliographical references and index.

Identifiers: LCCN 2024008121 (print) | LCCN 2024008122 (ebook) | ISBN 9780674247468 (cloth) | ISBN 9780674298187 (pdf) | ISBN 9780674298194 (epub)

Subjects: LCSH: Men'shagin, Boris Georgievich, 1902–1984. | Smolenskiĭ obkom KPSS. Partiĭnyĭ arkhiv. | Power (Social sciences)—Russia (Federation)—Smolenskaiā oblast'. | National socialism—Russia—History—20th century. | Smolenskaiā oblast' (Russia)—History—20th century. | Soviet Union—Politics and government—1917–1936. | Soviet Union—Politics and government—1936–1953.

Classification: LCC DK511.S7 D38 2025 (print) | LCC DK511.S7 (ebook) | DDC 303.30947—dc23/eng/20240405

LC record available at https://lccn.loc.gov/2024008121

LC ebook record available at https://lccn.loc.gov/2024008122

For Nico and Jacob,
pride and joy

CONTENTS

NOTE ON TRANSLITERATION

The Library of Congress transliteration system is used for Russian words, with the exception of some frequently used personal names (Menshagin, not Men'shagin; Asya, not Asia) and place-names (Viazma, not Viaz'ma; Roslavl, not Roslavl'; Yelnya, not El'nia).

CRUCIBLES OF POWER

PROLOGUE

THE CAPTURED ARCHIVE

AT 4:45 AM on June 22, 1941, the Wehrmacht crossed the Soviet border in an invasion that shook Joseph Stalin's Soviet Union to its very core. That was a Sunday. The following Saturday, an order was issued by the Bureau of the Smolensk Regional Committee of the Communist Party to evacuate key portions of the Smolensk Communist Party Archive and burn the rest. If this order had been fulfilled, Western understandings of Soviet history during the Cold War would have been far poorer. The collection that came to be known as the Smolensk Archive, which included some of the first available documentation on the establishment of Soviet rule, Stalin's collectivization of agriculture, and the Great Terror, would never have fallen into first German and then American hands.

The abandonment of the Smolensk Archive, left behind in a former church on a side street in the city center, is usually considered an accident of war. But a full explanation can plausibly be traced as far back as to the birth of Stalinism in the late 1920s. That was when thoroughgoing purges and promotions throughout the party-state left institutions everywhere, but especially in regions such as Smolensk, bereft of expertise. Throughout the 1930s, archival institutions in Smolensk were in a constant state of personnel turnover. The Communist Party Archive's location even switched three times in rapid succession before 1941.[1]

1

An additional factor was necessary for the capture of what became the only collection of Communist Party documents in the West during the Cold War: Russian collaboration with the Germans. A Smolensk archival official in the 1920s, Il'ia Morozov, fell victim to the ideological xenophobia of Stalinism. Accused of spying for Latvia and Poland, he was sent to the Gulag in 1932. After his return to Smolensk, Morozov pointed German intelligence to the site of the abandoned documents and became head of an archival bureau for the Task Force of Reichsleiter Alfred Rosenberg (Einsatzstab Reichsleiter Rosenberg, ERR). Headed by the Reich minister of the occupied eastern territories, this was the agency that looted art, books, Judaica, antiques, and archives of cultural, intelligence, and propaganda value. But Morozov, too, required help. He directed a team of thirty Russian women sifting through the treasure trove of documents.[2]

German officer and Russian librarian in the Smolensk City Library, March 1943. Photo credited to Otto Nerling from the Task Force of Reichsleiter Alfred Rosenberg. Yad Vashem Photo Archive, Jerusalem. 73/1/40, Item 79802.

In April 1943, the Smolensk materials, piled up in small mountains of thick bundles, were loaded onto trains for Vilnius. German archivists working for the ERR studied the plundered archive intensively there, and, in 1944, the Nazis continued their examination at the main anti-Bolshevik study center in Ratibor, Silesia, where the archive had been transported that same year.[3]

As the Red Army moved west, a fateful separation occurred—one that over seven decades later would prompt this book's investigation of the Smolensk Region. No one really knows exactly how the 538 archival folders of approximately 200,000 pages from the 1920s and 1930s that became known as the Smolensk Archive—perhaps 2 percent or less of the total transported—were detached from the bulk of the documentation. Nonetheless, a small portion of the files traveled with personnel from the Rosenberg Task Force to Bavaria. After the de facto division of Europe, these Communist Party documents reached the US Army's Offenbach Archival Depository near Frankfurt, where they fell into the hands of US Army intelligence. Intelligence agencies in Washington, DC, pored over the Smolensk files before they were declassified in the early 1950s.[4]

This cache of Communist Party records was the making of Smolensk's fame in Soviet studies. The names of the Smolensk Region's towns and rural districts, from Dorogobuzh to Belyi, became familiar to political scientists and historians. Harvard Sovietologist Merle Fainsod, who published his foundational *Smolensk under Soviet Rule* in 1958, became the first of a parade of Western scholars to interpret major questions of Soviet history on the basis of the Smolensk Archive. A good deal of what was known about Soviet history during the Cold War came from Smolensk.

But large gaps in the collection limited what could be known, especially about regional power relations with Moscow and Stalin's high-level party and secret police interventions. Not only was the archive relatively small and fragmentary, but it petered out after the year 1937. The documents could not shed any light on the monumental German-Soviet war or the regime changes of 1941 and 1943. The vast majority of Smolensk's looted archival files not diverted from Ratibor were recovered by Soviet troops in early 1945 inside three and a half railway freight cars at a train station near Oświęcim (Auschwitz) and repatriated to the USSR.[5] The vast bulk of

Transport of the Smolensk Archive from Vilnius, April 1943. Yad Vashem Photo Archive, Jerusalem. 73/1/42, Item 76932.

those materials, not to mention secret police files and other top-secret documents in Smolensk and Moscow, remained inaccessible until after the collapse of the Soviet Union. My investigation began with all those archival riches that returned to or remained in the USSR rather than traveled west with the fragmentary Smolensk Archive.

In the wake of the Soviet collapse, the "archival revolution" in Russia made the Smolensk Archive seem obsolete. New sources and new approaches transformed our understandings of Stalinism. Only in the 2000s did historians of the USSR launch into the history of the Eastern Front and wartime Stalinism in earnest. As the field was transformed, the Smolensk Region appeared to be the one place that was already familiar. Only rarely did Smolensk become the focus of international scholarship.[6] This book began with that vast corpus of rich materials beyond the captured Smolensk Archive that did not end up in the United

States after World War II and was made available after the end of the Cold War.

THERE IS ANOTHER REASON Smolensk's storied place in modern Russian studies makes it a particularly compelling focus for a new examination of power and power relations across the 1941 divide. In the entire library of studies of the regime that referred to itself as "Soviet power," in which considerations of power run like a red thread, there are surprisingly few works that make the workings of power into the primary focus, and even fewer that concentrate on power dynamics in a specific locale. Fainsod's 1958 *Smolensk under Soviet Rule* was one of the first and most important to do both.[7]

Fainsod's *Smolensk* was centrally about local power brokers and ordinary people during the rise of a new kind of revolutionary regime: Stalinism. The book very much went against the grain of his earlier *How Russia Is Ruled,* which was heavily deterministic. In that classic textbook studied by generations of students, he famously declared, "Out of the totalitarian embryo would come totalitarianism full-blown." *Smolensk,* by contrast, brought out the chaotic, far from inexorable workings of the levers of power in a revolutionary regime in a place far from Moscow. *Smolensk* was filled with human drama and contingency—even though, with his sources and his framework, Fainsod was not yet able to capture the crucial elements of choice, decision making, and agency. In his words, the files of the Smolensk Archive were "peopled with ordinary human beings trying desperately to lead normal lives in the midst of extraordinary and abnormal events."[8]

Fainsod, despite the pioneering nature of his work, was hampered by more than the lack of sources on the highest and most secretive levels of regime power. He wrote before successive revolutions in the human sciences in the late twentieth century exploded narrow definitions of when and where power is constituted. Understanding power in terms of state controls and resulting tensions, Fainsod uncovered some of the most distinctive traits of Stalinism as a totalizing, extremely violent regime standing apart from more run-of-the-mill authoritarianisms. In *Smolensk,* he penetrated the regime's monolithic facade to find chaos and improvisation. We can now perceive that these were two sides of the same coin. Radical "fantasies" of transformational state action enacted by imperfect levers of power spurred on ever more "hyper-planning" and centralization and, when that failed to work, paroxysms of violence.[9]

Fainsod became the first to discover the significance of the Smolensk Affair of 1928, the far-reaching purge of the Smolensk party organization held up by Moscow as an all-union model for other rural regions on the eve of collectivization. As the equivalent of the simultaneous Shakhty Affair in industry, the Smolensk Affair directly connected Smolensk to the end of the New Economic Policy (NEP) of 1921–1928 and made this rural backwater into an epicenter of the Stalin Revolution. Fainsod's implicit understanding of political power as unidirectional administrative control, however, was augmented by gaps in the Smolensk Archive. To him, this upheaval in the party-state apparatus simply showed how Moscow "slowly but inexorably" increased control from the 1920s to the 1930s. An oversimplified conception of power did not allow recognition of how the Smolensk Affair formed part of an exceptional, revolutionary conjuncture that scrambled the 1920s power hierarchy at the launch of Stalin's Great Break of 1928–1932, the first phase of Stalinism.[10]

Understanding power solely in terms of control, administration, and terror, Fainsod did not investigate how Stalin and the Moscow "center" acted simultaneously along several other dimensions to turn the lower levels of the power hierarchy against the entrenched regional elite. He did not explore the alternate reality created by propaganda as a form of power. He never saw ideology, language, culture, science, and expertise—all of which played similarly significant roles in the Smolensk Affair as well as the Great Terror—as distinct arenas of power relations. The gender order and sexuality, which in the Smolensk Affair figured through sensationalistic charges of sexual degeneracy against the regional leadership, went well beyond the scope of Fainsod's approach to politics. The Smolensk Affair, a deliberately induced disequilibrium in power relations, is a key to understanding the dynamics of a major Stalinist power play—and, by extension, the power-political methodology at the heart of Stalinism itself.

Archival records generated by the state reinforce the tendency to read power in terms of the political hierarchy and its agencies. Power, as I explore in this book, is not just top-down or hierarchical. It is multidimensional, flowing in many channels and directions among people, groups, political institutions and systems, and entire societies. Power is situational and contextual, in that its workings depend fundamentally on time and place.

Fainsod quoted Lev Tolstoy to the effect that the subject of history is the "life of humanity."[11] In the chapters that follow, the lives and experiences of a range of historical actors serve to open up the workings of power, not as a replacement but as a key supplement to the archive generated by the state. Any mono-dimensional conception of power deflects us from understanding how the very same people in extraordinary times could potentially become both victims and perpetrators, powerless in one area and powerful in another.

My study moves beyond the dichotomous "center-periphery relations" to excavate dynamic shifts among central, regional, and local levels of power. I do this not only for Stalinism, but for the German wartime regime on the Eastern Front. However, examining regimes and "systems" alone, I maintain, limits our understanding of Stalinism and Nazism, for that does not capture power dynamics as manifested in the lives of local and regional actors. Fainsod, invoking Tolstoy, pointed the way for us to understand that it is people—wielding, reflecting, deflecting, and succumbing to power—who hold the key to explaining how the two murderous, mass-mobilizing regimes worked at the moment of their monumental clash on the Eastern Front in World War II.

Merle Fainsod, and the field he did so much to create with his work on Smolensk, could not fully address questions about agency, choice, and power in the two most violent, revolutionary, and cataclysmic regimes in history. Nor could Fainsod take Smolensk into the most extreme and often most revealing conditions of its long history, when communism and fascism switched places twice, in 1941 and 1943, in the midst of their colossal clash. But he did raise the fundamental problem, critical today more than ever, of how radically illiberal, autocratic regimes rise and operate in intimate conjunction with the outlooks and actions of people immersed in locales such as Smolensk. My subtitle, *Smolensk under Stalinist and Nazi Rule,* is an homage to Fainsod's classic work.

INTRODUCTION

NOT ONLY DOES THE PAST INFORM the present, but the present opens up new ways of approaching and understanding the past. Today, the resonance of an age of extremes in which Stalinism and Nazism took root appears distinctly different than it did even only ten years ago. This no longer appears to be a tragedy that occurred in the far-off bloodlands, horrifying and significant yet distant from the modern age in which we live.[1] The dynamics of radically illiberal politics—especially how people reacted as the two regimes established themselves in times of unfolding crisis—now speak to us in novel ways. The exceptionalism inherent in the comforting illusion that "it could never happen here" no longer holds.

In the past decade, an increasingly hard-line dictatorship in Vladimir Putin's Russia became fixated on propagating a black-and-white, heroic mythology of the victory that legitimized Stalinism as well as defeated fascism. This brought a partial rehabilitation of the Stalinist past into the center of Russian politics in ways that prepared the launch of Russia's war of aggression in Ukraine in 2022. However, it is not only the historical mythmaking justifying a new war but also the return of harsh, radical political practices and extreme wartime conditions that compel us to reconsider an earlier era. Issues of war and occupation, empire and colonization, survival and atrocity, endurance and complicity, and, not least, perpetrators and enablers have moved to the center of attention.

The West, not just Russia, has also changed dramatically since the classic works about Stalinism and Nazism were written.[2] Far-right populist movements with lineages to fascism gained power in ways that make fascism no longer a fringe or defeated movement of the past. In the United States as elsewhere, extreme has become mainstream. The specter of authoritarianism looms over a troubled time of disequilibrium, with many outcomes possible. The most violent regimes of the twentieth century, and the conditions that shaped them, will not simply repeat themselves. But our present now speaks to this past with a new relevance.

In the history of highly ideological and repressive regimes and the people who live in them, wars and regime change are moments when much that was earlier ignored or concealed is exposed. In the Smolensk Region, a mostly ethnically Russian area roughly twice the size of Belgium now lying on the Russian Federation's western border with Belarus, fascist and communist rule traded places in the same locale twice in three years. My investigation focuses on the different levels of power in Stalinism and Nazism, as well as power relations among people operating within the two regimes. It picks up with the first rumblings of Stalin's Great Break circa 1927, before continuing through the German occupation of 1941–1943 and the restoration of Soviet rule in 1943–1944.

Those who read about the Great Terror or the Holocaust, even professional historians immersed in mountains of scholarship on fascism and communism, may intuitively wonder, What would I have done? It is in many ways an impossibly counterfactual and ahistorical query. Almost certainly, answering it engages psychological reflexes of wishful thinking. But it is not a question necessarily antithetical to scholarly analysis or rigorous archival research, insofar as undergirding it are questions about coercion and decision making, the dynamics of violent regime change and individual choice, the spread of radical ideologies and lived experience. The "dilemma of choice" within the almost unimaginable conditions of death camps and ghettos has long been crucial in Holocaust studies. It has been far less explored in regard to people and groups still facing extreme conditions but often with more room for maneuver under both Stalinist and Nazi rule.[3] We can approach the issue of choice, or agency, more closely only when we also discuss how it was always intertwined with all the constraints and pressures put in place in a specific time and setting, in this case framed by the two alternating and warring regimes of fascism and communism. In other words, weighing the actions of individuals and groups—including passivity, evasion, complicity, opposition, and, not least, attempts to maintain some sort of moral compass when faced with terrible alternatives— becomes vastly more revealing when the behavior is embedded in its deep historical context. This book provides a framework for how to think historically and analytically about power, lives, and choice.

Crucibles of Power

In the chapters that follow, the Smolensk Region, a place once so seemingly familiar in Soviet studies, becomes the site of a new investigation of power in the depths of the twentieth century's age of extremes. Instead of ending where the Smolensk Archive tapered off in the late 1930s, I integrate the history of the Stalin Revolution starting in the late 1920s with the German occupation of 1941–1943 and the subsequent restoration of Soviet power.

In the same post–Cold War moment when all the sources that never traveled west with the fragmentary Smolensk Archive became available, three hitherto largely distinct areas of inquiry—the histories of Stalinism, Nazism, and the Holocaust—moved into far more direct dialogue.[4] This book represents a new kind of entangled history: instead of studying Stalinism, Nazism, the Eastern Front in World War II, or the Holocaust separately, I seek out the insights to be had from bringing them all into a single frame. This approach does more than just leverage Russian and German materials in novel combinations and juxtapose the German / Nazi and Russian / Soviet "sides" throughout. It considers how Stalinism and Nazism were constantly interacting over time—whether at a distance, directly, or in the midst of an unprecedented total war. It probes how people in a largely Russian region made decisions, acted, and reacted under two alternating, radically illiberal regimes of the far Left and Right.

In the Soviet Union, power was multilayered and vastly more complex than Stalin or the Kremlin acting alone. The person in power in any autocracy, it goes without saying, is key. But any dictator is also dependent on—and, in part, the creature of—the system he attempts to shape. To this day, there is a small industry of Stalin biographies, many of which reinforce popular and scholarly fascination with the dictator rather than the dictatorship. The tendency to conflate a continental system of rule for its ruler remains popular; it is even more pronounced for a very different kind of authoritarianism in Russia today under Putin. A few of the best Stalin biographies have significantly advanced our understanding of the nature and contours of power at the highest level, as have a greater number of major studies of Adolf Hitler and top Nazis. Even so, in the entire library of studies of the regime that referred to itself as "Soviet power," in which considerations of power run like a red thread, there are few significant historical studies of specific locales that take power itself as their primary focus.[5]

Crucibles of Power flips consideration of the dynamics of power and politics from their pinnacles to the grassroots. At the same time, it aims squarely at the place where local and regional history meets the grand narrative. Moscow and Berlin are very much present throughout. Stalin, Hitler, and their lieutenants are crucial players, even though they had never heard of almost any of the people in the Smolensk Region who figure in this account.

Biographical Logics

Human decision making is intensively studied across the social and behavioral sciences, from sociology and economics to psychology and neuroscience. What historical research can offer is a retrospective grasp of life trajectories and their decisive turning points. It can place these within the wide range of particular political, cultural, and historical contexts that influence them. This, in turn, greatly illuminates people's self-presentations. What brought biographies and the question of agency to the center of this book were valuable new troves of autobiographical materials that emerged in the 2010s—ironically, in no small part because the Putinist myth of the Great Patriotic War made it into the number one topic of historical investigation in Russia. It became possible to track key crossroads in people's lives across the 1930s and 1940s in light of the broader arc of their biographies, clarifying how experiences under one regime conditioned what they did in another. I call this phenomenon biographical logics.

One major source for my investigation became the interview project launched in late 1941 by the Commission for the History of the Great Patriotic War, known as the Mints Commission, which tasked historians from the Soviet Academy of Sciences with conducting extensive interviews with figures deemed wartime heroes. But in the occupied territories, the commission's agenda was different: to record German atrocities and "accounts of the local population about life under occupation." Interviewees included women, non-communist physicians, underground members of the Communist Youth League (Komsomol), teachers, agronomists, and other professionals who lived through German occupation, among them Smolensk partisans fresh from the battlefield in 1942. The Academy of Sciences collection contains seventy substantial interviews from the Smolensk Region beginning as early as January 1942, long before official narratives about the war were set.[6]

Discovery of one other autobiographical source changed my project more than any other. In March 2017, I gave a talk about the Mints Commission interviews at the Higher School of Economics in Moscow. Afterward, I was approached by a colleague about the wartime memoirs of Boris Menshagin. The occupation-era mayor (*burgomistr*) of the city of Smolensk had also served as a defense attorney in Smolensk in the 1930s, where he first became famous for saving several defendants in the regional show trials during the Great Terror. His revelatory wartime recollections had never been published, nor had anything similar been seen from a Russian mayor under German occupation. I joined the editorial team that helped publish an 824-page annotated, critical edition of the memoirs in 2019.[7] Menshagin then became a central figure in my book.

The text of Menshagin's recollections has a unique history that affects how it must be read. After he retreated from Smolensk with the Wehrmacht and took on various collaborationist posts, Menshagin went to Berlin and then to Czechoslovakia at the end of the war. Taken by the Soviets in 1945, he was later sentenced to twenty-five years in prison for betrayal of the Motherland. A meticulous record keeper with a phenomenal memory for names, events, and dates, Menshagin had worked as an archivist before his legal career. He recorded his recollections in prison notebooks. But the Committee on State Security (or KGB, as the Soviet secret police was renamed) did not allow him to keep them when he was released from prison in 1971. Its successor, the Federal Security Service of the Russian Federation (FSB), denied having any record of these notebooks when queried in 2018. After his release, the elderly Menshagin was befriended by a group of Soviet dissidents interested especially in what he had to say about the Great

Terror. Menshagin reconstructed the notebooks by memory on cassette tapes smuggled out to Germany.[8]

For whom was Menshagin writing? Unlike many memoirs, his do not engage in introspective self-evaluation. The former defense lawyer wished to convince an invisible jury, perhaps even the court of history. But more immediately, Soviet accusations against Menshagin charged him with direct oversight—not indirect complicity—for all occupation-era atrocities in Smolensk, including the destruction of the ghetto. During his years in prison, Menshagin composed his memoirs while petitioning for a reduced sentence in requests to Premier Georgii Malenkov in 1955, First Secretary Nikita Khrushchev in 1962, and Procurator-General Roman Rudenko in 1968.[9] In his memoirs, Menshagin also mounted a case for his own defense. He did so adroitly and often subtly, in a manner that still disarms critics.

Like any good defense lawyer, Menshagin had to be at once convincing and selective in his presentation. His legal-political efforts conditioned his method of denying agency through episodes of silence or dissembling, while convincingly conveying verifiable and unique detail on a wide range of less sensitive matters.

Menshagin's activities under the German occupation bear an uncanny parallel to his behavior in the Stalinist 1930s. As a public defender during the Terror, Menshagin had to outwardly conform—even more studiously than under German rule—to the role the repressive regime required. Although my reconstruction of his choices reveals more pragmatism than his own self-presentation, he did stick his neck out in a fashion very rare for that era. At key moments in his life, he displayed unusual personal courage. His consistent religiosity and disillusionment with Stalinism certainly conditioned his decision to serve the Germans. Ultimately, however, Menshagin justified—likely even to himself—serving Berlin in precisely the same moralistic terms he justified serving Moscow. In both cases, he pointed to maneuvering that saved some victims but also gave him a measure of status and authority.

Past choices bias future decisions. The actions of the *dramatis personae* of this book, some whose lives are recounted across the chapters and others who make brief appearances, assume more meaning when examined under both regimes before and after 1941.

Menshagin's case is illustrative of power and choice in other ways. For one, untangling the complexities of his self-presentation required years of broader archival research. This informed how I approached the biographical and autobiographical materials woven into the fabric of *Crucibles of Power*. The discovery of Stalin-era diaries transformed the study of the 1930s, making those previously unknown texts the central focus of analysis, often in search of grand insights into the Soviet self. This book takes a different tack.[10] First, it interprets lives in tandem with a deep investigation of local, regional, and central levels of power. Second, while probing actions as sometimes more revealing than words, it examines autobiographical statements especially for insights into power relations. When looking up, Menshagin was subservient and highly constrained by German military authorities. When looking down, he acquired considerable authority over the civilian population of Smolensk, extending to and including the power of life and death.

Opportunity amid Cataclysm

Investigating biographical logics across 1941 and 1943 reveals another key issue: the replacement of Stalinism by Nazi rule, or the other way around, presented many people with the chance to dramatically alter their personal circumstances. Some found new opportunities or were transformed by new commitments. A second major figure in this book is the brash young Soviet loyalist Andrei Iudenkov. Stymied and frustrated in his ambitions before the war, Iudenkov found a new life within the Soviet partisan movement, committing himself to a difficult path in the face of initially widespread hostility from the rural population. For him, as for others, war and regime change created opportunities as well as dangers. Spectacular personal reinventions accompanied each power-political transformation in the region's history and the shifting fortunes of war.

All such transformations, by necessity, took into account the purification policies and classification schemes of either the Soviet regime (by and large around class and political categories, but increasingly also around nationality and patriotic state service) or National Socialism's new order in the East (first and foremost around antisemitism, race, anti-Bolshevism, and martial masculinity).[11] Everyone was affected by the way the two regimes enacted differing practices of promotion, purge, retribution, and extermination. For example, enemies of Soviet power gained favor in German recruitment policies, and Soviet methods of judging how locals acted under

German rule meant the difference between advancement and punishment on a mass scale.

One of the enduring paradoxes of Stalinism and Nazism is that even as their ideologies continued to exert sway and commitment on a mass scale, the harsh ways they classified everyone and the high stakes involved in ideological branding stimulated people to develop all sorts of strategies of evasion and advancement. Dissimulation was rampant and imposture common. Altering one's class background, personal history, and even ethnicity could change one's chances of survival. One of the most disturbing examples is the case of Mikhail Breitman, a Jewish political commissar who as a POW adopted the persona of a Ukrainian, Petrenko. He was trained by the SS to become a perpetrator in the Holocaust, only to declare his renewed loyalty to the Soviets in 1943 when uncovered as an agent sent by the Germans to infiltrate the partisans. Very different cases of identity switching emerged in the era of re-Sovietization after 1943. The profound destruction of the Smolensk Region and the creation of a substantially new regional elite made for some of the most outrageous successes in the long Soviet tradition of political imposture and economic corruption.[12]

Iudenkov was very different from his fellow partisan Fedor Gnezdilov, who also seized opportunities that opened up in 1941. A semiliterate "cadre of violence" and former executioner for the People's Commissariat of Internal Affairs (or NKVD, as the Soviet secret police was then called), Gnezdilov switched during the Great Terror to repairing escalators for the Moscow metro. He expressed great pride that as a "nobody" he rose to become a major partisan commander. Fighting alongside the partisan territories taken by Iudenkov's detachment in 1942, Gnezdilov named his unit "FD," after the first letters of his own name and patronymic as well as the initials of secret police (originally called the Cheka) founder Feliks Dzerzhinskii. In an interview, Gnezdilov boasted in direct and colloquial language devoid of party newspeak. Iudenkov, by contrast, first put pen to paper on December 13, 1942, to recount his own story, he said, "for myself personally" (*dlia sebia lichno*).[13] He rewrote that story over and over throughout the postwar period in sync with evolving versions of the Soviet past. As he emerged as a major party historian of the partisan movement and a bridge forward to the post-Soviet Russian myth of the war, Iudenkov essentially engaged in sanitizing and revising the difficult history he himself had experienced.

When the figures in this book faced crossroads in their lives or decided to fight for or against the Soviet or German side, they did not make their choices in a vacuum, but formed a part of larger groups and operated within specific institutional contexts and fields of power. Liudmila (Lyusya) Madziuk and Asya Shneiderman, for example, were among the young members of the Komsomol underground in Smolensk who wrote remarkable reports on gender and sexual relations between German men and local women, in which the power dynamics, pervaded by sexual violence, were distinguishable from but also overlapped with other major episodes of mass violence. By the same token, the key framework for understanding the partisan life of Iudenkov, as well as of his intelligentsia mentor Vasilii Kozubskii, was the intense partisan subculture that emerged in forest camps and nighttime raids. Elsi Eichenberger, a Swiss Red Cross nurse during the war, also became a unique chronicler, documenting her ongoing arguments with the Wehrmacht and SS men she treated in Smolensk in 1941.

Victims and perpetrators are conventionally treated as opposites, but multiple and conflicting roles are always possible, perhaps especially in times of extreme crisis. Many figures in this story became both victims and perpetrators at various times in their lives. Sometimes they were both at the same time. For those who became cadres of violence, as well as for those many Russians and Soviets who served the Germans, another key factor in biographical trajectories came into play: path dependency. Once certain fateful decisions were made or actions committed, particularly those involving political affiliations and war crimes, the road chosen was difficult to swerve from. At the same time, the high-stakes quest for survival made switching sides, and the attempt to do so, into a pervasive phenomenon.

Contingency and Life Chances

Vasilii Maslennikov, a third major figure in this book, devoted much of his postwar life to chronicling the mind-boggling changes he witnessed in a single village under Soviet and German rule in the Smolensk Region.[14] Cautious by nature, Maslennikov throughout his life was buffeted by events. He taught himself to read at an early age, and for him, a peasant determined to escape the village, literacy was his most precious asset. His trajectory in the 1920s and 1930s vividly illustrates the extent to which the Soviet system intervened in basic life chances connected to education and occupation. Set on a decade-long quest to cobble together an education, Maslennikov was deeply ambivalent about the consequences of the state violence he witnessed during collectivization and the Great Terror. But the only way out of the collective farm and to the more modern life he craved was to join the collectivizers and the Party. Maslennikov ultimately emerged as something of a peasant intellectual without a cause. Circumstances made him into a reluctant partisan, a forced laborer from the East (*Ostarbeiter*) in Germany, and a postwar repatriate grappling with stigma for decades.

Maslennikov's unique observations about his own village in the rural region of Smolensk offer one view of an agrarian population that was downtrodden and distant from the centers of power yet, because of its sheer numbers, decisive both to Stalinism and to the German occupation. For vast numbers of locals, rural and urban, there came moments when even indecision or inaction represented a choice. Maslennikov was an exceptional figure, recording his thoughts with the kind of historical acumen that made him rare among millions of peasants. But he, too, exemplifies the role of contingency for so many during the upheavals of the 1930s and 1940s.

People of virtually identical backgrounds—for example, Maslennikov and his two siblings—were sometimes judged in opposite ways politically because some element of pure chance determined their formal relationships to German and Soviet rule. Maslennikov himself was stigmatized but not punished because of his forced labor in Germany; his brother was accused of collaboration after being pressed to become a translator for the Germans; and his sister was deemed a suitable recruit to interrogate collaborators for the Soviet counterintelligence agency SMERSH.[15]

Despite all contingencies and constraints, at a key juncture Vasilii Maslennikov made one decision that was particularly far-reaching. In a German POW camp, surrounded by many others willing to promise anything to buy their own release, he refused to collaborate. Back in Smolensk after the war, this principled act gained him nothing but setbacks. Although he was tainted by forced labor in the land of fascism, it determined much of his subsequent life trajectory.[16]

The life stories explored in this book take us more deeply into what it meant to live and choose in moments of exceptional crisis. Consideration of people's experiences and agency, however limited and however tragic, deepens what can be learned from the political and military documents left by Soviet and German bureaucracies and provides very concrete examples of power relations. This insight, in turn, brings us to the Sphinx's riddle of all social and political inquiries: the nature of power itself.

Paradoxes of Power

The workings of power may appear overt and obvious, but they are also enigmatic and elusive. That is because power's many dimensions can be extremely tricky to gauge. In one common definition, power is the ability to get people to do things they otherwise would not do. "Hard power"—such as armed coercion, secret police repressions, forced deportations, and racial or class-based exterminations, all of which so clearly figured in the political violence of Nazism and Stalinism—produces visible, immediate results. Yet coercion and violence, especially in their extreme manifestations, may seem to succeed in the short term but then leave many unintended consequences. Stalin's unprecedented peacetime bloodletting, the Great Terror, created critical deficiencies on the eve of war. Arguably, it turned more people into enemies than its fabricated conspiracies eliminated. The unparalleled mass violence of Hitler's "war of extermination" in 1941–1942 in Smolensk and elsewhere produced a decisive turn in local attitudes that undermined what the invaders had not expected: a long-term occupation.

Many of the most important arguments about power under Stalinism and Nazism have revolved around Stalin and Hitler and address much about the nature of power. Both leaders, venerated in dictatorial cults and wielding the power of life and death over so many, at times have been rather perversely portrayed as "weak" dictators.[17] If that is the case, one might ask, what would a strong dictator look like? Repeated resort to repression in response to the cataclysms it unleashed, for example, may indicate Stalinism's weaknesses, in that it could not get its way by other means. There is a bit more validity to that notion. The kind of cohesion facilitating compliance was lacking in the multinational, continental, and still largely rural USSR. But violence, even as it was accompanied by an unprecedented level of mass persuasion (propaganda), was a deliberate choice and an ideological proclivity for a regime bent on excising enemies and remaking society. By the same token, Hitler was impulsive, lazy, and, after 1942, extremely isolated, but that too was not all about weakness. He expected his subordinates to battle it out in a kind of polycratic Social Darwinism. It makes little sense to label either the dictators or their dictatorships weak. Rather, in the interwar period as during the war, the dictators controlled extraordinarily repressive states and mobilizational mass movements that each featured distinct, even glaring, deficiencies.

One crucial metric in any analysis of power is state capacity. The Stalinist USSR and Nazi Germany, both murderous and ostensibly formidable, had to compensate for key deficits. They often did so through violence. In the vast rear administrations of the Eastern Front, for example, a relatively small number of Germans had to rely on huge numbers of armed and civilian collaborators to administer their new domain, even as the Nazis' all-encompassing racism and cult of domination hampered that effort. The Soviet political system was geared toward rapidly ramping up mass mobilization, and its command economy was capable of drastic reorientations demanded by the existential crisis of 1941–1942. But the Stalinist political and economic order also contained severe inefficiencies and drawbacks. Among the most conspicuous were the dysfunctions and shortages of the planned economy; others derived from the fact that urban-based Soviet power remained shockingly thin on the local level in the countryside. The forced collectivization of agriculture had turned the rural order into the regime's Achilles' heel.

The dimensions of "soft power" are diffuse, hard to measure concretely, and numerous. But this book shows that even in the historically violent forms of authoritarianism, these forms of power remain central. Power not only signifies political command, armed force, or political violence. It also figures in the guise of belief systems and mass persuasion, the selection of privileged loyalists, the role of experts and professionals, and the assertions of cultural-civilizational superiority crucial to Nazism and Stalinism. In the cataclysm of war on the Eastern Front, certain aspects of power took on potentially lethal significance on a sharply greater scale—for example, those related to information and disinformation, gender and crimes of sexual domination, and, not least, material and economic privileges, control over calories, and the quest for survival.

Core issues in the place and time investigated in this book became fundamental for both alternating and warring regimes and therefore unavoidable for the people who lived, served, and suffered under them. Two topics that hold particular significance are borders and geography and the region's Russianness. They inform how this book rethinks the classic

Nazi-Soviet comparison and the degree to which Smolensk was representative and unique.

Space and Power

Borders and territorial administration are intimately connected to power. The borders of Smolenshchina, as the Smolensk lands are informally known to this day in Russian, with its capital city of Smolensk, shifted throughout its long history, including after its designation as one of the Russian Empire's first provinces (*guberniia*) in 1706. But by far the most radical and politically far-reaching carousel of territorial reorganizations occurred between World War I and World War II. In February 1917, after the fall of the tsar, the large Western Region (*oblast'*) was created, uniting Minsk, Mogilev, Smolensk, and Vitebsk Provinces, with its capital in Minsk. After Soviet power was established in Smolensk in 1918, with German troops occupying Minsk, the capital moved to Smolensk. After the formation of the Belarusian Soviet Socialist Republic (SSR) and throughout the 1920s, the region shrank into a much smaller Smolensk Province, with a population of 2.92 million in the 1926 census. Then, in another dramatic reversal, in 1929 another giant Western Region, with its capital still in Smolensk, was expanded across western territories of the Russian Soviet Federative Socialist Republic (RSFSR). Suddenly, the area run from Smolensk had a population of over six million. In 1937, this giant territory was again broken up. A smaller, prewar Smolensk Region now contained 49 districts, as opposed to 125 in the Western Region between 1929 and 1937.

Even so, on the eve of 1941, the city of Smolensk was still the capital of one of the largest administrative-territorial units in European Russia. The Smolensk Region was restored in August 1943 when the Red Army drove the Germans out. After the war, it consisted of thirty-eight districts and four "regional-level" cities: Iartsevo, Roslavl, Smolensk, and Viazma.[18]

It was no coincidence that the region's two greatest administrative reorganizations, in 1929 and 1937, coincided exactly with the onset of the Great Break and the Great Terror. The giant new Western Region of 1929 was created to further Soviet socialism's grand transformation of the economy and society: it would turn a rural region of smallholders into an "agricultural-industrial" base for processing flax and other agricultural products. But the political motivations behind the region's rise and fall appear even more

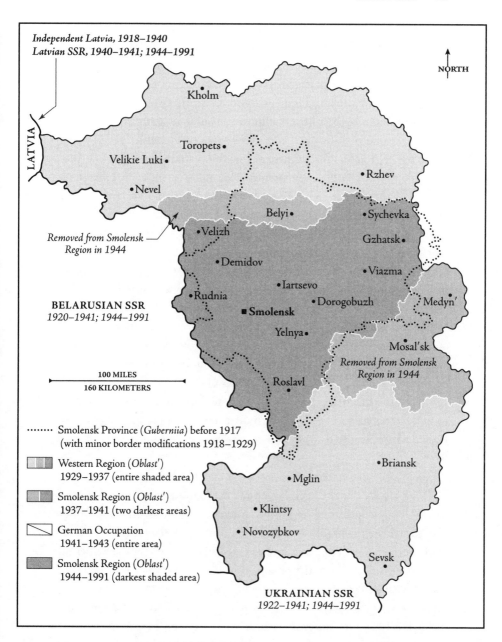

Independent Latvia, 1918–1940
Latvian SSR, 1940–1941; 1944–1991

NORTH

LATVIA

Kholm

Toropets•

Velikie Luki•

•Rzhev

•Nevel

Belyi•

•Sychevka

Removed from Smolensk Region in 1944

•Velizh

Gzhatsk•

•Demidov

•Viazma

•Iartsevo

BELARUSIAN SSR
1920–1941; 1944–1991

•Rudnia

•Dorogobuzh

•Medyn'

■ **Smolensk**

Yelnya•

Mosal'sk

Removed from Smolensk Region in 1944

100 MILES
160 KILOMETERS

Roslavl
•

••••••• Smolensk Province (*Guberniia*) before 1917
         (with minor border modifications 1918–1929)

▨ Western Region (*Oblast'*)
    1929–1937 (entire shaded area)

▨ Smolensk Region (*Oblast'*)
    1937–1941 (two darkest areas)

◫ German Occupation
    1941–1943 (entire area)

▨ Smolensk Region (*Oblast'*)
    1944–1991 (darkest shaded area)

•Briansk

•Mglin

•Klintsy

•Novozybkov

Sevsk
•

UKRAINIAN SSR
1922–1941; 1944–1991

Border changes in the Western / Smolensk Region, from before 1917 to 1991.

fundamental. The Western Region of 1929–1937 coincided exactly with the rule of the Old Bolshevik Ivan Rumiantsev, the prototypical "little Stalin," a term coined by the political scientist Merle Fainsod and now synonymous with regional strongmen or subnational dictators. "Borrowing a page from his master's book," Fainsod famously wrote, Rumiantsev "had made himself into something of a little Stalin in his home territory."[19] The Soviet system of cadre politics was a core component of Leninism, Stalin's own rise to power, and Stalinism. These major administrative-territorial restructurings were occasions, even pretexts, for massive shifts in party-state officials at the district and regional levels and for a long list of other key power-political metamorphoses.

A large factor made clear in a rural region such as Smolensk was just how sparsely staffed the Soviet regime—otherwise so effective at rapid mass mobilization in a way unexpected by Hitler and his generals in 1941—remained in the countryside long after collectivization. In the seventeen years before World War I, the urban population of Smolensk Region had grown 65 percent, more than twice as fast as the rural population, but it was still only 9.47 percent urban. Between 1914 and 1922, total war, civil war, typhus, and hunger not only reduced urbanization but led to overall population decline. By the 1926 census, the region was only 9.3 percent urban. By the 1939 census, that had grown to 18 percent—still more rural than surrounding regions and the eleventh most rural region of thirty-five in the RSFSR.[20] Below the district level of power, the Party had few effective levers.

The history of Smolensk illustrates just how fundamental to the course of Soviet history was the interplay among the four differing levels of power: central, regional, district, and local. The regional and district authorities needed one another badly, but they were often impotent at the very local level. Both blamed, criticized, and resented the other under the withering pressure emanating from the center. At moments of crisis, those levels became unstable. Power relations shifted as the center incited lower levels to attack the middle during major turning points. At the same time, the hierarchical chain of command within the party and state apparatus was routinely bypassed by powerful bureaucracies. These included, most notably, the secret police. In moments of crisis in particular, long-standing, informally constituted practices of directing specially tasked plenipotentiaries from Moscow were used to circumvent, even destroy, the regular

order. Soviet power relations were more complicated than the dichotomous notion of "center-periphery relations" suggests.

For Germany and its occupation regime on the Eastern Front, Smolensk
assumed importance first and foremost for another reason: military geography. Smolensk lay on the road from Minsk to Moscow, the same path
Napoleon traversed in 1812. That road was now the USSR's largest highway,
built starting in 1936 by Viazemlag, a traveling Gulag camp. The forced-
labor project constructed the Moscow-Minsk main highway along the same
route German invaders would shortly travel. As a result, the Wehrmacht's
Army Group Center, aimed through Smolensk toward Moscow, boasted
over 40 percent of all German divisions and over half the tanks.[21] The strategic importance of the Smolensk area made it a nexus of communications,
railway lines, and river crossings. After August 1941, Smolensk became the
headquarters of Army Group Center's Rear Area Command and a key
German economic base.

The three main Einsatzgruppen (deployment groups) led the turn to
genocide in the Holocaust and also played a role, neglected by previous
historians, in setting up the new occupation regime. Einsatzgruppe B,
headquartered in Smolensk after the city's capture in August 1941, contained the highest concentration of SS elites because it included an advance unit, Vorkommando Moskau, preparing to enter and purge the red
capital. Vorkommando Moskau was commanded by Franz Six, a major SS
perpetrator. On Soviet territory, Six reported to Arthur Nebe, head of
Einsatzgruppe B until November 1941 and longtime chief of the Reich
Security Main Office's (Reichssicherheitshauptamt, RSHA) Criminal Police (Kripo). Nebe had been involved in the involuntary "euthanasia" program to murder disabled children and psychiatric patients that began in
Germany and Poland in 1939. The method included the use of carbon
monoxide gas developed at Kripo's Criminal-Technical Institute. It was
later applied on the night of July 15, 1942, in the gas vans used to kill the
residents of the Smolensk city ghetto, which survived longer than any of
the seventeen other short-lived ghettos in the Smolensk Region, of approximately fifty in the RSFSR.[22]

Of the three Wehrmacht commands on Soviet territory, Army Group
Center became most centrally concerned with the partisan war in the occupied territories. General Max von Schenckendorff, from 1941 to 1943 head
of Army Group Center rear administration based in Smolensk, emerged as

the leading expert on counterinsurgency. In September 1941, Schencken-dorff convened the Mogilev Conference, which gathered military commanders and SS elites to propagate the message, to quote one attendee, "Where the Partisan is, there is the Jew. Where the Jew is, there is the Partisan."[23]

Of all occupied ethnically Russian territories, the forests of Smolensk and Briansk became the largest centers of the Soviet partisan movement, with roughly equal numbers of fighters. In forest bases they quickly created their own subcultures and communities, prosecuting political terror in what became a virtual civil war in the countryside. For units in the forests of Smolensk, closer to the home front than the marshlands of Belarus and Ukraine, the partisan war had different dynamics. Fueled by large numbers of Red Army soldiers escaped from huge encirclements in the battles of 1941, Smolensk partisans restored Soviet power in four partisan territories in mid-1942. At their height, these partisan territories incorporated in whole or in part twenty-five of the fifty-four prewar districts of Smolensk Region.[24] To a large extent, these Smolensk partisans came to power and ruled independently from Moscow, and they have never been investigated in depth. They restored a modified, rural, wartime version of Soviet power behind enemy lines, which I refer to as Stalinism without Stalin. The phenomenon not only reveals much about the history of the occupied territories but also sheds light on the varieties of Stalinism itself.

General Schenckendorff, architect of the novel wave of rural violence in the brutal anti-partisan war that overthrew these Smolensk partisan territories in summer 1942, paradoxically also emerged in that year as an advocate for an occupation regime that would win more hearts and minds. He and many others saw that the German war effort was threatened by rapidly deteriorating popular attitudes in Russian areas.

Even as Schenckendorff took the war of annihilation to new levels in the countryside previously disaffected by Soviet collectivization, he grasped the implications of heavy German reliance on large numbers of civilian and armed collaborators—including those needed for his anti-partisan operations. Wielding the stick, he advocated the use of carrots. It has long been known that the nature of Nazi racial colonization ultimately made a different kind of occupation regime impossible to create.[25] But how these German attempts to address the "Russian question" emerged in sync with the strivings and maneuverings of many Russian collaborators and local elites remained unknown, because they were not examined in tandem.

Differing Regimes

How, then, can we understand varied German initiatives aimed at creating a more effective occupation regime? Repeatedly dangling political incentives in front of Russians and collaborators in Smolensk and other regions defied Hitler's and Himmler's repeated inclinations. If Stalinist hypercentralization was compensation for weaknesses at the local level, it also fit the Stalinist USSR's party-centered, modernizing, mass-mobilizing, and scientist ethos. Nazi Germany, by contrast, is often dubbed "polycratic" because of its "jungle world" of competing power centers and personalistic fiefdoms. Chaotic political jockeying fit the impulsive proclivities of its dictator and the Nazi "Führer principle." At the same time, it meshed with ideology: biologized notions of the struggle of the fittest. Above all, in 1942 and 1943, German military and rear administration officials grappled with the widening gap between German war aims and Nazi ideology. Ian Kershaw famously made the phrase "working toward the Führer" central to explanations of how the Hitler cult acted as a political-ideological magnet across the Nazis' sprawling Social Darwinist state.[26] But far from Berlin, Schenckendorff and many others advanced repeated attempts to hold out some hope to the burgeoning number of Russian armed and political collaborators for a future in their own land that was not utterly servile, even if it was proffered only on short-term, Machiavellian grounds.

As Hitler's war of annihilation radicalized Nazism in 1941, working toward the Führer was accompanied by its polar opposite. The June 6, 1941, Commissar Order, throwing out conventional rules of war, justified summary execution of Communists attached to Red Army units, but opened the door to different treatment for others. Many thousands of party members were recruited as collaborators and spies. In August 1941, Schenckendorff personally interrogated Major Ivan Kononov, a Communist and career officer who defected with a large number of his soldiers. He then sanctioned one of the first units of Soviet armed collaborators fighting for the Nazis, against Hitler's clearly stated orders. This move was an early example of how occupation authorities on the ground frequently, if often temporarily, engaged in working away from the Führer.[27] This hardly made Nazism more lenient than Stalinism. Rather, those authorities were engaged in risky maneuvering within differing regimes of power relations.

Smolensk as Russian

Smolensk also assumed significance as an "ancient Russian city," a phrase that became so common in Soviet parlance that it was repeated in 1942 by the ardently anti-fascist Asya Shneiderman, who concealed her Jewishness in the communist underground inside the occupied city. Smolensk, one of the oldest settlements in ancient Rus', became the seat of a principality in 1054, two centuries before Moscow. The legacy of Rus' was claimed in all the East Slavic national narratives—Ukrainian, Belarusian, and Russian—in the nineteenth and twentieth centuries. Long after Muscovy incorporated Smolensk from Poland-Lithuania in the sixteenth century, it remained a contested borderland garrison with autonomist leanings. Decades after Tolstoy's *War and Peace* memorialized the patriotic Russian popular response to Napoleon in the Battle of Smolensk, the most prominent analysts of imperial space specifically did not include Smolensk in the Russian national interior, or imperial heartland. In 1890, the ethnographer Sergei Maksimov called Smolensk the Belarusian capital. In the Russian Empire at the time, seven of the province's districts were classified as Belarusian.[28] Only in the twentieth century did Smolensk become a quintessentially ancient Russian city.

Russians occupied the lowest rung of the Nazi racial hierarchy among the Slavs, below Ukrainians and Belarusians. The German racial order was an inversion of the Soviet national hierarchy that emerged in the 1930s, when Russians had assumed the status "first among equals" in Stalin's multinational USSR. In the interwar period, the Smolensk Region's population was classified as overwhelmingly Russian. But historically there was a sizable Belarusian minority, and throughout the modern period linguists and ethnographers debated the rural population's relationship to Belarusians. This issue would assume significance for a struggle between Belarusian and Russian nationalist collaborators during the war.

The 1939 census included a Jewish population in the Smolensk Region of 1.2 percent. In urban areas and the working class, even more so in the intelligentsia, however, Jews were more prominent than this figure suggests. Smolensk regional political elites, who typically circulated from postings around the country, featured some high-ranking Jewish and Latvian figures, as well as others, such as the occasional Ukrainian. In addition, the eastern parts of the region contained traditional religious Jewish communities that had migrated from Belarus shtetls after the end of the tsarist Pale of Settlement in 1917.[29] Needless to say, the invading Germans were inclined to wildly exaggerate the role of Jews in Stalinist rule in the region.

German military men in the region were well aware that the Soviet home front and the partisan movement had taken a hard turn to appeal to Russian national sentiment. So were their clients among Russian political collaborators, returning Russian nationalist émigrés, and Russophone propagandists in the region. In 1941 and 1942, recruiters "working away from the Führer" often simply renamed armed Russian collaborators Ukrainians, Cossacks, or Belarusians. But with huge numbers of civilian, police, and armed collaborators increasingly crucial to holding the vast territories, a reorientation justifying specifically Russian contributions to the German war effort was launched in late 1942. The move failed in part because it could not simply spirit away so many well-entrenched conceptions establishing Russians as "subhuman."

Wartime Smolensk also figured prominently in little-known attempts to create a Russian nationalist "third way" between German fascism and Soviet communism. This was the project of a right-wing Russian nationalist organization of young activist émigrés, the National-Labor Alliance of Russian Solidarists of the New Generation (NTSNP, after 1943 NTS), whose members were known as Solidarists. The national "solidarism" articulated by the movement, founded in Belgrade in 1930, was its distinctive term for a Christian corporatism that bore resemblances to fascist ideological currents in Austria, Italy, Portugal, Romania, and Spain. Portugal under Antonio Salazar proved most attractive to the Russian Solidarists because it combined authoritarian statism with Christianity and spiritual values. For that same reason, the Solidarists' founding platform displayed the vocabulary and influence of works by the far-right Russian religious nationalist philosopher Ivan Il'in (who became an officially promoted touchstone for Russian imperial nationalism in Putin's Russia, especially in the 2010s). Rejecting slavish Russian émigré aping of openly fascist models, Solidarism was youth-centered, accepting only those born in 1895 or after, and antisemitic, advocating a new Pale of Settlement. The movement seized on the German invasion in 1941 as a strategic opportunity, and hundreds took positions in local city and county administrations throughout occupied Russian territories.[30] Smolensk became the unofficial center of Solidarist operations in all the ethnically Russian occupied territories.

The Solidarists cultivated their network even as many joined German intelligence and propaganda initiatives. Many became significant perpetrators deeply implicated in German violence, including in Smolensk. Solidarist operatives attempted to recruit new members from a suspicious local population. The Solidarists' dreams of a Russian nationalist third way between Hitler and Stalin provoked German security forces to arrest about 150 NTS cadres starting in summer 1943. Even so, in 1943–1945 the Solidarists supplied a good part of the political personnel for Andrei Vlasov's German-sponsored Russian Liberation Army and German-sponsored training schools for Russian-language propagandists.[31]

Smolensk's Russianness assumed importance in a cultural and ideological sense. Competition for the loyalties of Russians lay at the heart of acrimonious wartime fights about whether fascism or communism was more barbaric and which was more European or advanced. These became prime arenas for a major propaganda war, collaborationist politics and counterintelligence, and even everyday encounters between occupiers and occupied.

The monumental clash on the Eastern Front in World War II has been dubbed a war of annihilation, an all-out war so total it was "absolute." In the occupied territories, it was also an unequal yet sustained cross-cultural confrontation.[32]

Stalinism and Nazism in One Region

The intellectual life of the twentieth century was shaped by debates over totalitarianism, but in scholarship their tendency toward balance-sheet comparisons of "regimes and systems" inevitably oversimplifies.[33] At the time Stalinism launched in 1929 and Nazism in 1933, the USSR and Germany were vastly different. Both "isms" evolved and took different forms in very different subperiods. In any comparison of their similarities and differences, everything depends on what is being compared, and then exactly when and where. In place of global comparisons, this book juxtaposes Stalinism and Nazism in one region, paying special attention to how they interacted with one another across the different levels of power. What new perspectives does this yield?

First of all, Soviet communism and German fascism both appear as revolutionary. The long-standing reluctance to see National Socialism as truly revolutionary comes in part from an inclination to view revolutions as all about liberation, not genocidal domination. But there are real advantages to taking the Nazis at their word and seeing fascism as a revolution of the Right. Revolutions come in stages—before, during, and after a regime change. Juxtaposing the revolutions of Left and Right highlights how interactions between Nazism and Bolshevism / Stalinism occurred at distinctly different turning points in their life cycles, above all when they went to war in 1941.[34]

The onset of a war of racial colonization in the land of Bolshevism triggered the most radical phase of the fascist revolution. The East was where the German drive for a European land empire converged with long-standing nationalist obsessions with backwardness and contagion, all of which were radicalized by Nazism. The Soviet East became the locus for the potential fulfillment of Nazi Germany's imperial-colonial dreams and the prospect of destroying the political and biological enemy. These two strands merged insofar as Jewishness and communism were imagined to be identical. As a result, the moment of the Nazi Revolution's greatest radicalization and the formulation of the Final Solution became the launch of the war for *Lebensraum* (living space) and against "Judeo-Bolshevism" on the Eastern Front.[35]

By contrast, the existential crisis of the war jolted Stalinism, still reeling from the Great Terror, toward results-driven, pragmatic reorientations— even as the onset of the wartime crisis in 1941 led to a ramping up of internal repressions. This move was the opposite of revolutionary radicalization. The regime was steadily turning away from the embrace of "leveling" and collectivism in the first years of the Stalin Revolution toward the highly stratified, hyper-statist, and increasingly entrenched social and political order of late Stalinism. The Soviet Union emerged from the war as a bizarre, radical-reactionary hybrid. This history of Smolensk encompasses the shift from Stalinist revolutionary revivalism to what can be seen as the midlife crisis of the revolution.[36]

Underlying these different stages of the Nazi and Soviet revolutionary trajectories lay parallel yet divergent drives of internal and external colonization. Unlike other European great powers, neither Germany nor the

USSR could rely on overseas colonies as motors of development and markers of global status. The revolutionary trajectories of Left and Right took shape in the midst of two colonizing projects: one primarily external, the other primarily internal. The Nazi Revolution, connected directly to perceived humiliation in World War I, militarism, and martial masculinity, chased its utopian fantasies in a new war of conquest and racial engineering. The Stalin Revolution's ersatz or political war took as its centerpiece a "class struggle" to remake society and an assault on backwardness. The countryside was the biggest internal colony of what might be called the Stalinist extraction state. In this sense, the Stalinist utopian fantasy of leapfrogging over imperialist capitalism took the form of a political war of internal colonization, launched more than a decade before the Nazi war of racial colonization.[37]

It is not surprising that the vast, impersonal forces of these different phases and drives were only dimly understood in Smolensk as they were unfolding. But one thing those who experienced both German and Soviet rule in Smolensk came to understand well was that the two regimes balanced hard and soft power in very different ways. Culture, education, and ideology were Soviet obsessions wherever communism was imposed, but the Germans had other concerns when it came to their Slavic underlings. The Nazi worldview was for Aryans.

Some peasant survivors of dekulakization—the violent expropriation and deportation of approximately 1.8 million wealthier peasants and those opposed to the collectivization of agriculture in the early 1930s—did, in fact, perceive uncanny similarities between the internal brutalities of the party-state during Stalin's Great Break and the foreign domination of the German occupation. But the vast majority did not grasp the nature of German rule, especially initially in 1941. To recover how choices were made as people lived through upheavals, we must also uncover the history of misunderstandings. The topic of incomplete information also holds significance for perceptions of violence at a time when not just its sheer scale but the very terms for such killing—genocide, ethnic cleansing, crimes against humanity, Holocaust—were as yet unknown.

To recover understandings during that time, we must first address gaps in our own. In contrast to thousands of detailed studies on the Holocaust, the centerpiece of Nazi violence, other large-scale Nazi crimes on Soviet

territory remain virtually unknown to all but specialists. The genocide
of the Jews included at least two million Jewish people living on Soviet
territory, most killed by bullets in ravines and trenches rather than in the
gas chambers of death camps. By March 1942, when the first death camp
in Bełżec began operations in the Generalgouvernement, on Polish territory, approximately two million Soviet POWs had already perished from
starvation, disease, bullets, and neglect in camps known as Dulags and
Stalags. Increasingly, this mistreatment facilitated the large-scale recruitment of a wide array of collaborators. By the war's end in 1945, as many as
3.3 million of 5.7 million POWs had perished. To this day, there is no
monograph in English about this war crime of genocidal proportions.[38] I
analyze this major atrocity as closely interconnected to the other overlapping waves of German political violence—the Shoah and the brutal anti-
partisan war in the countryside.[39] For popular perceptions, however, what
was also decisive were the casual, everyday brutalities of racial colonization, including rampant sexual violence and sexual barter. A pervasive
sense of humiliation, reinforced by the shocking reintroduction of whipping and flogging, which had been abolished in 1917, shaped contemporary
views of waves of mass violence as they were unfolding.

Smolensk as Microcosm

Whenever a single locale is investigated, questions arise about whether it is
representative. For the Smolensk Region in this period, there is no single
answer. As a very rural region, it was broadly typical of the Soviet countryside under collectivization and the regional level of power during the
Great Break and the Great Terror. In later periods of Stalinism and during
the German occupation, Smolensk provides a window into largely Russian
areas and the less-studied German rear units administered by the Wehrmacht. The Holocaust on Soviet territory had numerous variations connected to geography and timing, but, even so, Smolensk provides insight
into many dynamics of the Holocaust on the territories of the pre-1939
USSR. The Baltic countries and eastern Poland had different national politics, and the deprivation of sovereignty during the harsh Sovietization
following the Nazi-Soviet Pact in 1939 became a political resource for the
invading Germans in 1941. By contrast, areas that had been Soviet for over

two decades, including Smolensk, were marked by Soviet legacies that affected the German incitement of antisemitic violence. These included "friendship of peoples" propaganda and far greater caution toward participating in public activity.[40]

In other consequential ways, Smolensk was unique. Not only did the Smolensk Affair turn the region into an epicenter of the Stalin Revolution, but during the Great Terror it also became an early harbinger of what would unfold on an all-union scale. During World War II, the sheer concentration of Wehrmacht and SS forces, the proximity of Smolensk to Moscow, and the symbolism of the "ancient Russian city" made this a locale with its own distinctive dynamics.

Finally, the Smolensk Region itself was far from monolithic during the war and during the Soviet restoration after 1943. The territory was re-Sovietized in three distinct phases. Twenty percent of the eastern part was under occupation for only three to four months and thus was most typical of other briefly occupied parts of the RSFSR. Another 40 percent of the region was occupied for twenty-two months. After losing the Battle of Stalingrad and after the blockade of Leningrad was broken in January 1943, Germans pulled back in February from the Rzhev-Viazma field of operations, giving the Soviets superiority in a forward operation beginning in early March. A bombed-out Viazma was the biggest city retaken in spring 1943, but Soviet forces were stopped along the Moscow-Minsk highway before Dorogobuzh. Next, the westernmost part of the region was retaken after the August 1943 battle in Smolensk. This last 40 percent of the territory was under occupation for twenty-five to twenty-six months, making it more comparable to those western parts of the USSR that experienced extended German rule.[41] These substantially different wartime experiences within this one region became a key factor as Soviet power returned.

Temptations of Power

The figures explored in the chapters ahead, representing many groups and individuals connected to both Stalinism and Nazism, were almost never heroes. They fit only awkwardly into the black-and-white categories that diminish the horrors of war, including in Putin's Russia. Smolensk citizens were faced with often terrible alternatives. Historians have devoted great attention to victims and perpetrators, rulers and ideologues, collaborators

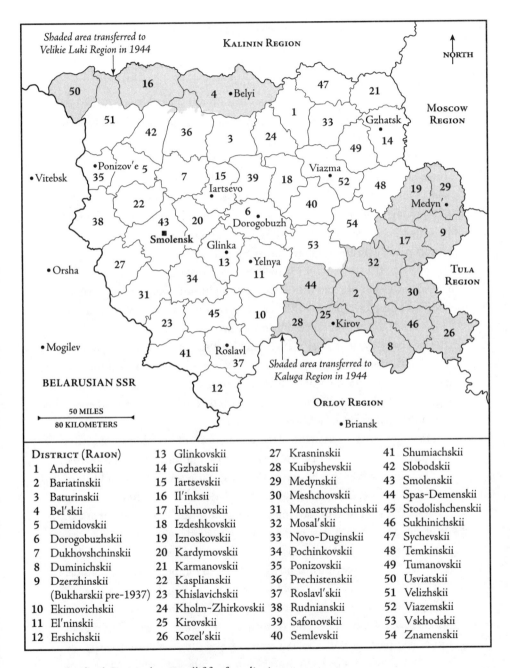

Smolensk Region showing all fifty-four districts, ca. 1940.

DISTRICT (RAION)			
1 Andreevskii	13 Glinkovskii	27 Krasninskii	41 Shumiachskii
2 Bariatinskii	14 Gzhatskii	28 Kuibyshevskii	42 Slobodskii
3 Baturinskii	15 Iartsevskii	29 Medynskii	43 Smolenskii
4 Bel'skii	16 Il'inksii	30 Meshchovskii	44 Spas-Demenskii
5 Demidovskii	17 Iukhnovskii	31 Monastyrshchinskii	45 Stodolishchenskii
6 Dorogobuzhskii	18 Izdeshkovskii	32 Mosal'skii	46 Sukhinichskii
7 Dukhovshchinskii	19 Iznoskovskii	33 Novo-Duginskii	47 Sychevskii
8 Duminichskii	20 Kardymovskii	34 Pochinkovskii	48 Temkinskii
9 Dzerzhinskii	21 Karmanovskii	35 Ponizovskii	49 Tumanovskii
(Bukharskii pre-1937)	22 Kasplianskii	36 Prechistenskii	50 Usviatskii
10 Ekimovichskii	23 Khislavichskii	37 Roslavl'skii	51 Velizhskii
11 El'ninskii	24 Kholm-Zhirkovskii	38 Rudnianskii	52 Viazemskii
12 Ershichskii	25 Kirovskii	39 Safonovskii	53 Vskhodskii
	26 Kozel'skii	40 Semlevskii	54 Znamenskii

and resisters, but there remains one very significant group that has not been given as much attention as it deserves. This was the ranks of ordinary people, far from the halls of power, who in an hour of crisis reached out to grab a slice of power for themselves.

World War II on the Eastern Front has often been called an ideological war. But despite the extraordinary impact of the ideological clash between fascism and communism, political ideas and affiliations were far from always the most overt motivations amid extreme conditions on the ground. These factors not only mixed and merged with many others but were often widely internalized and ingrained in subtle ways. This phenomenon, present among millions of German soldiers and local Soviet citizens, might be called banal Nazism or banal Stalinism.[42] Ultimately, the role of ideology under Stalinist and Nazi rule is a problem that cannot be uniformly deciphered. The ways in which their broader ideologies intersected or diverged with outlooks and identities is a complicated problem for every individual figure in this book. The crucial point is that both Stalinism and Nazism not only encouraged but in fact depended on the arrogation of a slice of power by their local agents. Jan Gross has put it best: the "minute, individual, spontaneous contributions" of these locals lay behind the institutional arbitrariness and "fearsome, incapacitating quality" of these regimes.[43] Both revolutionary regimes desired activists and true believers, not merely adherents just following orders.

Historians may have slighted the temptations of microdoses of power for ordinary people under radical dictatorships, but for some of the keenest intellectual observers of the age of the masses it represented a problem of acute importance. One such observer was Nadezhda Mandelstam. Writing about her difficult road to the Gulag during the Great Terror, she remarked: "It wasn't a question of just one dictator—anybody who had the slightest power, down to the humblest police official or doorkeeper, was also a dictator. We had not previously understood what a temptation power can be. Not everyone wants to be a Napoleon, but people cling desperately to what little power they have and will do their best to get all they can out of it." Another was Primo Levi, the Jewish Italian chemist who became an anti-fascist partisan, Auschwitz inmate, and writer. "Monsters exist," he said, "but they are too few in number to be truly dangerous. More dangerous are the common men, the functionaries ready to believe and to act without asking questions."[44]

There are two definitions of *crucible:* (1) a container in which metals or other substances can be melted, that is to say, transformed, and (2) a severe trial in which different elements interact, leading to the creation of something new. The crucibles that were the intersecting regimes of Stalinism and Nazism transformed people and shaped the USSR, Russia, and the world in ways that have lasted down to the present day.

1

AN EPICENTER OF THE STALIN REVOLUTION

NO ONE EXPECTED THAT the Smolensk Region would become one of the key launching points for the Stalin Revolution, least of all party leaders in Smolensk. Deeply involved in entrenching the party-state chain of command in the 1920s, they would suddenly be branded in May 1928 not merely as political enemies but, in lurid and inflammatory terms, as drunkards and sexual degenerates. The Smolensk Affair, an all-union signal triggering a far-reaching purge and transformation of regional cadres on the eve of the collectivization of agriculture, was a prototype of what Leon Trotsky later would call a Stalinist amalgam. It was a complex political scenario or plot, prepared by trusted emissaries from the center, twisting together far-flung political and ideological imperatives into a single bombshell to unleash the passions of the masses. The Smolensk Affair provides a key for understanding power dynamics in the Stalin Revolution.

The key plenipotentiary sent from Moscow to light the fuse was Iakov Iakovlev, a senior official from the party and state watchdog organizations, the Central Control Commission (CCC) and the Worker-Peasant Inspectorate. Iakovlev, born in Poland in 1896 to Jewish schoolteachers, joined the Bolsheviks in 1913 and, after studying and making revolution in Petrograd, developed a perfect profile for his assigned task. Iakovlev's areas of expertise were the western borderlands, the peasantry, and propaganda (he served as editor of the *Peasant Newspaper* and *Poor Peasantry* from 1924 to 1928). After his behind-the-scenes puppeteering in Smolensk, his rise was meteoric: Iakovlev became a central figure in the all-union purge of the state bureaucracy in 1929 and, as head of the People's Commissariat of Agriculture from 1929 to 1934, drove the cataclysmic collectivization of agriculture that reordered the entire Soviet countryside. His mission in Smolensk was integrally linked to these two epochal transformations.

More than a month before the Smolensk Affair became public, Iakovlev, at an April 14, 1928, meeting in Moscow of the Organizational Bureau (Orgburo) of the Central Committee of the Communist Party, laid out the charges that would later be broadcast to the world in *Pravda*. He built on scandals and problems on the local level in the Smolensk party organization, particularly those suggesting corruption and "family circles," or patronage networks, which were preventing a more aggressive "class line" in the countryside. The key move Iakovlev and his small team of Moscow colleagues made away from the public eye was to intertwine sensational revelations of "sick phenomena"—drunkenness, wife swapping, and sexual "perversions"—with an indictment of the entire regional leadership for political and economic sins. These transgressions ranged from bribe-taking to "covering up failures" in the promotion (*vydvizhenie*) of new cadres of humble origins. Above all, the regional leadership was blamed for the agricultural crisis of the previous two years, during which state procurements had declined. Ominously, Smolensk party leaders, none yet named, were accused of "cozying up to kulak elements." Iakovlev compiled a list of "the most vivid facts of degradation [*razlozhenie*]" and underlined the primary importance of "revitalizing and sanitizing the party leadership." Previously classified documents from the Smolensk Affair clarify his role in fomenting an upheaval in the regional power hierarchy in preparation for Stalin's Great Break.[1]

The charges were announced in the CCC's resolution of May 9, 1928, "On the Condition of the Smolensk Organization," which ran in *Pravda* at the same political moment that the sentences from the Shakhty Trial, a show trial of "bourgeois specialists" and non-party engineers from the coal-mining region of Shakhty, were handed down in the grand Hall of Columns in Moscow. The Shakhty Trial targeted industry on the eve of the industrialization drive; the Smolensk Affair targeted a rural area on the eve of collectivization. These two cornerstones of the New Economic Policy

(NEP), which created a long-term yet unstable paradigm for institutional-izing revolution after the breakneck violence of "war communism," were compromises with "bourgeois" technical specialists in industry and with the rural population. The political firestorm of 1928 in Smolensk Region would end the *modus vivendi* with the peasantry in this quintessential "bas-tion of NEP."[2]

In April 1928, Stalin also launched a campaign of "criticism and self-criticism" that would intentionally throw into chaos the party-state chain of command painstakingly built up during the 1920s. "We have internal enemies. We have external enemies," Stalin wrote. "We can never forget this, comrades, not for a single minute." In May, Stalin made his famous speech at the Institute of Red Professors declaring that collectivizing agri-culture was the surest method of extracting grain. When Stalin proclaimed in July that the road to socialism would involve an "intensification of class struggle," he was providing a doctrinal justification for a new era of violent upheaval. Stalin's "second revolution" had begun.[3]

Back in Smolensk, Fedor Liaksutkin and Boris Tseitlin, two more CCC plenipotentiaries from Moscow tasked with the "verification of the enact-ment of Soviet democracy in Smolensk region," had been gathering mate-rial since January 1928, long before Iakovlev arrived. Both Liaksutkin and Tseitlin were experienced in the ways of the District Party Committees (Raikoms) in the region. In a report to the Orgburo for its meeting on May 14, Liaksutkin and Tseitlin followed up on Iakovlev's opening salvo by revealing that the "sick" phenomena went far deeper than imagined. Now, the emissaries from Moscow did name names. Daniil Pavliuchenko, a longtime worker-revolutionary, with twelve years of experience on the bench of the textile factory "Katushka," had been rotated into the position of first secretary of the Smolensk party in 1926 and was about as sober and honest as a top regional party official could be. He had focused on meeting targets and building the regional apparatus during the quiet years of "high NEP" in the mid-1920s. A sacrificial lamb in the widening purge, he was now accused of taking part in drunkenness and "perversion," albeit "less than others." In the spring of 1928, Pavliuchenko and embattled regional party leaders desperately pointed to a range of structural, economic di-lemmas in NEP and agriculture that explained the procurements crisis in Smolensk. It was all in vain. The entire economic crisis of NEP was pinned on their political errors of being soft on the kulaks and other enemies. In a sign of what Moscow really thought of Pavliuchenko, he was transferred to another region and his party membership restored after a mere two months, in July 1929. Liaksutkin and Tseitlin acknowledged their debt for the incriminating evidence when they thanked the Smolensk regional secret police (then called the GPU, the State Political Administration).[4]

Clearly, the Smolensk regional GPU, which answered to secret police headquarters in the Lubianka in Moscow, had long been gathering compromising information on the Smolensk party organization. In spring 1928, this *kompromat* suddenly became useful in Moscow, when a destructive operation in the center aimed to unleash long pent-up discontentment in the localities. The whole party-state apparatus, from top to bottom, would be overhauled. A week after the scandal broke, a special regional commission began a purge of Smolensk state institutions in the most "soiled" districts.[5]

What became known to historians as the Smolensk Affair was given a different name at the time: the Smolensk "abscess" (*naryv*). It might seem odd that a political scandal was named with reference to a swollen area on the body containing an accumulation of pus. But the term was so normalized through constant use that to contemporaries it no longer seemed unusual. The foul, abnormal growth, the label suggested, had to be drained, excised, and healed. This medicalized terminology suggesting bodily disease, accompanying discoveries of extravagant yet hardly unbelievable acts of sexual and political corruption designed to inflame emotions, was an unsubtle bid to elicit popular outrage and disgust. In 1929 and 1930, it became a cliché to assert that the "abscess" had not been fully drained.

The link between behavioral and political disease showcased in the Smolensk charges was not merely deeply embedded in the language of ideology. It was institutionalized in the practices of party discipline, as exemplified in the entire history of party purges, discussions of "party ethics" in the 1920s, and the methods of the CCC, a kind of inner-party disciplinary police at the forefront of persecuting the successive political oppositions of NEP. Lifestyle deviations became a valuable political resource, because pretty much everyone was guilty. Until the right time, they could remain unpunished.

Stalin was a canny, long-term planner. As both the Smolensk Affair and the Shakhty Trial played out in 1928–1929, his jigsaw puzzle was slowly filled in. The last piece lay at the very top of the power pyramid: the "right deviation" headed by Stalin's erstwhile Politburo allies Nikolai Bukharin,

Aleksei Rykov, and Mikhail Tomskii. The ground for unmasking the moderates as rightist ringleaders was carefully prepared in 1928 at the same moment that the Great Break's radical course was set for forced industrialization and militant collectivization. Since January, the turn to "extraordinary measures" of grain requisitioning added to repressive actions started the previous year against private traders, the so-called NEPmen. One can argue that Bukharin and his allies were outmaneuvered, if not checkmated, early on when they went along with both the Shakhty and Smolensk operations. In the Smolensk party organization, far removed from the power struggles in the Kremlin, cases of true oppositionists in the mid- to late 1920s were few in number, consisting of scattered individuals. But here, as elsewhere, numerous "rightists" were quickly discovered: all those who, for any reason, shrank from fully jumping on the bandwagon of the massive, frenzied "socialist offensive."[6]

The Party's leading theoretical journal, *Bol'shevik,* pointed in May 1928 to the exemplary nature of the affair by referring to the "Smolensk signal." Pavliuchenko and nine other Smolensk party leaders were put on trial. Along with the better-known Shakhty Trial, these proceedings represented the first major Soviet show trials since 1922. A wide range of more minor "abscesses," dubbed blisters (*gnoiniki*), were uncovered around the country.[7]

All that remained was to bring in the rank and file and let the unintended consequences rip. Moscow's man on the ground, Iakovlev, presided over a joint plenum of the Smolensk Regional Party Committee (Gubkom) and Regional Control Commission on May 18 and 19. Over eleven hundred party members attended, 40 percent of them production workers and others drawn from district and local activists (*aktiv*)—a term in the Soviet political lexicon denoting the most committed, enthusiastic, and promising cadres. As the abscess was poked and prodded from all angles, Iakovlev openly incited these activists against the "hierarchy" imposed by the "hopeless bureaucrat" Pavliuchenko. Iakovlev slyly implied that the activists themselves might not be "healthy," since only one of ten thousand Communists in the region had sounded the alarm. "We will purge all dirt to the end," Iakovlev declared—in the same breath mentioning something equally on his mind, the imperative of boosting Smolensk's deliveries of flax.[8]

Suddenly, unbelievably, grievances could be aired. The chauffeur from the Regional Party Committee garage provided particularly salacious details: "They drove in with wives from the districts and got so disgustingly [*do takogo bezobraziia*] drunk that they mixed up their hotel rooms, they even mixed up the wives." In the memorable description by Merle Fainsod in *Smolensk under Soviet Rule,* criticism but not yet self-criticism hung thickly in the air. This was because worried district- and regional-level cadres still attempted to defend themselves, while the party "masses" expressed outrage. A large minority demanded harsher punishments for the leaders. Suddenly all sorts of cadres began to claim, as one speaker sardonically noted, that "I too was a whistleblower." Panicked regional authorities even urged that the CCC's damning resolution on the party organization be suppressed, on the grounds that its condemnations would discredit the authority of the Party. Iakovlev, in his concluding speech, roused the hall by saying the times demanded genuine revolutionaries, not bureaucrats. He declared they were a ruling party and must carry out a "genuine break" in their work in the countryside and in governance: "If in these quiet years, former red bannermen turned from Communists into paper-pushers, we will cut [them] out . . . We can replace one Pavliuchenko with ten workers, who will be 10–100 times better than Pavliuchenko (applause)." Some others, opening themselves to charges of the very "district patriotism" under attack, challenged the notion that the conditions uncovered by Iakovlev and Tseitlin were unique to Smolensk: "Things are probably far worse in the CCC." The region, they objected, was being made a scapegoat.[9]

Those skeptics were on target. The self-criticism campaign represented an attack launched at the top to devastate entrenched authorities and provoke a frenzy of ferment at levels below. Those in charge of the campaign quickly constructed a firewall around the top party leadership, with the exception of Bukharin's "right deviation." This intervention of the center to mobilize lower levels against the middle layers of the power hierarchy was not merely about "center-periphery" relations, if that implies a two-sided conflict. Not for the first or the last time, Moscow galvanized destructive activism at the grassroots to further its own dream of greater centralization. It did so deliberately to provoke disequilibrium in previously stable power relations. Moscow's agents were specially empowered plenipotentiaries such as Iakovlev and institutions, notably the secret police, whose chain of command bypassed the Regional Party Committee. The result was a general crisis of power relations strong enough to accompany a shift from one phase of the revolution to another.[10]

Chains of Command

The Smolensk Affair, then, was a political operation that signaled the beginning of what Stalin in 1929 dubbed the Great Break. During the "revolutionary offensive" of the Russian Civil War a decade earlier, Stalin innovated what came to be known as his "Tsaritsyn methods"—concocting counterrevolutionary plots by experts and wielding terror for political and economic goals.[11] Contemporaries immediately recognized in the Great Break's forcible grain requisitioning a return to the "war communism" of 1918–1920. The two martial stages of the revolution that sandwiched the unstable stabilization of NEP were indeed related. But there was never a simple return to a status quo ante. When the crisis of NEP arrived in the late 1920s, the social, economic, and political situation in the region had been vastly transformed.

Demographically, almost half the work-capable males in Smolensk Province had been called up in World War I by 1917. The effects of total war, revolution, civil war, and grain requisitioning, not to mention typhus, influenza, and migration east, reversed the steady population growth of the early twentieth century. By 1920, the population in the region had declined from its 1913 high point by 165,000 to 2.292 million. The same was true of the region's small urban population, which decreased from 9.47 percent in 1913 to 6.16 percent in 1920 (or about 180,000 urban residents, according to 1920 data). Smolensk remained an overwhelmingly agrarian region, with a 9.47 percent urbanization rate in 1913 compared to 17.4 percent in European Russia as a whole. The Bolsheviks' dilemma of building the proletarian dictatorship in a sea of peasants, a problem that Vladimir Lenin had tried to solve by capturing the state with a party vanguard and hoping world revolution would follow, was even more acute in a region with an industrial labor force of only fifteen thousand to twenty-five thousand. That figure included cottage industries and small industrial plants closer to the countryside.[12] In Smolensk Region, the Party was a ruling sliver searching for a base in a small minority.

From the early years of Soviet power, the small and flimsy Communist Party was very suspicious of its own members. The first provincial purge occurred from February to May 1919, with "flying auditors"—groups of three to five plenipotentiaries from the Regional Party Committee, totaling thirty-two and headed by a Central Committee member—who weeded out those held responsible for crimes among party, soviet, and military organs. The Party was hardly the only source of authority in the civil war years, and it had less clout on the ground than the "extraordinary" organs of power, the Regional Military-Revolutionary Committees (Gubrevkoms) and the provincial Cheka, the protocols of which show the agency was concerned above all with deserters, bandits, speculators, theft of government property, and political crimes such as "discrediting Soviet power." Indeed, one Communist and Red Army political commissar wrote the Regional Party Committee in June 1920 that local party cells existed only "on paper" and that the population looked on the requisitioning Bolsheviks as bandits or worse. Grain requisitioning made sowing plummet by spring 1921, as peasant rebels clashed with Red Army troops. But the bony hand of famine followed in the wake of an aggressive agrarian attack, something carried out on a far greater scale a decade later.[13]

Against this backdrop, it is possible to appreciate the magnitude of the achievement in Soviet state-building in the 1920s. Lenin had argued in 1921 that in the absence of international proletarian revolution, socialism in Russia could be achieved only by compromising with the peasantry. At the Tenth Party Congress, which ratified the NEP, Lenin pushed for compromise with petty capitalism of the kind based on small-scale trade. First, to achieve a desperately needed economic reconstruction, then as a long-term strategy for growing into socialism, NEP made a series of moderate social and economic compromises—with the peasantry, the non-party specialists, and the partially restored private sector. Politically, however, there was no strategic retreat from building the party-state and the cultural-ideological revolutionary drives taking place primarily within the Party. This was the inner cultural revolution of NEP, which would be militarized and directed outward when the floodgates opened at the end of the 1920s. The vanguard party had not been forged in order to ride into socialism on a "peasant nag."[14]

In the 1920s, the provinces run by fully forged institutions at the regional level were reliant on subordinate levels of power that became increasingly, even outrageously, imperfect down the line. If the regional-level organs of power were fully functioning by the early 1920s, institutions at the district (*uezd*) and especially county (*volost'*) levels "did not fully possess complete power in their territories." Still, the glass could be seen as half full: as opposed to the chaos of 1920–1921, a rough-and-ready chain of command had been consolidated. Party officials took advantage of a mid-1920s interlude of calm and gradualism, as opposed to the constant "atmosphere of crisis and urgency" that Fainsod observed of the Stalinist 1930s. With the economic recovery of NEP, the region's population surged 23.49 percent between 1920 and 1926. In the same period, urbanization increased from 6.16 percent to 9.3 percent.[15]

Vasilii's Village

The remarkable path of a lifelong observer of one Smolensk village began as a result of books, a fire, and a revolution. Vasilii Maslennikov, born in 1911 to peasants from the village of Filimony, centrally located within the Smolensk Region, spent the first six years of his life in Moscow because his father, Terentii, good with horses, found work as a horse cart driver delivering small packages for the Alekseevskii Military Academy. Maslennikov described his father as taciturn and obedient, qualities valued by the infantry officers who ran the institution. Terentii had completed three years of school, and Maslennikov's mother, Evfimiia, was illiterate, laboring at the school as a laundress. But the young Maslennikov taught himself to read by the age of five and, as it turned out, he loved it. Against the odds, reading scraps of newspapers and any other printed material he could find, Maslennikov became highly literate.[16]

The fire and the revolution came in 1917. During the December uprising in Moscow that followed the Bolshevik Revolution in October, the area around the Alekseevskii school was the site of some of the fiercest fighting between the Reds and conservative cadets. Collateral damage sparked a fire that destroyed the Maslennikovs' shack and with it the family's stored supply of food, a catastrophe that would shape young Maslennikov's life course. Through spring 1918, the boy frequently went hungry and begged for food, until his parents, whom he described as "fundamentally peasants" by nature, saw opportunity in the land seizures of the peasant revolution, and they returned to their home village. Such were the twists of fate that made Vasilii Maslennikov a commentator on the Smolensk countryside throughout the rockiest period of the twentieth century.[17]

After 1918, Maslennikov was raised largely by his grandfather Ignat, a "supporter of the old ways" who could piece together the words of his only book, the Bible, and, Maslennikov recalled, "instilled in me the notion that

Soviet power came from the devil." Ignat, born under serfdom, was thrifty and never touched vodka. He revered God and the landowner. Ignat worked a sizable tract of land outside the village of Kholmets (later merged with Filimony), a homestead he got when separating from the peasant redistributional land commune during the late imperial reforms of Petr Stolypin. In a manner typical of NEP-era Smolensk, Vasilii Maslennikov's village became dominated by homesteads in the 1920s.[18]

At first Maslennikov was teased as a Muscovite (he said *papa* and not *tata,* as in the local dialect, closer to Belarusian), but then an aunt taught him to speak in the rural way. He quickly became accepted as a local insider, living without books, newspapers, or radio from age seven to eleven. He did not go to a local school, because there was none. "People here still lived by the old ways," Maslennikov remembered, "quietly, with bread, milk, and lard." Finally, his family and three others with school-age children donated land so a local school could be built, and he began primary school. In the mid- to late 1920s, initially under the influence of anti-religious, activist young female schoolteachers, he began a second transformation away from his grandfather's influence. Maslennikov became a participant in the Komsomol and other Soviet initiatives, ultimately ending up as a party member, history teacher, and critical observer of both Stalinism and Nazism. It was this unusual, dual status as insider and outsider, as well as the disillusionments he harbored against internal and external colonization by two regimes, that led Maslennikov to devote much of his postwar life to a memoir chronicling the transformations he witnessed in his home village. As it turned out, the experiences of one ordinary, typical village from the 1920s to the 1940s were nothing short of extraordinary.[19]

Maslennikov's village was hardly a distant backwater. It was located a few miles from the railway town of Glinka, named in 1907 in honor of the composer, born nearby. Glinka itself was less than forty miles southeast of Smolensk and about fourteen miles west of the town of Yelnya. But Maslennikov's recollections of everyday life in the 1920s suggest how distinct and separate the peasantry remained within Soviet society. The village consisted of a series of extended households living in huts that were surrounded by individual homesteads. The huts did not have drapes, and in the evening one could see women inside spinning flax and men making sandals. On holidays, the women visited one another, recounting stories to the girls and singing songs; the men gathered separately to play cards, remember the war, and tell off-color anecdotes. Maslennikov never saw anyone with a watch, and for a "long time" the new Soviet calendar was ignored. Instead of the month and day, the villagers tracked time through the cycle of religious holidays. There were six churches within a few miles of the village, and as a boy Maslennikov knew all of them. The local priest, whose authority was great, kept track of improper, "godless" behavior.

The peasantry was not just an enormous, and far from monolithic, social mass that had strong regional variations and had been in accelerating motion especially since the mid-nineteenth century. It was a repository for a deeply rooted culture centered in the village. If urban Bolsheviks saw only backwardness and the "idiocy of rural life," party members who had rejected their own rural backgrounds could be even more visceral in condemning village culture.[20]

In the early years of NEP, noble lands expropriated in the rural revolution were now available and the assault of Stalinist collectivization was not yet on the horizon. During the rise of the homestead movement in Smolensk, there was some dissatisfaction and occasionally violent conflicts occurred over the division of land. Even though these disagreements often dragged out, they were adjudicated locally. In general, Maslennikov's village experienced greater prosperity after 1922. Maslennikov's father built a larger hut, and the family added land and livestock. Maslennikov remembered NEP as a most favorable time, when in the absence of compulsion his fellow villagers "willingly attempted to live better than they lived before."[21]

The Soviets notoriously used class analysis to understand the peasantry, dividing it up into kulaks, middle peasants, and poor peasants. Not only were these categories open to political manipulation, they ignored the cyclical fluctuations of extended households as they expanded or shrank. Despite some new political divisions, the rural revolution also largely strengthened peasant communities, as in a time of upheaval most peasants clung "all the more tenaciously to customary and conservative notions of household, family, marriage, and belief in order."[22]

Even as the new regime applied its class categories to the peasantry, ironically, the revolution produced a major leveling of socioeconomic differences as poorer and wealthier segments shrank. Peasant households in Maslennikov's immediate vicinity were now little differentiated: the area was dominated by homesteads and a broad swathe of "middle" peasants.

According to Maslennikov, in the seventy-five households in the vicinity of Filimony, only one used hired (*batrak*) labor in the summer, a key sign of prosperity. Elsewhere, however, hired labor was common and used not only by prosperous peasants. Official statistics for Smolensk Region in 1927 divided peasant households into 26.1 percent poor peasants, 71.3 percent middle peasants, and 2.6 percent kulaks. But the data, gathered in part at poor peasant meetings, was arbitrary and politicized from the outset. When these poor peasants identified "kulaks" at these meetings, they drew on long memories of household levels of prosperity from before the revolution that were not necessarily current. Attitudes toward Soviet power or levels of antipathy toward "speculation" could also factor into the judgment. What led middle peasants to become poor, Maslennikov noted about his own area, was when brothers split a father's household and became "weakened" or when an illness or death led to catastrophe. Some poor peasants took pride that they were the social "support" (*opora*) for Soviet power. Maslennikov remembered them with disdain and without sympathy: "They lived poorly either out of stupidity or out of following the traditions of their parents."[23]

Peasants and Cadres

Not only from the vantage of Maslennikov's village, but on the district and regional levels of power, the gathering storm could scarcely be discerned. This was because regional officials became skilled at diverting Moscow's priorities or merging them with their own. The July 26, 1926, Regional Party Committee meeting did discuss expectations for industrialization and the kulak danger, but the resolution on the first issue boiled down to raising educational budgets and the second to efforts to refrain from overburdening agronomists. As long as the chain of command appeared firm and the economy was doing reasonably well before 1927, Moscow took no unusual interest in Smolensk. A year before the lid blew on the Smolensk Affair, in 1927, the regional party conference blithely ignored a raft of problems that included an acute housing shortage and glaring weaknesses of the Party in the countryside.[24]

The agricultural downturn was related to a structural deterioration of economic relations between town and country (the "scissors crisis"). When the decline hit, along with the war scare of 1927, the glass could be seem more plausibly as at least half empty. Smolensk's bastion of NEP had considerable weaknesses. Above all, the Communist Party remained shockingly thin in the countryside. The rough-and-ready chain of command constructed in the 1920s, already shaky at the county level, essentially stopped there. The Party had virtually no institutional foothold in the village. In the 1920s, the rural soviets, or *sel'sovety*, "were forced to share power with the *skhody*," the village assemblies. These traditional organs of peasant self-governance even commanded their own, independently raised budgets, insofar as peasant households contributed funds to trusted elders for expenditures on firefighting, schools, and bridges. Sometimes the assemblies even replaced the rural soviets. Outside authority largely appeared in the guise of a parade of plenipotentiaries and periodic campaigns. Those conducting the campaigns were almost always outsiders, since nearly all party members in the region lived in cities and towns. Smolensk's especially low urbanization rates explain the fact that the overall number of party members was far less than the Soviet average (as late as 1940, on the eve of war, party members made up 1.04 percent of the population in the Smolensk Region, almost half the all-union figure). Class analysis may have reigned in the Soviet theory of politics, but in practice plenipotentiaries and the campaign mode were the most fundamental building blocks of Smolensk under Soviet rule.[25]

As the crisis of the late 1920s would starkly reveal, moreover, low-level state and economic officials in the countryside who made the system work were themselves often prosperous peasants and non-party local notables of rural origin. In far-flung rural areas, local state and economic officeholders mediated between local and peasant interests and those of higher authorities. Strikingly, the overwhelming majority of rural members of the Communist Party remained individual farmers even at the end of the 1920s and did not enter the collective farms. One of the sins ominously uncovered by the Smolensk Affair was "kulakization" (*okulachivanie*)—the term that preceded the notorious "dekulakization" denoting mass deportation of wealthier peasants and others opposed to forced collectivization in 1930–1931. "Kulakization" referred to wealthy peasants' corrupting of party members.[26]

The small inroads made by the Party in the countryside hardly meant, however, that the world of the peasantry had not changed dramatically in the 1920s. In many areas where peasant land seizures during the revolution had swept away the effects of the late imperial Stolypin reforms, the land commune (*obshchina*) reincorporated independent family homesteads (*khutory*) or enclosures (*otruby*) that were still part of the village but had separated from communal land tenure during what Petr Stolypin termed his "wager on the strong." The Smolensk Region, in contrast, embraced the homestead over the commune after 1917, becoming a bastion of *khutorizat-siia,* or "homesteadization."

"What Stolypin had failed to accomplish before the revolution," in the words of the Smolensk historian Evgenii Kodin, "was achieved by NEP." Kodin's data for the five years between 1922 and 1926 shows that homesteads dominated agriculture in Smolensk, constituting 50.3 percent of land tenure—as opposed to 18.9 percent enclosures and 14.8 percent villages with the traditional peasant land commune. In certain areas, the homestead dominated at much higher rates. At the central level of power in Moscow, agricultural policy making in the 1920s was marked by mixed signals, and in regional areas an acute paucity of Communists of rural background persisted. Smolensk peasants continued to favor the homestead over the commune, the tiny number of new collective farms, and other forms of land tenure.[27]

Crisis in the Countryside

While the consolidated homesteads initially showed a number of agricultural advantages over the commune, they were a far cry from the large-scale, mechanized agriculture that Soviet modernizers promoted. By the mid-1920s, moreover, homesteads became a victim of their own success. As more and more households wanted their own homestead, and as households divided and their number grew, *khutorizatsiia* began to interfere with productivity. Grain yields in Smolensk were lower than in the rich Black Earth regions. While Smolensk had made strides in livestock, it was known for its flax, which could be made into linens and exported. The procurement crisis in 1927, caused by crop failures and peasant reluctance to sell grain at low state prices, sent state grain procurements in the country as a whole into a tailspin. At the end of 1927, local leader Pavliuchenko reported a shortfall of grain deliveries from Smolensk one and a half times greater than the previous year. Flax deliveries from Smolensk also declined precipitously, in no small part because state prices for flax were also destructively low.[28]

Pavliuchenko's analysis of the "extremely serious" condition of the "grain market" for the regional leadership in 1927 was soundly economic, even apolitical. He noted the lack of manufactured goods for peasants to buy and the need to boost low state prices for grain. None of the eighteen points he raised made a single reference to kulaks or class conflict within the peasantry. This is why he was crushed by Stalin, who personally led the way to treating the procurement crisis as a political-ideological crusade, with kulaks and NEPmen enabled by unforgivably weak local leadership. Stalin shook up the central state agricultural leadership and, as the Smolensk Affair was being prosecuted in spring 1928, purged it of populist (former Socialist Revolutionaries), socially "alien," and "rightist" experts and personnel. Suddenly, homesteads were out; "extraordinary measures," another name for violence unleashed by the center, were in.[29]

The particular, top-heavy power structure of the Soviet system, so centralized in Moscow and so weak at the local level, explains much about the shift from the relative stasis of mid-1920s NEP to the coercive revolutionary tsunami of the Great Break. The center rotated in regional-level leaders frequently in order to prevent them from forming "clans" or "family ties" that blunted Moscow's influence. In Smolensk in the 1920s, Regional Party Committee members changed every two years on average, and Soviet Regional Executive Committee (Gubispolkom) leaders even more frequently. But this hardly changed anything. Regional-level cadres had common interests in deflecting pressures emanating from Moscow. They brought with them their own "teams" and networks and, in turn, pressured the level of the power hierarchy below them, the districts. Effective governance was also hampered by chronically low educational levels. Throughout the prewar period, the overwhelming majority even of regional leading cadres had only a primary education.[30] The lower levels of the power structure, with little leverage on the ground, especially in the countryside, in turn blamed or evaded their superiors.

In such a political system, it was not easy to enact major change. Empowering special plenipotentiaries to break through was a ubiquitous feature of Soviet power from the first. When things began to falter it was far easier to blame hostile sabotage than the intractable dilemmas created by the Soviet system itself. The "district patriotism" (*raionnyi patriotizm*) and protection of "one's own" (*svoi*) that occupied a central place in the gallery of political sicknesses the Stalinist leadership concocted in the Smolensk Affair were not invented phenomena. Nor were they merely about gaining material privileges or the corrupt practices of an emergent new elite. They were survival tactics, a defense evolved against constant and effective pressures from above. A central paradox of the Soviet system was that its everyday administrative and economic operations were highly ineffective, but in moments of crisis and the harsh glare of central prioritization, those pressures could be transformed into powerful mobilization tools.[31] Building socialism seemed to require, at least to Stalin and his team, nothing less than a cataclysmic onslaught.

Up from Backwardness

The young Maslennikov's attraction to Soviet power would shape his response to the coming upheaval in the countryside. Why would someone from his thrifty, religious background join the Party's cause just when it was gearing up to destroy his world? One reason was his early literacy and his education after 1925, which put him in contact with Komsomol members and young teachers who organized civic activities against the local priest, religion, and backwardness. One such person was Efrosin'ia Ivanovna, who was especially energetic and delivered fiery revolutionary speeches.[32]

Reading Maslennikov's memoir between the lines, there is compelling evidence that the young man's receptiveness to the work of the devil, as his grandfather called Soviet power, stemmed from the allure of urban civilization and, ironically, the greater access it brought to consumer goods. Among the most salient divisions in the peasantry were generational differences. The older peasants were satisfied with homesteads and land, but Maslennikov and his friends wanted the fruits of a more urban life, which were hardly at all available. Small-scale private trade legalized by NEP had led to the appearance of three private stores in Glinka: two owned by Jewish entrepreneurs, Itkin and Sonin, and the third by a Russian, Pronin. They were better stocked than the state cooperatives and had no lines, unlike the stores in Smolensk, where Maslennikov periodically went to the giant bazaar. Maslennikov's personal dream of acquiring a bicycle, which was completely unobtainable, preoccupied him not only as a youth but throughout the prewar years.[33]

Material goods were only one manifestation of a new, non-backward life. Even more important was "culturedness." Perhaps because of his Moscow childhood, Maslennikov was highly attuned to the differences in dress, speech, accent, behavior, and even gait that distinguished countrified youth from their urban counterparts. Maslennikov articulated a decidedly negative take on quintessentially peasant manners and behavior, especially among males, hinting that even when young he remained something of an outsider. Rural girls were shy and reserved; the boys, with their jovial mien, lacked all social grace. Peasant men he described as simply backward, including his very close childhood friends who never learned to read, spoke crudely, picked fights, and cultivated a type of bravado he perceived as typically peasant. Maslennikov was attracted to certain families in the village who prized education and seemed a bit more "cultured." In particular, he was drawn to two girls at the peasant school, Verochka and Zhenia, who he thought minimized their country "defects" (*nedostatki*) more than any of the others did. Even so, three of his four closest childhood friends remained illiterate and became collective farmers in the 1930s. Maslennikov was drawn to the Soviet project not as a convert but because he saw it as a counterweight to village backwardness.[34]

Promotion in the Provinces

Improbably, few words in the Soviet lexicon became better known among experts in Soviet history during the late Cold War than *vydvizhenie,* commonly translated as "social promotion" or "social mobility." These definitions are somewhat misleading, since *vydvizhenie* was just as centrally a form of political promotion. The phenomenon's importance comes from the discovery that far-reaching promotion policies launched at the start of the Stalin Revolution explained the long-term emergence of a new Soviet elite that owed its rise and loyalty to the dictator. The narrative we have inherited about *vydvizhenie,* however, has been unwittingly Moscow-centric. What was left out of the story was the immediate dynamics of a thoroughgoing replacement of the party-state apparatus at the regional and district levels. Promotion policies in Smolensk, in comparison to long-term fashioning of an all-union elite, were low-level and sudden. In the classic work on the topic, Sheila Fitzpatrick wrote that *vydvizhenie* "in retrospect must surely be seen as a very bold and imaginative policy which did in fact serve to consolidate and legitimize the regime."[35] Especially at the local and regional levels, however, promotion policies produced catastrophic, unforeseen political effects flowing from the meltdown of competence and expertise.

At the all-union level, the phenomenon of *vydvizhenie* came to stand in as a shorthand for movement into a large cohort of politically loyal, culturally conservative cadres that remained in power until almost the end of the USSR: the "Brezhnev generation." These *vydvizhentsy*, or promoted cadres, who were hastily educated primarily in engineering during the first Five-Year Plan, suddenly inherited dizzyingly high positions vacated during the Great Terror and became the dominant cohort in the party-state elite for decades to come. Fitzpatrick's work, pioneered mostly in Moscow archives, was so resonant because it elucidated arguments over the Soviet "ruling class" that went back to Trotsky's 1936 *Revolution Betrayed* and Milovan Djilas's 1957 *New Class.*[36]

Stalin and Viacheslav Molotov, his closest ally in the party leadership, originated a far-reaching policy in the Central Committee Secretariat around April–July 1928 in which "over 100,000 workers and Communists from the factories and apparats were mobilized and sent to higher technical schools." This plan, aiming at nothing less than forging a new ruling stratum, coincided with the same political moment as the Shakhty Trial and the Smolensk Affair, which set off attacks on old elites.[37]

The thoroughgoing renewal of cadres envisaged by Stalin and Molotov in Moscow not only drove the long-term, generational transformation of the elite *nomenklatura*. It had an immediate and jolting effect on the power structures of the party-state in regions like Smolensk. The preoccupation of students of Soviet politics with "elite" promotion may have derived from Fitzpatrick's original definition of a "promoted cadre": "A *vydvizhenets* may be defined as an adult student entering higher education after at least five years work experience. The term was normally applied to persons who had not completed secondary education and were of lower-class origin." The history of lower-level, provincial promotion policies suggests this definition was incomplete. No one in the late 1920s, least of all the promoted Smolensk cadres themselves, would have limited the phenomenon to higher or even secondary education. The far-reaching transformation initiated by Stalin's grand vision was as related to regional cadres as to the new elite, to agriculture as to industry, to the Smolensk Affair as to the Shakhty Trial.[38]

Iakovlev, the chief plenipotentiary sent from Moscow to manage the Smolensk Affair, included "insufficiencies in the promotion [*vydvizhenie*] of cadres" in his April 1928 list of the sins of the regional party organization. The new regional leadership, highly motivated to prove itself "healthy," plunged into the process of remaking regional officialdom. The promotion campaign immediately elevated 779 cadres between June and December 1928 into "responsible" positions. Over the next several years, as the pace increased, the promotion drive encompassed the entire gamut of party, state, economic, and trade union bureaucracies. By 1931, the number of promoted cadres in the Western Region reached about four thousand.[39]

Qualities of competence and cautious concern for prosperity belonged to a less militant era. A prime goal in promoting the new personnel was to eradicate narrow pragmatism (*deliachestvo*), understood as a "bureaucratized" attitude that impeded the "battle for the socialist reconstruction of the economy." A positive Central Committee resolution from July 5, 1929, about the successful Smolensk campaign, published in *Izvestiia,* once again made Smolensk into a "showcase [*pokazatel'nym*] for the entire country."[40]

The "battle" for cadres was part of a long-term war, but its effects were even more drastic on the periphery than in the center. At the higher echelons of power, Stalin's new elite underwent several years of breakneck training and took a further, deliberate push upward during the Great Terror before rising to the top in the mid- to late 1930s. Those promoted in the Smolensk drive starting in 1928 were immediately thrust into new positions, despite their desperate need of general education and basic training to address catastrophically low levels of literacy. Privileging loyalty and zeal dealt the regime a self-inflicted blow. The vast majority received training that was a far cry even from the watered-down higher education in new technical institutes and the like.[41]

In August 1929, the Smolensk Regional Party Committee gathered a group of *vydvizhentsy* to talk about their experiences moving from the factory to the office. Comrade Stepanova, who was promoted into the Textile Union, spoke emotionally about her difficulties: "I arrived almost completely illiterate, I could only sign my signature. I got myself a teacher . . . [I] studied a month and a half and learned a bit . . . When they promote you, they say all arrangements have been made, we will give you everything, and when they take you they give nothing, they throw papers at you and say look at all the directives and study them . . . One time I was crying, simply because it was hurtful that they promoted me when I was incapable and they demand[ed] a lot." Stepanova found a patron, a woman named Makurova, who taught her how to underline important passages in documents as a way of processing their meaning. Stepanova went to a general education course, one of hundreds of special courses set up for rapid training: "They show you all sorts of circles, hooks, and diagrams, and what the devil do I need those diagrams and circles for, I cannot become an engineer. I need general education courses, I have to learn reading and writing and arithmetic . . . I copy down the diagrams and circles from the blackboard, but when they ask about them I know nothing." Training overall was chaotic. Stepanova's course included those who had finished nine years of schooling and anyone who had merely gone through a "liquidation of illiteracy center" (*likpunkt*). "It is outrageous," Stepanova fumed. Her definition of success, achieved only after a year of misery, was to be able to "fulfill the directives that were given to [her]" and to "be useful in a certain way to the state."[42]

The sense of inadequacy of those struggling to keep up with their new jobs runs like a red thread through the hundreds of pages of documents on the promotion campaign. For one worker, used to moving around on the job at a proletarian bastion, the Katushka factory in Smolensk, "it was terrible to sit in a chair." A certain Babaev, promoted to assistant to the regional-level public prosecutor, was given an impossible workload: to receive up to fifty people a day and then wade through paperwork at night. Personnel shortages at the Procuracy had seemingly made it impossible even for the most energetic enthusiast to handle the job. But Babaev did not break down and cry, like Stepanova. Instead, he boldly asserted, "If we are going to frequently look up things in the legal code, it would be splitting hairs [*bukvoedstvo*]." Legal expertise was a waste of time. All one really needed was "proletarian instinct" in order to determine the nature of a case.[43]

The cocky Babaev, with his revolutionary embrace of class politics over the niceties of expertise in order to cut the Gordian knot of his new position, fit the profile of the kind of cadre the promotion campaign actively sought. Directives constantly spoke about "active and authoritative" cadres who would energetically prosecute the drive to socialism. In the typical campaign mode, the Regional Party Committee measured all progress in terms of percentages: Klintsovskii District had fulfilled the Regional Party Committee's plan for the number of promoted cadres by 64 percent as of July 15, 1929, while Viazemskii District had only reached 45 percent. As with poods of grain or tons of steel, hitting the quotas for sociopolitical promotion became the key indicator of success. In theory, large meetings of workers were supposed to discuss and acclaim candidates, but "administrative" promotion was common. So was simple mobilization by party cells. Reports sent to Moscow or public pronouncements held up the promotion drive as a successful model, while internal discussions bemoaned "campaign-administrative" methods.[44]

The promotion campaign, reshaping the state bureaucracy and economic apparatus and also the Party, was supposed to "decisively" target poor peasants, women, and non-Communists and also party members for higher positions. But the Regional Party Committee put lower-level party organizations in charge of the campaign, which appears to be one reason that recruitment of all those other groups remained "completely insufficient." Party organizations were able to rely on a rough-and-ready mobilization machine that reached down to party cells. In Roslavl County (okrug) in mid-1929, for example, at first an ad hoc and then a standing party commission was in charge of the promotion drive. In the entire area, only one peasant, one collective farm worker, and one woman were promoted. All the others promoted were urban men and political loyalists. Overall, rapid promotion in Smolensk in 1927–1931 boosted the political promotion of party members. The party contingent among those promoted jumped from 60 to 80 percent, with the sharpest rise in 1929.[45] Characteristically, the Communist Party was the only organization capable of mobilization in a time of severe dislocation.

If fortune favored the cocky Babaevs over the despairing Stepanovas, it raises the question of how the late 1920s conjuncture molded a new type of Stalinist cadre. At least in the short term, those who rode the wave of revolutionary chaos, disregarding technicalities and expertise, had a clear advantage. At the same time, fulfilling and overfulfilling orders at all costs may have seemed the simplest political survival tactic. In the event, lower-level cadres who committed "excesses" (peregibshchiki) were always blamed by the center when things got out of control. But it was the policies emanating from the top that made out-of-control excesses a reasonable strategy for inexperienced, severely underqualified parvenus in the first place. The making of Stalin's new elite came at the price of profound instability, devaluation of expertise, and a predisposition for coercion and subservience.

Fueling the Fire: The 1929 Purge and 1930 Reorganization

The acceleration of the promotion drive corresponded in 1929 with the purge of the Soviet state apparatus. Both processes were framed in "class" terms: one was designed to elevate allies, the other to eliminate "alien elements." Both ended up kneecapping specialists with rare qualifications and expertise.

A special regional purge commission was formed one week after the discovery of the Smolensk "abscess" to work in the most "contaminated" or "infested" districts. This medicalized language evoked sickness, infection, and infestation for a reason. It was intended to justify and facilitate the elimination of "socially alien elements," meaning former nobles, landowners, merchants, clergy, or, far more generally, white-collar personnel of intelligentsia or relatively elite backgrounds.[46]

What did the inflammatory language of class infestation really mean in practice? In the Smolensk aviation factory in August 1929, the sixty-four members of the technical-administrative personnel were deemed "contaminated" (*zasoren*) not only on the grounds that they were former officers or priests, but on the political grounds that they were connected to the Provisional Government or had belonged to Jewish socialist parties other than the Bolsheviks. Class and political categories became interchangeable. Combing through autobiographical questionnaires and interrogating suspects about them was the easiest and most mechanical way of purging, and in Smolensk it became a quick, default method for purge commissions. "Of what am I guilty, that I am the daughter of a former trader?" cried a peasant activist removed from a trade union. Up to that moment, she had very likely been loyally pro-Soviet. Mass participation and public pressure was a key part of the process. Purge commissions within institutions were encouraged to bring in large numbers of activists as audiences to unmask those guilty of covering up their "alien" backgrounds—which in at least some cases included members of the Worker-Peasant Inspectorate conducting purges. Those with exemplary social and political records could still be guilty of "bureaucratism," that is, opposition to the purge.[47]

It is likely that many employees who had been tolerated during NEP but were now targeted for dubious social and political backgrounds represented precisely that pool of qualified experts rare everywhere, but especially difficult to find in the regional context. The 1929 purge greatly contributed to the chaos of the Great Break moment. There was massive turnover in local state governance as a result, and in some districts, rural ones first and foremost, work became "almost paralyzed." At the height of the assault on cultural and educational institutions, a Komsomol firebrand with a middle school education was put in charge of the Smolensk Regional Museum, only to declare that a collection of old relics from the past did not deserve to exist.[48]

Losing one's position in a purge, in a fashion no less significant than gaining one in a promotion, carried significant economic and material implications far beyond the salary involved. Those purged in 1929 in the most severe "first category" lost not only their jobs, but their pensions and their apartments. The political stigma of purge came precisely at a time of plummeting standards of living, housing shortages, and the end of the private sector of NEP. Some administrators with high qualifications became manual laborers. For party members and those with party-approved (*nomenklatura*) positions, access to foodstuffs and manufactured goods, both very scarce during the lean years of industrialization and famine, was the most obvious way political and material well-being was intertwined in the Soviet system.[49]

It is true that the Soviet system privileged ideological and political considerations over purely economic rationales in many ways. But for local-level elites who stood to gain through the high-stakes political dramas of the initial phase of Stalinism, political-ideological and economic status could reinforce one another. Officials and party members in the region were hardly well-off in the early 1930s, but they were supplied above the norm. In the famine years of 1932–1933, a separate canteen fed 444 party activists in the city of Smolensk, and 247 received special rations in stores. District-level party figures constantly on the move came to expect produce, consumer goods, housing, and services as a prerequisite as much as a perk.[50]

The Making of the Western Region

The rapid-fire succession of political shocks—the Smolensk Affair, the promotion campaign, and the 1929 purge—continued with an even more massive administrative upheaval in mid-1929. On March 15, 1929, the creation of a new Western Region was announced, centered in the city of Smolensk and incorporating the former Smolensk, Briansk, and Kaluga Provinces along with parts of Tver' and Leningrad Provinces. With one stroke, the territory administered from the city of Smolensk was expanded from the 1920s Smolensk Province, with a population of about 2.3 million people, into the Western Region, with over 6 million people. The reorganization aimed to turn a primarily agricultural region into an "agricultural-industrial" base, in particular for producing and processing, as it was envisaged, as much as 50 percent of the USSR's flax.

If Stalinist forced modernization was one motivation behind the creation of the giant new territory, revamping the political system, the heart of which was cadres, was the other. Major opportunities for cadre appointments and cementing loyalties were inextricably attached to the administrative upheaval. Ivan Rumiantsev, the forty-three-year-old Old Bolshevik who was tapped as regional party first secretary, would oversee the next two stages of the revolution, a violent, massive "socialist offensive" dominated by a far-reaching calamity—the assault on the countryside during the collectivization drive—and a mid-1930s interlude of consolidation, stabilization, and entrenchment. Together, these two periods created the interlocking parts of an emergent Soviet system in the provinces—a society in which politics, economics, ideology, and culture were intertwined.

Taking charge of the giant Western Region in 1929 would catapult Rumiantsev into a dominant position in regional governance between the Great Break and the Great Terror. As he moved to mobilize a new army of cadres for the Great Break assault, he was able to cement his own patronage network and dominate Smolensk politics for the next eight years as the quintessential "little Stalin." In short, thoroughgoing administrative-territorial reorganization was the handmaiden of the new Stalinist order in the region.[51]

Scrambling the power hierarchy to squeeze out and transform the middle, regional level of power in a pincer action from above and from below was a quintessentially Stalinist power play. This political battle plan

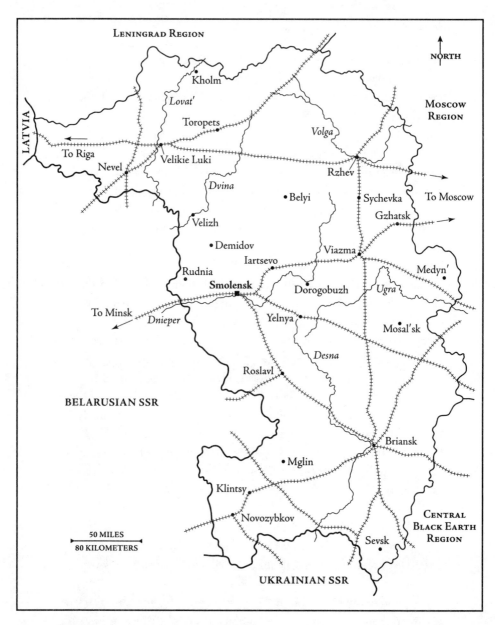

Western Region, 1929–1937.

was formulated in order to launch the collectivization cataclysm, the industrialization drive, and the making of a new elite. But the plan's success was also predicated on triggering mass fervor, which marked the first phases of Stalinism. It was reliant on the appropriation of slices of power by local activists, exemplified by the ideal of ruthlessly energetic cadres in the new army of the socialist offensive. This fundamental feature is what made the Stalin Revolution revolutionary. A decade before the war, millions of lives were reshaped by an ersatz or political war, the front lines of which were also continental in scope.

Vasilii Maslennikov was just one of those millions who struggled to reorient their lives in the wake of this upheaval and never truly succeeded. But his course was also affected by the meteoric rise of a close childhood friend from his village, Timofei Kuprikov, into the upper echelons of Stalin's new elite. This fellow villager, like Maslennikov, was a reader drawn to education and the opportunities that joining the Communist Party could open up. Kuprikov, energetic, outgoing, and curious, finished the same school for peasant youth that Maslennikov did. Then, Kuprikov was accepted into the nine-grade school in the nearby town of Yelnya. This created a path for him to Perm University, where he studied chemistry, and, later, prestigious party schools, Central Committee work, and an array of dizzyingly high postwar positions leading up to his appointment as deputy head of the Central Committee's propaganda department in 1965. Maslennikov, in a consequential twist, was rejected from the nine-grade school, making his educational path far more difficult. He blamed the setback on the fact that there were not enough spaces in the school for "middle peasants" like himself. For decades to come, Maslennikov would collect newspaper clippings about Kuprikov. The successes of his highly placed childhood companion remained a symbol of what might have been. Maslennikov's rise did allow him to escape rural backwardness, but ultimately only as a local schoolteacher almost always in the vicinity of his home village. Cultivating a special interest in history, Maslennikov found another calling as chronicler and critic of the historic upheavals he experienced.[52]

2

COLONIZING THE COUNTRYSIDE

AT THE HEIGHT OF Stalin's Great Break in 1930, the drive to force peasants into collective farms came to resemble the assault of an invading army. This was a domestic war spearheaded by the political police and waged in the name of building socialism. Anna Tsvetkova was three years old when agents of the Soviet secret police, then called the United State Political Administration (OGPU), burst into her village hut. They roared at her mother: "You are leaving, bitch! Get ready quickly." The innocent toddler piped up: "But Uncle, my mother's name is not bitch, you should call her Aunt Polia." The agents smiled. But harsh treatment continued as the family was taken to a building in the city of Viazma. It turned out to be a holding place for so-called special settlers slated for exile in the Urals, where most Smolensk "kulaks" were deported. The label justifying class war in the countryside, the centerpiece of Stalinist internal colonization, was flexible. Tsvetkova and her family were hardly wealthy. They owned a cow named Neshka, a horse named Bor'ka, and five chickens. The target of this "socialist offensive" was not a foreign country, but the rural interior.[1]

After much investigation later in life, Tsvetkova discovered that the years of suffering that began that day were collateral damage from the attack on the village order. Her family became the victim of a grudge from over a decade earlier. Her mother had feuded with a woman whose brother served in the Viazma OGPU. Now, that secret police agent had instructed his forces to cross the border from the Viazemskii District to Tsvetkova's village, which lay outside the directorate's jurisdiction, to abduct his sister's old enemy. When OGPU officials at the detention site learned the family had been taken from another district, they told Tsvetkova's mother to write a statement. There was no paper or pencil for her to use.[2]

A high degree of arbitrariness was a common feature of militarized Soviet violence in the name of socioeconomic development. Regional party chief Ivan Rumiantsev was informed on March 21, 1930, that meetings of poor peasants and new collective farmers were branding as kulaks those who were incapable of work, those they wanted to eliminate, or simply neighbors whom they looked upon with animosity. Collectivization "troikas," outsiders with no other information, frequently followed their lead without any verification.[3]

But for the generals in this battle for the countryside, the degree of randomness intrinsic to Soviet "extraordinary measures" was not crucial. Creating mechanized agriculture and destroying peasant backwardness were not the only goals. The special settlements for dekulakized peasants formed part of the nascent Gulag, the network of forced labor camps and colonies that expanded exponentially in those same years. Its creation after 1929 was driven not merely by the desire to "isolate" putative social and political enemies, but by the explicit mission of colonizing remote territories rich in natural resources.

In Tsvetkova's case, as in others, the actual results of the deportation initially resembled extermination more than colonization. Tsvetkova's family, along with the other arrested peasants initially held in Viazma, was sent to a remote part of the Urals in a journey that lasted a month. The arduous trip, just as in historical cases of ethnic rather than "class" deportations, itself produced many casualties. More fatal was the lack of supplies and infrastructure for the putative colonizers. Those living with Tsvetkova's family in one barrack in the special settlement were virtually the only ones out of hundreds to make it through the winter. When spring finally arrived in 1931, most everyone else had died or fled. Tsvetkova's father, who had been working in a Moscow factory when his family was deported, was rebuffed by the OGPU after trying to learn where his family was located. Eventually, Tsvetkova returned to her village. Determined to erase the stigma she faced as the child of deported kulaks, she became a model student in the late 1930s.

During the war, when the invading Germans were motivated by their own murderously utopian project of racial colonization, Tsvetkova served as a German-Russian translator for Red Army intelligence. In the fight against fascism, she made it all the way to Königsberg. There, reunited with her father, now a machine gunner, she celebrated Victory Day. "What a family of 'enemies of the people,'" she later observed with bitterness. "My whole adult life one thought has never left me: why did our beloved Motherland hurt our family this way?" Tsvetkova could not help comparing her experience of collectivization with Nazi German rule in Smolensk a decade later. Soviet deportations of peasant "special settlers" bore a haunting similarity to the German roundups of *Ostarbeiter,* or forced laborers from the East, who were seized from villages and deported to work in Germany. "It was the same way that the fascists drove Soviet people into slavery during the years of occupation."[4]

This chapter starts with the Stalinist assault on the countryside and ends with echoes of the Soviet cataclysm in Germany during the rise of Nazism. During the first phase of the Stalin Revolution, when the Soviet Union launched a form of internal colonization of its own countryside to create the Stalinist extraction state, leading "blood and soil" Nazis were viewing the unfolding catastrophe from Germany through the prism of their own funhouse mirror—the myth of an external empire ripe for the taking in the East. As National Socialism became a mass political movement in the early 1930s, Hitler and Nazi agricultural ideologues who would be influential during the invasion a decade later took a big step forward in formulating their utopian dream: an Eastern breadbasket for the Reich populated by German settlers and Slavic slaves.[5]

The Cataclysm Begins

The topic of the telegram that regional party second secretary Grigorii Rakitov sent to all District Party Committees on October 8, 1929, was the political importance of the potato. "The potato harvest in the Western Region," he explained, "is assuming the same exceptional political importance as the grain harvest." The reason was the "tense supply situation in the largest urban centers of the USSR (Leningrad, Moscow, and others)."

In mid-nineteenth-century Russian literature, the *khalat*, or house robe, became the symbol of arrogant and indifferent noble lords. Berating lower-level officials for their housecoat-like behavior (*khalatnoe otnoshenie*) toward "absolutely unacceptable" levels of potato procurement, Rakitov demanded "the most categorical measures." The pressure passed from the regional to the district level of power, however, was all too familiar. The party secretary of Krasninskii District complained about being bullied with three to four telegrams per day with the same content. Top regional officials, he charged, confused this machine-gun spray of paper fire with "effective leadership."[6]

Rumiantsev, Rakitov, and the head of the Soviet Regional Executive Committee (Oblispolkom), Il'ia Shelekhes, were themselves used to deflecting the well-nigh impossible demands from Moscow further down the power hierarchy. But gone were the days of the procurement crisis in 1927–1928 when higher deliveries alone might have satisfied the center. Moscow, not regional leaders, set the parameters of an escalating attack on the countryside to break peasant opposition to collective farms and guarantee food supply for the cities for the industrialization drive. The first benchmarks were the sanctioning of violent "extraordinary measures" for requisitioning teams to use against recalcitrant peasants starting in 1928, followed by a sustained effort to identify "kulaks" and break the resistance to collective farms in 1929. Wholesale collectivization was ratified in November 1929, followed by the first mass deportations of "kulaks" in winter 1930.

If the politics of deferred pressure Rumiantsev and his peers pursued were ubiquitous, they became a recipe for disaster in executing a major restructuring of the rural order. Collectivization became "the first of a series of bloody landmarks" that defined Stalinism's "complex and chaotic practices of violent transformation." In the country as a whole, the elimination of peasant smallholding provoked unrest, with some thirteen thousand riots and uprisings of two million participants by 1930 alone.[7] The Regional Party Committee was demanding results on the village level from an ineffective lower-level officialdom that was itself thrown into chaos in the wake of the Smolensk Affair.

Unexpected consequences began to show immediately in 1929. To meet quotas, district officials were extracting produce from poor rather than prosperous peasants. As peasant communities frequently banded together in light of the broadside from without, local authorities constantly failed to foment support of those classified as poor and middle peasants against the kulaks. A "kulak" literally meant a clenched or tight fist, and the peasant term became the Soviet epithet for the rural exploiting class. Now, it morphed into a notoriously flexible category that in practice encompassed peasants opposing collectivization. Local authorities tried to be creative: to "stimulate" deliveries, prosperous peasants were enticed with manufactured goods. As the harvest season reached its peak, the regional leadership incited subordinates in noticeably shriller tones to take "decisive measures with maximal force." At the same time, local party perpetrators were also blamed because they did not carry out "repressive measures" with "the strictest observance of revolutionary legality."[8]

After full collectivization and "liquidation of the kulaks as a class" became the order of the day in 1930, the lines of conflict became noticeably more fractured than a simple "civil war" of the urban-Soviet civilization against the peasantry. On the one hand, fights within the peasantry broke out into outright violence. Court records suggest that acts of reprisal from a variety of rural actors, including poor peasants and employees, rarely targeted agents of the Party directly. They took a less risky strategy: reprisals against peasants who had joined the collective farms or non-party local officials who enforced the policies of the center.[9] In other words, they aimed reprisals at those seen as collaborating with the collectivizers. As in the partisan war in the countryside of 1941–1943 that this situation in certain ways anticipated, the conflict played out both within rural communities and among entire villages forced to choose sides.

On the other hand, a second major clash broke out between district party authorities in rural localities and the so-called 25,000ers. The latter were urban, working-class activists mobilized by Moscow on an all-union scale to jump-start full collectivization at the very end of 1929. In the Western Region, these worker-Communists with extensive factory experience numbered eleven hundred. Some were mobilized by the Smolensk City Party Committee (Gorkom), but most were imported from the Ivanovo Industrial Region. As special representatives sent to disrupt local power relations, they might be considered plenipotentiaries—the term used for an informal yet ubiquitous Soviet political institution—except that they were not dispatched as individual emissaries but organized on a mass scale. The 25,000ers despised rural party-state authorities as "bureaucrats," their worst insult. The district party and state authorities they threatened could do nothing more effective than set up bureaucratic roadblocks, making the outsiders' lives miserable in terms of housing, rations, and material conditions. Rumiantsev and the regional leadership stood above these warring subordinates in the localities as the upheaval unfolded.[10]

Center, region, district—each level of power both blamed and needed the other. Only at the end of the chaotic year 1930 did Rumiantsev begin to ponder the implications of the flawed, warring levels of officialdom underneath him. At a plenum of Western Region party leaders, he spoke about how to fulfill the colossal tasks of building socialism and attempting to meet the control figures of the Central Committee—the two, by necessity, were interconnected if not identical in his mind. His answer was that "the entire focus" must be on the district level below the regional power structure. It was there, not in his own Smolensk offices, that "basic operational" work took place. Freely admitting to excesses and "crude mistakes, which led to much harm and the loss of material valuables"—a voice cried from the back bench, "Correct!"—Rumiantsev nonetheless maintained that the "root of all evil" lay in the ineffective district level of political power. For him, a more disciplined chain of command anchored in better party cadres was the cure to all that ailed regional governance. This simple political lesson Rumiantsev drew from collectivization not only bolstered self-preservationist buck-passing but served the interests of his own regional consolidation. Although the rising "little Stalin" succeeded in consolidating his own regional fiefdom, neither he nor any other regional Soviet political official ever created a genuinely effective chain of command.

Rumiantsev's preoccupation with the flawed district level was understandable. The buck stopped there: below the district level, party-state capacity was limited. But there was the rub; in 1930–1931, it was precisely at the district level that the race to boost percentages of collectivized households fueled rampant coercion and the creation of collective farms on paper alone. Erring on the side of excess took place even though the Western Region had not been scheduled by Politburo decree to complete collectivization until fall 1931. Combined with deportations of kulak households carried out primarily by the secret police, this made Rumiantsev's new fiefdom responsible for the largest decline in yields in the entire RSFSR, a total drop of 46.2 percent by May 1930. That disaster explained the all-union tactical retreat of Stalin's "Dizzy with Success" speech of March 2, 1930—a bombshell temporarily halting the collectivization drive and the accompanying anti-religious campaign, which in largely Russian regions focused on repression of Orthodox clergy and closing, often demolishing, churches. This became the founding and most dramatic example of an annual ritual of collectivized agriculture: introducing spring concessions at the time when peasant sowing was crucial, only to follow them with harsh "autumn ultimatums" in desperate pursuit of fulfilling the plan.[11]

Rumiantsev's preoccupation with flaws in the districts was logical, but superficial. Improving the District Party Committees would not solve the main issue: the district officials living in towns were themselves distant from the level of the collective farm, not to mention the village. Bullying the districts for results at the local level, where they had little leverage, was a root cause of those "excesses" in the first place.

War on Backwardness

Rumiantsev, the former worker turned high party official, and the 25,000ers, workers and Communist activists sent from the bench to coerce peasants into collective farms, shared a common misconception. They were certain that future farms would become factories and peasant backwardness would be eradicated once and for all. One activist sent into El'ninskii District expressed this view by reiterating the need to export to the backward peasantry current methods from the shop floor, "socialist competition" to fulfill plans and "shock work" to address urgent tasks. Many 25,000ers presented themselves as representatives of an advanced new world in a sea of kulaks, bureaucrats, and backwardness. They had internalized the industrial ideal in the utopian Soviet concept of collectivized agriculture at the end of the 1920s, in which every farm would become a factory and peasants would transform into proletarians. This was the vision justifying collectivization's cost.[12]

Addressing the 25,000ers, Rumiantsev also spoke the language of "culturedness." To him in this context, this watchword of the Stalin era implied modern labor discipline, keeping records, and managing inventories of farms just as the director of a factory would. He rejected the "primitive, compromising idea of communization," shared by radicals and glorified looters alike, in which everything would be socialized. The industrial or productionist ideal, to him, held out a more "materially prosperous, more cultured" future. Indeed, this was one of the Old Bolshevik's favorite themes of the 1930s. Rumiantsev told the 25,000ers a story of how he had personally visited an "unsightly, dirty" collective farm where no records were kept at all. Paperwork was absent even on the most fundamental metric: how much the farm had delivered to the state. The regional party chief, however, did not mention that the absence of basic recordkeeping, not to mention the production of annual reports, was more a rule than an exception in the chaotic, brutalized countryside of 1930. This fundamental fact makes all rural statistics, which generally underestimated land and livestock holdings at every level to minimize taxation, suspect from the ground up. It is also the prime reason that Rumiantsev's vision of the district controlling the grassroots was misconceived. His model ignored the villages and farms where peasants actually lived.

Over the long term, Rumiantsev's chain of command did improve significantly from the overt chaos of 1930. But collective farms never came to resemble factories. Instead, they formed part of a hybrid, Sovietized peasant world. The fields in the collective farms, on which peasants labored for little compensation, remained far less productive than the small household or private plots that peasants were able to cultivate. The large collective farms became the nodes through which the state extracted its agricultural deliveries, but motivation and productivity plummeted. In the decades that followed, local cadres were eventually peasantized. Once the violence subsided, peasant yearning for risk aversion was achieved. The result, which no one foresaw, was a permanently, disastrously underproductive agricultural sector and all that it implied.[13]

Vasilii's Vacillations

Vasilii Maslennikov was nineteen years old in 1930 when his village of Filimony experienced the onslaught of collectivization. The notion that there were kulak or prosperous exploiters among his neighbors was never something he accepted. Some peasants, he thought, possessed somewhat better farms and were more "experienced and resourceful." In fact, from the seventy-five homesteads in the vicinity of Filimony only one person was initially branded a kulak: Mikhail Dudinskii, whose father had run the landlord's estate before the revolution and who hired two laborers over the summers. But Maslennikov concluded that Dudinskii owned nothing "unnecessary" and would have willingly labored "more than many others" for the collective farm. It was Dudinskii's property that was required, not his life or labor. He had a connection in the District Executive Committee and avoided deportation by moving to the Donbass.[14]

Maslennikov also perceived little difference between those damningly categorized as "prosperous" and everyone else. In the locals' understanding, the prosperous were merely those who had enough grain to last from one harvest to another. Perhaps the axles on their carts were metal rather than wooden, or perhaps they owned a grain separator. In other words, class analysis was not primarily economic but political. Anyone who did not want to "socialize" the land and hand over the horse, the seed, the equipment, and a cow (if one had two), "all for free," risked being branded a "sub-kulak." During the second wave of dekulakization in 1931, five more kulaks from the area were suddenly identified and repressed. There was a new exodus of migrants out of the village.[15]

In the winter of 1929–1930, five of the six local churches near Filimony were closed during an attempt to create one large kolkhoz from all the households in five to six neighboring villages. Maslennikov witnessed at the local school agitational meetings where the male peasants (*muzhiki*) sat in silence as they were harangued to join. He was not able to distinguish among 25,000ers and district party officials, seeing them as identical in their push to match the fastest collectivization tempos. When a poor peasant at one of the meetings agreed to sign up for the collective farm, a loud voice shouted: "And what will you do in the collective farm, friend, if you couldn't even do anything with your own plot?" Another called out: "What are they going to do next, collectivize our women?"[16]

Maslennikov was ambivalent. He was young, his literacy was his strongest asset, and he felt a powerful pull to make himself more urban and more modern. That meant participating in the great projects the state had launched. "Personally, I did not want to be a backward young man lacking consciousness," he remembered. What choice did that leave him? The Soviet educational system, the Komsomol, and the Party were intertwined as a path out of the village. He was introspective and curious. In another time and place he might have even become a peasant intellectual or a critic of the political system. In rural Smolensk, the party-state had wrested much control over his life choices. But he was certain of one thing: "I was not prepared to live on the collective farm." All the same, Maslennikov believed the traditional, smallholding agricultural order was "irrational." As a result, he saw no choice—a recurring feature of his life story—but to "speak at meetings with the peasant men, giving explanations of party and state decisions aiming at collectivization." Later, he thought of himself as naive for initially thinking it would be possible to create collective farms voluntarily. "Above all I was disturbed by the use of pressure and the use of force to make peasants join the collective farm."[17]

Naked Dekulakization

The Party discussed the expropriation and deportation of a sizable segment of the population in abstract, ideological terms. In three years, mostly in two waves in 1930 and 1931, some 2.3 million "kulaks" were deported as families and approximately five million were expropriated as kulaks.[18] In practice, there were striking parallels between some of the ways urban collectivizers deliberately demeaned the backward peasants and the racially inspired German everyday violence was associated with humiliation of all backward Russians, urban and rural, during the occupation after 1941. In a haunting anticipation of antisemitic rituals enacted by invading German soldiers, for example, Soviet collectivizers forced peasants to dance during the closure of their rural churches. As in the Holocaust a decade later, expropriating the property of the victims became centrally caught up with the political violence.

Naked dekulakization was the term used not only for the unrecorded expropriation of kulak property, intended to start up the collective farms, but also for confiscatory targeting of "middle" and even poor peasants. Despite all sternly "categorical" bans on such looting, reports continued to reach the top about intimidation, theft, and trade in seized property. In the Smolensk Region, Red Army soldiers and commanders were deployed to close churches and carry out dekulakization, even though this militarization remained unauthorized. The "troika" of Rumiantsev, Shelekhes, and Lev Zalin (the OGPU representative) were in charge of dekulakization for the Bureau of the Regional Party Committee. In fact, Rumiantsev's numerous top-secret orders forbidding "excesses" contained deliberately mixed messages. In the same breath that he and other regional leaders warned about going too far, they also railed against right-wing "perversions" of the party line. The latter included accepting peasants into the collective farm but also allowing them to leave it or, more ominously, taking a "tolerant attitude toward the kulak such as 'better to wait than to overfulfill.'"[19]

During the state-sanctioned "liquidation of the kulaks as a class," it was entirely possible for the social or class category, as well as the "backwardness" of peasant culture, to function in similar ways as race and ethnicity in other forms of repression. There were cases of officials in this era, for example, referring to kulaks as a "breed." Despite the murky, easily changed boundaries dividing rural inhabitants on the ground, the tripartite "class analysis" of the peasantry was so ingrained that each group was essentialized and stereotyped in official directives, as in this statement: "It is necessary to explain to the poor peasant that the main task is to pressure the kulak." Some of those caught up in the anti-peasant zealotry of the era demanded that rural enemies be wiped off the face of the earth, while others declared that "we will make soap out of kulaks."[20]

"An Organized Pogrom"

The same party leaders who prosecuted the brutal war in the countryside became aghast when it spilled over into urban areas. The most infamous case of treating townspeople as kulaks—a debacle characteristically merging ideological and material motivations—occurred in late January and early February 1930 in the town of Medyn', not far from Viazma, in the district center. There a wide array of town and district authorities decided to "dekulakize" urban traders, not peasants, along with other "class aliens" in the town. In a raid sanctioned by the town soviet and District Party Committee, seventy-eight families were expropriated. Money, food, clothes, and even the possessions of a three-year-old child were seized with the participation of Red Army soldiers from the Eighty-First Rifle Division stationed nearby. Internal party investigations portrayed the victims as not "only" speculators—that would have been better—but "individual craftsmen, white-collar workers and their families, families of Red Army soldiers, and former workers." Evoking the legacy of antisemitic violence, a Regional Party Committee representative called it "an organized pogrom, only without murders."[21]

Only over a month later, on March 6, was the event condemned in the main regional newspaper, the *Workers' Path*. The timing was no coincidence. The press coverage and political documentation, which made Medyn' notorious and was later noted by historians, came exactly four days after Stalin's "Dizzy with Success" speech temporarily pulled back from collectivization's "excesses." There were, however, numerous other examples of expropriations of traders and craftsmen in non-rural areas that were never publicized, but about which the regional party leadership was well informed. Medyn' was far from unique. The fact remains that summary justice and forcible confiscations—"categorically" prohibited if only partially punished in such urban areas—were the sanctioned order of the day throughout the countryside.[22]

Material Motivations

At a time when standards of living were plummeting, Maslennikov was gripped by a determination to escape the countryside. The end of NEP created severe shortages of manufactured and consumer goods, as the "Russian and Jewish traders stopped trading at their stands in Glinka." State stores did not exist in the village, and there was "nothing to buy." Boots, hats, and clothes sometimes appeared in Smolensk stores, but enormous queues formed when they appeared. Maslennikov lacked the pants and shoes that he felt he needed to look halfway decent. Material concerns were reinforced by the demoralization that accompanied trauma. Almost all Maslennikov's young contemporaries lost energy and optimism, and he became confused and depressed. In early 1930, Maslennikov made another attempt to leave the village. He managed to enroll in an agronomy technical school (*tekhnikum*) in Kaluzhskaia Region. But because he had no relatives nearby who might supplement the starvation diet provided in the canteen, he quickly became so malnourished that he had to return home to Filimony. The headaches caused by his emaciated condition did not subside until the late 1930s.[23]

The best Maslennikov could do was to complete a three-month course in livestock breeding in nearby Sychevka, a town in a district touted for successfully creating new collective farms. Passing the class allowed him as of March 1931 to be certified as a livestock agrarian technician working for the kolkhoz center in Krasninskii District. In this new job, Maslennikov ran errands at numerous collective farms and had a bird's-eye view of the state of the countryside. He noticed that even in the model Sychevskii

District in 1931 the methods for collectivizing were always the same: dekulakize some households, seize their property, and exile them. If kulaks did not exist, they would have to be invented.

Collection of grain reserves and seed grain at gunpoint, on top of two bad harvests in 1931 and 1932, created near famine conditions. Smolensk did not experience mass famine in 1932–1933 as in Ukraine and the Volga region, but outbreaks of starvation were recorded and semi-starvation conditions were common. People survived by living off meager amounts of "second-class" produce from the private plots, which assumed an outsized role in collectivized agriculture. When no kulaks were left to blame, suspicion of sabotage fell on the kolkhoz leadership. Maslennikov's supervisors offhandedly told him to make up statistics in his district after he reported that farms were not keeping records. By spring 1932, a kind of "spontaneous uprising" was occurring as peasants took back the personal property they had released earlier to the collective farms. This was followed in August 1932 by Stalin's draconian decree on the theft of grain and kolkhoz property, according to which ten years in the Gulag could be given for petty theft. As an employee of the district administration, Maslennikov could now eat full and "normal" meals in a "closed canteen," alongside specialists and "responsible workers." But with his strong roots in Filimony, he remained struck by the "stupidity" of the name given to the collective farm in his home village: Liberation of the Serfs.[24]

Political Rewards

If the Stalin Revolution heightened material motivations as a result of extreme scarcity and hunger, the repressions of the era opened up opportunities for material enrichment for some. But for the 25,000ers, made up of party and working-class activists, it entailed short-term yet meaningful material sacrifices. They left the better-supplied cities for frequently miserable and dangerous conditions in the nascent collective farms in the run-up to the outbreak of the near famine conditions of 1932–1933 prevalent throughout the western RSFSR. They placed themselves in harm's way during a wave of anti-kolkhoz peasant violence. The 25,000ers' job was to direct collective farm gatherings, which were far more reminiscent of chaotic, brawling village assemblies than the stenographed sessions of an urban party cell. What motivated these foot soldiers of the political army invading the village? The answer was more complicated than only ideological zeal, the ubiquitously stoked "enthusiasm" of the 1930s.

Joining the 25,000ers mobilized in 1930, in theory, was voluntary. But when the Party in the guise of superiors called, it was difficult to refuse. In practice, workers from the factories were mobilized through party channels. Their reward was a special political status. Data on 862 of the 1,100 activists in the Western Region—800 of them men, since very few women were ready to "organize" the peasants in the patriarchal countryside—shows that over 86 percent of the 25,000ers remained in the countryside after the first wave of activism in 1930. The vast majority were rewarded with directorships or top posts in the new collective farms.[25]

On New Year's Day 1931, Rumiantsev presided over an extraordinary conference with the region's 25,000ers. The transcript of the discussion, which runs 168 pages long, shows how rank-and-file activists were obsessed with material conditions. This was understandable. Dubbed "commissars" by peasants, they were despised as the meddling agents of the center by many rural district-level party and state officials. The power struggle with embattled district officials prompted antagonistic local elites to wield distribution networks against the 25,000ers. This left the newcomers desperately scrambling for housing and access to promised rations. Try as they might, most were unable to receive a level of supply commensurate with their status as Moscow's favored party plenipotentiaries in the countryside. This was not what they signed up for.

In front of Rumiantsev and regional party officials, speaker after speaker among the activists complained bitterly about the "supply" question from every possible angle. Far more than kulaks or collective farms, it was their own living conditions that dominated the discussion: spoiled fish, lack of access to "closed distribution" points, and obdurate bureaucrats responsible for delays. No one, moreover, expressed surprise that the overwhelming focus of the gathering was on the absence of tobacco, not on Marxist-Leninism, Stalin, or socialism. The expectation that the party-state would provide a hierarchy of consumption commensurate with status was ubiquitous for everyone from Rumiantsev on down. To be sure, some activists did profess concern that their poor material conditions would compromise their "authority" and weaken 25,000er resolve to impose superior factory methods on agriculture. Ultimately, in the Soviet cadre system, political status, economic benefits, and ideological goals were always intimately interconnected, even in the breach.[26]

Serving in the front lines of the Stalin Revolution held out for the 25,000ers the prospect of political advancement, economic benefits, and a certification of ideological loyalty all at once. Joining the rampant coercion of peasants as they were stripped of independence and property presented to these urban party workers a recognition of their own superiority. It pointed to a path upward, a service that would be publicly celebrated for decades to come. In return for a slice of power, they helped prosecute one of the great cataclysms of the twentieth century.

Elusive Enemies

The assault on the village during the collectivization era sparked the most widespread popular opposition movement in Soviet history. Peasant women, less likely to be openly repressed if they protested than their brothers and husbands, were at the movement's forefront. In January 1930, Rumiantsev reported the proliferation of "peasant women's uprisings" (bab'i bunty) to Molotov. Hundreds of village women, many armed with pitchforks or stones, gathered for days in front of churches to prevent the removal of symbolically important church bells. The regional party first secretary did not conceal to Stalin's right-hand man how rural women themselves responded when instructed that poor peasants must organize against the kulak. "There is no kulak here, this is the poor peasant coming out," they cried. "Leave from here, we do not trust you, you strangled us with taxes, deliveries, plundered us. You are driving us into serfdom [barshchina], we will not join the kolkhoz. We will not give up the bells." But Rumiantsev still blamed a conspiracy of more elusive enemies, telling Molotov that the secret police concurred: kulaks and priests on the sidelines were the puppet masters.[27]

God also proved an elusive enemy. The assault on village culture and Orthodoxy encompassed closure of over half the churches open in 1929 and repressions of clergy that repeated during the Great Terror. The countryside, as a result, was gripped by religious sectarianism and apocalyptic rumors. High-level Regional Party Committee documents blamed these phenomena not on its own policies of persecution but on the collusion between internal and external enemies. Sectarians, believers, and their "promoters" were all "direct political agents of military-espionage organizations supported by the international bourgeoisie." The atheist party worker Mishin, a 25,000er working in Diat'kovskii District, appeared flummoxed by the pernicious influence of religion. "It is the most cursed affair . . . You come up against religion at every turn. Belief in God means it is hard to collectivize, since the peasants say that no matter what God will not allow it to happen."[28] Revealingly, Mishin spoke of "peasants" here in terms of the gulf between urban and rural, party and peasantry—not in terms of a separate rich peasant or "kulak" enemy.

In the Bolshevik imagination the kulak was at once ubiquitous and elusive, and that is one reason the term was so open to manipulation. Party documents referred to Stalin's warning that the kulak would attempt to conceal himself by divesting cattle. Throughout this period the term *prosperous* (*zazhitochnye*) was linked to kulaks, as in an October 1929 recommendation to "take all possible measures of social and penal pressure toward the kulaks and prosperous peasants." Some 25,000ers spoke of prosperous peasants "hiding" in the collective farms. At the Regional Party Committee plenum in 1930, in the wake of the "Dizzy with Success" speech, Rumiantsev voiced an obligatory restraint: "We cannot punish [prosperous peasants] like the kulak. Whether we call it dekulakization or elimination of the prosperous peasants, we must speak with them in a different way than with the kulak."[29]

Rumiantsev's declaration, however, was a very backhanded form of moderation. The term he used for "elimination of the prosperous peasants"—literally "de-prosperous-peasantization" (*razzazhitochivaniem*)—was so ungainly it was almost a caricature. In fact, it was coined as an obvious equivalent to "dekulakization." This implied that repressions against kulaks would be followed by finding "prosperous" peasants whose property could be expropriated for the new collective farms. Ominously, Rumiantsev provided an unofficial target figure: 3–4 percent of prosperous peasants were "tough" and could never be allowed inside the collective farms. He also declared that the kulak/prosperous peasant economy—he linked them together as being individualistic—must be totally eliminated. Such statements clearly stretched the notion of kulak to encompass prosperous peasants, foreshadowing the second wave of dekulakization in 1931. Peasants, however, did not simply accept these labels. The first step toward dekulakization, deprivation of voting rights, generated thousands of complaints.[30]

Pyrrhic Victory, Triple Burden

By 1933 and 1934, the collectivizers had won politically, but an economic and social malaise gripped the countryside. Maslennikov observed this with great clarity. Most of the kolkhozniki he observed had initially followed the old peasant custom of striving to "look no worse than the others," hoping that hard work and fulfilling norms would lead to a better life. But after two bad years and basically no return for their labor, the peasants did not rush off to work as they always had. Peasant absenteeism, indifference to kolkhoz labor, and rampant theft led to deplorable yields. As Maslennikov put it, the rural population was rife with rising "indignation." Once the state extracted its deliveries, there was almost nothing left behind. Women had no flax left over for themselves to weave. The "labor day," the basic unit of collectivized wage labor in agriculture, was paid by the state at cut-rate levels and, in hard times, sometimes not at all, once onerous taxes and fees were subtracted. It was widely seen as a kind of second serfdom.[31]

Within a few years of the cataclysm, a peculiarly hybrid, sovietized peasant world emerged. The hierarchies of the traditionally patriarchal peasantry were perpetuated but now intertwined with the new hierarchies of Stalinism. Women did the vast majority of the monotonous, back-breaking fieldwork of harvesting flax, a major crop in Smolensk Region; like beet production in Ukraine, it remained largely unmechanized. The small household plots—which commanded far more peasant effort than the collective farm land and produced a greatly disproportionate amount of food, and which peasants constantly pushed to enlarge legally or otherwise—were also a gendered realm. In an unstated acknowledgment that collectivized agriculture rested on women's backs, about 80 percent of rural Stakhanovites were women. These good-looking, vigorous young women overachievers, some selected to meet Stalin, were favored as symbols of the socialist countryside. It is well known that in the Soviet Union they and their sisters shouldered the famous "double burden" of housework and child-rearing combined with employment. Peasant women faced a grueling "triple burden": home and hearth; primarily manual labor on the collective farm; and, not least, the private plot and livestock for which they also cared.[32]

The exodus from countryside to town, both an immediate and long-term result of the assault on backwardness, plundered much of the rural manpower. From that point on, men were less than half the workforce. After the collective farm system stabilized in the mid- to late 1930s, it made economic sense for the most able-bodied men to do seasonal work (*otkhod*) in factories, lumber, or hauling. Yet men also dominated the mechanized positions and the farm leadership. Of the labor-day payments, two-thirds went to men and one-third to women. Policy and household dynamics together contributed to these inequalities, because women were the primary workers on the household plots and in the home. The luckiest extended peasant households in the post-collectivization countryside were able to strategize by sending a man to work in industry or seasonal work outside the collective farm, putting a woman in charge of the private plot, and keeping a less able-bodied person in the collective farm to maintain membership. For the rest, grinding poverty was endemic.[33]

Smolensk's Kolkhoz Poet

An entire generation was shaped by the dislocations and repressions of the collectivization era. This holds true even in the exceptional case of Smolensk's most famous peasant. The poet Aleksandr Tvardovskii grew up in the village of Zagor'e in Pochinkovskii District, southwest of Smolensk, and after Stalin died in 1953 emerged as the key literary figure of Khrushchev's Thaw, a period when cultural ferment accompanied and often pushed the limits of political de-Stalinization. Tvardovskii's relationship to his home in the countryside and to his father—who fled the village in 1930 after being denounced as a prosperous peasant, only to be deported as a kulak by the next year—proved fundamental to his life and literary work, first under Stalinism and then during de-Stalinization.

In the notorious Stalin-era propaganda myth of Pavlik Morozov, the Siberian boy hero denounced his peasant father to the secret police for helping kulaks, then became a martyr after being murdered by his family in 1932. Generations of schoolchildren learned about his renunciation of his family as a heroic feat. It remained unknown that the creators of the Pavlik cult had almost completely fabricated the facts of the slain boy's life. In the real-life case of the poet Tvardovskii, the young man also renounced his family, as did a number of other children of the repressed in the 1930s.[34]

Tvardovskii was twenty years old in 1930, living in the city of Smolensk, and already publishing poems and articles about rural life in local newspapers. Descended from a petty noble family on his mother's side, the budding poet had a complicated relationship with his successful, highly literate, and entrepreneurial peasant father, who apparently strongly opposed his literary career. In a remarkable episode, Smolensk party leader Rumiantsev personally advised the up-and-coming young writer to renounce his parents—a choice necessitated, the Old Bolshevik power broker told him, by the revolution itself. In January 1931, Tvardovskii took the first secretary's advice, refusing his father help even when he came to him after escaping exile.[35]

Still, the incident did not lift the stigma the young poet faced for being born to "kulak" parents, nor did it erase his complicated affiliation with his rural past. By 1934, he was being hailed for the success of his "kolkhoz poetry" and joined the regional branch of the Union of Writers. Tvardovskii was invited to read his work at the central Union of Writers in Moscow. He received this honor and publicity along with several of Smolensk's other rising literary figures. They included Konstantin Dolgonenkov, then affiliated with the journal Bolshevik Youth (Bol'shevistskii molodniak). During the war, Dolgonenkov became the main Russian-language propagandist in German-occupied Smolensk. The very same year the two young writers jointly achieved recognition in Moscow, Tvardovskii, the future cultural innovator and reformer, was ominously branded as a kulak "helper" in a Smolensk newspaper. Dolgonenkov, the future collaborator, had no skeletons in his closet.[36]

Success combined with stigma created an acute dilemma for the talented young poet. Like so many others, Tvardovskii attempted to address the issue by rewriting his own biography. This he did quite literally, through the diary he had kept from 1926 to 1932, the years of greatest trauma for him and his beloved countryside. In 1935, he copied certain entries into a new notebook and destroyed the old diary. He rewrote his autobiography as a renunciation of his father's peasant greed and depicted his own life's journey as a steady path to higher consciousness. Even after these drastic personal steps, however, Tvardovskii's break with his past was far from clean. During a visit to Smolensk in 1937, when his slight connection to Rumiantsev became a liability, he narrowly escaped arrest in a roundup of his peers.[37]

Tvardovskii uneasily retained a love for the countryside and his village, shaping his own ongoing sense of possessing an independent "nature" during his relocation to the elite literary institution in Moscow, the Institute of Philosophy, Literature, and History, after 1936. There is evidence that Tvardovskii was unsuccessful in his ideological efforts to grasp the necessity for the Great Terror. Nonetheless, in 1940 the writer became a full member of the Party, and in March 1941 he won the Stalin Prize for his 1936 narrative poem "The Country of Muraviia." But even as he climbed the ladder of the cultural hierarchy, Tvardovskii continued to develop a sense of autonomy rooted in his background in a rural Smolensk wracked by upheaval. The searing choice he made between his family and his career, just one of millions in the age of Stalinism, was formative for both his personality and his storied career. As editor of the crusading *Novyi mir,* the key literary journal of the Thaw starting in the 1950s, he set the pace for publications pushing the boundaries of cultural de-Stalinization.[38]

Collectivization as Precursor

In another kind of linkage, the era of collectivization in the early 1930s and the Great Terror of 1937–1939 were conjoined by many chains of historical causality. An entire generation of party members, cadres, and activists was shaped and promoted by the first great wave of violence and coercion. Promotion policies and the campaign mode advantaged those who fulfilled the mission at any cost and, especially for the duration of the upheaval, embraced voluntarism over expertise. In both periods of revolutionary revivalism, summary justice spearheaded by the secret police was at the forefront of political violence. The massive dislocations, population movements, and criminality set off by the assault on the peasantry, reflected even in Maslennikov's village, fed militarized forms of policing and governance that only intensified even during the short-lived stabilization of the mid-1930s. The invasion of the countryside formed a major part of "martial law socialism," a militarized set of extraordinary measures implemented by the party-state and the political police in the name of creating the new society. The practices of this first phase of Stalinism were a key precedent for the "mass operations" of the Great Terror.[39]

The collectivization era created no fewer preconditions for what occurred after the German invasion of 1941. As theft and shirking became prime peasant strategies during the mid-1930s stabilization of the rural order, peasants took advantage of greater state responsiveness to flood the system with agile petitions and complaints. But behind the scenes, rural hatred of the collective farm system was sown in widespread anti-Soviet statements. Foreshadowing behavior under German rule, peasants developed a "chameleon-like ability to adapt to changing rhetoric and campaigns." Throughout the late 1930s, rumors spread about imminent disbanding of the collective farms. Smolensk peasants were recorded anticipating war and speculating as to "whether Hitler would be a better leader than Stalin."[40]

As the post-collectivization rural order cultivated beneficiaries and loyalists, the countryside became fragmented and divided along many lines. Persisting divisions and resentments within the peasantry born in the collectivization drive would suddenly break out into the open after 1941 in a proxy war between supporters of German occupation and the partisans. The much-resented Stalinist extraction state deeply shaped rural responses during the 1941 collapse of Soviet power and initial responses to Nazi rule.

Finally, Stalinism required large numbers of boots on the ground to implement martial law socialism. Those "cadres of violence" would be "prepared for and ideologically committed" to brutalized conduct when the war arrived.[41] Further, the deep interconnections between political and ideological loyalty and privileged material conditions forged in the Stalinist economy of scarcity would inform life-and-death decisions about choosing sides during the war.

Stalinist internal colonization in the 1930s differed in many ways from the Nazi project of racial colonization on the Eastern Front in the period that followed. Anna Tsvetkova, deported as a toddler, could grow up to become a good Soviet citizen because Soviet social and political categories were often more mutable than Nazi racial hierarchies. A far less visible phenomenon, even to historians, has been how enmity between the two projects shaped their direction. A decade before Stalinism and Nazism went to war, the cataclysm of collectivization echoed in far-off Germany, making its mark in the aspirations of German fascism to acquire a colonial breadbasket in the East.

"We Cast Our Eyes on the Land in the East"

The onset of full-scale collectivization in the Stalin Revolution coincided with the rise of the Nazis as a mass party after 1930, and Hitler's seizure of power in 1933 came at the height of the Soviet famine that accompanied the assault on the countryside. On March 2, 1933, a few days after the burning of the Reichstag and the emergency decree suspending German civil liberties, Hitler was in the midst of a terror campaign against opponents and spoke at a rally at the Berlin Sportpalast. "Millions of people are starving," he declared, "in a country that could be a breadbasket for a whole world."[42] The formulation is revealing in several respects. As mass famine was unfolding in Ukraine, the Volga region, and elsewhere in 1932–1933, it remained an international political controversy rather than an established fact. A trickle of accurate journalistic, diplomatic, visitor, and refugee reports was largely contained by an effective Soviet information and travel blockade, reinforced by a flood of international communist propaganda. Hitler's bombast, ironically, was more accurate than most public information. Communist atrocities proved an effective weapon for the fascists, just as starting in 1941 the Soviets publicized shocking German crimes to major domestic effect.

During the Nazis' mass electoral expansion of the early 1930s, Hitler played on German anxieties about the specter of communist rule. He lumped his warring German Communist and Social Democratic rivals together as Marxists, tarring them both with the catastrophic human costs of Stalinism. In the election campaigns of 1930–1933, the Nazis chose not to propagate radical concepts of Judeo-Bolshevism and *Lebensraum* (living space) in the East, despite the central role they played for Hitler and the Nazi movement at other moments. Hitler and the Nazi Party were quite capable of tactical maneuvering when it came to Soviet communism.

The long-standing German "myth of the East" rested on images of Eastern Europe and Russia as the repository of backwardness, which highlighted the superiority of German *Kultur*. The image of the Soviet Union in Germany after 1933 manufactured fear with the tropes of a primitive, Asiatic order, but sharpened and transformed them with the threat of communist violence and impoverishment. School textbooks and mass propaganda racialized older stereotypes into fearful images of Jews and Bolsheviks, reaching millions of young German schoolboys who would later be mobilized for the Eastern Front. Yet it was not fear that motivated Hitler's 1933 formulation. Obliquely and almost wistfully, he hinted at the opportunities of the space that might become a "breadbasket for a whole world"—if only, to finish the Führer's sentence, it were subjugated and Germanized by the Reich.[43]

It is difficult to overstate the potency of this vision of continental empire within the Nazis' own far-right revolutionary trajectory. In the German nationalist movements shaping Hitler's outlook, dating back to the 1890s, the quest for a Greater Germany went hand in hand with antisemitism and prejudice against Slavs. The creation of *Grossdeutschland* topped the list of twenty-five points in the Nazi Party program of 1920. But as in so many other areas, these long-standing, durable nationalist ideas were revolutionized. Hitler championed the unification of Germans by wedding it to a racialized, utopian vision of continental empire and global dominance. The concept of living space (*Lebensraum*) dated to the eastward migratory colonialism and antisemitism pushed by the Pan-German League after 1891; the siren call of global German economic and great power dominance (*Weltpolitik*) found favor in political and industrial circles around the same time. Nazism merged and revolutionized both. The linchpin of its vision of German "greatness" led due east. It could be achieved only through subjugation of the Eurasian hinterland by a eugenically "healthy" master race.[44]

Hitler's stance toward the Soviet Union, unlike his antisemitism and dream of Greater Germany, was not fully fixed until he wrote *Mein Kampf*, which was published in 1925. Specifically, the allure of racial colonization in the Soviet space was increased by the newer concept of Judeo-Bolshevism. The association of Jews and revolution had a long history, including in Russia on the right wing of the political spectrum between the pogroms of 1881 and the Revolution of 1905. During the Russian Civil War, Russian émigré counterrevolutionaries helped propagate the concept of Judeo-Bolshevism in far-right circles abroad. Judeo-Bolshevism, nonetheless, was a key concept that was unevenly prominent in the history of German fascism.

Nazism got its start in Bavarian counterrevolutionary politics, which identified the short-lived Munich Soviet Republic with Jews and Russians. The flood of anti-Bolshevik writings in 1919–1920 was a significant influence on Hitler. Even more instrumental were the Baltic Germans in the Nazi Party, particularly Max Erwin von Scheubner-Richter, who fought with the Freikorps and was killed in the Beer Hall Putsch of 1923, and Alfred Rosenberg, the main ideologist of National Socialism in the 1920s. However, pure anti-Bolshevism was from the outset central only for some Nazis, such as a number of Baltic fascists. This contrasted with the covert fascination and admiration a number of leading party figures at times harbored for Bolshevism and even, before 1933, Stalin. Hitler, by contrast, connected the Social Darwinist "struggle for survival" (*Lebenskampf*) to a colonialist struggle for space (*Lebensraum*) specifically in the Soviet East. For Hitler, this crystallized a range of ideological postulates into a permanent constellation, which he then altered only in terms of tactics and emphasis. That linkage was also one reason Judeo-Bolshevism would come to the fore with a vengeance in 1941.[45]

Mein Kampf devoted an entire chapter to bashing the "Eastern orientation," a putative German-Russian alliance against the West so attractive to many German nationalists in the 1920s. Hitler argued that only the Germanic element had allowed an "inferior race" to create a Russian state in the first place. Now this state had been captured by the "international Jew," who had "robbed" the Russian nation of its own intelligentsia. The Soviet order stank of the "ferment of decomposition." The virile mission of National Socialism would be the Germanization of the "soil." This was the imperative of German living space, as argued in *Mein Kampf*: "We cast our eyes on the land in the East. We will finally end the colonial and trade policies of the prewar period and will take up the future politics of the soil."[46]

Hitler's take on Judeo-Bolshevism was contested within the Nazi Party and the wider "conservative revolution" by a broader strain of thought within German revolutionary nationalism after 1919 pushing for a geopolitical alliance in the East. A broad undercurrent of German fascination with Bolshevism, reflected within the Nazi Party as well, underscores how *völkisch* new nationalism (the German term has no direct equivalent, but carries the connotation of racialist populism and biological racism) represented a revolutionary phenomenon. The militants working for a new fascist order pictured themselves as national revolutionaries of the Right.[47]

In the Nazi context, national revolution was very tightly linked to war. The oversized role of martial values and militarized masculinity within both Nazism and the broader conservative revolution of the 1920s was shaped by World War I and, especially, its ignominious end. However ruthless and exploitative, Germany's military-bureaucratic occupation after 1914 differed greatly from the Eastern Front in the even more total war that followed. Antisemitism was not dominant in policy or ideology, and the Kaiser still spoke the language of national liberation. But the first push to the east prepared the ground for the second. Germany's military colony in

World War I, the Land Ober Ost, stretched from the Baltics to Russia's western borderlands. When Germany lost World War I on the Western Front in 1918, one million German troops remained in the east.[48]

The manner in which these visions of empire on the Eastern Front were snatched away in 1918 fueled sentiments of impotence and rage. The twenty thousand to forty thousand Freikorps guerrillas who fought a vicious frontier war in the Baltics following Germany's capitulation formed a stepping-stone rather than a direct precursor to the Nazi Revolution. Some fighters renounced German citizenship and found a freebooting freedom in the Baltics; others later joined the Nazis and became prominent in the war of annihilation and the Holocaust. But in general, the Freikorps phenomenon sparked resentment and persistent fantasies of future expansion.[49]

Blood and Soil

When Hitler in *Mein Kampf* referred to the future politics of soil, it represented not only a mystical notion connecting space with race. It also carried concrete connotations about agriculture, the ethnic German diaspora, and Germany's porous eastern border. As of the German census of 1925, fifty-eight thousand ethnic German immigrants from Russia remained in Germany of the approximately one hundred thousand who had emigrated there in 1914–1920. Ethnic German minorities in Volhynia and other parts of Ukraine were favored during the German occupation at the end of World War I. Hundreds of thousands of ethnic Germans in the Volga region, descended from settlers recruited under Catherine the Great, became a flashpoint for German outrage.[50]

During the Weimar period, the concept of the German nation routinely was understood to include Germans abroad, an expansion that was common not only on the nationalist right. The plight of the Volga Germans, played up by émigré groups and nationalist activists, became a prism though which Soviet agriculture and collectivization was viewed in Germany. In right-wing depictions, suffering national brethren in the East had also been stabbed in the back by the Jewish Bolsheviks. In Rosenberg's version of racial conspiracy, for example, the Volga Germans were being "robbed and raped" while Bolshevistic East European Jews (*Ostjuden*) flooded into Germany. The Eastern Jews had arrived in the migratory wave of 1914–1922; they came along with hundreds of thousands of Russians and tens of thousands of Germans from Russia, as well as over a million German citizens from formerly German territory in Poland and France. Expansionist fantasies of future imperial revenge were stimulated by visible symbols of impotence in Eastern Europe.[51]

In the "blood and soil" imaginings of the Right, Aryan warrior-farmers could take up the ancient Germanic push to the east, turning the influx of unwanted refugees on its head. In 1921, the young Heinrich Himmler, a year away from his degree in agronomy in Munich, heard Freikorps leader General Graf Rüdiger von der Goltz speak on the struggle for the Baltics. The future head of the SS and co-founder of its Race and Resettlement Office recorded in his diary: "If there's another eastern campaign I'll join it. The east is the most important thing for us. The west is liable to die. In the east we must fight and settle." In the late 1920s, Himmler failed as a chicken farmer around the time he took part in an antisemitic and anti-Slav youth group, the Artam League, which schemed to resettle urban Germans on rural soil and push Germany's ethnic frontier east. Himmler's comrade in this movement, Walther Darré, who took a doctorate in livestock breeding, emerged as a leading "blood and soil" theoretician. Darré published *The Peasantry as the Life-Source of the Nordic Race* in 1928 and became Himmler's co-founder of a new SS resettlement office in 1931. He took the post of Reich minister of food and agriculture from 1933 to 1942.[52] The "politics of soil" was an ideological concept that was deeply invested in actual soil, including the land that was collectivized in the USSR.

German diplomats in the USSR in the early 1930s were among the best-informed foreigners in the world on the Soviet crisis of collectivization and famine. German consulates in Kyiv and Kharkiv gathered information and generated relatively accurate reports. After the writings of the agricultural attaché in Moscow, Otto Aughagen, were picked up in the German press, the German government pressured the Soviets to grant exit visas to over five thousand Soviet Germans. German diplomats in Kharkiv had direct contact with the far Right as well. A hybrid left-right organization known as Arplan, the Working Group for the Study of the Soviet Russian Planned Economy, included both leftists and a group of nationalists, among them the Nazi Ernst zu Reventlow and a range of fascist intellectuals with "National Bolshevik" proclivities. An Arplan delegation passed through Ukraine from August 20 to September 15, 1932, and several of the rightists were briefed at the Kharkiv consulate. Some of them leaked reports about "monstrous hardship" to the press upon their return to Berlin. After the Nazi seizure of power, the German embassy in Moscow widely disseminated a September 18, 1933, report on the "starvation emergency" to ministries and other embassies.[53]

For a number of German revolutionaries of the Right, the human costs of collectivization only enhanced admiration for the violent ruthlessness of the Stalin Revolution. Famine would become a weapon of choice in the planning for colonization of Soviet land in the run-up to Operation Barbarossa. For others, armchair imperialists and the increasingly radicalized experts of German Russian studies (*Ostforschung*), the starving Soviet peasants were virtually invisible. The grand illusion of these strategists was that Germans could simply reshape "virgin land" capable of supporting "half a billion people," but which was currently only wasted on the racially inferior.[54] For Hitler and other Nazis who stoked fears of communism at home, the catastrophe of collectivization contributed to overconfidence about Soviet weakness. The misleading image of a colossus with feet of clay would be further solidified in the era of the Great Terror.

3

THE ENEMY WITHIN

BORIS MENSHAGIN, then a thirty-six-year-old defense attorney, walked into the Palace of Labor in downtown Smolensk on November 24, 1937. The grand building of the former noble assembly, built in 1855, had been enlarged at the end of the nineteenth century to include one of the city's largest concert halls. Now the hall was the scene of the trial of the workers of the Livestock Administration of the Western Region. The last of eight regional and district show trials, it coincided with the so-called mass operations marking the peak of Stalin's Great Terror. During the past year, a country still at peace had been caught up in a frenzy of denunciations and spy-mania akin to a state of war. Show trials were a key component of the bloodletting. Stalin and Molotov sent out telegrams ordering them to be held on the district and regional levels, and the secret police official sent from Moscow to Smolensk by NKVD chief Nikolai Ezhov in April to carry out the mass operations, Vasilii Karutskii, personally served as stage manager for most of the show trials in the region.[1]

The Smolensk regional newspaper, the *Workers' Path,* prepared the soil with shrill pretrial indictments of the "fascist hirelings" and "wrecker rabble." Four thick volumes prepared for the regional trial of eight agricultural specialists included demands for death sentences gathered from collective farms, factories, and schoolchildren. Menshagin remembered his reaction when he entered the hall: "Again it's packed to the gills. This is bad." He knew a guilty verdict was inevitable. But at that moment, he could not have predicted that he would become famous in Smolensk for getting the sentence stayed and the case reconsidered.[2]

As Menshagin understood perfectly well, he was playing the role of a minor actor in the performance. Soviet jurisprudence downgraded the significance of the defense counsel, who had no access to pretrial questioning or witnesses. When the Smolensk native began his legal career in the Central Black Earth Region during the era of collectivization, the legal system had lurched toward summary justice. Impatient judges had been known to intimidate lawyers for the defense. When Menshagin moved to the Smolensk Collegium of Defense Attorneys on the eve of the Great Terror, his closest colleagues were limiting themselves to pleas for reduced sentences.

From another point of view, however, Menshagin's role was not at all insignificant: his presence was crucial to upholding the facade of legality. Even during the Great Break and the Great Terror, the Stalinist state strove to maintain both law and terror as tools of state power. In fact, law and terror overlapped considerably, as the Terror itself was wrapped in legal trappings. When, without even a token defense, cowed and ingratiating defense counsels called for still harsher sentencing than the prosecution, it annoyed the head of the Procuracy in Moscow, Andrei Vyshinskii.[3] Menshagin was no rebel. He was a professional skilled at maneuvering in situations of intense pressure. Even so, he was about to achieve something extremely rare: a stayed sentence, a retrial, and, ultimately, an acquittal.

The Milkmaid and the Cow's Abscess

The livestock specialists Menshagin defended were accused of counterrevolutionary sabotage, or wrecking. But the Smolensk show trials were very different from the notorious Moscow trials of Old Bolshevik revolutionaries, where forced confessions and stage management were publicized around the world under a far brighter spotlight. One of Menshagin's clients, A. P. Iuranov, a brucellosis specialist from Moscow's Institute for Experimental Veterinary Medicine, retracted his confession. Iuranov denied infecting cattle with the disease he studied. All the same, an expert from Moscow was such an attractive villain in this rural region that Iuranov was actually featured in two such spectacles. One month before Menshagin met him in Smolensk, Iuranov appeared in a district show trial in Sychevka, a model livestock area whose delivery metrics had recently declined. There the chief witnesses against Iuranov were champion milkmaids, who appeared in court with the Order of Lenin pinned on their chests.[4]

As Menshagin looked on, the regional chief procurator heading the prosecution of the veterinarians, Georgii Mel'nikov, blamed all the area's shortages of milk products on sabotage. Only foreign, "imported" livestock, Mel'nikov charged, became the vehicles of infection against the proletarian state. Prudently, Menshagin did not directly defend the innocence of the accused. He rested his defense on a call for further scientific expertise that might determine whether cattle could be thus infected.[5]

The milkmaid gambit had worked so well in Sychevka that it was repeated in Smolensk. The main witness against the Moscow specialist Iuranov was once again a milkmaid, who testified that she witnessed him sicken one of her cows. The dairy hand evoked a kind of sorcery: "She was such a beautiful cow! He [Iuranov] somehow pricked her and the next day she was sick! A large abscess [*naryv*]."[6]

At the outset of the Stalin Revolution in 1928, when the political and personal sins of the Smolensk regional party organization had been branded an "abscess," the diseased growth had served as a lurid metaphor for what would need to be amputated in a large-scale political operation. When the deadly pustule reappeared in 1937, the infection was no longer metaphorical but literal. Only now its deliberate spread was invented out of whole cloth, attributed to traitorous experts guilty of creating local shortages. Other acts of wrecking announced at the June 1937 Central Committee Plenum by Ezhov, Stalin's diminutive, ultra-zealous secret police fixer now assuming the role of executioner in chief, included the deliberate spread of plague, anthrax, epizootics, and foot-and-mouth disease, not to mention the castration of pedigreed sheep.[7]

After a long legal odyssey, the livestock breeders' death sentences were reversed on June 21, 1939, and the convictions were changed from counterrevolutionary wrecking to negligence. Visiting his clients in prison, Menshagin told them they would be released for time served. They wept, he recounted, "and, to tell you the truth, I cried with them." By 1939, however, the reversal was significant but not unique. In late 1938 and 1939, after Ezhov was replaced with Lavrentii Beria at the helm of the secret police and the NKVD itself was purged, three trucks filled with legal documents arrived from Moscow at the Special Collegium of the regional court in Smolensk. These papers were necessary for the wave of reconsiderations of previous convictions that accompanied the end of the Great Terror.[8]

What was truly unusual was not the ultimate reversal but Menshagin's formal complaint that set it in motion at the height of the Terror in 1937. The basic facts behind his account are not in doubt. With his colleague S. S. Malkin, Menshagin traveled from Smolensk to present his complaint about the case to Vyshinskii himself at the Soviet Procuracy's pillared mansion on Bol'shaia Dmitrovka in central Moscow. On December 4, 1937, Vyshinskii telegrammed an order suspending the sentence pending further investigation, which ultimately led to the reversal of the sentence in 1939. What is doubtful is Menshagin's self-serving account of his dramatic audience with Vyshinskii in his palatial Moscow office, conveyed verbatim after many decades. In Menshagin's rendering, Vyshinskii was initially skeptical: "You come here and start to say, this is not right, this is not proper, the whole case is untrue. But what do you do back home? There you say 'I agree with the comrade prosecutor, but ask for a reduced sentence'—and you do not go any further." But the young Smolensk defense lawyer, in his response, bravely contradicted his superior—the Procurator of the Soviet Union, eminent jurist, and Stalin's main prosecutor at the Moscow show trials: "I said: this is not true, I raised the question of sending the case for further expert scientific investigation three times, and I wrote about that in the complaint."[9] Relegating his legal colleagues in Smolensk to the ranks of the cautious and the self-interested, Menshagin depicted his own actions as motivated by a spiritually informed altruism. "From childhood," he affirmed, "I firmly adhered to the rule: 'man shall not live by bread alone.'"[10]

The Smolensk historian Boris Makeev, who had access to the regional secret police archives in the 2000s before they were restricted, casts doubt on this pious self-presentation. "The conversation [with Vyshinskii] he describes does not correspond with the materials of the case. In the protocols of the legal procedures those episodes that Menshagin writes about in his memoirs do not appear, and the interventions he made appear much more modest." Similar discrepancies between the memoirs and the archives appeared in several of Menshagin's other cases. Menshagin, the legal historian ventured, either "did not hesitate to make things up, hoping to present himself in the eyes of his descendants in the best possible light, or he simply did not remember a number of nuances."[11]

Menshagin may have exaggerated his role in saving falsely accused victims of the Terror, but what he did is still notable in the context of mass fear. The question of his singularity is more complex than the specific differences between the archival documents and his memoirs. How was he brought to a moment when he decided to buck the great fear? How did his experiences under Stalinism set him on a path to becoming the mayor of Smolensk under the Nazi occupation regime?

Mass Participation in the Terror

The Terror forced virtually everyone, even in remote farms and villages, to make many choices, if only to swim with the venomous tide. Despite everything that historians now know, the phenomenon of the Great Terror remains one of the most mystifying and chilling cataclysms in a twentieth century full of atrocities. The case of Menshagin is one piece of a larger puzzle, a mosaic of politics, law, ideological passion, popular participation, and mass murder. What remains most in need of explanation is the relationship between the top-level design of this prolonged bloodletting and the paroxysm of mass popular participation, zeal, and conformism. Deciphering the enigma of this ersatz war, carried out in peacetime much like a military operation, helps explain the riddle wrapped up inside it—why and how one person took one action to save others at a time when few others could or would.

The show trials in the provinces scapegoated professionals, administrators, and local party elites as the sources of the countryside's most pressing animosity and discontent. The spectacles' messages were designed to be transparent to the masses. Years later, Menshagin concisely conveyed the gist of their political scripts. The trials in the Iartsevskii, Roslavl'skii, and Sukhinichskii Districts dealt with agricultural shortfalls and the poor harvest. Two others concerned another of Smolensk's agricultural concerns, cattle breeding. A trial of bakers blamed wreckers in the bakeries for bread lines and shortages in the city of Smolensk. Two others indicted experts in land redistribution (*zemleustroistvo*) for the haphazard, breakneck fashion that land claims were resolved as collectivization was completed in the mid- to late 1930s. Finally, the "counterrevolutionaries" indicted in two other show trials were district party leaders. The annihilation of party elites was a key novelty of the Terror, and the humiliation of local Communists was a surefire means of energizing rural inhabitants.[12]

Under Stalinism, it went without saying that mass mobilization and popular participation would be crucial tools in the elimination of enemies. Stalin, operating through party and NKVD channels, was instrumental in the design and most of the sentencing in the thirty-five provincial show trials launched around the USSR. Just after the dictator made the key decision to widen the scope of the Terror—with the turn to the mass operations that targeted for extermination swathes of the population and the regime's own cadres—he telegrammed regional party secretaries on August 3, 1937. He instructed them that it was "absolutely necessary to mobilize politically the *kolkhozniki* for the task of smashing the enemies of the people in agriculture."[13] Stalin's missive reflected a Bolshevik truism: agitprop, a neologism combining the genres of mass oral "agitation" and written "propaganda," represented not merely mass persuasion but mass mobilization. When Karutskii was named NKVD regional chief in Smolensk and thus took charge of the Great Terror in the region, he did not just become a central figure in the top-secret negotiations over the target numbers for the mass operations. He was also expected to devote his energy to whipping up public mass participation, including through the show trials. Each of the fictional narratives Karutskii helped roll out in these courtroom spectacles was anchored in the troubles and frustrations of an earlier period. The political earthquake of 1937 to which the trials belonged was even more deeply rooted in Soviet alternations of periods of revolutionary militancy followed by the respite of stabilizing yet untenable compromise.

Culturedness and Consolidation in the Mid-1930s

Sandwiched between the "socialist offensive" of the Great Break and the revolutionary revivalism of the Great Terror, the period between 1934 and 1936 was a time of consolidation and relative moderation. Quotas in agriculture and industry were moderated. Summary justice and extralegal arrests were minimized. Moves were made to destigmatize the children of kulaks and those with politically suspect social origins. Depriving citizens of the vote on the basis of their class origins was cut from the liberal-sounding 1936

Stalin Constitution.[14] The Great Break of the early 1930s had created chaos and disruptions in agriculture, education, and the professions. The mid-1930s interlude of consolidation that followed enabled a recovery. But just as in the mid-1920s before the Great Break storm, local and regional political leaders were able to entrench their positions.

A gathering of regional propagandists, for example, lamented in 1934 that "purely practical tasks" took precedence over self-criticism and the class struggle. In the mid-1930s, Smolensk regional courts were focused above all on supporting the state in economic administration. The most common crimes in the village in this period revolved around nondelivery of harvest quotas, deficiencies in animal husbandry, misuse of equipment, and theft of grain. Various systemic failures later prosecuted as counterrevolutionary crimes under the notorious Article 58 were handled within the conventional legal system. Vyshinskii and others moved to strengthen the role of defense attorneys like Menshagin. The Special Collegium of the Smolensk regional court, which became key to the jurisprudence of terror in 1937, was in previous years a dumping ground for the court's least qualified members. For lack of its own chamber, the Special Collegium met in the hallways.[15]

As turmoil of state-sponsored class war went on the back burner in the mid-1930s, the outlines of an emerging Stalinist civilization in the provinces took shape. It was centered in urban areas, where the Smolensk Region's population was growing, albeit more modestly than elsewhere. The Viazma-Briansk railway now connected two industrial centers. Plans for the region to become "agrarian-industrial" created dozens of new large industrial plants, including in machine building, textiles, and chemicals. Most of the 436 large industrial plants that existed in 1941, which employed from several hundred to up to ten thousand workers, were geared toward turning local raw materials, especially flax and hemp, into finished goods.[16]

The drive to rapidly expand the reach of education, culture, and propaganda was a centerpiece of the Soviet order. Here too, the mid-1930s period of consolidation marked a genuine shift. The year 1935 was the turning point for higher education in the Western Region, with four new institutions doubling the number in the region and serving six thousand students, along with thirty-three higher technical schools serving nine thousand.[17] In the cities and towns, factories and educational institutions, the "1930s generation," the first cohort that had never experienced prerevolutionary life, was most squarely incubated in the era's ethos of enthusiasm, political commitment, and culturedness (*kul'turnost'*).

This term, *culturedness,* stood for a kind of Soviet civilizing mission for the masses that was broadly disseminated and entrenched in the mid-1930s, flexible and capacious enough to be widely embraced by young activists of the 1930s generation and rising apparatchiki alike. The term encompassed education and political enlightenment as well as now sanctioned ideals of a prosperous, civilized lifestyle. Like its radical cousin of the 1920s and early 1930s, *cultural revolution,* it was the opposite of backwardness, which was slated for eradication. What was novel about the now dominant watchword of the period that followed was that it fused an intelligentsia embrace of enlightenment with a kind of Stalinist middle-class respectability.[18]

Stalin-era culturedness fused political literacy with clothes and hygiene, ideological correctness with a vision of the good life. Insofar as becoming cultured was a genuinely popular motivation for members of an urbanizing and newly literate society, it represented a carrot to the Terror's stick. The purchase of culturedness was broad enough that it was even attractive to ambitious young peasants trying to escape the village. One of them was Vasilii Maslennikov.

Maslennikov Chooses Culturedness

In another country, in another time, Maslennikov might have turned into a peasant intellectual critical of the social order. But in his repeated attempts to cobble together enough education to escape the collective farm from the 1920s on, the Komsomol and the Party had a lock on his life chances. He could not even conceive a path other than to join, to not stand apart from the regime. But his options were extremely limited and he remained fundamentally ambivalent about his choice.

Maslennikov tried first a radical step millions of other peasants took in this period. In September 1932, he uprooted and tried life as a worker in Moscow, hoping that a stint in industry would catapult him into a course of study as an engineer. Although he used the village contacts he had in the city, the best he could do was get a backbreaking job carrying heavy loads in a foundry. He realized he did not like the big city. "There was one other way out," he recalled. "Study more and become a first-generation member of the intelligentsia [*intelligentom*], if only a teacher." However, that was easier said than done. Only in 1935 did he garner an acceptance from a newly created institution founded the year before, the pedagogical institute in Novozybkov (now in Briansk Region).[19] It was not as a veterinarian, worker, or engineer that he would face the Great Terror, but as an apprentice history teacher.

It was the "cultured" part of the transformation from rural to urban that had always attracted young Maslennikov from the 1920s on. He embraced a package of traits, or a lifestyle, that included reading, knowing about the broader world, dressing well, and acquiring possessions (although in the 1930s economy, he never reached his dream of owning a bicycle). Briefly back in Filimony in 1933, he met a nineteen-year-old fellow schoolteacher, Zhenia Dmitrochenkovaia. Pretty and practical, she was also well-connected (her father was the collective farm chairman in neighboring Tishovo). Above all, she was literate, and he said, even there in the village, "I could also talk to her about literature and events in the world." To Maslennikov, there seemed to be only two choices: to raise himself up as a Soviet man or remain a "backward person" (*otstalyi chelovek*). In the late 1930s, the small town where he got a job, Ponizov'e, northeast of the city of Smolensk, along the Belarusian border, was attractive to him as a kind of "village that had become cultured" (*okul'turennaia derevnia*).[20]

Even as the outlines of a new Soviet civilization took greater shape in the region during the mini-thaw of the mid-1930s, the stabilization was fragile and temporary. The aftershocks of the Great Break overshadowed the rest of the decade. In the second Five-Year Plan of 1933–1937, for example, the collective farm system stabilized. Peasants abandoned open resistance and learned to use the Soviet system to their advantage. They flooded authorities with self-serving complaints and officials in the countryside became more responsive. In this non–Black Earth region, collectivized agriculture still only encompassed 59 percent of rural households in 1934, and a renewed drive to get rid of the remaining smallholders (*edinolichniki*) began in mid-1935. On the collective farms, the response to the Stalinist extraction state became virtually ubiquitous theft of grain and endemic foot-dragging. The result was a permanently underproductive agricultural sector. The Smolensk Region's bread and butter, animal husbandry, experienced a drop of about half in the number of horses, about three-quarters in terms of livestock, and about one-quarter in the number of fowl between 1928 and 1937.[21]

Under Stalinism, the number of human beings was also in decline. After the demographic recovery of the 1920s, a new demographic crisis resulting from mass migrations, an acute housing shortage, and food supply shocks could not be mitigated by a few years of 1930s stability between two up-heavals. In this region, a decline in birth rate, a rise in death rate, and an increase in child mortality accelerated dramatically toward the end of the decade. This demographic decline went well beyond the consequences of the Terror.[22]

Maslennikov, now from his more secure, small-town perch as an aspirational member of the Soviet intelligentsia, observed this new rural order and retained ties to his home village. He saw how the "labor day" system of payment left almost nothing to demoralized collective farmers. When kulaks were no longer available to scapegoat, the kolkhoz leadership took the blame. Smallholding farmers outside the collective farms were taxed out of existence, but the still mostly unmechanized collective farms did not represent the more rational order Maslennikov had imagined. He rationalized the ongoing difficulties as "growing pains."[23]

But in 1936, disaster struck the region's countryside again, this time in the guise of one of the worst crop failures of the century. Average precipitation was lower than in the famine year of 1891, and the average labor-day payments to farmers were lower than in 1932. Food was in short supply in the region for the first seven months of 1937, until a bumper crop saved the day. Unlike the man-made atrocity that capped the collectivization drive in 1932–1933, outright starvation was now avoided. In contrast to the early 1930s, the Soviet state curtailed grain exports at the start of the year. Ample food reserves served as de facto famine relief. Even so, the terrible harvest of 1936 contributed to a crisis of rural authority. In rural Bel'skii District, collective farmers simply refused to meet quotas. Even the despotic district party secretary Ivan Kovalev—purged in March the next year and accused of "rudeness" in fact typical of the bullying, foul-mouthed demeanor widely adopted by party bosses—admitted he would be driven out of the town of Belyi in a week if he attempted to extract the shortfalls.[24]

With their adversarial ideology and cataclysmic sociopolitical persecutions, the Bolsheviks had a talent for creating enemies where they had not existed before. The heavy-handed hunts for enemies gave everyone an incentive to camouflage and conceal, compounding the compulsion to go on the attack yet again. Former or escaped kulaks and all those with damaging social and political pasts were highly motivated to relocate and conceal their backgrounds, even as the state issued internal passports and tried to control urban space. In the wake of extreme social dislocation in the early 1930s, social marginals and repeat criminal offenders—concerns of "regular" policing—represented less masked opponents than groups outside the state's control. The repressive missions of the regular militia and the political police converged as the two were merged, also in 1934.[25]

In sum, the pragmatic if relative relaxation reflected in short-term social and economic policies of the mid-1930s was out of sync with ominous countervailing trends in the realm of politics, ideology, policing, and state security. This was the very same disjuncture that had engulfed the country when the NEP order was engulfed by the Great Break. History was repeating itself—the second time, to invert Marx, not as farce but as an even greater tragedy.

Unleashing the Masses

The quintessentially Stalinist plan at the pinnacle of power in Moscow, in a repetition of the power dynamics of the Smolensk Affair before it, was to let loose forces from below to facilitate an assault on the middle levels of power. The mobilizing spectacles of regional show trials were but one trigger for fomenting attacks on entrenched local and regional elites, now including party apparatchiki, as the terror snowballed into mass purging in mid-1937. Stalin and his lieutenant, Politburo member Lazar' Kaganovich personally intervened to install a new regional leadership after the fall of party first secretary Ivan Rumiantsev. Then, in summer 1937, this purge-era bureau of the Regional Party Committee took the lead, joining the regional NKVD and Procuracy in decimating the ranks of its own party organization.[26]

In 1937, mobilization worked to harness popular animosities to bring mass clamor for annihilating enemies to a bloodthirsty roar. Vigilance, accusations, denunciations, unmasking: this society-wide ferment, which Maslennikov likened to a buzzing nest of bees, was set in motion by sharp pokes from the party-state. Only this mass character was capable of making the cataclysm of the Great Terror so far-reaching.[27] The fact that mass participation was obligatory either has sometimes been confused with causal, politically determinative input "from below" or, by contrast, has never been fully reckoned with by those focusing at the top, on Stalin and Moscow.

The two dominant conceptual frameworks historians now use to understand the Great Terror—the elimination of a potential "fifth column," in expectation of coming war, and a monumental sociopolitical cleansing operation—are not, in fact, mutually exclusive. Both, however, ask about origins and explanations more than the actual power dynamics of the Terror. In a broad parallel to the best explanations of the Holocaust as a convergence of multiple historical agendas and practices of violence, each with its own pedigree, analyses of the Great Terror should recognize the convergence of overlapping strands of repression. Each of those streams, each with discrete roots and explanations, merged into a common waterfall in 1937.[28]

What brought them together was a reprise of the martial socialist offensive, an integral and already well-worn pattern of the revolutionary lifecycle. The revivalism was by now thoroughly statist, launched and ended by the dictator, and channeled through a specifically Stalinist form of mass mobilization. Yet it remained, in its way, revolutionary. Specially empowering the NKVD to go on a warlike footing was central to the mechanism of terror, but that was also prefaced and accompanied by inciting mass participation. As in the Great Break, an entrenched power hierarchy that had been consolidated in the previous period was a main target as the victim count skyrocketed.[29]

To this end, the master plot of all the regional and district show trials was that concealed "enemies of the people" had exploited and abused ordinary peasants and workers. Their unmasking explained not only all the shortages and unpopular policies, but offered something more: retribution. Authoritarian party officials, powerful "bureaucrats," and privileged professionals suddenly became vulnerable. According to the memoir of a Red Army general with roots in the local rural population, peasants in Bel'skii District viewed the Terror as retribution for earlier crimes against them during collectivization. The fall in March 1937 of Kovalev, Bel'skii's authoritarian district party secretary, raised expectations that other hated local bosses could be taken down. Local elites, especially those who had rammed through collectivization, were blamed for victimizing the common people and suppressing "democracy." As in the self-criticism campaign of 1929, for a brief moment entrenched power relations were inverted at the local level. Once again, this temporary subversion was intended to reinforce the power of the center.[30]

Unlike the era of collectivization, when the peasantry bore the brunt of mass violence, the countryside ended up with more autonomy and isolation in the late 1930s. But the Great Terror hit all elites and national minorities, urban or rural, especially hard. In the Smolensk Region, that included a third of collective farm chairmen. The remaining two-thirds were paralyzed by fear of denunciations. Paradoxically, therefore, the collective farm system in most ways continued its mid-1930s stabilization as the Party and the state, devoured by this new cataclysm, refrained from making significant new interventions.[31]

Perhaps the greatest legacy of the Great Terror was that revenge laced with *Schadenfreude,* whether in staged trials or in countless places of work, remained a potent cocktail. Even the educated city lawyer Menshagin, recording his memories, echoed in a more restrained fashion the sentiment of those ordinary Soviets and rural folk who reveled in the demise of their erstwhile oppressors. The first secretary of the Viazma District Party Committee, the Latvian Ian Iurmal'nek, had rejected Menshagin's legal defense. An Old Bolshevik since 1912, Iurmal'nek told the crowd that he would find a "common language" directly with the proletarian court. "You refuse," Menshagin remembered thinking, "well, so much the better for us." Recalling the party official's death sentence, Menshagin indulged in a restrained yet potent expression of ironic glee: "So it wasn't for nothing that he hoped to find that common language. He did find it. He was shot."[32]

Rise and Fall of a Little Stalin

Ivan Rumiantsev's eight-year stint between the Great Break and the Great Terror as party first secretary of the giant new Western Region made him the most powerful man in Smolensk. A skilled metalworker who joined the Bolsheviks in 1905, Rumiantsev gained crucial experience for the Stalin Revolution in the school of war communism in 1918–1920. Having demonstrated personal bravery in combat in the Russian Civil War, he was tapped for grain requisitioning and Cheka work in Kazan'. He was just as much a veteran of the NEP-era school of state building. For a decade after 1919, he rose up the ladder in successive party posts in a series of Russian regions, overseeing party purges while staunchly supporting Stalin throughout the inner-party struggles.[33]

Rumiantsev by necessity became skilled at exerting harsh pressure. He berated and cursed out people, demonstratively exhibiting command over underlings in the brutal style that became typical of the political culture of Stalinism. But like Stalin himself, he also knew how to turn on the charm. Unlike the *khoziain,* or big boss in the Kremlin, however, an effective little Stalin also had to know how to wheedle. After all, Moscow held him personally responsible for results. It was a high-stakes effort, for, as Merle Fainsod put it, the "little lords" of the provinces had to "cringe before the great lords of Moscow." Quite the opposite of Stalin, Rumiantsev moved around his districts to motivate as well as browbeat subordinates. "Rumiantsev spoke plainly, at times crudely," as one biographer put it, but with a certain "democratic" simplicity, "openly and comprehensibly."[34]

Moscow's quotas to the regions were impossible to fulfill. So were Regional Party Committee directives to the districts. The bar was always set too high not just for economic norms but also for cultural, educational, and ideological initiatives. The question then became how big the failure would be, as each level blamed yet reinforced the other. Designed to force results amid the fallout of deliberately induced failure, this system was bumbling, inefficient, and always ambitiously relentless.

In the first half of 1937, Rumiantsev struggled vigorously to keep one step ahead of the mounting pressures for purging his fiefdom without losing either the party organization's efficacy or his own power. In May 1937, he boasted that the inner-party "verifications" triggered by the assassination of Leningrad party chief Sergei Kirov in 1934 had purged 7,260 Trotskyists, spies, con artists, and "degenerates." What he did not mention was that his own regional elite had remained intact. Just one of those purged had been a district party secretary. Choosing his words carefully, the Old Bolshevik admitted to "grave political mistakes." Recent attacks on the Regional Party Committee leadership for living high on the hog, even if they were "demagogic," were "by and large correct." In a replay of the basic strategy of unleashing the hunt for unnamed "rightists" during the Great Break well before the "right deviation" was even revealed, even the future enemies of the people, Rumiantsev included, were forced to go along until the time was right. Smelling blood in the water, emboldened subordinates demanded to know why Rumiantsev and company had allowed those enemies he had purged to roam free rein in the past.[35]

A Recipe for Terror

In the decades since the first secret police documents on the Great Terror were studied by historians in the 1990s, the standard figures for overall number of arrests and executions (approximately 1.3 million NKVD arrests and 683,000 executions) have been revised upward. Oleg Khlevniuk writes: "As additional examinations of the statistics of the state security organs have shown, from October 1936 to November 1938, 1.7 million people were arrested in the USSR, and of them 1.5 million were convicted, including the 740,000 who were sentenced to death."[36] In terms of sheer scale, collectivization of agriculture in the early 1930s was no less murderous, given that dekulakization of five to six million peasants was followed by an avoidable, man-made famine in Ukraine and other regions in 1932–1933. In comparative terms, both episodes of mass violence were singular in that the regime launched such devastating waves of political violence against its domestic population during peacetime. What was different and even more unusual about the Terror was that one of its primary aims was to decimate the ranks of the regime itself. How can this be explained?

"The future bloodbath" of the Great Terror, Stephen Kotkin writes in his biography of Stalin, "was latent in Stalin's policy battles with what he called the right deviation in 1928 and especially 1929, when he took evident pleasure in humiliating Bukharin." It was far more than personal vindictiveness that linked the two violent "socialist offensives." The Smolensk Affair exemplified the mechanism for unleashing mass activism against the regime's own regional power structure and launching a far-reaching promotion of cadres. By actually exterminating large numbers of senior party officials a half decade later, along with every category of political, military, economic, and cultural elites, the Great Terror opened the door for a mass expansion of Stalin's Great Break program for wholescale political promotion. In other words, Stalin's own long-term vision of completing that generational renewal of the party-state proved a significant factor in 1936–1938. The *vozhd'* (or leader, as the General Secretary was known) gambled that a wholesale generational replacement would solve the system's bureaucratic pathologies. As Fainsod first noted, the Smolensk Archive contains "long lists of people previously occupying junior posts who found themselves lifted by the Purge of 1937–38" in an "undreamed of rapid rise."[37]

What has not received enough attention is that the Great Terror emerged out of the power-political methodology born in the opening phases of Stalinism. The basic Stalinist recipe for militant "socialist offensive" reappeared in a new guise to bring the mid-1930s consolidation to an end, that is to say, one revolutionary cycle later. Considering Smolensk on the regional level in both upheavals, rarely investigated together, brings this linkage into focus.

Emissaries and Beneficiaries

Rumiantsev's removal as regional party leader, in a new version of the earlier political operation that launched the Stalin period, allowed for newly appointed party and secret police plenipotentiaries to oversee a thoroughgoing purge of the regional party organization—a repetition of the very process that had made Rumiantsev into the prototypical little Stalin after 1929. The Old Bolshevik was recalled to Moscow on June 16, 1937, and arrested for his connection with the head of the Belarusian Military District headquartered in Smolensk, Ieronim Uborevich, a member of the Regional Party Committee. Uborevich had himself been indicted five days earlier along with his close associate General Mikhail Tukhachevskii, a native of Smolensk's Safonovskii District. They and others were accused of leading a "Trotskyist anti-Soviet military organization." Uborevich was interrogated longer than the others, because initially he would not implicate his friend Rumiantsev.[38]

Rumiantsev was replaced by Dem'ian Korotchenko. Born in a Ukrainian village in 1894, a party member from the Red Army generation of 1918, Korotchenko was a long-standing regional apparatchik who rose up to second secretary of the Moscow Regional Party Committee in early 1937 (along the way he Russified his name as Korotchenkov). He was a classic plenipotentiary, sent in from Moscow for only a few months in order to destroy Rumiantsev's regional elite and implement the mass operations. The day after the Politburo approved Rumiantsev's arrest, on June 17, Stalin's enforcer Kaganovich was already in Smolensk to meet with the Regional Party Committee bureau. The Politburo member's presence was deemed necessary to quash any missteps in the downfall of the erstwhile little Stalin. At an all-day meeting of the Regional Party Committee, Kaganovich, after speaking with each bureau member individually, "recommended" the arrest of Rumiantsev's closest associate, Grigorii Rakitov.[39]

Once again, as it was a decade earlier, Smolensk was a harbinger of what was to come on an all-union scale. Rumiantsev was one of four arrested Central Committee members who were regional party leaders that Ezhov mentioned at the fateful June 1937 Central Committee Plenum. This was the moment of Ezhov's "greatest triumph," when Stalin's loyal executioner developed the theory of a single, giant master conspiracy that, he insinuated for the first time, was present in every region and republic.[40]

Just as in 1929–1930, the mission of purging the regional *nomenklatura* was accompanied by a major territorial reorganization, again accompanied by the remaking of regional and district officialdom. This time, Stalin ordered the breakup of the giant Western Region born in the previous upheaval, creating smaller territories that included the new Smolensk Region. This territorial-political reorganization was launched in June 1937, the same month of Rumiantsev's downfall. The goal of downsizing was to produce smaller and less powerful regional party organizations more dependent on Moscow. Within short order, before leaving Smolensk in November 1937, Korotchenko replaced leading District Party Committee officials in twenty-five districts. In twenty of them, those removed were arrested. Korotchenko was rewarded for his short and bloody tenure in Smolensk with rapid promotions. At the end of the Great Terror, he moved up to top republican-level posts in his native Ukraine.[41]

"Every Communist is a *chekist*," Korotchenko declared at a meeting of party activists that took place shortly after he arrived in Smolensk to clean house. "Every party member must help the NKVD." The ascendancy of the secret police during the Great Terror disrupted the previous norms of the regional power hierarchy. Korotchenko worked in close tandem with Karutskii, newly arrived from Moscow to head the regional NKVD. The son of a Jewish petty trader born in Tomsk in 1900, Karutskii was also a "war communist," joining the Cheka in 1919 and rising up thereafter in far-flung posts in Turkmenistan and Kazakhstan.

As Smolensk regional secret police chief in 1937, Karutskii was also a man on a mission. He was out to redeem himself personally to his patron, NKVD chief Ezhov. Karutskii had been removed from his previous post in Western Siberia by Ezhov's predecessor Genrikh Iagoda, for "excessive alcoholism." In 1938, after presiding over the height of the Great Terror in Smolensk, Karutskii moved back to Moscow with a promotion to the all-union collegium of the NKVD. Perhaps it was the fallout from driving subordinates to torture and execute faster, perhaps it was stress Karutskii felt from a worsening position in an initial NKVD restructuring that weakened Ezhov's standing. Perhaps Karutskii's alcoholism never abated. As Stalin inched toward moving the Terror toward its close, on May 13, 1938, Karutskii became one of a series of NKVD perpetrators to commit suicide. He did not quite succeed in shooting himself, but he died later that day in a Moscow hospital.[42]

The destruction of the regional *nomenklatura* was deep and systematic. Two months after he arrived in Smolensk, Korotchenko reported directly to Stalin about the widening purge of party, state, and economic elites. What is striking about Korotchenko's assessment of the situation is the emphasis he put on the mass mobilization of forces from below. He emphasized the success of the campaign for "vigilance," which was spreading like wildfire. He promised that mass purging would address popular "discontent" (*nedovol'stvo*) over "everyday life," including long lines for bread and public baths, "extremely poor" services, agricultural shortfalls, deficit goods, and wasted resources.[43]

Predictably, however, the rampant dislocation and paralysis exacerbated preexisting economic problems. It led directly into an economic downturn, which only subsided on the eve of the war, with modest growth rates. A draconian prewar drive for labor discipline was pursued through the conventional legal system after the purges wreaked havoc with productivity.[44]

There was a major difference between the Great Break and the Great Terror in terms of the definition of the enemy. In place of dekulakization in the countryside, the Terror widened into roundups of numerous politically, socially, and ethnically defined groups, especially in the urban population. The production of victims proceeded much as with tons of steel in the Five-Year Plan, by issuing target numbers, although these deadly quotas were almost always overfulfilled.

Terror by Quota

The terror became "great" only because top-secret Politburo orders approved a dozen mass operations in summer 1937. These Politburo orders, signed by Ezhov and sent to regional NKVDs, planned mass arrests of groups in the general population defined in class, political, national, and social categories. For example, the largest mass operation, Order 00447, dated July 30 and targeting ex-kulaks, recidivists, and other "anti-Soviet elements," affected many former kulaks now in urban areas, radicalized long-standing policies toward social outcasts, and caught up a grab bag of internal enemies. Order 00486, issued on August 15, implicated wives and children of enemies of the people. The mass operations were responsible for the vast majority of victims of the Great Terror. The "limits" or target numbers in these orders, negotiated between the NKVD center in Moscow and regional party and NKVD leaders, recapitulated the practice of quotas set during dekulakization operations in 1930–1932.[45]

Smolensk (along with Omsk, a center for deported kulaks) was in the vanguard of the upward revision of "limits" for the quota for ex-kulaks. This reflected the initiative of the newly installed regional architects of terror, Korotchenko and Karutskii. By mid-June, Karutskii had arrested two thousand former kulaks slated for execution, and, by August 1, he reported to Ezhov about eleven thousand "counterrevolutionaries" and convicts. He cited Rumiantsev's supposedly soft-line approach to collectivization (in an area where there had been a great number of those classified as "middle peasants") and an influx of ex-convicts from other areas to justify higher quotas.[46]

Poles, Germans, Latvians, and Jews

After the passage of a 1991 law on the rehabilitation of the victims of political repression, Smolensk historians led by Evgenii Kodin, working with archivists at the regional secret police archive in Smolensk, created a database of arrests on the basis of the card catalog of secret police cases. Data for over twenty-nine thousand people politically "repressed" on Smolensk territory from 1917 to 1953 through secret police and judicial channels—if they were later rehabilitated, which generated detailed information—can be searched by sixteen categories, including reason for arrest, type of punishment, ethnicity, and party affiliation. In all categories, the numbers spike twice: during collectivization in 1929–1933 (primarily deportations and camp sentences) and the Great Terror in 1937–1938 (primarily executions by shooting).[47]

The Soviet "friendship of the peoples" doctrine and its strong ideological emphasis on multinational harmony always distinguished Soviet nationalities policy from the hard racism and genocidal eliminationism of
German fascism. At the same time, the national operations of the Terror
coincided with a cardinal shift in Soviet nationalities policy. In Smolensk
Region, small communities of national minorities—including those
identified as Polish, smaller numbers of Latvians, and a sliver of former
Volga Germans—were decimated in the national operations. Their cultural
and educational institutions created in the early years of the revolution were
folded into general Soviet organizations or shuttered.

In this largely Russian region, most of the cases with detailed information in the database (77 percent) were ethnic Russians, representing somewhere between 1 and 2 percent of the overall Russian population. While
the numbers of national minorities were small, in per capita terms they suffered far more. In the core months of those national operations in 1937–
1938, about 13 percent of the region's German population, 16 percent of its
Latvian population, and, incredibly, 17–20 percent of the Polish population were arrested.[48] A newly entrenched hierarchy of nationalities included
stigmatized and punished groups at the bottom.

By contrast, there was no national operation against the Jewish population. In the Smolensk Region, the group soon to be the special target of
annihilation under German occupation was victimized by the Great Terror
in roughly the same proportion of the overall population as ethnic Russians.
The Jewish population constituted 1.1 percent of the population of the region; in the database, Jews represented 1.7 percent of all those arrested by
the regional NKVD at the height of the Terror. Even as Jewish schools,
theaters, and collective farms were also subject to denationalization, their
members were not specially singled out. While antisemitism may have motivated individuals, Jews were not systematically targeted as Jews.

Even so, the Terror could not but have an outsized influence on Jewish
life, because Jews were strongly represented in the professions and the
intelligentsia. Purged Jewish party members included former Zionists from
the movement active in the region in the 1920s, high-level Communists associated with the purged Rumiantsev, and former members of the Evsekt-
siia, the Party's Jewish Section, disbanded in 1930. Popular antisemitism
may have been widespread, along with the association of Jews with control

of the Party. But popular prejudices did not dictate the targets of the Great Terror.[49]

Across the country, the percentage of the population repressed varied region by region. But by any account, the secret police operations in 1937–1938 constituted an extraordinarily intensive burst of violence. Records of executions in NKVD prisons in Smolensk, Viazma, and Roslavl show that the number of bullets in the back of the head averaged ten per day from August to September 1937, thirty by the end of September, forty by October, and up to sixty by December. Most of the shootings occurred not at night but in the late afternoon or early evening, as the executioners tried to finish by the end of the workday.[50]

A Breakdown of Trust

Maslennikov met the year 1937 finishing up his teacher's training in the pedagogical institute in Novozybkov. At his school, only three people that he knew of were actually victims of the purges. But for the rest of his life, he did not forget the atmosphere of suspicion and fear that the hunt for them provoked. In that small town, as everywhere else, the meaning of Stalin's speeches and the resolutions of the party congresses in early 1937 were crystal clear: large numbers of enemies had penetrated all organizations and had to be mercilessly eliminated. It followed that enemies must also be at the institute. The secretary of the party cell had to name someone.

Ivan Iudenkov was a top student. An energetic, "upbeat" young man, he was a convinced Marxist-Leninist. But he made a mistake. On hearing at a meeting that the famous revolutionaries Grigorii Zinoviev and Lev Kamenev were to be executed, he blurted out: "Is it really necessary to shoot them?" Maslennikov had no desire to condemn his classmate. Nor did anyone else at the meeting. Kseniia Ferapontova, a teacher of political economy, then applied a little pressure. Maslennikov remembered her as the school's ideological watchdog, a "real inquisitor" who serially denounced others in this era. "'Can such a person be a student in our institute?' The students kept silent. Then Ferapontova turned to one of the politically active female students. 'Well, so that's it. You, comrade Draichuk, what can you say about this question?' Draichuk was silent. 'Silence is a sign of agreement with Iudenkov. Is that it, then?' Facing this situation, Draichuk became confused and condemned Iudenkov."[51] Here as elsewhere, treating silence as a sign of guilt opened the floodgates of condemnation. "From that day on, Iudenkov started to become noticeably thinner . . . He did not know how to behave among the students." After a conviction for saving a copy of *Izvestiia* with a replica of Nikolai Bukharin's signature (the Old Bolshevik had been the newspaper's editor), the former model student was sentenced to five years. Iudenkov's girlfriend, Katya, was faulted for lack of vigilance—although Iudenkov had been president of the student union. She publicly renounced him.

The third victim turned out to be the ideological watchdog, Ferapontova herself. Maslennikov made derogatory comments about her physical appearance, saying she was "deprived of femininity" and ruined by a hunched back and nose of "rare construction." She had no friends or family; her only love was for Stalin, but it was the love of a "dog for its master." As with so many super-spreaders of terror who descended into serial denunciations, Ferapontova's hypervigilance was ultimately rewarded with the charge of using false accusations in the service of "wrecking." This came in late 1938, when Stalin signaled the end of mass purging. Accused of burning newspapers containing portraits of Stalin, Ferapontova wrote a suicide note declaring that giving her life for comrade Stalin would prove her loyalty. She hung herself in her apartment.[52]

The Smolensk party archives house hundreds of letters from the flood of denunciations, self-critical admissions, appeals, and pleas that resulted from the turmoil in virtually every place of work. Reading them, one sees how grudges, petty misdemeanors, legitimate grievances, and countless small acts of everyday life—preserving or throwing away a newspaper— were caught up in the state-sponsored, conspiratorial frenzy of the hunt for concealed enemies.[53]

If the avalanche of accusations seemed believable to many at first, especially of high-level political leaders far away, there is evidence that the allegations became increasingly implausible to others as they snowballed. The verbs and nouns in the political discourse of terror—*expose, destroy, unmask* and *lickspittle, toady, double-dealer*—entered the "language of the street." Initial exhilaration at the newfound ability to tear down the entrenched power hierarchy came to be replaced by "poisonous" distrust. If someone you knew became an enemy, the Party required you to write a statement. But this opened you up to interrogations. Not writing left you vulnerable to charges of concealment. The family unit, already buffeted by state-sponsored upheavals, was wounded by the requirement to renounce condemned spouses, children, and relatives.[54]

Trust, Geoffrey Hosking has argued, is as important as power in explaining the workings of society. If the Manichean ideology of Bolshevism and several waves of upheavals undermined preconditions for any culture of trust, the Great Terror was the last straw. The breakdown of social trust in Stalin's Terror was similar in effect to the religious revolution of early modern Europe in places where witch-hunting flared with great ferocity. Unlike the early modern era, the interwar years were a period of truly mass politicization. Millions of ordinary people now formed part of the political arena.[55]

Maslennikov, even in his quiet, far-off corner of a rural region, clearly grasped the suddenness of the destruction of bonds that were simultaneously part of the political system and everyday social relationships. All he had to do was look around his school. Everyone had started to "distrust one another." In the new atmosphere, "it was terrifying to utter anything that was not thought out beforehand." This is when Maslennikov likened his remote institute to a wounded, traumatized nest of bees.[56] It is an apt analogy for the Soviet Union writ large.

A Calculated Risk

When Menshagin prepared to travel to visit Vyshinskii in Moscow to appeal the show trial conviction of the counterrevolutionary veterinarians, his legal colleagues warned him of the petitions from around the region demanding harsh punishment. "The entire region!" he remembered them warning him. "Do you really not understand what kind of case this is?" Others urged him to back off: "You did your job." His superiors sent him a pointed warning: "Better to be a bad defense attorney but a good citizen."[57] Few Soviet citizens, not to mention defense attorneys, stuck their necks out when the mass operations were in full swing. Menshagin ignored the warnings. Why?

One explanation has to do with Menshagin's religiosity, which was combined with a relatively elite family history. His father, Georgii, an 1879 graduate of the St. Petersburg law faculty, was a member of the clergy who in the course of his legal career worked both in courts and as an ecclesiastical secretary. Throughout the 1920s and 1930s, Boris Menshagin himself never abandoned Orthodoxy. His biography provided some protection in the era of militant atheism. Menshagin served for eight years in the Red Army, for which he volunteered in 1919 after finishing the gymnasium in Smolensk the year before. Even though he always held noncombat posts in recordkeeping, this inoculated him against implications of anti-Sovietism. The experience as an archivist strengthened his meticulous nature and bureaucratic savvy.

Menshagin suddenly left the Red Army in 1927 because an anti-religious campaign revealed he was regularly attending church services. By that time, however, he had already completed legal education in the extension division of Moscow University. As he switched to a legal career, his religiosity again produced a setback: he was denounced, this time by the daughter of a cleric, for attending services in Smolensk's Uspenskii Cathedral. It seemed better to disappear for a while. Menshagin left Smolensk between 1928 and 1931 to work as a defense attorney in the Central Black Earth Region. He escaped unscathed because his Red Army service record omitted—why and how is not known—the reasons for his departure as well as his background in the clergy estate.[58]

Another explanation for Menshagin's purge-era action lies in his political judgments about Stalin and Stalinism. The period of relative relaxation in the mid-1930s lifted his "hope" for a continued path to moderation under Stalin's rule. This was the time Menshagin returned to Smolensk as a successful and well-off member of the regional Collegium of Attorneys. He dressed sharply and enjoyed a handsome salary matched by few in the city. One clue about how he was regarded comes from Fanni Khol'manskaia, the daughter of Menshagin's close colleague on the collegium, Isaak Frumkin, who also held a degree from the law faculty of Moscow University. The Frumkins had settled in Smolensk in 1929 with a group of Jewish families from Briansk. Frumkin shared many details of his professional life with his daughter. He later confided that he was very surprised when Menshagin became mayor of Smolensk under the German occupation. This was both because Menshagin was not antisemitic and because he never gave any indication of being anti-Soviet.[59]

Menshagin recalled that a new era seemed to be dawning when the draft of the new Constitution was publicized in June 1936. He even organized a "banquet" on December 5, 1936, in honor of the Stalin Constitution.

"I remember my sincere joy when . . . I raised my glass to the main author of that Constitution." During the Great Terror, the naivete of these hopes made Menshagin's disillusionment that much more intense. "I felt myself to be a hoodwinked simpleton."[60]

A final consideration for understanding Menshagin in 1937 was that the defense attorney, while taking a risk in appealing to Vyshinskii, was nonetheless playing an obligatory role in the Soviet system that Vyshinskii had long championed. The professionalization of law, of course, suffered a severe setback during the Great Terror, but it resumed in 1939–1941 and after 1945. Once the Terror was reversed in 1939, for example, thirty-two of sixty-nine cases involving party members convicted by the Special Collegium of the Smolensk regional court were overturned by the USSR High Court.[61]

Menshagin's bid to save the veterinarians in 1937 was undoubtedly a risk, but it was a calculated one. As he himself recalled with some pride, when Vyshinskii's telegram stopped the executions it "raised my personal prestige in the bar." The same conformist colleagues who had warned him off before now tendered their congratulations: "My man [*Okh, baten'ka*], you are so lucky!"[62] Menshagin excelled at maneuvering within the system; he succeeded because the system needed him.

Menshagin's prewar experience during the Great Terror holds striking parallels with his wartime tenure as mayor of Smolensk in 1941–1943. There too he used his position to save some lives in the broader context of putting his expertise in the service of another highly repressive regime. Both regimes, despite his calculated transgressions, valued him.

Police over Party

The Great Terror was predicated on an intentional destruction of the Communist Party hierarchy and the unprecedented empowerment of the secret police over the Party. Smolensk illustrates the extent to which the regional party organization had been decimated and weakened. In late 1937, in a "range" of districts, including Bel'skii, NKVD officials were actually carrying out party and state functions on the ground without Regional Party Committee approval. These NKVD officials were themselves party members, but they were usurping the institutional functions of the other two pillars of Soviet power, the Party and the state. The regional secret police was also promoting its own people into party and state posts without the sanction of the Regional Party Committee—something unthinkable before. Recruitment of new cadres into the Party was paralyzed because party officials were afraid to write the necessary letters of recommendation. They feared they would be blamed for backing anyone who might subsequently be unmasked as an enemy of the people.[63]

The beginning of the end came in late 1938. Party control commissions started reviewing appeals from purge victims. Kremlinologists observed that Beria had replaced Ezhov next to Stalin atop the Lenin Mausoleum during Revolution Day festivities on November 7, 1938. A decree signed by Stalin and Molotov ten days later ended mass arrests, blaming "excesses" on enemies who had infiltrated the NKVD and the Procuracy and "deliberately perverted Soviet laws." Beria succeeded Ezhov at the helm of the secret police by the end of November and began energetically targeting Ezhov's entourage. As the "purge of the purgers" spread in 1939, NKVD perpetrators who had become the most zealous torturers—many of whom were concealing their own compromising pasts—were put on trial by military tribunals. Throughout 1937–1938, victims of the Terror and their relatives had deluged regional and central party and legal authorities with hundreds of thousands of complaints. Now, many who had confessed retracted their confessions.[64]

As the once and future mortal enemies Stalin and Hitler partitioned Poland, the pact was accompanied by an awkward Soviet volte-face away from ideological anti-fascism. As with all turning points in Soviet history, 1939 was marked at once by internal and external reorientation. Internationally, the Nazi-Soviet Pact punctuated the end of the foreign policy pursuing collective security with the Western powers in Europe. Internally, Stalin's decision to end the Terror was accompanied by a political rebalancing of purge-era pathologies. Stalin was well aware that he had inflicted a grievous blow to the Party, Lenin's vanguard of the proletariat.

Over the course of Stalin's decades of rule, he calibrated the balance between the secret police and the Party by playing them off against each other. His systematic approach to *divide et impera,* both vertically by institution and horizontally by level of power, suggests how concrete power plays were integral to the recurring rounds of socialist offensive. The major power-political operations of the Great Break and the Great Terror instigated crisis and paranoia rather than being caused by them. Stalin took care not to allow even his own cult of personality, greatly strengthened by the Terror, to eclipse the Party as the bearer of sovereignty in the proletarian state. Indeed, editing the infamous *Short Course* history textbook even as the Terror raged, the "obsessively hands-on" *vozhd'* crossed out references attributing all agency to himself. He restored the Party to the central driver of history at the very time he was obliterating its members.[65]

The Threat of War

It was widely understood that the Western / Smolensk Region held special strategic and military importance in a coming war, and this gave Soviet ideological anti-fascism particular resonance. The Nazi German threat took center stage also because Rumiantsev was linked to the 1937 purge of Uborevich, one of the most innovative Soviet military theorists swept away in the ruinous decapitation of the Red Army. Others in the Soviet High Command had also maintained close ties with the German military during the clandestine alliance between the two outcasts of the Versailles system. But Uborevich had especially close connections with his Reichswehr counterparts and was a frequent visitor to Germany, studying at the War Academy of the German General Staff in Berlin as late as June 1933. His deep knowledge of German weaponry and tactics might have been useful in 1941.[66]

Accusations of a "military-fascist" conspiracy were rampant during the purge era in Smolensk. Rumiantsev himself, in his May 9, 1937, self-defense at the Smolensk city party conference, invoked proximity with "Polish and German fascism" and the "exceptionally important role" the region would play in the event of war. Kaganovich, during his sudden July 1937 appearance to monitor Rumiantsev's ouster, underlined the "front line" character of Smolensk. The area needed to serve as a solid rear when war began.[67]

Historians cannot agree about whether the threat of war was the trigger or the justification for the Great Terror. Even if we had access to unrecorded oral communications, which in the Soviet system were classified as higher than "top secret" documents, we cannot read Stalin's mind. Understanding the Terror as a preventative strike against a fifth column, a term attributed to Francisco Franco's general Emilio Mola Vidal that spread like wildfire on the Republican side of the Spanish Civil War in 1936, represents one dominant explanation for the cataclysm. In the late 1920s war scare and again in 1937, according to David R. Shearer, Stalin "radicalized internal policies of repression and mobilization (both social and economic) and sought to find diplomatic means to delay or avoid an invasion." Others emphasize the weight of the long pedigree of Soviet attempts to mold a society devoid of political and class enemies, which relied directly on the practices and dossiers of the secret police. Stephen Kotkin has suggested that Stalin himself slyly introduced the fifth-column explanation into circulation at the February–March 1937 Central Committee Plenum, the very moment the fifth-column factor began circulating inside the Party and became an explanation for what was happening in real time. In Smolensk, Rumiantsev's variation on the theme came directly after the plenum. The fifth column was a convenient, conspiratorial "story line," given that the Great Terror was about to wreck the military and heavy industry and plunge the country into a protracted security crisis.[68]

What can be firmly established is that in Smolensk, which in summer 1941 would bear the full onslaught of an invading army, the fifth-column talking point during the Terror was thoroughly disengaged from any immediate concerns about actual defense preparations. For one thing, the national operations against ethnic Poles, Latvians, and Germans, presumably related to destroying a potential fifth column, in actuality swept up rural communities, teachers in the national schools, theaters and clubs previously promoted by Soviet nationalities policy, and locals with Polish names dating back to the Grand Duchy of Lithuania. In terms of actual preparedness for a coming war, it became taboo even to contemplate military action on Soviet soil. An extensive planning operation for partisan warfare, for example, was shut down: "Bases and weapons caches were destroyed, and thousands of instructors were either shot or sent to the Gulag."[69]

The embattled Rumiantsev, on the eve of his downfall in 1937, made a startling declaration. When war did come, the Party could hardly be certain of the loyalty of the Soviet population. "It is very difficult," he asserted, "to calculate the political-moral condition of the rear, the political mood at the outbreak of war." Given what happened in 1941, this statement might be seen as prophetic. In the context of spring 1937, it might also be read as an advance justification for mass purging, offered up to stave off his own demise. No matter. Once he was condemned, his accusers divorced what he had said from any discussion of a possible war. The little Stalin who had dominated the Smolensk Region for so long was attacked for slandering the Soviet people and "attempting to sow panic in front of fascism."[70]

Restoring the Balance of Power

The power of the secret police to terrorize the Party turned out to be another extraordinary measure. Responding to signals from Moscow, party organs regained oversight of secret police appointments and replaced dismissed NKVD personnel with their own people.[71] By early 1939, with the secret police on its heels, the time was right for the Smolensk Regional Party Committee to go on the offensive. One pretext became the case of Aleksandr Maslov, a metalworker and party member since 1921 who had headed the political department of the Belarusian Military District headquartered in Smolensk. Maslov had been arrested on June 10, 1938, for membership in an armed "military fascist" conspiracy. In a letter conveyed to the Regional Party Committee by his wife, Ia. F. Maslova, he described torture, round-the-clock interrogations, false denunciations, humiliations, and face spitting as the most "liberal" part of an imprisonment that recalled the "history of the Middle Ages." In late 1938, the "physical measures" had ceased, but, he charged, NKVD "careerists" were trying to cover their tracks. He demanded a "verification" of the NKVD to correct the blow it had dealt to honest Communists. The Regional Party Committee formed a commission that confirmed the basic facts of the case. But it was only in March 1939, after more purging of the NKVD by Beria, that the Regional Party Committee dared to demand that the Central Committee send more prosecutors to speed up the legal reexamination of convictions.[72]

As 1939 drew to a close, the Regional Party Committee went on the attack. It appointed Georgii Manaev, a regional party secretary who had weathered the Terror as first secretary of the regional Komsomol, to go after "violations of revolutionary legality" in secret police investigations. Manaev uncovered "perversions" in the work of specific figures involved in the use of torture. This, as a Regional Party Committee report put it, "raised objections from the remaining 'old' NKVD officials," who did what they could to block Manaev's investigation.[73]

By 1940, the drastic weakening of the regional party organization had been recalibrated with the help of central authorities in Moscow. The Regional Party Committee was taken over by Dmitrii Popov, an energetic, up-and-coming forty-year-old graduate of the Agrarian Institute of Red Professors who had held his first major party post in Krasnodar only the year before. After the outbreak of war, his rump Regional Party Committee would emerge as one of the NKVD's rivals in the contest for the direction of the nascent partisan movement.

The restoration of the Party could not erase deep scars left by the Terror. The frenzy of vigilance against supposedly omnipresent enemies boomeranged against the system that unleashed it. Previously trusting loyalists experienced new doubts. After Maslennikov finished the teacher's institute at the end of 1937, he took a job in the town of Ponizov'e, the small seat of a deeply rural district, where all the buildings were wooden and of the "peasant type." Even at party headquarters, he recalled with satisfaction, one could order vodka at the canteen any time of day or evening without censure. It was a town, and he was finally freed from the village. The late 1930s were generally a happy time for him. But suspiciousness took root even in this out-of-the-way settlement, and rumors of inexplicable arrests reached him from near his home village in Filimony. He was certain innocent people were being purged. But he had made his choice. As the Terror wound to a close in 1939, Maslennikov was finally accepted as a candidate member of the Communist Party.[74]

Colossus with Feet of Clay

There was a supreme irony in Soviet justifications of terror as a means of eliminating a fifth column in the coming war. Nothing did more than the purges of political, economic, and military elites to disrupt Soviet readiness and create international perceptions of Soviet weakness—first and foremost in the ruling circles of Nazi Germany. Throughout all the geopolitical, diplomatic, and ideological gyrations that stretched from the demise of collective security to the double bluff of the Hitler-Stalin Pact and the Nazi-Soviet partition of Poland in 1939, the Terror formed the backdrop for Nazi Germany's disastrous underestimation of the Soviet system.

In certain ways, appearances were deceptive. The Terror had destructively rerouted the Soviet system's capabilities for mass mobilization to chasing invented conspiracies, injuring the backbone of the regime itself. The stereotype of a "colossus with feet of clay," a phrase repeated numerous times in German military documents in the key eighteen months of German war planning between July 1940 and the invasion of June 1941, was solidified with the disastrous Soviet performance in the Winter War against Finland in 1940. But years of ersatz or political warfare and the logistics of

internal colonization also created mobilizational capacity that could be har-
nessed with the arrival of a genuine enemy at the gates. The expectation
that feet of clay would crumble rested not just on a racial superiority complex, but on a profound underestimation of the "primitive" East's novel ca-
pacities for military, economic, and ideological mass mobilization. In the
run-up to 1941, Hitler and the German High Command gambled everything on the expectation that the Soviet Union would be knocked out
swiftly, thus sidestepping all of Germany's economic and logistical disad-
vantages in another two-front coalition war of attrition.[75]

Both regimes, in fact, showed great capabilities for misunderstanding
the other. If the Nazis fundamentally misunderstood Stalinism as a Judeo-
Bolshevik house of cards, weaker than the House of Romanov, the Soviets
and German Communists repaid the favor by mistaking National Socialism
as either another form of capitalism or a medieval throwback. Discounting
the modern and revolutionary forces shaping Nazism was a mistake as
fundamental as Stalin's blunder in discounting the warning signs of impending German attack.

German plans for the Soviet Union can be divided up into five broad
trajectories. These were military (encompassing strategic and security
dimensions); racial-demographic (involving longer-term plans for Germanization and engineering displacement of Slavs); colonial-economic
(including planning to secure agrarian, industrial, and labor resources and
the so-called Hunger Plan); antisemitic and genocidal (the formulation of
the Final Solution); and, least concretely but no less crucially, conceptual-
ideological (involving utopian visions and key concepts such as the East,
Lebensraum, and Judeo-Bolshevism). Within each of these overlapping
realms of advance planning, different institutions and figures took the lead,
although Hitler and the security apparatus under Reinhard Heydrich and
Heinrich Himmler were crucial to all. Even as the elements not infrequently
conflicted or even clashed within the sprawling Nazi system, there was an
interlocking logic animating all of them.

Military plans for Barbarossa in 1940–1941 centered around a knockout
blow. In the blueprints of Generalplan Ost (actually a series of never-finished
memoranda, the first of which dated to May 1940), the swift collapse of
the USSR would allow the colonial exploitation of Soviet western borderlands in order to win a world war and secure Germany's global dominance.
But Barbarossa also opened up fantastic new vistas for a new land empire

in the East, and Nazi euphoria fueled initial plans for longer-term demo-graphic engineering of Germans and Slavs as well as plans for genocide. Nazi antisemitism was both a fundamental ideological constant and part of a planning process for the most radical violence: the Jews were no ordi-nary "race" but the ubiquitous enemy behind capitalism and communism and the destroyer of other races.[76] Overall, Germany's global and imperial rise through conquest would necessitate reversing the entire direction of the Stalin Revolution, turning the land of forced industrialization into a rural arcadia. Stalinist internal colonization would be replaced by German racial colonization, making the USSR into a hinterland of farms, raw ma-terials, and "subhuman" laborers for the Reich.[77]

These plans were founded on a striking combination of technocratic ruthlessness and ideological delusions. That basic combination, despite the radically different content of their ideologies, was also visible in Stalinism. Utopianism and utilitarianism were both on full display in the Hunger Plan. The agrarian-economic planning process was driven by Herbert Backe, the second figure in the Reich Ministry of Food and Agriculture behind Walther Darré, the old "blood and soil" theoretician of the agrarian-racial resettlement of the East and Himmler's comrade from the days of the Artam League. Having watched Stalin's famine as a tool of collectiv-ization from their far-off ideological perch, the German agrarian radicals of the Right now readily turned to starvation as a collateral weapon of war. Although this vector of planning was also never fully completed before June 1941, it envisaged in cold-blooded, factual prose that tens of millions— perhaps thirty million Soviets—would "doubtless starve to death" so that food self-sufficiency could be preserved for the German population at home. The full extent of the Nazis' genocidal ambition is "staggering," in the words of Adam Tooze, but "what is less widely appreciated is that the Wehrmacht entered the Soviet Union intent upon not one, but two programmes of mass murder"—that is, the Holocaust and the Hunger Plan.[78]

In fact, there was a third: the so-called criminal orders constituted plans for waging a new, annihilationist form of war. These were a series of direc-tives also taken before the invasion in spring and summer 1941, which threw out the conventional rules of war then codified in the Geneva Convention of 1929. The best known is the Commissar Order, calling for summary ex-ecutions of political commissars, but the Martial Jurisdiction Decree was more far-reaching in that it authorized summary executions for all POWs without courts-martial. The decree's goal was twofold: to precipitate the military collapse of the USSR and to eradicate Jews and Bolsheviks, who were seen as virtually identical. Once again, the thrust was at once ideological and utilitarian.[79]

The worst atrocities in history have often been made possible after the advent of war or crisis. If a unique feature of Stalin's Terror was its self-destructiveness in peacetime, it is equally singular that cold-blooded Nazi advance planning for mass murder through starvation exceeded the actual capacity of the occupiers to achieve it. German forces, it turned out, were simply stretched too thin to contain savvy local populations and starve them on such a scale.[80] But the pitiless mental escalation of the first phase of Nazi radicalization on the Eastern Front in Poland in 1939–1940 blossomed into the euphoria of implementation with the invasion of the USSR in 1941. Not war in and of itself, but war in the East against Bolshevism triggered the most radical phase of the Nazi Revolution.

Several elements of the German preparations held particular significance for Smolensk. First, and most fundamentally, the necessity for a swift victory dictated a massive military thrust toward Moscow. The German High Command's war planning for troop movements was structured by the central transportation axis: Vilnius-Minsk-Smolensk-Moscow. In the troop plan of November 26, 1940, the path for the Army Group Center ensured Smolensk would receive the early brunt of the Blitzkrieg. Second, the expectation of mass starvation enabled the dire caloric crisis in cities such as Smolensk especially in 1941–1942 and, above all, the mass starvation of POWs in the great encirclements in the region. Third, in planning on the eve of war, "White Ruthenia" (a term that encompassed what became the Army Group Center administrative rear zone in eastern Belarus and western RSFSR) was expected to be a dumping ground for unwanted ethnic and "asocial" elements. This expectation was reflected in Alfred Rosenberg's memoranda and diary as he prepared to become Reich minister of the occupied eastern territories. It formed the general backdrop for planning the mass extermination that went on in Einsatzgruppe B's headquarters in Smolensk in fall 1941.[81]

The Ruthless Truth of War

If German conduct after June 22, 1941, built on the 1939–1941 radicalization of the Nazi revolution of the Right, so the course of prewar Stalinism directly influenced what happened in Smolensk during the war. In this rural region, collectivization and the kolkhoz system had created a large well of resentment against Soviet power. The series of economic and demographic blows sustained in the 1930s turned the struggle to overcome dire material hardships by any means possible into a mass phenomenon. At the same time, the 1930s consolidation of Stalinist civilization, with its long experience with mobilizing and motivating people and its compelling emphasis on becoming "cultured," ensured that numerous stalwarts—some young enthusiasts of the 1930s generation, others seasoned security personnel conditioned to hunt for internal enemies—would be primed for total war on a scale hitherto unimaginable. For loyalists, the new era after 1941 would herald a rocky transition from the imagined conspiracies of 1930s Stalinism to performing against a formidable occupying force. They would face what the great Soviet writer and war correspondent Vasilii Grossman called the "ruthless truth of war."[82]

As German legions massed upon its western border, Smolensk's divided population was only just recovering from the experience of the Great Terror, the deep scars of which corroded trust and paralyzed initiative. When individuals ranging from Boris Menshagin in Smolensk to Vasilii Maslennikov in Ponizov'e faced far-reaching decisions in 1941, they made choices that were deeply shaped by their experiences in the 1930s. As the people of Smolensk faced war and the German new order, they remained to no small degree rooted in the experience of prewar Stalinism.

4

REGIME CHANGE 1941

THE GERMAN INVASION of June 22, 1941, took even the best-informed Soviet people by complete surprise. That day found Vasilii Maslennikov vacationing in Krasnyi Bor, an idyllic wooded spot close to the city of Smolensk that was widely known for its dachas for the party and secret police elite. After many setbacks, Maslennikov had just secured his ticket out of the collectivized countryside: an appointment as a history teacher in the town of Ponizov'e. In this northeast corner of Smolensk Region on the border with Belarus, he had personally hit it off with the local district party leadership. His vacation at the sanatorium in Krasnyi Bor, a privilege for highly valued Soviet citizens, was a sign that he had finally made it.

He did not rest long. As the German troops stormed across the USSR's western border at 4:00 AM on June 22, Maslennikov was sleeping peacefully. At that moment, he had no idea that he was within walking distance of the killing field of Katyn, one of several NKVD execution sites where mass graves of thousands of Polish officers had been dug the year before. Still less could he have imagined that by the end of that summer, high-level Wehrmacht and SS officers would appropriate the party elite's dachas, renaming them "front villas," in the very place where he slept. In his wildest dreams he could not have believed that later that year, in November 1941, Adolf Hitler would visit the nearby Bärenhöhle bunker, the "Bear's Cave," as the Führer's headquarters was called, built the previous month for the ruler of a new eastern empire.

Teaching history overlapped with being a propagandist. Maslennikov had also taken on a party lecturer job approved by the Smolensk Regional Party Committee. He was versed in the official information available on the international situation. When the radio announced that morning in June that regular programming would be interrupted for a special announcement, Maslennikov had a premonition that it could be war. He was well aware that since 1939 war had overtaken Europe. Just over a year before, he himself had been asked by party authorities to "volunteer" for the Winter War with Finland, but the disastrous, costly Soviet victory of March 1940 had spared him from combat. Maslennikov heard rumors that Soviet POWs returned by the Finns had been sent straight to Siberia, since a Red Army soldier was not supposed to be captured under any circumstance. He also knew that the Soviets had carried out an especially large call-up to the Red Army without deferments. He even knew about recent reports in the Soviet press that German aviation had violated Soviet airspace. An instructor sent by the Regional Party Committee had pointedly conveyed to an audience of lecturers like Maslennikov that the pact Stalin and Hitler had made in 1939 was unreliable.[1]

Despite all this, it simply did not cross Maslennikov's mind that the news on June 22 would be about Germany. "If it were to be war," he remembered thinking, "it would be a small one, somewhere on the border, or even on foreign territory, with little bloodshed and rapid success." At noon that day, the sober, uninspiring, yet defiant commissar of foreign affairs Viacheslav Molotov, stepping in for a shell-shocked Stalin to make the announcement, invoked Napoleon's defeat, calling the *narod,* the people, to a new Fatherland War. At Maslennikov's sanatorium, no one slept that night. One comrade whispered about the hardships he had experienced in the Winter War. Deeply disquieted, all the men dispersed at the break of dawn.[2]

The depth of the chaos that ensued was due not only to apparent triumph of the Blitzkrieg gamble or Stalin's refusal to countenance any retreat. In Smolensk, unpreparedness was exacerbated by a widespread Soviet progression from complacency to shock, which for no small number turned into anger at the Soviet state itself. A cult of the inviolable socialist border and of the formidable Red Army formed key component parts of a

Stalinist superiority complex, assiduously embedded in ideology and culture. Exaltation was the correct register to convey the notion, dubious even to the most sympathetic foreign fellow-travelers, that the Soviet Union was supreme in every respect. Molotov, in his June 22 announcement of the invasion, pointedly linked the misguided arrogance of Napoleon and Hitler. But for years, Molotov's listeners had been bombarded by declarations about their own system's military invincibility. As regional party first secretary Dmitrii Popov revealingly mentioned in his Mints Commission interview, conducted in December 1943 by a Red Army major who was also a scholarly associate of the Soviet Academy of Sciences oral history project, a "large part of the population" of Smolensk did "not completely believe" what Molotov was saying. Perhaps it was just a sign that conflict with Germany had deepened, for "how could the Germans attack such a powerful country as ours?" Popov was openly admitting that large numbers of ordinary people were predisposed to perceive Machiavellian maneuvering behind even such a top-level official announcement.[3]

If the June 22 invasion produced widespread incredulity, the rapidity of the Blitzkrieg over the next three weeks, which moved German troops up to thirty miles per day and more, turned the world upside down for the entire population of the region. Army Group Center, massing along the Moscow-Minsk highway that led straight through Smolensk, boasted over 40 percent of all German divisions and over half the tanks. The brunt of the German attack thus led straight across the Dnieper-Dvina line, the Soviets' second strategic line of defense, to the very doorstep of Smolensk city. Spearheaded by highly mobile panzer forces, Army Group Center had advanced 370 miles in the first eighteen days of the invasion, decimating Soviet forward defenses, dismembering major parts of the Red Army, and virtually immobilizing Soviet command and control. The plan for Operation Barbarossa assumed that if the Germans smashed past both the outer and secondary military border districts, the Soviet state would wither away. Hitler believed the Red Army would collapse more quickly than the French had.[4]

Only on July 3 did Stalin make himself heard to the population in his famous "brothers and sisters" address. Even then, information remained scarce and needed to be deciphered. Around this time, Boris Menshagin was making his fateful decision to remain in the city, which led to his appointment as mayor of Smolensk from 1941 to 1943. He recalled: "Everyone, of course, was very interested in the course of military events. But official communiqués, conveyed by radio, were extremely meager. They spoke of difficult battles and beating back German attacks in various directions. To me one thing was clear: the battles were moving toward our territory, and the names of the directions in the reports spoke to the fact that our troops were retreating . . . Stalin's radio address on July 3 confirmed my conclusion."[5] The stream of news coming from the newly established wartime press agency, the Soviet Information Bureau (Sovinformburo), was opaque and often misleading. By the start of the Battle of Smolensk, which began on July 10, the Germans had inflicted over four hundred

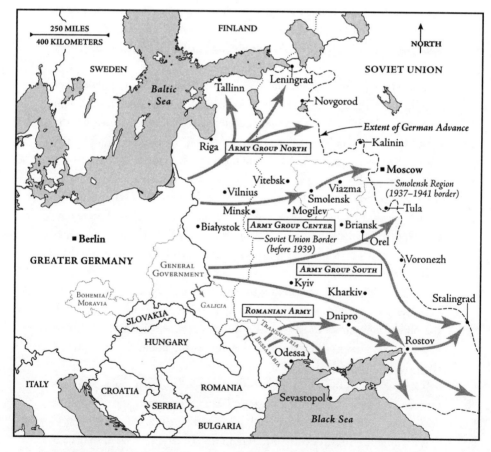

German invasion of the Soviet Union, 1941–1942.

thousand casualties and taken up to six hundred thousand prisoners. By July 16, the day Hitler appointed Alfred Rosenberg as Reich minister for the occupied eastern territories, the Führer assumed the war was all but won. Top military brass, including Fedor von Bock and Walter von Brauchitsch, were somewhat less sanguine, noting fierce Soviet resistance west of Smolensk in Orsha and Mogilev. Many Red Army soldiers were fighting to the death despite a woefully unready Soviet officer corps decimated in the Great Terror, which left soldiers and junior officers without direction. Despite disagreements with Hitler over strategy, the German High Command remained equally ignorant of the Soviet trump card: the powerful capacity for mass mobilization at the very core of the Stalinist system.[6]

During the military catastrophe of summer 1941, the civilian population found itself at a unique conjuncture triggered by the disintegration of Soviet power. Between the arrival of the Germans in the eastern part of Smolensk Region in early July and the stabilization of an established German occupational regime in the Army Group Center rear—which first began to take shape in Smolensk city in July, but in many areas to its east did not occur until the front lines moved after the fall of Viazma in October—there was a brief period widely known as *bezvlastie,* or power vacuum.

Power Vacuum

For all those who experienced this chaotic interlude, the contrast with the statism of prewar Stalinism was like night and day. Although there always remained room for maneuver even in the 1930s, decision making was seriously constrained. As Maslennikov knew so well, the Stalinist dictatorship commanded pervasive levers affecting people's life choices—education, socioeconomic status, and access to scarce goods and services. A common response was passivity or evasion along with activism, whether conformist or zealous. All of it was encapsulated in the classic Soviet saying: No initiative goes unpunished.

Suddenly, at this crossroads, initiative, indeed decisive action, became a matter of life and death. "With the arrival of the Germans," Menshagin rightly emphasized, "a question loomed in front of every resident of Smolensk: what to do?"[7] Far-reaching, often fateful decisions—to evacuate or to remain, to serve the Germans or to join the partisans, to register as a

Communist or to burn one's party card. To do nothing, or to wait and see, was also a decision.

As early as the evening of June 22, 1941, Smolensk citizens began loudly declaring at public meetings their support for the regime against the aggressor. But they hardly expected the Wehrmacht's arrival on their doorstep a mere three weeks later. Evacuation, chaos, and shock soon left the most fierce Soviet patriots and many other potentially loyal civilians without direction. As for the Communist Party, the district level itself was largely cut off from the Regional Party Committee with the end of telephone communications in mid-July during the Battle of Smolensk. "What to do next we will have to decide independently," the district party first secretary in Ponizov'e told assembled party forces, Maslennikov among them, on July 16. What the district leadership decided to do independently was to flee, abandoning the local population to its fate. The party officials, loaded down with family members and documents, took off on a truck guarded by an old policeman. It was quickly intercepted by Germans, and three district party secretaries were shot. Meanwhile, a fragmented regional party leadership left Smolensk and attempted to regroup in the city of Viazma to the east.[8]

Menshagin's Choice

Few choices were as consequential as Menshagin's acceptance of a position of authority as *burgomistr,* or the collaborationist mayor of Smolensk. To what degree was his appointment in July 1941 a deliberate choice? When it comes to his motivations during those critical days as German forces approached and entered the city of Smolensk, Menshagin's recollections are about as opaque as Sovinformburo communiqués.

Just as Menshagin himself heard those Soviet reports and was able to decipher the basic movement of German troops, so too can we read the train of events in his own life recorded in his memoirs. Menshagin's work in the courts ended on June 29, when the judicial building was hit in an air raid. The Germans began reorganizing the half-destroyed city on July 15. In his account, the defense lawyer simply omitted inconvenient facts, namely, the evacuation and, during the Battle of Smolensk, the mass flight of Smolensk citizens all around him from the city. The only time evacuation comes up at all is when it bolsters his image: he intervenes to convince a Jewish colleague, a fellow attorney, to leave the city, on July 15, 1941: "Suddenly the attorneys Gaidamak and N. Gol'tsova came up to me with luggage in hand. They said they did not know what to do. I said that it was dangerous for Gaidamak as a Jewish woman to stay, since the fascists' bad attitude to Jews was already well known."[9] Menshagin helped his Jewish colleague find a place on the last train out, hours before the Germans entered the city. He then returned to wait out the bombardment. As the bombs fell, he huddled with his family in a niche in the old city walls, built under Boris Godunov at the turn of the seventeenth century, which were adjacent to the yard of his house. In the context of mass flight and the ability of the well-connected to evacuate, as well as the decision of many others to take refuge in the surrounding countryside while aerial bombardment raged, Menshagin's choosing to remain in the city during the battle appears not only unusual, but highly considered. In another sense, however, his decision-making process was broadly representative. In discussing this period, Menshagin frequently mentions family, friends, local intelligentsia acquaintances, and colleagues, some of whom ended up in the city governance with him. His choice was not purely individual but made squarely in the context of his own personal and professional network. With the state largely absent, workplace, social, and personal networks were what people relied on when deciding next steps.[10]

There was another, perhaps decisive personal factor involved in Menshagin's decision, which is difficult to assess because he remained silent about the matter his whole life. Before the war, while still married, Menshagin had a child with another woman. Regime change coincided with the moment he left his first wife for his second. Before the war, Menshagin was married to Natalia Zhukovskaia, a typist in a Smolensk publishing house whom he had wed in 1922. They never had children. The marriage to Zhukovskaia began to unravel when he met Mariia Virenchikova, the wife of a former client. What is known about Menshagin's second marriage to Virenchikova comes not from Menshagin, but from a 2019 interview with their daughter, Nadezhda, or Nadia, born as the illegitimate child of Virenchikova and Menshagin on October 29, 1940—about eight months before the Germans reached Smolensk. Menshagin's lifelong silence on this matter was understandable. His essentially bigamous prewar relationship with Virenchikova violated both his legal and Orthodox sensibilities. Crucially, Menshagin made the fateful political decision to become mayor of occupied Smolensk around the very time he made a major change in his personal life, ending his marriage to Zhukovskaia and marrying Virenchikova, while also adopting his baby daughter Nadia's older sister.[11] World-historical change could facilitate highly intimate transformations.

Menshagin knowingly took serious risks by hiding during the battle and remaining in the city in those early days of occupation. On July 22, he was walking as usual in the city when he heard the German cry of "Halt!" Along with a group of others, he was briefly interned outside the city. In Menshagin's words, a POW serving as translator returned with a German junior officer, "pointed at me, and said: *'Jude.'* To this I answered: 'No, Russian.' Then the German asked about me and my occupation. The answer was attorney, but the translator gave it as *'Richter,'* that is, judge. I again spoke up: *'Rechtsanwalt'* [lawyer]."[12] Menshagin, who clearly knew enough German to make himself understood and was nothing if not savvy, was released.

Within days of being interned and accused of being Jewish, Menshagin became mayor of Smolensk. As head of the new city administration, he was tasked first and foremost with herding the remaining Jews into a ghetto and sorting the population.[13] On July 25, in keeping with the Germans' preference for appointing non-party members of the local intelligentsia to civil administrations, the new authorities had first settled on the older and, as it turned out, more weak-willed astronomer Boris Bazilevskii, a dean at the Smolensk Pedagogical Institute. Menshagin knew of the older man's appointment and—another clue about his intentions—took the initiative of meeting with him. He recalled several consultations around this time with Bazilevskii, other intelligentsia figures being recruited for the new city administration, and the new German authorities—represented by the figure of military administration counselor (Kriegsverwaltungsrat) Grünkorn, head of the seventh department of Field Headquarters (Feldkommandantur) 813, which was in charge of setting up the new civil administration in Smolensk. According to Menshagin, when Bazilevskii begged to be relieved of the post and recommended him in his place, "I was surprised and angry and said I also had no experience with administrative work." On July 30, Grünkorn decided the matter, saying that having legal experience favored Menshagin. Menshagin took the top post, and Bazilevskii was appointed deputy mayor.[14]

Menshagin, in other words, later very much wished to portray his appointment as mayor as a virtual accident of fate thrust on him, even though he had decided to stay in the city and joined local intelligentsia figures in talks with the German authorities. One thing is clear: whatever his calculations up until his appointment on July 30, there was no turning back. He was now in a new position of authority over the civilian population yet was fully subordinated to the Germans, with everything that set of power relations came to imply.

Commitment, Opportunity, Anger

Like Menshagin, the twenty-three-year-old party loyalist Andrei Iudenkov had access to Soviet radio reports in the days leading up to the German approach. But Iudenkov was in the town of Yelnya, fifty miles southeast of Smolensk, and unlike the shrewd urban professional, this low-level party activist, born to poor peasants in the village of Saliba in El'ninskii District, was far less equipped to interpret them. Iudenkov was a brash Soviet loyalist. Having finished primary school—a middle school simply did not exist in his rural district—he entered the Komsomol in 1934. Through grit and hard work he was able to become literate enough to gain access to the regional school for political-enlightenment work, which in turn allowed him to secure a job as inspector of political enlightenment at schools for the El'ninskii District's department of people's education. He secured full membership in the Party in 1940.

But as an ambitious, self-described hotheaded young man, Iudenkov felt stymied. He failed the state test to finish at the pedagogical institute. He was rejected from serving in the Red Army because of varicose veins in his right knee. In 1940, a personal tragedy led to a serious setback: his father died in a train accident, leaving him, as the oldest child, to help care for four younger brothers back in his home village. His first inkling of what lay in store came as he watched the city of Smolensk burning from German bombs far off in the night sky. He was in utter shock. "Smolensk burned. I thought it was like a dream, how could German planes be so deep in our territory?" he recorded the next year. "In my conception, the border was something that a fly could not go through."[15]

Just like Menshagin, Iudenkov seized what he saw as an unexpected opportunity opened up by the war. But his choice was the polar opposite of the former defense attorney's: Iudenkov joined the nascent partisans from the outset of the occupation. In less than half a year after his shock at the sight of Smolensk burning, this bold, newly minted young Communist would be catapulted to prominence as the political commissar of the Lazo Partisan Regiment, which played the key role in a six-month restoration of Soviet power in a swathe of territory around El'ninskii District. Iudenkov set down his first recollections on paper at the end of 1942, after the Wehrmacht had crushed the partisan territory with overwhelming force. The title page was marked "for myself," and he admitted that it was "devilishly hard to write" in the dark days of December 1942.[16] It was completely different from the series of postwar official writings and autobiographies he would write in the decades ahead.

In the chaotic period following the German arrival, Iudenkov fled his village out of fear that local "traitors" would denounce him as a party member. Moving around three districts during and after the Battle of Smolensk, he saw evidence of looting: "There was *bezvlastie*, people did not know what to do, everything connected to the state was falling apart, cattle were being looted." Previously hidden anti-Soviet expression in the population flared. In those early days of the war, he recorded, it was extremely rare to hear not just pro-Soviet but any anti-German talk.[17] The significance of popular anticipation of German rule, however, was not easy even for astute contemporaries to interpret. The power vacuum was a time shaped by the expectation of a new overlord, catastrophic Soviet retreat, and years of accommodation to all overweening authority.

The contours of popular response during the disintegration of Soviet power in Smolensk were likely very comparable to those in other predominantly ethnic Russian areas further east. Defeatism was most prevalent in rural areas and surged during battles when Soviet military defeat appeared imminent. Local activities in Riazan', where German occupation in fall 1941 lasted for a matter of weeks and not years as in Smolensk, were documented by returning secret police investigators. They recorded "staggering" amounts of looting of Soviet state property. There was also a resurgence of long-standing rural antipathy toward all authority, German and Soviet, as villages turned inward in a moment of crisis and opportunity. In towns, low-level petty notables in administration and industry who felt blocked by the Soviet system saw their chance for a fresh start under a new regime.[18]

After the Germans took Yelnya, Iudenkov made it to the city of Vi-azma in the eastern part of Smolensk Region. There he met an NKVD major attached to the Twenty-Fourth Army, and, as Iudenkov described, "somehow by itself the conversation turned to how I, in all likelihood, would be in a partisan unit and work in intelligence and sabotage." Iudenkov seized the chance to prove himself as a party member and overcome past obstacles. His determination to organize a partisan unit decisively altered his life trajectory.[19]

In some ways, deciphering the motivations of the young Red Army soldiers and their commanders who surrendered in 1941, *mutatis mutandis,* is similar to considering the civilian population. Motivations for both military and civilian Soviet subjects were affected by nationality, class, age, occupation, geography, and political-ideological orientations. The complex context behind individual decisions ranged from the basic urge to survive and save family, considerations of food and resources, to the disintegration of military or local political leadership. In the Red Army, active anti-Stalinism and anti-communist nationalism appear to have been significant parts of the mix. In the civilian population, NKVD reports from the period between July and September 1941 register "grievances" (*obidy*) against Soviet power from all parts of the population. "The Communists tortured us with their collective farms," one peasant from Gzhatskii District said and then gloated: "But now in response Hitler will drink their blood. He will bring us the good life. And I am waiting for him, so that he will destroy the collective farms and the Communists."[20]

Even as a considerable number of Soviet people rallied to the cause, the mood was different among the many Red Army soldiers who were trapped in the vast encirclements in this region, resulting in some of the largest numbers of POWs in the entire war. After they were captured, a bitter anger against the Soviet system flared precisely because of the long years of triumphalist Soviet propaganda. Vasilii Kozubskii was a school director from El'ninskii District who had joined the Party only in March 1941. He was also Iudenkov's mentor in the 1930s and, later in 1941, his close partner as military commander of the Lazo Partisan Regiment. One of the most introspective and thoughtful partisans later interviewed by Mints Commission historians, Kozubskii was the rare local intelligentsia figure who became a major partisan commander. He minced no words in describing the anti-Soviet anger of POWs in the Viazma encirclement in mid-October 1941.

He was one of the five thousand to six thousand captured Red Army soldiers forcibly marched east in a long column: "The mood of the column was altogether anti-Soviet. Conversations were as follows: now we see who lies and who tells the truth. Why was it necessary to drag the population into a war if you are incapable of beating an enormous military machine such as Germany. To speak up in defense of Soviet power would have meant being slaughtered on the spot." After days of hunger and with laggards subject to immediate execution, this forced movement east became one of the notorious death marches. Kozubskii escaped by pure chance. A woman watching the column turned out to be a staff member from his own school, and she hid him with relatives on the night of October 12–13, 1941.[21]

The First German Retreat

The period of regime change was prolonged in many parts of Smolensk Region by the course of military events. The failed Soviet defense in the Battle of Smolensk in July 1941 was more than just a bump in the road before the epochal showdown in the Battle of Moscow. For both doctrinal and situational reasons, the generals of the three Soviet armies leading the defense of Smolensk did not see holding the strategically important city as their top priority and "chose not to anchor the defense of the encirclement within city limits." Stalin had ordered a scorched-earth policy, but except for the bridges across the Dnieper, other major structures were spared. Some divisions of the Sixteenth Army, however, did fight block by block in the city, foreshadowing Stalingrad in 1943. Overall, the Battle of Smolensk damaged Army Group Center more than military historians earlier believed, and it directly contributed to the German failure to take Moscow in late 1941.[22]

After the fall of Smolensk, the Red Army attempted to relieve its encircled fighters with an offensive operation east of the city, centering on the German bulge at Yelnya. Yelnya was the very place where Iudenkov and Kozubskii would resist the Germans and, in fall 1941, help form a partisan movement, and it was quite close to Vasilii Maslennikov's home village near Glinka. The Yelnya operation represented the first Soviet counteroffensive and German retreat of the war. The war's first large-scale defense operation also occurred in the area outside Smolensk city, lasting into September.[23]

In the wake of the fall of Smolensk on July 16, first secretary Popov and the Soviet military engaged in a potentially deadly blame game over the defeat.[24] Despite this infighting between the generals and the regional party secretary, the crucial upshot was that the Soviets, with enormous losses of life and matériel, were able to seize an unexpected chance to mobilize and regroup. Hitler then overruled his top military brass, deciding in late August to redirect Army Group Center forces from the push to Moscow in order to take Kyiv in the south.

Hitler's cocky commandment meant, crucially for the Soviet defense, that the German drive on Moscow—Operation Typhoon—only recommenced on October 7. The great encirclements around Viazma and Briansk occurred in October. Tens of thousands of soldiers caught in them, known as *okruzhentsy*, escaped into the Smolensk partisan movement or to the villages. First secretary Popov, again sparring with the military, was on the mark when he defended those caught in encirclements to the Central Committee: "The disorganization of a part of the fighters and workers is considered the result of panic and cowardice. In fact, it is not so . . . Surrounded by the enemy, having not received instructions, the fighters had to find a way out as best they could or be exterminated or taken prisoner." There was no coherent Soviet strategy to deal with encirclement. NKVD special forces stationed behind the troops reportedly captured 657,363 soldiers fleeing their units from the start of the war until October 10, and 10,201 of them were reportedly shot.[25] Army Group Center's epochal defeat at the outskirts of Moscow in December led to a Soviet push west, liberating and re-Sovietizing parts of Moscow Region and eastern Smolensk Region in early 1942. After that, the front lines stabilized until summer of 1943.

Ghosts of 1937

The wartime emergency ushered in a new period of Soviet history. Now, the Stalinist system had to adapt its methods and approaches to a formidable German foe, as opposed to the phantasmagorical counterrevolutionaries of 1937 vintage. But when catastrophe struck, patterns set in 1937 were still exceedingly strong. Even as the seeds of a major shift were sown by reorientations in the state and army, it took until mid-1942 for generals and

German administration of occupied Soviet territory, with location of army groups and front lines, 1941–1943.

fighting units to be given more autonomy and for actual results to outweigh political fear and ideological conformity.

When the western front disintegrated, Stalin moved to punish military leaders responsible for their performance on the battlefield, which at least they had some hope of influencing, rather than treat them as enemies of the people. But recalibrating the balance between punishment and reward was also necessary. After being embedded for ten days with the Twenty-Fourth Army during the ill-fated Soviet advance at the Yelnya bulge, war correspondent Vladimir Stavskii wrote Stalin a revealing report dated August 15, 1941. His investigation disclosed that sticks had far outweighed the carrots: of those who fought at Yelnya, 480–600 were shot for desertion, panicking, and other offenses, but only 80 received medals. With regime survival on the line, the necessity of adjusting the balance between repressiveness and rewards for loyalists was uppermost on everyone's mind. "Right now," Stavskii wrote, using the negative Soviet term for unwarranted repression, "efforts are underway to eliminate these excesses."[26]

The instincts of 1937, even so, were exceedingly hard to overcome in 1941. When retreating east in summer 1941, Soviet security and party forces quickly executed prisoners and other figures caught up in the Great Terror, despite a June 24, 1941, NKVD order to evacuate them. Others, such as 274 people in Smolensk Prison No. 1, were left behind in the chaos. Far less well known is how "a wave of preemptive repression swept the entire country, carrying away 'suspicious elements' in regions located thousands of miles from the theater of war." Within the Soviet penal system, the result was a "little terror" that peaked in 1941 and early 1942 before being curtailed in a distinct shift starting in March 1942.[27]

During the power vacuum in Smolensk, Soviet authorities were in no position to shape popular reactions. It is therefore all the more striking that segments of party loyalists and, perhaps even more important, rank-and-file Soviet citizens and defeated soldiers were possessed by a deeply ingrained purge-era mentality. At a time when openly expressed anti-Soviet sentiment suddenly became widespread, those reared on the hunt for "enemies of the people" blamed traitors in their own midst. From the perspective of those who thought this way, popular anti-Soviet sentiment in 1941 had not been caused by collectivization or the Terror. In the alternate reality of popular Stalinism, the outbreak of anti-Soviet sentiment when the regime collapsed proved that repression had been fully justified all along. Previously hidden enemies of the people were morphing into open, identifiable traitors.

"We shot too few enemies of the people and traitors to the Motherland, that is why the Germans are beating us." That was the explanation given by a former Red Army officer hiding in the village of Filimony, Vasilii Sviatchenkovyi, in response to Maslennikov's wonderment that the Germans could have advanced so quickly. The officer's instinct to blame internal enemies, not uncommon at the time, spoiled relations between the two men. "This was not the time to seek these 'enemies,' more often than not imaginary," Maslennikov maintained. "The enemy was right in front of us, openly and brazenly entering our country."[28]

Among those who went over to the German new regime, Vladimir Melander, a forty-five-year-old zoologist born in 1896 to a noble family, was in the city of Smolensk when the Germans approached. The well-published professor and administrator at several higher educational institutions had survived the purges unscathed, despite his social origins. But in 1941, as Melander later told his interviewer for the Harvard Project on the Soviet Social System, "the spy-mania was terrific; I too was arrested for a few days." This is how, at least in retrospect, he justified his decision to remain under German rule: "When the Germans arrived, I remained there because I was afraid I would be arrested by the Soviets." He was recruited to the collaborationist local city administration, and served under Menshagin in several positions between 1941 and 1943, most notably as head of the housing department in 1942. After the bombing of Smolensk commenced in July 1941, he fled outside the city with many others. As Melander witnessed at one site, "the people greeted the Germans as liberators." Numerous portraits of Stalin's previously sacred image were defaced in hastily abandoned public spaces.[29]

The Soviet wartime ideological cliché of pinning the blame for anti-Soviet sentiment and collaboration on enemies of the people dated to the fleeting period of "power vacuum." This was the reaction of M. A. Bylenkov, an instructor from the Regional Party Committee military department tasked with organizing a partisan unit in the newly occupied city of Roslavl. Bylenkov arrived there in the midst of battle on the evening of August 1. The city fell August 8, and he reported on his activities on August 25. As Bylenkov described, goods were not to be had, as Russians looted the countryside and Germans looted the city. Bylenkov raised a partisan unit made up of thirty-two youths but only twenty rifles. His immediate instinct was to blame "the families of the repressed" for providing intelligence to the fascists. If the Germans could not be defeated, the internal enemy could be. "When detained these people are destroyed," he reported in the passive voice, and "measures are being taken to destroy" anyone else who became a collaborator.[30]

Einsatzgruppe B, in charge of "pacifying" the area in August 1941, viewed events differently. The more the security forces established control, the more committed enemies and looters ("sabotaging and vagabonding elements") took refuge in the countryside or forests. Most significant Soviet functionaries had fled and most documents identifying party and secret police figures had been destroyed, yet German forces were still able to recruit "significant numbers" of informers. All Jews, it was assumed, were in league with Soviet partisans.[31]

Both sides, in other words, identified enemies with deep-seated, ideological assumptions about how entire groups, whether anti-Soviet or "Judeo-Bolshevik," would act politically. Soviet partisans' preoccupation with betrayal and terror against traitors, which in the face of German military superiority provided a surrogate, proximate enemy much easier to target, took shape precisely in this period. Ideological zealotry, in turn, shaped reality in the guise of popular responses. To whom else would remaining Jewish residents go for aid except to the partisans? Possessing or inventing an "anti-Soviet" background, by the same token, helped locals find favor with the Germans.

In August 1941, El'ninskii District party secretary Iakov Valuev indulged in the Soviet political reflex of blaming all cooperation with the Germans on those "aggrieved by Soviet power." Valuev's list of internal enemies was made up of relatives of former kulaks, enemies of the people from the purges, priests, and the small number of ethnic German families in Smolensk. In fact, many erstwhile regime loyalists now changed their stripes. The head of the Smolensk NKVD along with a flood of party information-gatherers were already compiling lists of "traitors" among former Communists.[32]

Valuev's hackneyed explanation became standard for all those on the Soviet side inclined to embrace ideological oversimplifications. It avoided all personal and political gray zones and the devil's choice faced by locals. It discounted multiple motivations and situational opportunism and, in the years ahead, ignored side switching and the evolution of popular opinion. For Valuev, it also served to justify the past and ignore the failures of Stalinism. But that distorted view would have been difficult to believe if it did not contain a grain of truth. The moment of regime change in 1941 was the time not only when silenced enemies came out of the closet, but when anti-Soviet pasts proved one of many useful credentials in the German new order.

Evacuation, the Highest Stage of Sovietism

The invasion threw the regional party organization into overdrive. Back on June 22, 1941, the first day the Germans crossed the border, while Maslennikov still slept at the sanatorium in Krasnyi Bor, the party first secretary of the city of Smolensk, Ivan Mozin, was awakened nearby by a 4:00 AM phone call to his dacha. It was the Ministry of State Security: the Germans had invaded. Mozin received orders to make the evacuation of Factory 35 in Smolensk his top priority. The factory belonged to the People's Commissariat of Aviation Industry, but it produced tanks as well as planes. By early July, all the equipment and almost two thousand engineering and technical personnel from this factory had been evacuated to Kuibyshev (Samara), in the mid-Volga region. In the entire country, about fifteen hundred factories were transported to the Urals at a breakneck pace, often in near combat conditions. The mobilizational power of the party-state kicked into high gear. The Smolensk party organization mobilized several hundred thousand people for defense work, evacuation, and the military, with few desertions reported.[33]

Before June 22, Stalin had refused to countenance any plans for evacuation, considering it tantamount to defeatism. An evacuation council was created in haste only on June 24. But it was headed by a seasoned team under Politburo member Lazar' Kaganovich, a veteran of ruthless party-state social engineering drives since the first Five-Year Plan days. Starting with the Central Committee / Council of People's Commissars (Sovnarkom) evacuation order of June 27, the "most important industrial valuables" were prioritized. In terms of people, the most important were party-state apparatchiki, technical personnel, and priority workers, followed by women and children. Yet in a confirmation of the distinctive role of culture and the privileged intelligentsia in the Soviet order and in the war effort, precious resources at this critical juncture were devoted to evacuating cultural institutions. This, however, applied primarily to the elites of Moscow and Leningrad and to the arts, not to the professional or provincial intelligentsia in places such as Smolensk. Official estimates for the entire country of the number of people evacuated, totaling ten to twelve million, were almost certainly far lower than the real numbers of those who made it east. There were high rates of mortality along the way.[34]

The unprecedented emergency of 1941 displayed and furthered a feature of Stalinism honed during well over a decade of the "revolution from above": the uncanny ability to jump-start the party-state chain of command to concentrate on high-priority goals, relegating all else to the realm of unexpected consequences. On September 24, Popov informed the Central Committee that the "human resources" of the region had been "totally" mobilized. But for the many left behind—above all, the large rural population—Stalin's scorched-earth directive of July 10 to destroy remaining equipment and produce could not be anything but deeply unpopular. Evacuation of all large enterprises in the region's three biggest cities (Smolensk, Roslavl, and Viazma) as well as in other towns was carried out successfully. Only in Iartsevo was the evacuation of factories left half finished. On August 15, regional party secretary Popov reported that most peasants were not surrendering their cattle even as over nine hundred trains with products, raw materials, and valuables were evacuated. Inevitably, urban residents were far more likely to be evacuated than rural inhabitants, and in practice the whims of local officials could be of fateful importance.[35]

The overconfident Germans, fueled by fantasies of racial and cultural superiority, remained completely unaware of the well-honed potential of the Stalinist system to harness its political machinery for military goals. That "the evacuation was in many respects a triumph of the Soviet system of mass mobilization, the modus operandi of the Soviet state," is certainly a justified claim.[36]

Yet that is not the entire story. In 1941, the invasion also triggered the outsized initiative and self-mobilization of individual institutions and local leaders outside the party-state chain of command. Commanding local loyalties, non-party institutions worked around as well as through the official system.[37]

In keeping with the Party's Manichean worldview, Popov divided the entire population into heroic patriots and anti-Soviet elements. The party-state helped save itself in 1941 because it prioritized its material and human resources, but this left the remaining millions to their own devices.[38] In 1941, as in all previous and postwar population movements that were not entirely punitive or involuntary, calculation was involved when individuals weighed their strategies and personal circumstances. Those who uprooted and evacuated often had to make split-second decisions to pack in a few hours to leave for the interior, only to barter their belongings along the way for food.

A Rump Regional Party Organization

By October 1941, the Smolensk Regional Party Committee had no region left to run. In response to accusations made to the newly empowered State Defense Committee about Smolensk party members panicking and deserting, first secretary Popov scrambled to minimize the damage. In the blame game of fall 1941, Popov attempted to go on the offensive, bitterly indicting the generals for abandoning Smolensk city and military commanders for not giving instructions to encircled fighters. He did later admit that the head of the Regional Party Committee transportation section fled, "sowing panic among the population," and that two district party secretaries, instead of mobilizing party members, cried, "Save yourselves if you can!" Thousands of local party members were simply left to make decisions without any instructions at all. One of them was Ivan Bakaev, a party member and head of the electric station in the town of Sukhinichi (after 1944, in Kaluzhskaia Region), who later admitted under interrogation that because his family could not be evacuated, he "consciously" decided to remain under German rule: "I did not want to abandon my family."[39]

The previously powerful Smolensk Regional Party Committee itself barely existed as of October 1941. After the fall of Viazma by mid-month, the committee relocated east to Riazan', later moving to Moscow. During the German advance on Moscow in Operation Typhoon, the Regional Party Committee's lifeblood—cadres—was drained away. The formation of underground party organizations in the occupied territory was not a top priority, as they took second seat to the armed forces of the partisans. If the Regional Party Committee had eight secretaries before the war, by December it had only two, including first secretary Popov and one official in charge of propaganda. All its trucks and cars were given to the military. Only after the Soviet counteroffensive in the Battle of Moscow pushed back the Germans 60–155 miles west, and the eastern edge of Smolensk territory was liberated starting in January 1942, was Popov allocated a staff of six deputy party secretaries. Pro-Soviet initiative behind enemy lines inevitably fell into the hands of those actually on the ground. Aside from cowed local loyalists, these were mainly partisans and small numbers of party and secret police operatives.

Smolensk's Jewish Population

Few outcomes were more consequential than when Smolensk's Jews remained to face German occupation. In the 1939 census, Jews made up 1.23 percent of the region's population. Neither nationality nor level of threat from the Germans was part of Soviet criteria for evacuation, but non-evacuated Jewish residents who did move east on their own could, along with others, join the evacuation program. It is estimated that over 13,000 of the 14,800 Jews in the city of Smolensk managed to leave before the Germans arrived, in part because of the lengthy fighting during the Battle of Smolensk. In other locales, including Liubavichi—seat of the Orthodox Chabad-Liubavitch Hasidic dynasty before the revolution—about half the Jewish population in the town fled and the rest were confined to ghettos. Twenty such ghettos were created in July 1941 in the western part of the region. In territories of the occupied Soviet Russian republic (RSFSR), there were some 22,000 Jews in fifty ghettos. Almost all of these ghettos were short-lived and lasted only a few weeks or months. When the ghettos were destroyed, their residents formed part of the 70,000 to 120,000 from the Russian republic's territory who perished in the Holocaust. Many were unable to evacuate because they were not included in the Soviets' high-priority categories, unlike departing local elites, who might have given other residents instructions. Many Jews of various ages and levels of mobility, lacking information, attempted unsuccessfully to flee only when fighting began nearby. Indeed, in a fruitless bid to prevent panic, people in some localities were discouraged from leaving. In the district center of Shumiachi, seventy-five miles southeast of Smolensk, Jewish refugees from Poland were among 350 Jews trapped after evacuation and Red Army mobilization had saved the rest.[40]

Between 1939 and 1941, the period of the pact, the Soviet press omitted coverage of Nazi anti-Jewish policies, although in the 1930s there were certainly sources of information about Nazi antisemitism for those paying attention. Many people discounted Soviet propaganda or dismissed rumors stemming from Jewish refugees from partitioned Poland. Jewish testimonies later attributed decisions to remain to familiarity with German behavior from the period of German occupation on the Eastern Front during World War I, when members of the Jewish population often served as translators. This seems plausible. But Anna Shternshis, analyzing her own 198 survivor interviews and 229 others, concluded, however, that the "recurrent story of grandparents putting their faith in their positive experience with the German army during World War I seems to circulate in families as a sad yet comforting explanation of why the elders were left behind." Older relatives, who would have slowed the risky journey outside the confines of organized evacuation, did not survive to be interviewed.[41]

Chaos and Calculation

One keen observer of the brief power vacuum was Maslennikov. With the outbreak of full-fledged war in the area in mid-July, he fled with his wife southeast from Ponizov'e back to his home village of Filimony, where their children were staying with grandparents nearby.

Traveling across the eastern part of the region, Maslennikov witnessed a panorama of vivid, unforgettable scenes. At one group of collective farms, the Borodinskii sel'sovet, the authorities gathered all radio transmitters from the local population, so they would not hear about German military successes. All the confiscated devices, prized as rare and expensive in the countryside, were immediately destroyed by a bomb. Heading east, in Demidovskii District, they met a young Jewish woman "tragically frightened" of being caught, fully aware that the Germans were killing Jews indiscriminately. Kind words were all Maslennikov and his wife, Zhenia, had to offer. Next, a man claiming to represent the Soviet state—they had no idea what part—attacked them in their cart as panicking cowards. They fought him off. A desacralized image of Stalin, ripped and defaced, flapped from a wall.[42]

The Soviet order around them had collapsed, along with its monopoly on violence. Who could be trusted? How could one even tell which side strangers were on? In Kardymovskii District, Maslennikov met a fellow school director, who allowed him to sleep overnight in a school building. Maslennikov struggled to decipher from his host's cryptically cautious conversation whether this man was anti-Soviet and how he should respond. After a ninety-mile trek back to his home village, where he knew every byway and had picked mushrooms as a child, Maslennikov found himself in civilian clothes with a party card in his pocket. He was remembered and accepted by the villagers. But it was widely known that he had joined the Komsomol and the Party. What would they or the Germans do to him in the fog of war?[43]

The peasants around Maslennikov were also at a loss. As soon as the Germans arrived in the areas, work on the collective farm was paralyzed. "The kolkhozniki did not know what to do: should they continue to farm collectively or individually? . . . Meanwhile, the peasant women took the horses back to their households, trying to take their own horse that they had given to the kolkhoz ten years before—if it was still alive." In what would become a broadly determining factor in early German land policy, the existence of the collective farm was clearly very convenient for the invading army. Soldiers were able simply to requisition a portion of the collective livestock.[44]

Kozubskii, the future Lazo Partisan Regiment leader, was thirty-five in 1941. He was more urban, better educated, and a far more established school director in comparison with the parvenu Maslennikov, who was five years his junior. But they were both recent Communists, having been accepted as candidate members in 1939. Kozubskii, made a full member in March 1941, remained in El'ninskii District after June 22 while long-standing party members evacuated or fled. In July and August, before the Germans finally took the Yelnya bulge, he led emergency efforts to build anti-tank defenses at the Lesna and Ugra Rivers, all the while taking on the position of director of a group of collective farms. He was therefore in a prime position to observe the peasantry at the moment of regime change. Kozubskii was well attuned to the fact that the peasants surrounding him took a definite "interest in the enemy." They read the leaflets the German planes dropped in the area, but when he approached they would hide them in their pockets or pretend to use them for cigarette paper. Kozubskii saw how peasants in the area met their new overlords with bread and salt.

The First Partisans

Andrei Iudenkov was not so different from Maslennikov, although at twenty-three in 1941 he was seven years Maslennikov's junior. Their home villages were in neighboring districts, and they both pursued enlightenment work and education as a means of bettering their life chances. Both remembered the prewar years in the countryside, swimming and fishing and eating *shashlik,* as a kind of idyll. But the younger man, Iudenkov, had already made it to the district capital town of Yelnya and had found a friend and mentor in Kozubskii. Unlike the cautious and ambivalent Maslennikov, the hotheaded Iudenkov was raring for a fight. Described by his mentor Kozubskii as a "patriotic lad," Iudenkov threw in his lot with the Soviet cause as one of the first partisans even when it was most unpopular. He did not flee over to the Soviet zone during the fall of Viazma but, when the chance arose, accepted a mission to head back to El'ninskii District to organize a partisan unit in the face of an initially hostile rural population.[45]

Soviet wartime and postwar orthodoxies about an "all-people's uprising" begged the question of how a guerrilla movement crystallized in 1941 as fragmented, often self-appointed groups of local party, army, and secret police loyalists who found ways to survive a very hostile environment. Obsessed with traitors, spies, not to mention more basic issues of trust—partly from their Stalin-era background, partly by high-stakes necessity—the first partisans formed tight-knit groups and dominated them as they expanded. Living in forest camps, venturing out often at night to launch a reign of terror against pro-German traitors, commit acts of sabotage, and requisition food from the surrounding countryside, these original organizers remained the "elite" of the partisan movement even as its numbers swelled in 1942 and 1943.[46]

At the same time, a wide variety of partisan detachments emerged. They ranged from those sponsored by the Regional Party Committee or secret police to those completely off the Soviet radar and virtually indistinguishable from bandits and marauders. Partisan relations with the Soviet authorities and local populations thus varied significantly, as did internal dynamics within detachments. But what almost all of the units had in common at first was that they formed small, exclusive communities representing Soviet power in a sea of peasants and Germans. The word partisan

leaders used for this novel, wartime community remained the official Soviet one: *kollektiv,* or collective. Even as partisan leaders had unprecedented
autonomy behind enemy lines, their politics and culture remained recognizably Soviet despite a range of unique wartime innovations. What did it
mean for partisans to be Soviet in an area under Nazi rule?

The case of Iudenkov provides an important clue. He returned from defeated Viazma to occupied El'ninskii District by accepting an improvised
mission to work for the Soviet underground. Gambling on the nascent partisan underground and living in the forest, Iudenkov, it seems clear, found
an outlet for self-realization. In this he was not unlike others of different
backgrounds who were in some ways stymied in the prewar period but who
achieved success and recognition during wartime.

Iudenkov, as he explained in his Mints Commission interview, had
something of a rebellious streak and wanted more than anything else to see
action. Initially, he had taken a dislike to Kozubskii, his future partisan
commander, because when they met in the mid-1930s the older man was
supervising over a thousand students and thirty teachers. The young
Iudenkov dismissed him as a "bureaucrat." But after the young striver
realized how much he could learn from this comrade, Kozubskii became
his friend, mentor, and role model. Kozubskii's reserved and rational demeanor eventually impressed Iudenkov as a useful counterpoint to his
own overly "stubborn, energetic and at times not always desirably hotheaded" personality. After they reconnected in their home district in fall
1941, Kozubskii was the key figure encouraging Iudenkov and several
other of his former students to join him in starting a partisan detachment.
Iudenkov's skills were in "political enlightenment," so he became the
unit's political commissar.[47]

Once new units were formed, weapons gathered, and hiding places determined, a new partisan culture emerged very quickly. Partisans joined
units not only because of political and patriotic ideas. Some, including escaped soldiers, party members, and Jews, found a place to survive, and for
locals conscription certainly played a role. At the same time, the new situation started to weld the partisans into new, tight-knit communities. Even
when detachments were formed on Moscow's initiative, their distinctive,
freewheeling culture emerged independently, in forests far from Moscow.

In the late summer and fall of 1941 many partisans had little or no contact with Moscow or the Regional Party Committee. Some were ignorant

Andrei Iudenkov (front left) and Vasilii Kozubskii (front right) as political commissar and commander of the Lazo Partisan Regiment. In the back row are Natalia Iudenkova, Iudenkov's wife, and an unknown man. Smolensk State Museum-Reserve.

about basic news concerning the war. Ivan Fomchenkovyi, who came from a working-class family and joined the Party in 1926, later working as a newspaper editor in Smolensk and his home district of Iartsevo, wandered back to his home east of Smolensk city to organize a partisan group. Fomchenkovyi emphasized that he and his comrades had lost radio ties with Moscow for six to eight months in that period. They were so cut off from news that they initially did not even know about the Red Army's 1941–1942 winter offensive.[48]

To the degree their wartime communities remained recognizably Soviet or Stalinist, then, this was less imposed from above than from within. Iudenkov and other new partisan leaders hardly operated in a vacuum. Much of the partisan leadership emerged out of the party-state system of cadres. The earliest report I have found with Iudenkov's name was dated as early as August 26, 1941, shortly after El'ninskii District was taken by the Germans. It was a document signed by the district party first secretary Valuev and the district NKVD chief, a Lieutenant Puzanov. Iudenkov is listed as part of a unit in Mutishchenskii forest with access to a base containing 130 "Russian" rifles. The document demonstrates how the partisan movement at all levels, from the first, became preoccupied with violence and revenge against civilian collaborators. Its intelligence findings consisted of lists of individual "traitors" such as the daughter of a priest, a kulak, and a woman who "organized parties with the Germans" in her apartment.[49]

Iudenkov and his fellow partisans, while no less preoccupied with targeting collaborators, understood what official reports most often left out: much of the population, not just individual "traitors," was unsympathetic or hostile to their cause. As Iudenkov told his Mints Commission interviewer: "One must recognize that in those days defeatist moods were strong, and that was understandable, as our army had retreated and the Germans were hurtling forward, sweeping aside everything in their way."[50]

"Our partisans," as Iudenkov went on to say, "were people who in a range of cases were seized by panic, and in the period of the Viazma encirclement fled in entire groups from one German machine gun." He proudly claimed a role as political commissar in teaching them, using a quintessentially Soviet term connoting upbringing: "It was necessary to instill [vospitat'] a feeling of decisiveness, to show them that it was possible to hit the Germans."[51]

That formulation from the middle of the war in 1943, however, concealed the fact that in 1941 Iudenkov himself needed to learn a new, wartime way of life. Iudenkov did not know how to use a weapon before the war. But when he and his comrades ignored warning signs and shied away from executing a coward in their midst, despite "many reasons to do so," he quickly came to regret it. Soon after, the "waverer" panicked under fire. Iudenkov never forgot the time he executed his first collaborator. The man was a miller of Baltic German origin, and therefore part of a tiny ethnic German population in the region. The novice partisan scrawled a message in large letters and pinned it to the man's chest, so that the execution would serve a pedagogical function: "Shot as a betrayer of the Motherland and a German spy. We will do this with everyone who goes over to serve the Germans." Iudenkov became inured to ignoring the desperate pleas of collaborators about to die. "After that, I saw dozens of people before their execution. They wept, saying that they were not traitors, that they were good."[52]

A central, very practical problem remained: How could Iudenkov and other partisans know whom to trust? Even more striking than grown men crying was the brutally effective method Iudenkov personally devised for testing unverified partisan recruits. In his 1942 memoir, he recounted it with pride, in virtually the same breath that he expressed nostalgia for his idyllic prewar youth swimming and eating *shashlik*. In front of the untested recruit, Iudenkov would suddenly reveal that he was really a local policeman working for the Germans and that he was about to execute him. Some would break, immediately begging to join the German police. Others spat in his face—thus passing the test.[53]

Situation Report Smolensk: Einsatzgruppe B

As German forces pushed into Smolensk in the direction of Moscow, Einsatzgruppe B followed in the rear of the frontline troops, one of three main paramilitary "task forces" directed by SS chief Heinrich Himmler and subordinated to Reinhard Heydrich's Reich Security Main Office (Reichssicherheitshauptamt, RSHA). Einsatzgruppe B's commandos, totaling 655 men, entered Soviet territory between June 26 and July 1, 1941. Almost half the days that summer were march days. The rest were devoted to interrogations, securing urban centers, seizing Soviet documents, and recruiting local collaborators.[54]

In Einsatzgruppe B's most destructive and influential period of the occupation, from June 22 until November 1941, the task force was headed by Arthur Nebe. The son of a Berlin schoolteacher, Nebe was a World War I and Freikorps veteran. He launched a career in the criminal police in 1920 and joined the Nazi Party in 1931. His support for the Nazi seizure of power from inside the police led to a stint in the Gestapo and a meteoric rise to head of the RSHA's Criminal Police (Kripo), where in the late 1930s he took the lead on planning the deportation of Roma from Germany.

Because German forces expected to take Moscow, Einsatzgruppe B contained more high-level personnel than the other Einsatzgruppen. With Nebe overseeing Franz Six's Vorkommando Moskau preparing a total purge of the Bolshevik capital, Einsatzgruppe B was headquartered in Smolensk as of late August 1941. The task force's personnel records show it housed an administrative staff of 150, including twenty officers, totaling 16 percent of Einsatzgruppe B's size. Hundreds of pages of "situation reports" and other dispatches were sent to Berlin with the location line "Standort Smolensk," meaning the garrison or post. The first was dated August 29, 1941.[55]

The Einsatzgruppen were at the epicenter of a new stage in the Nazi Revolution. War ushered in new eras for both Stalinism and Nazism, but in differing directions. Already increasingly bureaucratic and entrenched, Stalinism was moving toward its more results-oriented wartime configuration. By contrast, the most radical energies of Nazism, directed outward toward racial domination and colonization, were intensified by war in the East. The occupation of Poland in 1939–1941 had already produced a distinct radicalization. Members of the SS training school in Fürstenberg, aimed at producing a "mindset" of "energetic ruthlessness" and "self-conscious determination," were seeded among the Einsatzgruppen troops at the outset of the invasion of the USSR.[56] Working in conjunction with other military and security forces, the Einsatzgruppen took the lead in the rapid launch of the Holocaust by bullets and a radical spike in mass violence in the broader war against "Judeo-Bolshevism." The wartime apotheosis of the fascist revolution was ushered in by a river of blood.

The imposition of German rule and the dynamics on the ground in Smolensk differed substantially from conditions in the Baltics and other areas occupied by the Soviets in 1939, where sudden loss of state sovereignty and Soviet mass repressions created intense resentment exploited by the invading Germans. The situation took a different form in Ukraine, where armed nationalists were initially a local ally. The occupation regime in the Belarusian lands of the Reichskommissariat Weissruthenien (White Russia), dominated by Nazi warlord Wilhelm Kube, differed from areas closer to the front run by the Wehrmacht rear area administration of Army Group Center, which included both eastern Belarus and predominantly Russian areas such as Smolensk. But in all formerly Soviet territories, the same intensive moment was marked by increasingly radical violence and the genesis of the Holocaust alongside the construction of new occupation regimes and the gathering of large quantities of new intelligence and information. As it confronted the Bolshevik East, Nazism was mutating.

This momentous shift to a new stage of Nazism in summer–fall 1941 was marked by distinct benchmarks that held direct relevance for the Smolensk Region. By July, after the existing rules of warfare were thrown out on the Eastern Front, mass shootings encompassed the murder of civilians, mostly Jewish women and children. This went along with an increasingly intimate association in ideology and political violence between Jews and potential partisan-communist resistance. By the time the push to Moscow was delayed in August, western areas of Smolensk Region were experiencing the establishment of local administrations and ghettos. By September, the brief interlude of a power vacuum shifted into what the Germans called "pacification." Next, the period roughly between September and Operation Typhoon's failure to take Moscow in December coincided with the complex yet decisive turn to the Final Solution (the best-known and most studied element), the mass destruction of POWs in starvation camps after the great encirclements at Viazma and elsewhere, and, in general, a sharp escalation in the entire victim count. This went alongside the lengthening time horizons for the war as it turned from Blitzkrieg to entrenched standoff. By the end of 1941, German rule was extended to the eastern parts of Smolensk Region, and the food crisis in the winter of 1941–1942 began.

In other words, the most unprecedented element of the radicalization associated with this new stage of Nazism, the first stages of the Holocaust, went hand in hand with a deadly spike in other forms of violence against POWs, partisans, and other "enemies of the Reich." It also corresponded with all the mundane practices and policies involved in apprehending, "pacifying," organizing, and ruling the "living space" in the east.

To explain the turn to the Final Solution, historians have emphasized the onset of German euphoria, Nazi "ideological intoxication," megalomania, and utopianism.[57] It is true that the rapid drive into the Soviet heartland seemed to many different Germans to confirm that a far-reaching, previously inconceivable racial-geopolitical reordering was possible. At the same time, the failure of the Blitzkrieg strategy, apparent to all by late 1941, exacerbated apprehension. The Holocaust and racial reordering, moreover, were pursued throughout the phases of victorious euphoria, stalemate, and defeat. The mental realization, first, that revolutionary goals might be achieved and, second, that they might well fail seemed to operate in tandem. Both euphoria and anxiety, never far apart, fueled Nazi radicalization.

Struggle and Control

The Einsatzgruppen are often described exclusively as mobile death squads at the forefront of the Holocaust. This is in no small part because Einsatzgruppen "action reports" (*Ereignismeldungen*), chronicling mass shootings with locations and numbers in a kind of rivalry among the mobile Sonderkommandos and the larger Einsatzkommandos up and down the front, were a written attempt by Nebe and the other commanders to provide Berlin with a deceptively exact bookkeeping of mass murder. By August 15, the reports were being circulated in at least forty-eight copies to Himmler, Heydrich, seven RSHA department chiefs, and a swathe of the security and police leadership. The reports' status as documentation on the Holocaust, giving insight into the "extermination dynamic" or feedback loop between Berlin and the Eastern Front, has ensured that they have been mined almost exclusively as part of the history of the Holocaust.[58]

The move to genocide, however, was unfolding simultaneously with the establishment of a harsh occupation regime and all the other security-policing functions associated with it. Given the rival, overlapping fiefdoms that made up the polycratic Nazi state, the arm of Himmler's RSHA had its hand in the pot of all sorts of other issues it associated with mastering "Judeo-Bolshevism" in the East.

By the time Einsatzgruppe B reached Smolensk in August, the task force was working jointly with Wehrmacht forces involved in rear administration. It took on an additional role as a key player in local regime-building and intelligence gathering—even as the army, for its part, played its own significant role in the Holocaust. Einsatzgruppe B's reports even included lengthy, interpretive digressions on the culture and history of the Russian "race" and the Soviet order.

Even as the fires of genocidal utopianism burned most brightly for Nazism at this very moment, in the sense that it was being driven forward by implacable and ultimately unachievable visions, it was no less defined by a pitiless, cold-blooded determination to implement these visions. The sense that goals and implementation were seemingly merging, that these visions were being achieved, was a crucial spark for radicalization.[59]

How can we explain this curious merger of revolutionary utopianism and ruthless pragmatism? The fallacy that ideological approaches are always impractical and impervious to rational calculation is especially misleading for both revolutionary movement-regimes of the far Left and far Right that fought this war. Bolshevism itself was the quintessential combination of utopianism and power-political ruthlessness. In the context of Nazi radicalization in 1941, the theories of Franz Six exemplify how the two strands came together. Six, one of the top officials in Einsatzgruppe B for the first three months of the war, was a brigade chief in the Vorkommando Moskau. Six came to the Eastern Front as head of the RSHA's Department VII, Ideological Research and Evaluation. A Nazi since 1930, Six held a doctorate from Heidelberg and developed close ties with the SS institute for racial studies (known as the Ahnenerbe). That was where he developed his theory of "enemy research" (*Gegnerforschung*)—a contested vehicle for advancing his own position within the SS. In one sense, his distinctive "theory" can be seen as representative. It made explicit a core feature of Nazism that animated all the various divisions of the SS: "struggle" and "control" were his twin guiding principles for identifying enemies. The first evoked revolutionary fervor; the second, exploitation and *raison d'état*.[60]

The SS and the New Order

August 1941 found Einsatzgruppe B at a moment when its mission was oscillating between violence, "pacification," and constructing the new occupation order. As its first reports from eastern Belarus began to include Smolensk in mid-August, they recorded sweeps for high-level Soviet apparatchiki, efforts to end looting, and seizure of political documents. This also meant acting on the information provided by newly recruited "networks of informants." The further east the task force moved, the more the element of surprise receded. More systematic, smaller-scale work was needed.[61]

Menshagin began acting as mayor of Smolensk in early August 1941, but his memoirs, despite his outstanding memory, never mention the SS or Nebe's Einsatzgruppe B. Later, Menshagin had no reason to give details about German security and police activities. Quite the opposite: he was motivated to address them only when they were specifically raised by Soviet authorities.

Nebe's reports, however, suggest that his forces were involved with a number of local activities in the city of Smolensk that directly impinged on Menshagin's newly constituted city administration and other areas. Nebe offered army field commandants support and reported that they required the "executive help" of security forces in such tasks as installing mayors, creating ghettos, registering Jews, and organizing obligatory civilian labor. Nebe reported that several Smolensk neighborhoods had been "systematically" swept "for functionaries and agents, criminals, etc." The August 29 report mentioned that former members of the Soviet-era Smolensk city administration would be invited to become confidential informants. The September 1 report approvingly noted the functioning of Menshagin's new civilian administration, along with the formation and activities of its order police (*Ordnungsdienst,* known popularly in Russian as the *politsai* or, in a local variation, *strazhniki*). The September 4 report noted Einsatzgruppe "initiative" in establishing "fruitful cooperative work" with army local and field headquarters (Orts- und Feldkommandanturen) in setting up collaborationist civilian administrations. Einsatzgruppe B's involvement in the takeover of Smolensk was extensive.[62]

Nebe candidly expressed great satisfaction that the genocidal zeal of his troops "could hardly have been expected" and should be credited to SS values and "ideological training." The coverage in the situation reports can be divided into four overlapping categories: violence, propaganda, information, and policy making. Indeed, these represented four central concerns of German racial colonization in the East more generally. In this sense, the Einsatzgruppen at the forefront of mass murder were not distinctive but representative. One of the most revealing aspects of Nebe's early Einsatzgruppe B reports was their descriptions of sustained encounters with local populations.[63]

"Simple and Primitive Russian People"

Army rear area authorities wished to stop spontaneous decollectivization of agriculture that might complicate requisitions as well as control over local populations, a stance that can be compared in its significance to

Napoleon's refusal to abolish serfdom as he invaded along a similar route in 1812. Rear administration reports from the Smolensk area in July and August 1941 not only warned against Russian looting as "arsonists, communists, agitators, commissars, etc." were apprehended, but identified "forbidden requisitioning by German soldiers" as a significant problem. It was in this context that Nebe's reports emphasized the potentialities for influencing the anti-Soviet and pro-German proclivities of the primitive peasantry as a matter of security for the troops. Sounding very much like a hopeful German "reformer" of 1942 or 1943 vintage, the head of Einsatzgruppe B immediately recommended in August 1941 that the Economic Inspection agency (Wirtschaftsinspektion) in Army Group Center's rear administration should produce leaflets proclaiming a new agrarian order. In other words, it was the head of the death squads who insisted that peasants would work without coercion if they could have the land, "if not right away, then in the foreseeable future."[64] At that time, top Nazi economic planners disagreed. Even after the key decrees proclaiming a new

A German officer addresses peasants about the harvest and political themes in the countryside outside the city of Smolensk, August 1941. Digital Picture Archives, Bundesarchiv.

agrarian order came in early 1942, they did not truly alter the pattern of delaying tactics.

Nebe also portrayed the opening of Orthodox churches as a major asset for the German new order. Church openings, Nebe wrote, were the "most visible sign of the changing times brought about by the German occupation." He cited reports that in places like Velizh (eighty-three miles north of Smolensk) even former Communists and Komsomols were attending services. In general, major divisions on religious policy persisted on the German side, as in other matters. For example, after the well-publicized opening of the Orthodox cathedral in Smolensk, Nebe's boss, RSHA chief Heydrich, complained "that it was not in the Reich's interest to have Germans help revive religion in the East." The security organs pushed for a more localized rather than widespread revival. What is significant about Nebe's account, however, is that Einsatzgruppe B reports assumed that the "mood" of the Russian urban and rural population was important to assess. By advocating for an SS role in matters having to do with popular opinion, Nebe was pursuing his own agency's institutional power. For example, he lobbied for the RSHA security police and intelligence arm to "alone and solely" become responsible for significant appointments among clergy members in order to make them useful for "security-policing" goals and intelligence-gathering.[65]

Although Einsatzgruppe B reports almost never indicated any specific sources of information, they were clearly based on interrogations and initial interactions with locals. The documents sent to Berlin form a kind of record of what was learned from, it was assumed, a simple, "intimidated," and "primitive" race. While other reports, including those from the Wehrmacht, could use far more blatantly ideological language of race, such as "Asiatic subhumans" (*asiatische Untermenschentum*), Nebe himself more typically wrote of "the mentality of the simple and primitive Russian people." His assumptions about backwardness seemingly led him to discount any possibility of strategic manipulation on the part of the population. He was aware that in the flood of denunciations to the region's new rulers, some false accusations about hidden Communists were advanced to settle scores. But he gave no hint that the performance of supplication, flattery and praise, caution about everything political, and the dogged pursuit of interests was informed by strategies honed for decades, even centuries in relation to Russian and Soviet superordinate authority. Seeing

Jewish conspiracy everywhere, Nebe displayed no small credulity toward the Russians and especially the peasantry.[66]

Manipulative supplication, a strategic invitation to paternalism, comes across very clearly in Nebe's reports—even if Germans puffed up by racial ideology were scarcely able to perceive it. The population wished above all to believe, Nebe reported, that the Germans were "seriously concerned with their care and the bettering of their situations." The police official noted widespread indifference to politics, yet locals were unlikely to be eager to parade political proclivities in front of their new overlords. Nebe's conclusion was as simple as it was categorical: the "wide masses" were "completely disinterested" in the change of regime and "only cared about the improvement of their personal economic relations." Already in August and September, fears of an "expected famine emergency" in winter were repeatedly mentioned. This very real concern, in fact, could explain both the supplication and the economic self-interest.[67]

A number of Nebe's ideas and proposals in 1941 anticipated General Max von Schenckendorff's equally contradictory conclusions in 1942 about the need to combine ruthless violence against enemies with winning hearts and minds among the primitive, gullible Russian people. Nebe, for example, pushed significantly to improve German propaganda. In conditions of a Soviet state collapse and power vacuum, wild and apocalyptic rumors spread rapidly, as they had especially during the cataclysms of the 1930s. German psychological warfare (*geistige Propaganda*) met great success in such conditions. Devastating rumors—Moscow had fallen, Stalin had fled to the United States, and so on—circulated with and without German involvement. On September 4, Nebe noted a current rumor—Stalin had declared the entire population remaining in occupied territories to be enemies of the state—to point out "a big area for German propaganda." German propaganda, he maintained, needed to address the issues of most concern to the population: the agrarian question, the church question, and issues of social security (*Sozialfrage*). In early September, Nebe advocated that the civilian administrations swiftly reopen elementary schools, a half year sooner than the German rear administration actually allowed. He digressed into a lengthy, surprisingly well-informed excursion into the history of the Soviet educational system that, it seems clear, rested on reports from local intelligentsia informants about Soviet policies. Grafted on were misleading exaggerations about the outsized role of both Jews and the tiny minority of *Volksdeutsche,* or ethnic Germans.[68]

As Nebe's barrage of reform proposals accompanied by his obsession with small minority groups suggests, the ideological framework of racial thinking did not prevent him from making policy recommendations that could be tactical or pragmatic as well as radical. At the same time, the Einsatzgruppe situation reports were permeated with severely misleading racial thinking. Speaking about the "Jewification" (*Verjudung*) of Soviet Smolensk, Nebe vastly exaggerated Jewish power and influence. The organs of Soviet power in Smolensk Region were overwhelmingly composed of ethnic Russians. Berlin was nonetheless informed that the Soviet party-state and all important positions within it were in Jewish hands. Since 1937, Jews had simply concealed themselves as Russian to hide their ubiquitous control.[69]

Judeo-Bolshevism, as this confirms, had become the main Nazi framework for identifying enemies. Yet this framework was not foreordained. At the outset of the war in the east in Poland between 1939 and 1941, targeting of the national intelligentsia of Poland worked alongside antisemitism as a major piece of German colonization. At that point in the war, it furthered the priority of breaking the Polish elite. This focus on the intelligentsia remained prominent during the preparation for Barbarossa and the initial weeks of the invasion. But in the slightly later Einsatzgruppe reports from Smolensk, the earlier focus on the intelligentsia, despite a few lingering references, was almost completely absent. In this region, the vast majority of those who would have been classified as members of the intelligentsia under the Soviets were professionals such as agronomists who were needed by the German regime. The Judeo-Bolshevik framework was now far more useful as a construct conflating Jews with Soviet agents, helpless civilians, partisans, and all other current enemies in the Soviet East. A standard rubric for the Einsatzgruppen reports was a variation on "Actions against Functionaries, Agents, Saboteurs, and Jews." The Jews were constant, but the other elements could vary.[70] The elastic Judeo-Bolshevik framework was murderously productive.

Legacies of the Interregnum

For a brief moment, as the Soviet state evacuated and German rule was incipient, both warring regimes were incapable of intervening in people's lives to the extent they did before and after. At this moment of regime change in 1941, everyone faced a choice and, once it was made, had to decide whom to trust and how to approach others. The three figures whose

choices have been tracked most closely during the 1941 regime change—
Boris Menshagin, Vasilii Maslennikov, and Andrei Iudenkov—expose a
range of decision making.

Menshagin, a non-party professional from the urban elite possessing
valuable skills and a readiness to turn against the Stalin regime, deliberately stayed in Smolensk and accepted a major post under German rule,
even as he fancied himself a paragon of morality. Buffeted by events, the
peasant teacher Maslennikov headed as fast as he could to his home village and family. Harboring significant doubts about Stalinism even while
it was clear he would never support German rule, he did what he could to
adapt to the new situation. The young striver Iudenkov had successfully
moved before the war from his home village to the town of Yelnya, but
when the Germans came he wanted to do more, both for himself and for
the Soviet cause. The wartime crisis for him was a moment of self-realization.
He unreservedly threw in his lot with the partisan movement while it barely
even existed.

Looked at from another perspective, however, these three very different actors were similar in one significant way. All three were careful
observers who in their own fashion recorded how the suddenness of the
collapse of Soviet power left them at a crossroads in their lives. This moment became seared into their memories. Each of them became dedicated
autobiographers.

What none of those three did for the duration of the war, however, was
to fundamentally alter their initial choices of 1941 by switching sides. Tens
of thousands of others—village elders who later covertly helped the Soviet
side, POWs and captured partisans conscripted as fighters by the Germans,
and many more—never left substantial biographical records or thoughts
about their lives. Motivated by highly situational factors, they could, after
some mixture of choice and coercion, switch sides repeatedly as well as
hedge their bets. Between the two poles of active collaboration and active
resistance, a vast, cautious, mass navigated in the middle, evolving as
German rule progressed. A 1944 party investigation found that about
12 percent of rural households in the Smolensk Region were tied closely to
the occupation administration, and a slightly lower number was affiliated
with the partisans. The vast majority, from the Soviet point of view typically labeled "passive," lay somewhere in between. The change of regime
in 1941 exposed stark divisions in the population.[71]

The brief moment of interregnum at the outset of the German new order left its mark on the subsequent course of the occupation. Even as the extent of German brutality would later shift popular opinion in an anti-German direction, those divisions apparent at the outset would only deepen. Conditions would approach a kind of civil war within the total war. But the exceedingly powerful, dictatorial states with their armies, agents, and ideologies remained intact. This distinguished the Eastern Front from the Civil War of 1918–1920, when the collapse of the old regime led to an array of nascent, potential, and failed new regimes and movements vying for supremacy. On the Eastern Front in World War II, Nazism and Stalinism always remained to shape the range of political choice available. In such conditions, survival and self-interest, often connected to obtaining and wielding whatever measures of local power could be seized, were surely among the most powerful motivators. But they were not the only ones. In this cataclysm, the people of Smolensk drew on strategies and reactions shaped by the experience of over two decades of life under the Soviets. As the short-lived power vacuum quickly filled, people in Smolensk turned to face a very different, wartime dictatorship.

5

MURDER AND HUMILIATION

AS AN ELEVEN-YEAR OLD BOY IN 1941, Evgenii Vakuliuk experienced a unique situation. His mother, Esfir, was Jewish, easily identified as such by her looks. His father, Ivan, was a Russian who spoke German well enough to enlist Wehrmacht soldiers' aid in the family's trek from Iartsevo to Smolensk after a failed attempt to evacuate. When the Vakuliuks reached their apartment in Smolensk, they found it had been occupied, with all their possessions, by the Gilinskii family, two Russian sisters and their mother. One of the sisters, who now worked for the German Field Commandant, threatened to denounce Vakuliuk's mother: "Your place is in the ghetto, you are Jews, get out of here!" Vakuliuk calmly recounted the story in a 2014 interview, at the age of eighty-four, speaking with a slight smile playing across his lips and only an occasional touch of bitterness. In Germany, if he had been half Jewish in the aftermath of the Nuremberg Laws of 1935, he would have faced curtailed rights as a "mixed-race person" (*Mischling*). But because his father was Russian, Vakuliuk's passport, according to Soviet practice, simply listed his nationality as "Russian." The young boy was so close to his mother that he chose to follow her into the Smolensk ghetto, created in early August 1941 in the Sadki neighborhood, on the far side of the Dnieper. "And thus we split up: my sister stayed with my father," settling in an unheated, vacant apartment in their old building, "and I went to the ghetto with Mama."[1]

As a boy, Vakuliuk did not grasp the dangers of his choice. As he put it, and his papers proved, "I was Russian." But in the coming months, the Gestapo relied on agents and denunciations to catch "Jews with Russian passports" living outside the ghetto, and later targets included children of mixed Russian-Jewish marriages.[2] Vakuliuk had vivid memories of constant humiliations inside the ghetto. But he did not discern the patterns of violence and atrocities conveyed by the only other Smolensk ghetto survivor, Vladimir Khizver, three years Vakuliuk's senior. Vakuliuk either did not know about or did not mention the series of confiscatory "contributions" overseen by Boris Menshagin's administration or the night Germans undressed and killed a row of young Jewish girls in the ghetto, prompting nightly patrols by older residents to protect them.[3]

Other survivors in twenty other ghettos on the territory of the former Smolensk Region and the approximately fifty on the territory of the Russian republic (RSFSR) have testified to a gamut of brutalities ranging from exploitation to sadism. Vakuliuk, for his part, simply wanted to be in the same place as his mother. In the atrociously overcrowded Smolensk ghetto, where between eighteen hundred and two thousand Jewish residents were crammed into eighty small houses, some had no room to sleep even on the floor. Even though the area was surrounded by barbed wire, it was a ghetto of the so-called open type. That meant its residents—mostly in work brigades accompanied by Russian policemen, known by the Russified German term *politsai*—could be marched outside its boundaries and around the city. Until the regime tightened two months before the ghetto's annihilation on the night of July 15–16, 1942, skilled craftspeople or professionals could also leave for work outside its territory.[4] Vakuliuk, however, since his documents stated he was Russian, managed to come and go unaccompanied. Alone of all the residents of the Smolensk ghetto, he experienced a kind of double life.

Sometimes, Vakuliuk chose to stay overnight with his father in his apartment; for some months he even went to an elementary school that opened for the Russian population. At the very same time that his mother languished in the ghetto, Germans quartered in the same apartment building as his father enjoyed conversing with a Russian in their native tongue.

If Ivan's marriage to Esfir had split their son's wartime existence, the heritage of his Soviet-era documentation also turned him into a middleman. As the desperate ghetto residents sold off all their valuables to buy enough food to survive, Vakuliuk was designated to deal with a Russian man, Dmitrichenko, who regularly stole flour at his place of work. Vakuliuk delivered gold to him and brought the flour back to the ghetto.[5]

As in other cities and towns under German rule, the very first steps of the occupation regime in Smolensk included the construction of a separated ghetto, registration of the city population for labor obligations, and the initiation of a population census. The German order to establish the ghetto came only three days after the Field Commandant office itself was set up in July. German orders and regulations prompted Menshagin's civilian city governance to carry them out at that same formative moment in August that his administration, the mayor noted with satisfaction, became a "well-ordered and rather well functioning apparatus." On August 19, 1941, Menshagin announced a general registration of city residents and the issuance of new identification papers. Clearing the Sadki neighborhood for the ghetto and sorting the civilian population were, in fact, the very operations that spurred the new city governance to take shape. The role that civilian town and city administrations played in the Holocaust through such micro-level population politics has been little observed.[6]

On the most local level, a new urban hierarchy was put in place. Street commandants (*komandanty ulits*) employed by the city governance gathered information on those non-Jews who were subject to register for their labor obligation in order to receive rations and identification papers. The ghetto was patrolled by Russian policemen under the aegis of the city administration. Menshagin recalled meeting with the dentist Painson (Peinsohn), the head of the *Judenrat,* the ghetto administration under German rule, on a weekly basis. If the Jews were at the bottom of the new urban hierarchy, the woman who appropriated the Vakuliuk's apartment and possessions, Gilinskaia, stood at the top. She worked for the German Field Commandant and was therefore not required to register at the labor market to receive ration cards, just like the personnel of Menshagin's city governance and its enterprises. In a time of acute material privation, those holding jobs with German institutions and Menshagin's administration had access to workplace canteens.[7]

The street commandants might be seen as in some ways continuing activities carried out in cities during the Stalin period by courtyard and building personnel, *dvorniki* and *vakhtery*. As during prewar Stalinism and the Terror, and as one of the period's legacies, wartime denunciations to the authorities from ordinary people like Gilinskaia were rampant. One Smolensk woman, Galina Moskovkina, lived on a street with two feared Russian policemen and a neighbor who regularly informed to the Germans. Moskovkina managed to hide one of her closest Jewish girlfriends in her basement until the very eve of Smolensk's liberation in 1943. But the *politsai*, finally tipped off about the basement, hauled them away in front of Moskovkina's young daughter. In the political and administrative circles in which Menshagin moved, denunciations and informing were, if anything, even more widespread.[8]

Beyond the Pale

A central fact of Jewish life in urban parts of the Smolensk Region was that the area was located just outside the eastern border of the former Pale of Settlement, beyond which Jews in imperial Russia faced legal restrictions on residence. Only a handful of Jewish merchants lived in Smolensk from the fifteenth century until the Great Reforms of the nineteenth century. After that, an influx of artisans, workers, clerks, and others came into the Smolensk Region from the overcrowded Pale. As Jews reached almost 10 percent of the city's population of 70,711 by 1914, they were leaving the Yiddish-speaking social and religious world of the shtetl for a predominantly Russian, urban milieu. The prerevolutionary Jewish population of Smolensk and other towns such as Roslavl was very stratified, ranging from a concentration of wealthy first-guild merchants to doctors and lawyers, clerks and poor artisans, and impoverished members of the poorest neighborhoods. Some Jewish socialists and labor activists who had dreamed the revolution would overcome the old exploitative world lamented in the 1920s that life in the Smolensk area had instead come to resemble that of the disbanded Pale.[9]

This situation was caused not only by a wave of new arrivals from the area of the Pale in Belarus, many of them Yiddish-speaking, religious Jews, but by the expanding boundaries of the Smolensk Region in all its interwar incarnations, which shifted slightly westward to incorporate a belt of former Belarusian shtetls east of Mogilev and Vitebsk and to the west-southwest of Smolensk and Roslavl. In the 1926 census, 1.5 percent of the population of Smolensk Province (38,285 people) was Jewish, with over half living in the more prosperous cities of Smolensk and Roslavl and almost a third in former Belarusian shtetls. The far larger Western Region created in 1930 had about 100,000 Jews, 1.6 percent of its population. While Russian areas outside the former Pale had relatively few Jews mostly concentrated in urban areas, the former shtetls to the west and southwest of Smolensk city had higher concentrations of Jewish residents. These included Liubavichi and Khislavichi, centers of Hasidic culture hostile to Zionism. In the neighboring Belarusian republic, early Soviet "indigenization" (*korenizatsiia*) policies promoting minority rights made Yiddish an official state language. Minsk in the 1920s became the Soviet "capital of Yiddish." In Smolensk and other cities of the Smolensk Region, Jews were more assimilated, Russian-speaking, and secular than in the former shtetls of the Pale. Although religious Judaism did not suddenly disappear and there was never any rigid, clear-cut dividing line between assimilated and traditional, these divisions were salient in a population that was already very heterogenous in socioeconomic terms.[10]

Vladimir Khizver was fifteen years old when the Smolensk ghetto was liquidated in July 1942. He and Evgenii Vakuliuk were its sole survivors. Khizver recalled in an interview in 1996 that he spoke no Yiddish, did not observe any religious holidays or Jewish customs as a child, and only felt his Jewishness when visiting his grandfather in Belarus. Until the war, his tight-knit friend group at school consisted of two Jewish and two Russian boys. He was hard-pressed to remember overt antisemitism in his life before the war, although everyone knew he and his family were Jewish.[11]

Blaming Jews for the revolutionary movement and Bolshevism, which animated pogroms in the Russian Empire and during the Civil War, gained powerful new impetus under Nazi rule on the Eastern Front. Judeo-Bolshevism could attract those perhaps not persuaded by antisemitism alone. The irony was that even after the Jewish masses gravitated to the Soviet order in part because every other armed force in the Civil War was implicated in pogroms, Jewish Communists still represented only a small and very distinct part of the Smolensk Region's diverse Jewish population. In general, Jews in the early Soviet Union benefited from the end of tsarist discrimination but now faced the new regime's anti-religious and anti-market orientation. Jews in Smolensk in the interwar period commonly resented rent-seeking local officials and harbored a wide range of opinions about Soviet power.[12]

Layered on top of all these linguistic-cultural, socioeconomic, and political divisions in the Jewish community were fresh ones resulting from Soviet evacuation and German deportations in 1941. Because of the protracted fighting, 13,000 of Smolensk city's 14,800 Jews, it is estimated, escaped before the city fell. In the former shtetls to the west of the city, only about half the Jewish population managed to evacuate, and in locations more isolated in the countryside the numbers were far lower than that. At the same time, however, an influx of Jews from Belarus, unsuccessful in fleeing further east, ended up in the Smolensk ghetto or others on Russian territory, almost all of which were created between August and October 1941. In addition, as many as 1,500 Jewish workers deported from the Warsaw ghetto and from Bobruisk were tasked with military construction work outside Smolensk city, almost all perishing from hunger and mistreatment. Only Nazi ideology and German policy, embodied in the topographical segregation of cities and the symbolism of the yellow star obligatory for all Jews over age sixteen, homogenized this highly diversified population.[13]

Feedback Loops between Berlin and Smolensk

Einsatzgruppe B figured prominently in precedents set in the progression from initial "actions" of the Holocaust by bullets in 1941 to industrial death camps after 1942. Its commandos, coordinating with army and local security forces, were at the forefront of "overfulfilling" formal remits on killing. After moving across Belarus, Einsatzkommando 9 at the end of July became the "first commando of *any* of the Einsatzgruppen" to expand mass shootings to include Jewish women and children. Individual commandos in Einsatzgruppe A in Lithuania and C in Ukraine mimicked the move in early August, before all others followed suit. For weeks, Einsatzgruppen units competed to outdo one another in victim counts even as pressure emanated from Berlin in the form of "displeasure over low execution figures reported." The escalation of extermination practices over the summer of 1941 was thus driven by a feedback loop between Berlin and perpetrators in the killing fields.[14]

The fall 1941 conjuncture, when German rule was extended into Smolensk and Russian territory, encompassed a number of key developments. In August, the Smolensk ghetto and Menshagin's governance began operating as Arthur Nebe shifted his headquarters east from Minsk to Smolensk. Ghettoization on Russian territory, therefore, was proceeding as the Einsatzgruppen and SS forces, aided by local policemen, were moving from shooting groups of Jewish men to annihilating Jewish communities in their entirety. As expectations of quick victory faded, the new occupiers faced a looming food supply crisis and the challenge of "pacifying" a huge expanse of territories. Finally, as the area under German control shifted east into Smolensk and adjacent Russian (RSFSR) regions, the capture and killing of increasingly large numbers of Jews was slowed. The fascists, at first fired up and euphoric, now radicalized and with much blood on their hands, quite simply had fewer Jewish victims to sate their genocidal ambitions.[15]

Nebe's report dated August 16, 1941, detailed a range of what were to him clearly frustratingly small shooting actions in the area. To be sure, in the specific belt of former Pale shtetls in Smolensk Region, including Liubavichi, Khislavichi, Monastyrshchina, Shumiachi, and Rudnia, concentrations of Jewish residents fell victim in greater numbers mostly after the Wehrmacht had secured the area in August 1941. But east of the former Pale, as Nebe explicitly noted, the numbers dropped. What he called "intellectual big city Jews" had plenty of time to evacuate. In this case, Nebe was right: on Russian territory there were many fewer Jews to be found. Of the 2.5–2.6 million victims of the Holocaust on Soviet territory, as estimated by Yitzhak Arad (including those territories in Molotov-Ribbentrop Europe that were sovietized in 1939–1941), 1.452–1.518 million came from within the borders of the former Ukrainian Soviet republic and 556,000–582,000 from the Belarusian republic. Far fewer, between 55,000 and 70,000, came from the Russian republic.[16]

At this crossroads, ghettos provided one means to continue the genocidal escalation while also addressing "pragmatic" considerations relating to the occupation regime. In this area, ghettos served primarily as a temporary prelude to more systematic destruction of the Jewish population, concentrating larger numbers of people while expropriating their valuables and exploiting their labor. In the entire span of occupied Eastern Europe, at minimum 1,150 ghettos were established. They differed greatly. In the words of one historian, "All ghettos were local." Sixteen ghettos in Smolensk

The twenty-one ghettos on the territory of the occupied Smolensk Region,
1941–1942.

Region were all destroyed between October and November 1941 (including Rudnia, Shumiachi, Roslavl, and Liubavichi) or during the first half of 1942, including four in close proximity to Smolensk (Gusino, Krasnyi, Pochinok, and Monastyrshchina).[17]

The major exception was the ghetto in Smolensk, located in a military, transportation, and economic hub where Jewish forced labor was in high demand. Flexibility could easily prevail over zeal in this case, since from the perpetrators' point of view the end result would ultimately be the same. Meanwhile, the liquidation of all the other ghettos around Smolensk did not go unremarked in the city, although Menshagin, who otherwise displayed familiarity with the civilian administrations of nearby cities and towns, unconvincingly feigned ignorance in his memoirs. By contrast, another eyewitness, the university professor B. Bazil'evich, recalled that local Russians "whispered more and more about the horrific atrocities the German brigands were carrying out on the Jewish population of various cities."[18]

Esfir and Evgenii Vakuliuk, Vladimir Khizver, the dentist Painson, and almost two thousand others inside the Smolensk ghetto also gained a temporary reprieve because the city lay directly on the Minsk-Moscow highway and was critical for the impending push to Moscow. The demand for Jewish workers in Smolensk, as Nebe complained in his September 3, 1941, report, "far exceeds" the supply, so that even nonessential skilled craftspeople were being diverted to hard labor.[19] This need explains the import of Jewish workers from Warsaw and points west, as well as the fact that the Smolensk ghetto alone in the entire region survived as long as it did, until the night of July 15–16, 1942.

Max von Schenckendorff, who as head of the Army Group Center Rear Administration area was Nebe's partner, had helped establish the exceptionally harsh approach to counterinsurgency adopted by the German military in World War I, well before the Nazis. As an antisemite who had embraced the "stab in back myth" to explain German defeat in the first war, he was able to form a bridge between the Wehrmacht, the SS, and the broader project of genocidal colonization. He viewed the Jewish population as a security problem and justified all German atrocities as a military necessity.[20] Small wonder that the general imbibed the ideology of Judeo-Bolshevism and saw the anti-partisan war as complementary to the Holocaust by bullets. The liquidation of ghettos during and after October 1941, when the

Army Group Center Rear Administration moved its headquarters to Smo-lensk, is indicative of how the Wehrmacht was indispensable to SS forces in carrying out the Holocaust.

But to fully understand the place of the Smolensk ghetto in the topog-raphy of the Holocaust, we must look to the Berlin-Smolensk feedback loop during the fall 1941 conjuncture. Heinrich Himmler, chief of the SS, visited Minsk on August 15–16. According to postwar trial testimony, he watched one of the many mass shooting operations of the Holocaust by bullets along with Nebe and Erich von dem Bach-Zelewski, head of the Higher SS and Police for the Army Group Center Rear Administration. The practical dif-ficulties of shooting hundreds or thousands of victims individually, the need for many units to put executioners on leave, the logistics of securing killing fields, and the lack of secrecy that went along with reliance on local aid were all perhaps no more significant to Himmler than the psychological effects on the perpetrators—possibly including himself.[21]

The launch of Operation Typhoon, the Wehrmacht's drive to Moscow, in the first days of October 1941 coincided with the destruction of sizable ghettos in the rear of Army Group Center. Notably, on October 2–3, the large ghetto in the Belarusian city of Mogilev was annihilated in the first of two major actions, with 2,273 people killed; 3,726 more were executed on October 19. October also marked the earliest destruction of ghettos on Russian territory and in Smolensk Region, for example in Tatarsk.[22]

The annihilation of ghettos between late fall 1941 and the last ghetto on Russian territory in Smolensk in July 1942 marked the onset of a new phase of the Holocaust. Mass executions remained a standard method throughout occupied Soviet territory. But after fall 1941, they were supple-mented by gas vans, used in the destruction of the Smolensk ghetto and elsewhere, and by the first mass industrial killings using Zyklon B gas in crematoriums. This began in the first Operation Reinhard extermination camps on Polish territory in Chełmno (December 8, 1941) and Bełżec (March 17, 1942).

Nebe, operating from his headquarters in Smolensk in fall 1941, helped lay the groundwork for implementing these new methodologies of mass murder. While commanding Einsatzgruppe B, Nebe remained head of the Criminal Police, returning to Berlin at the end of 1941. Before the war, Nebe had tasked Kripo's Criminal-Technical Institute with obtaining poison used in the T4 murder ("euthanasia") program designed by political and medical institutions to kill roughly seventy-thousand mentally ill patients, children, and others deemed "useless eaters" between 1939 and 1941. In those years, discussions of gassing as a more efficient and supposedly "humane" method of murder were discussed by numerous political and medical T4 perpetrators from Hitler on down. At the start of the T4 program, Nebe had directed Albert Widmann, an SS officer with a doctorate in chemical engineering and a member of the institute, to cooperate directly with the Führer's Chancellery.[23]

Now in Smolensk in 1941, Nebe directed a new push to get Widmann to develop new methods deemed necessary for the incipient Final Solution. In mid-September, Nebe brought Widmann to his Smolensk headquarters to plan a "special task." Patients from former Soviet state psychiatric wards in Minsk and Mogilev were used as test victims. After a "bizarre experiment" in dynamiting handicapped people in Minsk produced "macabre" results, Nebe and Widmann turned to a carbon monoxide van in Mogilev the next day. Initially termed *Sonder-Wagen,* or special car, in German, the vehicle became widely known in Russian as a *dushegubka,* or soul-killer. A model gas van was tested on Soviet POWs at the Sachsenhausen concentration camp at the end of October. By 1944, the overall victim count of fifteen gas vans operating on former Soviet territory had reached 350,000.[24]

Meanwhile, after meeting with high-level SS and police officials from the Generalgouvernement, Himmler approved the construction of the Bełżec extermination camp on October 13. In the days that followed, there was a flurry of activity in approving sites for other gassing camps. Plans for gas chambers in Mogilev, which never became operational, put them at the site of a recently created SS camp for "suspicious" civilians. Similar death camps, as confirmed by General Schenckendorff, were planned for nearby Vitebsk and Smolensk. It is an important demonstration of the synergies of overlapping violence on the Eastern Front that psychiatric patients, Soviet POWs, forced laborers, and suspect Soviet civilians were all first victims of gassing technologies that gained their widest application in the genocide of the Jews.[25]

Planning for both gas vans and gas chambers thus proceeded in tandem over the same stretch of fateful months. As this suggests, death camps with gas chambers, later virtually conflated with the Holocaust as a whole, were during the fall 1941 conjuncture planned much further east. They were expected to be built in Mogilev, Vitebsk, and Smolensk, with the latter two locations likely on the sites of projected SS labor camps. On September 17, Bach-Zelewski flew to Smolensk to hold talks with Nebe on these initiatives involving both mobile and stationary gassing. In late October, Himmler visited Mogilev and Smolensk with an entourage of SS officials. That this projected network of "transit and extermination camps" never materialized in Mogilev, Vitebsk, and Smolensk was not for lack of German design. They were cut off by intractable transportation difficulties and the fortunes of war.[26] Smolensk and its ghetto instead became a site for the deployment of gas vans.

The Mayor and the Ghetto

In September 1941, Smolensk's new mayor, Menshagin, received an elderly Jewish couple seeking to escape the Smolensk ghetto by Russifying their names on forged identification papers. They were recommended to him by the physician in the city hospital, P. I. Kesarev, as "good and harmless people." Menshagin, using his knowledge of the Soviet system, throughout the period regularly cross-examined a long parade of supplicants who needed residency or travel passes. Were they lying? Would they betray him? Were they sent by the Germans to test him? In this case, Menshagin evaluated the couple and rendered his verdict: "I liked them, so I signed both passports, stamped them and gave them back to them, asking that they tell no one about this." That little phrase—"I liked them"—is cause for reflection. Menshagin sent all others he did not like or trust "to the four winds." He did not agonize over these decisions. He displayed only satisfaction in wielding his newly acquired power over life and death.[27] In extreme circumstances like those on the Eastern Front, even an ostensibly humanitarian act can sometimes conceal an unexpected horror.

Describing his weekly meetings with the fifty-year-old head of the Judenrat, the dentist Painson, Menshagin was at pains to show how he had helped the ghetto. The mayor arranged a delivery of salt to the ghetto, which the residents exchanged for food. He produced licenses for individual residents, craftspeople, and medical colleagues of Painson, so they could work in the city, outside the ghetto. He apparently declined to impose at least one big confiscatory fine that could have been added to one taken by the German Field Commandant. These recollections, like so much else in Menshagin's memoir, can be corroborated by other documentary evidence (if, in this case, only fragmentary). As during his unusual visit to Vyshinskii at the height of the Great Terror, Menshagin took steps that either a passive or a zealous collaborator would not.[28]

What Menshagin neglected to add was that his humanitarian acts, as in 1937, represented calculated risks. Throughout his tenure as mayor he won the trust of his German overseers, who deflected all attempts to dislodge him and rewarded him with medals for his service. His caution when looking up to the Germans was now accompanied by heightened personal power when looking down on locals. As Vladimir Melander, head of the Housing Department and as of March 1942 the new Social Services Department in Menshagin's city administration, stated in a postwar interview for the Harvard Project on the Soviet Social System: "The mayor had in general quite arbitrary power of trying and convicting people: for instance, for assault, pillage, partisan activity; if necessary, cases were turned over to the Germans." Records from the city court no longer exist, but many cases of disputed property rights were considered and referred to the courts at Menshagin's weekly conferences with his administration's departmental heads. These disputes included rights to houses appropriated from Jewish residents in the ghetto (the derogatory term *yid, zhid/zhidovka,* appears in the protocols).[29]

Menshagin was disingenuous when he wrote that "no major events" occurred in the ghetto until he suddenly heard about its destruction. The regime had tightened up on November 6, 1941, in an order of the Field Commandant, "Concerning the Jews," which directed Menshagin and the police to oversee the confiscation of the tools and materials of Jewish craftspeople working outside the ghetto: "The *burgomistr* must, coordinating this with the Labor Market, distribute the tools to Aryan craftsmen." Two months before the ghetto's destruction, as the regimen around movement tightened further, Menshagin spoke of the potentialities of moving the ghetto outside the city boundaries to allow the cultivation of large garden plots for the "Russian population." We know from Menshagin's published orders that the mayor saw these city vegetable plots (*ogorody*) as of prime importance for the city food supply after the hunger crisis of winter 1941–1942. In fact, this space was used for plots to plant potatoes and vegetables after its residents were no longer alive.[30]

More directly, Menshagin's city governance was involved in coordinating confiscations of property, warm clothing, and valuables from the ghetto.

Buried deep in a September 11, 1942, report of the Economic Staff East (Wirtschaftsstab Ost) in the Smolensk Region is an entry confirming that the Smolensk city governance had overseen division of clothes and valuables from the ghetto's destruction. Menshagin's memoir explicitly notes that Georgii Gandziuk, his deputy mayor, told him, "Its property is being transferred to us." Asya Shneiderman, a Komsomol activist who concealed her own Jewish identity and indignantly reported on popular antisemitism, alleged that "clothing from the ghetto was brought by the Fritzes to the Gestapo and was worn by Smolensk prostitutes." According to the economic authorities, a quarter of the property went to the military hospital and half to the Wehrmacht, leaving another quarter for local Russian policemen (*Ordnungsdienst*). Other Jewish possessions such as furniture, dishware, and personal items were sold by the civilian administration in commission stores.[31]

After Menshagin's strategic silences in his memoir, the ghetto appears in one of the most openly duplicitous passages of his recollections. Gandziuk was one of several figures in the city administration who belonged to the far-right Russian nationalist movement of Solidarism. Gandziuk supposedly broke the news of the ghetto's liquidation to Menshagin after the fact: "'What do you mean, liquidated,' I asked. Gandziuk . . . gesticulated and stammered and said that the Jews had been killed. 'What, all of them? And Painson? What about the children?'" Menshagin reported that he refused to visit the site and sent Gandziuk in his place. "That was the word-for-word exchange of sentences between me and Gandziuk," he claimed emphatically. It stretches credulity that the deputy mayor would know about the massacre but the mayor would be left uninformed. The loading of up to two thousand ghetto residents into the gas vans was carried out by SS troops along with the Russian policemen. Mayors around the area were charged with creating these police forces and exercising general oversight. But these forces, who were involved in "actions" against Communists, partisans, Roma, psychiatric patients, and others, were generally headed by a Russian commander who reported not to the mayor but to German security forces. In the city of Smolensk, about 80 percent of these city policemen (eighty-eight guards and six agents in January 1942) were drawn from freed POWs from Dulag-126. As head of the city administration, Menshagin had general oversight—but not direct operational control—of the city police through his administration's security department (*otdel okhrany*).

Special operations involving police, violent actions, or armed anti-partisan expeditions were planned by Security Service (Sicherheitsdienst, SD), SS, and military administration authorities. The date of the destruction of the Smolensk ghetto was symbolically timed to coincide with the first anniversary of the German occupation of Smolensk.[32]

At the time of the ghetto's destruction, direct operational command of the city police lay in the hands of another returned émigré Solidarist, Nikolai Alferchik. He and his forces also worked alongside the SD on other major atrocities, including use of the gas wagons in January 1942 in the psychiatric hospital in Gedeonovka, east of Smolensk, and the shooting of 176 residents of the village of Aleksandrova identified as "gypsies" on April 24, 1942.[33]

Around nine o'clock on the night of the Smolensk ghetto's destruction, Evgenii Vakuliuk, now twelve years old, was about to go to sleep. Suddenly, he remembered that he had promised to meet some friends and left the ghetto. That coincidental outing saved his life. Loading of the residents into gas vans began three hours after Vakuliuk left, around midnight. As German forces and Russian policemen ran the operation, the ghetto's other survivor, Vladimir Khizver, was among those kept outside waiting in groups as the vans continued their round trips during the night. Khizver was a tiny, agile boy—"I am no giant," he joked during his 1996 interview. Suddenly, his mother noticed that both police guards were not watching, and Khizver sprang into a large pile of potatoes gathered nearby. He remained there, frozen in place, the entire night. Before dawn, he crawled out of the ghetto on all fours.[34]

Knowing full well that his mother and everyone on the vans had not survived, Khizver made his way to the house of a friend of his stepfather, the carpenter Grediushko. The carpenter became one of those people who, faced with a sudden decision, rescued Jews from destruction. Some, seemingly a small minority, were motivated by material gain. Grediushko acted as a friend of Khizver's stepfather, who was Jewish and was serving in the Red Army. Khizver did not know that his stepfather had been wounded near Viazma and succeeded—crucially, he did not "look Jewish"—in obtaining papers from the Germans that said he was Ukrainian. In an extraordinary coincidence, the stepfather made his way to his friend Grediushko only a few days after Khizver had arrived. The stepfather led Khizver out of the city, walking west at night, avoiding main roads, sometimes helped by peasants with food, sometimes run off in the villages. By sheer chance Khizver and his stepfather ran into a partisan unit, commanded by Nikita Gritskevich. They told the fighters who they were, as the young Khizver cried and begged to join the partisans. The two were brought before Gritskevich. After some indecision, the commander gave his consent, and Khizver became a partisan. Khizver lived out his life in postwar Smolensk, where he died in 2002.[35]

Such was the long chain of circumstances that saved one person's life. They were unobtainable to most, but hardly atypical for those few who escaped or survived ghettos across the occupied territories. Key factors for survival included skills and abilities, significant non-Jewish aid, appearances that did not immediately suggest Jewishness, and, not least, sheer coincidence and luck. As for Vakuliuk, as a survivor he could never forget the faces of the Russian policemen who had patrolled the ghetto. One day, a decade after the war, he was walking around the city of Smolensk and suddenly spotted one of them, now a civilian who had served out a ten-year sentence.[36]

POWs: The Largest German Atrocity on Soviet Soil

As one wave of Nazi violence temporarily crested, a second had already risen just behind it. The anti-Jewish shooting actions and ghetto destructions overlapped with the death marches and mass mortality in POW camps: Dulags (Durchgangslager), or transit camps, initially only holding areas with little camp infrastructure; Stalags (Stammlager), or stationary camps, and Oflags (Offizierlager), or officer camps. A total of 191 POW camps, typically mobile and operated in multiple locations, were created on the Eastern Front.

What transpired in these Dulags and Stalags held no small significance for the course of the war and the occupation in this region. "Never in history," writes the German historian Dieter Pohl, "have so many POWs died in such a short time as Red Army soldiers by German hands." As of March 1942, approximately 2 million Soviet POWs had perished in Dulags and Stalags. By the war's end in 1945, 5.7 million POWs had been taken and up to 3.3 million had perished. Arad estimated the scale of the Holocaust on Soviet territory at 2.509–2.6245 million Jewish victims, or 2.063–2.169 million on pre-1939 Soviet territory. In the European-wide genocide

A column of Soviet POWs in Roslavl in 1941. Yad Vashem Photo Archive, Jerusalem. 1288/8.

of the Jewish population of approximately 6 million people, about five of every six Jewish victims died on the Eastern Front (including in Poland, East Europe, and the USSR). Even so, in terms of Soviet territory alone, the scale of the Holocaust was exceeded by the mass murder of captured POWs.[37]

The Hunger Plan and the "criminal orders" set the stage for the mass destruction of POWs. The scale stemmed from the fact that the Blitzkrieg had immediately racked up astonishing numbers of captured Red Army POWs: 323,000 in the capture of Minsk in July and 348,000 in Smolensk and Roslavl in August. With the exception of the fall of Kyiv in September by Army Group South (665,000 POWs), the largest encirclements and largest numbers continued to go to Army Group Center on the road to Moscow. In summer and fall 1941 alone, there were a total of 2,465,000 Soviet POWs, with 1,413,000 of them captured by Army Group Center.[38]

The Battle of Moscow was nothing less than titanic. After the order for the Operation Typhoon advance on Moscow was signed on September 26, over 1.1 million Wehrmacht soldiers advanced along the Minsk highway between Smolensk and Moscow and the Warsaw highway from Roslavl to Moscow, facing an initial Soviet defense of 1.01 million Red Army soldiers. The Battle of Viazma slowed the Germans down enough to allow reserve troops from the Soviet interior to save Moscow, barely. In the huge encirclements of the Viazma-Briansk pocket, a staggering 662,000 soldiers were taken prisoner. After the fight for Moscow, the overall number of those captured had increased to the incredible number of 3.35 million.[39]

The most important and largest POW camps on Russian (RSFSR) territory all lay, with the exception of Pskov, in Smolensk Region—concentrated around Viazma, Roslavl, and Smolensk itself. Dulag-130 in Roslavl and Dulag-126 in Smolensk were large, with as many as 100,000 prisoners in 1941; along with Dulag-184 near Viazma, they were also among the longest-lasting and featured the most horrific conditions and death rates. POW camps and subcamps were also sprinkled throughout the region, in Dorogobuzh, Iartsevo, Sychevka, and Yelnya, and many other places, with a total of about sixty in the territory of prewar Smolensk Region.[40]

Even as the Holocaust remains central to public and historical discussions about the twentieth century, the number of historians who have written serious studies about the mass starvation of up to 3.3 million Soviet POWs can be counted on two hands. But as Donald Bloxham has observed, the Final Solution was carried out "in tandem" with other episodes of Nazi mass destruction. The most violent regimes always have multiple target enemies.[41] In Smolensk, as elsewhere, a multiplicity of episodes and forms of violence unfolded together and were interconnected in numerous ways. These synergies of violence, in turn, affect how we understand each one of them.

"The Nature of German 'Order'": Eyewitnesses and Perpetrators

Two people who survived some of the worst conditions in POW camps around Viazma were A. S. Pogrebnev and P. P. Erpylov. Red Army surgeons captured around Viazma in October 1941, they survived a march of eight days without food or water, drinking from puddles and eating falling snow, driven with sticks and blows. Those who could no longer walk were shot. At times, the German soldiers would simply open fire with automatic weapons on the columns of POWs. Red Army doctors were assigned the Sisyphean task of treating a mistreated population, but they sometimes saved lives and survived themselves, also becoming involved with underground organizations of POWs. "From the very first moment," the transcript of Pogrebnev and Erpylov's 1943 Mints Commission interview reads, "we saw that the Germans are trying to annihilate POWs by any means possible." How did the two doctors conceive what was happening? The terms that jurists, politicians, and historians have used since 1945—*genocide, Holocaust, crimes against humanity*—were still unavailable to them and were introduced into international usage only after World War II. Even now, none of the terms quite fit for this war crime, a massive but not systematic destruction of captured soldiers. With no readily available label, Pogrebnev and Erpylov were still able to speak powerfully and perceptively of mass atrocities, experiments in starvation, annihilation, and, simply, "the destruction of people."[42]

Those who experienced these POW camps and lived to tell the tale came to believe that Dulags deliberately aimed for increased mortality. Overcrowding in many camps was so intense that sometimes prisoners

SS guards supervise construction of a camp in Smolensk. Yad Vashem Photo Archive, Jerusalem. 4577 / 536.

could not even lie down to sleep. Survivors and eyewitnesses made many reports of cannibalism and "living corpses." Starvation, exposure to cold, as well as unsanitary conditions and rampant disease, notably typhus, were the main cause of death. Many Dulags were nothing other than holding areas surrounded by barbed wire. Until a certain amount of infrastructure was built, some could hardly even be considered camps. Each morning, special brigades of grave diggers would take the dead, numbering in the hundreds for each camp, to mass graves, which were later exhumed by the Soviets when they returned in 1943. In the words of one prisoner of Dulag-184, A. M. Peterburtsev: "That was how we learned the nature of German 'order.'"[43]

Making no preparation for POW camps to sustain life through food and housing, but rather making a concerted push for its destruction, represented an "astonishing break" with the rules of war, law, and tradition. The starvation camps did not register the names of prisoners, signaling to camp commandants the expectation of mass deaths. Even Nazi concentration camps at this time registered inmates. The death camps that became operational later in 1942, starting with Bełżec in March, also did not register names.[44] If the Einsatzgruppen were at the forefront of the escalation of the Final Solution, primary institutional oversight of the destruction of POWs lay with the military. The High Command of the Armed Forces (Oberkommando der Wehrmacht) was headed by Field Marshal General Wilhelm Keitel, who had issued the "criminal orders." The High Command of the Army (Oberkommando des Heeres) was headed by Field Marshal Walter von Brauchitsch, until he was dismissed in December 1941 for the failure to take Moscow. The quartermaster-general of the army, Eduard Wagner, was in charge of supplies and security in the rear areas. His office played a major role in the mistreatment of POWs, as did an array of economic and supply planners from Hermann Goering and Herbert Backe on down.

The mass destruction of POWs was at once an ideological, economic, political, and military decision. The advance expectation of mass starvation in prewar planning conditioned subsequent policies on food supply and rations. The deadly Nazi premise that the Wehrmacht must live exclusively on resources taken on Soviet territory excluded making the supply of Army Group Center a priority during the period of skyrocketing mortality rates. A different constellation of ideas and policies could have averted mass starvation. The atrocity was not inevitable, as it was portrayed at the time and in post hoc justifications from German military figures.

Just as economics was only one part of the process, starvation was only one means of destruction. Death marches racked up huge casualties before those weakened by battle even entered cold, disease-ridden camps ravaged by typhus epidemics and minimal medical care. Locals trying to feed the POWs were often turned away. Mortality rates in transit were atrocious but varied significantly by division and by date. The greatest casualties in this disaster came in the winter of 1941–1942, the time of the gravest, in large part intentional, food supply catastrophe.[45]

Within this overall context, not all were treated with equal brutality or dispatched with equal speed. This is where the SS forces played a role, in making a first separation of Jews, Communists, and "suspected partisans." This rough-and-ready sorting relied on crude methods of identification by appearances and denunciations, aided by large networks of German informers within the camps. In this aspect of the atrocity, generals and economic policymakers got a major assist from security and intelligence forces. The SS played a leading role in the "Special Commissions" in charge of filtration, but the Abwehr and other security agencies also took part. As in the Holocaust, a key dynamic to radicalization in the destruction of POWs was competition among agencies, such as between the SS and the army leadership, as they jockeyed for position in the greater Reich.[46]

Willi Weiss and Erich Müller, both soldiers in Security Battalion 335, shot laggards in the infamous POW death march from Viazma, which shocked residents while wending its way through the streets of downtown Smolensk on October 20, 1941. For a time, Weiss and Müller served as guards in Dulag-126 in Smolensk, which had an average population of about eight thousand. Both were interrogated by the Soviet counterintelligence agency SMERSH in 1944 before appearing in the Smolensk show trial of 1945. They spoke of orders to shoot all POWs who moved beyond a certain point in the camp. But they also shot POWs with contagious diseases, for trying to escape, or, in a phenomenon reported by many others, merely for sport or target practice. In the three weeks Weiss worked in the Dulag, about five hundred were shot and about 150 corpses were buried each day. Soviet interrogation records show that Weiss was born in 1899 in

a village in Lower Saxony, that he had a middle school education and belonged to no political party, and that he was a junior officer in the Third
Company of Security Division 335.

> Interrogator: To say it more exactly, this was the murder of
> unarmed people?
>
> Weiss: Yes, that is true, but those were our orders from above.[47]

Following orders: a familiar excuse. Historically, it is true that the scale of
victims is potentially far greater when armed military formations and discipline are involved. The "orders" would not have been there, of course,
without the extreme and widely shared Nazi ideology of biological racism
as the backdrop to German conduct. But a singularly extreme ideology
alone was not a *sine qua non* for armed troops treating Soviet POWs brutally or even as collectively disposable. Other Axis troops on the Eastern
Front, Hungarian and Romanian armies in particular, "approached the
level of callousness and cruelty toward their Soviet POWs that so many
Wehrmacht members displayed." Rather, advance planning for starvation,
military misconduct, and the broader genocidal context all came together
to produce the extraordinary scale of the destruction.[48]

Sofiia Anvaer, a third-generation Jewish doctor, had just graduated from
the medical institute before being captured in Viazma. She recalled the "pogrom" in a courtyard filled with POWs in November 1941 as the "the SS
men selected Jews and drove them to the right." She tried to hide: "I saw
how they were killing Jews, how the SS humiliated them by setting dogs
on them (I am not in any condition to describe it), and imagining what
they might do to a woman." Suddenly, a tall SS officer appeared in front of
her. "Although a half century has passed," she said, "I can see him now in
front of me as if it were yesterday."

> —Are you a Jewess?
>
> —No, Georgian.
>
> —Last name?
>
> —Andzhaparidze.

Anvaer had given the Georgian name of one of her classmates.[49] Muslim
POWs—who were circumcised and thus caught up in the most common

way of identifying Jews—were initially shot either as "Jews" or as "Asiatic" Red Army soldiers, until orders not to annihilate them came in September 1941.[50]

Jewish POWs summarily executed in POW camps can therefore be counted among the first victims of the Holocaust. This makes for an "astonishing" contrast with the Western Front, where the Germans showed leniency to over 60,000 Jewish POWs from France, Britain, and the United States. Arad estimates that on former Soviet territory, 5.5 percent of a total of 80,000–85,000 Jewish POWs survived by concealing their Jewishness. Joint security police and army guidelines on POW camps from July 17, 1941, slated all Jews, along with "politically intolerable elements," including civilians, for immediate execution. But identifying them was dependent on denunciations and prejudice, and thousands of Jews managed to conceal their names and ethnicity. The SS Special Commissions combed the Dulags seeking "unacceptable" POWs—political commissars, "fanatical communists," the partisans, and "all Jews"—to select and execute. In this mix, as Anvaer feared, misogyny also played its role. The Wehrmacht elite harbored a special abhorrence of Soviet women in combat, widely seen as "unnatural," and called them *Flintenweiber,* or "shotgun dames." While invalids and many civilians were released after filtration by security personnel, there were military orders to have female soldiers summarily shot, even though this was not systematically carried out.[51]

In sum, the entire gamut of interconnected racial, political, and other potential enemies of the regime—the hit list of Judeo-Communism—shaped the selection of victims for execution in Dulags and Stalags. This connection between the annihilation of Jews and the destruction of others on this enemies list is symbolized by the deportations of about 10,000 POWs to Auschwitz in October 1941 and the first test of Zyklon B there on 900 Soviet POWs. In fall 1941, some 40,000 POWs, depicted as bestial commissars and partisans, had been deported west to German concentration camps for execution, dwarfing previous killing campaigns and marking a turning point in the Nazi concentration camp system.[52]

Recruitment Grounds and Killing Fields

One other feature of the POW camps is especially salient for understanding their nature. Even as many contemporaries so clearly discerned a deliberately annihilationist intent toward prisoners, large numbers were slated for survival. In other words, the Dulags and Stalags were not only death camps but also major recruiting grounds. They provided all sorts of needed workers, urban and rural, skilled native speakers for intelligence work and propaganda, and, increasingly, military collaborators. The POW camps were of "enormous interest" for German counterespionage, according to Dmitrii Karov (Kandaurov), the rare Russian émigré Abwehr officer. They were sources for intelligence gathering and for "human material for recruitment of agents, spies, and later—anti-partisan troops." Karov recalled one German officer with the rank of major posted in the Smolensk Abwehr headquarters who, to forecast production trends, interviewed "many thousands" of POWs involved in Soviet tank production.[53]

Red Army soldiers in these camps came from all over the multiethnic USSR. Germans sorted the non-Jewish prisoners according to a malleable but meaningful racial classification. The most favored, reinforced by signals from the Wehrmacht High Command and Hitler in September 1941, were ethnic Germans ("Volksdeutsche"), Balts, and Ukrainians. Those from the Caucasus or Central Asia were called "Asians," and in general others were simply grouped under the flexible ethnonym "Russians." Crucially, however, this racial-ideological hierarchy was always combined with political and labor-related criteria. For example, in one July 1942 report on "Russian POWs" to the Army High Command, ethnic categories referred to "politically suspect elements," commissars, officers, and "other POWs." In practice, moreover, there was a great deal of manipulation of the German preference for Ukrainians in the hierarchy of Eastern Slavs. In places such as Smolensk, German recruiters on the ground often simply changed Russians into Ukrainians or Belarusians on paper.[54]

A former Red Army officer, who by summer 1943 was working under German command as part of General Andrei Vlasov's Russian Liberation Army, later described how he witnessed the selection of five hundred antipartisan fighters in the Roslavl Dulag. Although he was silent on his own role, he himself was clearly involved in the selection, since officers were held in different camps from soldiers. When the promise of "Ukrainian rations" was announced to recruits, "everyone who could move" surged forward. The verification of Ukrainianness was knowledge of how to say "bread" in Ukrainian; military fitness was evaluated by a German. Prisoners were desperate to sign up. The officer stated, "Imagine emaciated, half-dressed people in the remnants of Soviet military uniforms, often without shoes and feet wrapped in rags, half-starving (until the receipt of the so-called Ukrainian ration) . . . Add to this the complete hopelessness of any future that awaited them and you will understand the moral condition of these people." Those not selected were beaten back by truncheons.[55]

There was a practical and political calculus behind the preference for Ukrainians. Rural Ukrainians would have experienced mass famine in 1932–1933; the clear German expectation was that they would be more anti-Soviet than Russians. As one report from Dulag-240 in Smolensk from December 1941 explained, Ukrainians generally harbored a "stronger hatred" against Bolshevik elements and could be expected to treat political commissars and partisans with "greater hardness." The intent was to privilege those with anti-Soviet zeal when recruiting for auxiliary troops and policemen.[56]

Starvation in the POW camps created the conditions in which large numbers of prisoners, whatever their background, were willing to agree to anything to get out. Those who vowed never to serve the Germans under any conditions did not live to tell the tale. Once recruited and then released, policemen and anti-partisan "volunteer" troops from among the POWs—in significantly varying degrees trained, propagandized, armed, fed, and supplied in newfound positions of power over the population—were quickly tasked with the most violent brutalities of ghetto liquidations and anti-partisan warfare. They became notorious in the countryside in 1942 for looting, rape, and repression as they traversed the path from victims to perpetrators. Even so, some of these perpetrators later also switched sides a second time, going over to the partisans.[57]

There was a twisted, improvised, but increasingly settled logic to this duality of the Dulags and Stalags as death and recruitment camps at the same time. Starvation for those marked as enemies facilitated recruitment for those deemed capable of working and fighting. Those two major functions of the POW camps, moreover, were combined with a strong degree of deliberation. October 1941—a turning point in the radicalization of the Holocaust and the mortality of the death camps—also marked a shift at the highest levels to ratifying the exploitation of POW labor, a position toward which various agencies had already been moving since summer. In the usual off-the-cuff fashion, Hitler on October 15 spoke of "Russian POWs" as the "cheapest labor." Goering followed up in November with instructions for addressing labor shortages, conveying a strong signal to utilize this newfound pool of Soviet citizens in the German military economy.[58]

By January 1942, the Wehrmacht was issuing its own instructions about the usefulness and size of the "POW workforce" that could be used to free German soldiers for the front, along with long lists of useful professions. Thus filtration by racial and political categories was accompanied by selection of those with special skills, which according to spring 1942 reports in the Army Group Center Rear Administration area included "major professional groups" in agriculture, construction, and crafts. Released POWs staffed police forces and, increasingly after the partisan war heated up in 1942 after escapes from the encirclements, auxiliary military forces for operations against partisans. Throughout the occupied territories, POWs labored in agriculture, industry, and priority professions in the hundreds of thousands. The military understood best of all that holding vast territories behind the front lines was impossible without major involvement of local populations. "Special treatment" was ordered for technical personnel, tractor drivers and repair personnel, and administrative and technical staff in the critical realms of oil and coal, which were to be identified to the economic departments of the field commandants and the Economic Commandos (Wirtschaftskommandos) of the Economic Staff East.[59]

The direct connection between mass starvation and forced recruitment—that the first greatly facilitated the second—was made in a December 1, 1942, instruction from the Office of the Chief of the General Staff of the Wehrmacht High Command to the Ninth Army with the heading "Increased Utilization of POWs for the Goals of the Wehrmacht." It made the calculation between starvation and collaboration explicit: "Those fully exhausted and those dying of hunger among the POWs would consider themselves lucky if in this manner they could receive only two-thirds of the nourishment of German soldiers." It would be "advantageous" for Russians, the instruction continued, to learn German-style discipline and some German language so they could labor for the Reich after the war. As this suggests, the POW camps can be explained not only as a function of the war of annihilation and the escalation of mass killing but also as part of plans for racial colonization. The camps also reflected the distinct evolution in the military's realization of its reliance on the "Russian" population.[60]

Karel C. Berkhoff has argued that the mass starvation of up to 3.3 million Soviet POWs deserves to be called "genocidal," in the sense that it was "tending toward" an act of genocide against all those Red Army soldiers from the multiethnic USSR loosely labeled "Russians." As Berkhoff noted, it was hardly a secret among Germans stationed on the Eastern Front that up to two million "Russian" POWs had perished in 1941–1942. There is evidence that many shrugged the figure off, as if inferior Russians, the Slavic people deemed to be most infected with Bolshevism, were diseased "livestock."[61]

It does not make the mass destruction of Soviet POWs any less terrible that there is no convenient term for it. The 1948 United Nations Genocide Convention refers to genocide as the "intent to destroy, in whole or in part, a national, ethnical, racial or religious group." The moral, historical, and inevitably political concept of genocide, for better or for worse, has centered around the attempt to systematically annihilate a race or ethnicity (in part because the Soviets objected to including class collectivities that might have made Stalin's collectivization genocidal). Neither Hitler nor Himmler nor anyone else foresaw the liquidation of POWs "as a whole." Despite the ethnonym "Russians" casually and commonly applied to the multinational Red Army soldiers, German treatment was centrally about classification and filtration practices that distinguished among "racial," political, and economic categories. There is, therefore, good reason that Soviet POWs do not appear anywhere in Mark Levene's exhaustive compilation of major acts of genocide, sub-genocidal violence, and partial genocide throughout the European borderlands between 1912 and 1953, a full twenty-three of which were instigated by the Nazis in World War II.[62]

How, then, can we conceive of the phenomenon of the Nazi starvation camps? Crimes against humanity have been codified as crimes against civilians, not soldiers. This was undoubtedly a war crime, but its scale makes it an exceptional one. Even if it was not a genocide or genocidal, it was a war crime of genocidal proportions.

That said, buried deep in Christian Streit's classic study there is a chilling remark, made in passing. It was only the ad hoc German realization in late 1941 that POWs could solve the Reich's labor and occupation-related manpower shortages in a longer war that undercut the likelihood of their complete, "preventative" liquidation. A more total destruction was a distinct possibility, and Streit certainly did not find it inconceivable. But

with the expectations and needs of a large occupation, the genocidal potential in German treatment of POWs was undermined after 1941–1942 by
the need for greater recruitment.[63] Treatment of POWs remained brutal
and mortality high, but after the first winter of the war the POW camps
were tending away from, not toward, total destruction.

Reluctance to inflate the concept of genocide cannot diminish recognition of the enormity of what occurred. Indeed, the Dulags and Stalags
suggest just how closely antisemitism and the genocide of the Jews were
intertwined with other colossal acts of Nazi violence. This, in turn, allows
us to see how the greatest cataclysms of violence feed on the intersection of
many forms of enmity.

Repercussions

The POW camps had an outsized impact on the further course of the
German occupation. Sizable numbers of escaped or released soldiers in
the Smolensk Region quickly swelled the partisan movement. By early
1942, the forested areas of Smolensk and Briansk boasted two of the most
significant partisan movements anywhere, setting up the next, interconnected wave of German violence: the brutal anti-partisan war in the countryside starting in mid- to late 1942.

The Dulags and Stalags, like the ghettos, also had major implications
for collaborationist civilian administrations. In the city of Smolensk, Menshagin, like other Russians put in positions of authority, was in a position
to save numerous POWs from almost certain death in the camps. For one
thing, mayors generally had autonomy to select their own staffs, which
therefore were regularly padded; the mayor generally appointed the police
chief (*Polizeimeister*), who then put together his own force. In addition, in
late 1941 the Wehrmacht was willing to release—"with a security check
from the mayor of the locality"—significant numbers of civilians who could
show local connections, as well as women, children, and handicapped veterans incapable of fighting. It became German policy to allow craftspeople
and even schoolteachers to be subject to special sorting. Significant numbers were released to localities for labor needs, and at least a dozen of the
Smolensk city officials, doctors, teachers, and other professionals Menshagin
recalled in his memoirs had been interned for some amount of time. There
is plenty of evidence that these sorts of releases were common. In one of

many examples from the countryside, a peasant imprisoned in one of the Smolensk Dulags testified that he was released by the sanction of the elder (*starosta*) of his village.[64]

Menshagin did not claim to have arranged releases permitted by the Germans. He went further, taking credit for personally saving what he estimated as two thousand to four thousand lives of Soviet POWs in the course of the war. "I was categorically forbidden by a German instruction to give documents to those serving in the Red Army," he emphasized. In his 1955 appeal to Georgii Malenkov, building a case for his release from Soviet prison, he claimed that he had saved more POWs than any other mayor in the occupied territories, including Belarus and the adjacent Orlov and Briansk Regions. Menshagin rooted his memoiristic claim to moral superiority in these assertions about POWs. Recalling his 1945 interrogation by his antagonist, NKVD major Boris Beliaev, Menshagin righteously condemned the Chekist's questions about why he had certified an interned soldier, a certain Shlamovich, as Russian while knowing he was Jewish. The secret policeman "could not understand that people can do good without pursuing any kind of personal gain, that this in itself brings . . . great moral satisfaction."[65]

Menshagin's claim to have been connected to the release of large numbers of POWs is credible. So are the details he provides of falsifying legal papers for specific escaped Russians or Jews whom he decided to help. But the uniqueness of the city of Smolensk in deceiving German authorities about huge numbers of escaped POWs is difficult to believe. In the Smolensk Region alone, over three hundred thousand POWs were released in 1941–1943. There was, it is true, a brisk trade in false papers that included Menshagin's own forged signature. Corruption was rife within his own administration, as he well knew, and even underground communist operatives at times succeeded in paying off German authorities to see or release prisoners. But providing false papers was a very risky business, and amid the flood of denunciations providers and holders of such documents were often caught. Moreover, security within the city became extremely tight in 1942.[66] Did the cautious Menshagin provide papers to thousands of illegals, including fighting-age men, about whom the German military was unaware? It seems more likely that he conflated a smaller number he risked aiding behind the Germans' backs with all those others whom he was sanctioned to release. In another sense, both his risky philanthropy and his legal power of patronage to provide residency documents, jobs, and travel passes can be seen as two sides of the same coin. Both constituted his greatest wartime powers. Both were possible only by establishing his value and trust with his German overseers.

One display of public violence in Smolensk rivaled the destruction of the ghetto in its effect on the civilian population. There were several death marches of POWs in October 1941, but the one that had the most impact occurred on October 20, 1941. The massacre that took place that day was different from previous, demonstrative displays of public violence, such as hanging Jews, partisans, and "commissars" with signs in public spaces. Those acts were intended as symbolic, deliberate warnings. Public displays of this kind already distinguished wartime violence from, for example, the midnight knocks on the door during the era of the Great Terror. But on October 20, the message the public received was not intentional. It came from the path of the march that happened to lead through populated urban space. The physician Kesarev spoke of it as a day that, at a time of constant shocks, stood out for its display of "unbelievable cruelty" in front of the civilian population. When morning came, as another physician eyewitness put it, "Great Soviet Street was littered with the corpses of those Russian POWs who were shot in the night." Red Army officers documenting Nazi crimes in 1943 easily found twenty witnesses to help locate the mass graves that resulted. It was concluded that some five thousand POWs and officers were shot on the march from Viazma.[67]

To gauge how those who had lived through Stalinism experienced German wartime violence, and to relate that to the significant negative shift in popular opinion against German rule between 1941 and 1943, was far from Menshagin's agenda as he prepared his memoirs. It is interesting, therefore, that the October death marches through the city figure in his memoirs—in terms of local German authorities' own shock. Menshagin recounted a reception he attended with officials from the Seventh Department of the Field Commandant, which oversaw the city governance. Menshagin remembered the date as October 27, 1941, one week after the largest death march through Smolensk city streets. Perhaps he remembered correctly, because several such marches occurred that month. Sonderführer Oskar Hirschfeldt invited him into his private quarters afterward, where they drank red wine. "Well, the Germans have lost the war! Did you see what those donkeys did on the streets today?" Hirschfeldt, an ethnic

German born in St. Petersburg, had graduated from the legal faculty of Tartu University. He left Estonia for Germany when the Soviets arrived after the Nazi-Soviet Pact. The rank of Sonderführer signaled he was a specialist without military background hired by the Wehrmacht. It is possible that his shared legal background with Menshagin enabled the two to develop particularly good relations. Menshagin withheld comment, except to note the truth behind Hirschfeldt's prediction that Soviet soldiers would never surrender in such large numbers again.[68]

Lyusya and Asya Join the Underground

Two remarkable young women, committed opponents of German rule, left eyewitness accounts about occupation-era violence: Liudmila Madziuk (known to everyone as Lyusya) and Asya Shneiderman, who successfully concealed her Jewish identity. Both survived two Dulags. Both were among those who tried to aid the Jews of the Smolensk ghetto and the POWs in the camps. Both were Komsomolki, or members of the Communist Youth League, and both were shaped by the norms of Soviet urban civilization and the 1930s generation. When Madziuk and Shneiderman were released from the horrors of Smolensk's Dulag-126, they began conducting the first underground political work amid all the persecutions of the occupied city. They acted immediately and without the prospect of Soviet help or support, which came months later.

How Madziuk and Shneiderman got to that point is in itself a noteworthy story among the countless displacements brought about by the war. On hearing the first news of the invasion in June 1941, Madziuk dropped her engineering courses in Moscow and volunteered for training as a nurse. As a member of a citizens' militia (*opolchenie*), she joined the Siberian troops of the Twenty-Fourth Army in its Yelnya offensive southeast of Smolensk—the first substantial, if short-lived, setback experienced by the Germans. In October, the Twenty-Fourth Army, retreating east, joined the ferocious fighting in the Battle of Viazma. There Madziuk found herself, along with vast numbers of Red Army soldiers, caught in an encirclement. On October 10, in the village of Khar'kova, fifteen miles from the city of Viazma, she was taken prisoner, wounded and unconscious. When she awoke, she found herself in a building where Russian wounded were being held. This was where she first met Shneiderman, among the prisoners. Madziuk was only able to walk slowly, but she, Shneiderman, and a third person, named Klava, acquired civilian clothes and escaped, headed toward the Soviet side of the front. Three times they tried and failed to cross the front lines amid burned villages and German guards. Then "Klava quickly split off" from them, as "she became afraid because Asya was Jewish." Madziuk disregarded the danger.

On the third attempt, in the village of Staraia Ruza in Moscow Region, Madziuk and Shneiderman were arrested. Someone in the village had denounced them to the German security forces. Accused of being spies, both young women refused to admit to their interrogators that Shneiderman was Jewish. They were sentenced to death, but the execution was stayed. "Even now," Madziuk recorded, "I do not know why." Instead, they were sent to two POW camps, the first in Mozhaisk, the second in Smolensk.[69]

For five days in December 1941, the period of highest mortality, they faced the trial of internment in Smolensk's Dulag-126. In Shneiderman's words, "It was a gruesome picture: the barracks were completely unheated, people slept on the floor." Those who survived each day resembled no longer humans but "living corpses, hungry, dirty, and ever under the whips of the policemen." For someone reared on the values of the 1930s generation—including Soviet patriotism and internationalism, friendship of the peoples, women's liberation, and anti-fascism—the most bitter pill of all for Shneiderman was watching how newly appointed policemen in the camp, "our own Russian traitors," persecuted their own, "flaunting their whips and humiliating their own brothers."[70]

Popular Reticence for Antisemitic Pogroms

But when Einsatzgruppe B perpetrators reached Smolensk in August 1941, they were taken aback by popular civilian reluctance to join in the persecution. Nebe complained no less than twice, in August and October, that the Russian population was "surprisingly" unwilling to take part in attempts to provoke what were euphemistically called "self-help" actions— German-instigated pogroms. In his August 29 report, Nebe noted that in "old Soviet" areas the population appeared "passive" and too "intimidated" to participate.[71]

Nebe did not know how to explain this popular reticence within the pre-1939 borders of the USSR, as opposed to those parts of

Molotov-Ribbentrop Europe annexed by the Soviets in 1939, where large outbreaks of violence occurred with German incitement in 1941. Within the old borders of the USSR, official condemnation of antisemitism and two decades of multinational friendship were widely propagated as component parts of the regime. While there were incidents of antisemitic violence in the western borderlands in the 1920s and 1930s, they were not publicized. "The virtual disappearance of outbreaks of mass violence targeting Jews," in the words of one historian, "represented one of the most notable ruptures in manifestations of antisemitism from tsarist to Soviet times." The stigmatization and punishment of antisemitism in the early Soviet period may have prompted some to curtail antisemitic proclivities for fear of reprisal from the authoritarian state, while others may have accepted Jewish neighbors as equal citizens.[72]

When the Germans arrived in pre-1939 Soviet territory, Diana Dumitru has suggested, "long-time Soviet civilians," as opposed to armed units and local auxiliaries under military orders, "generally did not participate in anti-Jewish violence, unlike the populations of neighboring Eastern European territories." This was the case even though public participation was incited by Einsatzkommandos. Einsatzgruppe D, for example, which operated in southern and eastern Ukraine, reported a similar absence of civilian participation in antisemitic violence, despite the long history of antisemitism in the region. Some pogroms broke out in "old" Soviet territories, but it was uncommon.[73]

Nebe was puzzled. Eager to show local support for Einsatzgruppe actions, he touted popular associations between Soviet terror and the Jews. Citing "conversations" with German authorities around the region, he noted that Russians expressed "satisfaction" at the construction of ghettos "in most cases." But in a series of unusual and noteworthy passages concerning Smolensk, he even observed, for example, "Some individual voices have become loud in pointing out the treatment of the Jews as inhumane [*unmenschlich*]." Not only were people unwilling to take part in "self-help measures taken against the Jews," he continued, "but they even display a great lack of understanding for the measures taken by the German side against the Jews." Ultimately, Nebe, like his comrades in Einsatzgruppe D, rather unconvincingly attributed this reluctance to join in the persecution, at the height of German military success in 1941, to fear that the Soviets would return.[74]

The experience and perceptions of both the occupation and the Holo-caust differed significantly within the vast expanse of the Russian Soviet Republic. Some areas were like Smolensk, occupied for over two years; others further east were re-Sovietized after a mere six months. The timing and duration of the occupation led to different cost-benefit decision making both by the occupying authorities and by the populace. Areas along the Russian ethnic frontier, such as Crimea and the North Caucasus, with sig-nificant numbers of non-Slavs and Muslims, were shaped not only by local factors but by a noticeably more differentiated German approach toward population policies.[75]

But in terms of public behavior, the commonalities that confounded Nebe have another possible explanation. Two decades of Soviet rule and the Great Terror had inculcated the importance of lying low. There were mass denunciations during the Great Terror, but spontaneous participa-tion in public unrest on the streets was an entirely different matter. The dynamics in areas of the Soviet interior, including Smolensk, were strik-ingly different than in the areas further west that had been Sovietized only in 1939, such as Latvia or Bessarabia. Thus Nebe reported that in Smolensk, even "genuinely active elements" who aided the Germans in exposing hidden Communists and Jews did their best to remain "out of sight and unknown."[76]

The reticence of the general population to join public "actions" did not preclude antisemitic violence of remarkable cruelty on the part of individ-uals. Shneiderman's testimony is significant because her concealed Jewish-ness and anger at collaboration led her to record many details that others left out. She described the mistreatment of Jewish POWs by their fellow soldiers: "I myself saw how two Jews were held in a coop, in a den, where they were not given anything to eat and anyone who felt like it could hu-miliate them. Whenever they were taken out of the coop to relieve them-selves, a cry of 'hurrah' rose up in the barrack, someone would come up and spit in their faces, another would knock off their caps, and so on. It was all the more shameful that young people did this—'children of October,' who were raised by Soviet power and so quickly fell under the influence of the Fritzes."[77] For Shneiderman, fascist barbarism was a given. The true shock was when members of the "first Soviet generation," those born after 1917 and who had only known socialism, took the lead in the humiliation. She referred to them as unprincipled "henchmen," or *prikhvostniki,* a Soviet political term denoting followers, literally those attached to a tail.[78]

On December 19, 1941, both Madziuk and Shneiderman got the chance to do what they could to help the Jews in the ghetto and the POWs in the Dulag in Smolensk. Having successfully concealed Shneiderman's Jewish identity, they were released along with other women in Dulag-126. As Madziuk told it, "We blended into the general mass of people and received documents with the right to live in the city, where I settled together with Asya Shneiderman."[79]

By January 1942, Madziuk and Shneiderman had teamed up with Elena Mironovaia, a like-minded Komsomol member who sought out other activists. The group began to help the POWs and the ghetto population, even before forming an underground Komsomol organization. Red Army officers, held separately so they could not influence the troops, were less strictly guarded, so the young women brought them warm clothes and food. They were able to direct some POWs to partisans in the forests. Mironovaia told the Mints Commission: "We had ties to the Jewish population in Sadki. They did not let anyone in, especially Russians. There was a Jewish cemetery and a large ravine. Into this ravine we brought pamphlets and food. We handed over medicine."[80]

Vladimir Khizver, the survivor of the Smolensk ghetto, was asked about how neighbors and Russians looked on the ghetto laborers with their yellow stars. At first people stopped and stared, then they became used to it. But did they look with hatred or with sympathy? "There was some of everything," he answered. Then he thought a bit: "But more with sympathy, of course."[81] There are many examples of those, like Madziuk, who gave material aid or shelter to Jewish friends hiding from the ghettos, but they are overrepresented in oral histories and memoirs precisely because their authors were the ones who survived. Regional-level Soviet secret police (UNKVD) agents gathering intelligence on the occupied territory reported ample support for German persecution of Jews, including gleeful antisemitism: "The reign of the Jews has ended, now rule for us has begun." Shneiderman bitterly recalled the reaction of a former fellow member of the Komsomol at a workplace propaganda session: "When a German in front of us started to propagandize, saying the Jews must be destroyed as a lower race, that all evil comes from the Jews, she completely agreed with him and found nothing to do other than utter, 'Ah, those kikes.'"[82]

Many residents of cities and towns with ghettos or POW camps simply avoided those guarded areas at all costs. "We did not even look in that direction," exclaimed one Russian woman, nineteen years old in 1941, when asked about the Smolensk ghetto.[83] Yet one can easily find cases of those who studiously avoided trouble but, when suddenly presented with a concrete opportunity, gave aid to Jews, POWs, or party members. In this war, just as so many victims became perpetrators and so many collaborators became resisters, or vice versa, highly situational choices could prompt consequential decisions.

Humiliation and Everyday Violence

When Shneiderman spoke about Russian policemen in the Dulag "flaunting their whips and humiliating their own brothers," she invoked the term *humiliate* or *mock* (*izdevat'sia*). The associated noun, *humiliation* or *mockery* (*izdevatel'stvo*), became a red thread in popular testimony in Soviet war crimes documentation. Always more than a propaganda word, *izdevatel'stvo* implied mockery and bullying as well as brutality and humiliation. From the outset, the term informed the way Russian speakers described acts of violence or summary punishments for insignificant or imaginary transgressions. The use of the term organized people's emotions about the casual nature of German everyday violence and connected that to greater atrocities.

There was a pronounced symbolic dimension to mass violence in the Holocaust, ranging from the cutting of Jewish men's beards to the victims being forced to dance, the semipublic visibility of execution sites, and photography of violent acts as a demonstration of power.[84] Less known is the symbolic dimension of what might be called everyday violence under occupation. The dynamics were different in town and countryside, yet in both cases, Germans intended to send symbolic messages through those more quotidian performances. But as the spread of the term *humiliation* suggests, they could not dictate the nature of the messages received.

One peasant girl, sixteen years old in 1942, lived in the village of Serebrianka, near the district center in the town of Rudnia. She was unaware of the destruction of approximately one thousand residents of the Rudnia ghetto on October 21, 1941. But when interviewed in 2009, she still remembered walking five miles from the village to Rudnia to witness a hanging.

Villagers went out of a sense of solidarity with the victim, a peasant from her village caught in the forest. He had apparently gone to gather sap, but was arrested as a partisan. The hanging occurred near the church in the center of town. "There were many people there, and everyone cried."[85] Even when numbers were small, public visibility was a feature of everyday violence under German rule.

Another form of everyday violence was carried out in cities in the region by security forces out of direct public view, but with enough publicity to become widely known. In Smolensk, for example, it occurred in the notorious Gestapo headquarters, which took over the former NKVD building on what had been Dzerzhinskii Street. Daily beatings and torture by German interrogators were semipublic, in that many who saw or heard the abuse spread word about what occurred behind the walls. The prison's thirty rooms crowded in two hundred prisoners or more at a time. Attack dogs were deployed in special displays of sadism, especially on Jews. The head of the city police, Alferchik, was a constant presence. This form of demonstrative terror was hardly limited to Smolensk. Similar displays occurred in the Roslavl city jail, which at one time held up to twenty-five hundred people, as well as in Viazma and other cities and towns in the region.[86]

The brutality of everyday violence under occupation informed the way the major episodes of mass violence—inevitably only partially known and understood at the time—were perceived. "Humiliation" expressed Russians' sense that in the eyes of the German conquistadors, their lives were cheap and they were less than fully human. "The German executioners humiliated the peaceful population—women, old men, and children," three Viazma women testified. "They took away our human rights, incited lawlessness, and for the smallest suspicion shot completely innocent people without trial." When the three then recounted the German practice of leaving corpses hanging in public places for up to ten days as a means of instilling fear in the population, what they called humiliation encompassed public displays of violence. As a result, many urban residents tried to stay indoors as much as possible or avoided making eye contact on the street.[87]

"Give me a smoke, give it to me," a wounded POW in front of a clinic begged a German officer in one episode witnessed in Viazma. "The officer stopped, he must have been taken aback by such 'insolence' on the part of a Russian soldier. Not speaking a word, he put his hand in his pocket, took out his revolver and shot him. The wounded man crumpled up and the officer, not even glancing back, walked on." This account, recorded in a legal statement written in March 1943 by three physicians and signed by a Red Army captain, was but one of a litany of local testimonies, most from ordinary citizens, that invoked "humiliation [*izdevatel'stvo*]."[88]

German rule reintroduced the knout. Flogging was associated with serfdom and the tsarist order, and the Wehrmacht was well aware of this fact during the entire shift toward reliance on Russian labor and the civilian population in 1942 and 1943. A ten-rule set of instructions aimed at better treatment of Russians was seized from a dead German soldier and translated as a trophy document by the partisans. Rule 4 was "Avoid beating Russians." The tsarist system was hated because of the knout, German soldiers were taught, and the Bolsheviks had banned public corporal punishment and execution by hanging. "A Russian will never forget if you beat him," the leaflet continued; "beating in Russia is a sign of unculturedness." Other reminders—to speak calmly and without "haughtiness," to be "strict but just," and to "praise the Russian, if he does good work"—assumed German superiority but aspired to avoid open expressions of domination.[89] The very need to print up exhortations for better treatment showed how widespread such practices really were on the ground.

Such instructions showed awareness of how "humiliation" was effectively being used in partisan and Soviet home front propaganda, where it was linked to practices of beatings by whips and truncheons, the symbols of "feudalism" and the old regime. Even sorely needed Russian professionals who had been elites in the Soviet system were whipped. One agronomist working with thirty-five other agricultural specialists at a seed selection station on a former state-owned farm in Koshchino, near Smolensk, described how everyone wearing a German uniform carried "rubber whips on a wooden handle, with a strap on the handle"—"a real dog whip." The agronomists were given privileged salaries and rations, but Germans gave out beatings "for the slightest mistake." Russian women physicians and medical personnel in Sychevka described segregated bathrooms for non-Aryans, their demotion to sanitary aides and cleaners in a German hospital, and beatings. They stated simply: "The fascists humiliated us in every way possible."[90]

Another trophy document seized by the Soviets in 1943, "The Political Tasks of the German Soldier in Russia in Conditions of Total War," sermonized on the correct way to mobilize the seventy million people of occupied "Russia," forcefully asserting that final victory in the East would now hinge on whether "Eastern nations" sympathized with Germany. The trick was to engineer "voluntary cooperation" yet not truly strive to win over non-Germans "ideologically." Genuine conversion of those from other "races" was unnecessary in this struggle of "world views" between National Socialism and Bolshevism. But at the same time, Russians saw Germans as representatives of "European culture" and were not willing to "accept physical punishment by Germans." The worst insult and deepest "humiliation," the instructions concluded, was "to see in the Russian a person of a lower class, a half-human."[91] Did the authors of these Wehrmacht instructions to German occupiers realize how much their effort was undercut by the entire weight of the German-Nazi promulgation of the image of "subhuman" races in the barbaric "East"? Advocates of this "moderate" or strategic approach could not address just how much the humiliation associated with everyday violence was intertwined with their own atrocities. These could hardly be undone.

Abduction

In the countryside, major waves of violence and everyday humiliation were also connected, but the dynamics and timing of the correlation differed in urban areas. Hopes for decollectivization and the "new agrarian order" were only gradually dashed, and the food situation was better than in the hungry cities. Partisan terror, German reprisals, and peasant wariness toward all outside authority, not to mention great variation in local conditions depending on proximity to roads and partisan strongholds, created a fragmented and slowly shifting landscape. However, two major waves of violence in the countryside—the savagery of the anti-partisan war that spiked in mid-1942 and the deportations of women and teenagers for forced labor in the Reich, which were underway in 1942 but peaked in 1943—left major marks on rural responses to the occupation.

Those two waves of violence in the countryside were rooted in and in sync with the other major forms of violence and exploitation in the unfolding occupation. The rise of a strong partisan movement in late 1941 posed a threat to the city of Smolensk, now overflowing with German supply services and a home base for numerous staffs. Schenckendorff returned from vacation in February 1942 to oversee the massive anti-partisan offensive and a deeply contradictory shift to win the hearts and minds of newly important local populations. Security units involved, first, in the Holocaust by bullets and liquidation of ghettos and, then, in the death marches and POW camps, were now directed to the anti-partisan war. These connections are exemplified in the activities of Security Battalion 335 in this region, as seen in the cases of Willi Weiss, Erich Müller, and others captured and interrogated by the Soviets. The same period, as seen in the case of the Dulags, marked the shift to widespread exploitation of forced labor. The smallest units of the Economic Staff East, in charge of economic administration and exploitation of the occupied territories, were the Economic Commandos. In 1942, the Economic Commandos around the region focused on creating forced labor camps in order to foster "a more regulated employment of labor directly for the female population."[92]

The campaign for labor "volunteers" for the Reich, bolstered by propaganda and publicized trips, was from the start reliant on forcible abductions. As rural rumors spread about transport in cattle cars, hunger, and humiliations, it became increasingly necessary to rely on coercion rather than propaganda in order to meet deportation quotas. In April 1942, goals were set to exploit 1.4–1.5 million forced laborers from the East (*Ostarbeiter*). A resulting campaign in Smolensk began that month and culminated in a "hunt" for recruits, especially young women, reaching an initial peak in summer 1942. In November, for example, the Economic Commando from the Smolensk deported 375 men and 937 women. In December, in a measure taken to meet a failing labor recruitment quota, women and men held in the Roslavl Dulag as partisan bandits were deported in the place of volunteers. The turn to forced deportations on a mass scale prompted young women to seek exemptions by getting pregnant. Others fled to the forest to avoid being taken. As Abwehr officer Karov recounted, some POWs recruited from the Dulags for anti-partisan, "punitive" expeditions in the countryside refused to deport local women known to them. Bucking orders to round up local women could lead them to join forces with partisans. In total, at least eight hundred thousand people were recruited or forcibly deported as laborers from areas near the front. German and Soviet figures vary significantly, but between eighty-seven thousand and two hundred thousand residents from the Smolensk Region were deported as forced laborers.[93]

Just as the Holocaust and the Dulags paved the way for the violence in the countryside, the anti-partisan reprisals in Smolensk and Briansk in 1942, in turn, can be seen as setting the precedent for the deadly scorched villages policy later in the war. Further west, in Belarus, thousands of torched villages were partially or completely destroyed.

DECADES OF INTENSIVE and far-reaching scholarly debates about the Holocaust, its uniqueness and causation, have ultimately involved bracketing off the genocide of the Jews from other major forms of Nazi violence, which are studied separately. Disaggregating the causes of each form of violence leads to thinking about key factors as discrete rather than intertwined. The specific ways in which different forms of violence worked together have only rarely been at the center of interpretation. The case of Smolensk suggests that the major types of atrocities so often analyzed separately must also be considered in tandem. They were linked in their overlapping sequence and timing and in the identity of many of the perpetrators. In interconnected fashion, ideology, economics, warfare, and colonization all lay behind the escalation of the practices of mass violence. There is nothing preventing us from perceiving the singularity of the Holocaust while also recognizing how it is incomprehensible outside of the ways it amplified and overlapped with other forms of violence—against Communists, partisans, POWs, women, children, handicapped, Slavs, Roma, and all the colonized of the "East"— that were unfolding throughout the same historical conjuncture.

Synergies of violence were also strongly present in terms of popular response and the outlook of the largely Russian civilian population of Smolensk. All the major wartime atrocities were intertwined with public, everyday violence that came to be associated with humiliation. The effects of both extreme and casual violence shaped the experience of German rule. As during many occupations, large-scale aggregate, popular opinion in localities and regions could become a factor of great significance even when individuals had few if any rights. Russian awareness of German violence in 1941–1942 informed a popular shift against the occupation over the course of 1942 and 1943. But first, with the rise of a strong partisan movement, the battered region would also have to contend with partisan terror and the shock of short-lived re-Sovietization in several large partisan territories.

6

PARTISANS COME TO POWER

STARTING IN THE SUMMER OF 1941, the partisan and the political commissar became strands in a fascist tapestry of a fearsome, ubiquitous, yet elusive enemy. Nazi ideology had long linked Jews and Bolsheviks, albeit inconsistently and depending on the political conjuncture. With Judeo-Bolshevism ascendant on the Eastern Front, the partisan quickly joined that dyad in a kind of unholy trinity.

In the Soviet disarray after the fall of Smolensk, Soviet loyalists such as the young striver Andrei Iudenkov were roaming around in fragmented groups, surrounded by a largely hostile, cautious, rural populace. Soviet partisans had the capacity to blend into the population; their quintessential tactic was to strike suddenly under the cover of darkness. If German military triumphs in summer–fall 1941 fueled a kind of "megalomania" among Wehrmacht forces, why were the Germans obsessed with partisans even in the early days of the invasion, when a guerrilla movement barely even existed?[1] There was a grand disjuncture between the ideological image of the fearsome Jewish-Bolshevik-partisan threat and the weak, fragmented resistance that actually existed in 1941.

The answer lies in the interrelated purposes served by the specter of the partisan threat. Speaking in front of Hermann Goering, Alfred Rosenberg, Wilhelm Keitel, and other top brass as the Battle of Smolensk was raging on July 16, Hitler saw a marvelous opportunity in the fact that the "Russians" had ordered a partisan war: "It gives us the possibility of exterminating anything opposing us." Ever since the Napoleonic Wars, warfare in the midst of civilian populations, or incipient total war, had been increasingly caught up with guerrilla insurrection and counterinsurgency. In Belgium in 1914, the German army had famously committed atrocities against civilians in the name of fighting the threat of irregular insurgents. As with Stalin's Great Terror, there was a preemptive justification for Nazi violence in 1941. Ruthlessly striking the Judeo-Bolshevik enemy, even in the guise of seemingly helpless women and children, would secure the future living space. The most expansive possible identification of potential partisans helped overcome lingering inhibitions about the rules of combat.[2]

General Max von Schenckendorff, who on the Eastern Front in World War I had pioneered exceptionally harsh anti-guerrilla policies in the German-administered territories known as Land Ober Ost, convened a three-day Army Group Center conference in Mogilev in September 1941 that radicalized anti-partisan warfare and the Holocaust by bullets by linking the two together. Of the sixty-one officers who participated in what became known as the Mogilev conference, over 80 percent came from the roaming Security Divisions 221, 286, and 403, all of which were later active in the Smolensk Region. Arthur Nebe, the commanding officer of Einsatzgruppe B, and Erich von dem Bach-Zelewski, the SS Obergruppenführer whose role in "security" warfare later made him chief architect of anti-partisan warfare in the "dead zones" of Belarus, reinforced the message that was adopted by participants in the conference and spread far more broadly: "Where there is a Jew, there is a partisan." Conveying this to mostly junior officers who executed policy on the ground was an instrumental move. A "Jew-Bolshevik-partisan construct" became the means of bringing the weight of Wehrmacht forces into areas the Einsatzgruppen found logistically difficult to cover at the start of the Holocaust by bullets, and it continued on as a justification for targeting civilians.[3]

Schenckendorff quickly emerged as the chief architect of a new kind of annihilationist anti-partisan war. His injunction to destroy both "partisans and suspicious persons" repeated the refrain that Germans must act "mercilessly with complete disregard for any personal surge of emotion." As German rule was established in the eastern parts of the Smolensk Region in October, partisans were conflated with Communists and Jews as well as "German-hating agitators." There is no better illustration of the contradictions of German rule in the Army Group Center Rear Administration area than the fact that the general behind the Mogilev Conference was also the figure who, by spring and fall 1942, became most concerned with implementing a long-term occupation policy that might win support from the Russian population on which it depended.[4] By this time, it was abundantly clear that the Blitzkrieg march toward quick victory had transformed into a mission to "pacify" a vast rear of supply lines potentially vulnerable to Soviet guerrillas. This was the ideological and security-related synergy behind preemptive terror.

Victimizing potential insurgents and their potential helpers everywhere, the army and security apparatus created a self-fulfilling prophecy. A prime survival strategy for the huge numbers of military-age men caught in encirclement became to escape and join the partisans in the forest. The political commissar of one of Smolensk Region's largest units, the Dedushka Regiment, stated forthrightly in May 1942 that up to 80 percent of his partisans were escaped POWs who joined "thanks to the exceptionally harsh regime of the Germans."[5] Indiscriminate preemptive strikes against imagined enemies created real ones. This dynamic too was abundantly evident in Stalinism.

The deliberate German creation of a fearsome image of the partisan ran alongside the prosaic and quite effective monitoring of the strength of partisan activities, which became a large-scale undertaking. Radio transmissions were monitored, networks of agents were sent to infiltrate detachments, and reports constantly disseminated intelligence on the movements and strength of partisans in the localities.[6] The key German dilemma was generally not absence of information, but a lack of manpower to act on it in the vast spaces of the rear. The solution starting in 1942 was increasingly to rely on training anti-partisan forces from POWs and local policemen under German command. By then, the partisan movement was much larger. Given that the psychological effect of the partisans on the German occupiers was out of proportion to the military threat they posed, Nazi ideology was effectively empowering the Soviet partisan movement before it developed.

On the Soviet home front, the partisans quickly became an integral part of a massive patriotic-heroic propaganda drive. In January 1942, a *Pravda* article about the defiance of a beautiful eighteen-year-old partisan (*partizanka*), Zoia Kozmodemianskaia, who was tortured and hung behind enemy lines, touched a popular nerve. The press quickly created a full-blown cult of her martyrdom, purity, and loyalty to Stalin. By the time of the creation of the Central Staff of the Partisan Movement in fall 1942, the political narrative about partisan warfare came to center around the idea of an "all-people's struggle" in the occupied territories. The trigger was a top-secret order signed by Stalin, "On the Tasks of the Partisan Movement." It recalled the defeat of Napoleon's Grande Armée by peasant insurgents in the first Fatherland War of 1812. Panteleimon Ponomarenko, whom Stalin picked to direct the partisan movement, became the chief supporter of this line.[7]

This Soviet narrative of an all-people's struggle behind enemy lines emerged later than the German myth merging partisans, Jews, and Communists into a single enemy. But it, too, exaggerated partisan strength. Soviet public pronouncements concealed party-state concerns about a litany of partisan problems connected to insubordination, marauding, forcible conscription and requisitioning, "sitting out" (*otsizhivanie*) military action, and "degenerate" behavior violating communist norms.[8] Ponomarenko realized the need to curb this portfolio of partisan sins if the resistance was to attract more support. Especially after the tide of war turned in 1943, the "people's war" construct signaled hopes for a broadly based movement that was rooted in the Party and would expand partisan ranks to include more locals and women. An "all-people's struggle," discouraging partisan activities that would jeopardize popular support, was pushed with an eye toward preparing the ground for the return of Soviet power. The Soviet mythologization of the partisans thus held moderating implications, as opposed to the genocidal consequences of the German construct.

Nascent partisan detachments got off the ground best in those remote areas where detachments could create camps beyond easy German reach. In ethnically Russian areas, this was primarily in the forests of Smolensk and Briansk. Partisans flourished especially in the swamps and remote forest hinterlands of Belarus and were also present in the northern marshlands and non-steppe areas of Ukraine.[9]

"Too Many Nursemaids"

De facto autonomy on the ground was not the only factor fragmenting the early partisan movement and making oversight so spotty. For over a year after the invasion, the NKVD, the Red Army, and the Party sparred vigorously to make the partisan movement into their own fiefdom. Behind enemy lines, there was great room for independent maneuvering. "When there are too many nursemaids," as the first secretary of the Orel Regional Party Committee put it, "then the child [goes] unsupervised."[10]

In the three-way contest for control of the partisans in 1941–1942, the political police initially held the dominant position. Pavel Sudoplatov, head of the NKVD's Department of Special Tasks, later the Fourth Directorate, was in charge of covert operations in the occupied territories. Many of the first partisan detachments were jointly organized by local party activists and NKVD personnel together. Secret police chief Lavrentii Beria was the first to push for more centralized command over the partisans, with the unrealized hope that the NKVD's strong initial role would grant it primacy. The Red Army, both its High Command and its political chief, Lev Mekhlis, also launched attempts to direct many partisan activities, but in the second half of 1942 seems to have lent support to the NKVD.[11]

Ponomarenko, a beneficiary of sociopolitical promotion (*vydvizhenie*) policies starting in the First Five-Year Plan when he was rapidly trained as a transport engineer, was a dilettante in military matters. But it was he who emerged victorious as head of the new Central Staff of the Partisan Movement. Stalin met with the former head of the Belarusian party organization five times in September 1942 as a more centralized direction for the partisan movement was put in place. The formula of a supposedly mass, "all-people's" movement was thus the public narrative that corresponded with Stalin's internal emphasis on the party-political element in directing the partisan struggle. For Stalin and Ponomarenko, the political and patriotic direction of the partisan movement was the key factor. Their thinking came into accord with Carl Schmitt's later observation that "the political character of the partisan is crucial," since for any guerrilla movement it becomes imperative to distinguish the guerrilla from a bandit.[12]

Ponomarenko's triumph came at the same time that Stalin moved to grant Red Army generals more autonomy in military decision making, in part by abolishing the office of political commissar in the Red Army on October 18, 1942. But Stalin's empowerment of Ponomarenko actually led to the reinstatement of political commissars in partisan detachments, demonstrating that Stalin envisaged the partisan movement as a party-political as well as a military phenomenon. While the role of these commissars varied by unit, the Central Staff maintained ties especially with them. The rump wartime Smolensk Regional Party Committee on the Soviet side of the front lines also claimed a significant role in oversight of units in the Smolensk Region.

If the Central Staff minimized infighting among the "nursemaids," it could not eliminate it for the duration of the war. A typical example of this came in January 1943, when the Smolensk Regional Party Committee's first secretary, Dmitrii Popov, who at the time also worked for the Central Staff, wrote Ponomarenko that the Smolensk partisan leader Sergei Antonenko refused to recognize Regional Party Committee authority. Antonenko would only report to the NKVD's Fourth Directorate, and the NKVD's Sudoplatov, "having taken Antonenko under his protection, deceived [Popov], communicating that Antonenko and his detachment went behind enemy lines on a special task." The commander's insubordination occurred even though this unit had actually been formed not by the NKVD, but by the Regional Party Committee. For good measure, Popov accused the partisan commander of "sitting out" military activities and "sneaking" triple allocations of food and financial support from army, NKVD, and party sources. Far from carrying out a special operation, Antonenko was on vacation in a village near Moscow, having reassigned as "reinforcements" to the Red Army all those fighters within the unit who opposed him.[13] Such interagency infighting was very common, and continuing patronage of units among the sparring agencies remained an important factor. Competing allegations illustrate just how difficult it was for non-partisan overseers to find out what was really happening in the forests behind enemy lines.

Party-state and NKVD cadres instrumental in forming many detachments—the core of what might be called the partisan elite—pushed back against Ponomarenko's expansion of the partisan movement. As the Central Staff argued for more political oversight, charismatic, warlord-like military commanders with their own mini-cults and followings evaded supervision, some more skillfully than others. Most adopted patriarchal wartime pseudonyms—*dedushka* (grandfather), *diadia* (uncle), *batia* (father)—that became synonymous with their units. Despite their autonomy, the proximity of Smolensk to the front lines allowed for more oversight missions and interactions with what partisans called the Soviet mainland (*bol'shaia zemlia*) than, for example, with remote areas of Belarus or Ukraine.

As the partisans quickly emerged as the primary representatives of Soviet power behind enemy lines, the partisan elite dominant in many units was able to re-create elements of Stalinism—understood simply as Soviet-ness in its Stalin-era incarnation. They did so in the midst of wartime exigencies and adaptations, which by necessity meant incorporating many features of rural life. The Soviet order on the other side of the front lines also evolved quickly during the wartime emergency, and yet in a wide array of different settings across the multinational, multicultural Soviet "mainland" it remained recognizably Stalinist.[14]

That elements of Stalinism were perpetuated within partisan communities behind enemy lines hardly implies that every partisan fighting fascism deserves the label "Stalinist." Partisans were motivated to fight for many different reasons—to repel invaders in their land, for Russian or Soviet patriotism, to simply survive as military-age men under occupation, or, most mundanely, because they had been conscripted. Partisan subculture included many rituals, practices, and policies derived from the partisan elite's grounding in the prewar party-state. In this sense, far from Moscow, the partisans forged a unique phenomenon: Stalinism without Stalin.

A Society in Miniature

Like revolutionary and mass conscription armies, the partisans brought the strains and conflicts of prewar society into new wartime configurations. But unlike the Red Army, partisans lived in closed communities governed not by regular institutions but by commanders whose authority rested on relations with the elite and the rank and file in detachments (*otriady*)—the primary unit with which partisans most identified. The partisan movement was in some ways very stratified and in others extremely cohesive. This basic duality shaped both the internal dynamics of the partisan movement and its relations with Moscow.

Groups of partisans, entrenched for long periods in camps and then suddenly mobile, forged a kind of pro-Soviet society in miniature behind German lines. This microcosmic society had its own rulers, the military commanders; a ruling class, drawn especially but not exclusively from former party-state cadres; a younger generation, dominated by Komsomols; a population made up of rank-and-file fighters; and a marginalized underclass of women, minorities, peasant conscripts, and defectors from German counterinsurgency forces. The currency of the partisans' forest realm was weapons, equipment, food, and moonshine, as well as the prestige of martial prowess and practical skills. It elevated its commanders, who held a patriarchal authority. But makeshift headquarters could not substitute for a kremlin. Rather, the commanders' leadership was enacted in close quarters with the elite and inside egalitarian, freebooting communities.

Partisan communities in their forest camps were divided in political, social, national, and gender terms. They drew from local populations and former Red Army soldiers who came from all over the USSR. Those with skills useful for military and rural life often dominated the rare white-collar professional and intelligentsia types who held high status in prewar urban Soviet civilization. In national terms, Slavs dominated over Jews and other national minorities. The predominant martial ethos was masculine. While a million women served in the Red Army on the Eastern Front, an unprecedented number, there were at most twenty-eight thousand *partizanki* (female partisans) out of hundreds of thousands of people in the movement. There was no military role that women did not play in the partisan war, but as a whole they remained marginalized.[15]

The partisan elite was largely drawn, with notable exceptions, from party officials, the secret police, and the Red Army—the three pillars of the Soviet regime vying for control over the movement as a whole. But it was hardly identical to the prewar party-state elite, most of whom had evacuated. Those in command positions had to adapt to radically new wartime circumstances and stood in between military commanders and the rank and file. For example, the commander and the political commissar of the Smolensk City Partisan Detachment operating near the city of Smolensk in August 1942 discussed how its leadership strongly distrusted fighters who had lived under fascist rule before joining. Of the detachment's fifty-two members, thirty-three were non-party; political commissar Ivan Mozin, the former secretary of the Smolensk City Party Committee, begged the Smolensk Regional Party Committee to send more "verified" cadres from the other side of the front lines, including "city party and soviet workers."[16] Not unlike many parts of the Soviet "mainland," there was a gulf between the leadership and the "ordinary" rank and file. In units such as this, the partisan elite set the tone and the leadership was deeply shaped by the prewar Party.

A good example of a member of the core partisan elite with an NKVD background is Feoktist Demenkov, born in 1903 and a party member since

1927. Demenkov worked for the security organs for fourteen years before the war, rising up as the head of the Dorogobuzh district division (*raiotdeleniia*) of the NKVD. He was thus a veteran of the Great Terror and remained at the job after the "purge of the purgers" in 1939. At the outset of the war, in July 1941, months before Dorogobuzh was occupied, Demenkov was named commander of a future partisan detachment. His commissar was supposed to be the former secretary of the District Party Committee, I. A. Buleiko. The two feuded furiously as a result of fateful events that led to the death of Demenkov's family during the evacuation.

Demenkov did not even try to contain his bitterness. A year later, he devoted a good portion of his Mints Commission interview to denouncing the sneaky "scoundrel" (*prokhvost*) Buleiko, whom he accused of responsibility for the deaths of his wife and son because Buleiko had abandoned them during the evacuation. Buleiko opposed an offensive partisan military strategy in Dorogobuzh as utopian, Demenkov alleged, but the real reason was that he was such a coward that he came within an inch of being summarily shot by partisan commander "Dedushka" (Vasilii Voronchenko). As Demenkov told it, he saved the life of the man he hated by telling the commander, "You can't do that, he is the secretary of a District Party Committee." Secret police and army personnel often looked on the party cadres as timid dilettantes when it came to security and military affairs. Buleiko himself, needless to say, contradicted Demenkov in his own reports, claiming full credit for the "mass development of the partisan struggle" in the area.[17]

Regional- and district-level NKVD and party officials such as Demenkov and Buleiko, launching partisan activities in their home areas, possessed important local knowledge. This was not necessarily about forests or rural networks, however. It was about their fellow party-state cadres. Demenkov mentioned that he personally knew about forty party members remaining in the district. Clearly, he saw everyone outside the leadership group and local party loyalists, including the 80 percent of his fighters who had escaped from encirclement, as less reliable.[18]

Demenkov held forth on the verification of cadres. One had to monitor concrete tasks, incrementally increasing in importance, he said, until the moment neophytes could be brought into the *aktiv*, the group of leading activists and cadres—the notion ubiquitous in the interwar period for all party collectives. "Here there is riffraff from the entire Soviet Union, you can't find out everything about a person immediately," he remarked. "You must verify him."[19] The word for verification, *proverka*, was also a Soviet term for purge. Shortly after he said these words, Demenkov was killed in action during the major German anti-partisan offensive in Smolensk Region in September 1942.

The Making of a Partisan Elite

The prominence of secret policemen and party cadres in forming units was not unique to Smolensk. In the first year after the German invasion, the NKVD took the lead in organizing partisan detachments and was clearly the dominant force among the three main groups in the movement. In Minsk Region, for example, the first fourteen partisan detachments had 1,162 members, including 539 from the NKVD, and were commanded by state security officers; in areas closer to the Soviet zone such as Smolensk and Briansk, the NKVD was even more active. Throughout the war, "special forces" (*osobisty*) often drawn from partisans with NKVD backgrounds, maintained the role of verifying partisans for political loyalty and, like their counterparts in the Red Army, worked in security roles inside detachments.[20]

The army element was also especially prominent in Smolensk and Briansk, where the Blitzkrieg of Army Group Center caught hundreds of thousands of soldiers in giant encirclements. Partisan commanders who were military men evolved away from the Red Army, which tried to enmesh them in conventional operations, but retained a sense of hierarchy and professionalism. By the same token, party cadres were bolstered by Ponomarenko's stress on the political dimension to the partisan war and often saw themselves as the natural leadership. The three "corporate" loyalties dominant in the partisan leadership—the NKVD, the Party, and the army—formed the core leadership in many detachments.[21]

An example of a figure from the party-political wing of the movement, but with an army background, was Gaian Amirov, twenty-five years old in 1941. A Tatar from Ufa who became the political commissar of a major partisan battalion that drove the Germans out of Dorogobuzh in the first half of 1942, Amirov was an unusual figure in the predominantly Slavic partisan leadership. His experience straddled party and army training and postings in Kyiv and Moscow in the 1930s. When he was captured near

Vitebsk, Amirov expressed pride that he did not destroy his party card but concealed his status as a political commissar only by donning a "simple Red Army uniform"; if the Germans "found out I was a *politruk*," he said, "they would have shot me immediately."[22] His success as a partisan came through two lucky breaks. First, he teamed up with a resourceful local peasant Communist to gather weapons and fighters; then, he hit it off with his future commander, the executioner turned partisan, Fedor Gnezdilov.

Amirov deliberately heroicized his peasant partner with the rustic name Potap Avvakumovich Panenkov in several autobiographical accounts from 1942 to 1948. But it is also clear Amirov held him in great esteem and affection. Panenkov, a local peasant without a party-state background, was the exception who proved the rule in playing an outsized role among the nascent partisan elite. Born poor, Panenkov credited his success to Soviet power and the Party. In the fall of 1941, when Amirov met Panenkov for the first time, he saw a man "of medium height, broad-shouldered with black hair, dressed in a black jacket, a shirt with a broad collar, and peasant boots." He was, Amirov enthused, "basically a wonderful person. The whole district loved him." Talkative, outgoing, and playing up the role of the merry peasant to the full, Panenkov had been deemed unfit for military service. Amirov's usual verification process did not apply, he recalled: "I don't know why, but I immediately felt like I trusted Potap and began to tell him everything . . . Maybe I trusted him because I already had some experience. After all, I was a political commissar."[23]

Panenkov knew the villages as an insider. He had a wide network of relatives and friends who provided safe houses and food, and they helped collect weapons and fighters to support the partisans. He could identify Komsomols and recruit trustworthy peasants. The critical role Panenkov played can be judged by the fact that his home village of Zamosh'e and the cluster of villages surrounding it in El'ninskii District became an unofficial partisan capital in late 1941. In sum, this beneficiary of the post-collectivization countryside knew the rural population in a way former party-state officials, even those from the same district, could not. Panenkov was never interviewed. He was killed during a German raid on April 22, 1942.

The second decisive moment for Amirov came after months of organizing, when the small detachments in the area combined forces and became a regiment. Amirov recalled the moment when he joined forces with Fedor Danilovich Gnezdilov, commander of the unit "FD": "He said: let's unite.

I said: let's do it [*davai*]." Amirov took credit for the new regiment's orientation, claiming he told Gnezdilov: "We must carry out a military system, so there won't be partisan feuding [*partizanshchina*] or haggling at the bazaar." They even adopted the ungainly name Twenty-Fourth Anniversary of the Red Army Regiment in an attempt to imitate army organization, unlike other partisan units. Amirov became Gnezdilov's political commissar, and within two months they were in charge of several thousand fighters.[24]

Demenkov and Amirov suggest how, in practice, the major experiences and institutions feeding the nascent partisan elite overlapped. Demenkov was an NKVD figure, but his work for the secret police in the Dorogobuzhskii District also placed him within local party networks. Amirov had roots in the Komsomol and was a party-political figure, but served in the Red Army before the war. The secret police, the army, and the Party feuded at the top and commanded different types of corporate loyalties, but on the ground they were just as often intertwined.

Partisan commanders, standing above both the elite and the rank and file, were often older, maintaining positions at once authoritarian, patriarchal, and repeatedly tested from below and from the mainland. The meteoric rise of Gnezdilov suggests how the harsh challenges of the 1941 cataclysm allowed a number of enterprising men to climb to the top as partisan military commanders from entirely outside the party-state elite.

Cadre of Violence

FD, as Gnezdilov became known, came to the partisans shaped by the entire era of total war, revolution, civil war, and Soviet state repression. He was "not only mentally, but practically prepared" for the brutalization of the war on the Eastern front—a quintessential Soviet cadre of violence.[25] Semiliterate, clever, brutal, and brash, Gnezdilov, who was born to a poor peasant family in the Voronezh region, was a professional executioner before the war.

Long before becoming a famous partisan in Smolensk, Gnezdilov worked in counterinsurgency in the borderlands of the Russian Empire. At the age of eighteen, he joined the tsarist troops fighting the 1916 uprising in Turkestan. During the Russian Civil War, he fought with the Red Army in the south, then returned to Soviet Central Asia to "liquidate bands" of rebels in the early 1920s. Many Civil War veterans were rewarded with advancement in the early Soviet state and brought the martial values of "war communism" with them. Gnezdilov was rewarded with an invitation to study at a party school, which would have advanced his career. But he was too illiterate to take advantage of the opportunity. Instead, after demobilization at the end of 1922, he began work as an executioner for Soviet courts in Central Asia. "Eleven years I shot enemies of the people who were sentenced by our Soviet court," he proudly told the Mints Commission in May 1942.[26]

By 1929, the executioner had "gone psycho" (*zapsikhoval*), as he readily admitted, but claimed to have been cured by six months in a psychiatric institute. He moved to Moscow and found work in the department of prisons of the NKVD. In his interview, Gnezdilov did not give any details about his work for the NKVD between 1933 and 1937. In the opening year of the Great Terror, he quit working for the secret police. One can only speculate that he found it safer or more bearable to become a repairman of equipment and trucks for the city—a skill that served him well during the war when his unit fixed up tanks.[27]

The outbreak of the war found Gnezdilov mobilized as part of the militia (*opolchenie*) of the Kirov section of Moscow, guarding an airfield and a segment of roads. When the Germans opened fire, his comrades panicked and fled. "I cursed them for cowardice," he tellingly remarked, "but at that time I was a nobody [*malen'kii chelovek*]."[28] Gnezdilov's self-description, along with the phrase "at that time," was revealing. Wounded twice in encirclements, hiding in a trench for twelve days, Gnezdilov eventually reached a village in El'ninskii District determined to start up a partisan detachment. At first it was made up only of "eight guys" he trusted. He named the unit "FD"—after his own initials, but also after Feliks Dzerzhinskii, linking his own wartime moniker with the founder of the Cheka. By the time he spoke to the Mints Commission a year later, in 1942, FD was no longer a nobody. He was a partisan commander who had liberated a territory. Like so many other partisans, he seized the calamity of 1941 as a moment of opportunity. After his success in Dorogobuzh, he was awarded the Order of the Red Banner by Marshal Georgii Zhukov himself.

Giving his interview in an earthy, colloquial voice that differed markedly from the more official tone usually taken by party officials, Gnezdilov peppered his extraordinary tale with boasts about his ruthlessness in liquidating prisoners, marauders, and Germans. The first-person singular underlined his newfound status: "If I go on a nighttime raid, then I destroy 200–300 Germans." But Gnezdilov knew full well that there was a time to build himself up and a time to pay fealty to the center's cult of personality. He attributed the destruction of three anti-partisan punitive detachments sent against him by the Germans to an almost mystical boost in morale created by the text of a speech by Stalin, received from the heavens in the form of pamphlets dropped by Soviet aviation. "We read it, studied it," he intoned.[29]

Ten years older than Gnezdilov, Vasilii Voronchenko, known as Dedushka (Grandfather), also seized on the outbreak of war to transform his life and become a legendary partisan commander. In Voronchenko's case, that meant reversing an exclusion from the Party twenty years before. Born in a village in Dorogobuzhskii District, Voronchenko was educated in Orthodox schools before working in timber and sugar factories in Moscow. After serving in a railroad battalion in World War I, he joined the Bolsheviks in 1919, but he was expelled in the 1921 general party purge. As he recounted his life in June 1942, this setback had haunted him for two decades. His many attempts to rejoin the Party failed, but the war finally gave him the opportunity to come in from the cold. Sporting a magnificent handlebar mustache and a trimmed beard flecked with gray, Voronchenko took Demenkov as his political commissar and led one of Smolensk's largest detachments. He was wounded in an air attack on his headquarters and on April 5, 1942, was airlifted to Moscow. The next month, Voronchenko's party membership was restored. He survived the war and lived to see his ninety-eighth birthday.[30]

The soldier-turned-executioner Gnezdilov and the ex-communist worker-turned-engineer Voronchenko were vastly different in terms of educational level and the ways they expressed themselves. But they had one thing in common: both left Moscow after the outbreak of war to seize new opportunities in Smolensk, and both found a means of overcoming their unrealized prewar aspirations as partisan leaders.

Stalinism without Stalin

Even as the partisan movement forged its own wartime communities and distinctive culture, it drew on a great many Soviet constituencies and hierarchies. Party bean counters calculated a total of 120 partisan units with

62,000 people in Smolensk Region during the entire war. The better-known Briansk forest area in nearby Orlov Region exceeded that number, with 156 units but a roughly equal 60,000 partisans. Together, Smolensk and Briansk held almost half the partisans of the predominantly ethnically Russian territory of the RSFSR, with its reported total of approximately 1,000 units and 250,000 partisans. Those numbers conceal very different types of detachments; some were in regular radio contact with Soviet authorities, but especially in 1941 and 1942 others were not. A representative of the Smolensk Regional Party Committee admitted "a big mistake" to the Central Committee in February 1942: it had made no arrangements for communications with eleven of twenty-four partisan units in the eastern districts of the Smolensk Region.[31]

A significant party element was a crucial component of the partisan movement. Seasoned party-state cadres can be distinguished from newly minted Communists and a large Komsomol cohort. For example, the overall composition of Belarus partisans for the entire war (a number of Smolensk detachments either crossed the border or ended up there) included 10,055 party members and 11,869 candidate members, which represents 7.8 percent combined. Half were new Communists accepted in unregulated admissions during the war, just as the gates of the Party were opened wide to Red Army soldiers with distinguished military service. However, the Belarus partisans included another 54,928 Komsomol members, or an additional 19.44 percent of the total. In terms of the rural element, Belarus partisans included over 39 percent peasants. But the figures also include 12.26 percent white-collar workers, 12.16 percent students, 2.51 percent teachers, small numbers of professionals, and 17.1 percent workers. Further east in Orlov and Smolensk Regions, both closer to the Soviet mainland, partisans included noticeably higher numbers of party members, candidate members, and Komsomols: in 1943, they constituted about 48 percent of the total.[32]

As partisan ranks were swelling and their fortunes riding high in several areas of Smolensk Region in early 1942, Voronchenko spoke to leaders from about forty detachments on January 26. He distinguished the Soviet "friendship of peoples" from Nazi racial ideology: "We are supported by a rock-solid rear of the entire Soviet people regardless of nationality, without enmity among those nationalities, about which the fascists and their troubadours in the guise of Goebbels are dreaming . . . We do not consider the multinational nature of the Soviet state its weakness." Perhaps Voronchenko considered it necessary to address this issue because non-Slavs, as many sources attest, were generally low in the hierarchy of partisan society. Jewish partisans who fled ghettos or Nazi persecution to join the armed resistance commonly faced antisemitic attitudes in the partisan leadership and suspicions that the Germans had planted them as spies. Leonid Gol'braikh, who survived the war by joining the partisans, took his commander's recommendation that he change his last name to a Slavic one, a common practice.[33]

A Komsomol instructor conducting political work in the partisan regiment under the command of Sergei Grishin and operating east of Smolensk city reported "incorrect" opinions about the Jews and prejudices against Crimean Tatars and Ukrainians among partisan youth in March 1943. In response to the widespread antisemitic prejudice that Jews had tried to avoid frontline fighting, she was able to point to Jewish partisans who had won medals and distinguished themselves in "their very own partisan unit." Antisemitism was just one of a long list of partisan infractions of proper Soviet behavior that Komsomol activists in particular attempted to rectify.[34]

War and politics both reinforced the masculine ethos of the partisans. Partisan women cursed just like the men, violating a taboo for women still very much in force in Soviet society. It was useless to struggle against it, one *partizanka* remarked; it had become "partisan chic." Dominant values were masculinized in a world in which prowess in battle and practical skills for remote rural living trumped other values. Like the village itself, Stalinism was patriarchal, and the big cult of Stalin trickled down to the mini-cults of the military commanders. The commander is the partisans' "father and friend," exhorted a handwritten partisan newspaper in October 1942, criticizing those who disrespected their duty by ignoring him.[35] Worship of the far-off dictator in the Kremlin and the immediate authority of the commander were different, but the two reinforced one another.

Partisan women served as soldiers, snipers, and political operatives as well as cooks and concubines—the phenomenon of "front wives" was also common in the Red Army. These very different roles and backgrounds not infrequently made different groups of women hostile to one another. Young women serving in the Komsomol, secret police, and military intelligence had special opportunities for assignments as spies and saboteurs. Outside combat, women made outsized contributions as medical personnel and formed the core of the partisan radio network. Other women cleaned, cooked, and served as "mobile wives" for commanders and partisan leaders. A young woman in the Komsomol contingent sounded a typically critical note of these types in January 1944: "There are several girls who are very content that nothing is demanded from them. They marry, live in their huts, wash dishes, wear short skirts and shoes with high heels and are happy with their life."[36] Women without political or military skills occupied the lowest rungs of the partisan social hierarchy. But women fighters were also expected to cook and clean, experiencing the same "double burden" as in broader Soviet society. The divisions among women in the partisan society-in-miniature reflected the fragmented Soviet gender order itself.

Among men, freewheeling partisan culture fueled an erosion of constraints when it came to women. Even as women were honored as heroines and fighters in the war, in the words of one historian, "Female sexuality had also come to be seen as dangerous and treacherous, and thus a legitimate trophy item, which could be taken with impunity."[37] Suspicion of female treachery was not invented out of whole cloth, as teenage girls and young women were used as spies on both sides, contributing to widespread distrust.[38]

Partisans' liberation from prewar constraints was potentially always in conflict with communist codes of proper behavior, so often honored in the breach. "Debauchery" and sexual "licentiousness" were commonly paired with accusations of lack of vigilance toward women suspected as German agents. It was one more infraction authorities and informants commonly placed alongside other accusations such as insubordination, marauding, and military shirking. Since more or less all partisans were open to accusations of some violation of official communist ethics, this became one more arrow in a quiver of political weapons to be pulled out when needed. Such lifestyle "deviations" commonly detained the Smolensk Regional Party Committee, NKVD, or Central Staff when they were accompanied by insubordination, politicized as part of a feud, or assumed such scandalous proportions that they affected partisan effectiveness. Rarely did extended discussion of such problems reach officials at the very top levels, who were concerned with military and logistical updates, demands for resources, and statistics on enemy casualties—which, Soviet-style, were routinely and significantly inflated.[39]

A sanitized image of the partisan society was supported not only by political commissars tasked with sending off reports but also by the rank and file. Reports of some Komsomol women, for example, glorified partisan commanders as unvarnished models of heroism with the same tropes in vogue in press propaganda.[40] This was a perennial urge of both war and politics: to whitewash methods and means in light of the nobility of the ends.

A Wartime Subculture

If the various divisions within partisan society stratified the movement, it was at the same time brought closer together by a distinct wartime culture that merged Stalinist rituals and habits with wartime thirst for revenge against "traitors" and wartime freebooting. The partisan spirit was at once mythologized and condemned as *partizanshchina,* a pejorative term with implications of ideological unorthodoxy and political insubordination, yet also holding connotations of the rough egalitarianism of the red and anarchist partisans of the Russian Civil War, from which a number of partisan units took their names. The Civil War represented a distant model for the partisans of the Great Patriotic War, even if that was often filtered through the immensely popular 1934 film *Chapaev.* Stalinism itself, which merged with many cultures and subcultures across the vast Soviet space, was itself descended in one strand from the heroic period of "war communism," with its rough-and-ready commissars in leather trench coats.

Folkloric and rural notions of liberty also played a role in the wartime partisan communities. "In the popular imagination," in the words of Kenneth Slepyan, the partisan ethos was "customarily associated with autonomy from the state, wildness, spontaneity, and the freedom to pursue the 'good life'—to enjoy wine, women, and song." Even political commissar Amirov proudly gestured to this reputation: "Sometimes we had to go into battle with the accordion. You would have a party [*vecherinka*] going on and the German shows up, so you drop the accordion and begin the battle."[41]

The war offered a way to fight for the Soviet side and escape the centralized norms of 1930s Soviet modernity, which promoted status in the new urban hierarchy and a heavy stress on "culturedness," the written word, and political enlightenment. No matter how autonomous partisan units could be from the Moscow-centric mainland, many made use of rituals paying fealty to the Stalin cult.

Commissar Amirov vividly evoked the mass celebration that had occurred soon after Soviet power had been declared in the Dorogobuzh and Yelnya partisan territories. It took place on March 18, 1942, the day of the Paris Commune. It was a bright, sunny afternoon in Zamosh'e, the home village of Potap Panenkov. German aviation was visible in the sky overhead. More than a hundred party and Komsomol activists, with partisan representatives dressed in their patchwork of irregular uniforms, gathered outside the village school to celebrate the restoration of Soviet power. Delegations from collective farms from each liberated district had sewn red flags and arrived with eggs, butter, milk, and honey that appeared as both gifts and a kind of tribute. The height of the ceremony came when the banners of the new partisan regiments, recently combined from smaller detachments, were ritually unfurled. Commissar Amirov proffered the banner to his commander, "FD" Gnezdilov, who enjoined the assembled commanders and commissars to swear that they would "defend the honor of the Motherland." No vodka was involved, Amirov hastened to add, but all solemnly drank just one glass of moonshine to the health of comrade Stalin. Villagers signed an oath-like letter to Stalin, later published on the front page of *Pravda* in the name of seven hundred male and female collective farmers and partisans.[42] Such rituals served a dual purpose: they signaled political loyalty to the Soviet cause as represented by the Stalin cult while augmenting the authority of the partisan commanders.

The Mystique of Batia versus the Cult of Stalin

The barrage of political-enlightenment work among partisans enumerated by the political commissars in countless bureaucratic reports was, no less than statistics on German casualties, prone to hyperinflation. But doctrinal instruction took a backseat to boosting morale by any means possible. For example, Grisha Gitin, a former ideologist from the Institute Marx-Engels-Lenin-Stalin who worked in the Twenty-Fourth Anniversary of the Red Army partisan regiment's Political Department founded in February 1942, translated and distributed excerpts of letters captured from German soldiers that expressed fear of their impending demise.[43]

In the small subdivisions of the partisan regiment, Soviet-style shaming tactics became personal. In the wall newspaper of the Third Company of the detachment called "Death to the German Occupiers," the political commissar publicly rebuked partisans who served poorly, listing their names and misdeeds in an article exhorting all to "equal the front rank."[44] This quintessentially Soviet tactic was more likely to succeed than arid doctrinal postulates.

The fragile balance between the freewheeling partisan community and the bureaucratic Soviet system clashed most dramatically in the Smolensk

Boevoi listok (Fighting sheet), handwritten newspaper from the Third Company of the partisan detachment "Death to the German Occupiers," October 4, 1942. BA MA MSG 137/15, by permission of Bundesarchiv-Militärarchiv, Freiburg.

Region in the case of the partisan commander Nikifor Koliada. One of the most effective and charismatic warlords operating in the northwest with a base in Demidovskii District, he became known as "Batia"—an at once affectionate and respectful old East Slavic term for father that, in the famous diminutive-intimate form *tsar'-batiushka,* "little father," had been used to denote the tsar. In the course of 1942, Koliada's local mystique and commander cult grew in proportion with his insubordination and his rivalries.

The overconfidence that led Koliada down this ruinous path seems to have been at least partly a product of his unusual resume, which included a first stint as a partisan over two decades before. When the war broke out, the charismatic warlord was fifty years old. He had roots in rural society and the military, having grown up in a poor peasant family in Kharkiv Province and studied before the revolution at a Moscow school for ensigns. He had served in World War I and as a pro-Bolshevik partisan in Ukraine and in the Russian Far East in 1920, the year he joined the Party. He studied at the Far Eastern University from 1925 to 1930, and his work selling timber for hard currency for the Soviet foreign trade apparatus sent him traveling around the USSR and abroad. He saw Smolensk for the first time only when he was sent there by the NKVD's Sudoplatov after the outbreak of war.

If some partisan commanders dressed up in capes or special costumes, and others had fighting songs composed about their "feats," Batia / Koliada elevated himself by almost never appearing in front of his troops. In Moscow for a conference of partisan commanders in July 1942, he talked at length to the editors of *Komsomol'skaia Pravda,* demonstrating the ego-centric bluntness that got him into trouble. He boasted that his detachment had succeeded with almost no contact with Moscow authorities. He avowed that the Germans feared partisans more than the Red Army "because the partisans don't take prisoners but simply destroy them." Back in Smolensk, Koliada refused to coordinate his activities with the Red Army. He brazenly declared: "I did not and will not carry out the decisions of the [Smolensk] Regional Party Committee, we got along and will get along without the Regional Party Committee." Koliada pointedly expressed scorn for apparatchiki who sat out the war in the Soviet rear.

Small wonder retaliation came sooner rather than later. An NKVD "special communication" of May 8, 1942, enumerated a long list of infractions: "sitting out" military activities, lack of party-political work, unauthorized shootings, and marauding. That summer's open insubordination triggered concerted retaliation. "To tolerate such a 'commissar' and give him political leadership over three thousand people is impossible," former Smolensk party secretary Mozin, now a political commissar in a detachment operating not far from Koliada, wrote regional party first secretary Popov in July 1942. Inside the units, rifts between Koliada's loyalists and "military comrades" erupted. Koliada now stood accused of having multiple wives, becoming infected with venereal disease, and hosting lavish feasts at his headquarters.[45]

Mozin knew that Koliada was not unique. "It is necessary to also say that recently on the territory of our region there have appeared many other 'wild' partisan detachments . . . They obey no one," Mozin admitted. What made Koliada an extraordinary case was his unconcealed, demonstrative defiance. The mini-cult of Batia, insofar as it affected his own outlook and actions, had come into conflict with the big cult of Stalin, which stood for the Soviet system. Stalin stood above the Party; Koliada could not be allowed to do so. He was urgently summoned from the battlefield to Moscow at the end of September 1942. On October 7, Stalin signed his arrest warrant. Sentenced to twenty years in the Gulag, Koliada was one of the first to be rehabilitated after Stalin's death—only to collapse and die from a heart attack shortly after his release in 1954.[46]

Partisan Terror

The German invasion reoriented the Soviet system from the fabricated fifth-column plots to staving off a very real fascist enemy at the gates. But the partisans' twin obsessions with local traitors to the Motherland and infiltration by fascist spies preserved the nexus between internal and external enemies at the heart of Stalinism. The cause of "revenge," central to partisan identity and action, was in sync with the Soviet wartime propaganda drive, although Moscow and Red Army authorities would have preferred more partisan military action against the Germans. "We are Stalinists," declared Voronchenko. Smolensk's surging partisan movement carried out a local terror against "traitors to the Motherland" greater in scope than in areas with strong national movements such as Ukraine and the Baltics.[47]

Voronchenko added a penetrating and chilling remark. "If there were not traitors among us," he said, "there would also not be loyalists." In other words, it was not merely destroying German-appointed village elders and policemen "especially mercilessly" and "without red tape" that helped create partisan unity. What Voronchenko called "deeply conspiratorial work" against internal "traitors and cowards who wormed their way into [the partisans'] midst or [tried] to do so" to his mind played a priceless role in strengthening the collective.[48] The pursuit of traitors was not merely an unpleasant necessity but a positive means of binding brothers-in-arms. His comment evokes the bonds holding perpetrators of political or criminal violence together.

The fear of infiltration of the partisan wartime "collective" (*kollektiv*), the word partisan leaders routinely used to signify the affective ties in their detachments as well as the most basic building block of Soviet life, was real. Dmitrii Karov, the Russian émigré officer in German military intelligence, considered it easy to place into partisan ranks agents who had memorized detailed biographical "legends." But it was extremely difficult to maintain communications with them. "Partisans always stayed together," he explained, "and leaving the unit even for a short time, of course, raised suspicions." Partisan women were monitored with special intensity by female comrades in positions of authority, given the danger of sexual assault from male comrades and official Komsomol puritanism toward female sexuality. "*Partizanki* always complained that it was very difficult for them to wash. Even then they were always in view."[49]

The group bonds within partisan units can be understood in part as a replacement for the institution of the family, badly strained and broken during the war. In the horrifically drawn-out starvation in Leningrad under the blockade, for example, it was not uncommon for family members to seek or find replacement families in other institutions.[50] Partisans fighters routinely left their families for extended periods or had lost them in the war. Both German and partisan forces targeted families and relatives of their enemies. Partisan detachments became for many a kind of ersatz family. When the Red Army liberated Briansk in 1943, one commander recalled how his demobilized fighters wept out of a feeling of emptiness and horror at being left alone.[51]

In the first phase of the partisan movement in 1941 and early 1942, terror against collaborators became the primary mission. The observant commander of the Lazo Regiment, Vasilii Kozubskii, posited this as a simple statement of fact: "The partisan movement developed its activities mainly through the destruction of traitors, German hirelings." What even the acute Kozubskii neglected to add, and Stalinist vocabulary obscured, was that this partisan terror was fueled by deeply local and situational concerns that welded it to other facets of partisan life. Poorly armed irregular fighters in initially small groupings were much safer focusing on rural civilians as opposed to German targets. The places and times of partisan executions correlated directly with partisan recruitment of locals into the ranks—either from conscription or from the violent winning over of partisan-friendly villages. If a commander did not order the execution, partisan tribunals, modeled on the troikas used in the red terror during "war communism" in 1918–1920, meted out summary justice.[52]

Partisan reprisals against entire villages were directly connected to the nature of partisan requisitioning, an all-important enterprise that greatly strained relations even with cooperative villages. All partisans lived off the countryside; Moscow's consistent policy was only to provide equipment and weapons. Peasants, of course, were also subject to German taxation while their land and livestock in areas near the fighting were ravaged by war. The line between requisitioning and plunder from both partisans and Germans was not at all clear-cut, as "legal" requisitioning in both cases involved merely handing over a receipt, some signed and stamped, others scrawled in pencil on scraps of paper. Wehrmacht troops also resorted to this practice to avoid the appearance of mere theft.

There were direct material incentives for partisans to target collaborators. As Petr Shmatkov, a District Party Committee secretary turned partisan commander in Znamenskii District, recounted in May 1942: "When we shot and destroyed traitors, all of their property was confiscated and went to the detachment." The Germans, for their part, offered confiscated partisan property and desirable plots of land to the local policemen, not to mention bounties for information about the partisans.[53]

Traitors to the Motherland

But how, exactly, were traitors identified? The task was not simple, because the Germans sometimes coerced rural policemen and elders into serving, and at other times those officeholders switched sides when partisans were in the area. Interested locals became crucial for identifying "traitors" to partisans or, to German forces, identifying hostiles who abetted partisan "bands." Consider the July 1942 account of Konstantin Romanov from the village of Chernyshino in the Duminichskii District, northeast of Briansk. When German units first reached his village on October 7 and 8, 1941, "their first question was, where is the leadership of the rural soviet and the collective farm?" Later, an anti-partisan punitive expedition of conscripted POWs under German command arrived in the village to root out pro-Soviet elements. All who were captured were shot. It did not take long for villagers to direct these reprisals to their own ends. In January 1942, villagers targeted a certain Orlov, who actually wished to work for the Germans. As Romanov told the story: "[Orlov] was not one of us [*nash chelovek*]. The Germans were told that he knew where the partisans were. He did not know where the partisans were. Someone informed on him, saying he himself was connected to the partisans. They hung him."[54] Thus did the locals replay tactics from the collectivization era, when outsiders by necessity were dependent on local testimony to identify who was, for example, a "kulak" sympathizer.

When partisans drew on local youths as recruits and operated in areas where their families and friends still lived, revenge against local collaborators became even more intimate. Karov, the Abwehr officer, noted that it was not uncommon for partisans to have relatives working for the Germans as policemen. Party and Komsomol members who had concealed their pasts under occupation were vulnerable to blackmail to join the partisans. The refusal of the Batia partisans to coordinate with the Red Army stemmed not from the arrogance of their commander Koliada alone, but from the fact that, according to Central Staff statistics from May 1942, 90 percent of his troops were from the local population. This compares with 40–50 percent of the Dedushka partisans. Entering into a local war against collaborators in Prechistenskii and Iartsevskii Districts, Koliada's locals recruited the remaining male population from their home villages and attacked other villages as "enemies." The Red Army dismissed their internecine local obsessions as a "waste of time."[55]

By July 1942, when Koliada's conversation with Komsomol journalists was transcribed in Moscow, the freewheeling commander, clearly a loose cannon, was openly expressing an unorthodox enthusiasm for recruiting from the ranks of "traitors." In Slobodskii District, he recounted, his Batia partisans shot about two hundred policemen, elders, and mayors. In the process, he came to realize that the Germans had forced them to assume those positions "willingly or unwillingly." He then conversed for three hours with forty-eight policemen he recruited: "I cursed them out, saying, what are you doing, you are fighting your own. They told me: I was mobilized, they took me, they forced me, etc." The Germans had threatened them or their families with execution. Koliada, whose reign of terror had disrupted the entire area of his operations with reprisals, now belatedly enthused that the vast majority of collaborators constituted an "unsteady" (*shatkii*) element that could be won over. In fact, former policemen did become partisans but were among the most mistrusted of all the groups making up partisan society. Koliada's logic might have been convincing to those immersed in the local politics of the occupied countryside. Advanced in the shadow of the Kremlin, it sounded heretical.[56]

Partisans Come to Power

Numerous partisan detachments across the Eastern Front, dependent on the rural population for food supplies, gave assurances of one kind or another that after a Soviet victory the collective farm system would not return. Sometimes they even helped peasants to divide up the land—in one case reportedly distributing it in the name of Stalin. The intelligence unit of the Wehrmacht's Security Division 221, operating in Smolensk Region in spring and summer 1942, had informers inside partisan units, including the Lazo Regiment. It reported how "a better life after the war is being promised ('Stalin had no knowledge that the population was living so badly')."[57]

In refusing to defend the hated collective farms, partisans were acting pragmatically on a question with direct implications for their own food supply. Does that flexibility change anything about our understanding of the partisan phenomenon? Hopes that great wartime sacrifices would be rewarded with postwar concessions, fueled by rumors, were also widespread in the Red Army. These popular aspirations were not spun out of whole cloth. On the home front, restrictions on private plots were loosened and the wartime crisis strengthened "pragmatists" over "ideologues."[58]

But what actually happened when the fortunes of war allowed partisans not only to drive the Germans out, but to restore Soviet power for a significant amount of time? In this instance, once again, actions spoke louder than words. The phenomenon of partisan territories, where partisan forces actually restored a version of Soviet power, reached its peak in the middle of 1942. When given the chance, these partisans fashioned a recognizable if crude wartime version of Soviet power in its Stalin-era model. The partisan territories represent one of the most revealing illustrations of Stalinism without Stalin.

In all former Soviet occupied areas, two of the largest partisan territories, sometimes styled republics, were launched from the forested parts of Briansk and Orlov Regions. The Smolensk Region, which boasted four, was transformed even more. The largest partisan territory in Smolensk Region was centered in Dorogobuzh, a district seat seventy-seven miles east of Smolensk along the Dnieper, but it partially or completely included land from nine other districts. It was connected by a fragile land corridor with the El'ninskii territory to its south, centered on the district seat of Yelnya, a town on the Desna River fifty-one miles east of Smolensk. The other two were the Vadinkskii partisan territory north of the Smolensk-Viazma railroad line and the northwest partisan territory near Vitebsk Region, which included a slice of the Smolenskii District. None posed an immediate military threat to the Germans, as the partisan territories were not near communications or defensive positions. But they held obvious political significance to the occupation regime and potentially represented a future military-strategic problem. As a result, the partisan restoration of Soviet power, which in the largest territories rested on at most five thousand to six thousand partisan troops in each, was short-lived. They formed no earlier than January 1942 and were crushed by the Germans by the summer, in Dorogobuzh and Yelnya starting in June. At their height in March 1942, twenty-five of the fifty-four prewar districts of Smolensk Region were liberated in part or in whole.[59]

A top-secret, hand-drawn map of partisan actions in Smolensk as of April 30, 1942, signed by the deputy head of the Fourth Directorate of the Smolensk Region NKVD, colored the partisan-held areas in red. The bright color jumped off the page, reflecting the hope partisan victories inspired on the Soviet side in that hard and bitter year. The Dorogobuzh territory in the north included the regiments FD (Gnezdilov and Amirov) and Dedushka (Voronchenko and Demenkov), while partisans in the smaller El'ninskii territory to the south included the Lazo Regiment (Kozubskii and Iudenkov). The northwest partisan territory around Sloboda, the base of the Batia regiment (Koliada), formed a third prominent area.

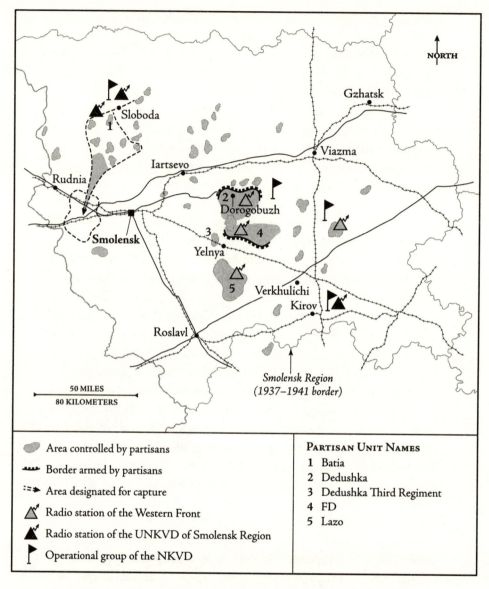

NORTH

Gzhatsk

Sloboda

1

Viazma

Iartsevo

Rudnia

2
Dorogobuzh

3   4

Smolensk

Yelnya

5   Verkhulichi

Kirov

Roslavl

Smolensk Region
(1937–1941 border)

50 MILES
80 KILOMETERS

Area controlled by partisans	**PARTISAN UNIT NAMES**
Border armed by partisans	1 Batia
Area designated for capture	2 Dedushka
Radio station of the Western Front	3 Dedushka Third Regiment
Radio station of the UNKVD of Smolensk Region	4 FD
Operational group of the NKVD	5 Lazo

Partisan territories in occupied Smolensk Region as of April 30, 1942. Re-created from "Diagram of the Areas of Operation of Partisan Units in Smolensk Region on 30.4.1942," signed by Deputy Chief of the Fourth Section of the Smolensk UNKVD Fadeev. GANISO f. 6, op. 1, d. 936, l. 72.

This short-lived yet far-reaching partisan triumph in the first half of 1942 was dependent on the military conjuncture. The Wehrmacht's failed attempt to take Moscow between October and December 1941 brought German forces to the front, allowing partisans behind enemy lines breathing space. During the Red Army counteroffensive, stalling only in late spring 1942, captured and escaped Red Army soldiers created an influx of men with military training into the hitherto weak partisan movement. Partisans benefited from greater support from Soviet aviation. In the first two months of 1942, the number of partisans in Smolensk Region tripled, and by May 1, 1942, they stood at 16,583 in forty-four detachments. In summer 1942, Smolensk and Orlov Regions' partisans were made up of soldiers escaped from encirclements at the level of 40–60 percent, as opposed to less than 30 percent in Leningrad Region.[60]

What happened inside the partisan territories has remained virtual *terra incognita,* but much can be deciphered especially about Dorogobuzh and Yelnya. Various partisan leaders spoke about the same events in Mints Commission interviews soon after their defeat in summer 1942, and what they said can be tested alongside documentation preserved from those two short-lived "partisan republics." It is clear that Smolensk partisans restored Soviet power for the most part on their own. The Red Army, NKVD, and Regional Party Committee made key contributions, but the decisive factor in the partisan restoration was not orders from above. It was common assumptions among the partisan elite about the nature of Soviet power.

The main elements of outside input can be succinctly established. The "raid" of Lieutenant General P. A. Belov's famed Cavalry Corps after the Red Army's Rzhev-Viazma offensive starting January 1942 brought regular troops into the Yelnya-Dorogobuzh areas. Partisans coordinated operations with Belov, sent him recruits from the villages, and even fought battles jointly as Belov fought his way out of the rear. More importantly, the Smolensk Regional Party Committee arranged for six district leaders who had evacuated from the region in 1941 to be airlifted back to Yelnya on April 1. The group included Iakov Valuev, who became a district party first secretary in the newly established partisan territory. Finally, NKVD emissaries arrived in all such territories with checklists of instructions: replace German-appointed cadres, make lists of party members, investigate theft of collective farm property, and establish medical care and schools.[61]

The crux of the restoration of Soviet power in Yelnya and Dorogobuzh was the open establishment of civilian, that is, party-state institutions of power—District Party Committees (Raikoms) and Executive Committees (Raiispolkoms). Communists from the partisan units and underground party committees emerged to staff these offices. The barrage of decrees they produced reveal the contours of their endeavor. Haphazard partisan terror against traitors and irregular requisitioning was succeeded by a more systematic renewal of cadres, a major purge of German rural appointees, and the more regularized extraction of resources through taxation and exhortation. A propaganda blitz and attempts to conjure up a rudimentary welfare infrastructure accompanied the restoration of Soviet power. What actually emerged, however, was a kind of civilian-military dual power, since the commanders of large, newly combined partisan regiments hardly ceded their authority to the now legal party committees.

For Amirov, who remained political commissar in the Twenty-Fourth Anniversary partisan regiment, it was all hands on deck, whether one was in a partisan regiment or the new civilian power structure. "I was occupied there not just with military questions, but economic issues, the restoration of Soviet power, political questions, issues of discipline, educational questions." Amirov understood what he was doing neither in terms of sovereignty nor civil-military relations. Instead, he asserted that the "single most important thing" connecting all his efforts "was to carry out a selection of cadres and their promotion [vydvizhenie]."[62] Amirov and other members of the partisan leadership did not need to take direct orders from Moscow, or even quote Stalin's dictum that "cadres decide everything." Their entire worldview had been formed by the centrality of the cadre system and social-political promotion policies at the core of Stalinist rule.

Re-collectivization

The very first extant written decree in the Yelnya partisan territory, put out by District Party Committee secretary Ivan Gusev on March 20, 1942, stipulated that restored collective farm chairmen should be drawn first and foremost from the ranks of those who had held positions before the war and, more generally, from "patriots of the Motherland who have proven their dedication to the Soviet people through active struggle with the Hitlerite bandits." Those who staffed the new power structures on the district level were all drawn from those who had worked in local party and state posts before the occupation.[63]

One of the most powerful hidden connections between the partisan leadership and the Soviet mainland was an understanding of politics and policy through the prism of selecting, promoting, and purging cadres. Partisans, Komsomols, and underground party members were entitled to Soviet salaries and could transfer them to family members on the home front. The Smolensk Regional Party Committee in Moscow, inundated with requests, secured this funding from the Central Committee. In other words, the freewheeling partisan ethos in the partisan camps hardly made fighters less invested in the material rewards, medals, prestige, and career prospects on the other side of the front lines. One reason documentation from Yelnya on the partisan territory was preserved was precisely because party members were so concerned about maintaining their credentials.[64]

The purge of collaborators in the liberated territories was more thorough-going, better reported, and more juridical than the earlier partisan terror. The new civilian judiciary now overlapped with those of the summary justice troikas of the partisan detachments. But even when the purging of "enemies of the people," as party secretary Valuev somewhat anachronistically termed "traitors to the Motherland," was carried out by the NKVD special forces within the regiments, the restoration of Soviet power resulted in a more systematic process and better documented charges. Later, Amirov claimed that not all were shot; some were sentenced to eight to ten years and kept under guard. After the fact, his was one of many partisan voices insisting that "revolutionary legality" had been scrupulously upheld. "Not one punishment connected to the investigation of traitors of the Motherland was carried out without the [regiment] Special Department [Osobyi Otdel] and not one sentence was carried out without . . . the approval of the military troika that included FD [Gnezdilov], me, as commissar, and Potap Panenkov, as secretary of the party organization."[65]

Amirov protested too much. As late as 1948, he was still defending Gnezdilov and other partisan leaders from accusations of feuding, grudge murders, and generally acting, in his own sarcastic caricature, like "a collection of bandits, shooting this way and that." However, partisan commanders were in a tough bind. They were now trying to run networks of villages and towns in an area with large numbers of armed fighters, who did not suddenly abandon many features of partisan life. Party secretary Valuev in Yelnya charged that "at first" Gnezdilov and Amirov even helped the Twenty-Fourth Anniversary Regiment distill and sell moonshine (*samogon*). A March 31, 1942, NKVD report from this region explained that moonshine brewing helped with requisitioning. This happened in a context in which there were no forces for a militia, and deserters posing as partisans seized foodstuff from the villages. The "unreliable" element among the partisans deserted to become bandits. Voronchenko openly admitted that many of his own Dedushka detachments, when they went from fighting to resting in the rear, descended into banditry. Persuasion was his only tool in his attempt to restore discipline. Indeed, Amirov's own accounts suggested that some partisan commanders accused others of being traitors to the Motherland or of planning to murder one another. Kozubskii, vividly describing the feuding and conflicts among the various partisan units, put it differently: "In the Dedushka Regiment there was absolutely no discipline. There were cases when one battalion attacked another over tobacco." Unsurprisingly, Kozubskii had nothing negative to say about his own Lazo Regiment.[66]

The Dorogobuzh and Yelnya partisan territories were established around the very moment the Germans promulgated their decree on land, publicized on February 26, 1942. After many internal German debates over whether to revise the collective farm system, the proclamation held out the promise—but, crucially, not the reality—of thorough decollectivization.[67] At the very time the Germans were proclaiming a new agrarian order, the new partisan territories set about reversing the spontaneous moves away from the collective farms that had occurred when Soviet power disappeared. Inevitably, this set off a veritable tug-of-war of disputes and reassessments.

Misleadingly, Moscow was simply informed that collective farms had been restored. In fact, it was not possible simply to put them back together again immediately, especially since in many districts the Germans had seized much cattle and property. Local party authorities made significant concessions to wartime reality, such as allowing private plots to be exempted from collective sowing and giving compensation to those who had engaged in individual plantings. These coincided with conflicts over deliveries in kind recorded on scraps of paper and Soviet-style exhortation ("Every household must clothe and shoe one partisan!"). Despite all complications, however, the partisan territory was clearly attempting to reintroduce "labor days"—the heart and soul of the kolkhoz system, in which *corvée*-like labor obligations to the collective farms were only rewarded with meager compensation later, if at all. For these partisans, reestablishing Soviet power could not be done without re-collectivizing agriculture.[68]

Surrounded by the Germans, plagued by feuding, the newly liberated partisan territories nonetheless launched significant initiatives in the realms of "political enlightenment," putting in place a makeshift welfare system and propagandizing everyone involved as much as possible. All these undertakings went beyond measures that can be considered highly practical and connected to the war effort, such as agitprop to counter fascism, sanitation to prevent outbreaks of disease, or the opening of meat plants and flour mills. Rather, they represented an explicit, if only partially realized, goal to restore "public-social-cultural institutions." Temporary schools were organized on collective farms to avoid aviation attacks, and six hundred prewar Komsomol members in the Dorogobuzh partisan territory were mobilized to conduct agitprop. Local members of the intelligentsia and refugees from other districts were given partisan rations. Ideology and welfare were also indispensable ingredients in any recipe for Soviet power. This formed a stark contrast with the priorities of German racial colonization, since most Nazis did not even consider Russians or Slavs fit to "enlighten" in the first place.[69]

Wehrmacht Counterinsurgency

In a series of major operations against Smolensk and Briansk partisans starting in spring 1942, the German military tried to square the circle of crushing the partisan surge and creating more viable occupation policies. General Schenckendorff, head of Army Group Center Rear Administration, embodied the contradictions involved. He was at once the architect of large-scale anti-partisan operations of exceptional brutality and one of the most prominent advocates of enacting more viable occupation policies to win over the Russian population. The threat of partisan-controlled territories so near the front lines alarmed Schenckendorff and the High Command. Axis forces, including Hungarian troops, launched the biggest counterinsurgency campaign of the war on the Eastern Front, with nine divisions committed by May 1942. In the Smolensk areas, Security Division 221, together with the Tenth and Eleventh Panzer Divisions, engaged in "fast-moving combat, in atrocious conditions, against partisans largely trained and equipped to military standards."[70]

While Security Division 221 was plagued by inferior manpower, its intelligence unit, like others elsewhere, took the lead in supporting Schenckendorff's attempt not to alienate the civilian population. In March 1942, reflecting a widespread nostrum, the intelligence unit touted "propaganda of the deed." This was the not unreasonable notion that demonstratively decent behavior on the part of German troops would be more effective than any words. On April 10, it called for handing over prisoners for questioning while forbidding summary executions. Partisan defectors must be "noticeably better treated than normal POWs and as much as possible better treated than they were among their own troops." Summary "retribution measures" such as burning of villages could only be ordered by battalion commanders, while "wild plunder" would be strenuously restricted and "female honor" defended. When such restraint was shown, in fact, notable results were registered. But those were the exceptions. Crushing the partisan territories in the end produced a new and significant wave of mass violence, this time in the Russian countryside.[71]

This was, in part, because Schenckendorff's own instructions alternated between offering the carrot and brandishing the stick. These contradictory impulses were mimicked lower down in Security Division 221's intelligence unit. For example, a laconic instruction conveyed that among those rounded up for suspected partisan activity, children under age ten should not be shot, signaling that no one else was exempt. Most importantly, one can trace a direct line between the mass shootings of Jews in 1941 and the ever clearer anti-civilian reprisals of the big anti-partisan operations in Smolensk and Briansk in 1942. Many of the same German forces carrying out the Holocaust by bullets in 1941 later engaged in atrocities in the rural areas further east while fighting the partisans in 1942. In 1941, for example, Security Division 221 was located in the same genocide locations as SS troops on thirty-three occasions, even more than other rear area troops. Their mass reprisals against civilians around Smolensk and Briansk Regions in 1942, in turn, followed directly into the devastating "dead zones" policy of laying waste to "pro-bandit" areas in rural Belarus after 1943.[72]

The inconsistent move to policies favoring the carrot over the stick ran up against the widespread contempt of the *Landser,* or rank-and-file German soldier, for the primitive East and inferior Slavs. Seeing the grinding poverty of the Soviet villages as they were quartered in peasant huts seemed to confirm ingrained ideological messages about the primitive, repulsive, Asiatic Russians. But there were also more immediate motivations involved. When forty-three-year-old Willi Weiss, a sergeant in the Third Company of Security Division 335, went on a requisitioning expedition south of Smolensk near the Smolensk-Briansk railway line in April 1942, his unit searched a village. The German soldiers found themselves unable to reach their cattle and grain targets. Weiss and a small group of comrades then rounded up a group of villagers and hung them with signs around their necks: "friends of the partisans." When this act did not produce the desired result, his company set fire to the village houses and left. Of the ten such operations in which he admitted to participating, six resulted in the burning of entire villages. In this case, the element of frustration and scapegoating was an immediate spark behind the reprisals: available civilians suffered in place of elusive partisans. Revenge for partisan ambushes was another common motivation behind the most brutal reprisals.[73]

The German response, with its very heavy reliance on terror tactics, was in sync with the methods of the war of annihilation. It reflected the readiness of the German military-security apparatus to turn to mass reprisals to compensate for deficits of manpower in the rear. Schenckendorff's contradictory push for a different kind of occupation appears to have been actively supported by a number of military and intelligence officers under his command. But on the ground, highly mobile units such as Security Division 221 ultimately had no stake in long-term stability in this or any other locale. There are also numerous indications that the conscripted POWs and Soviet fighters used on the front lines of the anti-partisan actions were poorly equipped and controlled.[74] The message sent to the Smolensk population by brutal mass reprisals was not substantially altered by Schenckendorff's half-hearted discovery of the virtues of moderation. The propaganda of the deed did turn out to speak more powerfully than the written word.

Aftershocks

In June and July 1942, the Wehrmacht reconquered the partisan territories. Partisans and inhabitants of entire villages hid in the forests for extended periods. Numerous partisan elites from the territories made often harrowing escapes to the Soviet side of the front, where they gave their Mints Commission interviews and received medals. The Twenty-Fourth Anniversary Regiment was dispersed, and most of the Dedushka Regiment was destroyed. Some of its troops ended up working as policemen for the Germans in towns and villages. Numerous others from Dorogobuzh served in a German anti-partisan battalion commanded by Vladimir (Waldemar) Bishler, an émigré nobleman from Saratov who oversaw fifteen hundred fighters for the Germans. Devastatingly, the overturned restoration of Soviet power had revealed the members of the underground party committees for all to see. Never again would the Smolensk partisans strive to create sovietized territories.[75]

For the partisan movement that had surged in Smolensk in 1942, the rout of late summer and early fall 1942 was a significant but not a fatal setback. Many partisans escaped and dispersed over the area, and the partisan movement was substantially rebuilt. When the partisans regrouped in fall 1942, it was a different phase of the struggle, corresponding to the creation of new detachments and less overt, intra-agency infighting due to the creation of the Central Staff. Yet the partisan territories left a legacy. In prominent and decisive fashion, partisan fighters had established themselves as the representatives of Soviet power behind enemy lines. Despite all their autonomy on the ground, along with the rough partisan ethos that evoked guerrilla groups from earlier periods of Russian history, the partisan movement as a whole had demonstratively ensured that Soviet power never fully disappeared from the region.

The partisan surge of 1942 brought the conflict inside peasant families and into entire villages forced to choose or switch sides. Internecine conflict was heightened because the unfolding of the partisan war in 1941–1942 remained politically ambiguous for civilians making choices in this region. On the one hand, the Red Army advance and the creation of partisan territories made the prospect of potential return of Soviet power and its rural order a distinct and imaginable possibility in this area—long before Stalingrad turned the tide of war in 1943. German mass reprisals could not but alienate the rural population. On the other hand, victorious German power remained the dominant reality. For the rural inhabitants in the Smolensk Region, the future was murky and the price for everyone remained exorbitantly high.

7

COLLABORATION AND THE RUSSIAN QUESTION

VASILII MASLENNIKOV'S PRIMARY MISSION was to keep his family intact. Just as he had finally established himself as a history teacher in the town of Ponizov'e, the outbreak of war pushed him back to his home village during the 1941 power vacuum. The reason was clear: Maslennikov, his wife, Zhenia, and their two children were staying nearby with his in-laws, and his own parents continued to live quietly on the collective farm. During the Battle of Smolensk, Maslennikov's younger siblings, Tonia and Ivan, both students in the Smolensk Pedagogical Institute hoping to follow their brother's footsteps and become teachers, also hiked on foot to the parental peasant hut. So many thousands of families were broken up at the moment of the war's outbreak, Maslennikov later reflected. "In our family, the war forced us to first gather all together, and only later tore us apart."[1] Circumstances not only separated them physically, but shaped the diametrically opposed ways they were judged politically.

By the time the Maslennikov family gathered, frontline German officers and soldiers, intimidating peasants just by virtue of their well-fed and athletic builds, set about establishing a new regime in the countryside. They appointed a village elder (*starosta*), Leon Aleksin, and three policemen well known to all the villagers. The first policeman, Yermak, whom Maslennikov judged an unscrupulous "con" (*zhulik*), knew some German from his service in World War I. The second, Izot, had long cultivated hatred for all "commissars," his term for anyone Soviet. The third, Khariton, was semiliterate, inscrutable, and always silent. His qualification for the village *politsai* was that his father had been branded as "prosperous" during collectivization. Maslennikov was a civilian and respected by the villagers. But he was in a precarious position: everyone knew he had joined the Communist Party. As in many other villages, the new elder, Aleksin, chose not to serve the Germans zealously. He did not expose party members or escaped soldiers. "Who knows what the future will bring," he made a point of telling Maslennikov, hedging his bets in case the Soviets were ever to return. But Aleksin thought the Germans would almost certainly be victorious, and he "naively and stupidly hoped that when the war ended the Germans would give him land and he would become rich." The elder's demeanor shifted like a weathervane along with the movement of the troops: he was careful not to offend pro-Soviet sensibilities during the Soviet offensive in nearby Yelnya in late summer, he became bolder when the Germans advanced on Moscow, and he turned cautious again after Operation Typhoon failed to take Moscow in January 1942.[2]

Maslennikov's village was typical of the German new order in the countryside. Each village was run by a male elder, and much could depend on his fulfillment of German commands. Each elder commanded one to three policemen and sometimes a scribe. These positions involved salaries, food rations, and payments for families in event of death. They also brought freedom of movement at a time when it was increasingly restricted at night and outside the village. In Maslennikov's village as in others, evidence of enmity toward Soviet power or repression, such as dekulakization in the 1930s, was an advantage for these posts. "As a rule," opined Dmitrii Karov, the Russian émigré who had returned as an Abwehr officer involved in police recruitment, dekulakized peasants and others repressed under the Soviets made poor policemen: their main goal of "revenge" against those who had denounced them led to "unbelievable viciousness" that only aided partisans and Soviet propaganda. Rural policemen were motivated by what Karov considered the "most unbelievable" grudges, such as the theft of a piglet a decade before. Former collective farm chairmen and party members were also appointed as elders, in keeping with similar exceptions regularly made in towns and cities.[3] Claims to have been persecuted under Stalinism were therefore a factor, but they were not necessarily determinative. German reliance on armed and appointed locals grew over the course of the occupation, but Germans' endemic distrust of their own collaborators would never abate.

Maslennikov and his siblings, gathered in their village at the war's outset, took divergent paths. Accidents of geography and the whims of circumstance, far more than morality or political convictions, were the determining explanation—at least at first glance. After October 1941, Filimony lay at the edge of the nascent partisan territories that for several months after February 1942 would restore Soviet power in Yelnya and Dorogobuzh. Even though Maslennikov was a military-aged man, as a native resident of the village he could have lived there legally under German rule. But with partisans ascendant in the area in early 1942 and as a known party member, he became worried the Germans would not make fine distinctions. The village was divided: a woman with sons in the Red Army, for example, berated him for not serving at the front. By February 1942, with the partisan territories established, Filimony lay right on the border between partisans and Germans. Both the village and the risk-averse Maslennikov were still neutral, but he was acutely aware that for him it was a "dangerous moment." His passive formulation explaining how he threw in his lot on the Soviet side says it all: "It became necessary to go to the partisans and worry about family left behind." The reason it became necessary was because a partisan commander from Glinka arrived in the village, convened a meeting of all men aged seventeen to thirty-five, and ordered them to form their own partisan unit. That left little choice, but, even so, some men managed to disappear before the meeting. Maslennikov, along with fifteen other locals and escaped Red Army soldiers, signed up. As a history teacher, he was even named the unit's political commissar.[4]

Maslennikov thus joined the partisans, if a bit late and because he saw little other choice. His brother and sister faced different situations. After Maslennikov departed, his family left the hut in Filimony and moved in with acquaintances inside the rear of the Yelnya partisan territory, in order to avoid the fighting. Maslennikov's brother, Ivan, twenty-two in 1941, had been exempt from military service because of a disabled left arm. In his new village, Ivan helped "serve and feed" the partisans and was initially arrested as a partisan when the Germans crushed the partisan territory after June 1942. But it was not hard to prove he was handicapped, and when German authorities discovered he knew German "fairly well" Ivan was enlisted for the duration of the occupation as a translator at the Glinka commandant's headquarters. This job, serving the German military, earned him arrest as a collaborator upon re-Sovietization in late 1943. Tonia, Maslennikov's sister, survived German occupation and was enlisted by advancing Soviet army forces to work for SMERSH, in military counterintelligence—a position that, Maslennikov observed elliptically, she hated and left as soon as possible.[5]

The three siblings, whom the outbreak of war had gathered in their home village, thus took three paths. Their paths diverged even though the siblings seem to have been quite similar: young, literate peasants who, through education, were trying to better their lives in one of the sole ways open to them. None of them were pro-German, and they were hardly zealous Stalinists. Each of them seems to have taken a wartime stance reluctantly and for lack of perceived alternatives. Despite all these similarities, the roles for which they would be judged were radically divergent: Maslennikov became a partisan, Ivan worked for the German occupation regime, and Tonia served as an agent of Stalinist retribution.

Army Group Center Rear Administration area (Korück) reports on the rural population from Smolensk Region and eastern Belarus often reflected the impressions of the compilers. But one commonality running through assessments from many different localities across the entire period of occupation was the equation between Red Army or partisan proximity and popular willingness to serve the Germans. "The Russian population no longer believes in the strengths of our Wehrmacht," a February 25, 1942, report lamented. "They have seen the retreat of our troops and see now that we are also in the rear areas no longer master of the situation." Mayors, elders, policemen, and anti-partisan troops were portrayed as fearful about the return of Soviet rule, which, another report claimed, would mean "he who works or has worked with us is a dead man."[6] This functioned as a convenient explanation for the Germans whenever locals were reluctant to cooperate. Even so, areas close to the front lines differed from the rest of the Soviet Union and the European theater, where calculations about which side would emerge victorious revolved around initial impressions of overwhelming German superiority and then underwent a significant shift only after the Battle of Stalingrad in 1943. In Smolensk, the smaller Soviet advances after the Battle of Moscow in late 1941 and the restoration of Soviet power in partisan territories in 1942 made for more frequent fluctuations of calculations about military victory in the localities.

Can the Maslennikov siblings' divergent fates really be explained entirely by circumstances alone? The dichotomies that have so often structured thinking about collaboration in World War II—voluntary versus involuntary, structural versus situational, material versus ideological—are in concrete cases such as Maslennikov's often impossible to fully disaggregate. After German counterinsurgency crushed Maslennikov's partisans in summer 1942, he faced another decisive moment. He mentioned it almost in passing in his memoirs, as he was never proud of his innate cautiousness, but in his life story it was a consequential event.

Maslennikov was incarcerated in the enormous German concentration camp in Roslavl, deprived of his shoes in exchange for wooden clogs, and, he wrote, "humiliated and without rights in my own land," when he was approached by the camp officer. Maslennikov and ten other men were offered the chance to serve as volunteers for the German military. In return, they would get a ticket out of the Dulag, good rations, and even a weapon. Other inmates jumped at the chance. Maslennikov turned it down. The reasons he recorded are of interest. "I, of course, did not imagine myself to be a hero of the resistance," he said in his self-deprecating way. Yet the notion of serving the Germans repelled him. He was well aware that others may have simply wanted a way out of the camp in order later to escape. "But that," he observed gravely, "entailed great risk. And not everyone is capable of that." Maslennikov made that choice not merely out of caution. Although much of his life he was buffeted by events, in those moments in the Roslavl camp Maslennikov made a decision: not to become a collaborator. Something about the camp commandant's offer to serve the Germans repulsed him. His words convey a sense of bitterness at the servile role he was contemplating: "As if it were not enough I had ended up in captivity, now I was going to voluntarily serve them?"[7]

Maslennikov's choice was costly: he spent over two years in captivity and forced labor. He almost died of sickness and malnutrition after he was evacuated out of Smolensk Region with the Germans in 1943, ending up as a forced laborer in Saxony until the end of the war.[8] The man's outlook and agency at that instant determined his path, even if his choices all along were greatly constrained. Entire categories of victims subject to mass annihilation, in particular Jews but also POWs, were not offered the option he was. Others were given a choice either to comply or not to survive. But as this key moment in Maslennikov's life also suggests, many others were never truly choiceless.

Collaboration East and West

The modern meaning of the term *collaboration,* to work with the enemy during a wartime occupation, derives from Vichy France. It was used by Marshal Philippe Pétain in the sense of "an openly desired co-operation with and imitation of the German regime" in order to further an anti-parliamentary "national revolution."[9] That usage quickly turned it into a politicized term of opprobrium. In the war of annihilation on the Eastern Front, Soviets and partisans simply used "traitor" (*predatel'*) and "betrayer of the Motherland" (*izmennik rodiny*). Self-styled partisan "avengers" and implacable Stalinists in Moscow, when it suited them, may have implicitly recognized the long continuum of gray zones between active collaboration and resistance that was so salient in the occupied territories. But, quite unlike in Europe, everyone on former Soviet territory deciding what to do knew that it could provoke Stalinist retribution. While very few entered the war desiring to serve either Germany or fascism, a great many would become complicit with what transpired.

In terms of the choices faced both by elites and by ordinary people, there were other fundamental distinctions between Western and Eastern Europe. Opportunities for collaboration were greater in West European states where Germany tolerated national-level governments and coercive but profitable forms of economic integration. This created rationales and rewards for business, industrial, and agricultural interests, not to mention the political classes. In the East, by contrast, outright political domination and economic plunder were to pave the way for colonization and racial re-ordering. Unprecedented German mass murder on the Eastern Front and the exceptionally brutal nature of Stalinism raised the stakes considerably for all decisions relating to sustenance and survival. It would be a fallacy, however, to think that the German occupation regime on the Eastern Front did not need or want collaborators. On the contrary, large numbers became indispensable to the regime's very existence.[10]

There were other distinctions among Russian and non-Russian former Soviet territories. In Smolensk and other pre-1939 Soviet territories, the political ideas motivating cooperation—so-called ideological collaborationism—rarely if ever included coherently pro-fascist proclivities. Rather, motivations almost always revolved around anti-communism and anti-Stalinism. But unlike the Baltics, Ukraine, and, even to a lesser extent, nearby Belarus, occupied Russian territories had no significant, aggrieved nationalist movements eager to turn the Nazi war of racial colonization into the moment of their own national independence. General Andrei Vlasov's Russian Liberation Army (ROA) was a propagandistic attempt to capitalize on the allure of a "third way" of Russian national independence, and its widely distributed propaganda did attempt to fan the flames of Russian nationalism, but it remained a symbolic rather than actual Russian force virtually until the end of the war. A Russian path between fascism and communism did become important mostly for returning Russian émigrés and local elites under occupation, but ended up stillborn.

Whereas Hitler's Machiavellian "moderation" in France in June 1940 facilitated exploitation of an independent Vichy, the Führer took a hard line by implacably and repeatedly denying any long-term concessions to nationalist movements or autonomy that would modify German racial domination in the East. Alfred Rosenberg, at the height of his influence when first appointed Reich minister for the Eastern Territories, advocated for a subordinate, rump Russia and—with the explicit goal of stimulating Belarusian nationalism—expanding Belarus within 250 miles of Moscow, with Smolensk as its capital. Rosenberg, a weak politician, quickly became a second-tier player in Nazi power politics, although he was still significant in the occupied East. He never directly addressed how his own anti-Russian crusade squared with his support for wartime concessions to political autonomy in Russian territories. This represented his own brand of Machiavellianism. "Pacifying" Russians would be important only until buffer states could be created after the war.[11]

The plans of Rosenberg's Eastern Ministry quickly "fell foul of Himmler's policy of maximum repression" and "Göring's aims of total economic exploitation." Hitler, for whom eradicating "Judeo-Bolshevism" was key, never forgot to disparage Nazism's initial common cause in the early 1920s with far-right Hungarian, Ukrainian, and Russian émigré nationalists. The drive toward destruction at the crux of Hitler's power, epitomized by the genocidal premise behind the war of annihilation, made compromise impossible.[12]

At the same time, the Third Reich's personalistic "Führer principle" encouraged chaotic competition over policy. Throughout 1942 and 1943, debates over a more effective mode of treating the population and proposals for creating a puppet regime to do so repeatedly percolated at various levels in the military administration, the economic organs, and Rosenberg's ministry.[13] Army Group Center's architect of the brutally successful anti-partisan war in Smolensk and Briansk in spring–summer 1942, Max von Schenckendorff, made perhaps the most high-profile attempt. Schenckendorff mobilized widespread recruitment of local armed forces and, despite all contradictions, supported occupation policies that brandished carrots as well as sticks. By the end of 1942, with the war not going well, he concluded that carrots alone were not enough. For Russians, it was necessary to offer a political goal.

"A Kind of Protectorate"

The headquarters of Rosenberg's Eastern Ministry was located in a long building on Berlin's grand avenue, 63 Unter den Linden, the same address of the Soviet embassy in Berlin before the war and in East Berlin afterward. On December 18, 1942, top military brass and economic administrators mingled with Rosenberg's staff to hear the veteran general hold forth on the characteristics of the Russian population. General Schenckendorff, then sixty-seven, with his stiff military bearing and closely cropped gray hair, spoke about how primitive Russians nonetheless possessed "intelligence" and were capable of grasping hard yet just measures. Grateful to Germany for the opening of Orthodox churches, Russians should be easy to govern. But continually harsh economic conditions and hunger led to a "noticeable deterioration of relations." The rural population was demoralized by forced labor deportations, "wild requisitioning," burning of villages, and what he euphemistically termed mistreatment (*falsche Behandlung*), an allusion to atrocities such as the mass starvation of POWs. Soviet adoption of Russian national themes was becoming increasingly effective in partisan propaganda. German war aims in Russia had been "clearly" set on creating a "colonial system," Schenckendorff continued, but now it was no longer feasible to take "political goals" and a central "Russian" government off the table. In a vague yet evocative formulation, he proposed "something like a kind of Protectorate."[14]

Rosenberg and General Kurt von Tippelskirch greeted Schenckendorff's proposals with open enthusiasm. General Otto Stapf, head of Economic Staff East (Wirtschaftsstab Ost) since August, agreed that in the interests of German economic success "the Russian" should be given "a

clear political goal as soon as possible." Rosenberg took the positive response as vindication of his savvy leadership. To his diary, the old Nazi
ideologue vented his frustration about being branded by other power brokers as a weak-willed "philosopher," adding: "The entire debate showed
one thing: that the approach of solely governing 'the Slavs with a strong
hand' has been the wrong one."[15]

Creating Collaborators

All programmatic proposals to change the direction of German racial colonization, needless to say, ended in failure. Hitler rejected them out of hand
in this case, and his contempt for Rosenberg seemed only to increase as the
war wore on. Many military and administrative authorities acutely perceived that the Führer's zealotry came with palpable costs to the war effort.
This alone ensured that the constant political and bureaucratic jockeying
over when and how to use non-German forces in the East did not cease.[16]

All hard-line declarations, moreover, flew in the face of the basic fact
that, using its own and Axis forces, Nazi Germany would simply not have
been capable of prosecuting the war at the front and holding its vast Soviet
territories, where an estimated 68.4 million people (over 40 percent of
the prewar Soviet population) experienced German rule. Collaboration in
Western Europe was primarily administrative and economic and, to a lesser
extent, military. On the Eastern Front, local "volunteers" immediately became crucial manpower for the Holocaust by bullets, with over one hundred
thousand guard units aiding Germans within eight weeks of invasion.
Armed police and anti-partisan units gained greatly in size and importance
in 1942. At the Battle of Stalingrad in 1943, up to one in ten soldiers captured
by the Soviets were former Red Army soldiers. By September 1943, the
overall number of Soviet citizens in German uniform had risen to between
eight hundred thousand and one million. In the course of the war, as many
as 1.3 to 1.6 million Soviet citizens served as armed troops under a vast pan-
oply of names and organizations: policemen in town and countryside, in
larger anti-partisan units, and under Wehrmacht, Abwehr, and SS command. The number of Soviets militarily serving the Third Reich was far
greater than citizens from all the countries of Europe combined. Hitler's
preference for non-Russians such as Ukrainians notwithstanding, concessions to military necessity were made, one step after another.[17]

Most of the military conscripts were recruited from the POW camps. Research in German sources—*contra* post-Soviet and Putin-era memory mythology in Russia itself—suggests that by far the largest number were of Russian nationality (51 percent), followed by peoples of the Caucasus (18 percent), Ukrainians (16 percent), and Balts (12 percent). Such statistics on the Eastern Front are especially difficult to establish with certainty, and despite the line for nationality in Red Army soldiers' military identification booklets, national identity was far from always clear-cut. But the booklets were the basis for the information collected, and if documents were missing, German interrogators asked. Since identifying as Ukrainian, for example, rather than Russian would increase chances of release and survival, the likelihood is that German records rather underestimated the percentage of Russian collaborators. Without Soviet citizens—including Russians—fighting on the German side, a German military historian has concluded, the Wehrmacht could not have continued the war after the Battle of Stalingrad.[18]

Some of the most notorious Holocaust perpetrators were POWs recruited from the Dulags: the first contingent of about 2,560 of the almost 5,100 men trained for guard detachments at the Trawniki Training Camp near Lublin. The number of POWs who became "Trawniki men" increased between the end of 1941 and summer 1942. It was a very multinational group. While some Russians may have identified as non-Russians especially in 1941, detailed data suggest that Russians (including twenty born in the Smolensk Region) were the second-largest group after Ukrainians. It is hard to imagine that any of them, regardless of nationality, anticipated the role they would play. Between March 1942 and November 1943, the SS deployed the Trawniki men in death camps to carry out the mass murder of approximately 1.7 million European Jews in German-occupied Poland. Operation Reinhard, "perhaps the most skillfully coordinated mass murder operation in history," never involved a staff of more than 150 Germans.[19]

Moscow was well aware of the massive numbers of armed collaborators from among its own citizens, even as Stalin and the Soviet state increasingly tilted toward invoking Russian patriotic and nationalistic themes. An analysis from the Central Headquarters of the Partisan Movement in July 1943, for example, estimated the size of the order (auxiliary) police— in Smolensk termed *strazhniki,* or guards, but most often simply called *politsai*—in the entire occupied territories as "no less than" 350,000.

Historical scholarship now puts the number as at least 400,000, half in military formations and the other half in police forces in town and countryside.[20] Ultimately, however, Hitler's implacable insistence to avoid any and all concessions that might turn propaganda into "deeds" proved as significant as moves toward widespread exploitation of armed collaborators. In Russian areas, this stance emanating from the top demoralized those forces, nipped in the bud any potentially popular Russian "third way" between Nazism and Stalinism, and informed the significant popular turn away from German rule in the course of 1942–1943.

At the same time, Stalinism itself played an outsized, even decisive role in creating collaborators. The legacies of the 1930s that in rural areas created the most antipathy toward Stalin and the Soviet system were collectivization, famine, and the suppression of religion. To those were added the Great Terror and mass operations, widespread reliance on repressed forced labor in the Gulag, the immiseration of the population during forced industrialization, and repression of national minorities. But even leaving all those legacies aside, Soviet decision making after the war began— evacuation of the privileged, scorched-earth orders, insistence on no retreat—arguably had an even larger impact. Stalin's public statements that soldiers and officers in captivity were traitors to the Motherland openly equated loyalty with death alone. German and Soviet interrogation records suggest that few Soviets entered the war ready to take up arms against their own country. All the same, Stalinism represented a powerful, structural "push" factor behind collaboration.[21]

A Russian from Paris in German Counterintelligence

Dmitrii Karov, born Kandaurov, was in a unique position to understand the recruitment of police and anti-partisan armed forces in the mostly ethnically Russian occupied territories. Having fled Russia in 1919 during the Civil War, he was educated in Russian émigré educational institutions in Paris. He was thirty-eight years old in 1940 when France capitulated to Germany and he took a job as a German-French-Russian translator in Hannover's Deutsche Edelstahlwerke, a plant producing aircraft engines. Within a month, he was recruited to German military intelligence. In December 1941, he was assigned to Intelligence Unit 1c of the Wehrmacht's Eighteenth Army in Army Group North. In 1943, he also served at the Abwehr field headquarters in

Vitebsk. Karov thus observed Army Group Center Rear Administration territories from 1942 on, especially the Surazh forest area and eastern Belarus. He also passed through Smolensk city and parts of Smolensk Region. A Russian Abwehr officer was unheard of. There were plenty of other émigrés and locals working as translators and interrogators, but Karov's officer status always provoked great surprise in 1941 and 1942. This only abated with the German decision to recruit greater numbers of military collaborators in the so-called Eastern battalions in 1943 and 1944. Like so many émigrés who had served the Nazis, Kandaurov became known by a pseudonym after the war—Karov.[22]

The covert battle that Karov joined between German and Soviet intelligence agencies assumed a scope unmatched in any other theater of World War II. Under the auspices of the German High Command, the Abwehr contained units in intelligence gathering, counterintelligence, and sabotage. Karov held a high opinion of the institution that trained him, and he later absolved it of complicity in Nazi crimes. In 1952, he called it a "good school" of counterespionage that Hitler disliked for its "apolitical" bent. In fact, a number of Abwehr figures, from Admiral Wilhelm Canaris down, were anti-Nazi; Canaris was involved in several of the attempts to assassinate Hitler. Yet the organization's World War II record was mixed: it was ineffectively decentralized, penetrated by the NKVD, and locked in destructive rivalries with the SS and the Security Service (Sicherheitsdienst, SD). The Abwehr set up field headquarters that were among the first and most deeply involved agencies recruiting armed military commandos from POWs and local populations. Karov's activities included interrogating captured Soviet agents (often youths and even children) and recruiting clandestine networks of agents for counterespionage and the anti-partisan war. Karov's work placed him squarely in a murky, suspicion-filled shadow war in the occupied territories that immediately touched all those recruited as collaborators.[23]

In the quasi-scholarly, memoiristic works of history that Karov penned in Munich after the war, he strove for an objective tone critical of both Germans and Soviets, endeavoring to explain German defeat and Soviet realities to new audiences in émigré Sovietology and the Cold War United States. His accounts sometimes misinterpreted internal Soviet affairs. But these narratives also feature insights drawn from his direct experience in the recruitment of police and anti-partisan collaborators from local populations.[24]

Karov felt a strong affiliation with the anti-communist Russian contingent working specifically in German counterintelligence—even as he often expressed disdain for other Russian émigrés serving Axis forces as opportunistic and incompetent. He made sharp distinctions within the invading German forces as containing people vastly different "in political and moral terms." The needless brutality inflicted by the Germans, he repeatedly concluded, was a "stupid" error. It is not hard to detect professional pride in his own activities and, more broadly, the Abwehr. He depicted himself as fully on board with Abwehr feuds with the SS and SD, reserving special ire for their "absence of any moral or ethical principles." Karov believed the Soviet Russian population was widely "infected" by Bolshevism, but he could not stand many of his own German colleagues' racial prejudices about inferior, primitive Asiatics. He was delighted, for example, when a captured Russian intellectual surprised his captors by discussing the philosophy of Immanuel Kant in German. He expressed disdain for antisemitism while professing Christian values; he thought highly of those Russian compatriots who avoided servility.[25]

Karov's superior in Vitebsk in September 1943, a Captain Schultz, made a habit of insulting Russians' "Asiatic mugs" in his presence. Karov took the bait. "I got angry and told him that I was also Russian, I would never become German," he recalled. Then he went a step further. Karov told Schultz that "those 'Asiatic mugs' had driven the Germans from Stalingrad, and it would soon be necessary to leave Vitebsk if there were many other officers like him." Their resulting feud became so dangerous for Karov that he only escaped alive by arranging to be transferred to another unit.[26]

Russians into Ukrainians: Working Away from the Führer

How Karov selected policemen underlines the extent to which the murderous population politics of Stalinism and Nazism undergirded a new wartime politics of identity that profoundly shaped the recruitment of collaborators. "The author of these lines," as Karov frequently began his autobiographical anecdotes, personally "verified a huge number of people who called themselves [Soviet] political prisoners of the 58th Article [of the

Soviet penal code]." In other words, Soviets vied for German favor by presenting themselves as victimized counterrevolutionaries. Karov was eager to show he was not fooled. He dismissed these claimants as "petty people, frequently drunkards and in any case never part of any serious anti-Soviet organizations."[27] The returning émigré may or may not have been right. During the Great Terror, Article 58 was applied on a mass scale for fantastical rather than genuine conspiracies. But the point is that he remained certain about falsified self-presentations and rampant deceptions.[28]

If those repressed by Soviet power had a leg up with the Germans, many thousands of former Communist Party members also ended up in German service. German attitudes toward ex-Communists varied, but collaborators in this category were subject to repeated verifications and loyalty tests as the partisan war and the counterintelligence shadow war heated up after 1942. An NKVD official, reporting to Dmitrii Popov at the Smolensk Regional Party Committee–in-exile, slanted intelligence on collaborators to bring out their "counterrevolutionary" characteristics, attributing the defection of party members to prewar "unreliability." German military intelligence, for its part, recorded arrests of "NKVD agents" tasked with identifying collaborators and documented disputes about those denounced as Soviet agents but quite possibly "loyal" to the Wehrmacht.[29]

It was a topsy-turvy world, created by the sudden regime change from communism to fascism and both sides' frenetic search for leverage. Karov described the case of a party figure associated with the NKVD whom the Germans put in charge of local police. To prove his loyalty in September 1941, this former Communist rounded up Jews and Roma with zeal. But locals, outraged by his NKVD ties, tried to lynch him. He was simply moved to a different locality for the same job. Historians of the Holocaust, most famously Jan Gross in his work centering on the destruction of Jewish villagers by their Polish neighbors in Jedwabne, have suggested how antisemitic zeal could serve as a means to conceal earlier cooperation with Soviet power in 1939–1941. In Smolensk, betraying partisans could serve a similar function. In Yelnya, for example, the Communist Tarasenkov betrayed hidden partisan storage places for weapons in order to ingratiate himself with German authorities.[30]

Race (to use the German category) or nationality (to use the Soviet) played a major yet obfuscated role in recruitment. Following the proclivities of the Nazi leadership, Russians became the least-favored nation—at least publicly and on paper. The new hierarchy in the Army Group Center region was highlighted by the general instructions for the creation of city and town administrations in 1942, calling for "order police" under mayoral oversight to be formed from the small minority of ethnic Germans (*Volksdeutsch*), Belarusians, Ukrainians, and Russians. That order both inverted and scrambled the Soviet hierarchy of nationalities. Russians, the first among equals in the Stalinist "friendship of peoples," were now beneath all others save those slated for genocide, Jews and Roma, while, to put it in Soviet terms, a suspect subtitular nationality, ethnic Germans, was moved from the bottom to the top. Belarusians topped Ukrainians only because they were more numerous in the population of Army Group Center's Rear Administration. An order not to arm policemen in ethnically Russian regions such as Smolensk remained salient for the duration of 1941. This, however, only prompted German recruiters to classify police enlistees as Ukrainians or Belarusians, often, in Karov's words, "without their approval." Other reports suggest that identification in POW camps of Ukrainians and Belarusians for larger police units starting in late 1942 remained highly arbitrary.[31]

National categories were not always manipulated. In largely Russian regions such as Smolensk, Ukrainians tasked with forming police, guard, and fighting units were observed using knowledge of Ukrainian language as the litmus test of ethnicity. A shift occurred in January 1942 when instructions from the German army undercut policy favoring Ukrainian POWs. Significantly for the future of Russian-Ukrainian relations, widespread German practices of reclassification were not flagged in Soviet reports on German preference for Ukrainian collaborators, which were taken at face value.[32]

In occupied Smolensk, renaming Russians as Belarusians held particular political significance. For decades, linguists and ethnographers had debated the relationship of Smolensk peasants to Belarusians. But by the 1926 Soviet census, the vast majority identified as Russians. Prewar counts showed only about twenty thousand ethnic Belarusians in the Smolensk Region. Now, those who acknowledged or claimed their "true nationality" as Belarusian, for example, might be freed from starvation in POW camps. In spite or perhaps because of the history of the Belarusian national movement as late forming and relatively weak starting in the early twentieth century, émigré nationalists who followed the invading Wehrmacht now dreamed about

Smolensk as a prize component of a future independent Belarus. For example, nationalist activists Dzmitryj Kasmovič (in Russian, Dmitrii Kosmovich) and Michał Vituška (Mikhail Vitushko) arrived in the area in 1942, forming and directing the Smolensk County (*okrug*) police and also taking part in police, SS, and anti-partisan armed forces in other locations, from Briansk to Mogilev. Both were nephews of the new *burgomistr* of Smolensk County, the nationalist leader Radasłaŭ Astroŭski (in Russian, Radislav Ostrovskii, also known as Ostrovskii-Kalish). With Boris Menshagin firmly ensconced as the competent Russian mayor of Smolensk city, a Belarusian-Russian power struggle was set in motion. Astroŭski quickly became Menshagin's nemesis.[33]

Material Incentives and Path Dependency

There were two types of armed collaborators: policemen in town and countryside and fighters for larger armed units under German command, initially used in anti-partisan operations (known as Eastern troops or battalions and to locals as "punitives"). As local police grew in number in 1942, their provisioning and weapons improved. But even as the need for Russian collaborators grew by leaps and bounds, German officers remained authorized to beat them. They faced constant German suspicion that their ranks contained "unfit, criminal, and Bolshevik elements."[34]

In the civilian population, there was widespread hatred for both types of armed collaborators. That was because whenever policemen faced poor conditions, as Karov put it, "as always in such cases," they took bribes and resorted to "illegal requisitioning." In Smolensk and Vitebsk, military rations were given only for participation in concrete military operations. In the countryside, "punitives" felt free to loot during anti-partisan operations and to declare any village "partisan" as a pretext, which "rather frequently" provoked outrage and drove the rural population to the partisans. To defend villages from assaults by these brutalized outside forces, armed local village policemen sometimes teamed up with their ostensible partisan foes, with whom they could be bound by community and kinship. Profoundly local imperatives were of constant salience within the larger war.[35]

In March 1943, SMERSH investigators attached to the Soviet Twentieth Army interrogated one of these armed collaborators, a POW camp guard named Kirill Klishin. A former Red Army soldier, Klishin had been caught in an encirclement on November 17, 1941, sent to a POW camp, and selected by the camp commandant to join the police. He was sent to work at a POW camp in Spassk, Tumanovskii District, northeast of Viazma, on February 15, 1942, where he joined six other policeman and a head of police in guarding POWs within the camp. His job of "enforcing discipline" included taking sick or infirm prisoners out of the camp for execution. In Spassk, Klishin became a notorious sadist. Now, in captivity, NKVD investigator Captain Goshchenko interrogated Klishin:

> *Question:* From whom did you receive orders to beat the POWs with a rod?

> *Answer:* I was ordered to beat the prisoners with a rod for violations of order by the commandant of the camp.[36]

Such questioning was routine. But the investigation took a dramatic turn on April 23, 1943. That was the day Klishin was confronted by a witness, Aleksandra Berezina, a villager in Spassk who had known the policeman by his adopted pseudonym, Grisha. Berezina was a collective farm worker with four grades of education. During the occupation, her apartment building looked over a former church where POWs were kept. "I was forced to see the whole picture of bestial humiliation of the Russian POWs by the policemen," she stated. Grisha was known for relishing his power of beating and humiliating the starving prisoners. Berezina saw these beatings and how Grisha picked up a rifle each time he drove POWs out of Spassk for execution. When his workday was done, the policeman frequented Berezina's apartment, where Russian-German translators from the camp were quartered. "Grisha frequently visited during that time and I talked to him, I asked him the question: 'why are you destroying the soldiers, they are the same Russians as you are.' Grisha just loved being a policeman, and he said: 'and why do you pity them, just give our brother the chance and he will smash you on the head.'" Now, face-to-face with Klishin in captivity, Berezina concluded her testimony: "In material terms, the policeman 'Grisha' lived well. I saw him wearing two watches."[37]

Grisha cynically justified his taste for violence against his countrymen. But his case illustrates not only how some armed collaborators came to relish their power over others. It also indicates a certain path dependency. Once the choice was made to join the Germans, even if only to survive, it led the decision-maker further down a dark road increasingly difficult to reverse. This was true not only of those like Grisha who took pleasure in inflicting pain, but for many others not at all eager to serve the occupiers. Path dependency was reinforced by fear of Soviet reprisals, by indoctrination once recruited, and, not least, by meaningful material privileges in a time of extreme scarcity.

In routine situation reports from localities around the area, German military and economic authorities consistently made an equation between what they deemed positive attitudes in the local population and survival rations and wintertime fuel. This crude correlation was routinely noted not just for police and larger anti-partisan units, but for the towns' general population, which was subject to mandatory labor obligations. There was another equation, equally well noted in German reports, between fewer calories and growing unrest. As the Smolensk Economic Commando pithily put it in May 1942, "halfway" decent (*halbswegs ausreichend*) conditions produce "loyalty." After the harshest hunger in winter 1942, rations for the urban population in Smolensk city and other towns improved somewhat. Around the same time in 1942, Army Group Center orders made more urgent demands to supply anti-partisan troops "by all means necessary," in the words of an August 8, 1942, order, so they would be noticeably better clothed and armed than the partisans they fought. In addition to rations, policemen began to receive vodka, tobacco, coveted items such as chocolate and razors, and, in some areas depending on missions fulfilled, "German rations" that included some meat, sugar, and ersatz coffee. In addition to police participation in forced requisitioning and looting, it became commonplace after summer 1942 to entice armed collaborators with better housing, land, and bonuses.[38]

In the larger armed formations under the SD, SS, and Abwehr, it was forbidden to leave a unit and, in fact, it was extremely difficult to do so. As Karov pointedly mentioned, those who had committed crimes and atrocities, including genocidal acts against Jews and Roma, "were interested in not leaving witnesses to their acts among the living." The majority of recruited or conscripted fighters, he observed, realized that their lives were cheap and almost certainly short. They "let themselves go completely" and "found comfort in vodka, women, and cards."[39]

"Active Collaboration of the Russian Population"

The initial decision to collaborate could be reinforced not only by material privileges and the power over civilians that armed status implied. Indoctrination also played a role. The establishment of the General of Eastern Troops in the Army High Command at the end of 1942 reflected a retreat from the most hard-line stances on the "Russian question" in German leadership circles. It opened the door to recruitment of greater numbers of armed collaborators.[40] After a separate Inspectorate of Eastern Troops was also created in December 1942, attempts to indoctrinate these "volunteers" in courses and schools entered a new phase.

Until this point, courses for policemen recruited from the Dulags had been taught by junior officers or civilians with military rank and focused on tactical preparation, German language, and practical information such as German ranks and insignia. The ideological side, according to an account of courses for recruits from the camp in Roslavl, was boiled down to Hitler's biography, German war aims, and glorification of Germany and the German race. The inspectorate, by contrast, made a concerted attempt to justify collaboration ideologically. The "Basic Guiding Principles on the Education of Volunteer Units," disseminated as printed instructions, argued that Russians were not "subhuman" and the nation was not identical to Bolshevism. It made numerous caveats: the Russian was a "master at lying," consumed by an inferiority complex, prone to drunkenness, and always had an excuse for everything. Under good German leadership, innate qualities of courage and intelligence—even the basis for a "new Russian governance" (*Verwaltung*)—would come to the fore. There was also an appeal to pragmatism: "Everyone who knows the East has learned that without the active collaboration [*Mitarbeit*] of the Russian population the German *Volk* will never solve its tasks in the East." Ten "rules of conduct" captured by partisans from a killed German soldier even repeated Russian-language press propaganda in the occupied territories by granting Russians Aryan status. It recommended avoiding expressions of racial superiority, since "the Belarusians, Ukrainians, and Great Russians of the North belong to the Aryan race, in their blood flows that of Vikings."[41]

Transforming the subhumans of yesterday into the little brothers of today was an impossible enterprise halfway into a war of racial colonization. In a school formed at the Ninth Army's Headquarters of Volunteer

Troops for former Red Army officers in a village near Smolensk, a Russian junior officer was reportedly outraged by a German officer's lectures: "You say that Germany . . . will provide machines, technology, and specialists after the war, and in return Russia will give grain, meat, produce, and raw materials. Therefore, you will not give Russia a chance to develop further and grow its technology, culture, and civilization? Therefore, you wish to turn Russia into a colony of Germany? Therefore, my son will have to plow the land, and not study at university?" After Russian officers in training were made to apologize for this outburst, the German lecturer was quietly replaced by another.[42]

Émigré Russian Nationalists and Greater Belarus

No sooner had German rule been established in Smolensk than a flow of émigré anti-communists appeared. An influx of re-immigrant nationalists, carpetbaggers, ideologues, and covert "third way" activists all attempted to ride the Nazi tiger for their own ends. Some former nobles even succeeded in reestablishing landed estates in the Smolensk countryside; other political returnees sought and for a time received support from locally powerful German patrons. In October 1941, two young nationalists presented themselves to Menshagin in Smolensk as Solidarists, representatives of the National-Labor Alliance of Russian Solidarists of the New Generation (NTSNP, after 1943 NTS). They were D. P. Kamenetskii and Nikolai Alferchik, the first arriving from Yugoslavia, the second from Poland. Alferchik was twenty-four years old in 1941. Menshagin listened with interest to firsthand accounts of the interwar Russian emigration, something unimaginable a few months before. He also learned about Solidarism, read the political brochures he was given, and saved them in his apartment. Both Alferchik and Kamenetskii made "a good impression" on the new mayor. Menshagin had already been inundated with complaints about the new city police. These two, he thought, would be far more competent.[43]

Its activist stance catapulted Solidarism into a significant position in occupied Russian territories, and Smolensk became its base of operations. The Solidarist Georgii Gandziuk, an engineer by training who had grown up in Stuttgart, arrived from the group's European headquarters in Prague in January 1942 and became Menshagin's deputy mayor, after the early exit of Boris Bazilevskii. Georgii Okolovich, born in Riga and active in German-occupied Poland after 1939, headed Solidarist underground operations in Smolensk and Orsha while holding positions in those city administrations. In Smolensk, the Solidarist cell acted like a little colony. Okolovich's apartment was its informal center of operations; the home of a well-known actress and theater director was its informal club. Its members formed a pillar of support for Menshagin as head of the city governance. In October, another group of Solidarist agents passed through Smolensk and Roslavl on their way to taking up governance positions in nearby Briansk, arriving there only days after it was taken by German troops.[44]

In that first October 1941 encounter between the Smolensk jurist turned mayor and the young Solidarist émigré activists, it seems hard to imagine that any of them perceived the path down which their choice to collaborate would so quickly take them. Alferchik, in particular, became a major perpetrator. The young man who made such a good impression on Menshagin was quickly transformed into a particularly cruel interrogator spearheading anti-partisan punitive expeditions out of the city. He was the chief of the Smolensk policemen on the night of July 14, 1942, joining German security forces in killing at least eighteen hundred Jewish inmates from the Smolensk ghetto. Alferchik also was in charge of the "actions" murdering hundreds of Roma in the Smolensk countryside.[45]

Émigré Belarusian nationalists became active in Smolensk only some months after the Russian Solidarists, in mid-1942. That is because they arrived as part of the entourage of their patron Günther-Erich Kraatz, who first traveled from Minsk to set up the new governance in Briansk in October 1941, only taking up in April 1942 the post of field commandant of the Seventh Department in charge of civilian governances in Smolensk. He was accompanied by Radasłaŭ Astroŭski, born in Slutsk in 1887, who his entire adult life was involved in Belarusian politics and gymnasium education in Poland. Astroŭski began his career as a politician in June 1917, when as a young man he became a member of the Central Committee of the Belarusian Socialist Hromada, the largest Belarusian political party. In the Civil War, he fought with Anton Denikin's White army. In the decades that followed, he underwent several political transformations: briefly a member of the Communist Party of Western Belarus in 1926, he recanted in order controversially to promote Polish-Belarusian cooperation. By

1940, he began to cooperate closely with the Germans, whom he saw as the key to an independent, greater Belarus. Kraatz, his patron, installed him as mayor of Smolensk County.[46]

With émigré adherents of the late-forming Belarusian nationalism scattered after World War I, Belarusian nationalists remained "a small, detached circle of intellectuals, treated with indifference or suspicion by the peasantry on whose part they claimed to speak." Although they had long been pawns in the interwar geopolitical jockeying among Berlin, Moscow, Warsaw, and Kaunas, Lithuania, that competition also created opportunities for them. Shortly after the German invasion, Astroŭski and Kasmovič, in a secret meeting in Minsk, helped found the Belarusian Independence Party, which resolved to use Germany for their own goals while striving to remove Russians and Poles from administrative posts in the occupied territories. Both considered Smolensk and Briansk to be ethnographically Belarusian and a key component of their future state. Astroŭski's background in education was also key to their aspirations. If they could not yet realize their dream of an independent Belarus, they could at least turn the local schools Belarusian.[47] Or so they thought.

The newly arrived Belarusians lumped the Solidarist activists, Menshagin, and, later, of course, Vlasov together as hopeless Russian chauvinists. Astroŭski, using the pseudonym Kalush in 1964 and speaking about himself in the third person in a hagiographical *apologia pro vita sua,* wrote that in the "town" of Smolensk, as opposed to the supposedly ethnographically Belarusian countryside, "the attitude toward him, as a Byelorussian, was very hostile. The mayor was Menshagin, a former Soviet lawyer and a fierce Russian chauvinist . . . All the offices in the town were staffed with Russians who, more often than not, were hostile towards Byelorussians."[48]

Menshagin, for his part, called the German field commandant official protecting the Belarusians, Kraatz, a self-centered "German chauvinist, who believed a bad German was better than a good Russian." The officious Kraatz loved using his prewar title of "Oberrat," an honorific roughly meaning "senior official." Menshagin expressed even greater antagonism for Astroŭski, but tempered it with grudging respect. Astroŭski was a "hardboiled politician, for whom the idea he proclaimed of a 'greater Belarus' represented in the final analysis the key to his personal career, a person far from stupid, but amoral."[49]

The feud in Smolensk between Menshagin and Astroŭski was at once personal, bureaucratic, and political. Astroŭski arrived to set up a Smolensk County civilian administration that would oversee eight districts and the city of Smolensk. The parallelism was likely from the start to involve a conflict, and the two clashed over personnel and oversight. Astroŭski had lived much of his life in Vilnius and Lodz. Cultural differences with Soviet Russians accompanied those caused by his Belarusian nationalist aspirations and drive to subordinate the city administration. To make a long story short, Astroŭski tried to import Belarusian textbooks from Minsk in order to open Belarusian schools. All educational institutions had been closed since the invasion in 1941, and they were only reopening in 1942 at the elementary level after many local efforts in the face of German indifference. Menshagin openly opposed Astroŭski's Belarusian projects, and the Belarusian activist entered into an internecine battle to have the Russian mayor removed.[50]

Despite Kraatz's patronage and a formally higher position than his Russian rival, Astroŭski failed in all his efforts. His deputy director of the county school department, Savva Khatskevich, a non-party mathematician who taught for a decade at the Smolensk Pedagogical Institute before the war, greatly admired Astroŭski as a cultivated, experienced pedagogue. Khatskevich did credit Menshagin for doing much to reopen schools, but saw the latter's opposition to his own boss, Astroŭski, as insubordination. In a Mints Commission interview, Khatskevich, darkly alleging that Menshagin bribed German authorities, admitted that the Smolensk mayor continued to enjoy their confidence: "Menshagin was so successful in gaining the sympathies of the local German authorities that he felt no dependence on the county executive." Astroŭski maneuvered to bring a fellow Belarusian nationalist from Poland, Stanislav Stankevich, now the mayor of Borisov, to Smolensk to replace Menshagin. Stankevich was directly implicated, along with his chief of police, in the extermination of sixty-five hundred to seven thousand Borisov Jews in October 1941. He arrived in Smolensk but inexplicably departed the next day.[51]

The whole episode sheds light on Menshagin's involvement in the "Russian question." The mayor never conceived of himself as a politician acting in the political sphere. When he wanted to disparage his bitter rival, he referred to him as a "hard-boiled politician." Instead, he depicted the world in terms of personalities and personalism, upright and immoral interlocutors, even as he was revealing just how much his position of *nachal'nik goroda,* city boss, held in terms of local power and patronage in times of danger and scarcity. Menshagin always avoided discussions of politics in the sense of a pursuit or clash of political principles, as opposed to administrative intrigues. It was not only that this was in his best interests, both under the Soviet and the Nazi regime; he saw and presented himself as an educated professional. However, when faced with a challenge to Smolensk's Russianness in the form of Astroŭski's Belarusian nationalism, he pushed back hard and was proud to do so.

If the rivalry with Ostrovskii took place behind the scenes, Menshagin also developed a widely propagated public persona in Smolensk with his wartime directives, radio addresses, and newspaper articles. Menshagin often had to deal with the German Propaganda Department of the Smolensk field commandant's section responsible for overseeing the local city and regional administrations. It was through that office that German occupation authorities exercised oversight of the Smolensk newspaper *New Path* (*Novyi put'*) through a former German Moscow correspondent and press attaché. A good portion of the newspaper was filled up with articles and reports prepared in Berlin for all the occupied Russian territories: rosy-colored military news or propaganda pieces about Jews, Judeo-Bolshevism, and Hitler. Yet a significant part was produced by a stable of Russian journalists, including its editor, Konstantin Dolgonenkov, and some Solidarist émigrés. This produced a distinctive stream of local Russian commentary, which was anti-Soviet, frequently antisemitic, and, occasionally, Aesopian in its subtly nationalistic evocations of the difficult position of Russians under German rule.[52]

Menshagin's public presence during the war does not completely contradict the impression of a practical, managerial type conjured up later in his memoirs. Aside from the publication of his orders, Menshagin appears rarely in its pages to mark ceremonial occasions connected to the work of the city governance, such as anniversaries of German rule. On these occasions, he concentrated for the most part on the improvements, albeit with far more than a little exaggeration, that his governance had made in city life in the face of the difficulties the administration inherited.

Yet Menshagin did not, and could not, appear merely as a technocrat. His published writings, as one might expect, praised the Germans profusely, particularly when those statements were made as speeches with German overseers present. He repeated those antisemitic tropes dominant in the Smolensk Russian-language press, which above all revolved around the concept of Judeo-Bolshevism. Menshagin pointedly associated Jews with Marxism and referred to the Soviet home front "on the other side of the Judeo-Bolshevik wall." The mayor also repeatedly endorsed a theme hammered home with great frequency in both German and collaborationist propaganda in the occupied territories: Germany would lead "a new, cultured Russia" to become part of "a New Europe." In July 1943, Menshagin wrote that German soldiers were not "the raging, mystical 'barbarians' of Judeo-Bolshevik propaganda—no! They turned out to be highly cultured, sensitive, and to the greatest degree orderly people." In the name of this higher culture, the mayor urged Russians to work for Germany, praised Vlasov's ROA, and enjoined "total war against Judeo-Bolshevism."[53]

After all he had witnessed, Menshagin was far from naive. Did he really foresee a future Russia somehow free from both Stalinism and the German yoke? He was intimately acquainted with the bloodthirstiness of both regimes that stood in the way of any solution to the Russian question. Astroŭski, for his part, liked to remark that if the Third Reich would only extract tribute like the medieval Mongols while giving his homeland local autonomy, the Germans would win the war. He often complained bitterly that his position as mayor of Smolensk County gave him less power than any German junior officer, according to his colleague Khatskevich. "This was an educated, cultivated, ambitious person who strove for power," Khatskevich concluded. "He was not a bribe taker or an intriguer. He strove for power."[54]

Vlasov and the Russian Question

Around two o'clock in the afternoon on December 14, 1942, mayor Menshagin was visited by Sonderführer Hesse, a translator for the Seventh Department of the field commandant. He was told to report to the Army Group Center headquarters, housed in the old technical college building in downtown Smolensk. There he was received by Lieutenant Colonel Wladimir Schubuth, a former military attaché in Moscow before the war, who was now Schenckendorff's top intelligence officer coordinating the recruitment of national military formations for Army Group Center.

According to Menshagin: "They took me into a room where two German officers who spoke good Russian were sitting . . . They asked me to read a document." Menshagin had only known about the July 1942 capture of General Andrei Vlasov, the deputy commander of the Volkhov front south of Leningrad, because it had been reported in the Smolensk newspaper *New Path*. Schubuth received Menshagin, asking him to sign the document if he agreed with its contents. It was the text of what came to be known as the Smolensk Declaration. Apparently drafted by Vlasov's ghostwriter, the murky ex-Soviet operator Miletii Zykov, and signed by Vlasov after long negotiations involving Wehrmacht propaganda authorities, it proclaimed: "Germany does not wish to encroach on the living space of the Russian people or its national and political liberties . . . The place of the Russian nation lies in the family of European nations; its place within the 'New Europe' will depend on the degree of its participation in the struggle against Bolshevism." "I gave my assent and signed the declaration," Menshagin recalled. "With that our conversation ended and I left."[55]

Boris Menshagin (sitting) as mayor of Smolensk, while a German overseer looks on.
National Digital Archives, Poland.

This perfunctory signing ceremony in Smolensk turned out to be a sham. The massively distributed leaflet calling for the unification of the Russian people around anti-Bolshevism, dated December 27, 1942, was given the symbolic place-name of Smolensk and thus became known as the Smolensk Declaration. But the published declaration did not include Menshagin's name. Another, second signing ceremony was actually held in Dabendorf, a village twenty-five miles south of Berlin. That was where the main training camp for the ROA was set up under the control of the German High Command's Propaganda Department.[56]

Vlasov did visit Smolensk on March 3, 1943, as part of his tour of the occupied territories. Accompanied by Schubuth and met by Schenckendorff, the renegade general delivered an address at the city theater. But there is no evidence that he ever met the mayor, his sometime co-signer of the so-called Smolensk Declaration. Through the machinations of Vlasov's sponsors, Vlasovite propaganda was distributed not only to the Red Army but all around Smolensk and the perimeter of the front. In response, the Soviets quickly launched a major counterpropaganda campaign against Vlasov that peaked in summer 1943. As the NKVD and partisans mounted a veritable hunt to assassinate "Raven" (Vlasov's code name) and gather information about the Russian committee in summer 1943, they believed Smolensk was actually a center for the movement.[57]

The fiction of the signing ceremony launched what was in essence a fictional army. The Russian committee and Vlasov's ROA never in fact existed as independent entities (only in January 1945 was Vlasov finally allowed to form two divisions). The notoriety of Vlasov and Vlasovites during and after the war—and in Russia down to the present day—has eclipsed their actual role. This can be attributed to the propaganda war over Vlasov starting in 1943, the Stalinist obsession with "betrayal," and postwar émigré politics. The ROA and "Aktion Wlassow" (Project Vlasov), as the Germans called the operation, was devised as a recruitment tool to reverse military setbacks. ROA propagandists in POW camps and population centers would recruit armed collaborators and, it was hoped, prompt defections from the Red Army. Recruitment grew apace. But, as in 1941–1942, all units remained under German command.[58]

Crucially, however, the propagandistic nature of Project Vlasov was not immediately apparent in spring and summer 1943. Even Vlasov himself and his supporters, as well as some key German military men, seem to have found it possible to believe that allowing this large-scale propaganda initiative might presage a change in policy toward the Russian population that many thought necessary, especially in Army Group Center.[59]

Vlasov had loyally served Stalin as one of the Red Army's most talented generals until the moment his ill-equipped and poorly prepared Second Shock Army on the Volkhov front was sent into a dubious offensive operation approved by Stalin and almost completely destroyed. Tall, gaunt, with horn-rimmed glasses, pursed lips, and a slightly scholastic air, Vlasov initially appeared to believe that he and his fellow defecting officers could reroute a German propaganda initiative into actual policy shifts.[60]

That calculation was reinforced by some of Vlasov's chief handlers, including the Baltic German officer Wilfried Strik-Strikfeldt, born in Riga and trained in St. Petersburg, who kept assuring Vlasov that he would get his armed force and even a political organization. Given Schenckendorff's warmly received December 1942 report calling for a new engagement with the Russian question, this did not seem far-fetched. German "national-conservative" members of the secret military opposition to Hitler, such as Henning von Tresckow and Claus von Stauffenberg, supported a potential "German-Russian alliance" and hoped the Vlasov movement would lead to a "new orientation" of German policy. Tresckow's supporters were concentrated in Army Group Center and were behind the failed March 13, 1943, attempt to assassinate Hitler, who stopped in Smolensk on his way from Vinnitsa to East Prussia. The striker pin of the delay igniter on the bomb, disguised as a bottle of Cointreau, hit the percussion cap but failed to ignite.[61]

The Smolensk Declaration sent shock waves through the occupied Russian territories. Vlasov's massively disseminated writings were strikingly and openly nationalist. Calling for a Russian "national revolution," the Vlasov movement entered the fray against Stalinism over the wartime claim to Russian national themes. Soviet appropriation of tsarist military heroes was branded a "despicable deception." Vlasov's speaking tours through the occupied territories in spring 1943, which in addition to Mogilev, Bobruisk, and Smolensk included a trip through the northwest, including Pskov, was met with acclaim by his adherents and German military propagandists, who portrayed Russian popular response as a wave of excited support. Partisans and Soviets depicted locals as indifferent or hostile. In reality, few volunteers for Vlasov's cause materialized among local populations, but, unsurprisingly, more men harshly interned in POW camps were willing to sign up. In Smolensk, Khatskevich retrospectively dismissed Vlasov's visit as inconsequential: "It was well known that somewhere General Vlasov existed, that he had a committee and gathered Russian officers around him . . . But he could do only what they ordered him. Vlasov visited Smolensk. Many saw him, but he had no power and, therefore, no influence."[62] Even so, Vlasov's apparent strivings to transform propaganda into policy crossed the line for top Nazi hard-liners. Eduard von Dellingshausen, who first encountered Vlasov as his interpreter and High Command minder during the three-week trip, was present when Vlasov made what became an infamous remark. Thanking his German military hosts for their hospitality, Vlasov magnanimously expressed the hope that he would welcome them with equal courtesy as his guests in Moscow![63] To Nazi leaders, including Hitler and Heinrich Himmler, reports of such pretensions to future independence were like waving a red flag in front of a bull. In a meeting with Field Marshal Wilhelm Keitel and other top brass on June 8, 1943, Hitler ranted that concessions to a Russian national army or any kind of future Ukrainian state were "pure fantasy." Vlasov was forbidden to return to the occupied territories and confined outside Berlin to virtual house arrest.[64]

Himmler staunchly backed up Hitler's hard-line stance, as the prim-looking genocidaire emerged as one of the strongest opponents of concessions to national sentiments. To SS officers in Poznań in October 1943, in a speech that became infamous for its open justification of the Holocaust, Himmler disparaged Vlasov and added: "I don't care in the least what happens to the Russians or the Czechs . . . Whether other nations are prosperous or die of hunger only interests me in so far as we have slaves for our culture."[65]

Despite Vlasov's novel symbolic significance, there was one way his defection marked a continuation rather than a break in the patterns of collaboration. Once he and fellow officers threw in their lot with Nazi Germany, it inexorably pulled their movement down a path shaped by their devil's pact. The training schools in Dabendorf and other locations preached elements of Nazi ideology. The Vlasovite press mimicked Nazi-sponsored antisemitism, and Vlasov's top officers were among those implicated in anti-partisan and racial atrocities. "It is increasingly implausible," in the words of one historian, "to draw a line separating the Vlasov Project from the core power structures and agendas of Nazism in the East."[66]

The Lokot' Statelet: From Russian Self-Governance to Heart of Darkness

On one territory, the Germans from the outset did grant Russian nation-alist actors a far greater measure of internal political autonomy. This was the Lokot' Republic or Lokot' Self-Governance, centered in the district capital of Lokot' in Orel (Orlovskaia) Region, 56 miles south of Briansk and 217 miles south of Smolensk. At its height after a late 1942 expansion, it comprised a territory stretching across eight districts in Orel and Kursk Regions and had a population of 581,000 residents. For almost two years between 1941 and 1943, the Lokot' statelet boasted its own government, military force, laws, and school system. Its founder was Konstantin Vos-koboinik, a veteran of anti-Soviet peasant uprisings in the area. A charis-matic member of the local intelligentsia, Voskoboinik had been an in-structor at a technical school before the war. After German forces appeared in Lokot' in October 1941, he emerged as a fiercely anti-partisan, unabash-edly pro-German mayor with greater Russian political ambitions.[67]

In December 1941, Voskoboinik sent his deputy, Bronislav Kaminskii, chief engineer at a local distillery, to negotiate with the commander of the German Second Panzer Army, General Rudolf Schmidt. The territory was at once economically unimportant to the occupation and militarily signifi-cant because of its concentration of railway and communication lines serving Army Group Center. An autonomous Lokot' served as a buffer suc-cessfully fighting the partisans concentrated in Briansk forests. Schmidt became the key German figure supporting its autonomous status.[68]

The Lokot' Self-Governance rested on deeper social roots than its red equivalents, the partisan territories that briefly declared independence in 1942 because of a fleeting concentration of military and political forces. Peasants in the area had lived on the estates of the Grand Duke Mikhail Romanov, brother of the last tsar, and experienced unusual prosperity. The area recorded no disturbances in 1905 and 1917 and was treated as anti-Soviet long before collectivization. Both Voskoboinik and Kaminskii, who took over after January 8, 1942, when Voskoboinik was treacherously killed during negotiations with partisans, harbored their own animus against the Soviet order. Voskoboinik had been exiled in the 1930s for his role in the area's 1921 peasant uprising; Kaminskii had been expelled from the Party in 1935 and exiled in 1937 for Trotskyist associations.[69]

For a fleeting moment in late 1941, self-governance took on a democratic direction. Voskoboinik recruited local professionals to an initially collegial administration. They oversaw policies hearkening back to the NEP, abolishing collective farms and legalizing private enterprise but retaining administrative control of larger industry. Voskoboinik, however, aspired to make the territory into the kernel of a new Russian national state. He took the lead in publishing on November 26, 1941, a manifesto of the People's Socialist Party of Russia (Narodnaia sotsialisticheskaia partii Rossii), also known as "Viking" (in May 1943, it became the National-Socialist Party of Russia). Its open antisemitism and praise of Hitler, also features of the Lokot' newspaper *Voice of the People,* clearly aimed at currying German favor for a Russian brand of national socialism. The manifesto itself, however, did not contain fascist or racial ideology but outlined a program for a non-communist Russian state: just as the invasion of Vikings had led to the rise of Rus' in the ninth century, so the German conquest would create a new Russia. Voskoboinik's successor, Kaminskii, launched an initiative to distribute the manifesto in Smolensk and adjacent areas. It was met with indifference and suspicion.[70]

German officers visiting Lokot' noted with approval its efficient military-administrative *Ordnung;* its tricolor Russian flag with the image of Saint George and, flying alongside it, a banner with a swastika; and the "hard and exceptionally energetic" activity of the man they nicknamed the King of Lokot', despite his short, sickly, and nondescript appearance. In 1942, Kaminskii's rule quickly turned dictatorial. It merged civilian and military leadership and prosecuted an increasingly brutal anti-partisan war that included forced conscription, hostage taking, and forced resettlement. Voskoboinik's original "people's militia" of eighteen volunteers grew to a height of over nine thousand fighters as the Russian Liberation People's Army (RONA) in 1943, equipped by the German rear area (Korück) 532 Quartermaster. RONA joined ferocious German anti-partisan operations in 1942–1943.[71]

The notion that Kaminskii's fiefdom could expand and even serve as some sort of model for occupied Russian territories was fostered by political activity both within Lokot' and on the German side. Schmidt openly fueled Kaminskii's ambitions. He even succeeded in protecting the Lokot' autonomy arrangement after an audience with Hitler at his East Prussian

"Wolf's Lair" in July 1942. With Rosenberg's support, Schmidt signed an order dated July 19 firming up Lokot''s autonomous status. On January 8, 1943, Rosenberg wrote to Hitler to suggest that expanding Lokot'-like "experiments" on a larger scale would not endanger German control. Control, in fact, was never jeopardized. The absence of Wehrmacht troops and the presence of Kaminskii's brigade, with their white armbands and Saint George's cross, was merely the "illusion of autonomy." The less visible presence of SD, Abwehr, and military administration infiltration and oversight of Lokot' ensured that the experiment in Russian autonomy could have been terminated at a moment's notice.[72]

Well before the Smolensk Declaration, Lokot' emerged in 1942 as a possible precedent for addressing the "Russian question." Among Russian collaborators in Smolensk and adjacent areas, if hardly the beleaguered population at large, it attracted attention. There was some traffic between the Solidarist colony in occupied Russian territories and Lokot', and the Solidarists managed to recruit some adherents inside Kaminskii's territory.[73]

Broader interest in the Lokot' model in the course of 1942 testified to a remarkable, previously unknown synergy between Russians yearning to harness national sentiment and those German military and political figures hoping to harness the Russian population. Both sides were dancing around what Hitler had called "pure fantasy." In April 1943, letters written by Schmidt were discovered criticizing Hitler's prosecution of the war and the Nazi Party. The patron of Lokot' was relieved of his command of the Second Panzer Army.[74]

Even as broader German and Russian interest grew, Lokot' was becoming an experiment less in Russian national autonomy than in ultra-violent warlordism. The dictatorial Kaminskii exhibited an increasingly "Kurtz-like penchant for violence."[75] As one of his executioners, Kaminskii selected the troubled Antonina (Ton'ka) Makarova, born in 1920 near Sychevka, in the Smolensk Region. A Komsomol member who volunteered to serve in the Red Army in 1941, Makarova escaped German captivity after the Viazma encirclement with a man who used her as his "field wife," and after a traumatic falling out with him she worked for a time as a prostitute. Ending up at Lokot', armed by Kaminskii with a Maxim machine gun and fueled by alcohol, she executed approximately fifteen hundred partisans, civilians, women, and children. Makarova's Red Army heroine was Anka the Machine Gunner from the famous 1934

Soviet civil war film *Chapaev.* She became notorious as Ton'ka the Machine Gunner.[76]

As for Kaminskii's brigade, with the collapse of the German central front in summer 1943 some went over to the partisans, others continued to fight Soviet power until 1946, and ten thousand or more followed Kaminskii into some of the worst atrocities of the Belarusian theater. In August 1944, Kaminskii's brigade formally became the "29. Waffen-Grenadier-Division der SS RONA." It teamed up with the ultraviolent, sadistic war criminals in Oskar Dirlewanger's larger anti-partisan SS commando, responsible for more mass atrocities than any other. Kaminskii and Dirlewanger were at the forefront of the horrific "urbicide" in Warsaw in reprisal for the Warsaw Uprising of 1944. After Kaminskii was executed by Erich von dem Bach-Zelewski, then the top German commander in Warsaw—for mass plunder rather than mass murder and rape—some remnants of Kaminskii's troops were incorporated into Vlasov's army as it was finally given its own command. General Vlasov, whose movement had always distrusted the "little Russian leader" of Lokot', contemptuously rejected most of them as mercenaries.[77]

Hired Pens

Like the broader German military effort itself, the massive propaganda war that pervaded everyday life on the Eastern Front could not have taken place without large numbers of Russophone collaborators. While its effectiveness is not easy to ascertain, both regimes took it as a given that they must invest very large amounts of scarce resources, paper, and manpower into written propaganda. The number of leaflets dropped by aviation, which in the occupied territories dominated over radio and film, was astronomical. The total number of propaganda pieces created by both sides dwarfed World War I and numbered in the hundreds of millions.[78]

Altogether, 230 newspapers and journals were published in Russian on German-occupied Soviet territory. For a three-month period in 1942 alone, the single Propaganda Department of just Security Division 286 produced 700,000 posters, 40,000 brochures, and 3,500 portraits of Hitler. *Mein Kampf*, however, with its withering contempt for the Russian race and eagerness to create German "living space" in the East, was never translated or excerpted.[79]

On the key theater of the world's most total war, Soviet and German propaganda entered into an odd kind of covert, deep-seated dialogue. They were able to do so because the two efforts were part of an international "propaganda revolution" underway since World War I and overlapped in many ways. This was the case even though the specific ways in which propaganda fit into both regimes and their ideologies of course differed both in general and over time.

It is true enough, as Peter Kenez claimed, that there was "no Bolshevik Goebbels," in the sense of a single mastermind fascinated by the techniques of mass manipulation. But this observation does not take us very far. The enduring image of Joseph Goebbels as master manipulator was itself propaganda (or narcissistic self-persuasion) promoted by Goebbels himself. It is also the case that there was an unusually strong didactic, dogmatic streak in Soviet propaganda, which in the Social Democratic tradition was conceived as part of an entire ladder of genres stretching from agitprop and "political enlightenment" to scholarship and culture. But as time went on, the Soviets increasingly relied on propaganda as a tool for mass mobilization. During and after the war, they became more heavily invested in techniques of disinformation (*dezinformatsiia*), which served them well in the military conflict. Such particularities should not obscure commonalities stemming from the intensive transnational circulation of methods and approaches. Goebbels himself, more than most, was arguably attuned to the genuine innovations of revolutionary Bolshevism.[80]

Both Nazism and Stalinism, despite all their major cultural and ideological divergences, used propaganda to propagate ideas or elements of ideology, as a key tool for mass mobilization and as a vehicle for disinformation (or, as the Germans called it, psychological propaganda). During the war, the German effort shifted dramatically from a heavy emphasis on psychological warfare in expectation of a quick victory. As winning collaborators became important in 1942, this was recalibrated in favor of depicting a positive image of Germany and obfuscating plans for racial colonization.[81]

Both propaganda establishments were impressed with the scope of the enemy effort. Both had experts and practitioners who studied the other side. Both responded to specific campaigns with counter-campaigns. The German turn in 1942 to more recruitment of Russians led to a reorientation toward more long-term initiatives. These included elementary school openings, theater, film, and radio—although the investment in "soft power" or cultural initiatives always remained tiny compared to the unparalleled Soviet commitment. Along with Schenckendorff in Smolensk, Goebbels in Berlin also saw the need for a new course in 1942 in the occupied east that would include "pseudo-governments," until Hitler cut that off. From this dynamic, however, German policy initiatives such as the revival of Orthodoxy and land policy in 1942–1943 were propagated with large-scale propaganda components.[82]

Journalists, writers, and propagandists formed by the Soviet system—intelligentsia collaborators—helped shape the enterprise in the occupied territories. POW camps were the prime recruiting grounds for these literary figures. That was how, for example, Vlasov's ghostwriter Zykov was first recruited. The Vlasov movement led to an expansion of recruitment and opening of schools for propagandists, including ROA courses training forty to sixty propagandists in Smolensk from late 1942 to mid-1943.[83]

In Smolensk, regulars in the Russian-language press such as Konstantin Dolgonenkov ensured that pro-German propaganda used language and tropes familiar from Soviet times. Born in 1895 in Roslavl, this poet, journalist, and Western Regional Union of Writers member from its founding in 1934 was in the company of Aleksandr Tvardovskii and other up-and-coming young literary figures in the Smolensk Region in the 1930s. As editor of *New Path*, Smolensk's main newspaper from 1941 to 1943, Dolgonenkov was one of those pens for hire who supplemented publications prepared in Berlin with local input. Directed but likely not preliminarily censored by the rear area Propaganda Department, Dolgonenkov's Germanophilic agitprop was clothed in polished Russian and dwelled on antisemitic and Russian national-patriotic tropes. The distinct contribution of the "native" intellectual collaborators in the Smolensk press, itself a model for other areas in Army Group Center Rear Administration territory, was to inject a local and hence more persuasive element into the occupation press.[84]

Dolgonenkov refocused former Soviet themes of the radiant future and "new life," now touting the Third Reich's construction of an advanced and modern regime for a Europe that would include Russia. Enthusiastic reports of trips to see the wonders of the Reich evoked an earlier era of pro-Soviet fellow-travelers. In the midst of war, death, and hunger, ex-Soviet intellectuals such as Dolgonenkov promulgated a barrage of familiar images of prosperity, modernization, and advance, only this time in service of Germany's new Europe.[85]

Inside the occupied Russian territories, the unacknowledged dialogue between the German and Soviet propaganda machines was particularly deep on two thematic issues. The first concerned which regime could represent genuine Russianness; the second concerned whether Nazi Germany or the Stalinist USSR was culturally more advanced. Even as these two polemics ran like a red thread through the propaganda war, each was also a preoccupation for many of the various nationalists and collaborators advocating solutions to the "Russian question" inside the occupied territories.

On the Soviet home front, the Stalinist deployment of Russian national themes reached such heights during the war that even "traitors" to the Motherland who were ethnically Russian, such as Vlasov, received far less play than non-Russian collaborators. In response, pro-German propaganda in Russian consistently aimed to deny its veracity: "Bloody Stalin has not changed!" Only a Russian "national revolution" against Stalin would liberate Russia from collective farms and "Judeo-Bolsheviks." The Germans' stage-managed revival of Orthodoxy in 1941–1942, with fourteen major churches and cathedrals in the Smolensk diocese opened in 1941 and thirty-seven more in 1942, was a visible and popular development. Army Group Center monopolized religious policy in rear areas, and, as in tsarist times, sermons regularly featured heavy-handed political messages. It took two full years for Stalin to answer with his wartime rehabilitation of the Orthodox Church, when leading prelates issued their September 8, 1943, "Condemnation of Traitors to the Faith and the Fatherland."[86]

Around the claim to civilizational superiority, on the Soviet side, writers and mass propaganda alike depicted fascist barbarism and backwardness as a bitterly ironic reversal: a "civilized country of slave owners," vainly trying to push "great Rus'" to its knees," had forfeited all claims to possess a higher culture. Intelligentsia collaborators in the occupied territories, in response, constantly played the European card. Dolgonenkov and other Russian-language propagandists repeated that Russia would not fruitlessly strive to "catch up and overtake" the West but actually form an integral part of a prosperous, civilized Europe. A strain of antisemitic propaganda even implied that Russians were also Aryans. Fyodor Dostoyevsky, for example, was included in a European pantheon of antisemites, alongside the notion that Jews had always been hated by Aryans; the Jewish race must be banished from "European" nations, which included Russia.[87]

Indicative of just how intensively Soviet propaganda specialists studied German methods is a 1942 memorandum, "Political Work on Degrading German Troops." It originated in the political administration of the Soviet Third Army, which had fought in the Battles of Smolensk and Moscow. The gist was a strong advocacy of broadening the anti-Wehrmacht propaganda enterprise in place of the inflexible hyper-centralization of the Red Army's Main Directorate of Political Propaganda. Can it really be the case, it asked, that "one to two master compilers of leaflets [*listovki*]" from the directorate were sufficient for all military theaters? Instead of blanketing the Germans only with written propaganda dropped from the air, the Soviets should harness underground agents in operations, recruit captured Germans such as ex-Communists, and empower propaganda agents in the occupied territories.[88]

In addition to the imperative of shifting away from rote and wooden Stalinist didacticism, the report, forwarded to Stalin, expressed an almost glowing admiration for German methods. When troops from Central Asia appeared, the Germans immediately produced propaganda in Uzbek, Kazakh, Turkmen, and Bashkir; the Soviet side was incapable of reaching Axis forces around Vitebsk that included French, Italian, Hungarian, and Spanish troops. The Soviets urgently needed to imitate Goebbels's enterprise, which had developed a whole range of "psychological approaches" to reach the rank-and-file soldier. The Soviets required new approaches to reach people "with a German psychology," such as the kind of humor and satire that Soviet political enlightenment establishment traditionally considered politically "primitive." What most fascinated the Soviets were the tricks of disinformation. The report admired German fakes "that look like our leaflets," using slogans that were familiar to Soviets.[89]

Propaganda succeeds best over long periods of time in conditions allowing it to reinforce an alternate reality. As it evolved on both sides in the course of the conflict, how effective was propaganda in recruiting adherents? The population in the occupied territories did not, with the partial exception of the cities, have access to newsreels and film, this era's most persuasive media combining spoken words and images. Karov, immersed in the murky world of counterespionage, disparaged the efficacy of propaganda, because collaborators were so motivated by material and practical incentives.[90] But the Abwehr officer was no historian of propaganda. One thing he failed to consider was that in conditions where propaganda saturates the information ecosystem or works in conjunction with other factors, it may subtly affect even those who ostensibly reject it. Even the most skillful propaganda will work best in reinforcing other motivations, as opposed to overcoming them.

As Karov also noted, Soviet *deza*—disinformation—played a big role in occupied Russian territories. It was spread both by agents and by disseminated materials with false information, for example, on partisan troop movements or alleged German evacuation plans. The murky, violent world of distrust and counterintelligence, which pervaded the entire enterprise of recruiting adherents, fostered an emphasis on psychological pressure and manipulation. The Soviet experience of war, in turn, prompted the integration of propaganda into increasingly elaborate covert operations. In this sense, the titanic struggle on the Eastern Front thus left a strong legacy for the further development of Soviet "active measures" in the postwar period.[91]

The Tragic Agency of Breitman–Petrenko

Both sides in the propaganda war regularly pledged full amnesty to defectors even as they distrusted them greatly as suspicious elements and possible double agents. "The hour of payback is near," one Soviet leaflet promised in February 1943. Soviet power will "forgive you and not touch one of the hairs on your head."[92] The Soviet-German clash is often called an ideological war, and the revolutionary regimes of Right and Left did remain highly ideological. This hardly meant that ordinary people's motivations were all about ideas or doctrine. In the propaganda war, appeals to high-minded ideals mingled with crudely pragmatic calculations about switching sides.

One of the most disturbing documents generated in the entire history of side switching on the Eastern Front is the April 1943 "Testimony" of Mikhail Breitman. A Jewish party member and political commissar born in 1918 in Bila Tserkva near Kyiv, he was captured on August 11, 1941, in the Battle of Smolensk when his tank division was destroyed. Imprisoned in a makeshift Dulag on the banks of the Dnieper near Orsha with tens of thousands of POWs, facing immediate execution both under the

Commissar Order and as a Jew, he identified himself by the Ukrainian name Petrenko. In September, most likely to escape death by starvation, he volunteered to join the Forty-Sixth Ukrainian Auxiliary Police Battalion formed by the SS. He became a guard. Such were the decisions that kept him alive, but pushed him down a tragic path.[93]

Breitman recalled in his "Testimony" Jewish children and mothers killed by raucous Germans at the first mass shooting of sixty-five hundred members of the Minsk ghetto on November 7, 1941, Revolution Day, along with other gruesome atrocities. He omitted the role that his own and two other police units played in supporting the Einsatzgruppen. A half year later he was unmasked as Jewish in the police unit and faced another choice: between execution and recruitment for German counterintelligence operations. He chose the latter. In July 1942, he went through operational training, German-language courses, and political indoctrination in a three-month SD school near the camp and killing fields of Malyi Trostinets. By this time, numerous other espionage schools had been established around the occupied Soviet territories and in German-occupied Poland, the Generalgouvernement, to infiltrate partisan units and convey intelligence about their movements. For example, one nineteen-year-old Smolensk woman from a village in Mosal'skii District, captured near Sevastopol in June 1942, was recruited with the promise she would study "West European culture" at her Crimean training center.[94]

The circumstances of Breitman's case may have been extremely unusual, but it was grounded in a widespread phenomenon. Imposture spread so widely in Soviet times and during the war in part because it offered an escape from the deadly politics of identity—the complex negotiation of political, national, and class categories at the heart of Stalinist social engineering. Breitman had become Petrenko to escape certain death from Nazi antisemitism, and in this he was not alone. Another Jewish recruit, Samuil Rabinovitch, captured with a group of mostly ethnic Russian POWs, was later interrogated by the NKVD in September 1942. Like Breitman, Rabinovitch also concealed his Jewish identity when deported to a holding camp in Stuttgart. There he was recruited as an agent, visited Berlin with 120 other recruits, and trained near Lublin. There is also evidence about concealed Jewish policemen. One Smolensk policeman named Friedman, passing himself off as Ivanov, reportedly took part in the destruction of the Smolensk ghetto.[95]

The discussion of so-called Jewish collaboration with the Nazis has focused on postwar Soviet trials and prosecution of ghetto auxiliary police or controversial members of the ghetto administrations (*Judenräte*), the latter often implicated during the impossible attempt to protect their own in dealings with German authorities on matters of life and death. Less well known are those who concealed their Jewish identities and became perpetrators, or whose Jewishness was known when Germans used them as trained anti-partisan agents.[96] The major impediment for more such cases was not the urge to survive as a factor prompting collaboration, but Nazi hatred and murder of Jews.

Breitman, exposed by the Germans as Jewish and accompanied by seven other German-trained spies, succeeded in joining the "Diadia Vasia" partisans then operating in the Minsk Region. After one of his co-collaborators gave himself away in a drunken indiscretion, Breitman once again found himself compromised. The former Red Army political commissar (*politruk*) was again placed under arrest, this time by the partisans. Once again, his life was at stake.[97]

Interrogated by an NKVD officer, Breitman wrote out two detailed autobiographical documents by hand, one about German atrocities, the other about the "Gestapo School 12" (in Russian, "Gestapo" was often used as the umbrella term for the Nazi secret police and was conflated with the RSHA, SS, and SD). Leaving out the chain of circumstances that now forced him to confess, Breitman declared: "Together with everyone else I gave my oath [to the Nazis], because I wanted to save my own life. Joining the partisan unit, I decided to exculpate myself, to wash away this shame with my own blood. The fascist reptiles miscalculated. They can extract any promise with the threat of death, but they were mistaken about its fulfilment. I ask you to give me my life, I will justify myself."[98]

This declaration is striking for its language of ideological appeal to the Soviet side, which appears passionate in tone but under the circumstances takes on an undertone of desperation. By his own admission a collaborator for the sake of survival, Breitman began with his wish to testify to the hypocrisy of German claims to "civilization and culture." He was "a witness to the so-called 'builders of the New Europe.'" He saw Germans berating Soviet POWs as subhumans and instructing them to adapt to German *Kultur*. "To have only a crust of bread is uncultured," he wrote with the pointed sarcasm typical of Soviet propaganda; "to shoot people is 'culture.'"

The "Testimony" ended with a rousing declaration that could have come from any Soviet newspaper: "You, Hitlerite dogs, will be damned by the whole world . . . Remember, the Russian [*russkii*] people have never been under the yoke of outlanders [*inozemtsev*] and never will be." Breitman's April 13, 1943, "Testimony" was written out, signed by hand, and countersigned by the head of the partisan brigade that arrested him. Typed copies were carefully labeled "not for publication." The documents were signed Mikhail Iosifovich Breitman. But Soviet copies and correspondence thereafter renamed him Breitman-Petrenko, as if underlining his two-faced identity. After Breitman had been interrogated and conveyed his information in writing, his NKVD interrogator—who was also Jewish, judging by his last name Ber—took him out and shot him.[99]

After experiencing the darkest sides of human nature in the Holocaust and the war of annihilation, it would be understandable why Breitman's thoughts turned to culture and civilization. But as a party member and political commissar, he surely knew very well just how he was invoking a leitmotif of propaganda and the ideological war. He did so in an hour of extreme need, hoping that a convincing declaration of political loyalty could save his life another time. In order to survive, he had abandoned his previous ideological commitment; now he summoned it back for the same end. As Jeffrey K. Hass has observed: "We assume 'agency' is positive and involves capacity to realize oneself. It might be less so when it is *compelled* and involves thinking the unthinkable." Breitman's odyssey is a disquieting reminder of the lengths that can be traveled in order to survive. For Breitman, to collaborate with the Nazis required hitherto unthinkable improvisations. The kind of decisions he took are prime examples of what can be called compelled or tragic agency.[100]

8

SEX CRIMES AND A CLASH OVER CIVILIZATION

ELSI EICHENBERGER RECALLED the moment she first learned that her destination was Smolensk. The twenty-nine-year-old, German-speaking nurse from Bern, Switzerland, was heading east in mid-October 1941 on a Swiss Red Cross medical mission to German field clinics on the Eastern Front. The train conductor suddenly announced that "General Winter" had already arrived in the Russian city, which lay under two feet of snow. "Smolensk? We all pricked up our ears. Would Smolensk be our future place of work?" She and the thirty-one Swiss surgeons and physicians and thirty nurses had not known they were traveling so deep into occupied territory. All Eichenberger knew about Smolensk was that it had a cathedral and ancient city walls and that, a few months before, the Battle of Smolensk had "overnight made it tragically famous around the world."[1]

Eichenberger's first glimpse of occupied Smolensk was shocking. Houses left standing were the exception in a place that looked like a "pile of rubble." The plucky, idealistic Eichenberger had worked in England as an au pair in 1931–1933 and trained as a pianist in the Bern Conservatory for three years after receiving her nursing degree in 1936. She was distressed that the Swiss medical mission had become notorious for what her compatriots thought of as its "damned pro-Nazism." Was the Red Cross duty to help everyone "tortured by hate and war" not justification enough for saving wounded German soldiers?[2]

The Swiss mission, in fact, represented an attempt to placate Nazi Germany, which was increasingly annoyed by the "studiousness of Swiss neutrality." Its organizer, the prominent Swiss surgeon Eugen Bircher, was close to pro-German circles. But those who signed up had a range of motivations, including surgeons' professional desire for wartime field experience. What made this strong and sensitive young woman stand out from her Swiss colleagues was that her increasingly disturbed fascination kept returning to the worldview of the German soldiers and their attitudes toward Russians. Eichenberger's opportunity to speak with German men on the Eastern Front was unique. At the Military Clinic 4 / 531 in the northern part of the city, she was in charge of caring for one hundred wounded men, with new ones arriving every two to three days. She worked alongside German doctors, socialized with Wehrmacht officers, and was propagandized by zealous SS men. Transferred to the Military Clinic 606, in a nineteenth-century building that had housed a university surgical facility, she took dictation for letters from soldiers who could not hold a pen.[3] Her travelogue brings to life a wartime, German Smolensk, coexisting with and overshadowing the depleted, downtrodden native population. In this huge armed camp and transportation hub, large numbers of soldiers, officers, and administrators were coming, going, and always on the move.

Elsi's Travelogue

What the German men told Eichenberger from October 1941 until her departure from Smolensk on January 19, 1942, was more frank than their letters home, which were often guarded. It was in certain ways more open than the conversations later surreptitiously recorded among soldiers and Nazi Party members in Allied prisons long after the 1941 moment of radicalization had vanished. After Eichenberger left Smolensk, arriving home from a journey that included a chauffeured drive through the Warsaw ghetto and the experience of Nazified Berlin, she used her diary to write a travelogue geared toward the Swiss public, including details of her thoughts and conversations. After it was edited by the publisher and appeared in 1945, she did not preserve her original notes. Yet Eichenberger's account remains, in the words of the medical historian Reinhold Busch, the "only report from a neutral observer in World War II who conveys the state of the [German] troops on the Eastern Front and their mental makeup in such unvarnished form."[4]

Eichenberger confronted the German obsession with race right away on the train ride east. The German medical officer accompanying the Swiss, a gynecologist in civilian life, held forth on racial mongrels (*Mischlinge*). A Swiss physician drily noted that Italians, Germans, and French in Switzerland all felt themselves Swiss and said, "I don't think that we Swiss are a bad race." Eichenberger's own arguments with German soldiers at first centered on her defense of Swiss neutrality in the war. A captain from Leipzig mocked Swiss mobilization: "Ha, a mouse against a lion, a louse against an elephant!" She noted the "stubborn bigotry" of "so many Germans." Soldier after soldier "tactlessly" demanded to know why she was there to help them and why the Swiss were against Germany, questions that became "as old as Methuselah" and "as daily as bread." Her answer: "Can you not accept that we came to help the injured and the wounded, and that we prove that every day? Why can't you believe in the decent humanity of others? Why is it always about you, you, and always you?"[5] Fascism was relentlessly self-obsessed.

These discussions of Swiss neutrality quickly opened up a Nazi German *Weltanschauung,* a term that in the Nazi period came to signify not only worldview but ideological outlook. Eichenberger brought out its two-sided obsession with ruthless power, on the one hand, and victimization by racial conspiracy, on the other. The soldiers, "as if from one mouth," insisted that "they" had attacked "us," that plans had been found, that "the Führer literally said . . ." The twenty-year-old Erich Funke from Heideland, a member of the Waffen-SS, invariably kept coming back to the pestilence of the Jews. "What is communism? Nothing but poverty, misery, dirt, and the masses. And who leads the masses? The Jews." Eichenberger countered with the dangers of dictatorship: "But Funke, how can one single man"—Hitler—"be responsible for so many dead people? It is madness!"[6]

As their German-speaking caregiver, Eichenberger was treated only partially as an outsider. Linguistically, culturally, and through her work in the clinic, she appeared as a proximate, Germanic relative. To her shock and dismay, in her presence soldiers felt free to display their atrocity photographs of hanged Soviets and captured partisans swinging from trees.

A commercial industry sprang up around soldiers' amateur photography, including the sale of cameras and photo albums embossed with the swastika. Trophy photographs included the dismembered corpses of Slavic women and even, in one example discovered by a historian, the camaraderie of fifteen German soldiers in a semicircle, bonding over the sexual subjugation of a supine, anonymous woman. To Eichenberger, however, the wounded soldiers under her care who displayed photos of partisan corpses were not only asserting their prowess and domination. Importantly, she had no trouble detecting a current of fear underlying their revulsion. "They seem to have a downright fear of the [women] partisans, even as they disdainfully call them '*Flintenweiber.*'" She asked, "Why are you showing me these?" On the defensive, they felt it necessary to justify the hangings on military grounds. "'A deterrent!' they answer coolly and laconically." Her thought instead was, "Victims."[7]

The German embrace of this deterrence narrative to justify disproportionate brutality is corroborated by one of the most revealing sources on Wehrmacht soldiers. British and US intelligence surreptitiously taped the conversations of thousands of German POWs, many of whom had served on the Eastern Front. The tapes were mined for intelligence and selectively protocolled. Mass reprisals against civilians, women, and children came up in records of casual conversations from a wide variety of Wehrmacht soldiers. Soldiers "basically saw eye-to-eye" with their military and political leaders in justifying drastic, highly disproportionate reprisals against the civilian population by invoking the notion of "psychological deterrence." The widespread perception that armed women perverted the natural gender order provoked a visceral, emotional response.[8]

Much as with the chilling phenomenon of "ghetto tourism," which Eichenberger later experienced when visiting the Warsaw ghetto, in Smolensk she and a Swiss doctor, accompanied by a German colleague, were freely given a tour of the notorious Gestapo prison on the former Dzerzhinskii Street, previously the headquarters of the NKVD. In this "haunted hell" of thirty rooms holding two hundred people or more, Eichenberger was shaken by the attack dogs and sadistic guards. The soldier who was their tour guide explained that many would soon be shot. "They are all partisans and Jewish vermin. Watch out!" He showed them a "Jewish broad" (*Judenweib*) awaiting execution the next day. "What did she do?" Eichenberger asked. "'Do? Bah, she's a Jewess!' The man said it with equanimity, as if it was the most natural thing in the world to slaughter a woman, single and alone, because she had come into the world Jewish."[9]

Eichenberger was most struck not merely by the violence, but by the Nazi cult of pure power: "It makes an unspeakable impression to witness the results, over and over again, of a one-sided, purely power-political upbringing [*machtpolitischen Erziehung*] . . . Men who have been processed by propaganda year after year lack not only any other yardstick but any capability for making comparisons." The "Aryan worldview," utterly absorbed in its own "racial community," saw nothing in the suffering of the individual, and everything in the will to power, behind which stood the "power of the party and the state."[10]

The depth of Eichenberger's insights into German soldiers was matched by the superficiality of her contacts with Russians. Here there was a language barrier, for she only learned a few words from a Latvian Russian teacher. Even so, Eichenberger could not but observe the subordinate position of the Russian medical personnel, who despite their medical degrees washed floors and bathed patients. She was "astounded" at the small portions they received, mostly potatoes and onions. The Germans at the clinic said only that the Russians there had it good.[11] Given the near starvation conditions in Smolensk that winter, this was painfully true.

The genre of the travelogue, edited by the Swiss publisher, affected Eichenberger's account in several ways. It led her to exoticize Russia, including a long search at the end for a balalaika to take home—"a little piece of the Russian soul!" Her anti-fascist convictions, the 1941 moment of German ideologically informed euphoria mixed with anxiety, and the literary need to convey her message all pushed her toward homogenizing her depiction of German soldiers.[12]

Even when it came to Russians at Clinic 606, Eichenberger gave only a part of the story. In this war of annihilation, things that appear improbable today did occur. At least four doctors from the clinic recalled in detail the half-Jewish Anastasia, a "strikingly pretty" medical student in her early twenties, who returned to the city after the bombings of the Battle of Smolensk to care for her sick mother. A Swiss physician explained that there were no Nazi Party members among the clinic's medical personnel, except for one orderly. His colleagues ("of course") arranged for him to be sent off to the front. Lacking food and work, Anastasia returned to her former medical school and found the German field clinic. She was taken in by the

Swiss surgeon Wolfgang Rückert, who helped her complete her training as an anesthesiologist while they worked together daily at the operation table. Wounded and starving POWs released from the two Dulags in Smolensk were treated in a "Russian room" in the clinic, listed on paper only as an emergency space. Some of them even lived in barracks near the clinic, getting their fill to eat and, after starving in the POW camps, feeling "contented as pigs." This "Russian room" was created, Rückert wrote in a 1995 recollection, after he found Anastasia outside the clinic treating a POW with a frostbitten foot. His whole life Rückert remembered how Anastasia acted with equal part professionalism and kindness toward the German soldiers for whom she cared: "Assja [Anastasia] never made a distinction between friend and enemy. She treated all who were in need as her neighbors." Taking her in was not without danger: a Jewish woman similarly found working in a Wehrmacht military clinic in late August 1941 in Minsk was executed by the SS in an Einsatzkommando sweep.[13]

Some sources suggest that Wehrmacht soldiers directed their misogynistic, sexualized acts of brutality at Russian and Soviet nurses. Nurses found already dead were denuded, dismembered, and defiled. One member of a German armored division who saw such acts, accompanied by crude, mocking taunts, became ashamed of his compatriots. With bitter irony, he referred to the perpetrators as "bearers of culture."[14] Invoking the supposedly higher German *Kultur,* called into question by acts of sexual brutality, signaled how on the Eastern Front sex crimes, the gender order, and assertations of civilizational superiority became deeply intertwined.

Banal Nazism

Eichenberger's depiction of German soldiers did not confront the problem of martial masculinity. When it came to the officers, she recalled only chivalrous and traditionally sexist treatment. Studies of perpetrators suggest that extreme violence can be accompanied by a pressing need "to reinforce a sense of their own humanity."[15]

Other accounts of nurses' experiences with wounded German soldiers were very different from Eichenberger's. Willy Peter Reese, a bookish, twenty-three-year-old budding poet when drafted in 1941, left a harrowing "confession" of the horror and degradation of Wehrmacht life as he passed through "Vitebsk, Smolensk, Vyaz'ma, and a thousand other villages and hamlets" that remained "cameos in the endless journey." A sensitive, literary type, Reese was unusual, and he was no Nazi or racist either. Observing the war as a rank-and-file draftee, he brooded about what he clearly understood to be his own degradation. He reserved a special venom when talking of "comradeship," the concept central to positive German depictions of the bonds among frontline soldiers since the Great War. This was, he wrote in a troubling passage, perverted into "sadism, gallows humor, satire, obscenity, spite, rage, and pranks with corpses, squirted brains, lice, pus, and shit, the spiritual zero."[16]

Yet even Reese's brutally frank depictions were short on specifics. He was disgusted with the barbarization of warfare, but avoided many details. His account of befriending a night nurse when convalescing in a Warsaw hospital is worth juxtaposing with Eichenberger's. "They followed her, watched her walk, groped under her dress . . . the soldiers didn't recognize the limits. The animal in them grew stronger. They desired any woman, and there was only the nurse . . . [Their] hatred at not obtaining the booty expressed itself in foul tirades." What this nurse told him about this sexual harassment resonated, because, Reese said, "I had seen it all for myself."[17]

Eichenberger, stressing the power of ideology, was struck by how the Germans in Smolensk spoke "as if from one mouth." Yet a large degree of variegation is only to be expected among the seventeen million men who served in the Wehrmacht on all fronts, differences exemplified by Reese. Military men were drawn from urban and rural backgrounds, different generations, and all political and ideological camps. A number of Jewish men hid their identities in the army.[18] Others, such as the Russian underground activists in Smolensk, perceived many differences among German soldiers. How can we explain the seeming contradiction between the heterogeneity of the Germany army and Eichenberger's perception of ideological uniformity?

The concept of "banal nationalism" denotes the everyday, endemic ways in which assumptions are reinforced and naturalized without any explicit reference to the dogmas of a belief system. The massive German army exhibited what might be called banal Nazism—and, by extension, it is useful to think about banal Stalinism. The secretly taped Wehrmacht soldiers almost never discussed ideology or politics directly. Passing the time in their cells, soldiers brought up rape, killing, and chilling reprisals in terms of adventure, sport, and "chest-puffing" tales, some of them invented. Among the soldiers, some hated Jews but expressed shock at genocide; others perpetrated acts of extreme violence but were critical of Nazism. Despite all these differences, a common feature emerged across the POWs' conversations. Soldiers discussed extreme acts calmly, because they had become routine. They rarely argued about rapes and other violations of peacetime taboos. What is striking from this point of view is not their differences but how the experience of war and indoctrination created a shared mentality. The fact that this "banal Nazism" was implicit, embedded in ordinary soldiers' attitudes, only made it more powerful.[19]

Sexual violence was one component of the synergies of violence that connected the Holocaust with other waves and forms of Nazi violence on the Eastern Front, but there are compelling reasons to examine it separately. Sexual violence, far broader than rape alone, is distinguishable and distinct from other forms of violence in part because the intensity and intimacy of sex is embedded within especially powerful taboos. The vast majority of victims of wartime sex crimes, but not all of them, were women. Many victims were fearful or had compelling reasons not to speak openly about what they had experienced. Postwar Soviet trials and investigations did not target sexual violence explicitly, and Article 6 of the Charter of the International Military Tribunal, in its definition of crimes against humanity, did not include it. For virtually the duration of the twentieth century, the historical profession marginalized the topic. All this created special problems of sources and source analysis.[20]

Sexual violence has finally begun to be examined extensively in studies of the Holocaust, but it also formed the backdrop for a different, less scrutinized set of wartime relationships between German men and Russian women. In a manner different from other forms of violence, violent and coercive sexuality could overlap with or shade into sexual barter and consensual relations.[21] Gender roles were one area where fascism and communism diverged most sharply. In a context of military and sexual conquest, unequal power relations between German soldiers and civilian Russian women informed a wartime clash over which culture and political system was more civilized.

Militarized Masculinity

"Fascism," George L. Mosse wrote, "based itself on the continuity of the war into peacetime and presented itself as a community of men." Martial prowess became central to far-right concepts of the New Man that arose in the German new nationalism between the wars, from Oswald Spengler's "new barbarians" to Ernst Jünger's "soldier-workers." The quintessential fascist revolutionary was the paramilitary storm trooper, not the proletarian steelworker of Soviet iconography. Nazism in power incorporated bourgeois values of restraint and discipline, home and hearth, but only partially. That sort of respectability was in tension with right-wing revolutionary values glorifying a destructive, subversive "energy and virility" in the service of a "racially sanitized state."[22]

The onset of the most radical stage of the Nazi Revolution in 1941 strengthened the imagined bonds between military-ideological and sexual conquest. That connection, common in many military cultures, was accentuated in the specific context of Nazism. In the Nazi worldview, war and sexual conquest appeared the quintessence of human and male existence; virility was linked to fertility and therefore to race and the racial community. The ideal soldier was not just strong, but aggressive and manly. This explains German assumptions that a sterile person could not be a good soldier.[23]

German acts of sexual and nonsexual violence, which often occurred together, took place in the context of the large, complex organization of the army, but they also frequently varied according to the specific dynamics of small groups, which promoted hazing rituals and demonstrations of masculine prowess. Rape was often committed where others could see and was part of the performance of conquest and humiliation.[24]

This heightened expectation of military-sexual domination created a contradiction: Aryan mixing with inferior races violated the precepts of "racial hygiene." To Reichsführer Himmler, the SS was his own elite "community of men" (*Männerbund*); in a prewar speech he even referred to Nazi Germany as a *Männerstaat,* or a male state. Himmler in particular had a long history of hard-line views on German sexual relations with Eastern "races" as a threat to racial reordering of Europe. This is what Eichenberger picked up on when she observed that sexual "relations between Germans and Russian women is strongly forbidden."[25] In practice, however, the prohibition was very widely ignored.

There is no open-and-shut case that Wehrmacht authorities strategically used sexual violence as a weapon of war, in the manner of mass rape and sexual enslavement by Serb forces toward Bosnian women or the mass rape and sexual mutilation by Hutus in Rwanda toward Tutsi women and children in the 1990s. The German military selectively punished sex crimes when they seemed to threaten military effectiveness. What debates over this issue have shown is that the authorities, on the one hand, expected and condoned rape on the Eastern Front while, on the other, acted on concerns about the breakdown of discipline and the spread of venereal disease. Since Russian girls and women were routinely deployed both by Soviet partisans and by security agencies for intelligence missions, spy-mania heightened German military authorities' fears about German liaisons with Russian women. The German High Command approved the widespread establishment of military brothels, attempted to regulate prostitution, and paid much attention to children of mixed marriages. But beyond these policies, it largely turned a blind eye. Racial ideology and military calculations converged in the military and security apparatuses' joint fear that long-term German relationships with local women would soften the pitiless determination needed to win the war.[26]

Impunity and Opportunity

There was little sanction against sexual violence, ample opportunity to pursue it, and minimal incentive to cultivate the civilian population. Each of those three factors is key to explaining significant historical variations in the prevalence of wartime rape and sexual violence. Since Section 2 of the Barbarossa Jurisdiction Decree abolished prosecution of German soldiers for crimes against enemy civilians, essentially nullifying the military penal code, military units rather than courts-martial decided cases involving soldiers' crimes. As a result, much came to depend on individual commanders. Of the 17 million serving the Wehrmacht on all fronts during the entire war, a mere 5,349 were convicted of "acts of indecency," including homosexual acts. Furthermore, the hyped-up threat of partisans provided justification or excuse for sexual crimes from the start of the invasion in 1941. An Army Group Center order specifically allowed for "any means," even torture, to be applied when interrogating partisans, "including women."[27]

The two most substantive sources on German sexual violence are the Soviet Extraordinary Commission that gathered local testimonies about German atrocities, including from Smolensk, and German trial evidence from military courts about those cases that were considered. In both cases, there were taboos and euphemisms in discussing sexual matters. In the Soviet case, neither the Extraordinary Commission nor the 1943 Soviet decrees on punishments for crimes by "traitors" made sexual crimes a consistent focus of investigation. Sexual issues tended to be filtered out during the compilation of central, synthetic Extraordinary Commission reports based on local testimonies. But locals stepped forward with information of rape and sexual violence across many contexts, and this resonated with Soviet atrocity propaganda. The German trial sources were scattered and made unsystematic by lax enforcement, while the courts' focus on military effectiveness created gaps in evidence.[28] Yet the Soviet and German sources, despite their limitations, have not been considered together. When they are combined, they reveal commonalities that allow us to speak with some approximation about sexual violence across the broad spectrum of practices recorded.

Male Bonding and Gender Traitors

Many Extraordinary Commission reports on German atrocities included rape and sexual violence as one line in longer lists of other acts. For example, a report on the Dzerzhinskii District in Smolensk Region, which was liberated in January 1942 (and moved to Kaluzhskaia Region in 1945), gave an accounting of the three-and-a-half-month occupation that had led to the deaths of 1,119 civilians, including 112 women, by suffocation, torture, and mass shootings. The typology of atrocities did not include rape, but one particularly graphic line included sexual torture and murder: the "breasts of the bodies of tortured and shot women" were visible among charred corpses. A later report from the very same district, however, gave a different, more detailed account of rapes by drunken soldiers. Some were carried out in front of children in villages; some raped women were taken to serve as sex slaves in an army brothel (near the town of Kondrovo); some raped women were subsequently killed, while four cases of rape and torture were detailed at the end of the report. If they fit the purpose, some individual testimonies were approved for publication by the Central Committee's Agitprop Department and the Sovinformburo.[29]

More detailed and systematic reporting came from medical professionals living under occupation. A gynecologist from Smolensk city, P. I. Kesarev, for example, included both the events he had heard of secondhand (gang rapes and mass rapes in villages) and those he saw personally at the civilian hospital where he worked. These illuminated an additional, ubiquitous range of gender violence, that is, acts not involving sexual contact, such as the case of a German head doctor who regularly ordered women undressed and observed them washing. Kesarev reported the rape of a seventy-year-old woman, who died three days later. "Violence toward women was a common occurrence," he concluded. "But, of course, it is not possible to give a precise figure."[30]

When Soviet testimonies are analyzed in conjunction with material about sex cases stemming from German military court cases, the picture suggests the central importance of violent male bonding. First of all, rape and gang rape regularly occurred in the same locations as other crimes and atrocities committed by groups of soldiers—including other assaults of a sexual nature, such as sexual mutilation and torture of men and women and nonsexual violence involving large numbers of civilians, including looting, arson, murder, and mass executions. In this war as in others, rape in and of itself was not necessarily the most atrocious fate a victim could meet. Many of these outbreaks of terror that encompassed sexual violence were associated with the partisan war, requisitioning, and security operations in the countryside. Opportunity presented itself especially when soldiers carried out actions in the villages or were quartered alongside Russians in urban and rural areas. From drinking bouts to married men seeking adventure all the way to gang rapes, the group rituals of militarized masculinity could present ways of escaping the strictures of military discipline and flouting the norms of civilian life.[31]

It may have even seemed to the male perpetrators committing sexual assaults that their actions were prompted more by what was going on in their immediate group than by the tenets of any belief system. Yet male bonding in the small group became linked to large constructs such as the German "racial community" (*Volksgemeinschaft*) in ways both subtle and profound. The euphoria of military conquest in 1941 seemed to provide proof of racial superiority; the conditions of the grinding, dirty poverty of Stalin's USSR, which German soldiers constantly spoke about, seemed to confirm the dominance of German *Kultur* and the primitive, yet threatening, alien civilization of the Judeo-Bolshevik East.[32]

A key connection between the individual and the small group to the overarching Nazi order was ideas about the proper place of women. These were challenged by the fact that women fought in large numbers in the Red Army and that the partisans included women fighters. This appeared as a fundamental challenge to the gender order upheld by the Third Reich, which above all propagated a clear-cut, unambiguous gender binary. In official conceptions, gender roles were both natural and under threat from Jews, homosexuals, and other deviants. Misogyny was further ideologized by depictions of Jews as feminine or sexually deviant, a staple of antisemitic propaganda, and branding *Flintenweiber,* Red Army and partisan women, as traitors to their gender. Among the SS men who staffed the concentration camp system, those reluctant to kill were derided as soft and feminine. As one Sachsenhausen executioner later put it, "No one wanted to be seen as a 'limp dick.'"[33]

Sexual Barter and Long-Term Relationships

Both German and Russian men routinely denied that rape and sexual violence were widespread. One soldier, Otto Pauls, was typical in his boast that the Wehrmacht was greeted with open arms, so that "we did not even need to" resort to rape. Lev Dudin, an intelligentsia collaborator in occupied Kyiv, concurred: "They did not have to rape women; women themselves made it unnecessary. Who knows, maybe it was the curiosity for all things foreign, or plentiful wine and foodstuffs, or simply the absence of men and loneliness, but the Germans did not have to complain about the availability of our women."[34]

One reason these men were able to downplay or deny mass sexual violence was that during the occupation cohabitation between Russian women and German men became "virtually a mass phenomenon." Partial Smolensk data from local governances in 1942 is supplemented by partisan intelligence reports of German soldiers and officers marrying Russian young women in the countryside, facilitated by evening vodka parties among village youth and soldiers. Large numbers of children born to German fathers and Russian mothers were the subject of extensive Wehrmacht discussions in general and in the Smolensk Region specifically. After the German retreat, in the first half of 1944, the NKVD reported that almost a third of sixty-three murder cases recorded in the Smolensk Region were infanticide: children born to Russian mothers and German fathers.[35]

Evidence of widespread sexual contacts between German men and Russian women also comes from the outbreaks of venereal diseases. The

Smolensk gynecologist Kesarev noted that, before the war, cases had been so rare that his dermatological-venerealogical clinic had difficulty finding examples to show medical students. During the occupation, patients with syphilis and gonorrhea overflowed from the city's clinics like "never before."[36]

German soldiers' memoirs boasted that women were easily enticed by luxury goods such as salami, chocolate, and cognac, demand for which spiked throughout the occupied territories by 1942. But undoubtedly, the greatest motivation for civilian women was basic caloric needs. During the winter of 1941–1942, the nadir terms of food supply, civilians faced semi-starvation conditions in urban areas throughout the Army Group Center Rear Area. In a February 12, 1942, letter to the garrison headquarters (*Ortskommandatur*) in Smolensk, mayor Boris Menshagin reported that the 500 gram norm of bread per person that had been set from August to December 1941 had been reduced by German order to gram norms of 200 per worker, 150 for nonworkers, and 75 for children. Even these drastically reduced amounts were violated, prompting Menshagin, almost always outwardly compliant, to call the situation "completely unacceptable."[37]

Dudin's remark about "curiosity for all things foreign" evoked women's personal motivations, as well as perhaps the insecurity of "native" men that fueled the shame surrounding the topic on the Soviet side. Consensual relations can be seen as part of a continuum that included semi-coercive, forced, and violent encounters. It is probable, for example, that for some women living under occupation, a long-term relationship with a German became a form of protection from other Germans. For men and women, relationships could serve as wartime islands of domesticity. Many Russian women did not know whether their husbands serving in the Red Army were alive. Long-term relationships come up in numerous testimonies. A librarian for the Task Force of Reichsleiter Alfred Rosenberg, in the words of a Russian colleague, "conducted herself badly" (a euphemism for sexual relations) with a German official. The couple left Smolensk with the retreating Wehrmacht in September 1943.[38]

Barter of all kinds, including sexual barter, accompanied the weakening of the money economy in 1941. It became prevalent in local commerce, especially between town and countryside and especially involving food. Sexual barter, the trading of sex for food and scarce commodities, could be present in brief exchanges tantamount to commercial sex as well as in long-term relationships or marriage. Those instances where historians of

World War II have been able to analyze extensive oral and written records of sexual barter in places of extreme scarcity, such as the Theresienstadt ghetto and concentration camp in occupied Czechoslovakia, convey the vast range of activities such exchanges could encompass.[39]

Unlike the sexual barter in Theresienstadt, which occurred within the Jewish society of that ghetto, the exchange in Smolensk was between German military men and Russian women (who rarely spoke much German) in a military-dominated zone. These Russian women were making a decision infused with political and ideological implications. The stigma at the time in the politically polarized civilian society against *nemetskaia podstilka*—a derogatory term that can be translated as "German bedding" or "German mattress"—blossomed at the end of the war. At the moment of German retreat from the region, women became targets once again, now out of a Russian-Soviet desire for revenge.

In conditions of extreme scarcity and a barter economy, it may be difficult to draw a line between sexual barter and prostitution. Laurie R. Cohen, a historian conducting an oral history project in Smolensk over a half century later, found only a single informant on sexual matters, whom she dubbed Nadia to protect her identity. In an interview, Nadia mentioned Russian women who were "beautiful, made-up." "They lived perfectly well. Some lived on our street; two were even in our building. We knew perfectly well the kind of work they did." Nadia qualified any mild condemnation her remarks implied by adding: "Generally, you worked wherever you could."[40]

The interview with Nadia is suggestive of how rare it has been to hear the voices of women about German-Russian sexual relations. Two groups of women who were watching left their reactions in the historical record: professional women, such as physicians and teachers, and young women activists conducting underground political work in the occupied city of Smolensk.

Lyusya's Journey

Liudmila (Lyusya) Madziuk, the twenty-one-year-old Komsomol activist released from Smolensk's Dulag-126 along with her Jewish friend Asya Shneiderman, began conducting political work among German soldiers in Smolensk around the same time Eichenberger was working in her clinic, in the harsh winter of 1941.[41]

What set Madziuk apart in occupied Smolensk was her good knowledge of German. Working in a canteen run by a pro-Soviet Russian woman, Madziuk was able to initiate frequent conversations with German soldiers and agitate among her fellow Russian laborers. Her Komsomol cell, one of three active in Smolensk when it began functioning in January 1942, was made up of three other women and five men. Its members sought out residents who might reveal themselves as sympathetic to the Soviet cause amid what underground activists uniformly described as a mostly indifferent or hostile civilian population. The group gathered and used propaganda leaflets dropped by Soviet aviation, hung up homemade posters, and tried to evade arrest, far from always successfully. The young people took on these small-scale activities on their own initiative.

Throughout 1942, the Germans oversaw a significant tightening of security in cities and towns in the region. In Smolensk, the city police force, which coordinated with German security, included some former Komsomol members, who recognized their prewar comrades if they appeared in public spaces. The security crackdown had significant effects in Smolensk, especially after a group of at least 130 pro-Soviet residents and underground party members were rounded up and executed in July 1942. This virtually sealed the city off from regular contact with Moscow. Only in March 1943 were the ranks of the underground Komsomol supplemented by a mission of nine women agents in the so-called Mozin group. The group was named after the former Smolensk city party secretary, Ivan Mozin, who was now a partisan commander outside Smolensk and had organized the mission. Shneiderman had been sent on a mission from the city to connect the Mozin group to the existing underground. The whole time, from January 1942 up until the liberation of Smolensk in summer 1943, Madziuk was conversing with German soldiers.[42]

Unlike Eichenberger, who emphasized the uniformity of Nazification, Madziuk immediately noticed very different outlooks among the German men. "It is harder to work among the German youth than among the older men, by the way," she told her Mints Commission interviewer. "The youth are fanatics. Fixed formulas have been beaten into their heads and they do not desire to understand and know anything else. Among the older people one finds those who were members of the Communist Party [of Germany]. You can talk to them . . . They relate to us with sympathy and read Russian leaflets with pleasure." In her written report produced two months earlier, however, Madziuk put it somewhat differently, not drawing such a

City of Smolensk in April 1942, with the Cathedral of the Assumption in the background. Digital Picture Archives, Bundesarchiv.

categorical generational or political division. It was not only older former Communists who were reachable, she clarified, but also those Germans most "dismayed" by the course of the war: "I worked in one German canteen, peeling potatoes, and gradually began to observe the Germans. It turns out they were not all of the same mindset. Some were simply dismayed by the situation: the end of the war was not visible, families in Germany were hungry, and especially in 1943 the soldiers themselves started to feel the lack of food supplies." Madziuk's efforts revolved around convincing Germans of the superiority of the Soviet system. Differences in Germans' outlook, she thought, centered on the unshakable belief of the "fanatics" that Soviet life was nothing more than repressiveness and exploitation, that everyone wallowed in "dirt and cold." To "wake up" such hostile men, she said, "cost great effort."[43] Significantly, she never implied that their very nature as fascists or Germans made the task impossible. Madziuk remained optimistic they would be won over.

In fact, Madziuk scored some successes that seem remarkable today. Interested German soldiers allowed her to use the soldiers' radio at the canteen at 5:00 AM to listen to transmissions from Moscow and translate what she heard. Others expressed interest in the partisans. "I already knew how to approach the Germans," Madziuk remarked with pride. Madziuk even obtained a copy of the second volume of Karl Marx's *Kapital* for a German soldier named Leo, a former Communist now fighting for Hitler. "I asked him, to what party do you belong? 'I am not fascist and not communist.' I asked him what prompted him to leave the Communist Party and go over to the side of Hitler. He said that he was corrupted by the widespread agitation and went along with the tide, which he now regrets." Other Smolensk residents able to speak with Germans—male and female, party and non-party—reported war-weariness, arrests for desertion, and poor morale especially after 1942. Madziuk claimed that three Germans she had propagandized deserted to join the partisans. There were, in fact, cases of Wehrmacht soldiers who joined the partisans. Fritz Paul Shmenkel (1916–1944), who was sardonically dubbed "Ivan Ivanovich" by the partisans of the "Death to Fascism" partisan group active in Smolensk and Kalinin Regions, was posthumously declared a Hero of the Soviet Union in 1964.[44]

Imagining the Wehrmacht soldier Leo and the Komsomolka Madziuk poring over an edition of Marx underscores how this conflict, often called an ideological war or a war of annihilation, also involved significant cross-cultural interactions, however fraught or unequal. Improbable connections were sometimes made as Russians and Germans observed one other. That we even know about Leo is likely because Madziuk felt obliged to recount the episode for a particular reason. It established that she herself was a good Komsomol activist carrying out proper political-enlightenment work with a German man, after which in her report she embarked on a delicate topic: how to explain the extensive sexual relations between German men and young Russian women.

Madziuk's unusual emphasis on different types of Germans and her overt sympathy for "good" or redeemable Germans was made in the spirit of communist internationalism. But it certainly went against the grain of wartime thirst for revenge and an avalanche of Soviet propaganda demonizing Germans. What was even more remarkable was that Madziuk openly spoke about reaching the more sympathetic Germans more easily than her Russian civilian co-workers. "The mood of the Russian population, of the young women [*devushki*] was completely different. It was very difficult to work among them." In the canteen, women bustled to demonstrate their "eagerness" to please the Germans. When she told them to slow down, they replied: "What for?" Some of them did read her Soviet leaflets, but others "reported to the authorities that Madziuk [was] disrupting work and going against the German authorities." She managed to get away only by switching jobs several times.[45]

"Everything Depended on the Girls Themselves"

Madziuk, a quintessential member of the 1930s generation, shared her enthusiastic Soviet patriotism and her ideas about gender as one of those Soviet urban youth of the first generation to be raised entirely under Soviet power. Her experiences in higher education and the Komsomol in particular shaped her outlook and made her representative. Born in the city of Kozlov (now Michurinsk), Tambov Region, Madziuk joined the Komsomol in 1939, the same year she began studies at the prestigious Moscow Institute for Transport Engineers, with a specialization in aviation. The conventional view of the Soviet gender order is that the agendas of Bolshevik feminist revolutionaries and early Soviet policies aimed at women's emancipation were rolled back with the end of the Central Committee's Women's Section in 1930 and reversed in the mid-1930s "retreat" on the family, motherhood, and abortion. In fact, the situation was more complex than a simple reversal from the 1920s positions to those of the 1930s and beyond. Madziuk herself is an excellent case in point.

The model "new Soviet person" of the 1930s generation was an ideal for the emerging urban, Soviet civilization: enlightened, enthusiastic, ready to fight for the cause, and moral, in the sense of anti-hedonistic and a willingness for self-sacrifice. Both in the 1930s and during the war, those young women striving to embody some version of this ideal type embraced the drive to become "cultured," a pillar of the Soviet political-enlightenment state in its 1930s configuration. Culturedness (*kul'turnost'*) carried the connotation of civilized and included political literacy, proper behavior, avid learning and broad knowledge, rational restraint, and self-improvement. When the war came, many members of this generation that had been born too late to fight in 1917 or the Civil War, including young women, leapt to make their own sacrifice. Madziuk volunteered as a nurse in 1941, but many tens of thousands of young women clamored to fight with the Red Army. When many of them were initially discouraged in recruitment centers at the local level, some volunteered to join the partisans or risky underground missions into occupied territory for the organs of state security.[46]

Despite the 1930s turn to glorifying motherhood along with the Motherland, then, Madziuk and many other young women of the 1930s generation remained fiercely committed to pursuing traditionally male endeavors, whether in their careers or in waging war. Institutionally, the Komsomol and higher education were both places where female activism and jettisoning traditional gender roles were still pursued, even as the male leadership of those institutions sometimes articulated a newly emboldened male chauvinism.[47]

The war itself was also a means to break out of gender constraints. In Madziuk's case, her ability to study aviation engineering clearly informed her belief in the superiority of Soviet socialism. She had the following to say about sexual barter in Smolensk: "The girls were drawn to the Germans by the fact that the Germans brought them bread, candy, and so on. They were satisfied. One girl lived next to us. She reasoned in this way: what more do I need? I have my own room, it is warm in the room, and I have bread. That is my ideal. I don't need anything else. The Germans could supply all that she needed for a 'happy life.' There were very many girls like that." This, to Madziuk, was a clear-cut case of putting petty-bourgeois acquisitiveness over political and social commitment. Against the backdrop of widespread sexual violence and brutal material conditions, however, it could also be interpreted as a practical-minded quest for stability and material security. Madziuk reported, "Many explained their liaisons with the Germans by the fact that they needed to feed their children: 'who can help me with that? Of course, the Germans. Where can I do it, what can I get?'" Madziuk did not approve of this hardheaded, acquisitive pragmatism, which had many roots in the Soviet economy of shortages. She initially remarked: "I would say that everything depended on the girls themselves. If they did not want to, they would not do it. True, it would have meant going hungry and walking around in poor clothes, but in the end they would have remained honest." But Madziuk was not unsympathetic. She realized the sacrifice she favored was not an easy choice. She immediately added: "Work conditions were bad. They paid 18 marks a month. What could you do with them, when a loaf of bread cost 20 marks." Madziuk, characteristically, expressed a degree of empathy even if she eventually condemned these women. To her, ultimately, there always remained a choice.[48]

Four other Komsomol young women activists and a number of non-party women professionals living under occupation also alluded in Mints Commission interviews to sexual relations between German men and Russian women. Seemingly unprompted, they volunteered their various remarks in the course of their conversations. For example, twenty-four-year-old Vasilisa Agil'iarova, the secretary of the Mozin group, was originally from a village near Smolensk and had completed two years of higher education in a communist university. She told her interviewer how she recruited two young women hairdressers into the underground. She then broke off, it seems clear, because she had suddenly thought about the sexual issue in association with the hair stylists, and then made the following comment: "A great number of Smolensk girls behaved badly [*plokho sebia veli*] and went out with [*guliali*] the Germans. You look around, and they walk along the street holding hands with Germans, and they are talking in the German language." In contrast to the clear disapproval she had just conveyed, Agil'iarova then noted that one of the hairdressers had carried out clandestine tasks and had become a "good Komsomolka."[49] To "behave badly" is clearly a euphemism for sexual relations and was the polar opposite of being a good Communist. Agil'iarova's resort to colloquial expressions shows the difficulty in openly discussing sexuality in general and liaisons with the fascist invaders in particular.

It did not take membership in the Komsomol, however, to disapprove of German male chauvinism and aggression. The accounts of the non-party teachers and physicians dovetailed with those of the agents and activists. But the professional women were in an even better position to observe the arrogant entitlement and assertion of domination that the occupiers made no effort to conceal. As Larisa Bazykina, a first-grade teacher, put it: "They looked at every woman as if they were examining a good [*tovar*]. You walk along and hear 'Hey, Liuba!' There was no other kind of talk."[50]

Menshagin recalled meeting as early as mid-September 1941 with German and Russian physicians, experts in venereal disease, and his military overseers from the Seventh Department of the 813 Field Commandant. He was asked, as were other new local administrators, to provide a suitable city building for a brothel. Describing himself as "surprised and angry," Menshagin, likely anticipating popular outrage, explained to the Germans that prostitution in the forms that had existed before 1917 had disappeared. The German garrison physician shrugged his shoulders and said that a brothel would serve the health interests of both soldiers and women. Likely with his reputation in mind, Menshagin claimed in his memoirs that a brothel was not opened in Smolensk. There are reports of three.[51]

One Komsomol operative who passed through Smolensk in summer 1942, V. P. Boldinaia, discussed the Wehrmacht-organized brothels. The NKVD took particular interest in this topic, partly because the brothels offered opportunities for intelligence gathering and partly because widespread popular indignation about them in the occupied territories and on the home front offered fodder for effective propaganda. Creating separate brothels for officers was standard practice, and an elite bordello for German Luftwaffe officers in the city of Smolensk was housed in a former hotel. As in other locations in the occupied territories, brothels were all in great demand. Without giving a source, Boldinaia reported that there were 1,860 women in brothels in Smolensk Region. She also reported that 1,867 Jews from the Smolensk ghetto were killed in gas vans, a suspiciously exact figure but one that does fall into the range of what historians estimate. There were at least 50,000 women in military brothels in the greater Reich, and brothels were also created in labor and concentration camps.[52]

Tellingly, Boldinaia's report to the Komsomol Central Committee gave all her observations about German-Russian gender relations squarely in the context of her discussion of brothels and commercial sex. She then discussed how "girls who are connected with the Germans walk around with painted lips and curled hair, all cleaned up [chisten'kie] and wearing shoes with 11-cm. heels." Like many other women, she emphasized how Germans at the central labor market routinely selected the best-looking women for jobs: "They must wear their best dress to work for the Germans."[53] The unstated implication was that those who did not strive to satisfy the Germans would be coerced into doing so.

Zinaida Namatevs, the Mozin group's second-in-command, was a twenty-year old geology student in Moscow when the war broke out. She had joined the Komsomol in 1938. She recalled entering Smolensk dressed as a village girl, hinting at unwanted attention from German men: "It was a bit strange, there were Germans everywhere. You walk along the street, and it seems that each German is looking at you." After a long accounting of her mission in the underground, Namatevs returned to the sexual issue. The German women in Smolensk, most of them nurses, hated Russian women, she reported. This was because "the German men really liked"—the word

"But the summer in Smolensk still has its charms." From Friedhelm Kaiser, *Smolensk: Kleiner Wegweiser durch Geschichte und Sehenswürdigkeiten* (Smolensk, 1942), 40, in BA MA 36 / 645, by permission of Bundesarchiv-Militärarchiv, Freiburg.

she used was *uvazhali,* which can mean "respected," but in this context it means "rated highly"—"Smolensk girls." German men said that the locals would tolerate a lot more things than "our own women" would.[54] How did Namatevs know? She did not elaborate. But her remark is suggestive of the new power relations that German men took for granted as conquerors in the East.

A cartoon about summer clothing revealing a shapely young Russian woman can be found in the back of a German-language guide to the history and monuments of occupied Smolensk. This guidebook was put out by the propaganda office of the Smolensk commandant in 1942 and clearly intended for rank-and-file soldiers. Signed by the Nazi-era poster artist Peter Landhoff, it presented young Russian women in the city as a tourist attraction, ignoring the official Wehrmacht discouragement of soldiers' relationships and the Nazi ban on "racial defilement."

"On the Culture of the Germans"

German assumptions of racial superiority were made as they strutted around the East, traditionally associated with backwardness. The Soviet political and professional women who observed their behavior, however, related it to a shocking reversal of preconceived notions of Europeanness, which even in the Soviet period was broadly associated with culture and advanced development. When they called the German men uncultured, it was not merely a quaint way of censuring them. They turned to a familiar concept as a means of asserting the European invaders' inferiority, indeed barbarism.

The German notion of *Kultur* had served as a marker of national distinctiveness since the nineteenth century, and the concept was radicalized as confirmation of racial superiority under the Nazis. The Russian-Soviet concept of *kul'turnost'* (culturedness) became a keyword only in the Stalinist 1930s. It was widely popularized starting in the middle of the decade as a means to link political and cultural literacy with behavior promoted as civilized, modern, and desirable. Yet this mass popularization was but one milestone in a longer history. The notion had been deployed in debates in the 1920s by Bolshevik intellectuals who wished to contest the traditional Russian reverence toward European "bourgeois" culture. After the 1930s, because *kul'turnost'* reflected a merger of intelligentsia and Soviet outlooks, it was widely internalized for decades to come as a marker of cultural level for the rapidly expanding urban and educated classes. Throughout, this Soviet conception of civilized values always held distinct international implications, and in the Stalin period it formed part of an assertion of outright Soviet superiority. Such assertions often overlay a strong undercurrent of anxiety. If the intelligentsia émigré Lenin had viewed Russian culture as "semi-Asiatic," seeing the need for Soviets to catch up with bourgeois culture before surpassing it, the 1930s ratified a Stalinist superiority complex. Built socialism was declared superior in all respects, including in the realm of culture. As Il'ia Ehrenburg later wrote, these loud paeans betrayed underlying fears of inferiority.[55]

At the same time, medieval barbarism had been constantly invoked in Soviet treatments of fascism from its origins in the early 1920s, even as fascism was also ideologically conflated with capitalism and imperialism. During the war, the Soviet press, including the military newspaper *Red Star*, widely publicized rapes and the humiliation of Russian women as part of atrocity propaganda, which picked up markedly in early 1942 when the German retreat from Moscow liberated areas that had experienced the occupation. As Jeffrey Brooks has noted, during the war the Soviet press became deeply invested in broadcasting the humiliation of

Soviet women, families, and children—as opposed to the setbacks faced by the state, the Party, or Stalin. "The appeal to men to save women from sexual violation and children from mistreatment is one of the most powerful and personal constructions of honor. It had been lacking in Soviet official culture since 1917."[56]

Madziuk, Shneiderman, and the other Komsomol women took these concepts of barbarism and culturedness from the Soviet public sphere and internalized them in personal ways. Their recurrence in the context of German men's behavior demonstrated that for the women these were hardly formulaic slogans, but notions with real meaning that were tested in the harsh realities of wartime survival.

Madziuk chose not to explain how much her reports on German men were based on observation of other women and how much she experienced herself. She never mentioned outright sexual violence. She simply charged that German men rudely accosted and handled women in an uncultured way [nekul'turno]. "I asked, do Germans really treat girls that way?" Madziuk referred twice more to the concept of culturedness, conveying emotion and animus: "A more uncultured people I have never met, they were uncultured to a degree that was horrible." In addition to their behavior toward women, Germans were "stingy to an unbelievable degree." Their goal in life was merely to own "a small home, a cow, a pretty garden." While stinginess opposed traditional Russian values, and petty-bourgeois lust for property opposed Marxist-Leninist principles, both implied German inferiority.[57]

The last section of Madziuk's interview was unique among the seventy Mints Commission interviews from Smolensk Region. It was flagged with a subtitle: "On the Culture of the Germans." Here she used the shocking lack of "culturedness" among these supposedly superior Europeans as the key to explaining an interconnected litany of flaws, including domineering sexual behavior, philistine acquisitiveness, and reactionary views about women in the workplace. Madziuk did not explicitly relate these behaviors to German war crimes, but these "cultural" attributes were described in the midst of a litany of German atrocities.[58]

What outraged Madziuk about German attitudes was that even "the best of them" could not believe that she was training before the war to become a transportation engineer. "In their understanding, what should a woman do? Bear children and keep the home." They could picture a woman as a

doctor or an artist, but a woman engineer was simply beyond their imagination. "I asked what a girl could achieve in Germany, and they replied
that you have a lot of promise, you know German, you could become a
secretary in an office."[59]

Madziuk's criticism of German anti-feminism was echoed by the Komsomol and non-party professional women alike. Soviet women doctors in
particular were furious and insulted by the way German medical personnel denigrated them as ignorant subordinates. One of the most detailed commentators was Antonina Semenova (b. 1906), a non-party pe-
diatrician. The German attitude, Semenova said, was, "You do not know
anything. You are a Russian doctor." This reflected a much broader German
repudiation of the worth of Soviet science and culture: "They had the idea
that our universities are not worth anything, that we are all uncultured
[nekul'turnye] people, that we do not possess an elementary level of cultural attainment [elementarnykh kul'turnykh navykov], that our education
does not impart anything."[60] Even those Germans in minor positions of
authority, Semenova emphasized, took pleasure in roaring at subordinates.
They dedicated great effort to cultivating an imperious, "commanding tone."
As for Russian women, "They did not consider us women to be people. It
was a lower race."[61]

Asya's Fury

Unlike Eichenberger, who lambasted the long arm of Nazification while
interacting with many officers and soldiers as individuals, or Madziuk, who
was repelled by fascism while empathizing with Germans open to her
political work, Asya Shneiderman was enraged. She gave no quarter to
anyone in her long report to the Komsomol, titled "Occupied Smolensk"
and dated September 14, 1942. She never spoke about how she concealed
her Jewish identity. But once she and Madziuk were issued identity papers
when they were released from the Dulag, she appears to have been safe from
denunciations in a city where she was not known. Having lived through
the two greatest Smolensk atrocities, the starvation of POWs in the camp
and the murder of eighteen hundred to two thousand Jewish residents of
the Smolensk ghetto by gas vans in mid-July 1942, Shneiderman could not
even bring herself to use the word "Germans" in the report. Instead,
she used the derogatory term *nemchura,* a Russian synonym for Fritzes.

She saved her most bitter, sarcastic epithets for their lackeys, the Russian collaborators.[62]

Shneiderman, like Madziuk, said nothing of her own autobiography. But she, like Madziuk, gave many indications that she was a committed member of the 1930s generation. Thoroughly atheist, she ridiculed a priest's "hallelujahs" when describing an evening spent at the house of one former employee of the House of Soviets. This "utterly unprincipled, opportunistic, lickspittle element" had replaced a portrait of Stalin in his luxurious apartment with icons in one corner and a portrait of Hitler in the other. Shneiderman remained proudly Soviet, referring to those few Smolensk civilians who helped the underground and preserved the collected works of Marx, Lenin, and Stalin as "true patriots." Like Madziuk, she was thoroughly committed to her generation's project of becoming enlightened and spreading enlightenment. "People with higher education, teachers, doctors, students, all work as cleaning women for the Fritzes—and not just as cleaning women, they sell themselves to the Fritzes."[63] To Shneiderman, there was no distinction between sexual barter and prostitution. Both were tantamount to treason.

While Madziuk expressed some degree of empathic understanding for Smolensk women who consorted with Germans, Shneiderman pictured any such relationship as voluntary self-subordination. She was particularly bitter about Galina Fokina, an eighteen-year-old former Komsomol member in the city. Trying to win her over, Shneiderman invoked the name of the Soviet pilot Valentina Grizodubova and her appeal to both the women of the world and the partisans. This was Shneiderman's way of raising the topic of resistance and female heroes. Grizodubova, born in 1909, became famous in 1939 as the captain of an all-female crew that broke aviation distance and speed records with a twenty-six-hour flight from Moscow to Komsomol'sk-na-Amure in the Soviet Far East. She was particularly revered by the younger women of the 1930s generation, who yearned to follow in her footsteps. In response, Fokina merely branded the partisans as "bandits" who robbed the civilian population. "When in front of us a German propagandized the destruction of the Jews as a lower race, saying that all evil stems from the Jews, she fully agreed with him and could not find anything else to say except pronounce, 'Ah, those kikes [*Akh eti zhidy*].'" Shneiderman's words conveyed a degree of bewilderment: "[This] was spoken by a child of October, who studied for 10 years in a Soviet school."[64]

Like other assimilated Jews fully committed to the Soviet project,
Shneiderman gave no hint of a specifically Jewish as opposed to Soviet
identity. She even appeared open to the merging of Russian and Soviet
patriotism advancing in the USSR since the 1930s when she referred to
"our Russians" and to the ruins of Smolensk, "an ancient and beautiful
Russian city." Yet there was nothing like living among Nazis to remind
Shneiderman of her own Jewishness. She devoted more space to popular
antisemitism than any of the other eyewitnesses. Rumors spread among
Smolensk's Russian population, she reported, about large amounts of food
supposedly found in the starving ghetto after its Jewish inhabitants were
killed.[65] Shneiderman's fury appears representative of many Jewish survivors of varied backgrounds.

When Shneiderman spoke of German men and Russian women, she revealed the link between sex and conquest that made this issue so explosive
for her and so many others. She too recounted episodes of rampant, brazen
sexual harassment by Germans in the workplace. An eighteen-year-old co-
worker in her canteen kitchen, Tamara, for example, refused to give herself to the fifty-year-old German cook and was fired. When the same cook
made Shneiderman a gift of chocolate, hoping to meet her after work, she
retorted: "Russian girls do not sell themselves for chocolate." But Shneiderman was forced to admit that her defiant declaration had in fact been
false: "They sell themselves to the Fritzes, and the Fritzes mock and hu-
miliate our girls. When they meet a Russian girl for the first time these
coarse, impudent Fritzes make gestures for them to go sleep with them [*itti
s nimi spat'*]." Shneiderman overheard a German officer tell a Russian
young woman that she would find work conditions excellent if she would
also sleep with him. In Shneiderman's rendition of her response, she boldly
intervened to deliver a stinging rebuke: "In our army no rank-and-file soldier, not to mention a commander, would allow himself to speak so un-
ceremoniously to a girl—come sleep with me. It is just uncultured."[66] It is
possible Shneiderman was unaware of the widespread Red Army officer
practices of picking "mobile field wives" (*pokhodno-polevye zheny*) from the
ranks of their own subordinates, a practice so widespread it was known by
its acronym (*ppzh*). Early on in the war, the issue had been downplayed
by party and army authorities, but not the Komsomol. Did Shneiderman
retrospectively present her exchange with the officer in a way that turned
her into a fearless defender of Soviet culture? We cannot know.

In the Soviet context, the claim to culturedness implied superiority. In Shneiderman's depiction, the European, so often seen in both Russia and the USSR as culturally advanced, was revealed as the barbarian. The officer reacted only with amused contempt, and it is this incredulity that gives Shneiderman's account the ring of truth: "He laughed and answered me: you should not even speak about culture, you need 100–200 years to even reach the level of German culture. I said to him that we do not even strive to reach German culture, because Germany has become an uncultured country."[67] Soviet culturedness had collided with German *Kultur*. The argument between the Komsomol activist and the Wehrmacht officer quickly turned from the treatment of Russian women to the German-Soviet contest over civilizational superiority.

"More a Soldier in a Skirt than a Woman"

"We wanted to get rid of Dolgonenkov," wrote Elena Mironovaia, a prewar instructor in the regional Komsomol. The act of revenge Shneiderman and the entire underground Komsomol in Smolensk would have loved to carry out more than any other was the assassination of Konstantin Dolgonenkov. Highly prominent on the radio and as editor in chief of the Smolensk newspaper, renamed from the *Workers' Path* to the *New Path* (*Novyi put'*), Dolgonenkov was a principal Russian-language political propagandist during the occupation. What enraged Shneiderman and the underground was that he had been a well-known Komsomol poet, member of the Smolensk Regional Union of Writers, and professional journalist before the war. With no weapons or training, they never succeeded—unlike Mariia Osipova, trained by the NKVD and Soviet military intelligence, who carried out the spectacular assassination of Wilhelm Kube, the Reichskommissar of Weissruthenien in Minsk on September 22, 1943. Shneiderman was left only to mock Dolgonenkov's "little newspaper" for its absurd lies about the "Judeo-Bolshevik yoke," singling him out as a "talentless scoundrel" (*bezdarnaia svoloch'*).[68]

In fact, the experienced propagandist ran a rather professional operation. In the pages of *New Path* and other wartime publications, *Kultur* and Germany's advanced economic system were portrayed as beneficial to Russians. The "woman question" was also alive and well. Many of the same issues that preoccupied Madziuk and Shneiderman, and what the role of women implied about Russia / the USSR's relationship with "cultured" Europe, were also addressed by Smolensk's pro-German commentators. For example, two front-page commentaries in *New Path* in February and May 1942, unsigned but possibly written by Dolgonenkov, sharply criticized Soviet positions. The first, "Woman and Her Rights," began with the issue of the Soviet "double burden," about which Madziuk and Shneiderman never spoke. Because Soviet women could not choose to stay at home, Soviet promises of equal rights were worthless. Previously, women were slaves of men; now, Soviet women were simply slaves, not to their husbands but to the Soviet state. The second article, "Rebirth of the Russian Woman," criticized the Soviet system for forcing women to work and now to fight. The Soviet system impoverished them, while the German new order would satisfy their consumerist desires (in the bright future, presumably). "Girls want to dress better," it argued, not to save up for months for "some sort of Soviet junk."[69]

Occupation press criticisms of the false nature of Soviet equality for women actually appeared to champion a genuine parity that supposedly would arrive under the German-led new order—a boldly distorted sleight of hand. At the same time, the articles also upheld the fundamental tenet of the Nazi German gender order, that biological difference made for different roles for men and women that must not be defiled. The "highest appointment for a woman is her motherly duties" and the "real calling of woman is the family," the Viazma newspaper *New Era* insisted in 1942. The German form of gender equality was supposedly realized in separate but equal spheres. *New Path* condemned the mixing of gender roles that was the source of the greatest scorn and anxiety in the Nazi German context: "The new type of woman Communist resembles more a soldier in a skirt than a woman."[70] The discourse on women articulated by Russian collaborators in the stunted wartime public sphere created around local Smolensk media paid homage to Nazi German orthodoxies and sharply condemned Soviet positions. But by touting equality, it also reflected a noticeable assimilation of the Soviet experience.

If Madziuk and Shneiderman concluded that German brutality and ignorance were a prime reason to invert Germany's high place on the cultural gradient, the Viazma publication called for Russians not to "catch up and overtake" the West, as in the Stalin-era slogan, but to seize the chance Germany was offering to actually join "the great family of peoples of

Europe." The Nazi racial hierarchy, conveniently, went unmentioned in this condemnation of Soviet lack of culture (*bezkul'tur'e*). Combining a quintessential Soviet concept with anti-Soviet religiosity, the article ended with the exhortation to "purge ourselves spiritually" (*ochistit'sia dukhovno*).[71]

Shorn Women and "German Bedding"

In France after the defeat of the German occupiers, approximately twenty thousand women accused of collaborating were subject to a twentieth-century descendant of the charivari, a folk ritual of shaming wrongdoers, including adulterous women, that stretched back to medieval times. In public, facing large and hostile crowds, women's heads were shaved. No court sentenced them. The vast majority of these *femmes tondues,* or "shorn women," were not political collaborators; their crime was sexual relations with German men. Humiliation rituals or beatings expressing popular rage took place in other parts of Central and Western Europe, too. No directive or ruling existed, of course, defining sex as an act of collaboration. Prostitutes were considered "professionals" and treated leniently, and shorn women were also targeted for their political sympathies or collaborationist activities. As Fabrice Virgili pointed out in *Shorn Women,* the classic work on the topic, these violent and collective acts of public vengeance were always carried out by men. The outrage about consorting with representatives of the conquering power concealed "innumerable daily acts of cowardice": the flood of denunciations the French had made to German authorities during Vichy. Stigmatizing sexual collaborators with shears and scissors allowed people to "move from a position of being victims of violence to one where they inflicted it, and thereby reasserted their patriotic identity."[72]

A very different dynamic played out in Smolensk and occupied Soviet territories. When there were reprisals against "horizontal collaborators," they were often far more severe than shaving heads. Upon liberation of occupied areas, NKVD and SMERSH operatives swept in with wide leeway to arrest those considered dangerous traitors to the Motherland. While we have more to learn about how women associated with Germans were sometimes caught up in these repressions, there are many known cases in which they were sent to the Gulag. Wide variations in the timing and severity of those reprisals between the war years and late 1940s, however, suggest that much depended on how local party authorities and the secret police approached the issue. Sometimes no action was taken at all; in other locales, women were sentenced to forced labor, exiled, accused of moral crimes or prostitution, or fired from jobs. The crucial point is that generally these were not, as in France, instances of popular or public retribution. They were administrative, political, police, and sometimes judicial actions carried out by armed representatives of the Red Army and the party-state in reestablishing Soviet power.[73]

In the Stalinist context, the fact that women slept with fascists or Germans specifically was actually not the primary concern. The crucial consideration was the political implications of the sexual act: intimate relations with any foreigners were a sign of disloyalty and unreliability. Only this can explain the fact that, during the war, women involved with British and US sailors in Arkhangel'sk and US airmen in Poltava—at the time allies, not enemies—were subject to hostile suspicion and, in the former case, exile and harsh repression. Soviet reprisals during and after the war were heavily shaped by the 1930s model of Soviet repressive practices, in which identification of "socially alien elements" reinforced the longtime linkage between social profile and political-ideological loyalty. Since the punishments of the state were determined and carried out by its representatives on the ground—who appropriated their own slice of power—public perceptions about the comportment of women were not necessarily the decisive factor. In France, by contrast, it was the very ostentatiousness or public nature of French women's attachment to Germans that most frequently made them targets of public shaming.

Why was the popular response in Smolensk and other occupied territories so different than in France? Popular anger certainly existed, and emotions also ran high. Young Russian women who worked in German institutions or who socialized with German or Axis soldiers and had sexual relations with them were insulted with names such as "German bedding" and "German shepherd." However, spontaneous public action had become virtually unthinkable under Stalinism.[74]

Aleksandr Solzhenitsyn, as he wrote in his magnum opus *The Gulag Archipelago,* was familiar with the popular condemnation of "horizontal collaboration" from his time in the advancing Red Army, where he served as a twice-decorated officer. He also witnessed Red Army soldiers carry out mass rapes in East Prussia, which had their own set of multiple motivations—including tacit military and political approval from above, conquest, and rage at German prosperity. Additionally, Soviet mass rapes were intended as acts of punishment and revenge in response to German brothels, rapes, and humiliation of Soviet women, which were all trumpeted in the Soviet press. Solzhenitsyn wrote about the incarceration in the Gulag of Soviet women who had consorted with the enemy, specifically in the women's camp division in Mine 2 in Vorkuta. Epithets such as "German bedding" were used against them, he claimed, and came as much from Soviet women as from men. He enumerated many reasons, including hunger, that women in wartime may have entered into relations with foreign soldiers, but noted widespread postwar approval of condemnation: "We hear the words 'German bedstraw' and nod in agreement." The presence of these women in the camps ironically meant that supposedly emancipated Soviet women were told "your body is, first and foremost, the property of the Fatherland." The dissident writer preferred his audience to confront a different question: "What was it in *us* that made the occupying troops much more attractive to our women?"[75]

Stalin-era anathemas, in the end, extended not only to open discussions of sexuality but to any open consideration of the gray zones of morality and behavior of all those left behind when the Soviets evacuated. The stigma of occupation spread steadily to encompass entire populations that had lived under German rule, and not just certain women. The civilian population itself knew all about extreme material and caloric deprivation. Some may have preferred to cast the first stone if given the opportunity, but they were in no position to do so. On the Eastern Front, the extent of the violence and hardship was such that its trauma, in the midst of a transition back to Soviet rule, was handled very often by repression, suppression, and taboo.

Madziuk, Shneiderman, and the other young women of the Smolensk Komsomol underground expressed different levels of empathy and anger at German soldiers and the young women of Smolensk. But they were united in their loyalty to a Soviet Union that they believed gave them freedom to pursue traditionally male occupations, condemned nationalism and antisemitism, and abhorred overt degradation of women. Many of their Komsomol reports treating those values as axiomatically Soviet, in a bitter historical irony, were addressed to Aleksandr Shelepin, then secretary of the Komsomol Central Committee.

Shelepin was promoted to that post in 1943 after he came to Stalin's attention for his underground work recruiting youth to the partisan movement, including the famous Soviet martyr Zoia Kozmodemianskaia, whom Stalin selected as the heroine of a massive propaganda campaign. Building on ideological shifts within Stalinism in 1943–1945, Shelepin became leader of a group of hard-line apparatchiki from the wartime generation that assumed prominence in the era of the postwar anti-cosmopolitan campaign. These *shelepintsy* drove the emergence of a "Russian party" in late Stalinism and after, which injected elements of Russian nationalism and, for the first time, open antisemitism into communist ideology.[76] The brave young Soviet women of the underground participated in the debate over culture and civilization to deflect and counter the brute force of military and sexual conquest. What they assumed to be the bedrock of the Soviet order was crumbling beneath their feet.

9

SOVIET POWER RETURNS

A PERSONABLE MAN IN HIS MID-TWENTIES arrived in destroyed and hungry Smolensk on June 12, 1944. He had two thousand rubles in his pocket next to a party card and a clutch of medals from the defense of Stalingrad. Once again the seat of Soviet power in the region, Smolensk had been liberated by the Red Army in an offensive operation lasting from August to October 1943. The Regional Party Committee had set up in the city center, bringing along an influx of party-state officials and high-priority construction workers. Huge quantities of rubble were cleared with manual labor, and reconstruction funds were flowing from Moscow. But after eight thousand of Smolensk's nine thousand buildings were destroyed by the time of the German retreat, there was still no electricity or telephone service. Bread shortages were common, and only two reliable sources of water were available for the whole city. For an exhausted population hoping German defeat might lead to a better time, instead poverty, hardship, and hunger were the order of the day.[1]

But for the restored party and secret police officials in the provincial capital, feting a top fighter ace and hero of Stalingrad was exactly what they needed. Between June 12 and August 13, Pavel Golovachev made radio addresses, gave newspaper interviews, and launched into a whirlwind of meetings with leading workers and decorated partisans. At a banquet in his honor on July 23, he mingled with top regional elites. Several of them had already become his friends and drinking partners.

The only problem was that the Hero of the Soviet Union was actually a two-time deserter and, it turned out, a very talented con man. His real name was P. T. Matveenko, and he was born in 1918, a year after his mark. He was also an officer and a pilot, but after crashing a plane he deserted to escape the sentence of a military tribunal. He fled to Moscow, where he befriended his fellow aviator Golovachev. Three days before he arrived in Smolensk, Matveenko robbed Golovachev of his medals, party card, documents, and money.[2]

In Smolensk that summer, the swindler used his celebrity status to wander Regional Party Committee and secret police headquarters without proper ID, taking meals at the cafeteria for leading cadres. Although every high-level party meeting of this period was punctuated by ominous warnings by secret police officials about vigilance and infiltration, friendly top officials had the imposter fitted for suits, paid a stipend, and supplied like a member of the *nomenklatura*. Matveenko frequented the apartment and drove the car of an NKVD colonel who headed the military procuracy for NKVD troops in the Smolensk Region, a certain Vasil'ev. Matveenko went on fishing trips with his new drinking partners in the secret police. He even got engaged to Vasil'ev's daughter Zoia.[3]

The NKVD remained silent about how the imposter was exposed in August. But an investigation revealed that he had already been sentenced for desertion to ten years in the Gulag by a military tribunal. It was not only the secret police leadership that was fooled. After the banquet, regional party first secretary Dmitrii Popov invited him to a dacha vacation with the region's top officials.[4]

Impersonating Heroes of the Soviet Union was a wartime variant on political identity theft. But such high-profile cases and professional con men, as well as the brisk market for forged internal passports, were the proverbial tip of the iceberg. Imposture was a large-scale feature of Soviet life in part because there was so much to gain in conditions of endemic shortages, ideological and bureaucratic rigidity, and social turmoil. Il'ia Il'f and Evgenii Petrov's satires, with their celebrated anti-hero Ostap Bender, were still sanctioned in the 1940s. The fictional "great schemer" appeared compelling and entrepreneurial, modifying his names with comical frequency. In reality, the scale and success of imposture stemmed from the fact that the illegal "shadow economy" paralleled and intersected with legal state-run structures, and *nomenklatura* elites were active in both. Political imposture mimicked and exploited official ideological and cultural norms, just as the shadow economy fed off state economic structures.[5]

The turmoil of the Civil War and the Great Break were, if anything, matched or exceeded in a place like bombed-out Smolensk, and this led to a spike in forged identities. In the city of Smolensk before 1945, the prewar party-state elite was off fighting, killed, or dispersed: of 1,037 members of the prewar District and City Party Committees, only 178 were present after Soviet power was reestablished. Over twenty thousand new appointments around the region by February 1945 came from an influx of cadres sent from the Soviet interior, thousands of returnees from the 1941 evacuation, and new recruits. This steady turnover continued for at least three full years. Like other imposters, Matveenko audaciously acted his role by tapping into Stalinism's worship of decorated, titled, and hyperbolically overachieving heroes. "Control over the selection of cadres" was so lax and chaotic, regional NKVD chief Aleksei Pechenkin predicted just months before Matveenko pulled off his spectacular scam, that "it is not at all impossible that our institutions will be filled with people like Ostap Bender of Il'f and Petrov's *Golden Calf*."[6] The dilemmas of restoring Soviet power in 1943 were far from all about retribution, anti-fascism, and political restoration. They were also deeply embedded in the Soviet economic order and its primary beneficiaries, the Stalinist new elite.

Rubble

At the outset of re-Sovietization in October 1943, the overall population of Smolensk Region had plummeted more than half, from 1.98 million in the 1939 census to 983,000. In the immediate aftermath of 1943 battles, the urban population had shrunk by over seven times its former size to a mere 50,000. Popov tallied up the extent of the devastation to infrastructure for the Smolensk Regional Party Committee on December 23, 1943. A total of twelve cities and thirteen district center towns had been mostly destroyed along with all 236 electrical stations, 1,491 miles of railways, and the entire telephone and telegraph network. Of 900 enterprises, 870 were destroyed. Approximately 300,000 civilians had been killed and as many as 200,000 deported to forced labor in Germany. Several districts, including

Civilians leaving Viazma during the German evacuation, 1943, Yad Vashem Photo Archive, Jerusalem. 7904/254.

Iartsevskii, Prechistenskii, Slobodskii, and four others, had been depopulated by 70–80 percent. About 400,000 citizens were homeless. A half year later, in June 1944, an estimated 25,000 were still living in earthen dugouts, with twice that number crammed into a hut with two to three families.

Statistics about infrastructure, of course, told only part of the story. Depopulation, absence of adult males, a dismantled educational system, migrations and high levels of labor desertion, and a catastrophic food situation all figured in reports from late 1943 and 1944. As in the Civil War, "bagmen" from Moscow roamed the area buying up produce and selling finished goods as soon as the railway connection was restored. Crime and moonshine production shot up.[7]

Ideological "contamination" and acute personnel shortages after two years of fascist rule were, therefore, only a fraction of the dire problems faced by those charged with restoring Soviet power. Many economic crimes were simply a function of restoring the planned economy, insofar as it made markets illegal. Yet the regional-level NKVD was preoccupied with elaborate corruption schemes, many involving falsified documents. Pechenkin detailed cases of interlopers from other areas with false identities working with trade organizations or in the distribution system in order to siphon off state goods on a significant scale.[8]

In 1943, the wartime reliance on bonuses and material incentives began to be portrayed as quasi-corrupt, a sign of heightened official awareness of endemic corruption and weakened institutions in the USSR as a whole. With monumental crises in housing, food, and transportation, Smolensk created rich soil for shadow activities. More fundamentally, Soviet entrepreneurial behavior, always needing to successfully navigate the cumbersome, bureaucratic Soviet system, had increasingly entrenched itself in practices of self-enrichment.[9]

Carrots and Sticks

Popov now faced the greatest challenge of his career. The man who had become the party first secretary of the Smolensk Region on the eve of war, now additionally tasked with heading the Smolensk City Party Committee, was born in 1900 into a peasant family in Tambov. Popov had been rotated into Smolensk as second secretary of the Regional Party Committee in 1939, moving up into the top slot in 1940—the period when the Party was being bolstered in the wake of its decimation during the Great Terror. He fit the profile of young, postwar provincial first secretaries whose careers took off when they filled the gap created by the Terror. Most of them were in their thirties and products of the Stalinist 1930s. Slightly less than half were promoted to their positions on the eve of war, the rest during the war years.[10]

Popov was shaped by three formative experiences: war, the Stalinist 1930s, and the party system of education and propaganda. Unlike many postwar first secretaries who served at the front as military officers or political commissars, Popov had received his military experience much earlier, on the Civil War's Southern Front. Even so, unlike many, he never adopted a truly militarized disposition, and this can be attributed to the rest of his background. Unlike so many politically and socially promoted cadres, Popov did not get his start with rapid-fire engineering courses and the Stalinist school of industrial politics. As befitted the future head of a rural area, Popov spent collectivization in three districts in the Central Black Earth Region and went on to train as a rural economist at the

Institute of Red Professors' Agrarian Institute in 1933–1936. Popov was no cadre of violence. He weathered the purge years as a specialist on Leninism at the Central Committee's Higher School of Propagandists. In the end, always more the persuader than the stereotypical, boss-like bully of the 1930s, Popov by nature gravitated more toward the carrot than the stick. A critical dossier prepared on him in 1947 judged him "more of a teacher than an organizer" who was "insufficiently tough and hands-on."[11]

Popov was neither as flamboyant nor as ruthless as the Old Bolshevik Ivan Rumiantsev, Smolensk's original "little Stalin" until his fall in 1937. The war had led to cyclical change in the perennial Soviet seesaw between ideologues and pragmatists, so that while the battles raged and reconstruction loomed it became geared more toward results. These were times of stark alternatives: either the fascists would be defeated or they would destroy you; either infrastructure would be restored quickly or it would remain in ruins. Under late Stalinism, there would be yet another turn of the wheel toward the primacy of ideology, as the anti-cosmopolitan campaign and the Doctor's Plot coincided with the incipient Cold War.

Throughout these shifts, the Stalinist system of power relations remained recognizably in place. Popov, the man Moscow held responsible for reconstruction, was as reliant on the middle level of power, the District Party Committees, as he had been in the prewar period. As much as ever, the Regional Party Committee swamped the lower levels with orders and resolutions, but Popov admitted there was "no systematic accounting about whether the decisions [were] fulfilled." The District Party Committees, in turn, continued to possess too few levers of influence over the very local level and, ensconced in the towns and district centers, did not pay much attention to it. Popov accused officials of ignoring the primary unit of economic production in the countryside, the collective farm. Anyone listening to Popov attempting to hector and cajole in his speeches to party officials and activists between 1943 and 1945 would have been forgiven for wondering whether the German occupation had changed very much at all.[12]

The return of Soviet power signaled an uncanny resurrection of the regional system of power relations. Comrade Shul'ts, first secretary of the Gzhatskii District Party Committee, perpetuated the hoary tradition of inverting the criticism by blaming the higher level, the Regional Party Committee. "I consider it my obligation to note that the Regional

Party Committee leadership, even now, makes the mistake of barraging the District Party Committees with every kind of telegram on questions large and small . . . You get 5–6 telegrams a day and don't know which one to address."[13] Despite all the changes war had brought, the structural antagonisms and dysfunctional relations among the levels of Soviet power—central, regional, district, and local—were, as if set in amber, preserved from the prewar era.

Popov, in the face of the broad-based devastation of his region, was forced to rely on the same elite that had happily bestowed its privileges on the imposter Matveenko—an emergent ruling class that itself was a regular patron of the black market. Over one thousand leading officials from thirty regional organizations charged with rebuilding the economy were crowded into one central hotel in downtown Smolensk, Popov railed in September 1943. They spent two hours a day at the canteen and quit work early, using lack of electricity and telephones as an excuse. "Is this really work, comrades?" But at this moment of serious need, it was possible to push the privileged regional elite only so far. Party officials, he ended plaintively, did not get their hands dirty organizing, preferring to issue commands "on paper." Somewhat heretically, the first secretary went so far as to complain that Smolensk citizens who had worked hard under German rule were now lazing around eating "white bread" and complaining about the lack of vodka. The exasperated Popov was implying that without coercion the Soviet system was unable to motivate sufficiently, either by incentive or by mobilization.[14]

Popov, like all regional party first secretaries, did wield the usual pressure points of cadre department dossiers, compromising material (*kompromat*), and patronage. But nothing could get around the fact that Popov was reliant on a ruling stratum that was invested in a lifestyle, even in the chaos and ruin of war, that was vastly elevated above the ordinary people it was tasked with motivating. The scandal of the imposter Matveenko cracked open a window into the lifestyle and privileges of the Stalinist new elite: the apartments and the dachas, the special canteens and clothes, the accessibility of scarce automobiles and weapons, and everything else the swindler had enjoyed that summer.

Popov, although he could not have known it, was living through a hinge period in the history of the Soviet regional elite. The *nomenklatura*, not fully secure in its positions and hence privileges until after the Thaw, certainly did not rest easy so soon after the Terror. But the beneficiaries of the purges were never subjected to the kind of political decimation that occurred in 1937, nor was the secret police empowered over them in the same way. In the far more stable postwar period, the new party elite became distinctly less revolutionary as the social and political hierarchy of the regions stabilized.[15]

Fundamentally, Popov could scarcely address the deeper forces at play in shaping how Soviet rule was restored. In most ways, the regional first secretary was merely following as best he could a recipe he did not invent for restoring Soviet power. One influential factor in 1943, and a window into how the most essential features of the socialist order were defined in practice, was the model of re-Sovietization established in the eastern districts of Smolensk in early 1942.

The First Re-Sovietizations

First came the Red Army. Five eastern districts of the Smolensk Region— Dzerzhinskii, Il'inskii, Kozel'skii, Medynskii, and Meshchovskii, as well as slices of fourteen others recaptured by the end of 1941—were now to undergo, as Popov reported on December 26 to Georgii Malenkov in the latter's capacity as Central Committee secretary, the "work of restoring the Soviet order and economy." Local residents "warmly greeted their liberator-warriors, commanders, and political workers in the Red Army," offering drink, rest, and "active aid to the special organs to uncover traitors to the Motherland." Joyous public welcomes of "our own" would be repeated in 1943 and in 1944 in Belarus, and small wonder.[16] They came after an intense wave of German atrocities. The sheer depth of intentional devastation seemed to shock even party officials in their first reports and, when immediately publicized across the Soviet home front, became a major factor in rallying the population in the rear. But few locals would have forgotten that the Wehrmacht had initially been widely greeted with bread and salt.

Popov's caveats to the celebratory theme of patriotic reunification came, as it were, not in the headline but in the footnotes. Among the materials Popov forwarded to Malenkov was a report from the secretary of the Medynskii District Party Committee detailing Red Army "outrages" against the locals, including "chaotic misappropriation" by "individual troops" of large amounts of precious seed grain and horses. Red Army mass rape and looting in Germany and Europe is well known, but depredations against the Soviet population on Soviet soil, which began at the start of the war, remain virtually unstudied.[17]

A second caveat came from the voices of the liberated that surveillance uncovered for the Party. For example, one letter perlustrated by the NKVD and distributed through party channels came from a woman working in the Troitskaia factory in the town of Kondrovo, the administrative center of Dzerzhinskii District (in 1944 transferred from Smolensk to Kaluzhskaia Region). Its lack of punctuation hardly prevented G. A. Krivenkova from expressing her anger and trauma:

> People here have suffered terribly, we have survived a horrible amount . . . Unlucky is he who has been occupied too much has been necessary to live through in this cursed time, it is hard to forget, but how to forget when everywhere you get a rebuke for working for the Germans, but how are we guilty, we were cast away and they only said save yourself as you can and everyone drove off somewhere, but to leave you needed money, and they didn't even pay us wages owed, we were left to die, but death took pity on us and passed us by.[18]

Krivenkova's home, Dzerzhinskii District, was fully in Red Army hands on January 19, 1942, after a three-and-a-half-month occupation. By the end of January, district party-state authorities were reporting Dzerzhinskii District "completely purged" of the fascist occupation. One of the two highest Soviet priorities that month was inventory. Long before the first steps to establish the Extraordinary State Commission on Nazi Crimes, which started only at the end of 1942, practices of immediately compiling an inventory of human and economic losses were launched jointly by Red Army officers, party-state officials, and the NKVD. All of them were reliant on the aggrieved local population for information. Contacting and canvasing locals willing to cooperate, whatever their motivation, became crucial both for documenting atrocities and for identifying collaborators.[19]

The other Soviet priority was purge. The regional NKVD chief expressed the goal of "total cleansing of the [liberated] districts of enemy elements." The key question, of course, was how exactly to define and punish enemies. The mood among newly appointed District Party Committee secretaries was vengeful, especially against former party comrades who had collaborated: "We must take the most decisive measures up to and including physical destruction, while there still is the possibility—[given] the absence of juridical organs [*laughter in the hall*]."[20]

The NKVD, with only four officials and ten operatives on the ground in these eastern districts when re-Sovietization began, was itself scrambling to reestablish its own "apparat" and informant networks. Petr Kondakov, the Smolensk regional NKVD chief at the time, outlined the methods used in these initial sweeps of the reconquered districts, which were repeated in 1943. In this eastern slice of Smolensk Region between January and March, 1942, the NKVD arrested 1,136 as spies and traitors, 240 as policemen for the Germans, 321 as anti-Soviet, and 575 as working for the Germans—this last category was usually applied to those who directly aided the German war effort or occupation regime. More than half, 621 of them, were sent to be tried by military tribunals. Forty of the arrested collaborators were former Communists. Over 800 more remained under investigation.[21]

While NKVD chief Kondakov, predictably, bandied about the hard-line goal of "uncovering and exterminating" all traitors, a number of party officials were more pragmatic, even blaming the Party for poor prewar preparation and chaotic evacuation. Unsurprisingly, the officials advocating relative moderation were those now responsible for the daunting tasks of reconstruction. Given acute shortages of badly needed categories of workers, including physicians, teachers, and agronomists, the purity of the NKVD's categorical hard line was impossible to maintain.[22] These early divergences were the harbinger of maneuvering and compromises for several years to come.

A Recipe for Restoration

The priorities in Popov's reports from 1942 reveal much about the formula for re-Sovietization. In his December 26, 1941, report to Malenkov, he flagged the very first issue as propaganda and "political-mass" work, that is, blanketing the districts with tens of thousands of copies of the regional newspapers and brochures with Stalin's speeches. Another issue was triage in the realms of infrastructure, economic institutions, and transportation. This included satisfying the "basic needs" of the "workers"—hospitals, social and sanitary services such as bathhouses, and, in particular, "cultural-enlightenment institutions." The Soviet commitment to culture and welfare was a distinct priority in the guise of schools and libraries, movie houses, and "houses of socialist culture," which were among the first pieces of infrastructure to be rebuilt. The final issue Popov flagged to Malenkov was the identification of traitors, including the hot-button topic of Communist Party members who had betrayed the Motherland.[23]

Even amid horrific devastation, the Soviet order privileged ideology, culture, and propaganda to such a degree that it was impossible not to include them among the highest priorities during wartime restoration. The head of the Political Department of the Sixteenth Army spearheaded cultural initiatives, including concerts and film screenings in the districts. The contrast with fascism was clear: "With special glee they destroyed cultural institutions. Dumb and cruel, they hate culture and science—they drive out schools, turn theaters and museums into stables, burn libraries, and destroy the monuments of history, culture, and art that are dear to the Soviet people."[24]

After 1945 and 1947 when the Sovietization of Eastern Europe was launched, the replication of a recognizably communist system, despite very significant national and historical variations, advanced despite the absence of a master plan. Instead, deep-seated assumptions on the part of the Sovietizers were reinforced by the interlocking logic of an all-encompassing Soviet system.[25] Even when Soviet power was not exported abroad but put back in place in the Russian heartland, it is the unstated assumptions of actors such as Popov that stand out. For example, he spoke of all "organizational and political work" in the same breath, regularly tacking back and forth among economic, political, and ideological-cultural institutions. It was precisely the checklist of the quantifiable that was key, whether it be number of economic or cultural-enlightenment institutions or the number of cadres.[26]

There was also much that Popov perforce left out. While maintaining that housing, child homelessness, and "care for the population" were exceptionally important for the party organization, he admitted almost in passing that the districts re-Sovietized starting in early 1942 had no light industry at all. "Not one functioning enterprise of the Commissariat of Light Industry exists in our region, not one shoe factory, not one clothes factory. There are plans, conversations, but none have materialized in a year and a half." Production and politics, even more than ever during the wartime emergency, had completely dominated over consumption.[27]

In a rural area like Smolensk, the restoration of Soviet power was deeply shaped by the peasantry and agriculture. Popov, the former agrarian red professor, grappled with restoring a collective farm system that had been deeply altered by spontaneous decollectivization and German reordering of the countryside. Every one of Popov's pronouncements on agriculture after 1943 related to what had transpired under the Germans in different parts of the region. To understand what he faced in the countryside, we first consider what German rule had changed.

Legacies of the "Agrarian New Order"

Vasilii Kozubskii, the schoolteacher turned Yelnya partisan commander, mentor of the young partisan striver Andrei Iudenkov, refused to flee with most local party officials when the Germans approached Smolensk. Son of a landless peasant from Volhynia, Kozubskii joined the Komsomol in 1922, rising up as a school administrator and joining the Party in 1939. For a brief time in 1941, Kozubskii headed a group of collective farms in the very same territory he liberated in 1942 when he became a rare intelligentsia partisan commander. Kozubskii left some of the most insightful extant observations on the spontaneous decollectivization of agriculture he witnessed when Soviet power collapsed in 1941.

The local peasants Kozubskii observed were intrigued by German propaganda promising land and freedom. The peasants who pushed for decollectivization, including those the Germans named as elders, at first started the division of property in small ways. Given shortages of common feed for horses, for example, they divided the horses up with the argument that otherwise the animals would perish. Once the horses were divided, it meant hay would be too. Soon, in Kozubskii's immediate locality, "the countryside was seized by a fever." Everything in the collective farm was put up for division. Even that group of peasants inclined to preserve the collective farms "came into the orbit of the division and was included in it."[28] Decollectivization came from below. But this was no peasant revolution, as in the mass seizure of noble land in 1917. The German new regime, prioritizing easier food requisitioning for its army, forestalled any full dismemberment of the collective farms.

"Do not carry out an arbitrary division of land!" German propaganda in the countryside screamed.[29] Even so, rural disillusionment with the new overlords came slowly. While the familiar, Soviet brand of internal colonization still evoked much resentment in the countryside early in the war, it took time before disillusionment with German racial colonization set in.

The net result of the period of German occupation was a significant setback to the Soviet collective farm system. Local patterns of decollectivization, as well as how far the long-promised German "land reform" was taken in 1942 and 1943, varied greatly depending on the inclinations of local Germans and the dynamics of local peasant communities. Even in some districts neighboring Kozubskii's, the division of kolkhoz property was far less widespread than the schoolmaster turned partisan witnessed in his area.[30]

In other words, what Kozubskii described was a complex process, spurred on but hardly completely controlled by the regime change, within a conflict-ridden rural population. Rural communities, despite internal conflicts, could still act as part of a discernable rural ecosystem. Peasant solidarity cohered or fractured depending on the situation. The triumph of the "private tendency," Kozubskii observed, led directly into all sorts of new disputes over how kolkhoz property was divided.[31]

Alfred Rosenberg's New Agrarian Order, proclaimed with a propaganda blitz and a flurry of decrees in February 1942, for the most part preserved collective farms under a new name—"communal" farms—while holding out two more stages to turn agriculture into individual landholding. The whole process on the German side formed part of the more general "tug-of-war" between those pushing concessions for a viable occupation and others speaking the language of merciless exploitation. These hard-liners included not just the usual Nazi leaders but top agrarian policymakers, such as food policy chief Herbert Backe and his assistant, SS-Gruppenführer Hans-Joachim Riecke. In Smolensk, Russian-language decrees from spring 1942 reinforced the obvious: deliveries to the military were sacrosanct. Military authorities set them according to "local circumstances"—a flexible and capricious formulation that deliberately carved out rewards for collaborators and anti-partisans. It fell to ex-Soviet professionals, the agronomists, to play the key role of adjudicating disputes.[32]

The German land reform did create a flurry of activity and significant changes. In the Smolensk Region, there is evidence that the land devoted to private or household plots within the renamed communal farms doubled. But the second stage of "reform" stalled, the third stage of individual landholding even more so. In Smolensk, the result was a middle ground between the Russian northwest under Army Group North, where there was a uniquely widespread implementation of the last stage of individual plots and relaxed taxation in 1943, and the harsh requisitioning in Reichskommissariat Ukraine under the brutal Erich Koch.[33]

Comparative Exploitation

During the occupation, Popov was closely watching the loud German promises and slow-walked implementation in the Smolensk Region, which he had presided over before the war. In a top-secret October 1942 report, Popov captured the strong element of German instrumentalism when he called the agrarian new order nothing more than an effort to capitalize on the "private-property tendencies of the peasantry." He rightly asserted that "the Germans have not succeeded in gaining full control of agriculture," and he was spot on in emphasizing that a year of unrealized German promises had inflamed peasant skepticism to "all these 'new orders,' 'laws,' and 'resolutions.'" But the party functionary was doctrinaire in describing all of German policy as relying on "kulak elements" and tendentious when positing the complete anti-German disillusionment of the "predominant mass of the kolkhoz peasantry."[34]

Popov's "class analysis" omitted something taboo even in a top-secret document: an assessment of the actual levels of German agricultural requisitioning and, above all, how those compared with Soviet extractive practices. Peasants, by contrast, were acutely aware of this all-important metric of rural exploitation under German and Soviet rule. To the Solidarist Aleksandr Kazantsev, who visited the countryside around Smolensk, it was not even close. "In comparison to the 'worker-peasant' state," he wrote in his 1952 memoirs, "the Germans were downright dilettantes in the art of plundering the countryside." Kazantsev was no agrarian expert, and his journalistic writing was prone to sweeping political exaggerations. But the well-known quotation does vividly evoke how a combination of peasant subterfuge and German incapacity made the German rear administration in the Russian countryside feel less onerous than the Stalinist collective farm system.[35]

Agronomists with more expertise described a complex situation with numerous local particularities. Peasants opposed divisions that bypassed traditional calculations about the number of household "eaters," and German economic administrators tried to block increasing those household plots not subject to the military taxation. One non-party agronomist credited harsh requisitioning and casual violence in 1941 for "sharply" worsening peasant attitudes toward the occupiers, even as in subsequent years the Germans took a "somewhat different" approach.[36]

The German economic administration in Smolensk also consistently identified food supply and diet as decisive for the outlook of the population. Just how important the German-Soviet comparison appeared to peasants was underlined by Security Division 221 shortly after it had helped crush the partisan territories in Yelnya and Dorogobuzh in July 1942. Above all, the situation report observed shrewdly, peasants were preoccupied with how high their delivery quotas would become. If they ever had to be raised above Soviet levels, the report warned, it would be "urgently necessary to emphasize in a special propaganda campaign its necessity as a wartime measure." A comparison with Soviet levels of extraction in many areas likely remained favorable through 1943. Even the half-hearted, stymied German agrarian reform may well have appeared preferable to the kolkhoz system and therefore remained a political factor for the rural population.[37]

The religious revival under occupation also provided another sharp contrast with the Soviet order and demonstrated the extent to which many, especially in the rural population, remained pious. The Soviet anti-religious drive had closed or destroyed 99.5 percent of the prerevolutionary Orthodox churches in Russian areas that fell under German occupation. Church repairs and openings followed the German invasion, and partisan reports registered a significant response in the countryside. Peasants were likely to notice the widely propagandized ceremonial reopenings, including the cathedral in Smolensk. They were far removed from the divide-and-conquer confessional policy of the Germans, surveillance of clergy, and the widespread pressure for clerical collaboration. There were, however, incidents of negative popular reactions to portraits of Hitler and anti-Soviet political messages at services. From the start, Nazi hard-liners opposed the religious revival, and like agrarian reform it was half-heartedly pursued. The results were modest if measured in number of churches reopened. They numbered 2,150 in all the occupied RSFSR, about 3 percent of the prerevolutionary total (although schools or other buildings were sometimes used for worship). Much of the revival, in fact, was driven locally by clergy and believers maneuvering in the new situation. At a very local level, this brought attempts to ban divorce and divisive efforts to inject anti-evolutionary teaching, corporal punishment, and prayer into schools.[38]

From the perspective of the rural population, any gains accrued from the "new agrarian order" and the end of official Soviet atheism were balanced out by violent German destructiveness in the anti-partisan war, forced labor and deportations, and, not least, ubiquitous violence. Peasants had jumped from the frying pan into the fire. In 1943, it was the familiar frying pan that awaited them yet again.

Rural Russia under the Restoration Regime

According to analysis by Popov and other high-level officials starting in 1943, very different situations had emerged in different parts of the Smolensk Region. The occupation and destructive German retreat left a number of districts severely depopulated. In particular, areas near major roads and battles in 1941 and 1943, as well as the anti-partisan operations of 1942, were hit disproportionately. The briefly occupied easternmost districts, re-Sovietized first, did not display the rampant "anti-kolkhoz" and "anti-Soviet" attitudes observed further west. But even there, collective farms were weak and family plots were producing the bulk of the produce. Northwest districts liberated in fall 1943 were also in bad shape, having lost between 60 and 80 percent of agricultural output. Those returning from evacuation needed assistance, but those peasants who remained had appropriated land and were better-off materially. Finally, the group of southwest districts liberated in fall 1943, which included Kozubskii's Yelnya, were in the best position economically, but, from Popov's point of view, the worst off ideologically. The first secretary did not mince words: the Party was confronting an almost complete return of "individual farming." There was a direct correlation between those southwest locales that were doing better economically than before the war and the most "anti-kolkhoz moods" after collective farms were restored in November–December 1943. Family plots outside the collective farms were responsible for over 90 percent of livestock production. There lay the rub. Collective farms, as officials frequently noted, allowed peasants to sow greater acreage for state procurements, but their productivity was terribly low.[39]

The inverse relationship between ideological success and agricultural productivity was never directly confronted by Popov and his officials. The

matter was not open to discussion: the collective farm system was synonymous with Soviet power and it would return with it. Speaking in
December 1943, Popov tolerated no ambiguity about what the peasantry
needed to hear: "The Red Army drove out the German occupiers, Soviet
power is restored, and with it we are restoring the kolkhoz system and
not only formally, but in substance." The thinly spread layer of party-
state forces plainly feared forcing the issue. "The peasants, or the basic
mass of them, are set against the collective farms," Popov admitted, and
"are still hoping for a return to individual cultivation." Many collective
farms, as in the early days of collectivization, existed more on paper than
anything else. Horses that had been "socialized," for example, in reality
remained with their previous owners. Local authorities fearing difficulties were content with moving slowly. No sooner had Popov rallied his
party troops, moreover, than the region was hit with a very bad harvest in
1944, exacerbating a serious food crisis and bringing widespread reports
of hunger and malnutrition.[40]

There is no question that the Smolensk party first secretary was un-
flinchingly confronting an almost impossible situation compounded by a
series of interlocking crises. As the hunger crisis became acute in mid-1944,
Popov was forced to beg the Central Committee in Moscow to approve
forty-six hundred tons of grain per month to be sent to the region. Scant
wonder, however, that the Central Committee plenipotentiaries sent to
evaluate him criticized Regional Party Committee officials for not working
in emergency mode. The work ethic of party officials was lax, and Popov
himself was "not demanding" and incapable of tough measures.[41] This soft-
line reputation, registered in his dossier, would pursue him into the more
stable postwar era.

Cadres Do Not Decide Everything

From Leninist "appointmentism," first disputed in the early years of the
revolution but codified in Stalin's 1935 slogan "Cadres decide everything,"
the new elite had internalized a veritable philosophy of rule revolving
around cadres. In March 1944, acting chief of the regional secret police
K. Stal'nov, his very name evocative of the words *steel* and Stalin, illustrated
the faith that virtually all problems could be solved by cadre appointments. "If we correctly decide the question [of cadres]," Stal'nov declared,

"we shall succeed in preparing and distributing cadres in a Stalinist way [*po-stalinski*] and thus solve nine-tenths of the tasks that the Smolensk party organization faces."[42]

Stalinist cadre politics drove much in the era of reconstruction. But in this period of extreme flux and reconstruction, personnel appointments were hobbled by not one but two Achilles' heels: the enduring weakness of the party in rural areas and a desperate shortage of even modestly qualified experts.

Former partisans, celebrated and trusted politically, became first-choice candidates for appointments, but few were capable or inclined to become collective farm chairmen. Cases abounded of occupation-era policemen, elders, or prewar holdouts for individual landholding (*edinolichniki*) who still became directors of collective farms.[43]

Beginning in 1944, a contested, drawn-out process at the lower rungs of rural society began in local soviets and courts. Moscow's policy aimed at a redistribution of collective farm cattle and property away from occupation-era policemen, mayors, and elders in favor of families of partisans and Red Army soldiers. But local organs were rebuked for favoring an egalitarian, insufficiently punitive approach.[44]

But at the higher levels of rural society, what the party-state lacked in efficiency it made up for in relentlessness over longer periods of time. The number of party members serving as collective farm directors jumped from 3 percent in 1944 to over 16 percent in 1946. In the same period, the number of directors who had lived through the occupation fell from over 84 percent to 53 percent, made up by a large increase in the number of demobilized Red Army soldiers, who had now replaced partisans in the most favored status.[45]

In the collectivized countryside before and after the war, women were relegated to manual labor while men took charge of machines and tractors. In the memorable words of Liubov Denisova, the "uncontested supremacy of the male breadwinner in the village family was reinforced economically, legally, socially, and by the 'fist.'" But now, as a result of a glaring new gender imbalance, discontinuity reigned. Before the war, only a miniscule number of women became collective farm directors. Peasant women in Smolensk, as on the Soviet home front, were the prime force keeping the countryside going during the war. When the Soviets returned in a highly anomalous moment in this patriarchal rural society, women in large numbers became kolkhoz directors. As of January 1946, one document showed an unprecedented 22 precent of Smolensk collective farm directors (1,218 of 5,451) were women. That striking development would, as everywhere else in the postwar countryside, prove short-lived.[46]

Agronomists in a rural region were simply too scarce and valuable to be dismissed, despite the key role they had played under the occupation. The Germans had humiliated and even whipped them, but nonetheless favored them with good salaries, privileged rations, and land. Agronomists and foresters regularly made reports to German authorities as informers (*V-Leute*) in rural areas. Popov revealed in June 1944 that these very same experts were shaken. Now they were forced to serve as formally appointed "agitators" for the party line. They "fear to go to the collective farms, they fear being selected as agitators." He explained why: "Teachers, agronomists, veterinarians and other cultured forces in the village are afraid to open their mouths . . . You know why? Because 99 percent of these agitators lived on occupied territories together with the population and the majority worked for the Germans . . . Many of them went to the peasants to speak about German policy, and it is awful for them now to have to go to them with Soviet policy."[47] The regime remained spread so thin in the countryside that it had no one else available to dish out agitprop except for the same nonparty professionals who had worked under the German occupation.

Former partisans, initially favorites for appointments, did have the credentials for political reliability. But freewheeling wartime forest communities of violence had hardly prepared them for the demands of Soviet bureaucratic centralization. In the distinctly more results-oriented period of reconstruction, partisans did not fare well. They were underqualified even as the Soviet elite was gradually becoming more credentialed. Many former partisans had become accustomed to conscripting, requisitioning, and, not least, terrorizing locals. In positions of rural authority, the regional Procuracy concluded in August 1944, many of them "go partisan, conducting illegal searches, seizing grain and property from collective farm workers, including Red Army families."[48]

Stigmatizing the Occupation

The region's new rulers had difficulty understanding those who had survived German rule. Higher-ranking regional party cadres, as before circulated from the interior by the Central Committee or returning from evacuation and the Red Army, had not experienced life under German occupation. By 1945, Red Army demobilization eased the acute shortages of personnel. Those who had "proven themselves in battle" were now the go-to favorites for appointments. Demobilization in Smolensk Region swelled the ranks with over forty-five thousand personnel placements in industry and state institutions, including over seventeen hundred placed as collective farm and rural soviet directors, while repatriation from German forced labor and returnees from the 1941 evacuation in particular increased the number of teachers.[49]

Popov attempted in vain to mitigate the stigma now associated with working in any capacity under the occupation regime. "Why should teachers who honestly conducted themselves," he asked rhetorically in front of regional party activists in June 1944, "be afraid that they lived under the occupation?" One clue lay in the statistics Popov reported to the Central Committee about the 1943–1944 school year. Smolensk Region was employing 9,949 teachers in 2,442 schools with 268,625 pupils. It was reported that 9,000 more children did not go to school for lack of shoes and clothing; by comparison, before the war there had been well over half a million schoolchildren. Among these 9,949 teachers, there were a mere 59 Communists and 532 Komsomol members. A full half of their number, by contrast, had worked as teachers under the occupation—as even Popov put it, in "German" schools. Popov never explained how "honest" conduct could be determined. The stigma of occupation began with the purges of those who had "worked for the Germans"—which could be defined narrowly in terms of positions as collaborators and those working in jobs that directly aided the military or, more broadly, to many more who remained in other jobs, including teachers. Popov justified a necessary reliance on such teachers. But he described how returnees and other loyalists were already weaponizing the stigma of occupation: "Some are saying, 'servants of the fascists, we know what you were doing here.'"[50]

German rule, in fact, wrecked almost the entire educational system either deliberately or through indifference. With the exception of vocational training, only elementary schools were reopened in 1942, often through the insistence or initiative of local governances. Portraits of Hitler and removal of communist symbols were mandatory, but by necessity Soviet-era textbooks were still used. Teachers described a situation in which there was little oversight, clerics sporadically tried to introduce religious instruction and ban evolutionary theory, and teachers of various views engaged in political maneuvering. Even when it meant giving up the food security of jobs in kitchens and canteens in the hungry city of Smolensk, all but two women teachers returned to their jobs.[51]

Popov and various regional authorities in 1944 were therefore on firm ground in saying that local teachers under the occupation had not worked for the German regime directly, but rather had served their own people and the children.[52] But in this case as in others, those who had lived under German rule—survivors of the brutal occupation who never collaborated and were never tried—forever had to explain their life under fascism in concrete ways such as personnel questionnaires. Their status was low and their life chances reduced.[53]

As party first secretary, Popov spoke a good game of prioritizing ideology along with industry, supplying Moscow with seemingly impressive statistics on numbers of political lectures alongside square meters of living space restored. What was impossible to voice was that despite all intentions, the dissemination of ideology and the political acclaim the regime demanded were extremely difficult propositions not only amid the ruins in 1943 and early 1944, but also during the severe hunger of mid- to late 1944 and a major famine of 1946–1947. Both directly affected Smolensk and all the western agricultural regions of the USSR. In the midst of severe deprivation, as during the wartime emergencies on the home front, the elaborate obligations of "mass-political work" in practice moved toward the back burner. In the sense that immediate emergencies took priority, reconstruction represented a continuation of the war that continued to rage in the west.[54]

Even so, despite the crisis-ridden conjuncture of 1943–1947, it is quite clear that Soviet power in Smolensk succeeded in restoring the symbolic universe of Stalinism. It reintroduced its rituals, official celebrations, newspeak, and, not least, its political expectations. In this sense as well, the nascent myth of a heroic "people's war" against Nazism as the barbaric essence of unculturedness and the myth of reconstruction as a popular restoration of the Soviet system were interconnected. They were propagated together after German defeat. Officially, the period of reconstruction was declared over at the outset of the Cold War in 1948. In fact, recovery and rebuilding from wartime devastation continued well into the 1950s.[55]

Ultimately, despite drastic social change and a noticeable evolution of both the elite and the political system, the Soviet order was rebuilt by checking off the boxes to resurrect the model of prewar Stalinism.

Inside the Purge of Communist Collaborators

Nothing demonstrated that Soviet power was back more than punishment and purge, which now took the form of identifying traitors to the Motherland. Judging traitors represented a far-reaching legal, political, and ideological mobilization carried out by the army, the secret police, the Party, and, not least, the people.

In the public sphere, rough-and-ready military tribunals set up by the entering Red Army were pedagogical, demonstrative, and local. More scripted were the prominent war crimes show trials, the first of which was produced in Krasnodar, where Soviet power returned in February 1943 and collaborators were tried for treason in July. Smolensk's own show trial of ordinary German perpetrators such as Willi Weiss from the 335th Security Division, following the first show trial of Germans in the Kharkiv trial of December 1943, followed later. SMERSH interrogations and evidence gathering, comprising thirteen thick volumes, began in January 1944, almost two full years before the trial was staged on December 15–20, 1945. A leading documentary film director, Esfir Shub, captured the results in a 1946 documentary, *Courtroom Trial in Smolensk.*[56]

Behind the scenes, differing political, administrative, and secret police tracks were put in place for another retribution—one that was quiet, quick, and secretive. It began with the initial sweeps, interrogations, and extrajudicial trials of high-level collaborators by the NKVD. Hidden from the public eye and even today little known, a parallel process of inner-party "cases" of communist collaborators disciplined and verified the base of Popov's power, the regional party organization.[57]

For the party leadership, one of the most disturbing and challenging wartime revelations was the "passivity" and willingness to collaborate shown by well over half of local Communists living in Smolensk under German occupation. Once again, the eastern districts liberated in early 1942 provided the first experience with the matter. "The large majority" of local party members in town and countryside who remained under German rule, the final Regional Party Committee study concluded, "acted completely passively during the occupation, not showing itself in any way and not giving aid to the partisans and Red Army."[58]

The discovery of large numbers of "passives" and "traitors" came at a hinge moment in the Party's historical trajectory. The Party had become a mass organization by the end of the Civil War but throughout the 1920s remained a kind of elite order, hard to join and much easier to leave involuntarily. In the 1930s, its ranks were expanded further: by the eve of the war, the Communist Party comprised about 2 percent of the all-union population. In the decades ahead, this expansionist trajectory created a society in which almost all important careers of any kind required party membership. But because of its especially rural nature, in Smolensk Region at the end of 1940 party membership was almost half the all-union norm: only 1.04 percent of the population of 2.686 million in the 1939 census. The vast bulk of Smolensk Region's party members lived in cities or towns: 67 percent were classified as "white collar" personnel and 15.5 percent as workers, and the rest, rural Communists, represented fewer than two people of every thousand in the countryside. Party membership in Smolensk was rooted in the state bureaucracy, the economic organs, and the party apparatus itself.[59]

Those party members left under German rule, however, were not representative of this largely urban elite. Of just over 32,000 party members in the region in June 1941, over 11,000 joined the army and 12,000 were evacuated, leaving over 8,000 party members in occupied Smolensk. Although final statistical data on everyone evaluated are elusive in the mountain of materials generated by the purge, it is clear that a large majority of those verified were new Communists admitted in the 1930s, including rural Communists admitted in 1939–1941. Rural party members were less likely to have been evacuated; more than a third of party members left behind were rural, and even more than that were women. The rest were cadres given assignments to form partisan units or go into underground party committees.[60]

Given the Communist Party's long-term expansionist trajectory, these three groups who remained under occupation—rural party members, new party members, and loyalists—could be considered key demographics for anyone thinking about the cohesion and strength of the ruling party. The results of the verification of the region in 1944, therefore, were sobering: only about 38 percent of party members who had lived under occupation were deemed to have "fulfilled their duty" in one way or another, which included helping partisans or perishing at the hands of the Germans. Over 30 percent were "passives," and the rest were "traitors" working in some way for the German administration or military effort, including "outright betrayers of the Motherland" who evacuated with the Germans. As of summer

1944, 66 percent of the "party cases" had resulted in expulsion from the Party. What was revealed to the Regional Party Committee between 1942 and 1944 was the size of an "unreliable element" that had "wormed its way into the Party." These Communists, and by extension district officials who had not shown the "necessary leadership" of them, had failed their "very first serious trial by combat."[61]

One part of the regional reaction to this moment of truth was manifested in the mechanics of the "verification" itself. The gathering of information, which was taken seriously and dragged out well into 1944, accompanied the simultaneous canvasing of locals to document fascist atrocities. This was itself an influential part of the re-Sovietizing process. The mountain of material it generated was part of an ongoing interaction of new authorities with those who had remained, showing that the Party was still heavily reliant on a mobilized citizenry even while favoring the testimony of "verified Communists and non-party members who carried out work for the good of our Motherland."[62]

The heightened pragmatism that came to the fore after the German invasion, especially in 1942, continued to be on display during the inner-party housecleaning after re-Sovietization. For example, reliance on pro-Soviet local opinion was balanced out by information of other kinds. The party member's own attitudes under interrogation—especially "lack of candor," sometimes lack of contrition—could become decisive. Great weight was paid when scarce written documentation was available, such as letters revealing political attitudes or signatures on documents. Pro-Soviet family relations, especially if a rural woman had a son serving in the Red Army, could be decisively positive; the reverse was true when there was evidence of women consorting with Germans. Post-occupation behavior, such as taking no part in "social-political work" after the return of the Soviets, also figured into discussions. In general, a noticeable moderation of the politics of retribution after the initial sweeps for traitors, replicated later in Belarus and Ukraine, reflected pragmatic considerations about the acute shortages of personnel. More severe definitions of betrayal would have generated a destabilizing number of repressions.[63]

Despite some role for personal persuasiveness and personal connections, and a perhaps surprising degree of flexibility on the part of the Regional Party Committee in carving out exceptions to punishment, the thousands of "party cases" were interpreted according to a crude division of the local

Communists into loyalists, passives, and traitors of various stripes. This tripartite division had become standard in Soviet "class analyses" of "proletarian" allies, "bourgeois" enemies, and waverers in the middle (or in terms of kulaks and middle and poor peasants). The categories were abstract standards of loyalty to the Soviet cause and had little to do with the real-life situations people faced under German occupation. Fear, pressure, danger, the quest for survival, extreme violence, changing attitudes, and the initial hopelessness of the first phases of the war did not figure in this schema. Soviet classifications did not account for the actual gray zones people inhabited during the occupation. As time went on, more and more people simply fell silent, stigmatized by the brush of collaboration merely because they had endured the harsh trial of German rule.[64]

What lessons would be learned from the wartime "passivity" of Communists under Nazi rule? Given that the Party was the linchpin of the Soviet order, the answer to this question would say much about the trajectory of the Soviet order in the postwar period. The short answer is that while individual transgressors were taken to task, the broader implications were swept under the rug.

A Lack of Reckoning

In an attempt to get off the hook, a number of the party members who appeared in front of their superiors turned to a combination of contrition and excuses. Most common was the old tactic of pleading ignorance and lack of leadership: "We are semiliterate, no one worked with us, we did not know what to do, we destroyed our party cards and did not justify the calling of member of the Party," one not unsympathetic report summed up the reactions in Dzerzhinskii District, one of the first-liberated eastern districts. It was true enough that local party members had been hastily abandoned by district and local leaders and had received few if any instructions as the Germans approached in 1941. The condemned who excused their conduct by crying out for more paternalism, more directives from above, were received with some sympathy at the top of the regional hierarchy.[65]

The Party's disciplinary system comprised an alternative to the regular courts, as well as to military tribunals, secret police investigations of collaborators, and high-profile show trials. The Party's own prerogatives, wrecked during the Great Terror, were now guarded jealously against both the secret police and the Procuracy. The problem with ordinary party members was not inaccurately diagnosed as self-interest and lack of commitment. Yet the solution was merely a ritualistic call for more Marxist-Leninist doctrine and more "daily care" for the "ideational-political upbringing" of new party members. In other words, the answer to the crisis exposed by the war was more instruction from above, as if a direct order not to do so would have prevented the rank and file from losing their party cards. The relative mildness of the party disciplinary system toward its own was no anomaly but part of a "double standard" for party members. This would become especially apparent in the realm of economic crimes, and particularly after the draconian 1947 law against theft of state property, which came in the midst of famine and sent over one million citizens throughout the USSR to the Gulag through the regular courts.[66]

From Popov on down, one searches in vain for any deeper, more systemic diagnosis of the problems the Soviet order and its political elites confronted. The victory over the Germans in World War II is commonly seen as the moment when Soviet communism, at unbelievable cost, finally legitimized its rule, gaining a renewed lease on life for almost half a century. The most secure, long-lasting one-party regimes, the social science literature on authoritarian durability tells us, "are those rooted in a period of sustained, violent struggle." Revolutions, civil wars, and victory over foreign invaders produce "elite cohesion" and the ability to mobilize the populace.[67] The USSR had experienced not only a revolutionary civil war but also the domestic civil war of Stalin's second revolution and the titanic struggle on the Eastern Front. It had large numbers of zealous loyalists and cadres of violence and, as war and reconstruction both proved, retained rare mobilizational capabilities. But did it have elite cohesion?

In the localities and the regions, the case of Smolensk shows, elites were drawn from places with glaring and lasting weaknesses in the collectivized countryside, which had crippled initiative and liquidated talent in the Great Terror. Postwar elites in a region such as Smolensk had very different wartime records—some had fought, others had evacuated. Then, in the face of popular aspirations upon emerging victorious from an incredibly costly war, the regime only tinkered with a hyper-statist economic system that generated formidable amounts of discontent and corruption.

As the postwar system was rebuilt on the prewar model, victory cemented a regime whose durability masked a host of enduring weaknesses.

As a Marxist might say, the conditions of future crises were already growing within the womb of victorious Stalinism.

Katyn: The Local Goes International

In March and April 1943, the last spring of the German presence in Smolensk, the first signs of thaw were appearing in the frozen earth not far from the Krasnyi Bor dachas of the past and future party elite. As the ground softened, mass graves were uncovered. They dated from the 1940 NKVD executions of Polish officers deported east after the Nazi-Soviet Pact partitioned Poland. No single event in Smolensk Region would haunt the victorious Soviets as much, or affect the Soviet Union on the international stage for so long, as the German discovery of 4,421 executed Polish officers in the Katyn forest, twelve miles west of Smolensk.

As Nazis in Berlin and Smolensk prepared a bombshell announcement about Stalinist mass murders, their own activities on Polish territories dwarfed the horrific atrocity they condemned. In March, the Germans liquidated the Jewish ghetto in Krakow; on March 22, the four large gas chambers under construction since 1942 went into operation at Auschwitz-Birkenau. In the Katyn forest, mass graves of Polish officers began to be exhumed on March 29, and on April 13 the discovery was announced on Berlin radio and in newspapers for the first time. No matter how many atrocities the Germans had committed, the Soviets would find out the hard way that a crime of this scale was difficult to falsify. The propaganda coup spearheaded by Goebbels was the most priceless of the war precisely because it was grounded in verifiable fact. It was bolstered by the forensic experts of the technical commission of the Polish Red Cross supervised by the Germans after April 15, by the papers found on the soldiers dating up to the 1940 day of their execution, and by circumstantial evidence that would mount for years to come.[68]

The first inkling Smolensk mayor Boris Menshagin got of the discovery, which would irrevocably change not only Polish-Russian relations but the course of his own life, came just before the public announcements on April 12 or 13. Some days later, he was asked by the head of the Propaganda Department of the Wehrmacht Rear Administration to travel to the mass grave site the next day. At 2:00 PM on April 18, the mayor was driven from downtown Smolensk along with two members of his city administration, an officer from Andrei Vlasov's Russian Liberation Army, and the editor of the Russian-language newspaper *New Path,* the former Komsomol poet Konstantin Dolgonenkov. "Our car turned off the Vitebsk highway around the 15 km sign from Smolensk, turning left into the forest, and right away a terrible stench hit our noses, making it difficult to breathe. We soon saw corpses lying in stacks on the edge of a long, zigzag trench. All these corpses were dressed in the gray uniform of the Polish military."[69]

The exhumation of the mass graves launched three long-lasting processes. First, on April 15, 1943, Radio Moscow announced the Soviet Information Bureau's rebuttal of Goebbels, blaming "German fascist henchmen" for the atrocity. This began an elaborate propaganda blitz of staged publicity and disinformation that has aptly been dubbed a "war of the perpetrators." Second, the international political and diplomatic fallout began, starting immediately with Stalin's April 25 break of diplomatic relations with the Polish government-in-exile. Third, evidence gathering and investigation commenced, although for several years it was slow-walked by the Western Allies to forestall a rift with their Soviet ally—Germany's intent all along. The onset of the Cold War transformed those dynamics. Research was furthered by a major 1952 US congressional investigation and detective work involving techniques such as aerial photography.[70]

The decisive turning point, when the legacy of the propaganda war begun in 1943 finally took a backseat to firmer historical understanding, came only after a half century of Soviet cover-up. In the late 1980s, Mikhail Gorbachev's reforms led to opening of key Soviet archives, and, in 1992, Russian Federation president Boris Yeltsin declassified top-secret NKVD and Politburo documents from the Presidential Archive in the Kremlin. This included NKVD chief Beria's 1940 memorandum proposing the shooting of "14,700 former Polish officers, officials, landowners, police, intelligence agents, gendarmes, [military] settlers, and prison guards" in the three special camps and 11,000 other "sworn enemies of Soviet power" in NKVD prisons. It was approved by the Politburo on March 5, 1940. To this day, however, the 1943 German propaganda coup fixed the association of the executions in Polish and international memory of the crime with the word "Katyn" and the NKVD execution site near Smolensk. The 4,421 officers executed in the Katyn forest were sent from an officer's camp in the Smolensk Region, in Kozel'sk, southeast of the city of Smolensk. A total of 21,857 other prisoners were in fact executed in different locations: near two other special NKVD camps, one in Starobel'sk, southeast of Kharkiv, the second in the Ostashkov camp in Kalinin Region, west of Kalinin (Tver'), as well as in NKVD prisons in the territories of western Ukraine and Belarus annexed in 1939.[71]

Stalin's exact motivations, as always, are hard to pinpoint, but far from all the Poles he sentenced to death with the Politburo decision were officers or elites, nor is there evidence of collusion with the Nazis, who were also decapitating the elite in their part of partitioned Poland. At the Kozel'sk camp, Vasilii Zarubin, an erudite, polyglot NKVD expert, led a filtration and information-gathering operation among the POWs. For Stalin and the Soviets, characteristically, the Poles' political outlook was central. The "vast majority" clearly remained immune and resistant to sustained NKVD attempts at political reeducation in the special camps. Their bedrock commitment to a future independent Poland "automatically made them counterrevolutionary and anti-Soviet, as Beria claimed they were." Exceptions to the rule were four hundred pro-Soviet POWs, including officers deemed willing to serve Soviet interests, who were spared their countrymen's fate.[72]

Menshagin's tour formed part of the German propaganda offensive. A kind of excursion bureau was set up in Smolensk, along with an exposition at the gravesite itself, for visitors ranging from international news correspondents to local peasants. One such visitor was fourteen-year-old Dmitrii Khudyk from the village of Serebrianka. His father, a railway worker in 1940, had already told him about locals seeing the train cars of Poles transported to the site. Indeed, locals had pointed the Germans to the initial discovery of the remains as early as 1942, and then again in early 1943. Khudyk, against his cautious father's wishes, joined ten others from his village in a truck that brought them to the Katyn forest. "The Germans took us up to the trenches, and, showing the corpses, spoke in broken Russian: 'Look. This was done by Russians, and not by us.' Not far from the forest, along the Dnieper, the Germans organized something like a museum exhibit of the personal effects of the Polish military officers." Locals had turned from key witnesses and informants about the atrocity to an audience for the publicity campaign. Starting later in 1943, local testimony also figured in Soviet counterpropaganda efforts as grassroots "evidence" of German guilt.[73]

Foreign correspondents examining the German exhibition about the
mass graves uncovered at the site of the Katyn massacre, April 1943.
Digital Picture Archives, Bundesarchiv.

Smolensk readers of the Russian-language occupation newspaper the
New Path, in a long account immediately published by Dolgonenkov on
April 18 about his tour with Menshagin, were informed that "Judeo-
Bolshevism" was the culprit. Over thirty other pieces on Katyn published
in the Smolensk newspaper between April 18 and July 15 blamed Jewish
NKVD officers for the executions.[74]

No sooner was Smolensk recaptured than the Soviet counteroffensive
began. An NKVD "operational-investigative group" was put under a high-
ranking counterespionage expert overseeing Polish matters relating to

344   CRUCIBLES OF POWER

Katyn. This was Leonid Raikhman, a close associate of Pavel Sudoplatov, chief of "special tasks" in the occupied territories. The brief of Raikhman's group, later subject to its own investigation by the Soviet Military Procuracy in 1990–1991, was to develop evidence for a counternarrative accusing the Germans of the Katyn atrocity. This included planting forged documents on the bodies dated later than May 1940, to show that Germans could have perpetrated the killings after they arrived in 1941. Raikhman's secret police team was on-site for over three months, working from October 5, 1943, to January 10, 1944. Exactly two days after Raikhman's team completed its work, on January 12, a special commission of elite forensic physicians headed by the chief surgeon of the Red Army, the academician Nikolai Burdenko, was officially charged to begin its task. All of the eminent and experienced experts on his team came from Moscow and the best medical institutions. All were "unambiguously loyal Communists or had shown their trustworthiness in close cooperation with the NKVD."[75]

The Burdenko Commission's work proved extraordinary in a different sense of the word. Between 1943 and 1945, the Extraordinary State Commission on Nazi Crimes produced twenty-seven communiqués in Russian and English. It was a truly massive effort: approximately seven million citizens were involved during the compilation of its 54,000 official reports and over 250,000 eyewitness statements. The work of the Extraordinary Commission later became the foundation of the broader Soviet case at Nuremberg. As with the citizen interviews conducted by Red Army investigators in the Smolensk Region before the Extraordinary Commission was up and running, which were then folded into its collections, an endeavor so large could hardly be stage-managed. The evidence it created, in fact, could not even be fully assimilated at top levels. It was certainly possible for this resulting flood of materials to be misleadingly summarized and presented, and how it was synthesized depended on the conjuncture and the people involved. However, among all the Extraordinary Commission reports, the communiqué produced by the Burdenko Commission was unique. Its investigation was completed the fastest; its report, published in *Izvestiia* after its release on January 26, 1944, was far longer than the others. It was the only report that was not submitted for back-and-forth review by top Soviet leaders. It was the only one that left no archival trace about its creation in the files of the Extraordinary Commission secretariat.[76]

Dress Rehearsal

When Raikhman's group appeared in Smolensk in 1943, Menshagin was gone. He had evacuated with the retreating Germans shortly before, on September 20, 1943. After several interrogations, Boris Bazilevskii emerged as the key witness for the Soviet counternarrative on Katyn. Bazilevskii was an astronomer who, for a little over two months, served as Menshagin's deputy mayor at the start of the occupation in 1941. The crux of the evidence he agreed to provide was that Menshagin, a favorite of the German authorities and a morally compromised drunkard to boot, confided to him in 1941 about a German massacre of Poles.

Bazilevskii, initially charged by the Soviets under Article 58.1 for betrayal of the Motherland, debuted his story in front of Western journalists arriving by train in Smolensk to visit the grave site in Katyn on January 22, 1944. This "Katyn junket" had been organized by the Sovinformburo chief, the witty and urbane Solomon Lozovskii, a veteran propagandist involved with the cover-up from the start. Lozovskii and Goebbels, it was rumored, studied each other's public pronouncements. The very next day after appearing in front of the press, Bazilevskii, in a manner highly anomalous for the Soviets, was exonerated for his activities under German occupation "for lack of evidence of a crime." To at least some members of the international audience, the news conference and Bazilevskii's testimony appeared to be a scripted "show." Even so, the resulting 1944 press coverage of the Burdenko Commission evidence emboldened the Soviets brazenly to include the Katyn massacre among the charges they brought against the Germans at Nuremberg. Bazilevskii later reiterated his testimony in Moscow and testified at the Nuremberg trials on July 1, 1946. For his service, he lived out his days as a professor of astronomy in Novosibirsk. His personnel file was even wiped clean of his 1941 collaborationist activity.[77]

In addition to securing Bazilevskii's oral testimony, Raikhman's secret police team falsified written evidence. The result was the so-called Menshagin Notebook. It consisted of seventeen pages of notes in pencil in Menshagin's handwriting. In fact, genuine notebook pages did indeed exist and were discovered by the NKVD in October 1943. They dated to the outset of the occupation in early August 1941, when the newly installed mayor was summoned by German authorities to the former NKVD building, ordered to set up the Smolensk ghetto, and told to record his instructions in a notebook. It seems probable that only two specific parts of two of the pages were doctored by the Soviets by merely altering several words. The result was a passage on page 11 referring to Polish prisoners and a reference on page 13 to German killings in "Koz. Gor.," denoting the village of Koz'i Gory near the Katyn forest.[78]

Smolensk at Nuremberg

The Nuremberg trials in late 1945 to early 1946 simultaneously marked the last major moment of cooperation among the wartime allies and the onset of the Cold War. In the words of Francine Hirsch, the Soviets had won the war but at Nuremberg "lost the victory"; the way the Katyn affair played out at the trial was the linchpin of those unexpected consequences. Among the Allies, it was the Soviets who had insisted on the necessity of a major trial. The USSR had played a major role in developing and prosecuting Nuremberg's legal innovations on the international stage, notably the central charge of "crimes against peace." Yet the Soviet leadership had also insisted on including Katyn among the charges, gambling against the advice of the skeptical chief US prosecutor, Justice Robert H. Jackson. It is ironic that those brought up with the bedrock belief of Leninism and Stalinism that both law and history were fundamentally political were caught flat-footed by Nuremberg's potent combination of justice and politics. Even the most able Soviet prosecutors were used to predetermined show trials and unused to Western-style legal procedure. They were unprepared for effective counter-witnesses challenging their evidence, and the hyper-centralized Stalinist command structure hamstrung nimble responses. While Bazilevskii's hearsay evidence about Menshagin was challenged, the Soviet presentation of its case on Katyn was no catastrophe in and of itself. But more than enough lasting doubts about the Soviet version were created in open court by the defense that Stalin and his lieutenants may well have regretted introducing Katyn into the trial in the first place. Katyn was completely omitted from the final verdict of the International Military Tribunal. Nor did it figure in the dissenting opinion of the Soviet judge, Iona Nikitchenko.[79]

When Menshagin's name was invoked in front of the judges, lawyers, and journalists at the trial, it was declared that the ex-mayor of Smolensk had vanished without a trace. The world did not know that shortly before the trial began in 1945 the ex-mayor had suddenly and on his own initiative fallen into Soviet captivity. As Menshagin was discussed in

Nuremberg, he was interned in central Moscow, in the NKVD's notorious Lubianka Prison.

Menshagin in Captivity

After evacuating Smolensk with the retreating Germans, Menshagin was appointed mayor of Bobruisk, in eastern Belarus, from October 21, 1943, to June 26, 1944, abandoning that second mayoralty three days before Bobruisk was captured by the Red Army. Sometime later, he resurfaced in Berlin as an instructor for POWs working for the political branch of the Vlasov movement, the Committee for the Liberation of the Peoples of Russia, which began functioning in November 1944. Toward the end of the war, in late February 1945, Menshagin was evacuated to Karlovy Vary, in Czechoslovakia, with about a hundred members of the committee. That was where his personal tragedy occurred.

On May 11, Menshagin was separated from his family outside Karlovy Vary when he was picked up by a US patrol and temporarily placed in a US camp. As it happened, the spa town was turned over to the Red Army the very day he was processed. When he rushed back, he assumed his missing family had been taken by the Soviets. On May 28, Menshagin turned himself in to Soviet authorities with the hope of reuniting with his family. In his personal life, as in his political life, Menshagin miscalculated. His wife and children had made it to the American sector.[80]

Thus began Menshagin's long journey of incarceration. On August 9, 1945, he found himself in the NKVD prison on Dzerzhinskii Street in Smolensk. There had been two regime changes in Smolensk since Menshagin had maneuvered within the legal system as a defense attorney during the Great Terror, appealing successfully on behalf of defendants facing fabricated legal accusations. It turned out that the secret police had long memories. When he was interrogated as a high-level collaborator on the day of his arrival, he recognized the handwriting of the Smolensk regional UNKVD official who interrogated him, Boris Beliaev, from prewar legal cases. The very first point in Beliaev's indictment, which ended up imprisoning Menshagin for twenty-five years, was that before the war the former defense attorney during the Great Terror had "incited those accused to recant the admissions they had made during preliminary investigations."[81]

On November 30, 1945, on the eve of Menshagin's departure for the Lubianka in central Moscow, he was paid a visit by party first secretary

Dmitrii Popov. What did they discuss? We may never know. Menshagin spent no less than six years in the Lubianka while his case remained "under investigation," long after his interrogations had ceased. In the first years of his imprisonment, Menshagin was interrogated by Beliaev in Smolensk and several others in Moscow, including Akhmed Meretukov, who had been a member of Raikhman's secret police team in Katyn. "They asked me what I knew of the Katyn affair," Menshagin said. Each time, Menshagin recounted how he first learned about Katyn in April 1943. "After that they said: we won't write that down right now, we will return to this question later."[82]

Why was Menshagin's life spared when so many other high-level collaborators were executed? On the one hand, the Menshagin Notebook and Bazilevskii's testimony about Menshagin had figured prominently in the Soviet counternarrative of German culpability for Katyn. Perhaps no one dared to eliminate him, in the event he might be needed or useful at some point in the future. On the other hand, if the maintenance of the Katyn fraud were truly the top priority, would he not have been more useful dead than alive? The evidence available now consists only of Menshagin's own brief account of what happened to him in the Lubianka. He claimed he was only interrogated after 1947 and that in 1949 he was told his case was no longer being investigated, after which he was more or less forgotten.[83] We may never know the full story unless the Lubianka archives become available.

The German discovery of Katyn in the spring of 1943 was not the only extraordinary event that would keep the Smolensk Region a focal point of international attention for the duration of the Cold War. In May 1943, the Communist Party documents that comprised the future Smolensk Archive were transported to Vilnius. Seized by the United States and studied by the Central Intelligence Agency (CIA) for years after the war, they would keep the Smolensk Region near the forefront of Sovietology for the duration of the Soviet period. In 1990–1992, the 1940 Soviet documentation about Katyn was finally released and the massacre returned to the spotlight of international attention. At that very moment, the "archival revolution" prompted a historical gold rush for new sensations. Students of the Soviet past and the German occupation, all too quickly, largely forgot about Smolensk.

EPILOGUE
AFTERLIVES

IN THE YEARS FOLLOWING THE WAR, Vasilii Kozubskii, the schoolmaster turned partisan, proved as anomalous as a politician as he had been as the rare intelligentsia partisan military commander. For his role in leading the Lazo Partisan Regiment in liberating the El′ninskii partisan territory in 1942, Kozubskii was awarded the Order of Lenin. After the fall of the partisan territory in summer 1942, he served for the rest of the occupation in the regional apparatus of the Central Headquarters of the Partisan Movement. A beneficiary of the recruitment of partisans into political posts in the initial phase of reconstruction, Kozubskii went on to become a district party secretary in 1944. He thus became one of regional party first secretary Dmitrii Popov's underlings in the economically and socially calamitous postwar years.

While vastly different from the cadres of violence among the partisans, such as the former executioner Fedor "FD" Gnezdilov, Kozubskii had one thing in common with many others who had lived through the war in free-wheeling partisan communities. He was never happy pushing paper or dealing with cadre politics. He wanted to work with people—a message he managed to convey, if not in so many words, to his Mints Commission interviewer. From 1947 until his death in 1958, Kozubskii became the representative of the Council for Religious Affairs in the Smolensk Region.

There he devoted much time working with surviving Jewish communities in local efforts to memorialize the Holocaust.[1]

Kozubskii was, therefore, in rapid succession, a public figure in the prewar local intelligentsia, a collective farm official, a partisan commander, a wartime bureaucrat, a party politician, and, in his work with local Jewish communities, a humanitarian. His path was hardly typical of partisan commanders. But it underscores the fact that there was significant diversity among the many people and units constituting the partisan movement. More than that, Kozubskii exemplifies how identifying biographical logics under Stalinist and Nazi rule can reveal twists and turns that defy neat social and political categories. The postwar trajectories of the other main protagonists in this book are equally revealing.

BY THE WAR'S END IN 1945, Dmitrii Popov had served as party first secretary in the region during two of the most devastatingly difficult periods in Smolensk's long history: the years of German occupation and the first years of postwar reconstruction after 1943. Anyone serving as the top regional political leader during the Stalin period, of course, had to be able both to wield and to weather pressure, coercion, violence, and intrigue. But Popov, the old red expert on agriculture, was always more of a persuader than the "little Stalins" among his domineering and ruthless peers. Popov did not last long into the postwar period. In 1947, the regional elite united against him and appealed to Moscow for his removal.

In October 1947, the Cadres Department of the Central Committee in Moscow prepared a dossier on Popov for Aleksei Kuznetsov, a rising functionary who had distinguished himself as a regional party leader during the Siege of Leningrad. As in previous high-level political machinations, Central Committee plenipotentiaries sent to investigate the Smolensk Regional Party Committee were involved in the ouster. The Popov dossier drew on their accounts. The justification for removal homed in on the Smolensk leader's weaknesses, in his case a lack of ruthlessness. Popov was "insufficiently tough and hands-on," as well as "too trusting" and "insufficiently resolute." The actual source of Popov's "undoing," in the words of a study about postwar regional party first secretaries, was his "failure to bring together a tightly knit and obedient ruling circle."[2] Perhaps Popov's personal qualities were responsible for this, but the Smolensk regional elite had been in too much flux to band together against him before.

As regional party chief, Popov was far less dominant and flamboyant than Smolensk's quintessential "little Stalin," his predecessor Ivan Rumiantsev. The historical roles Popov was called on to play in facing the existential crisis of total war and epic devastation during reconstruction were no smaller than those played by Rumiantsev in the Stalin Revolution of the 1930s. But Popov was always a more bureaucratic, behind-the-scenes player than his charismatic predecessor. He was also markedly less revolutionary. Whether or not he was tough enough, the regional first secretary in this sense reflected a great transformation of the Soviet elite across three distinct periods—prewar, wartime, and postwar Stalinism. As leaders in Smolensk, Rumiantsev and Popov both lived and worked, rose and fell within the years of the Stalin period. But each represented distinctly different phases in the life cycle of the revolution.

THE YEAR OF POPOV'S DOWNFALL, 1947, marked the onset of the Cold War and the division of Europe that would last until 1989. The deterioration of relations between the erstwhile allies and their rapid pivot to a new, global ideological conflict greatly affected the postwar fate of the Belarusian and Russian nationalists active in occupied Smolensk. As they again became émigrés, these peripatetic collaborators formed part of a veritable sea of displaced persons. Overall, at war's end, according to a 1946 Soviet Repatriation Administration assessment, Germany and the Axis powers had deported almost seven million civilians and POWs as forced laborers. Non-returners subject to repatriation to the USSR numbered at least three hundred thousand on top of at least a million who were either dead or missing. Soviet displaced persons in Europe at the war's end included a wide range of POWs, Holocaust survivors, forced laborers, voluntary exiles, and erstwhile collaborators. Soviet clashes with the Western Allies over refugees counted among the first diplomatic conflicts of the incipient Cold War.[3]

Neither Michał Vituška nor Dzmitryj Kasmovič, the two Belarusian nationalists involved in setting up local police units in Smolensk, was brought to account for the numerous atrocities each perpetrated. Vituška could not be, for he did not survive the war. In 1943–1944, he became a major in the volunteer battalions of the Belarusian Central Rada, the puppet administration in occupied Minsk. In 1944, he took part in intelligence and sabotage operations as head of a special SS unit known as Black Cat, whose fighters were parachuted behind Soviet lines. After the Germans left, Vituška's partisans remained to fight the Soviets. He was killed by Soviet forces in January 1945, although rumors circulated that he had escaped to the West.[4]

Both Vituška and Kasmovič were nephews of Belarusian nationalist leader Radasłaŭ Astroŭski, the sometime Smolensk County mayor who became Boris Menshagin's rival. Astroŭski, having left Smolensk with the retreating Germans, got a significant promotion in the German occupation regime in Belarus in 1944. Appointed president of the Belarusian Central Rada in Minsk, the cultivated schoolmaster, who local educators in Smolensk had thought resembled a genteel Pole, oversaw the substantial 1944 military conscription of young Belarusians to form the Belarusian Home Defense Force, which later joined the Waffen-SS.[5]

In emigration after the war, both Astroŭski and Kasmovič became leaders of one wing of the Belarusian national movement, sparring with other émigrés after 1948 in their effort to turn a resurrected Central Rada into the recognized Belarusian government-in-exile. Their prominence was directly facilitated by Cold War politics and the boost it gave to anti-communist émigrés. For example, Kasmovič was also active in the World Anti-Communist League and the Anti-Bolshevik Bloc of Nations, headquartered in Munich, while Astroŭski was a member of the latter's Central Committee. In 1956, Astroŭski moved from Germany to New Jersey. He died in 1976 in Benton Harbor, Michigan. Kasmovič passed away in Stuttgart in 1991.[6]

MANY SOLIDARISTS, those Russian right-wing émigré activists who turned Smolensk into a headquarters for their wartime operations in occupied Russian territories, also found a lifeline in the Cold War conflict. Nikolai Alferchik, head of the Smolensk city police during the occupation, had a substantial amount of blood on his hands. He was on-site or in command during the destruction of the Smolensk ghetto and many other atrocities, including the murder of psychiatric patients and Roma. Along with mayor

Menshagin, he retreated with the Germans when they lost Smolensk in 1943. As Menshagin served his second posting as mayor in Bobruisk, Alferchik was promoted to direct a department of the SD in Minsk, where he was also linked to atrocities. After Smolensk, Menshagin and Alferchik, colleagues in the Smolensk wartime city administration, would cross paths three more times. The first was in Borisov after their evacuation from Smolensk, in late 1943. The second meeting came in Minsk, when Alferchik was awarded a medal by the SD in 1944. They met for the third and last time at Menshagin's Berlin apartment at a birthday party for his niece in December 1944.[7]

Solidarism remained in the service of anti-communism, now in a new, Cold War context. The émigré organization NTS reestablished its pre-1940 ties with British intelligence and succeeded in becoming a key client of the CIA. It was funded to carry out covert operations in East Germany and the USSR, activities that barely materialized because the Russian nationalist organization had a limited presence in the former and virtually none in the latter. Solidarists relied on "posturing and misinformation" to build their reputation among the Western powers, even as they fell into internal bickering in the postwar decades. Ideologically, the movement's corporatism, faith in national revolution, and cult of action had given it a clear family resemblance to interwar fascist movements. Now, Cold War propaganda portrayed it as a group of democratic, anti-communist freedom fighters. It appears the CIA was content with this situation: despite the Solidarists' lack of success, they could be used as a weapon of psychological warfare to demoralize the United States' Cold War rival. It is even possible that the Soviets, because they had penetrated the émigré organization, were satisfied to have these Russian émigrés as their enemy's client. The Solidarists' wartime immersion into the murky, paranoid world of espionage and counterintelligence in the German-Soviet war thus continued in new guise, as the Cold War settled into a decades-long, in some ways strangely stable, conflict.[8]

In this situation, many former collaborators and perpetrators changed their names, denied as communist propaganda all Soviet accusations that arose, and leveraged their anti-Soviet experience and skills to serve new masters in the Cold War. Alferchik, for example, resided in Salzburg until 1950 under the name of Nikolai Pavlov. Like many others, he was protected by his postwar career as a recruit for Western intelligence agencies. Starting in the 1980s, a tenacious Australian journalist, Mark Aarons, investigated Alferchik's case along with many others. Aarons found that the Soviets had requested Alferchik's extradition as early as 1945. It made no difference that during Alferchik's half decade in Austria between 1945 and 1950, American and British knowledge of his role in atrocities in Smolensk and Minsk was "obviously" detailed and accurate. As with other police and SS collaborators, the former Smolensk police chief was deemed particularly qualified for anti-Soviet operations. Alferchik is known to have been recruited by US intelligence in 1948 and by Australian intelligence in 1951. It is possible he worked for British intelligence as well in 1945, along with other Solidarists released from Allied camps, but almost no British intelligence records are publicly available. Aarons, the investigative journalist, devoted his career to questioning the competence, and even basic loyalty, of many such perpetrator recruits in their anti-communist intelligence activities. He noted "intriguing hints" that the Soviets used Alferchik as a double agent.[9]

Aarons's investigative reporting led to the creation of a new, governmental Special Investigations Unit in Australia in the late 1980s. The Nazi hunters in the unit made Alferchik one of their highest-priority investigations. But he was never prosecuted. By that time, most eyewitnesses were not alive, and in 1992 Alferchik was paralyzed by a stroke. He passed away in 1995. So many parts of the Australian security file on Alferchik have been blacked out that much of his postwar role in intelligence operations remains obscured.[10]

KONSTANTIN DOLGONENKOV, the Komsomol poet who became editor of the German-sponsored newspaper *New Path* in occupied Smolensk, outdid those Solidarist émigré nationalists who transitioned from serving the Nazis to working for the Americans in the name of anti-communism. In rapid succession, Dolgonenkov achieved success under not two but three ideologies: communism, fascism, and liberalism. An up-and-coming litterateur in party publications in the Stalinist 1930s, he became not only the most prominent propagandist in occupied Smolensk but a man of many pseudonyms. He pursued his literary career in a number of Smolensk occupation-era journals that published poetry and prose along with political essays. For example, he appeared as Avdei Avdeev in the satirical journal *Scourge* (*Bich*). He published in *The Bell* (*Kolokol*) and *At the*

Turning Point (*Na perelome*), the former given the name of Alexander Herzen's influential nineteenth-century Russian "thick journal" published in Europe. In Munich after the war, he tweaked his name, becoming Domanenko. When the liberal prerevolutionary journal *Russian Thought* (*Russkaia mysl'*) was resurrected under the same name in newspaper form in Paris in 1947, he wrote for it under the name K. Akimych.[11]

Across the realms of publishing and propaganda, culture and politics, Dolgonenkov pursued one profession as a writer. But he did so under the successive banners of communism, fascism, and liberalism, all within the space of about fifteen years. Given the number of ex-Communists who became German collaborators and were active in emigration during the Cold War, this kaleidoscopic series of reorientations was not unique. Dolgonenkov died in Munich in 1980 at age eighty-five.[12]

FOR ALL THOSE WHO REMAINED IN THE USSR, the profound impact of the war on the postwar course of Soviet history can hardly be overstated. Demographically, socially, and economically, the trauma and sheer devastation on the Eastern Front took decades to overcome. The approximately twenty-seven million Soviet losses created a long-standing gender imbalance and labor shortages in the population, which regained its 1941 size of some two hundred million only in 1956. Ideologically, victory over fascism gave the Soviet regime a new jolt of legitimacy and in certain ways even came to overshadow 1917. Geopolitically, the Soviets acquired the "outer empire" in East Europe and emerged as a superpower in the bipolar world. A less obvious impact came in the realm of social psychology.

Even as postwar Stalinism dashed many popular hopes that victory would lead to a loosening of the harsh regime in town and countryside, the "front generation" of soldiers as well as other survivors were tough and not easily intimidated. Many had experienced great wartime autonomy. As earlier geographical and social boundaries evaporated in the wartime trial by fire, they experienced and observed much that was new. For the duration of the Stalin years, the wartime necessity to make choices and comparisons led more to psychological, as opposed to political, ramifications. As Elena Zubkova has put it, the experience of war itself did not necessarily change attitudes toward the regime. In her explanation, it "awoke in people the capacity to think in unaccustomed ways, to evaluate a situation critically, and never again to accept uncritically any exclusive version of the truth." Perhaps. Those in the occupied territories experienced a fascist regime at the peak of its right-wing revolutionary destructiveness, not the kind of quasi-spontaneous "civic spirit" present on the home front. Undoubtedly, the phrase "never again" in Zubkova's formulation was overstated. As she herself pointed out, a new "awareness of the multiplicity of ways of life and the value of personal choice" brought by the experience of war was balanced out with a countervailing tendency: the import into civilian life of the "custom of command and submission" present in the army and already a feature of barracks Stalinism.[13]

The war further strengthened the resilience and independence of spirit of Liudmila (Lyusya) Madziuk, the 1930s generation feminist and underground activist in occupied Smolensk. In 1943, when she so keenly analyzed the patriarchal traditionalism of the German soldiers she worked to

Liudmila (Lyusya) Madziuk (first row, first from the left) among a group of students and staff from School No. 1 in Moscow, 1937. Viacheslav Madziuk, her brother, is in the middle of the top row, without a tie and with a pin on his shirt; her other brother, Gennadii Madziuk, is in the bottom row, third from left, with the model airplane. Studio "Luna."

convert, she was only twenty-two years old. In the Smolensk underground, her anti-fascist outrage was inflamed by her German interlocutors' inability even to imagine a woman achieving her dream of becoming an aviation engineer.

After the war, Madziuk successfully realized the career she had always imagined as a professional woman whose qualifications put her in a productive position of authority. This was an outcome very much connected to the aspirations she displayed in her trenchant wartime commentary on German culture and "unculturedness." According to those who knew Madziuk later in her life, she returned to Moscow in 1943 to finish her education. She did not become an aviation engineer, but went on to have a successful professional career as a chemist. Just as much as prewar experiences so deeply shaped wartime choices, wartime experiences in turn shaped postwar trajectories.

Madziuk achieved her dream far from Moscow, however. It appears that after her father was repressed, she and her younger brother, Gennadii, another model student in prewar Moscow who survived the war to become a geologist and cartographer, settled in the far north in Ukhta, Komi Republic. There she became head of the chemistry department at the district energy directorate Komienergo. As for so many other families, the war deprived the Madziuks of close family members. Her older brother, Viacheslav, a geology student who fought with the Red Army from 1942 on, perished near Königsberg / Kaliningrad in East Prussia in 1945. Liudmila Madziuk died in 2002 at the age of eighty-one.[14]

VASILII MASLENNIKOV LIVED OUT THE REST of his life in the Smolensk Region, never far from where he grew up. The keen observer of his home village of Filimony had been determined to avoid becoming a "backward" person and instead, in his own hopeful yet self-deprecating words, raise himself up to be "a first-generation member of the intelligentsia, if only a teacher."[15] His refusal of German offers to collaborate in the POW camp in Roslavl cost him two years of forced labor in Germany between 1943 to 1945. After all he had suffered, he then faced the stigma attached to captivity abroad.

Maslennikov was one of the approximately two million Soviet citizens liberated by the Red Army by early 1945. Soviet troops found him in Zittau,

Saxony, along with his group of forced laborers vying for the chance to guard their former German captors. One liberated young prisoner in Maslennikov's group politely inquired if he could have permission to kill one of the Germans, but the sergeant would not allow it. On a series of freight trains with open platforms, loaded down with people and trophy goods, Maslennikov made his way back to Smolensk, using a few purloined items himself to ease his trip into the Soviet interior. For a second time, he "fell in love" with the quality of the roads in Germany and Poland and marveled at a trophy American Studebaker car. His journey back to the Motherland was unexpectedly fun—and revealing. The men in his forced labor unit traveled alongside young, rural Russian women who had been deported from the countryside to Germany, most of whom had worked as cleaning women for the wives of German military men. Conversations, relationships, and even love affairs ensued between them and Maslennikov's "brothers." What struck Maslennikov most was not just that the women were "young and pretty" but that they "had acquired European habits and manners of conversation and behavior."[16]

If travel restrictions and terror had made the prewar Soviet Union highly isolationist for all but high-level elites in the 1930s, the war and its massive demographic dislocations brought tens of millions out of their villages and millions of Soviet citizens into Europe. Even those who never did fight, face deportation, flee, or travel were affected by a sea change in material culture. A massive influx of looted and trophy Western material goods arrived especially after Stalin's so-called package decree of 1944 legalized sending items home. The degree to which 1930s Stalinism was a "closed society" has often been overstated. But "trophy Westernization" opened up a taste of the outside world and greater familiarity with its material culture on a far wider scale than before. In 1950, one-third of all cars in Moscow were foreign; in 1951, three-fourths of films in distribution in the Soviet Union were foreign trophy films taken from abroad. At the same time, Soviet political and security ruling circles, led by Stalin, were haunted by the historical ghost of "Decembrism," the 1825 Decembrist constitutionalist uprising against tsarism by army officers who had experienced life in Paris during the Russian victory in the Napoleonic Wars. Soviet citizens' hopes for a postwar relaxation of the regime were dashed, then reversed entirely in the harsh ideological crackdown associated with Andrei Zhdanov after 1947. Nonetheless, the long-term aftereffects of the war on Soviet society, including the outlooks of all those who, like Maslennikov, had rarely if ever before left their home districts, were profound.[17]

Having been liberated by the Red Army, Maslennikov avoided the Soviet filtration camps in which over three million other repatriates from holding camps in the British, American, and French zones of occupation in Germany were put. Even so, Maslennikov observed with some bitterness, he was returning home with "stigma" attached. "I knew from the experience of prewar life how traumatic it was to be stigmatized as an alien class element, or one of the many other common labels, and now I myself was experiencing stigma."[18] This comment suggests he understood very well how the labels themselves frequently evolved or changed even as the phenomenon of branding and stigmatization remained.

Every time Maslennikov tried to get a job, no matter how much in demand teachers were, the ever-present questionnaire required he reveal his time in fascist Germany. If a friend or contact helped him by leaving out his inconvenient past in a recommendation, they got in trouble if and when it came out. Back in the still mostly ruined city of Smolensk in 1945, Maslennikov was rejected for teaching posts several times. Only through a chance encounter with an old acquaintance did he secure a job. He did so well that after three years, in 1948, he was tapped to become director of a school. He decided not to attempt to conceal his time in Germany. When Iakov Valuev, head of the Smolensk city soviet, learned about Maslennikov's ideological taint, he vetoed the appointment.[19]

Valuev was the very same party secretary from the El'ninskii District, Maslennikov caustically noted, who had been evacuated from the occupied territories in 1941. He had only returned from the home front by airplane to visit the El'ninskii partisan territory in 1942, taking off again for Moscow in advance of its collapse a short time later. For over a decade, Maslennikov taught geography, because he was banned from teaching a "patriotic" and political subject such as history. His workplace tribulations, including a traumatic firing because of his past in 1954, plagued him until attitudes eased during Khrushchev's Thaw. This occurred only around 1960. Maslennikov never forgot the harshly "categorical" words of one hostile supervisor whose son had died in the war. "Now you, Maslennikov, sat it out somewhere in captivity and returned home alive and healthy."[20]

Unable to support his family, Maslennikov quit the city of Smolensk in 1948. He got a teaching position in the Glinkovskii District and once again found himself back in the very same area as his native village. Back in the countryside he had observed so acutely his whole life, Maslennikov had an overriding impression that the small collective farms of the region remained heartbreakingly "poor." But unlike in the 1920s, now "the collective farmers were used to poverty. They seemed only to fear getting even poorer than they were." Peasant women harvesters, still earning virtually nothing from the labor-day system, made do by concealing grain under their skirts, practices sanctioned and even regulated by any brigade supervisor who was "not a fool." The "real theft" in the long history of postwar agricultural reforms, Maslennikov avowed, was punitive state taxes in money and in kind aimed at strengthening "collective" labor and preventing peasants from working their private plots.

"In agriculture," Maslennikov stated the obvious, "it was clear that everything was not on the right track." Referring to the Khrushchev-era attempt to reverse the course of Siberian rivers, he recounted a witticism he heard about the sorry state of affairs: "But to make up for it, we are building rockets, we are conquering the Yenisey [River], and we are the best on the planet in ballet." Clearly, in his sympathies, Maslennikov remained close to the peasantry. He had witnessed and weathered much—including collectivization, the Great Terror, and the war. Even as he had many reasons and a long time to hone his criticisms of Stalinism and the collectivized countryside, after the war he continued to teach and speak at public events to the satisfaction of local party authorities. Bitter about much, including the stigma he faced, he nonetheless avowed that the witticism he repeated was in fact "true." He watched as a new Smolensk slowly, painstakingly emerged by the 1950s along with all the rest of the Soviet superpower's military and industrial achievements. The great ballerinas and other cultural Soviet accomplishments did make him proud. Having recounted this, Maslennikov made a most interesting declaration. Soviet achievements on the world stage, he declared, "were significant and they unwillingly attracted our attention, somehow taking our thoughts away from the failures of agriculture."[21]

Maslennikov had put his finger on Russia's old imperial complex, now in Soviet guise. This was the hoary dynamic by which local hardships and oppression were vindicated even for the suffering masses by the great power stature of the state. As he evoked the allure and the illusions of the Soviet superpower during what was in many ways its height in the 1950s, he spoke about the deflection not of others' but of "our" thoughts. In other words, he pointedly included himself.

Maslennikov's long postwar work on his memoirs themselves formed part of a war memory of a distinctly unofficial, non-statist variety. Until his death in 1998, he loved to read and travel, and he visited Moscow every year to go to museums and the theater. He had not only become "cultured," but had produced an authentic grappling with his personal life and fate under two regimes in one of the world's most consequential wars. But the account was published locally in a tiny print run by his relatives only in 2014. The fact that he ended his memoirs with a subtle, typically self-deprecating moment of introspection seems significant. Ambiguous to the end about the regime that both helped and hurt him, Maslennikov at the end abandoned his historian's detachment by including himself in the Soviet version of Russia's imperial mentality. Victory in the war and the superpower status it brought, he acknowledged, seemed to partially paper over the festering problems he witnessed in his own life and the life of his home village.

BORIS MENSHAGIN FINALLY LEFT the Lubianka in Moscow in 1951 when he was sentenced to twenty-five years in prison, including time already served. He served out his quarter-century term in the Vladimir Prison of Special Designation, a facility for prisoners deemed politically significant. Perhaps because of fears he might somehow be contacted during ongoing investigations into Katyn in the United States and elsewhere, Menshagin spent many of those years in isolation, without a cellmate. He was even instructed at the beginning of his term that he had been "deprived" of his name and should only identify himself as "Number 29."[22]

Among the other "special" prisoners in Vladimir Prison were *chekisty*, incarcerated secret police operatives from the Stalin era. These were among the only cellmates it was deemed safe for Menshagin to have for much of his sentence; they could be counted on to consider him an enemy. Ironically, Menshagin briefly shared his cell with Pavel Sudoplatov, head of the NKVD Fourth Directorate in charge of diversion and espionage in the occupied territories. The spymaster had been arrested after the assassination of Lavrentii Beria following Stalin's death in 1953.[23] Soviet history made for strange bedfellows.

Menshagin started writing the first version of his memoirs in 1952. After his notebooks were confiscated upon his release in 1970, at the age of sixty-eight, he used his improbably powerful memory to reconstruct them. By this time, the young dissidents who got to know him especially as a source of information on the Terror, including Gabriel Superfin, observed his reticence to discuss his tenure as wartime mayor of Smolensk. Superfin recalled in 2019 that Menshagin often spoke in front of others "like a machine, without stopping, without including any movement of his eyes." What impressed the human rights activist above all was Menshagin's pronounced equanimity. Evidently, after everything Menshagin had experienced, "he was already past all emotions." Especially when it came to the Katyn massacre of 1940, discovered by the Germans in 1943 when Menshagin was mayor, he replied reluctantly, with stock phrases. Menshagin had been so isolated during a quarter century in prison that he knew nothing about his onetime deputy mayor Boris Bazilevskii's testimony at the Nuremberg trials, which upheld the Soviet version of Katyn and invoked Menshagin as proof of German guilt for the massacre. Only in 1971, when Menshagin took up residence in a home for the elderly—one reserved for released convicts—did he begin to understand his own role in the Soviet denial of culpability. A hostile neighbor, citing the third volume of the 1958 Soviet edition of the protocols of the Nuremberg trials, no less, attacked Menshagin for personally carrying out the execution of the Polish officers.[24]

KOZUBSKII'S PROTÉGÉ, the young striver Andrei Iudenkov, had been stymied before the war but found a new identity in the partisan movement. While Iudenkov was still in the midst of the conflict, he grappled with such difficult topics as the hostility of the local population in the early days of 1941 and his own emotions when he executed traitors in the local partisan terror. His extensive postwar writings about the war were very different. In 1955, at age thirty-eight, he graduated from the Central Committee's Academy of Social Sciences, the top institution of "party-minded" scholarship, and he defended his doctor of sciences dissertation in 1970. His life's work in his decades at the party institution, essentially, was to sanitize what he himself had seen and experienced in his youth. As author of four autobiographical works on the Lazo partisans written across four decades, as well as many other publications about the war, Iudenkov both reflected and helped shape the evolution of the war myth.[25]

The initial memorialization of the war after 1945 flowed directly from Soviet wartime propaganda. This was very much on display in Iudenkov's earlier works, including his 1960 book on the Lazo partisans. Themes of pride and sacrifice, heroism, martyrdom, Russian nationalism and Soviet patriotism, and the unified "people's war" against fascism were ever-present drumbeats both during and after the war years. Another familiar pillar of Iudenkov's work was the leading role of the Party, which supposedly directed the partisan movement at all key moments. The Party was sometimes personified by Stalin or the Central Committee and, on the district level of power, by Yelnya party secretary Valuev. This was the same Valuev who torpedoed Maslennikov's appointment as a school director in 1948, whom Maslennikov derided for being airlifted in and out of the partisan territory. Iudenkov had himself worked under Valuev for the Smolensk city party organization for several years after the war. In 1960, Iudenkov even claimed that "not one person" among the district party activists had left the fight for the Soviet rear.[26]

Textbooks and patriotic histories routinely whitewash the past. But in this case, Iudenkov had lived through the very history he was revising. Given what he personally had experienced, the details as well as the big picture of his auto-revisionism are instructive.

Writing about rural Smolensk in 1960, Iudenkov made no mention of the peasantry or the local population outside statements about general support for the Soviet cause. There was nothing about collaboration. Nor was there any hint of nonmilitary violence or the partisan mission of vengeance against traitors. The decisions, trials, and experiences that ordinary people faced during the war were nowhere to be found. Iudenkov had been one of the leaders of the partisan territory in Yelnya. Remarkably, his readers in 1960 would never have known that the partisan territory had existed or that Soviet power was restored there for almost half of 1942. Instead, the narrative referenced only those battles with the Germans marking the territory's rise and fall, operations dubiously presented as preparing the soil for the Red Army to liberate Smolensk in 1943.[27]

Iudenkov's text, like much of the teaching of the Great Patriotic War in the educational system throughout the late Soviet period, was all about battles, logistics, and leaders. It was a strangely technocratic, statist mode of teaching the history of an unprecedented, catastrophic, total war of annihilation. Solemn phrases about the scale of the conflict could not disguise a lack of empathy for the actual people in the "people's war." Indeed, ordinary people, as opposed to leaders, heroes, nations, and classes, did not figure as historical actors. This deeply anti-humanistic mode of official history continued to have great currency in post-Soviet Russia.

At the same time, one key difference between Iudenkov's narrative and what the public had heard during the war itself was the complete excision of hate propaganda, which had been such a powerful and emotional, if blood-curdling, cornerstone of mass mobilization starting in 1941. Rather, in the postwar years, the cult of war encompassed the Soviet "struggle for peace" against the new Western warmongers. In Iudenkov's work from the era of "peaceful coexistence," Soviet heroes had taken up arms only out of necessity. Jarringly, however, Iudenkov pointedly glorified Valuev for demanding "vigilance," a Stalinist term ubiquitous in the era of the Great Terror. Evoked after Khrushchev's de-Stalinization launched in the Secret Speech of 1956, this seems to place Iudenkov in the conservative rather than the reformist wing of the Party.[28]

Another major aspect of the postwar myth was historical inevitability. The sections on the war written by Iudenkov in the 1964 *Against the Falsification of the History of the CPSU* repudiate any hint of contingency in the German-Soviet war that might explain victory by anything but the "superiority of the socialist system." That said, in his more specialized academic work, Iudenkov's wartime experience did allow him to make distinct contributions. In a 1971 monograph, he became one of the first Soviet historians to investigate the anti-Soviet press, German wartime propaganda, and the role of collaborators in the Nazi propaganda machine.[29]

In Iudenkov's contributions to the war myth in the late Soviet period, references to a unified, multinational "Soviet people" run like a red thread. In this he was merely reflecting the general direction of the Soviet narrative. Immediately after the end of the war, Stalin had modified his hard wartime turn toward elements of Russian nationalism, which he had pushed aggressively during the regime's existential crisis. In the postwar years, the Soviet-era multinational friendship of peoples—as opposed to continuities in the history of the Russian state and nation—emerged as a mainstay of the war myth. This accelerated after Khrushchev's de-Stalinization, because singling out the Russian national contribution to Soviet victory was associated with

Stalin. In realms outside of war memory, the group around Aleksandr Shelepin and other Russian cultural conservatives more successfully advanced Russian national themes within the confines of the ideologically possible.[30]

Despite these shifts, however, both the imperial and the national always remained intertwined in the Soviet myth of the war. Even in the mainstream versions of the war myth, the supranational Soviet and the national Russian were almost impossible to disaggregate. A good example of this is the 1985 book *The People's War* put out by a group of authors headed by Iudenkov. Popular support for the partisan struggle was discussed in terms of the "Soviet people," but the book was about the "ancient Russian" land of Smolensk. Thus the work opened with the failure of all foreign invaders throughout the centuries, including Mongol and Polish invaders, Lithuanian princes and Polish landowners, and Swedish and Napoleonic armies. Referring to the hero warriors of ancient Rus', it boasted that all invading armies had faltered in Smolensk as they came up against "Russia's outpost of bogatyrs."[31] In the postwar period, the Soviet system continued to become simultaneously more imperial and more national.

Nonofficial war memory after 1945 was filled with still-raw grief and trauma often suppressed in official versions. With an estimated twenty-seven million war dead, how could it not be? Only with some distance, during the Leonid Brezhnev era in the 1970s and 1980s, did the cult of victory take on a massive scale and an officious, sacral aura. As the victory over fascism emerged as a full-blown civic religion with its own relics, rituals, artwork, and monuments, suffering was further suppressed by the "smooth surface of official memory." Under Brezhnev, who as a young man was deeply shaped by the war, over twenty "super-shrines" were constructed. These memorial ensembles included the 560-ton Motherland Monument *cum* war museum that after 1981 loomed over Kyiv from the right bank of the Dnieper. The Brezhnev era also witnessed the reconstruction of urban space in "hero cities." This term was used during the war and the immediate postwar period, but became formalized under Brezhnev in a hierarchy of heroism symbolizing Brezhnevian stability. Hero City status also brought with it significant municipal resources. Publication of Iudenkov's *People's War* in 1985 coincided with the conferral of Hero City status on Smolensk, where the eternal flame is still tended at the outskirts of the reconstructed city gates.[32]

Iudenkov's *People's War*, released in twenty thousand copies, exemplified a newfound professionalization of the war cult. It was replete with a far more detailed array of names and dates, facts and figures. This time, the 1942 Smolensk partisan territories and the Yelnya restoration of Soviet power were discussed at some length. Even so, they were interpreted only in light of aiding the military effort, as a "base for the further development of the armed struggle"—that is, not in terms of their rise and fall inside the occupied territories but as part of a single-stream, triumphal march to victory. Without discussion of rural support for the German occupation regime or requisitioning and marauding on both sides, the contributions local populations gave to the partisans within those territories were presented as proof of the all-people's struggle against fascism. The "whole history of the people's struggle on occupied Soviet territory" testified to "the most noble care on the part of the Party for the civilian population."[33] This was a story of paternalist generosity extended by the party-state even behind enemy lines, a wishful harmony projected retrospectively on wartime state and society.

It was certainly possible in literature, film, art, and even memorials to express pain, grief, and personalized suffering, seemingly within the constraints of the late Soviet sacralization of the war. But by the time of Mikhail Gorbachev's perestroika and glasnost of the late 1980s, a quarter century of "military-patriotic upbringing" had lost its grip. A drumbeat of perestroika-era revelations, ranging from the decimation of the Soviet military in the Great Terror to the Nazi-Soviet Pact, Katyn and other mass graves, and all the other crimes of Stalinism, quickly sparked a mass desacralization of the war.[34]

The result was a raucous, freewheeling cacophony. No single new war myth replaced the Soviet one between the late 1980s and the 2010s, when the hardening of Vladimir Putin's dictatorship led to its systematic reformulation. Nonetheless, the Soviet legacy was essential to that Putinist resurrection, despite all the major differences between the two regimes, their ideologies, and their wars. In both the Soviet and Putin-era patriotic narratives, the national and the imperial dimensions of statism remained intimately intertwined. After 1991, specifically socialist ideological formulations lost their grip. But those earlier, minority Soviet-era strands of the war myth that promoted elements of Russian nationalism, and the general Soviet glorification of a mighty state, remained as resource and legacy.

So did the victory's inextricable association with Stalinism and the leader's strong hand, intertwined with a patina of imperial glory always on the surface of the war myth.

Some of the mechanisms by which such reformulated legacies reemerge across historical ruptures, even the regime change of 1991, are exemplified in Iudenkov's last, post-Soviet memoirs. His 1998 *The Happiness of Difficult Roads: Toward a Biography of My Generation* was published in two hefty tomes. This was a much more personal, detailed narrative about his own life, chock full of conversations and details that would never have made it into official Soviet commemorative writing. Yet even in this newly personalized genre, Iudenkov still followed the political conventions of the Soviet war myth: the embattled partisan movement he had helped get off the ground from the start was directed by the (largely absent) district and central party leadership. Iudenkov was appointed to serve under Valuev in the Smolensk city party organization when Soviet power was restored in fall 1943. It comes out that there he met party secretary Dmitrii Popov, academician Nikolai Burdenko, and secret police chief Petr Kondakov as they took charge of the investigation of Katyn. After Gorbachev's 1990 release of the original NKVD orders proving Soviet culpability for the 1940 massacre, an additional collection of Soviet documents was presented to Poland by Boris Yeltsin in 1992. In Poland and East Europe, as well as for anti-Stalinist Russians, the toponym "Katyn" became a potent symbol for all the other killing fields. At the same time, the Soviet version of Katyn lived on as a visible, post-Soviet Russian strand of Katyn denial that included high-ranking politicians as well as trained historians. Iudenkov, the now elderly doctor of historical sciences, sided with the deniers. He continued to argue the Stalinist position about German culpability for the massacre until the bitter end.[35]

DURING THE SOVIET COLLAPSE in the late 1980s and early 1990s, Russian émigré Solidarists started to return to Russia, taking advantage of the political relaxation and a fascination with noncommunist ideas after so many decades of Marxist-Leninist dogma. The free-for-all surrounding the desacralization of the official Soviet war myth included the strong presence of Russian nationalist commemoration, constrained or semi-submerged before.[36]

It was in this context that Solidarist leader Roman Redlikh returned to Russia in 1991, taught philosophy in Moscow, and visited Smolensk in 1993. Redlikh had joined the young right-wing émigré nationalist movement in 1940, the same year he received a philosophy degree in Berlin. He had worked as a propagandist in German POW camps in 1941–1942 and visited Smolensk and Roslavl in 1943. He went on to hold a position as head of one of the training groups for the Vlasov movement in Dabendorf, where he taught propagandists by assigning the works of philosopher Ivan Il'in on Russian statehood. He and other Solidarists, part of a movement in decline since its heyday in the 1950s, now hoped in the 1990s that recruiting adherents inside Russia would create a strong new organization. They found some adherents, but struggled to gain traction.[37]

In Smolensk, however, Redlikh succeeded in sparking a debate about Menshagin, whom he had met in 1943. In an interview, he called the mayor "an exceptionally good and talented man," whose "heritage" was wasted. "Who were they in Stalin's eyes? Traitors and betrayers! . . . Menshagin was a traitor because he tried to help the population. This is what Menshagin and Menshagins did throughout the occupied territories."[38]

Redlikh's version of the wartime past was strongly countered by a party archivist and historian, the Smolensk native Leonid Kotov. As a teenager, Kotov lived through the German occupation, and in December 1943, shortly after the Soviets retook the city, he signed up for the Red Army. At fifteen years old he fought in battles on the First Ukrainian Front. In later decades, Kotov became a party archivist, loyal to the heroic Soviet mythologization of the war to the point of denying Stalin's culpability for the 1940 Katyn massacre even after the secret police documentation was released under Gorbachev. Kotov responded by publishing a series of anti-Menshagin articles indicting the mayor as culpable in all the major wartime atrocities in Smolensk. The essays featured tendentious readings of Menshagin's apparently genuine correspondence with German army authorities, documents Kotov reproduced at length but not in full. Unfortunately, the leading Soviet historian of wartime Smolensk and former archivist failed to follow standard citation methods about the provenance of the sources. This could not have been an accidental oversight. Were the apparently genuine documents selectively presented, or was other evidence omitted? To my knowledge, the documents he published have not surfaced since.[39]

The Redlikh-Kotov debate in Smolensk in the early 1990s was one drop in a veritable ocean of post-Soviet polemics and reconsiderations about the war, Stalinism, Russian history, and fascism. In this case, participants and partisans from that era were still confronting one another after the fall of communism. Kotov's political manipulation of archival documents was one small precursor to the methods of the memory wars that would blossom in Russia and Eastern Europe in the twenty-first century.[40]

Kotov quoted in the course of his polemic some of the written questions he received from regional history buffs at a 1994 conference for educators. One of them was brilliantly on point in questioning the lack of "literature on how the population lived under the occupation." A second was justifiably puzzled: "How should we think about General Vlasov and was there a 'Vlasov movement'?" A third could have opened up a long discussion about a key issue: "Is it right to call the war Great and Patriotic, since millions of Soviet people fought on the side of the Germans? . . . It seems more like a Second Civil War." Especially given the paucity of information available at the time, these were remarkably important and pointed questions. Just like his political enemy Redlikh, however, Kotov viewed history in terms of black and white. Redlikh had literally used the word *good* for the "Menshagins" of the occupation; Kotov deployed the adjective *evil* for anyone who portrayed the years of occupation of Smolensk in a positive light.[41]

Even though the émigré Solidarists, as during the war itself, failed to gain much of a foothold at all inside Russia, certain public and academic trends in Russia in the 2000s and 2010s echoed Solidarist positions, including a positive approach to anti-Stalinist Russian nationalism in the Vlasov movement and the occupied territories. But the role of émigrés across the years from the occupation to the post-Soviet period is emblematic of another phenomenon. It was perhaps inevitable that when a new type of ideology arose in post-Soviet Russia, it would be on the right wing of the political spectrum (as well as far less doctrinal and far more eclectic in the digital age). After the Soviet period, the Right was what was new and different. Even as Solidarist returnees met little practical success, a reclamation of the entire legacy of the Russian interwar and wartime emigration—in all its wings, from humanistic to fascistic—proceeded intensively in the 1990s and after. Even when elements of the late Soviet and then the Stalinist past were resurrected in the 2010s, there was no going back openly to the status quo ante. The long and tangled genealogy of the new right-left, red-brown syncretism that emerged within decades of the end of the USSR remains to be excavated by future historians.

ON FEBRUARY 24, 2022, Russia's invasion of Ukraine transformed Russia's relationship with the world and launched a dark new chapter in Russian history. History politics was initially front and center in justifying a war of aggression that brought three decades of relative Russian openness to the outside world to an abrupt end. Central to justifying what was euphemistically called Russia's "special military operation" in Ukraine, especially in the war's first year, was a new, Putin-era war myth entrenched in the 2010s and radicalized in the run-up to the crossing of the Rubicon. As the decade progressed, it remained unclear where Russia's increasingly radical domestic crackdown might lead. As I researched this book throughout that decade during extended stays in Moscow and Smolensk, I was not naive. But the deliberate destructiveness—and self-destructiveness—of the subsequent war of aggression and atrocities in Ukraine was hard to imagine.

In the contradictory decade of the 2010s, the Great Patriotic War became by far the number one historical topic in Russia. But that preoccupation encompassed wildly divergent and, as it turned out, incompatible trends. The Russian annexation of Crimea in 2014 not only launched a long-simmering military conflict in eastern Ukraine. It escalated a history-propaganda war that moved to the center of the Putin dictatorship.[42]

BECAUSE OF THE WAY the Putin regime initially justified the Russian war in Ukraine as if it were a continuation of the German-Soviet conflict on the Eastern Front, the two wars will now in some ways always be linked. The ironies of the Russian presentation of the invasion of Ukraine almost as a historical reenactment are immense. Unlike in 1941, when Stalin and the USSR were caught unaware, Putin's imperial grab across international borders looked very much like a throwback to the Nazi German invasions of its neighbors. In the late 1940s, communism, for better or for worse, commanded a great deal of ideological sympathy; the strength of the Soviet order was its ability to mobilize the masses. As it launched into war in 2022,

Russia possessed far less ideological allure and struggled to motivate and mobilize its people—although, in another throwback, this time to Stalinism, it did not hesitate to treat its large numbers as cannon fodder. Then, the Nazis carried out an unprecedented annihilation of civilians, including Jews, POWs, and peaceful women and children. Now, in the name of de-Nazification, Russia began targeting civilians, setting up occupation regimes, and creating mass graves for its erstwhile Slavic brothers. In a matchless irony, the resulting civic activism and national unity in Ukraine made the resistance there into a veritable "people's war," the designation invented under Stalinism to paper over its own deficiencies. A number of different echoes of the past could be detected as the invasion turned into a grinding war of attrition. A Winter War scenario emerged: that Russia, as in the Soviet fight against Finland in 1940, might "eke out a victory at tremendous cost." One of Russia's sacrifices appears to be its own domestic future. Just as the Eastern Front in World War II created profound legacies, Russia's revanchist attempt to re-enact the Great Soviet Victory will profoundly alter Russia's course for decades.[43]

History does not repeat itself, but it often rhymes. Both the differences between the mid-twentieth-century war in whose name this horrific 2020s war of aggression was waged and the historical parallels have been striking. Three-quarters of a century after the end of World War II, the world was once again watching the movements of the front lines in a war with trenches, tanks, looting, and rape—even if it was also replete with drones, cell phones, Telegram channels, and satellite imagery. Putin, truly, was no Stalin. But the way he doubled and tripled down in the face of the unexpected setbacks to his reckless gamble resembled nothing if not Stalin in the 1930s.

Almost all the trends and figures involved in the 2010s in creating a new Putinist war myth remained to make it more extreme at the outset of the invasion of Ukraine in 2022. The Putinist myth, like the old Soviet one, rested on a mirage of unadulterated heroism and historical inevitability that obscured, if not completely elided, the practices, horrors, and choices of actual war. To this, an emergent new ideology steeped in far-right, statist intellectual precursors from the age of extremes added its own cult of ruthless "geopolitical" thinking.

In the Putin-era myth of the war starting in the 2010s, the crude version of Marxist-Leninist determinism to which those like Iudenkov had resorted was replaced by historically far-right ideas about the primacy of geopolitics and the superiority of Russian civilization. Despite all altera-tions, it was still not hard to discern a genealogy connecting this new Russian statism to the earlier, long-familiar Soviet trope of the political logic of history and the superiority of Soviet socialism. In this new version of the Stalinist superiority complex, now popularized on gladiatorial television talk shows, the preemptive, state-sponsored defense of Russian civilization justifies the sacrifice and immiseration of people, even of mil-lions. The very juxtaposition of Stalinist and Nazi rule pursued throughout this book became a prosecutable crime. A 2021 Russian law, following on numerous precursors and precedents, criminalized any public attempt to "equate" the "purposes, decisions and actions" of the Soviet leadership and military with those of Nazi Germany during World War II.[44]

All works of history, including this one, are shaped by the context in which they are created. The catastrophic consequences in Putin's Russia of a newly weaponized mythmaking about the war made the complexities of actual lives caught in the crucibles of Stalinist and Nazi rule seem more than ever important to recover.

ARCHIVAL ABBREVIATIONS

BA MA—Bundesarchiv-Militärarchiv, Freiburg am Breisgau (German Federal Military Archive)

GANISO—Gosudarstvennyi arkhiv noveishei istorii Smolenskoi oblasti (State Archive of Contemporary History of Smolensk Region)

GARF—Gosudarstvennyi arkhiv Rossiiskoi Federatsii (State Archive of the Russian Federation)

GASO—Gosudarstvennyi arkhiv Smolenskoi oblasti (State Archive of Smolensk Region)

NA IRI RAN—Nauchnyi arkhiv Instituta rossiiskoi istorii Rossiiskoi akademii nauk (Scholarly Archive of the Institute of Russian History, Russian Academy of Sciences)

NARA—National Archives and Records Administration, US National Archives

RGASPI—Rossiiskii gosudarstvennyi arkhiv sotsial'no-politicheskoi istorii (Russian State Archive of Social-Political History)

RGASPI (Arkhiv VLKSM)—Rossiiskii gosudarstvennyi arkhiv sotsial'no-politicheskoi istorii, Arkhiv Vsesoiuznogo Leninskogo Komsomola (Russian State Archive of Social-Political History, Archive of the All-Union Leninist Communist Youth League)

SA—Smolensk Archive

USHMM—United States Holocaust Memorial Museum

NOTES

PROLOGUE

1 S. L. Solodovnikova, *Istoriia arkhivnogo dela v Smolenskoi oblasti (1908–2004)* (Smolensk: Svitok, 2004), 33–69; Patricia Kennedy Grimsted, "Displaced Archives and Restitution Problems on the Eastern Front in the Aftermath of the Second World War," *Contemporary European History* 6, no. 1 (1997): 33.

2 P. V. Khoroshilova et al., eds., *Svodnyi katalog kul'turnykh tsennostei, pokhishchen-nykh i utrachennykh v period Vtoroi mirovoi voiny*, vol. 4, bk. 2, *Utrachennye arkhivnye fondy. Arkhivy VKP(b)* (Moscow: Ministerstvo Kul'tury Rossiiskoi Federatsii, 2005), 54–58; K. A. Dmitrieva et al., eds., *Vozrashchenie "Smolenskogo Arkhiva"* (Moscow: ROSSPEN, 2005), 30–31; Hanns Christian Löhr, *Kunst als Waffe—Der Einsatzstab Reichsleiter Rosenberg. Ideologie und Kunstraub im "Dritten Reich"* (Berlin: Gebr. Mann Verlag, 2018), 58, 167; Peter M. Manasse, *Verschleppte Archive und Bibliotheken: Die Tätigkeiten des Einsatzstabes Rosenberg während des Zweiten Weltkrieges* (St. Ingbert: Röhrig Universitätsverlag, 1997), 109–13, 128–37.

3 Patricia Kennedy Grimsted, *The Odyssey of the Smolensk Archive: Plundered Communist Records for the Service of Anti-Communism*, Carl Beck Papers in Russian and East European Studies, no. 1201 (Pittsburgh: Center for Russian and East European Studies, University of Pittsburgh, 1995); Patricia Kennedy Grimsted, "Roads to Ratibor: Library and Archival Plunder by the Einsatzstab Reichsleiter Rosenberg," *Holocaust and Genocide Studies* 19, no. 3 (2005): 390–458.

4 Patricia Kennedy Grimsted, "Reconstructing the Record of Nazi Cultural Plunder: A Survey of the Dispersed Archives of the Einsatzstab Reichsleiter Rosenberg (ERR)," IISH Research Paper 47 (Amsterdam: International Institute of Social History, 2022), https://www.errproject.org/guide/ERR_Guide_Germany .pdf; Patricia Kennedy Grimsted, "Spoils of War Returned: U.S. Restitution of Nazi-Looted Cultural Treasures to the USSR, 1945–1959," *Prologue: Quarterly of*

the National Archives and Records Administration 34, no. 1 (Spring 2002): 27–41; Grimsted, "Displaced Archives," 39–43.

5   V. N. Shepelev, "Sud'ba 'Smolenskogo arkhiva," *Izvestiia TsK KPSS,* no. 5 (1991): 135–38; Evgenii Kodin, "*'Smolenskii arkhiv' i amerikanskaia sovetologiia* (Smolensk: SGPU, 1998), 6–18, 23; Grimsted, "Odyssey," 4–5, 71, 73, 76–77, 128n213.

6   Amir Weiner, *Making Sense of War: The Second World War and the Fate of the Bolshevik Revolution* (Princeton, NJ: Princeton University Press, 2000). One exception is the important study of the city of Smolensk by Laurie R. Cohen, *Smolensk under the Nazis: Everyday Life in Occupied Russia* (Rochester, NY: University of Rochester Press, 2013).

7   Merle Fainsod, *Smolensk under Soviet Rule* (Cambridge, MA: Harvard University Press, 1958). The major exception is Stephen Kotkin's *Magnetic Mountain: Stalinism as a Civilization* (Berkeley: University of California Press, 1995).

8   Merle Fainsod, *How Russia Is Ruled* (Cambridge, MA: Harvard University Press, 1953), 59; Fainsod, *Smolensk,* 446. See also David Engerman, *Know Your Enemy: The Rise and Fall of America's Soviet Experts* (New York: Oxford University Press, 2009), 180–205, 209–11, 230. Fainsod's formulation anticipated the subtitle of Sheila Fitzpatrick's 1999 magnum opus, *Everyday Stalinism: Ordinary Life in Extraordinary Times: Soviet Russia in the 1930s* (New York: Oxford University Press, 1999). On continuities across successive "schools" of totalitarianism, revisionism, and post-revisionist scholarship, see Mark Edele, "Soviet Society, Social Structure, and Everyday Life," *Kritika* 8, no. 2 (Spring 2007): 349–73 (368n82 on Fainsod).

9   Lynne Viola, "The Aesthetic of Stalinist Planning and the World of the Special Villages," *Kritika* 4, no. 1 (2003): 101–28; Peter Holquist, "New Terrains and New Chronologies: The Interwar Period through the Lens of Population Politics," *Kritika* 4, no. 1 (2003): 169–72.

10 Fainsod, *Smolensk,* 48–52. See Michael David-Fox, "Re-reading Fainsod in Smolensk," *Kritika* 22, no. 4 (Fall 2021): 811–38.

11 Fainsod, *Smolensk,* 446.

INTRODUCTION

1   Timothy Snyder, *Bloodlands: Europe between Hitler and Stalin* (New York: Basic Books, 2010).

2   A kind of *summa* of the classic comparative scholarship is found in Michael Geyer and Sheila Fitzpatrick, eds., *Beyond Totalitarianism: Stalinism and Nazism Compared* (New York: Cambridge University Press, 2009).

3   Lawrence L. Langer, "The Dilemma of Choice in the Deathcamps," *Centerpoint* 4, no. 1 (1980): 50–53; Evgeny Finkel, *Ordinary Jews: Choice and Survival during the Holocaust* (Princeton, NJ: Princeton University Press, 2017).

4   Inter alia, see Michael David-Fox, Peter Holquist, and Alexander Martin, eds., *The Holocaust in the East: Local Perpetrators and Soviet Responses* (Pittsburgh: University of Pittsburgh Press, 2014).

5   Stephen Kotkin, *Stalin*, vol. 1, *Paradoxes of Power, 1878–1928* (New York: Penguin, 2014), and vol. 2, *Waiting for Hitler, 1929–1941* (New York: Penguin, 2017); Oleg Khlevniuk, *Stalin: New Biography of a Dictator*, trans. Nora S. Favorov (New Haven, CT: Yale University Press, 2015); Ian Kershaw, *Hitler*, vol. 1, *1889–1936: Hubris* (New York: W. W. Norton, 1998), and vol. 2, *1936–1945: Nemesis* (New York: W. W. Norton, 2000); Peter Longerich, *Heinrich Himmler: A Life*, trans. Jeremy Noakes and Lesley Sharpe (New York: Oxford University Press, 2012).

6   Transcripts of these interviews were too frank to be published after the war, and the closed collection only became available after 2015. D. D. Lotareva, "Komissiia po istorii Velikoi Otechestvennoi Voiny i ee arkhiv: Rekonstruktsiia deiatel'nosti i metodov raboty," in *Arkheograficheskii ezhegodnik*, ed. S. O. Shmidt (Moscow: Institut Slavianovedeniia RAN, 2014), 123–66; Jochen Hellbeck, *Stalingrad: The City That Defeated the Third Reich*, trans. from the Russian by Christopher Tauchen and Dominic Bonfiglio (New York: PublicAffairs, 2015), 68–82; "Instruktsiia Komissii chastiam o sostavlenii istorii," undated, NA IRI RAN f. 2, r. XIV, op. 1, ed. khr. 7, l. 27, l. 28.

7   B. G. Men'shagin, *Vospominaniia: Smolensk . . . Katyn' . . . Vladimirskaia tiur'ma* (Paris: YMCA Press, 1988); *Boris Men'shagin: Vospominaniia. Pis'ma. Dokumenty*, ed. Pavel Polian et al. (St. Petersburg: Nestor-Istoriia, 2019). An original typescript of the wartime memoirs in the 2019 volume is in the Archiv der Forschungsstelle Osteuropa (FSO), 01-030.148 Levitskaja, University of Bremen.

8   See Pavel Polian's contributions in Men'shagin, *Vospominaniia* (2019), 215–53, 217n5, 254–64, 613–89.

9   Reprinted in Men'shagin, *Vospominaniia* (2019), 587–612.

10 Michael David-Fox, "Nachal'nik goroda: B. G. Men'shagin v istoricheskom kontekste," in Men'shagin, *Vospominaniia* (2019), 173–214. Cf. Jochen Hellbeck, *Revolution on My Mind: Writing a Diary under Stalin* (Cambridge, MA: Harvard University Press, 2009); for a different approach, see Alexis Peri, *The War Within: Diaries from the Siege of Leningrad* (Cambridge, MA: Harvard University Press, 2017), 7–14.

11 Christopher R. Browning and Lewis H. Siegelbaum, "Frameworks for Social Engineering: Stalinist Schema of Identification and the Nazi *Volksgemeinschaft*," in *Beyond Totalitarianism: Stalinism and Nazism Compared*, ed. Michael Geyer and Sheila Fitzpatrick (New York: Cambridge University Press, 2009), 231–65.

12 On Breitman-Petrenko, see Chapter 7. For a fresh discussion of imposture, subjectivity, and agency, see Timothy Blauvelt and David Jishkariani, "Deciphering the Stalinist Perpetrators: The Case of Georgian NKVD Investigators Khazan, Savitskii, and Krimian," in *The Secret Police and the Soviet System: New Archival*

Investigations, ed. Michael David-Fox (Pittsburgh: University of Pittsburgh Press, 2023), esp. 168–79.

13 GANISO f. 8, op. 1, ed. khr. 243, l. 1. Unless otherwise noted, all translations are my own. The study of perpetrators, so prominent in Nazi and Holocaust history, remained "largely uncharted territory" in Russian and Soviet studies until the 2010s. Lynne Viola, "The Question of the Perpetrator in Soviet History," *Slavic Review* 72, no. 1 (Spring 2013): 1.

14 Vasilii Maslennikov, *Bez tsenzury. Smolenshchina. Voina. Plen. Avtobiografiia* (Mozhaisk: Mozhaiskii poligraficheskii kombinat, 2014). Maslennikov died in 1998; the book was published in 2014 by his relatives in a print run of three hundred copies, one of which is in the Library of Congress.

15 SMERSH was the name coined by Stalin in 1943 as a portmanteau of the Russian words *Smert' shpionam,* meaning "death to spies."

16 See Chapter 7 and the Epilogue.

17 Hans Mommsen, the "functionalist" most associated with arguing that Hitler was a "weak dictator," apparently first used the phrase (*ein schwacher Diktator*) in a footnote in 1966. See Hans Mommsen, *Beamtentum im Dritten Reich* (Munich: De Gruyter, 1966), 98n26. On Stalin, see James Harris, "Was Stalin a Weak Dictator?," *Journal of Modern History* 75, no. 2 (2003): 375–86; Oleg Khlevniuk, "Top Down vs. Bottom-Up: Regarding the Potential of Contemporary 'Revisionism,'" *Cahiers du monde russe* 56, no. 4 (2015): 837–57.

18 R. V. Anoshkin and A. P. Katrovskii, *Dinamika naseleniia Smolenshchiny* (Smolensk: Universum, 2009). In 1944, Smolensk Region lost some thirteen districts to Kaluzhskaia Region and three to Velikie Luki Region.

19 Merle Fainsod, *Smolensk under Soviet Rule* (Cambridge, MA: Harvard University Press, 1958), 59–60.

20 Anoshkin and Katrovskii, *Dinamika naseleniia,* 19–21, 90.

21 Oksana Kornilova, *Kak stroili pervuiu sovetskuiu avtomagistral' 1936–1941* (Smolensk: Svitok, 2014); David M. Glantz, *Operation Barbarossa: Hitler's Invasion of Russia 1941* (Stroud, UK: History Press, 2001).

22 Andrej Angrick et al., eds., *Deutsche Besatzungsherrschaft in der UdSSR 1941–1945. Dokumente der Einsatzgruppen in der Sowjetunion* (Darmstadt: WBG, 2013), vol. 2; Robert Proctor, *Racial Hygiene: Medicine under the Nazis* (Cambridge, MA: Harvard University Press, 1988), 190.

23 Waitman Beorn, *Marching into Darkness: The Wehrmacht and the Holocaust in Belarus* (Cambridge, MA: Harvard University Press, 2014), 104; Jörn Hasenclever, *Wehrmacht und Besatzungspolitik in der Sowjetunion: Die Befehlshaber der rückwärtigen Heeresgebiete 1941–1943* (Paderborn: Ferdinand Schöningh, 2010), 202–3.

24 There were also two partisan territories in Briansk and five in other regions. See
I. P. Shcherov, *Partizany: Organizatsiia, metody i posledstviia bor'by (1941–1945)*
(Smolensk: Universum, 2006), 129–36; Dmitrii Komarov, *Smolenskaia oblast' v
ogne Velikoi Otechestvennoi: Voina, narod, pobeda* (Smolensk: Svitok, 2015), 155–73;
Leonid D. Grenkevich, *The Soviet Partisan Movement, 1941–1944* (London: Frank
Cass, 1999), 187–92.

25 Alexander Dallin, *German Rule in Russia 1941–1945: A Study of Occupation
Policies,* 2nd ed. (Basingstoke: Palgrave Macmillan, 1981); Timothy Patrick
Mulligan, *The Politics of Illusion and Empire: German Occupation Policy in the
Soviet Union, 1942–1943* (New York: Praeger, 1988).

26 Mulligan, *Politics of Illusion,* 2–3, 10; Ian Kershaw, "'Working toward the Führer':
Reflections on the Nature of the Hitler Dictatorship," *Contemporary European
History* 2, no. 2 (1993): 103–18.

27 Jeffrey Burds, "'Turncoats, Traitors, and Provocateurs': Communist Collabora-
tors, the German Occupation, and Stalin's NKVD, 1941–1943," *East European
Politics and Societies and Cultures* 32, no. 3 (2018): 606–38; Mark Edele, *Stalin's
Defectors: How Red Army Soldiers Became Hitler's Collaborators, 1941–1945*
(Oxford: Oxford University Press, 2017), 4, 128.

28 Asya Shneiderman, "Okkupirovannyi Smolensk. Sov. Sekretno," September 14,
1942, RGASPI f. 1M, op. 53, d. 246, l. 75; Leonid Gorizontov, "The 'Great Circle'
of Interior Russia: Representations of the Imperial Center in the Nineteenth and
Early Twentieth Centuries," in *Russian Empire: Space, People, Power, 1700–1930,*
ed. Jane Burbank, Mark von Hagen, and Anatolyi Remnev (Bloomington:
Indiana University Press, 2007), 84; Laurie R. Cohen, *Smolensk under the Nazis:
Everyday Life in Occupied Russia* (Rochester, NY: University of Rochester Press,
2013), 7–8.

29 T. I. Novosel'tseva and N. F. Pikalova, "Provintsial'naia vlast': Ot obshchikh
kontorov k sistemnoi vertikali," in *Provintsial'naia vlast': Sistema i ee predstaviteli,
1917–1938 gg.,* ed. E. V. Kodin (Smolensk: SGU, 2005), 10–31.

30 A. V. Okorokov, *Fashizm i russkaia emigratsiia (1920–1945 gg.)* (Moscow: Rusaki,
2002), 458–60; *Rannye ideinye poiski rossiiskikh solidaristov* (Moscow: Posev, 1992);
Marc Raeff, review of *Novopokolentsy* (1986), by Boris Prianishnikoff, *Slavic
Review* 48, no. 2 (1989): 305–6; Dallin, *German Rule,* 523–32; Sebiast'ian Shtopper
[Stopper] and Andrei Kukatov, *Nelegal'nyi Briansk 1941–1943: Nelegal'naia
deiatel'nost' razlichnykh sil v okkupirovannykh Brianske i Ordzhonikidzegrade s 6
oktiabria 1941 po 17 sentiabria 1943 goda* (Briansk: Bukvitsa, 2014), 41–43.

31 Benjamin Tromly, *Cold War Exiles and the CIA: Plotting to Free Russia* (New
York: Oxford University Press, 2019), 44–47; A. V. Okorokov, *Osobyi front:
Nemetskaia propaganda na vostochnom fronte v gody Vtoroi mirovoi voiny*
(Moscow: Russkii put', 2007), 136–38; Shtopper and Kukatov, *Nelegal'nyi Briansk,*
252–56.

32 Chris Bellamy, *Absolute War: Soviet Russia in the Second World War* (New York: Vintage Books, 2007).

33 Katerina Clark and Karl Schlögel, "Mutual Perceptions and Projections: Stalin's Russia in Nazi Germany—Nazi Germany in Stalin's Russia," in *Beyond Totalitarianism: Stalinism and Nazism Compared,* ed. Michael Geyer and Sheila Fitzpatrick (New York: Cambridge University Press, 2009), 399–402.

34 George L. Mosse and Roger Griffin embraced the notion of a fascist revolution, but this was more a metaphor for zealous radicalism than a move to incorporate insights derived from the study of other revolutions. George L. Mosse, *The Fascist Revolution: Toward a General Theory of Fascism* (New York: Howard Fertig, 1999); inter alia, see Roger Griffin, "Fascism's Modernist Revolution: A New Paradigm for the Study of Right-Wing Dictatorships," *Fascism: Journal of Comparative Fascist Studies* 5, no. 2 (2016): 105–29; Jack A. Goldstone, *Revolutions: A Very Short Introduction* (Oxford: Oxford University Press, 2014), 38. Goldstone originally had a chapter (later cut) on revolutions on the right, in which he discussed Germany, Turkey, and Egypt, places where nationalism became the overriding revolutionary motivation. Correspondence with Jack A. Goldstone, January 14, 2023. See also Jeremy Noakes, "The Nazi Revolution," in *Reinterpreting Revolution in Twentieth-Century Europe,* ed. Moira Donald and Tim Rees (New York: St. Martin's, 2001), chap. 6; Jean-Denis Lepage, *Hitler's Stormtroopers: The SA, the Nazis' Brownshirts, 1922–1945* (Barnsley, UK: Frontline Books, 2016), 229–33; Donald Bloxham, *The Final Solution: A Genocide* (New York: Oxford University Press, 2009), 5–6.

35 Gerd Koenen, *Der Russland-Komplex: Die Deutschen und der Osten 1900–1945* (Munich: C. H. Beck, 2005); Vejas Gabriel Liulevicius, *The German Myth of the East: 1800 to the Present* (Oxford: Oxford University Press, 2009); Paul Hanebrink, *A Specter Haunting Europe: The Myth of Judeo-Bolshevism* (Cambridge, MA: Harvard University Press, 2018); Timothy Snyder, *Black Earth: The Holocaust as History and Warning* (New York: Tim Duggan Books, 2015).

36 Michael David-Fox, "Toward a Life Cycle Analysis of the Russian Revolution," *Kritika* 18, no. 4 (Fall 2017): 741–83.

37 Den Khili [Dan Healey], "Nasledie GULAGa: Prinuditel'nyi trud sovetskoi epokhi kak vnutrenniaia kolonizatsiia," in *Tam, vnutri: Praktiki vnutrennei kolonizatsii v kul'turnoi istorii Rossii,* ed. Aleksandr Etkind et al. (Moscow: NLO, 2012), 684–728; Lynne Viola, *The Unknown Gulag: The Lost World of Stalin's Special Settlements* (New York: Oxford University Press, 2007), 185–86; Alexander Etkind, *Internal Colonization: Russia's Imperial Experience* (Cambridge, UK: Polity Press, 2011).

38 I am indebted for this formulation to Mark Edele's commentary at the 2023 Association for Slavic, East European, and Eurasian Studies (ASEEES) annual convention in Philadelphia.

39 Dieter Pohl, *Die Herrschaft der Wehrmacht: Deutsche Militärbesatzung und einheimische Bevölkerung in der Sowjetunion 1941–1944* (Munich: R. Oldenbourg, 2008), 203; Christian Streit, *Keine Kameraden: Die Wehrmacht und die sowjetischen Kriegsgefangenen, 1941–1945,* rev. ed. (Bonn: Dietz, 1997), 10, 20. A new reference work is *The United States Holocaust Memorial Museum Encyclopedia of Camps and Ghettos, 1933–1945,* vol. 4, *Camps and Other Detention Facilities under the German Armed Forces,* ed. Geoffrey P. Megargee et al. (Bloomington: Indiana University Press, 2022).

40 See Chapter 5; also see, inter alia, Alexander Brakel, *Unter Roten Stern und Hakenkreuz: Baranowicze 1939 bis 1944* (Paderborn: Ferdinand Schöningh, 2009). On loss of sovereignty and Sovietization as a political resource for the Germans in 1941, see Snyder, *Black Earth.*

41 "Stenogramma Zasedaniia XIII-go Plenuma Smolenskogo oblastnogo komiteta VKP(b) ot 23–25 dekabria 1943 goda," RGASPI f. 17, op. 43, ed. khr. 1717, l. 225; Komarov, *Smolenskaia oblast',* 445–70.

42 The terms are adopted from Michael Billig, *Banal Nationalism* (London: Sage, 1995); see Chapter 8.

43 Jan Gross, *Revolution from Abroad: The Soviet Conquest of Poland's Western Ukraine and Western Belorussia* (Princeton, NJ: Princeton University Press, 1988), 232.

44 Nadezhda Mandelstam, *Hope against Hope,* trans. Max Hayward (New York: Modern Library, 1999), 268; Primo Levi, interview, *New Republic,* February 17, 1986.

1. AN EPICENTER OF THE STALIN REVOLUTION

1 "Dokladnaia zapiska otvetstvennogo instruktora TsK VKP(b) t. Iakovleva ob obsledovanii Smolenskogo gubernskogo partorganizatsii," no later than May 19, 1928, GANISO f. R-5, op. 1, d. 192, ll. 58–79; Evgenii Kodin, *"Smolenskii naryv"* (Smolensk: Smolenskii gos. ped. institut, 1995).

2 Daniel R. Brower, "The Smolensk Scandal and the End of NEP," *Slavic Review* 45, no. 4 (Winter 1986): 702.

3 Kodin, *"Smolenskii naryv,"* 15, citing *Pravda,* April 18, 1928; Brower, "Smolensk Scandal."

4 "O polozhenii v Smolenskoi organizatsii VKP(b) (Dokladnaia zapiska tt. Liaksutkina i Tseitlina)," no later than May 14, 1928, GANISO f. R-5, op. 1, d. 192, ll. 79–109; Aleksei Zhukov, "Sotsial'no-ekonomicheskie i obshchestvenno-politicheskie protsessy na Smolenshchine na zavershaiushchem etape novoi ekonomicheskoi politiki: 1925–1929 gg." (candidate of sciences diss., Briansk State University, 2008); Brower, "Smolensk Scandal," 698.

5   Brower, "Smolensk Scandal," 702; K. G. Markevich, "'. . . Iavliaetsia absoliutno chuzhdym elementom' (Iz istorii chistok gosapparata v 20–30 gg. XX veka)," *Vestnik Katynskogo memoriala,* no. 2 (2003): 30–31.

6   See, e.g., GANISO f. 5, op. 1, d. 277, l. 78; RGASPI f. 17, op. 21, ed. khr. 4060, l. 1; SA T87 WKP 33, 208; Lynne Viola et al., eds., *The War against the Peasantry, 1927–1930: The Tragedy of the Soviet Countryside,* trans. Steven Shabad (New Haven, CT: Yale University Press, 2005), 9–117; Kodin, *"Smolenskii naryv,"* 11; Brower, "Smolensk Scandal," 703–6.

7   B. Feigin, "Smolenskii signal," *Bol'shevik,* no. 10 (May 31, 1928): 14–22; Kodin, *"Smolenskii naryv,"* 13–14.

8   "Protokol No. 3 Zasedaniia Ob"edinnenogo plenuma Smolenskogo Gubkoma i Gubernskoi kontrol'noi komissii VKP(b) XVII sozyva s aktivom ot 18–19 maia 1928 g.," SA T87 WKP 33, 363–66.

9   Merle Fainsod, *Smolensk under Soviet Rule* (Cambridge, MA: Harvard University Press, 1958), 48–52; Kodin, *"Smolenskii naryv,"* 34–35; SA T87 WKP 33, 386.

10 Cf. J. Arch Getty, *Practicing Stalinism: Bolsheviks, Boyars, and the Persistence of Tradition* (New Haven, CT: Yale University Press, 2013), esp. 233; James Harris, "Resisting the Plan in the Urals, 1928–1956: Or, Why Regional Officials Needed 'Wreckers' and 'Saboteurs,'" in *Contending with Stalinism: Soviet Power and Popular Resistance in the 1930s,* ed. Lynne Viola (Ithaca, NY: Cornell University Press, 2002), 201–27, esp. 201n1.

11 Stephen Kotkin, *Stalin,* vol. 1, *Paradoxes of Power, 1878–1928* (New York: Penguin, 2014), 300–307.

12 R. V. Anoshkin and A. P. Katrovskii, *Dinamika naseleniia Smolenshchiny* (Smolensk: Universum, 2009), 20–22, 90; William Rosenberg, "Smolensk in the 1920s: Party-Worker Relations and the 'Vanguard' Question," *Russian Review* 36, no. 2 (1977): 130–31.

13 T. I. Novosel'tseva and N. F. Pikalova, "Provintsial'naia vlast': Ot obshchikh kontorov k sistemnoi vertikali," in *Provintsial'naia vlast': Sistema i ee predstaviteli, 1917–1938 gg.,* ed. E. V. Kodin (Smolensk: SGU, 2005), 11–13; Fainsod, *Smolensk,* 39; Markevich, "'. . . Iavliaetsia,'" 27; S. V. Aleksandrov, "'Sovetskoi vlast'iu pochti ne pakhnet': Smolenshchina v 1920–1921 gg. po dokumentam Smolenskogo arkhiva," *Vestnik Katynskogo memoriala,* no. 15 (2015): 78–103.

14 Martin Malia, *Russia under Western Eyes: From the Bronze Horseman to the Lenin Mausoleum* (Cambridge, MA: Harvard University Press, 1999), 302; Michael David-Fox, "What Is Cultural Revolution? Key Concepts and the Arc of Soviet Cultural Transformation, 1910s–1930s," in *Crossing Borders: Modernity, Ideology, and Culture in Russia and the Soviet Union* (Pittsburgh: University of Pittsburgh Press, 2015), 122–28.

15 Novosel'tseva and Pikalova, "Provintsial'naia vlast'," 14, 24; Fainsod, *Smolensk,* 72; Anoshkin and Katrovskii, *Dinamika naseleniia,* 90.

16 Vasilii Maslennikov, *Bez tsenzury. Smolenshchina. Voina. Plen. Avtobiografiia* (Mozhaisk: Mozhaiskii poligraficheskii kombinat, 2014), 3–5, 21.

17 Maslennikov, *Bez tsenzury,* 21–26, 45; Lynne Viola, *Peasant Rebels under Stalin: Collectivization and the Culture of Peasant Resistance* (New York: Oxford University Press, 1996), 6, 8.

18 Maslennikov, *Bez tsenzury,* 25–37.

19 Maslennikov, *Bez tsenzury,* 26, 31, 38.

20 Maslennikov, *Bez tsenzury,* 26, 31, 38; Viola, *Peasant Rebels,* 6, 8.

21 Maslennikov, *Bez tsenzury,* 37, 43.

22 Viola, *Peasant Rebels,* 6–7.

23 Smolensk peasants in the mid-1920s to 1930: SA WKP 292 (1926–1927), WKP 295 (1927–1929), WKP 218 (1929–1930); Kodin, *"Smolenskii naryv,"* 26, citing GANISO f. 3, op. 1, d. 3840, ll. 224–25; Maslennikov, *Bez tsenzury,* 38, 43.

24 RGASPI f. 17, op. 21, ed. khr. 4061, l. 56, l. 57, l. 96 (1926 Regional Party Committee protocols); Kodin, *"Smolenskii naryv,"* 11.

25 Novosel′tseva and Pikalova, "Provintsial′naia vlast′," 14; Dmitrii Komarov, *Smolenskaia oblast′ v ogne Velikoi Otechestvennoi: Voina, narod, pobeda* (Smolensk: Svitok, 2015), 10.

26 GANISO f. R-5, op. 1, d. 189, l. 74; E. V. Kodin, "VKP(b) kak partiia-gosudarstvo," in *Provintsial′naia vlast′: Sistema i ee predstaviteli, 1917–1938 gg.,* ed. E. V. Kodin (Smolensk: SGU, 2005), 115, 123; Lynne Viola, *The Best Sons of the Fatherland: Workers in the Vanguard of Soviet Collectivization* (New York: Oxford University Press, 1987), 103–5; Viola, *Peasant Rebels,* 22; Kodin, *"Smolenskii naryv,"* 26.

27 Kodin, *"Smolenskii naryv,"* 20–32, quotation 21; James W. Heinzen, *Inventing a Soviet Countryside: State Power and the Transformation of Rural Russia, 1917–1929* (Pittsburgh: University of Pittsburgh Press, 2004), 163–66.

28 "Protokol zasedaniia biuro Smolenskogo Gubkoma VKP(b)," December 29, 1927, SA T87, WKP 33, 20; Brower, "Smolensk Scandal," 692; Viola et al., *War against the Peasantry,* 9–56.

29 Heinzen, *Inventing a Soviet Countryside,* 195–219; James W. Heinzen, "'Alien' Personnel in the Soviet State: The People's Commissariat of Agriculture under Proletarian Dictatorship, 1918–1929," *Slavic Review* 56, no. 1 (Spring 1997): 73–100.

30 Novostel′tseva and Pikalova, "Provintsial′naia vlast′," 27–31.

31 Kodin, "VKP(b) kak partiia-gosudarstvo," esp. 113.

32 Maslennikov, *Bez tsenzury,* 48, 52–56.

33 Maslennikov, *Bez tsenzury,* 43, 50, 71, 163.

34 Maslennikov, *Bez tsenzury,* 61–65.

35 Sheila Fitzpatrick, *Education and Social Mobility in the Soviet Union, 1921–1934* (Cambridge: Cambridge University Press, 1979), 17.

36 Even "neo-totalitarian" historians not only accepted Fitzpatrick's empirical breakthrough but took away a focus on the Stalinist political elite. See Martin Malia, *The Soviet Tragedy: A History of Socialism in Russia* (New York: Free Press, 1994), 539n25.

37 Sheila Fitzpatrick, "Stalin and the Making of a New Elite," in *The Cultural Front: Power and Culture in Revolutionary Russia* (Ithaca, NY: Cornell University Press, 1992), 149–82.

38 Fitzpatrick, *Education and Social Mobility,* 16–17, 187.

39 Iakovlev, "Dokladnaia zapiska," l. 63; T. I. Novosel'tseva, "Vydvinem upravlentsev iz naroda!," in *Provintsial'naia vlast': Sistema i ee predstaviteli, 1917–1938 gg.,* ed. E. V. Kodin (Smolensk: SGU, 2005), 202–55.

40 "Postanovlenie po dokladu ob itogakh vydvizheniia 600 rabochikh i krest'ian v gosapparat po Zapadnoi oblasti," undated, 1930, GANISO f. R-5, op. 1, d. 74, ll. 124–25; Novosel'tseva, "Vydvinem," 206.

41 Higher technical education in the Smolensk Region was limited to one polytechnical institute; in the late 1920s, there were forty-three lower-level *proftekhshkoly* with agricultural and industrial specializations. Higher education in Smolensk Region was expanded only in 1935. E. Ivanova, "Stanovlenie i razvitie sistemy vysshego obrazovaniia v Zapadnoi oblasti (1929–1937)," *Krai Smolenskii,* no. 9 (September 2007): 18–22.

42 "Stenogramma soveshchaniia vydvizhentsev pri Obkome VKP(b)," August 28, 1929, GANISO f. R-5, op. 1, d. 74, ll. 142–70.

43 "Stenogramma soveshchaniia vydvizhentsev," ll. 170–72; "Pis'mo rabochego-vydvizhentsa," in *"Proverkoi zaiavleniia ustanovleno . . .": Povsednevnaia zhizn' liudei v pis'makh i obrashcheniiakh k vlasti. 1930-e gody,* ed. E. V. Kodin (Smolensk: Svitok, 2013), 10.

44 "Informatsionnaia svodka. O rezul'tatakh vydvizheniia po Zapadnoi oblasti," no earlier than July 15, 1929, GANISO f. R-5, op. 1, d. 74, ll. 128–31; GANISO f. R-5, op. 1, d. 189, l. 78; GANISO f. R-5, op. 1, d. 189, ll. 58–61; GANISO f. R-5, op. 1, d. 277, ll. 58–61; GANISO f. R-5, op. 1, d. 74, d. 189, l. 277.

45 GANISO f. R-5, op. 1, d. 277, l. 58; GANISO f. R-5, op. 1, d. 189, l. 78; GANISO f. R-5, op. 1, d. 74, ll. 112–13; Fitzpatrick, *Education and Social Mobility,* 182; Novostel'tseva, "Vydvinem," 226.

46 Markevich, "'. . . Iavliaetsia.'"

47 GANISO f. R-5, op. 1, d. 192, l. 13; Markevich, "'. . . Iavliaetsia,'" 30, 32.

48 "Vsem okruzhkomam," August 10, 1929, GANISO f. R-5, op. 1, d. 189, l. 16; Ivanova, "Stanovlenie," 21; K. G. Markevich, "Chistki gosudarstvennykh uchrezhdenii na Smolenshchine v 1920–1930-e gody," in *Provintsial'naia vlast':*

Sistema i ee predstaviteli, 1917–1938 gg., ed. E. V. Kodin (Smolensk: SGU, 2005), 189; Vladimir Anikeev, "Chistka," *Krai Smolenskii,* no. 5 (2012): 41–49.

49 Markevich, "'. . . Iavliaetsia,'" 39.

50 Kodin, "VKP(b) kak partiia-gosudarstvo," 133–36; Kodin, *"Proverkoi zaiavleniia ustanovleno . . . ,"* 19.

51 E. G. Karelin, "Istoriia sozdaniia Smolenskoi oblasti i ee politiko-administrativnoi sistemy," in *Vsia zhizn' Smolenshchine* (Smolensk: Smolenskaia gorodskaia tipografiia, 2011), 17–23, quotation 18; Fainsod, *Smolensk,* 52–61.

52 Maslennikov, *Bez tsenzury,* 51–56, 63, 65–67.

2. COLONIZING THE COUNTRYSIDE

1 A. N. Tsvetkova, "Iz istorii sem'i N. S. Tsvetkova," *Vestnik Katynskogo memoriala,* no. 8 (2008): 93–113.

2 Tsvetkova, "Iz istorii sem'i," 99–101.

3 S. V. Aleksandrov, "Dokumenty rasskazyvaiut: Raskulachivanie Smolenskoi derevni (Arkhivny materialy 1930–1931 gg.)," *Vestnik Katynskogo memoriala,* no. 12 (2012): 181. The term *developmental violence* is discussed in Christian Gerlach and Nicolas Werth, "State Violence—Violent Societies," in *Beyond Totalitarianism: Stalinism and Nazism Compared,* ed. Michael Geyer and Sheila Fitzpatrick (New York: Cambridge University Press, 2009), 151.

4 Tsvetkova, "Iz istorii sem'i," 101.

5 Alvin W. Gouldner, "Stalinism: A Study of Internal Colonialism," *Telos* 34, no. 5 (1977): 4–48; Den Khili [Dan Healey], "Nasledie GULAGa: Prinuditel'nyi trud sovetskoi epokhi kak vnutrenniaia kolonizatsiia," in *Tam, vnutri: Praktiki vnutrennei kolonizatsii v kul'turnoi istorii Rossii,* ed. Aleksandr Etkind et al. (Moscow: NLO, 2012), 690, 694; Lynne Viola, *The Unknown Gulag: The Lost World of Stalin's Special Settlements* (New York: Oxford University Press, 2007), 21, 25–29.

6 GANISO f. R-5, op. 1, d. 192, ll. 27–28; RGASPI f. 17, op. 21, d. 4079, l. 62.

7 Gerlach and Werth, "State Violence," 175–76; Lynne Viola, *Peasant Rebels under Stalin: Collectivization and the Culture of Peasant Resistance* (New York: Oxford University Press, 1996), 3–4.

8 October 1929 telegrams from Grigorii Rakitov to county party organizations, GANISO f. R-5, op. 1, d. 192, l. 22, l. 25, ll. 27–28, ll. 29–31; RGASPI f. 17, op. 21, d. 4079, l. 61.

9 Tat'iana Novosel'tseva, "Sudebnaia vlast' v bor'be s 'kontrrevoliutsionnym terrorom': 1930-e gody," *Krai Smolenskii,* no. 7 (2012): 13–17.

10 "Stenogramma oblastnogo soveshchaniia 25-tysiachnikov," January 1, 1931, GANISO f. R-5, op. 1, d. 1174, l. 37; Lynne Viola, *The Best Sons of the Fatherland:*

Workers in the Vanguard of Soviet Collectivization (New York: Oxford University Press, 1987).

11 Nellie Ohr, "Collective Farms and Russian Peasant Society, 1933–1937: The Stabilization of the Kolkhoz Order" (PhD diss., Stanford University, 1990), 5.

12 GANISO f. R-5, op. 1, d. 1174, l. 122; Viola, *Best Sons,* 153, 163–64; Deborah Fitzgerald, "Collectivization and Industrialization: Learning from the Soviets," in *Every Farm a Factory: The Industrial Ideal in American Agriculture* (New Haven, CT: Yale University Press, 2003), 157–83.

13 GANISO f. R-5, op. 1, d. 1174, ll. 25, 35–37; Viola, *Peasant Rebels,* 239–40; Mark Tauger, "The 1932 Harvest and the Famine of 1933," *Slavic Review* 50, no. 1 (Spring 1991): 77.

14 Vasilii Maslennikov, *Bez tsenzury. Smolenshchina. Voina. Plen. Avtobiografiia* (Mozhaisk: Mozhaiskii poligraficheskii kombinat, 2014), 80.

15 Maslennikov, *Bez tsenzury,* 81, 83, 105–6; Sheila Fitzpatrick, *Stalin's Peasants: Resistance and Survival in the Russian Village after Collectivization* (New York: Oxford University Press, 1994), 80–127.

16 Maslennikov, *Bez tsenzury,* 76, 97–99.

17 Maslennikov, *Bez tsenzury,* 86, 90, 97, 112, 101–4.

18 Nicolas Werth, "Dekulakization as Mass Violence," *Mass Violence and Resistance—Research Network,* Sciences Po, September 23, 2011, https://www .sciencespo.fr/mass-violence-war-massacre-resistance/en/document /dekulakisation-mass-violence.html, accessed March 21, 2024.

19 Ivan Rumiantsev, "Vsem sekretariam okruzhkomov VKP(b)," February 5, 1930, GANISO f. R-5, op. 1, d. 555, l. 17; "Dokladnaia zapiska. Ob izvrashchenii linii partii po raskulachivaniiu," February 1930, GANISO f. R-5, op. 1, d. 555, ll. 30–35; Bureau of the Regional Party Committee instructions to the District Party Committees, no later than February 30, 1930, GANISO f. R-5, op. 1, d. 555, l. 68; Regional Party Committee correspondence with NKVD, GANISO f. R-5, op. 2, d. 918.

20 GANISO f. R-5, op. 1, d. 192, l. 25; Ivan Rumiantsev to Viacheslav Molotov, January 26, 1930, GANISO f. R-5, op. 1, d. 555, ll. 1–5.

21 "Korni i uroki 'Medynskoi istorii,'" March 6, 1930, GANISO f. R-5, op. 1, d. 566, ll. 11–14; "Protokol zakrytogo zasedaniia biuro Viazemskogo okruzhkoma VKP(b) ot 13 fevralia 1930 goda," GANISO f. R-5, op. 1, d. 555, l. 12; GANISO f. R-5, op. 1, d. 555, l. 68.

22 "O peregibakh v raskulachivanii," no later than February 2, 1930, GANISO f. 5, op. 2, d. 548, ll. 36–39; published in S. V. Aleksandrov, "Dokumenty rasskazyvaiut: Raskulachivanie Smolenskoi derevni (Arkhivnye materialy 1930–1931 gg.)," *Vestnik Katynskogo memoriala,* no. 12 (2012): 160–65.

23 Maslennikov, *Bez tsenzury,* 79, 91, 101–4; Fitzpatrick, *Stalin's Peasants,* 81.

24 Maslennikov, *Bez tsenzury,* 99, 112, 113, 114, 127.

25 "Svodka ob ispol'zovanii '25000' po Zapadnoi oblasti," no exact date, 1930, GANISO f. R-5, op. 1, d. 277, ll. 29–32; GANISO f. R-5, op. 1, d. 700, ll. 74–82.

26 GANISO f. R-5, op. 1, d. 1174, ll. 17–20, 41, 45, 48–53, 122–45; cf. Viola, *Best Sons.*

27 GANISO f. R-5, op. 1, d. 555, ll. 1–5; Viola, *Peasant Rebels,* 37; Lynne Viola, "*Bab'i Bunty* and Peasant Women's Protest during Collectivization," *Russian Review* 45, no. 1 (1986): 23–42.

28 GANISO f. R-5, op. 1, d. 108, ll. 3–4; GANISO f. R-5, op. 1, d. 1174, l. 125; Lynne Viola, "The Peasant Nightmare: Visions of Apocalypse in the Soviet Country-side," *Journal of Modern History* 62, no. 4 (1990): 747–70; Victoria Smolkin, *A Sacred Space Is Never Empty: A History of Soviet Atheism* (Princeton, NJ: Princeton University Press, 2018), 45–49.

29 GANISO f. R-5, op. 1, d. 555, l. 19; GANISO f. R-5, op. 1, d. 192, l. 22; RGASPI f. 17, op. 21, d. 4079, l. 112.

30 R. V. Shamilin, "Zhaloby krest'ianstva kak istoricheskii istochnik po izucheniiu politiki raskulachivaniia, 1929–1931 gody (na primer Zapadnoi oblasti)," in *Istoriia stalinizma: Repressirovannaia rossiiskaia provintsiia,* ed. E. V. Kodin (Moscow: ROSSPEN, 2011), 97–103.

31 Maslennikov, *Bez tsenzury,* 101, 103–4, 106–14, 130; Ohr, "Collective Farms," 27–34, 86; Fitzpatrick, *Stalin's Peasants,* 128–51.

32 Liubov Denisova, *Rural Women in the Soviet Union and Post-Soviet Russia,* ed. and trans. Irina Mukhina (London: Routledge, 2010), 2, 9–10, 13–23.

33 Ohr, "Collective Farms," 371, 406–7.

34 Catriona Kelly, *Comrade Pavlik: The Rise and Fall of a Soviet Boy Hero* (London: Granta Books, 2005).

35 "Aleksandr Trifonovich Tvardovskii," Smolensk Regional Universal Scholarly Library, http://www.smolensklib.ru/sites/default/files/old%20str/tvardov/biogr/history1.htm?fbclid=IwAR1uPvMDSjdBgd1HiZW5cCIjEnfz9WQ4NUXOoB bryWnhCbEngEhFzYmllUk, accessed June 10, 2023.

36 A. T. Tvardovskii, *Sobranie sochinenii,* vol. 6, *Pis'ma (1932–1970)* (Moscow: Khudozhestvennaia literatura, 1983), 330, 604; Denis Kozlov, *The Readers of "Novyi Mir": Coming to Terms with the Stalinist Past* (Cambridge, MA: Harvard University Press, 2013), chap. 5.

37 Anatoly Pinsky, "The Origins of Post-Stalinist Individuality: Aleksandr Tvardovskii and the Evolution of 1930s Soviet Romanticism," *Russian Review* 76, no. 3 (2017): 458–83.

38 Pinsky, "Origins," 465–69.

39 David R. Shearer, *Policing Stalin's Socialism: Repression and Social Order in the Soviet Union, 1924–1953* (New Haven, CT: Yale University Press, 2009).

40 Ohr, "Collective Farms," 178, 345.

41 Mark Edele and Michael Geyer, "States of Exception: The Nazi-Soviet War as a System of Violence, 1939–1945," in *Beyond Totalitarianism: Stalinism and Nazism Compared,* ed. Michael Geyer and Sheila Fitzpatrick (New York: Cambridge University Press, 2009), 350.

42 Hitler quoted in Timothy Snyder, *Bloodlands: Europe between Hitler and Stalin* (New York: Basic Books, 2010), 61.

43 Gerd Koenen, *Der Russland-Komplex: Die Deutschen und der Osten 1900–1945* (Munich: C. H. Beck, 2005), 413–15; Wolfram Wette, "Das Russlandbild in der NS-Propaganda: Ein Problemaufriss," and Hans-Erich Volkmann, "Das Russlandbild in der Schule des Dritten Reiches," in *Das Russlandbild im Dritten Reich,* ed. Hans-Erich Volkmann (Cologne: Böhlau, 1994), 55–78 and 225–55; Vejas Gabriel Liulevicius, *The German Myth of the East: 1800 to the Present* (Oxford: Oxford University Press, 2009).

44 Manfred Weissbecker, "'Wenn hier Deutsche wohnten . . .': Beharrung und Veränderung im Russlandbild Hitlers und der NSDAP," in *Das Russlandbild im Dritten Reich,* ed. Hans-Erich Volkmann (Cologne: Böhlau, 1994), 14; Mark Mazower, *Hitler's Empire: How the Nazis Ruled Europe* (New York: Penguin, 2008), 2, 15; Timothy Patrick Mulligan, *The Politics of Illusion and Empire: German Occupation Policy in the Soviet Union, 1942–1943* (New York: Praeger, 1988), 9.

45 Weissbecker, "'Wenn hier Deutsche wohnten . . . ,'" 14–16; Paul Hanebrink, *A Specter Haunting Europe: The Myth of Judeo-Bolshevism* (Cambridge, MA: Harvard University Press, 2018), 85; Walter Laqueur, *Russia and Germany: A Century of Conflict* (New York: Little, Brown, 1965), 135; Michael Kellogg, *The Russian Roots of Nazism: White Émigrés and the Making of National Socialism, 1917–1945* (Cambridge: Cambridge University Press, 2005).

46 Adolf Hitler, *Mein Kampf. Eine kritische Edition,* ed. Christian Hartmann et al. (Munich: Institut für Zeitgeschichte, 2016), 2:1657, 1661, 1675; Laqueur, *Russia and Germany,* 145–47.

47 Michael David-Fox, "A 'Prussian Bolshevik' in Stalin's Russia: Ernst Niekisch at the Crossroads between Communism and National Socialism," in *Crossing Borders: Modernity, Ideology, and Culture in Russia and the Soviet Union* (Pittsburgh: University of Pittsburgh Press, 2015), 185–220.

48 Vejas Gabriel Liulevicius, *War Land on the Eastern Front: Culture, National Identity, and German Occupation in World War I* (Cambridge: Cambridge University Press, 2000); Liulevicius, *German Myth,* 147; Mazower, *Hitler's Empire,* 24–29.

49 Annemarie H. Sammartino, *The Impossible Border: Germany and the East, 1914–1922* (Ithaca, NY: Cornell University Press, 2010), 58, 203–4.

50 James E. Casteel, *Russia in the German Global Imaginary: Imperial Visions and Utopian Desires, 1905–1941* (Pittsburgh: University of Pittsburgh Press, 2016), 144–53.

51 Sammartino, *Impossible Border,* 2, 203–4.

52 Peter Longerich, *Heinrich Himmler: A Life,* trans. Jeremy Noakes and Lesley Sharpe (New York: Oxford University Press, 2012), quotation 53, 100–103, 109–10.

53 Casteel, *Russia,* 158–60; GARF f. 5283, op. 6, d. 172, l. 11; Michael David-Fox, *Showcasing the Great Experiment: Cultural Diplomacy and Western Visitors to the Soviet Union, 1921–1941* (New York: Oxford University Press, 2012), 249–62.

54 Casteel, *Russia,* 131–33; Hanebrink, *Specter Haunting Europe,* 128.

3. THE ENEMY WITHIN

1 Roberta T. Manning, "Massovaia operatsiia protiv 'kulakov i prestupnykh elementov': Apogei Velikoi Chistki na Smolenshchine," in *Stalinizm v rossiiskoi provintsii: Smolenskie arkhivnye dokumenty v prochtenii zarubezhnykh i rossiiskikh istorikov,* ed. Evgenii Kodin (Smolensk: SGPU, 1999), 235–36, 242–44.

2 Boris Makeev, "Deiatel'nost' organov prokuratury i suda po rassledovaniiu ugolovnykh del o kontrrevoliutsionnykh prestupleniiakh v 1937–1938 gg. (po materialam Zapadnoi i Smolenskoi oblastei)" (candidate of sciences diss., Smolensk State University, 2007), 165–67; *Boris Men'shagin: Vospominaniia. Pis'ma. Dokumenty,* ed. Pavel Polian et al. (St. Petersburg: Nestor-Istoriia, 2019), 31, 293.

3 Peter H. Solomon, *Soviet Criminal Justice under Stalin* (New York: Cambridge University Press, 1996), 1, 135, 177, 183, 212, 221, 236, 358; Eugene Huskey, *Russian Lawyers and the Soviet State: The Origins and Development of the Soviet Bar, 1917–1939* (Princeton, NJ: Princeton University Press, 1986), 212–13, 221.

4 Makeev, "Deiatel'nost' organov prokuratury"; Manning, "Massovaia operatsiia," 244–45.

5 Men'shagin, *Vospominaniia,* 31, 266–84.

6 Men'shagin, *Vospominaniia,* 297.

7 Marc Jansen and Nikita Petrov, *Stalin's Loyal Executioner: People's Commissar Nikolai Ezhov, 1895–1940* (Stanford, CA: Hoover Institution Press, 2002), 20, 76, 174, 202.

8 Solomon, *Soviet Criminal Justice,* 231–34; Men'shagin, *Vospominaniia,* 289, 314.

9 Men'shagin, *Vospominaniia,* 304, 341; Makeev, "Deiatel'nost' organov prokuratury," 176.

10 Men'shagin, *Vospominaniia,* 266, 281, 300, 301.

11 Makeev, "Deiatel'nost' organov prokuratury," 177–79, quotation 178.

12 Makeev, "Deiatel'nost' organov prokuratury," 146–91; B. V. Makeev, "Deiatel'nost' mestnykh sudebno-prokurorskikh organov po rassledovaniiu del o kontrrevoliutsionnykh prestupleniiakh vo vremia massovykh politicheskikh repressii 1937–1938 godov," in *Provintsial'naia vlast': Sistema i ee predstaviteli, 1917–1938 gg.,* ed. E. V. Kodin (Smolensk: SGU, 2005), 281–330; Men'shagin, *Vospominaniia,* 285–90; Manning, "Massovaia operatsiia," 244, 253–54, 254n85.

13 Sheila Fitzpatrick, "How the Mice Buried the Cat: Scenes from the Great Purges of 1937 in the Russian Provinces," *Russian Review* 52, no. 3 (1993): 306; Michael Ellman, "The Soviet 1937 Provincial Show Trials: Carnival or Terror?," *Europe-Asia Studies* 53, no. 8 (2001): 1221–33.

14 Sheila Fitzpatrick, *Everyday Stalinism: Ordinary Life in Extraordinary Times: Soviet Russia in the 1930s* (New York: Oxford University Press, 1999), 131.

15 GANISO f. 5, op. 2, d. 727, ll. 3–4; Tat'iana Novosel'tseva, "Sudebnaia vlast' v bor'be s 'kontrrevoliutsionnym terrorom': 1930-e gody," *Krai Smolenskii,* no. 7 (2012): 13–17; Solomon, *Soviet Criminal Justice,* 164, 177, 231.

16 R. V. Anoshkin and A. P. Katrovskii, *Dinamika naseleniia Smolenshchiny* (Smolensk: Universum, 2009), 21; Dmitrii Komarov, *Smolenskaia oblast' v ogne Velikoi Otechestvennoi: Voina, narod, pobeda* (Smolensk: Svitok, 2015), 11–18.

17 E. Ivanova, "Stanovlenie i razvitie sistemy vysshego obrazovaniia v Zapadnoi oblasti (1929–1937)," *Krai Smolenskii,* no. 9 (September 2007): 18–22.

18 Vera S. Dunham, *In Stalin's Time: Middleclass Values in Soviet Fiction,* rev. ed. (Durham, NC: Duke University Press, 1990), 19–23; Michael David-Fox, "What Is Cultural Revolution? Key Concepts and the Arc of Soviet Cultural Transformation, 1910s–1930s," in *Crossing Borders: Modernity, Ideology, and Culture in Russia and the Soviet Union* (Pittsburgh: University of Pittsburgh Press, 2015), 104–32; Sheila Fitzpatrick, "Becoming Cultured: Socialist Realism and the Representation of Privilege and Taste," in *The Cultural Front: Power and Culture in Revolutionary Russia* (Ithaca, NY: Cornell University Press, 1992), 216–37; Vadim Volkov, "The Concept of *Kul'turnost':* Notes on the Stalinist Civilizing Process," in *Stalinism: New Directions,* ed. Sheila Fitzpatrick (New York: Routledge, 2000), 210–30; Catriona Kelly and Vadim Volkov, "Directed Desires: *Kul'turnost'* and Consumption," in *Constructing Russian Culture in the Age of Revolution, 1881–1940,* ed. Catriona Kelly and David Shepherd (Oxford: Oxford University Press, 1998), 291–313.

19 Vasilii Maslennikov, *Bez tsenzury. Smolenshchina. Voina. Plen. Avtobiografiia* (Mozhaisk: Mozhaiskii poligraficheskii kombinat, 2014), 122–51; quotations 122, 143.

20 Maslennikov, *Bez tsenzury*, 124, 167, 171.

21 Nellie Ohr, "Collective Farms and Russian Peasant Society, 1933–1937: The Stabilization of the Kolkhoz Order" (PhD diss., Stanford University, 1990), 7, 86, 347, and chap. 5; Makeev, "Deiatel'nost' organov prokuratury," 153–55.

22 Komarov, *Smolenskaia oblast'*, 14–19 (the number of births declined almost 34 percent and deaths rose 10 percent between 1937 and 1940).

23 Maslennikov, *Bez tsenzury*, 109, 127, 130–31, 164.

24 Roberta T. Manning, *Government in the Soviet Countryside in the Stalinist Thirties: The Case of Belyi Raion in 1937*, Carl Beck Papers in Russian and East European Studies, no. 301 (Pittsburgh: Center for Russian and East European Studies, University of Pittsburgh, 1984), 5–6, 35; I. G. Kovalev to Ivan Rumiantsev, April 7, 1937, GANISO f. 5, op. 2, d. 1798, ll. 156–66.

25 See esp. David R. Shearer, *Policing Stalin's Socialism: Repression and Social Order in the Soviet Union, 1924–1953* (New Haven, CT: Yale University Press, 2009); Marc Junge, Andrei Savin, and Aleksei Tepliakov, "The Origins of Stalin's Mass Operations: The Extrajudicial Special Assembly, 1922–1953," in *The Secret Police and the Soviet System: New Archival Investigations,* ed. Michael David-Fox (Pittsburgh: University of Pittsburgh Press, 2023), 42.

26 RGASPI f. 17, op. 21, d. 4109, ll. 250–61 (protocols of the Bureau of the Western Regional Party Committee [Obkom] from September 1937); GANISO f. 6, op. 1, d. 28 (Special Files [*osobye papki*] of the Bureau of the Regional Party Committee and Presidium of the Regional Executive Committee [Oblispolkoma]).

27 Maslennikov, *Bez tsenzury*, 161.

28 Oleg Khlevniuk, *Master of the House: Stalin and His Inner Circle,* trans. Nora S. Favorov (New Haven, CT: Yale University Press, 2009), chap. 5; Yoram Gorlizki and Hans Mommsen, "The Political (Dis)Orders of Stalinism and National Socialism," in *Beyond Totalitarianism: Stalinism and Nazism Compared,* ed. Michael Geyer and Sheila Fitzpatrick (New York: Cambridge University Press, 2009), 68; Sheila Fitzpatrick, "Varieties of Terror," in *Stalinism: New Directions,* ed. Sheila Fitzpatrick (New York: Routledge, 2000), 258.

29 Michael David-Fox, "Toward a Life Cycle Analysis of the Russian Revolution," *Kritika* 18, no. 4 (Fall 2017): 741–83; Michael David-Fox, "Razmyshleniia o stalinizme, voine i nasilii," in *SSSR vo Vtoroi mirovoi voine: Okkupatsiia. Kholokost. Stalinizm,* ed. Oleg Budnitskii and Liudmila Novikova (Moscow: ROSSPEN, 2014), 176–95.

30 Manning, *Government,* 44, citing the memoirs of P. G. Grigorenko; Fitzpatrick, "How the Mice Buried the Cat," 316, 319; Ellman, "Provincial Show Trials," 1231; "Telegramma i.o. sekretaria Zapadnogo Obkoma VKP(b) D. S. Korotchenkova I. V. Stalinu," August 26, 1937, and "I. V. Stalin D. S. Korotchenkovu," August 27, 1937,

in *Tragediia sovetskoi derevni: Kollektivizatsiia i raskulachivanie, 1927–1939,* ed. V. P. Danilov et al. (Moscow: ROSSPEN, 2004), vol. 5, bk. 1, 400–401.

31 Ohr, "Collective Farms," 96–105.

32 Men'shagin, *Vospominaniia,* 311.

33 Merle Fainsod, *Smolensk under Soviet Rule* (Cambridge, MA: Harvard University Press, 1958), 59–60; "Ivan Petrovich Rumiantsev," in *Rukovoditeli Smolenskoi oblasti (1917–1991 gody): Biograficheskii spravochnik,* ed. N. G. Emel'ianova et al. (Smolensk: GASO, 2008), 144–46.

34 Fainsod, *Smolensk,* 78; N. F. Pikalova, "Ivan Petrovich Rumiantsev," *Vestnik Katynskogo memoriala,* no. 8 (2008): 31–37, quotation 35; T. I. Novosel'tseva and N. F. Pikalova, "Provintsial'naia vlast': Ot obshchikh kontorov k sistemnoi vertikali," in *Provintsial'naia vlast': Sistema i ee predstaviteli, 1917–1938 gg.,* ed. E. V. Kodin (Smolensk: SGU, 2005), 31.

35 "Stenograficheskii otchet V-i oblastnoi partkonferentsii Zapadnoi oblasti," May 18–26, 1937, RGASPI f. 17, op. 21, d. 4072, ll. 25, 32–33, 260–70.

36 Oleg Khlevniuk, "Top Down vs. Bottom-Up: Regarding the Potential of Contemporary 'Revisionism,'" *Cahiers du monde russe* 56, no. 4 (2015): 838.

37 Stephen Kotkin, *Stalin,* vol. 2, *Waiting for Hitler, 1929–1941* (New York: Penguin, 2017), 440–42, 463–64, 483, 488–89; Fainsod, *Smolensk,* 60–61; Moshe Lewin, "Bureaucracy and the Stalinist State," in *Stalinism and Nazism: Dictatorships in Comparison,* ed. Ian Kershaw and Moshe Lewin (Cambridge: Cambridge University Press, 1997), 53–74.

38 Manning, "Massovaia operatsiia," 232–34.

39 RGASPI f. 17, op. 163, d. 1153, l. 10; E. G. Karelin, "Istoriia sozdaniia Smolenskoi oblasti i ee politiko-administrativnoi sistemy," in *Vsia zhizn' Smolenshchine* (Smolensk: Smolenskaia gorodskaia tipografiia, 2011), 19; "Dem'ian Sergeevich Korotchenkov," in *Rukovoditeli Smolenskoi oblasti (1917–1991 gody): Biograficheskii spravochnik,* ed. N. G. Emel'ianova et al. (Smolensk: GASO, 2008), 146–48; Manning, "Massovaia operatsiia," 235.

40 Jansen and Petrov, *Stalin's Loyal Executioner,* 75–77.

41 Karelin, "Istoriia sozdaniia"; "Dem'ian Sergeevich Korotchenkov," 147.

42 "Karutskii Vasilii Abramovich," in *Spravochnik po istorii Kommunisticheskoi partii i Sovetskogo Soiuza, 1898–1991,* https://web.archive.org/web/20141106044857/http://www.knowbysight.info/KKK/07881.asp, accessed March 22, 2024; Marc Junge and Rol'f Binner, *Kak terror stal "bol'shim": Sekretnyi prikaz No. 00447 i tekhnologiia ego ispolneniia* (Moscow: AIRO-XX, 2003), 42; Jansen and Petrov, *Stalin's Loyal Executioner,* 142–44; Alexander Vatlin, *Agents of Terror: Ordinary Men and Extraordinary Violence in Stalin's Secret Police,* ed. and trans. Seth Bernstein (Madison: University of Wisconsin Press, 2016), 43, 75–76.

43 D. S. Korotchenkov to I. V. Stalin, August 10, 1937, GANISO f. 5, op. 2, d. 1728, ll. 1–14.

44 GANISO f. 5, op. 2, d. 1728, l. 83; Kotkin, *Stalin,* 2:442.

45 Vatlin, *Agents of Terror;* Nicolas Werth, *L'ivrogne et la marchande de fleurs. Autopsie d'un meurtre de masse 1937–1938* (Paris: Taillandier, 2009); V. V. Krasheninnikov, "Iz istorii politicheskikh repressii na Brianshchine, 1937–1938 gg.," in *Istoriia stalinizma: Repressirovannaia rossiiskaia provintsiia,* ed. E. V. Kodin (Moscow: ROSSPEN, 2011), 104–13; Korotchenko to Stalin, August 10, 1937, ll. 1–14; N. N. Il'kevich, "Grigorii Braginskii: Gibel' redaktora 'Rabochego puti,'" *Vestnik Katynskogo memoriala,* no. 6 (2007): 44–49.

46 Junge and Binner, *Kak terror stal "bol'shim,"* 41–42, 128.

47 E. V. Kodin, "Elektronnaia baza dannykh zhertv politicheskikh repressii Smolenskoi oblasti kak istoricheskii istochnik," in *Istoriia stalinizma: Repressirovannaia rossiiskaia provintsiia,* ed. E. V. Kodin (Moscow: ROSSPEN, 2011), 41–52. See "Elektronnaia kartoteka zhertv repressii Smolenskoi oblasti, 1917–1953gg.," https://websprav.admin-smolensk.ru/repress/, accessed April 4, 2023.

48 Kodin, "Elektronnaia baza." Cf. better-documented statistics: Marc Junge and Bernd Bonwetsch, eds., *Bol'shevistskii poriadok v Gruzii,* 2 vols. (Moscow: AIRO-XXI, 2015); Melanie Ilic, "The Great Terror in Leningrad: A Quantitative Analysis," *Europe-Asia Studies* 52, no. 8 (2000): 1515–34.

49 This discussion draws on excellent research by Michael C. Hickey, "Jewish Institutions and Stalinist Terror in Smolensk" (unpublished paper, 2021); cf. Elissa Bemporad, *Becoming Soviet Jews: The Bolshevik Experiment in Minsk* (Bloomington: Indiana University Press, 2013), 176–210; and Arkadii Zel'tser, *Evrei v sovetskoi provintsii: Vitebsk i mestechki, 1917–1941* (Moscow: ROSSPEN, 2006).

50 S. V. Aleksandrov, "Rasstrel'nye akty 1937 g. (po materialam arkhivno-sledstvennykh del UFSB Smolenskoi oblasti)," *Vestnik Katynskogo memoriala,* no. 14 (2014): 46–56. In the case of Georgia, far better documented than Smolensk, historians have calculated that altogether "no less than 3 percent" of the population was victimized. Marc Junge, "Kolichestvennyi analiz massovykh operatsii NKVD," in *Bol'shevistskii poriadok v Gruzii,* ed. Marc Junge and Bernd Bonwetsch (Moscow: AIRO-XXI, 2015), 1:71–73.

51 Maslennikov, *Bez tsenzury,* 157.

52 Maslennikov, *Bez tsenzury,* 145, 158–59, 162.

53 For example, GANISO f. 5, op. 2, d. 1798, ll. 109–13.

54 O. L. Leibovich, "'Individ razoblachenii' v terroristicheskom diskurse v 1937–1938 godakh," in *Istoriia stalinizma: Repressirovannaia rossiiskaia provintsiia,* ed. E. V. Kodin (Moscow: ROSSPEN, 2011), 16–41; Wendy Z. Goldman, *Inventing the*

Enemy: Denunciation and Terror in Stalin's Russia (New York: Cambridge University Press, 2011), 2–4, 48–52, 72, 144–46.

55 Geoffrey Hosking, "Trust and Distrust in the USSR: An Overview," *Slavonic and East European Review* 91, no. 1 (2013): 1, 4; Cynthia Hooper, "Trust in Terror? The Search for a Foolproof Science of Soviet Personnel," *Slavonic and East European Review* 91, no. 1 (2013): 26–56.

56 Maslennikov, *Bez tsenzury,* 159–61.

57 Men'shagin, *Vospominaniia,* 300–301.

58 Pavel Polian, "Fenomen Men'shagina: Biograficheskii ocherk," in *Boris Men'shagin: Vospominaniia. Pis'ma. Dokumenty,* ed. Pavel Polian et al. (St. Petersburg: Nestor-Istoriia, 2019), 23–30, esp. 24n2, 29; Men'shagin, *Vospominaniia,* 275.

59 Men'shagin, *Vospominaniia,* 268–78; F. I. Khol'manskaia (Frumkina), "Chto pomnitsia," in *Arkhiv evreiskoi istorii* (Moscow: ROSSPEN, 2016), 8:19–21.

60 Men'shagin, *Vospominaniia,* 266.

61 Solomon, *Soviet Criminal Justice,* 1, 6, 164, 177; T. V. Kozlova, "Arkhivy otkryvaiut tainy," *Vestnik Katynskogo memoriala,* no. 1 (2002): 34.

62 Men'shagin, *Vospominaniia,* 307.

63 RGASPI f. 17, op. 21, ed. khr. 4123, l. 2, ll. 24–25.

64 Solomon, *Soviet Criminal Justice,* 257; Jansen and Petrov, *Stalin's Loyal Executioner,* 160–89; Lynne Viola, *Stalinist Perpetrators on Trial: Scenes from the Great Terror in Soviet Ukraine* (New York: Oxford University Press, 2017), 168–69; J. Arch Getty and Oleg V. Naumov, *The Road to Terror: Stalin and the Self-Destruction of the Bolsheviks, 1932–1939* (New Haven, CT: Yale University Press, 1999), 527–52; Kotkin, *Stalin,* 2:587–89; Timothy Blauvelt and David Jishkariani, "Deciphering the Stalinist Perpetrators: The Case of Georgian NKVD Investigators Khazan, Savitskii, and Krimian," in *The Secret Police and the Soviet System: New Archival Investigations,* ed. Michael David-Fox (Pittsburgh: University of Pittsburgh Press, 2023), 152–85.

65 David R. Shearer and Vladimir Khaustov, eds., *Stalin and the Lubianka: A Documentary History of the Political Police and Security Organs in the Soviet Union, 1922–1953* (New Haven, CT: Yale University Press, 2015), x, 309; David Brandenberger and Mikhail Zelenev, eds., *Stalin's Master Narrative: A Critical Edition of the History of the Communist Party of the Soviet Union (Bolsheviks): Short Course* (New Haven, CT: Yale University Press, 2019), 8–14; Kotkin, *Stalin,* 2:576–79, 586.

66 Sally Stoecker, *Forging Stalin's Army: Marshal Tukhachevsky and the Politics of Military Innovation* (New York: Routledge, 2018), 84.

67 GANISO f. 5, op. 2, d. 1783; Manning, "Massovaia operatsiia," 235.

68 David R. Shearer, *Stalin and War, 1918–1953: Patterns of Repression, Mobilization, and External Threat* (New York: Routledge, 2024), 51; David R. Shearer, "Stalin at War, 1918–1953: Patterns of Violence and Foreign Threat," *Jahrbücher für Geschichte Osteuropas* 66, no. 2 (2018): 188–217; Junge, Savin, and Tepliakov, "Stalin's Mass Operations," 24–27; Kotkin, *Stalin,* 2:351, 428–35.

69 L. A. Kachulina, "Gorod Velizh. 1937 god," *Vestnik Katynskogo memoriala,* no. 3 (2004): 19–21; "Iz istorii kolkhoz im. F. E. Dzerzhinskogo Smolenskogo raiona Smolenskoi oblasti," in *Dorogami pamiati* (Smolensk: Memorial Katyn', 2015), 12:3–11; Kenneth Slepyan, "Why They Fought: Motivation, Legitimacy, and the Soviet Partisan Movement," NCEEER Working Paper (National Council for Eurasian and East European Research, Washington, DC, 2003), 4; Sabine Dullin, *La frontière épaisse: Aux origines des politiques soviétiques (1920–1940)* (Paris: Éditions de l'EHESS, 2014).

70 "9-ia Gorodskaia Partiinaia Konferentsiia g. Smolenska. Vechernee Zasedanie," May 9, 1937, GANISO f. 5, op. 2, d. 1783, ll. 182–88; "Stenogramma doklada Rumiantseva V-i oblpartkonferentsii," July 23, 1937, GANISO f. 5, op. 2, d. 1783, l. 201.

71 Oleg Khlevniuk, "Archives of the Terror: Developments in the Historiography of Stalin's Purges," trans. Simon Belokowsky, *Kritika* 22, no. 2 (Spring 2021): 382.

72 "Ot zakliuchennogo Smolenskoi tiur'my, byvshego komissara 109 st. d. BVO—Maslova Aleksandr Vasil'evich. Zaiavlenie," no earlier than June 10, 1938, GANISO f. 6, op. 1, d. 312, ll. 69–73; "Zasedanie biuro Smolenskogo Obkoma VKP(b). Protokol No. 4, punkt No. 5 ot 7/III-1939 g. O rezul'tatakh proverki zaiavleniia zakliuchennogo MASLOVA," March 7, 1939, GANISO f. 6, op. 1, d. 312, ll. 445–49.

73 "Spravka po delu sekretaria Smolenskogo Obkoma VKP(b) t. MANAEVA G. G.," no earlier than September 14, 1938, GANISO f. 6, op. 1, d. 312, l. 449; Obkom *osobaia papka* materials on Manaev: GANISO f. 6, op. 1, d. 312, ll. 92–93, 445–49.

74 Maslennikov, *Bez tsenzury,* 162–71, 176.

75 Rolf-Dieter Müller, *Enemy in the East: Hitler's Secret Plans to Invade the Soviet Union,* trans. Alexander Starritt (London: I. B. Tauris, 2015), 208, 231; Adam Tooze, *The Wages of Destruction: The Making and Breaking of the Nazi Economy* (New York: Viking Penguin, 2007), chaps. 13–14.

76 Inter alia, see esp. Czeslaw Madajczyk, ed., *Vom Generalplan Ost zum Generalsiedlungsplan* (Munich: K. G. Sauer, 1994); Mechtild Rössler und Sabine Schleiermacher, *Der "Generalplan Ost": Hauptlinien der nationalsozialistischen Planungs- und Vernichtungspolitik* (Berlin: Akademie Verlag, 1993); Tooze, *Wages of Destruction,* 429–85; Alex J. Kay, *Exploitation, Resettlement, Mass Murder: Political and Economic Planning for German Occupation Policy in the Soviet Union, 1940–1941* (New York:

Berghahn Books, 2011); Michael Wildt, *An Uncompromising Generation: The Nazi Leadership of the Reich Security Main Office,* trans. Tom Lampert (Madison: University of Wisconsin Press, 2010); Christopher R. Browning, *Origins of the Final Solution: The Evolution of Nazi Jewish Policy, September 1939–March 1942* (Lincoln: University of Nebraska Press, 2004); Christian Gerlach, *Kalkulierte Morde: Die deutsche Wirtschafts- und Vernichtungspolitik in Weissrussland 1941 bis 1944* (Hamburg: Hamburger Edition, 1999); Peter Longerich, *Heinrich Himmler: Eine Biographie* (Munich: Siedler, 2008); Peter Longerich, *Hitler: Biographie* (Munich: Siedler, 2015); Alexander Dallin, *German Rule in Russia 1941–1945: A Study of Occupation Policies,* 2nd ed. (Basingstoke: Palgrave Macmillan, 1981).

77 Timothy Snyder, *Bloodlands: Europe between Hitler and Stalin* (New York: Basic Books, 2010), 161–63.

78 Alex J. Kay, "'The Purpose of the Russian Campaign Is the Decimation of the Slavic Population by Thirty Million': The Radicalization of German Food Policy in Early 1941," in *Nazi Policy on the Eastern Front, 1941: Total War, Genocide, and Radicalization,* ed. Alex J. Kay et al. (Rochester: University of Rochester Press, 2012), 101–29, quotation 108; Tooze, *Wages of Destruction,* 476–80, quotation 476.

79 Felix Römer, "The Wehrmacht in the War of Ideologies: The Army and Hitler's Criminal Orders on the Eastern Front," in *Nazi Policy on the Eastern Front, 1941: Total War, Genocide, and Radicalization,* ed. Alex J. Kay et al. (Rochester: University of Rochester Press, 2012), 73, 77, 93.

80 Gerlach, *Kalkulierte Morde.*

81 Jürgen Matthäus and Frank Bajohr, eds., *The Political Diary of Alfred Rosenberg and the Onset of the Holocaust* (Lanham, MD: Rowman and Littlefield, 2015), 259–51; V. A. Zolotarev, ed., *Natsistskaia Germaniia protiv Sovetskogo Soiuza: Planirovanie voiny* (Moscow: Kuchkovo pole, 2015), 31, 87; Müller, *Enemy in the East,* 225. Einsatzgruppe B: see Chapter 5.

82 Antony Beevor and Luba Vinogradova, ed. and trans., *A Writer at War: Vasily Grossman with the Red Army, 1941–1945* (New York: Pantheon, 2005), 355.

4. REGIME CHANGE 1941

1 Vasilii Maslennikov, *Bez tsenzury. Smolenshchina. Voina. Plen. Avtobiografiia* (Mozhaisk: Mozhaiskii poligraficheskii kombinat, 2014), 178–81; Roger R. Reese, *Why Stalin's Soldiers Fought: The Red Army's Military Effectiveness in World War II* (Lawrence: University Press of Kansas, 2011).

2 Maslennikov, *Bez tsenzury,* 182.

3 "Stenogramma besedy s t. Popovym D. M. Smolensk," December 16, 1943, NA IRI RAN f. 2, r. III, op. 8, d. 1, l. 1. Border: Sabine Dullin, *La frontière épaisse: Aux origines des politiques soviétiques (1920–1940)* (Paris: Éditions de l'EHESS, 2014); Michael David-Fox, *Showcasing the Great Experiment: Cultural Diplomacy*

and Western Visitors to the Soviet Union, 1921–1941 (New York: Oxford University Press, 2012), chap. 6.

4   Dmitrii Komarov, *Smolenskaia oblast' v ogne Velikoi Otechestvennoi: Voina, narod, pobeda* (Smolensk: Svitok, 2015), 49–58; David M. Glantz, *Operation Barbarossa: Hitler's Invasion of Russia 1941* (Stroud, UK: History Press, 2001); Sergei Amelin, "Tochka nevozvrata," in *Boris Men'shagin: Vospominaniia. Pis'ma. Dokumenty,* ed. Pavel Polian et al. (St. Petersburg: Nestor-Istoriia, 2019), 161–65.

5   Men'shagin, *Vospominaniia,* 345.

6   David M. Glantz, *Barbarossa Derailed: The Battle for Smolensk 10 July–September 1941* (Solihull, UK: Helion, 2010), 1:20, 28, 33, 148; Reese, *Why Stalin's Soldiers Fought,* 308; Richard J. Evans, *The Third Reich at War* (New York: Penguin, 2009), 179–88, 310.

7   Men'shagin, *Vospominaniia,* 371.

8   Komarov, *Smolenskaia oblast',* 22–23; Maslennikov, *Bez tsenzury,* 188–89.

9   Men'shagin, *Vospominaniia,* 347.

10 Men'shagin, *Vospominaniia,* 346–50. NKVD intelligence noted personal and professional networks: GANISO f. 6, op. 1, d. 742, l. 7.

11 Pavel Polian, "Fenomen Men'shagina: Biograficheskii ocherk," in *Boris Men'shagin: Vospominaniia. Pis'ma. Dokumenty,* ed. Pavel Polian et al. (St. Petersburg: Nestor-Istoriia, 2019), 27–29, citing 2019 interview with Nadezhda (Nadia) Borisovna Men'shagina.

12 Men'shagin, *Vospominaniia,* 352.

13 See Chapter 5.

14 Men'shagin, *Vospominaniia,* 353–59; Amelin, "Tochka nevozvrata," 166–72.

15 "Vospominaniia komissara Partizanskogo Polka im. 'Lazo' Iudenkova A. F. za period iiun' 1941 po iiul' 1942," GANISO f. 8, op. 1, ed. khr. 243, ll. 1–237, ll. 1–6; "Stenogramma besed s komissarom polka im. Lazo tov. Iudenkovym," May 22, 1943, NA IRI RAN f. 2, r. II, op. 2, d. 31a, ll. 1–39.

16 Iudenkov, "Vospominaniia," l. 1.

17 Iudenkov, "Vospominaniia," ll. 34–37; "Stenogramma besed s . . . Iudenkovym," l. 9.

18 Oleg Budnitskii, "The Great Patriotic War and Soviet Society: Defeatism, 1941–42," *Kritika* 15, no. 4 (Fall 2014): 767–97; Seth Bernstein, "Rural Russia on the Edges of Authority: *Bezvlastie* in Wartime Riazan'," November–December 1941," *Slavic Review* 75, no. 3 (Fall 2016): 560–82.

19 Iudenkov, "Vospominaniia," ll. 19, 35–37; "Stenogramma besed s . . . Iudenkovym," ll. 3–9.

20 Komarov, *Smolenskaia oblast'*, 28–29; Mark Edele, *Stalin's Defectors: How Red Army Soldiers Became Hitler's Collaborators, 1941–1945* (Oxford: Oxford University Press, 2017); Mark Edele, "'What Are We Fighting For?' Loyalty in the Soviet War Effort, 1941–1945," *International Labor and Working-Class History* 84 (Fall 2013): 248–68; Reese, *Why Stalin's Soldiers Fought.*

21 "Stenogramma besedy s. t. Kazubskim V. V. Shtab partizanskogo dvizheniia, d. Ratkevshchina Smolenskogo raiona Smolenskoi oblasti," December 9, 1943, NA IRI RAN f. 2, r. II, op. 2, ed. khr. 31b, l. 4. After the war, Kozubskii often spelled his name Kazubskii.

22 Glantz, *Barbarossa Derailed*, vol. 1; Stenogramma besedy s. t. Mozinym I. P.," December 12, 1943, NA IRI RAN f. 2, r. VI, op. 2, d. 24, ll. 2–3; Komarov, *Smolenskaia oblast'*, 49.

23 Glantz, *Barbarossa Derailed*, 1:15, 77, 195.

24 D. M. Popov to A. A. Andreev, August 15, 1941, GANISO f. 6, op. 1, d. 740, ll. 20–22.

25 "Sekretariu TsK VKP(b) tov. Andreevu A. A. ot sekretaria Smolenskogo Obkoma VKP(b) Popova D. M. Dokladnaia zapiska," November 24, 1941, GANISO f. 6, op. 1, d. 741, l. 1; Komarov, *Smolenskaia oblast'*, 111; Reese, *Why Stalin's Soldiers Fought*, 309; Edele, *Stalin's Defectors.*

26 Reese, *Why Stalin's Soldiers Fought*, 60; Stavskii quoted in Budnitskii, "Great Patriotic War," 792.

27 GANISO f. 6, op. 1, d. 28, ll. 230–35; Oleg Budnitskii, "The Great Terror of 1941: Toward a History of Wartime Stalinist Criminal Justice," *Kritika* 20, no. 3 (2019): 447–80; Budnitskii, "Great Patriotic War," 791; Glantz, *Operation Barbarossa*, 54–55.

28 Maslennikov, *Bez tsenzury*, 187, 213.

29 Harvard Project on the Soviet Social System, Schedule B, vol. 11, case 439, interviewer A.D. [Alexander Dallin], interview conducted February 10, 1951, Widener Library, Harvard University, http://nrs.harvard.edu/urn -3:FHCL:965255, accessed August 5, 2019 (Melander identified from internal evidence). Defacement of Stalin portraits: GANISO f. 8, op. 1, d. 36, l. 5.

30 "V Obkom VKP(b) ot instruktora voennogo otdela Obkoma VKP(b) Bylenkova M. A. Dokladnaia zapiska," August 25, 1941, GANISO f. 6, op. 1, d. 28, ll. 219–22.

31 "Bericht Einsatzgruppe B über die polizeiliche Tätigkeit vom 9.–16.8.1941," in *Deutsche Besatzungsherrschaft in der UdSSR 1941–1945. Dokumente der Einsatz-gruppen in der Sowjetunion*, ed. Andrej Angrick et al. (Darmstadt: WBG, 2013), 2:104–5.

32 "Smolenskomu Obkomu VKP(b). Ot sekretaria El'ninskogo RK VKP(b) Valueva Ia. P.," no earlier than August 20, 1941, GANISO f. 6, op. 1, d. 28, ll. 228–29;

inter alia, "Nachal'nik Upravleniia NKVD SSSR po Smolenskoi oblasti Maior gosbezopasnosti Kondakov. Dokladnaia zapiska. O faktakh izmeny i predatel'stva so storony otdel'nykh chlenov, kandidatov v chl. VKP(b) i komsomoltsev," February 21, 1942, GANISO f. 6, op. 1, d. 742, ll. 32–36.

33 "Stenogramma besedy s t. Mozinym," l. 2; GANISO f. 6, op. 1, d. 740, ll. 14–15; Glantz, *Barbarossa Derailed,* 1:27; Sergei Maksudov, "K probleme izucheniia razmerov i kharaktera evakuatsii v gody Velikoi Otechestvennoi voiny," *Rossiiskaia istoriia,* no. 3 (2019): 44–48.

34 Rebecca Manley, *To the Tashkent Station: Evacuation and Survival in the Soviet Union at War* (Ithaca, NY: Cornell University Press, 2009), chap. 2; Erina T. Megowan, "For Fatherland, for Culture: State, Intelligentsia, and Evacuated Culture in Russia's Regions, 1941–1945" (PhD diss., Georgetown University, 2016); Komarov, *Smolenskaia oblast',* 31.

35 GANISO f. 6, op. 1, d. 740, l. 16; D. M. Popov to A. A. Andreev, "Dokladnaia zapiska," September 24, 1941, GANISO f. 6, op. 1, d. 741, ll. 4–5.

36 Glantz, *Barbarossa Derailed,* 1:28; Manley, *Tashkent Station,* quotation 3; Glantz, *Operation Barbarossa,* 60.

37 Dmitrii Popov, "Nachal'niku Upravleniia propagandy TsK tov. Aleksandrovu," no exact date, USHMM RG-22.015M, frame 159; M. N. Potemkina, *Evakuatsiia v gody Velikoi Otechestvennoi voiny na Urale: Liudy i sud'by* (Magnitogorsk: Magnitogorskii gosudarstvennyi universitet, 2002), 17; Manley, *Tashkent Station,* 3–5; Megowan, "For Fatherland, for Culture."

38 GANISO f. 6, op. 1, d. 741, l. 5.

39 GANISO f. 6, op. 1, d. 741, ll. 1–3; D. M. Popov to A. A. Andreev and G. M. Malenkov, no earlier than March 1, 1942, GANISO f. 6, op. 1, d. 741, ll. 73–87.

40 Iosif Tsynman, ed., *Bab'i iary Smolenshchiny: Poiavlenie, zhizn' i katastrofa Smolenskogo evreistva* (Smolensk: Rus', 2001); *The United States Holocaust Memorial Museum Encyclopedia of Camps and Ghettos, 1933–1945,* vol. 2, *Ghettos in German-Occupied Eastern Europe,* ed. Martin Dean (Bloomington: Indiana University Press, 2012), 1728, 1820.

41 Evgeny Finkel, *Ordinary Jews: Choice and Survival during the Holocaust* (Princeton, NJ: Princeton University Press, 2017), 51–68, quotation 54; Anna Shternshis, "Between Life and Death: Why Some Soviet Jews Decided to Leave and Others to Stay in 1941," *Kritika* 15, no. 3 (Summer 2014): 477–504, quotation 502.

42 Maslennikov, *Bez tsenzury,* 190–93.

43 Maslennikov, *Bez tsenzury,* 193–99.

44 Maslennikov, *Bez tsenzury,* 199.

45 "Stenogramma besedy s t. Kozubskim," l. 50b. Their joint recollection from 1944 is more formulaic: A. F. Iudenkov and V. V. Kozubskii, "Vozniknovenie i boevaia

deiatel′nost′ otdel′nogo partizanskogo polka im. Sergei Lazo," October 12, 1944, GANISO f. 8, op. 1, d. 36, ll. 5–67.

46 Kenneth Slepyan, *Stalin's Guerrillas: Soviet Partisans in World War II* (Lawrence: University Press of Kansas, 2006); Masha Cerovic, *Les enfants de Staline: La guerre des partisans soviétiques (1941–1944)* (Paris: Seuil, 2018); Michael David-Fox, "Syncretic Subcultures or Stalinism without Stalin? Soviet Partisans as Communities of Violence," *Russian Review* 78, no. 3 (July 2019): 486–501.

47 "Stenogramma besed s . . . Iudenkovym," ll. 1, 10b; "Stenogramma besedy s t. Kozubskim," l. 50b.

48 "Stenogramma besedy s sekretarem Iartsevskogo raikoma VKP(b) Smolenskoi oblasti tov. Fomchenkovym Ivanom Illarionovichem," April 19, 1942, NA IRI RAN f. 2, r. II, op. 2, ed. khr. 24a, l. 19.

49 "Dokladnaia zapiska El′ninskogo RK VKP(b) i RO UNKVD Smolenskoi oblasti. Ob operativnoi rabote v raione voennykh deistvii po sostoianiiu na 26 avgusta 1941 g.," GANISO f. 6, op. 1, d. 28, ll. 226–27; "Stenogramma besed s . . . Iudenkovym," l. 8, l. 9.

50 "Stenogramma besed s . . . Iudenkovym," l. 9.

51 "Stenogramma besed s . . . Iudenkovym," l. 23.

52 Iudenkov, "Vospominaniia," ll. 36, 42, 235, 237.

53 "Stenogramma besed s . . . Iudenkovym," l. 21.

54 Alex J. Kay, "Transition to Genocide, July 1941: Einsatzkommando 9 and the Annihilation of Soviet Jewry," *Holocaust and Genocide Studies* 27, no. 3 (Winter 2013): 411–42; Christian Gerlach, "Die Einsatzgruppe B 1941/42," in *Die Einsatzgruppen in der besetzten Sowjetunion 1941/42: Die Tätigkeits- und Lageberichte des Chefs der Sicherheitspolizei und des SD,* ed. Peter Klein (Berlin: Edition Hentrich, 1997), 52–70.

55 Ereignismeldungen UdSSR (hereafter EM) 65, August 27, 1941, in *Die "Ereignismeldungen UdSSR" 1941. Dokumente der Einsatzgruppen in der Sowjetunion,* ed. Klaus-Michael Mallmann et al. (Darmstadt: WBG, 2011), 1:368–76; Gerlach, "Die Einsatzgruppe B," 53; Christian Ingrao, *Believe and Destroy: Intellectuals in the SS War Machine,* trans. Andrew Brown (Cambridge, UK: Polity Press, 2013), 162–63.

56 Jürgen Matthäus, "Anti-Semitism as an Offer: The Function of Ideological Indoctrination in the SS and Police Corps during the Holocaust," in *Lessons and Legacies,* vol. 7, *The Holocaust in International Perspective,* ed. Dagmar Herzog (Evanston, IL: Northwestern University Press, 2006), 116–28, quotations 119.

57 Christopher R. Browning, *Initiating the Final Solution: The Fateful Months of September–October 1941* (Washington, DC: USHMM, 2007); Christian Ingrao, *The Promise of the East: Nazi Hopes and Genocide, 1939–43,* trans. Andrew Brown (Cambridge, UK: Polity Press, 2019); Thomas Kühne, *The Rise and Fall of*

Comradeship: Hitler's Soldiers, Male Bonding, and Mass Violence in the Twentieth Century (Cambridge: Cambridge University Press, 2017), chap. 5.

58 Klaus-Michael Mallmann et al., "Die Optik der Täter: Quellenkritische Vorbemerkungen," in *Die "Ereignismeldungen UdSSR" 1941. Dokumente der Einsatzgruppen in der Sowjetunion,* ed. Klaus-Michael Mallmann et al. (Darmstadt: WBG, 2011), 1:7–38.

59 Michael David-Fox, "The Blind Men and the Elephant: Six Faces of Ideology in the Soviet Context," in *Crossing Borders: Modernity, Ideology, and Culture in Russia and the Soviet Union* (Pittsburgh: University of Pittsburgh Press, 2015), 75–103; cf. Matthäus, "Anti-Semitism as an Offer," 119.

60 Ingrao, *Believe and Destroy,* 100, 230.

61 "Bericht Einsatzgruppe B . . . vom 9.–16.8.1941," 104–5; EM 67, August 29, 1941, in *Die "Ereignismeldungen,"* 1:376.

62 "Bericht Einsatzgruppe B . . . 9.–16.8.1941," 110; EM 67, 376; EM 70, September 1, 1941; EM 73, September 4, 1941, in *Die "Ereignismeldungen,"* 1:385–86, 399.

63 Mallmann et al., "Die Optik der Täter," 27; EM 90, September 21, 1941, in *Die "Ereignismeldungen,"* 1:516; Babette Quinkert, *Propaganda und Terror in Weissrussland 1941–1944: Die deutsche "geistige" Kriegführung gegen Zivilbevölkerung und Partisanen* (Paderborn: Ferdinand Schöningh, 2009), 70.

64 "Trudiashchiesia! Rabochie! Krest'iane!," German propaganda poster, NARA T-501, serial 42, frame 1112; "Tätigkeitsbericht. Kdt. R. A. 559. Ic A. O. St. Q.," August 31, 1941, NARA T-501, serial 42, frame 1110; EM 67, 369, 374.

65 EM 73, 398; EM 122, October 23, 1941, in *Die "Ereignismeldungen,"* 1:722–23; Alexander Dallin, *German Rule in Russia 1941–1945: A Study of Occupation Policies,* 2nd ed. (Basingstoke: Palgrave Macmillan, 1981), 478; Daniel Peris, "'God Is Now on Our Side': The Religious Revival on Unoccupied Soviet Territory during World War II," *Kritika* 1, no. 1 (2000): 97–118.

66 EM 65, 368–69; EM 106, October 7, 1941, in *Die "Ereignismeldungen,"* 1:634, 636; NARA T-501, serial 48, frame 916; EM 97, September 28, 1941, in *Die "Ereignismeldungen,"* 1:596; EM 73, 406.

67 EM 73, 395; EM 90, 519; EM 67, 368; EM 106, 636.

68 EM 73, 395; EM 78, September 9, 1941, in *Die "Ereignismeldungen,"* 1:424–27; EM 90, 519; Quinkert, *Propaganda und Terror,* 140–200.

69 EM 78, 428–29; "Otchet o sostave partorganizatsii po . . . natsional'nosti," January 1, 1941, USHMM RG-22.015M.0001, 345; RG-22.015M.0002, 50–146.

70 EM 97, 495–96.

71 Komarov, *Smolenskaia oblast',* 219–20.

5. MURDER AND HUMILIATION

1   Evgenii Ivanovich Vakuliuk, July 12, 2014, Jeff and Toby Herr Oral History Archive, USHMM RG-50.653.0023 (hereafter Vakuliuk interview).

2   NA IRI RAN f. 2, r. VI, op. 2, d. 9a, l. 13.

3   Vakuliuk interview; Vladimir Khizver, Visual History Archive, University of Southern California Shoah Foundation, VHA Interview Code 20183, October 13, 1996 (hereafter Khizver interview); Vadim Dubson, "Getto na okkupirovannoi territorii RF (1941–1942 gg.)," *Vestnik evreiskogo universiteta v Moskve* no. 3 (21) (2000): 157–84.

4   Dubson, "Getto"; Leonid Kotov, "V Smolenske okkupirovannom," *Krai Smolenskii,* no. 7–8 (1994): 53–73; Iosif Tsynman, ed., *Bab'i iary Smolenshchiny: Poiavlenie, zhizn' i katastrofa Smolenskogo evreistva* (Smolensk: Rus', 2001).

5   Vakuliuk interview.

6   *Boris Men'shagin: Vospominaniia. Pis'ma. Dokumenty,* ed. Pavel Polian et al. (St. Petersburg: Nestor-Istoriia, 2019), 360–61; Menshagin city ordinances, August 19, 1941, and September 1, 1941, GASO f. 2573, op. 1, d. 1, l. 2; GARF f. 7021, op. 44, d. 66, l. 14. Cf. Yuri Radchenko, "Accomplices to Extermination: Municipal Government and the Holocaust in Kharkiv, 1941–1942," *Holocaust and Genocide Studies* 27, no. 3 (Winter 2013): 443–63; Michaela Christ, *Die Dynamik des Tötens: Die Ermordung der Juden von Berditschew, Ukraine 1941–1944* (Frankfurt am Main: S. Fischer, 2011).

7   Vakuliuk interview; Michael David-Fox, "Nachal'nik goroda: B. G. Men'shagin v istoricheskom kontekste," in *Boris Men'shagin: Vospominaniia. Pis'ma. Dokumenty,* ed. Pavel Polian et al. (St. Petersburg: Nestor-Istoriia, 2019), 173–214.

8   Yahad-In Unum interview with Vera Moskovkina, December 1, 2009, USHMM RG-50.653.0022; Yahad-In Unum interview 67R, USHMM RG-50.589.1331; Yahad-In Unum interview 45R, USHMM RG-50.589.1310; David-Fox, "Nachal'nik goroda"; Leonid Kotov, "Kak bylo unichtozheno Smolenskoe getto," *Krai Smolenskii,* no. 2 (November 1990): 40–48.

9   This section draws on Michael C. Hickey, "Revolution on the Jewish Street: Smolensk, 1917," *Journal of Social History* 31, no. 4 (1998): 823–50; and esp. Michael C. Hickey, "Sown with Tears: Jews and the State in Smolensk" (unpublished manuscript, 2021), chaps. 7–10.

10 Yitzhak Arad, *The Holocaust in the Soviet Union* (Lincoln: University of Nebraska Press, 2009), 185–98; Michael C. Hickey, "Jewish Institutions and Stalinist Terror in Smolensk" (unpublished paper, 2021); Elissa Bemporad, *Becoming Soviet Jews: The Bolshevik Experiment in Minsk* (Bloomington: Indiana University Press, 2013), 81–111.

11 Khizver interview.

12 Zvi Gitelman, *A Century of Ambivalence: The Jews of Russia and the Soviet Union, 1881 to Present,* 2nd ed. (Bloomington: Indiana University Press, 2001), 64–86, 119; Hickey, "Sown with Tears."

13 NA IRI RAN f. 2, r. VI, op. 2, d. 9a, l. 16; Khizver interview; Martin Dean, "Occupied Russian Territory," in *The United States Holocaust Memorial Museum Encyclopedia of Camps and Ghettos, 1933–1945,* vol. 2, *Ghettos in German-Occupied Eastern Europe,* ed. Martin Dean (Bloomington: Indiana University Press, 2012), pt. B, 1782–1785; Arad, *Holocaust in the Soviet Union,* 287; Laurie R. Cohen, *Smolensk under the Nazis: Everyday Life in Occupied Russia* (Rochester, NY: University of Rochester Press, 2013), 122–28; Christ, *Dynamik,* 92.

14 Alex J. Kay, "Transition to Genocide, July 1941: Einsatzkommando 9 and the Annihilation of Soviet Jewry," *Holocaust and Genocide Studies* 27, no. 3 (Winter 2013): 425–27.

15 Dean, "Occupied Russian Territory," 1785; Arad, *Holocaust in the Soviet Union,* 126–33; Jürgen Matthäus and Frank Bajohr, eds., *The Political Diary of Alfred Rosenberg and the Onset of the Holocaust* (Lanham, MD: Rowman and Littlefield, 2015), 426.

16 "Bericht Einsatzgruppe B über die polizeiliche Tätigkeit vom 9.–16.8.1941," in *Deutsche Besatzungsherrschaft in der UdSSR 1941–1945. Dokumente der Einsatzgruppen in der Sowjetunion,* ed. Andrej Angrick et al. (Darmstadt: WBG, 2013), 2:103–5, 109–10; Arad, *Holocaust in the Soviet Union,* 525.

17 Waitman Beorn, *The Holocaust in Eastern Europe: At the Epicenter of the Final Solution* (London: Bloomsbury, 2018), 151–78, quotation 156; Vadim Doubson, "Smolensk," in *Encyclopedia of Camps and Ghettos,* vol. 2, pt. B, 1821; Dubson, "Getto," 159.

18 "Vospominaniia prof. B. Bazil'evicha," September 28, 1943, in *Bab'i iary Smolenshchiny: Poiavlenie, zhizn' i katastrofa Smolenskogo evreistva,* ed. Iosif Tsynman (Smolensk: Rus', 2001), 29.

19 "Bericht über die polizeiliche Tätigkeit in der Zeit vom 24. bis 30. August 1941," in *Deutsche Besatzungsherrschaft in der UdSSR 1941–1945. Dokumente der Einsatzgruppen in der Sowjetunion,* ed. Andrej Angrick et al. (Darmstadt: WBG, 2013), 2:130.

20 Jörn Hasenclever, *Wehrmacht und Besatzungspolitik in der Sowjetunion: Die Befehlshaber der rückwärtigen Heeresgebiete 1941–1943* (Paderborn: Ferdinand Schöningh, 2010), 185, 202–4, 564–65.

21 Arad, *Holocaust in the Soviet Union,* 137.

22 Dubson, "Getto," 159.

23 Henry Friedlander, *The Origins of Nazi Genocide: From Euthanasia to the Final Solution* (Chapel Hill: University of North Carolina Press, 1995), 54–56.

24 Friedlander, *Origins*, 86–89, 141–42; Mathias Beer, "Die Entwicklung der Gaswagen beim Mord an den Juden," *Vierteljahrshefte für Zeitgeschichte* 35, no. 3 (1987): 403–17; Christopher R. Browning, *Initiating the Final Solution: The Fateful Months of September–October 1941* (Washington, DC: USHMM, 2007).

25 Christian Gerlach, "Failure of Plans for an SS Extermination Camp in Mogilev, Belorussia," *Holocaust and Genocide Studies* 11, no. 1 (1997): 60–78, quotation 62; Arad, *Holocaust in the Soviet Union*, 137–39; Joshua Rubenstein, "Unearthing the Holocaust on the Russian Front," *Kritika* 20, no. 2 (2019): 415.

26 Dieter Pohl, *Die Herrschaft der Wehrmacht: Deutsche Militärbesatzung und einheimische Bevölkerung in der Sowjetunion 1941–1944* (Munich: R. Oldenbourg, 2008), 252–53; Gerlach, "Failure of Plans," 62–65, 69, 74n48, quotation 64.

27 Men'shagin, *Vospominaniia*, 364–65, 394–95.

28 Men'shagin, *Vospominaniia*, 401; see also 51, 195, 249.

29 Harvard Project on the Soviet Social System, Schedule B, vol. 11, case 439 (interviewer A.D. [Alexander Dallin]), 3, 4, 5, interview conducted February 10, 1951, Widener Library, Harvard University, http://nrs.harvard.edu/urn -3:FHCL:965255; Smolensk city administration housing records, 1941 and 1942, GASO f. R-2573, op. 1, d. 5; GASO f. R-2573, op. 1, d. 174, ll. 2–3.

30 "Rasporiazhenie No. 24 nachal'nika goroda Smolenska," July 28, 1943, GARF f. 7021, op. 44, d. 66, l. 23; "Rasporiazhenie polevoi komendature mestnoi komendature," November 6, 1941, in *Boris Men'shagin: Vospominaniia. Pis'ma. Dokumenty*, ed. Pavel Polian et al. (St. Petersburg: Nestor-Istoriia, 2019), 715–16, and extant reports from Men'shagin to German authorities, 693–71.

31 "KDO im Bereich der Kommandatur Smolensk. Kriegstagebuch für die Zeit vom 1.9.–10.9.1942," BA MA RW 31/788; Asya Shneiderman, "Okkupirovannyi Smolensk. Sov. Sekretno," September 14, 1942, RGASPI f. 1M, op. 53, d. 246, l. 79; Kotov, "V Smolenske okkupirovannom," 72n10.

32 Men'shagin, *Vospominaniia*, 467–68; A. A. Kostiuchenkov, "Organizatsiia i struktura vspomogatel'noi politsii (strazhi) na okkupatsionnoi territorii Smolen- skoi oblasti 1941–1943 godov," *Izvestiia Smolenskogo gosudarstvennogo universiteta*, no. 2 (2012): 210–19; "Protokol doprosa obviniaemogo GUDIIAN Kurta ot 10 ianvaria 1944 goda," USHMM RG-06.025, reel 40, frame 5; Abt. 1c/A.O. Stu. Qu, "Bericht über den russischen Ordnungsdienst in rückwärtigen Armeege- biet," April 30, 1942, NARA T-501, serial 72, frame 1014; NARA T-501, serial 72, frame 1060; D. Karov (Dmitrii Petrovich Kandaurov), "Russkaia politsiia v okkupirovannykh nemtsami oblastiakh SSSR v voinu 1941–1945," 19, box 20, Research Program on the USSR, Bakhmeteff Archive, Columbia University Rare Book and Manuscript Library. On Gandziuk and returning émigré Solidarists, members of the NTSNP, see Chapter 7.

33 Pavel Polian, "Fenomen Men'shagina: Biograficheskii ocherk," in *Boris Men'shagin: Vospominaniia. Pis'ma. Dokumenty,* ed. Pavel Polian et al. (St. Petersburg: Nestor-Istoriia, 2019), 43–48; see also 793–94.

34 Vakuliuk interview; Khizver interview.

35 Khizver interview.

36 Beorn, *Holocaust in Eastern Europe,* 265–71; Evgeny Finkel, *Ordinary Jews: Choice and Survival during the Holocaust* (Princeton, NJ: Princeton University Press, 2017); Vakuliuk interview.

37 Pohl, *Herrschaft,* 201; Christian Streit, *Keine Kameraden: Die Wehrmacht und die sowjetischen Kriegsgefangenen, 1941–1945,* rev. ed. (Bonn: Dietz, 1997), 10, 20; Arad, *Holocaust in the Soviet Union,* 525; Donald Bloxham, *The Final Solution: A Genocide* (New York: Oxford University Press, 2009), 9–10.

38 *The United States Holocaust Memorial Museum Encyclopedia of Camps and Ghettos, 1933–1945,* vol. 4, *Camps and Other Detention Facilities under the German Armed Forces,* ed. Geoffrey P. Megargee et al. (Bloomington: Indiana University Press, 2022), 8–38; Streit, *Keine Kameraden,* 83; Dmitrii Komarov, *Velikaia Otechestvennaia voina na Viazemskoi zemle* (Smolensk: Universum, 2009), 179.

39 Komarov, *Velikaia Otechestvennaia voina,* 138, 142–43.

40 *Encyclopedia of Camps and Ghettos,* 4:39–42, 79, 82–83; Dmitrii Komarov, *Smolenskaia oblast' v ogne Velikoi Otechestvennoi: Voina, narod, pobeda* (Smolensk: Svitok, 2015), 216.

41 Bloxham, *The Final Solution,* 10.

42 "General-leitenantu meditsinskoi sluzhby professor N. N. Burtsenko ot b. voennoplennykh vrachei Pogrebneva A. S., Erpylova P. P.," no exact date, 1943, NA IRI RAN f. 2, r. VI, op. 2, d. 9a, ll. 22–25; Pavel Polian, *Zhertvy dvukh diktatur: Zhizn', trud, unizhenie i smert' sovetskikh voennoplennykh i ostarbaiterov na chuzbine i na rodine,* 2nd ed. (Moscow: ROSSPEN, 2002), 226.

43 *AD-184: Sovetskie voennoplennye, byvshie uzniki viazemskikh "dulagov," vospominaiut,* ed., E. A. Ivanova (Moscow: Algoritm, 2017), 68, 94.

44 Timothy Snyder, *Bloodlands: Europe between Hitler and Stalin* (New York: Basic Books, 2010), quotation 256; Christian Gerlach, *Kalkulierte Morde: Die deutsche Wirtschafts- und Vernichtungspolitik in Weissrussland 1941 bis 1944* (Hamburg: Hamburger Edition, 1999), 142–56, 781–819.

45 Gerlach, *Kalkulierte Morde,* 796–802; Karel C. Berkhoff, *Harvest of Despair: Life and Death in Ukraine under Nazi Rule* (Cambridge, MA: Belknap Press of Harvard University Press, 2004), 95–101; Cohen, *Smolensk,* 103–13.

46 NARA T-501, serial 8, frame 10; Polian, *Zhertvy,* 83–91, 217–29; Streit, *Keine Kameraden,* 55, 154–59, 187–88; Pohl, *Herrschaft,* 208, 218.

47 GARF f. 7021, op. 44, d. 41, ll. 21–22; "Protokol doprosa obviniaemogo VAIS Villi," January 11, 1944; "Protokol doprosa obviniaemogo MIULLER Erikha," January 9, 1944, USHMM RG-06.025, reel 40.

48 Bloxham, *The Final Solution,* 6; Berkhoff, *Harvest,* 112.

49 *AD-184,* 115.

50 Yahad-in Unum interview 67R, USHMM RG-50-589.1331; Polian, *Zhertvy,* 83–91; Kay, "Transition to Genocide," 414.

51 Arad, *Holocaust in the Soviet Union,* 381; Pohl, *Herrschaft,* 201–5; Berkhoff, *Harvest,* 92; Johanna Jacques, "A 'Most Astonishing' Circumstance: The Survival of Jewish POWs in German War Captivity during the Second World War," *Social and Legal Studies* 30, no. 3 (2020): 362–83.

52 Streit, *Keine Kameraden,* 25, 223; Nikolaus Wachsmann, *KL: A History of the Nazi Concentration Camps* (New York: Farrar, Straus and Giroux, 2015), 260–62, 270.

53 D. P. Karov, "Nemetskaia kontrrazvedka v okkupirovannykh oblastiakh SSSR v voinu 1941–1945 gg.," December 12, 1952, 14, box 20, Research Program on the USSR, Bakhmeteff Archive, Columbia University Rare Book and Manuscript Library. Dulag release documents: GASO f. 2573, op. 1, d. 4, ll. 1, 42.

54 Berkhoff, *Harvest,* 106–7. See also Chapter 7.

55 "Kak formirovali nemtsami dobrovol′cheskie chasti iz inostrantsev," BA MA MSG 149 / 3, 103–11.

56 NA IRI RAN f. 2, r. VI, op. 2, d. 9a, l. 24; NARA T-501, serial 48, frame 886; Men′shagin, *Vospominaniia,* 68.

57 Inter alia, USHMM RG-22.015M, reel 2, frames 489–99.

58 Streit, *Keine Kameraden,* 201–2, 238–39.

59 *Encyclopedia of Camps and Ghettos,* 4:9, 30; BA MA RH 26–221 / 40; BA MA RW 31 / 787; BA MA RW 31 / 788; BA MA W 31 / 790; NARA T-501, serial 48, frames 915–17; NARA T-501, serial 48, frames 882–85; NARA T-501, serial 8, frame 714.

60 "Vermehrte Heranziehung von Kriegsgefangenen für Zwecke der Wehrmacht," December 1, 1941, NARA T-501, serial 48, frames 915–17; cf. NARA T-501, serial 66, frames 296–300; NARA T-501, serial 51, frames 748–51; frames 802–5; Gerlach, *Kalkulierte Morde,* 458, 809.

61 Berkhoff, *Harvest,* 3, 90.

62 Mark Levene, *The Crisis of Genocide,* vol. 2, *Annihilation: The European Rimlands, 1939–1953* (Oxford: Oxford University Press, 2013), 415–19.

63 Streit, *Keine Kameraden,* 188, 210.

64 NARA T-501, serial 72, frame 1014, frames 1055–62; "Armeeoberrkommando 9. O.Qu. / Qu.2, Betr.: Zivilisten in Gefangenenlagern," December 30, 1941, NARA T-501, serial 51, frame 739, frame 751; NARA T-501, serial 8, frames 710–16;

Karov, "Russkaia politsiia," 13; "Stenogramma besedy s t. Kesarevym P. I.," undated, prob. December 1943, NA IRI RAN f. 2, r. VI, op. 2, d. 32, l. 2; NA IRI RAN f. 2, r. VI, op. 2, d. 26, l. 1; "Stenogramma besedy s t. Novikovoi A. G.," December 17, 1943, NA IRI RAN f. 2, r. VI, op. 2, d. 22, l. 1; copies from TsA FSB, Osobyi fond, delo "Smolenskii protsess nad nemetskimi voennymi predstupnikami," USHMM RG-06.025, reel 41; Pohl, *Herrschaft*, 213, 216; Igor' Ermolov, *Tri goda bez Stalina. Okkupatsiia: Sovetskie grazhdane mezhdu natsistami i bol'shevikami, 1941–1944* (Moscow: Tsentrpoligraf, 2010), 57–67.

65 Men'shagin, *Vospominaniia*, 394–99, 592; quotations 395, 398.

66 RGASPI (Arkhiv VLKSM), f. 1, op. 53, d. 247, l. 37; d. 263, l. 45, ll. 49–52; d. 252, l. 83; Mariia Sementsova, "Vospominaniia," undated, GANISO f. 1721, op. 1, d. 10, l. 2, l. 4. Over 300,000 POWs released: Kostiuchenkov, "Organizatsiia i struktura," 312. Corruption: NA IRI RAN f. 2, r. VI, op. 2, d. 16, l. 10b; Harvard Project on the Soviet Social System, Schedule B, vol. 11, case 439, Widener Library, Harvard University, http://nrs.harvard.edu/urn-3:FHCL:965255, accessed July 14, 2021.

67 GARF f. 7021, op. 44, d. 1095, ll. 1–4, l. 11; V. Raevskii, "Organizatsiia i sostoianie kozhno-venerologicheskoi bol'nitsy g. Smolenska, zverstva i proizvol nemtsev vo vremia okkupatsii," October 6, 1943, NA IRI RAN f. 2, r. VI, op. 2, d. 9a, l. 20; NA IRI RAN f. 2, r. VI, op. 2, d. 9a, l. 12.

68 Men'shagin, *Vospominaniia*, 37n3, 358, 398–99.

69 "Stenogramma besedy s t. Madziuk L. Ia. Besedu provodit nauchnyi sotrudnik Komissii t. Fedosov," December 14, 1943, NA IRI RAN f. 2, r. VI, op. 2, d. 15, ll. 1–3, quotation l. 10b; L. Madziuk, "Dokladnaia," October 22, 1943, RGASPI f. 1M, op. 53, d. 263, ll. 41–46, quotations l. 43.

70 Shneiderman, "Okkupirovannyi Smolensk," l. 74.

71 Ereignismeldungen UdSSR (hereafter EM) 67, August 29, 1941, in *Die "Ereignismeldungen UdSSR" 1941. Dokumente der Einsatzgruppen in der Sowjetunion*, ed. Klaus-Michael Mallmann et al. (Darmstadt: WBG, 2011), 1:368–69.

72 Elissa Bemporad, *Legacy of Blood: Jews, Pogroms, and Ritual Murder in the Lands of the Soviets* (New York: Oxford University Press, 2019), 107; Diana Dumitru, *The State, Antisemitism, and Collaboration in the Holocaust: The Borderlands of Romania and the Soviet Union* (New York: Cambridge University Press, 2016), 7, 17.

73 Dumitru, *The State*, 182–83, 186–89; Diana Dumitru and Carter Johnson, "Constructing Interethnic Conflict and Cooperation: Why Some People Harmed Jews and Others Helped Them during the Holocaust in Romania," *World Politics* 63, no. 1 (2011): 1–42; Bemporad, *Legacy*, 117n52.

74 EM 106, October 7, 1941, in *Die "Ereignismeldungen*," 1:635–39; Dumitru, *The State*, 183.

75 Arad, *Holocaust in the Soviet Union,* chap. 32; Kiril Feferman, *The Holocaust in the Crimea and the North Caucasus* (Jerusalem: Yad Vashem, 2016).

76 EM 106, 637.

77 Shneiderman, "Okkupirovannyi Smolensk," l. 74.

78 Shneiderman, "Okkupirovannyi Smolensk," l. 74ob, l. 75ob; "Stenogramma besedy s t. Madziuk," l. 20b.

79 Madziuk, "Dokladnaia," l. 43.

80 "Stenogramma besedy s chlenom Komsomol'skoi podpol'noi organizatsii v Smolenske Mironovoi E. S.," December 4, 1943, NA IRI RAN f. 2, r. VI, op. 20, l. 1.

81 Khizver interview.

82 Arad, *Holocaust in the Soviet Union,* 428; "Sekretariu Smolenskogo Obkoma VKP(b) tov. Popovu. Dokladnaia zapiska o polozhenii v okkupirovannykh nemtsami raionakh Smolenskoi oblasti," Viazma, October 1, 1941, GANISO f. 6, op. 1, d. 742, l. 25; Shneiderman, "Okkupirovannyi Smolensk," l. 77ob.

83 Interview 45R, USHMM RG-50.589.1310.

84 Christ, *Dynamik,* 106–23, 266.

85 Yahad-In Unum interview 55R, USHMM RG-50.589.1320.

86 "Svidetel'skie pokazaniia o zverstvakh, istiazaniiakh i istreblenii sovetskikh grazhdan za stenkami nemetskoi tainoi politsii 'Gestapo' v gorode Smolenske," October 1, 1943, NA IRI RAN f. 2, r. VI, op. 2, d. 9a, ll. 27–29; Cohen, *Smolensk,* 128–31; Zinaida Namatevs, "Dokladnaia," October 22, 1943, NA IRI RAN f. 1, op. 53, d. 263, ll. 50–51; GARF f. 7021, op. 98, d. 43, l. 27.

87 GARF f. 7021, op. 44, d. 43, l. 10; cf., inter alia, USHMM RG-22.015M, reel 2, frame 242; Cohen, *Smolensk,* 132.

88 "Akt ot 16 marta 1943 goda," GARF f. 7021, op. 44, d. 43, l. 3.

89 "Pamiatnyi listok dlia nemetskikh voennykh," undated, 1943, RGASPI f. 625, op. 1, d. 49, ll. 332–33.

90 "Stenogramma besedy s t. Korotkovym I. V. Smolensk," December 18, 1943, NA IRI RAN f. 2, r. VI, op. 2, ll. 1–2; GARF f. 7021, op. 44, d. 43, l. 2.

91 "Perevod s nemetskogo. Politicheskie zadachi nemetskogo soldata v usloviiakh total'noi voiny," May 30, 1943, RGASPI f. 625, op. 1, d. 49, ll. 356–61; similar documents, ll. 363–65.

92 Monthly reports of Wi Kdo Kommandatur Smolensk, January–December 1942, BA MA RW 31/788; BA MA RW 31/789; BA MA RW 31/790; BA MA RH 26-286/6; BA MA RH 26-286/12; NA IRI RAN f. 2, r. VI, op. 2, d. 9a, l. 12.

93 Pohl, *Herrschaft,* 310–15; Hasenclever, *Wehrmacht,* 379–412; Cohen, *Smolensk,* 113–16; Karov, "Russkaia politsiia," 136; "Stenogramma Zasedaniia XIII-go Plenuma Smolenskogo oblastnogo komiteta VKP(b)," December 23–25, 1943, RGASPI f. 17, op. 43, ed. khr. 1717, l. 26.

6. PARTISANS COME TO POWER

1   Thomas Kühne, *The Rise and Fall of Comradeship: Hitler's Soldiers, Male Bonding, and Mass Violence in the Twentieth Century* (Cambridge: Cambridge University Press, 2017), chap. 5.

2   Hitler quoted in Richard J. Evans, *The Third Reich at War* (New York: Penguin, 2009), 225; Alex J. Kay, "Transition to Genocide, July 1941: Einsatzkommando 9 and the Annihilation of Soviet Jewry," *Holocaust and Genocide Studies* 27, no. 3 (Winter 2013): 418–19; David Bell, *The First Total War: Napoleon's Europe and the Birth of Warfare as We Know It* (Princeton, NJ: Princeton University Press, 2008); Carl Schmitt, *The Theory of the Partisan: A Commentary/Remark on the Concept of the Political,* trans. A. C. Goodson (East Lansing: Michigan State University Press, 2004).

3   Sönke Neitzel and Harald Welzer, *Soldiers: German POWs on Fighting, Killing, and Dying,* trans. Jefferson Chase (New York: Vintage Books, 2013), 330; Waitman Beorn, *Marching into Darkness: The Wehrmacht and the Holocaust in Belarus* (Cambridge, MA: Harvard University Press, 2014), 6–8, 60, 92–118, quotation 92; Kay, "Transition to Genocide," 425–26. See also Himmler's November 18, 1941, order among captured German documents housed in the Kremlin's Presidential Archive, in S. V. Kudriashov, ed., *Partizanskoe dvizhenie v gody Velikoi Otechest-vennoi voiny* (Moscow: Istoricheskaia literatura, 2015), 587–89.

4   Quoted in Beorn, *Marching into Darkness,* 108; Mark Edele, *Stalin's Defectors: How Red Army Soldiers Became Hitler's Collaborators, 1941–1945* (Oxford: Oxford University Press, 2017), 127; NARA T-501, serial 42, frame 1110, Korück 559 intelligence reports, August 31, December 14, and December 30, 1941: NARA T-501, serial 51, frames 739, 751; Ereignismeldungen UdSSR (hereafter EM) 65, August 27, 1941; EM 90, September 21, 1941; EM 97, September 28, 1941; EM 108, October 9, 1941, in *Die "Ereignismeldungen UdSSR" 1941. Dokumente der Einsatzgruppen in der Sowjetunion,* ed. Klaus-Michael Mallmann et al. (Darmstadt: WBG, 2011), 1:373, 516, 594–96, 656.

5   "Demenkov Feoktist Nikolaevich," May 16, 1942, NA IRI RAN f. 2, r. II, op. 2, ed. khr. 7b, l. 29.

6   D. P. Karov, "Nemetskaia kontrrazvedka v okkupirovannykh oblastiakh SSSR v voinu 1941–1945 gg.," December 12, 1952, 34–37, box 20, Research Program on the USSR, Bakhmeteff Archive, Columbia University Rare Book and Manuscript Library.

7   Petr Lidov, "Tania," *Pravda,* January 27, 1942; "Prikaz Narodnogo komissara oborony. O zadachakh partizanskogo dvizheniia," September 5, 1942, RGASPI f. 69, op. 1, d. 3, ll. 12–16; "'Partizanskoe dvizhenie dolzhno stat' vsenarodnym.' Dokumenty AP RF o deiatel'nosti Tsentral'nogo shtaba partizanskogo dvizheniia. 1942–1943 gg.," *Istoricheskii arkhiv,* no. 3 (2015): 3–25.

8   NKVD reports from Smolensk Region in early 1942: GANISO f. 6, op. 1, d. 936.

9   Masha Cerovic, *Les enfants de Staline: La guerre des partisans soviétiques (1941–1944)* (Paris: Seuil, 2018), 59–66.

10 Quoted in Kenneth Slepyan, *Stalin's Guerrillas: Soviet Partisans in World War II* (Lawrence: University Press of Kansas, 2006), 110.

11 Bogdan Musial, *Sowjetische Partisanen 1941–1944: Mythos und Wirklichkeit* (Paderborn: Ferdinand Schöningh, 2009); Alfred J. Rieber, *Stalin and the Struggle for Supremacy in Eurasia* (Cambridge: Cambridge University Press, 2015), 269–70; *Organy gosudarstvennoi bezopasnosti SSSR v Velikoi Otechestvennoi voine: Sbornik dokumentov,* 5 vols. (Moscow: [various publishers], 1995–2007).

12 Musial, *Sowjetische Partisanen,* 149; Schmitt, *Theory of the Partisan,* 10.

13 Dmitrii Popov to Panteleimon Ponomarenko, January 10, 1943, RGASPI f. 69, op. 1, d. 301, ll. 1–2.

14 Compare, *mutatis mutandis,* new patriarchal norms in the Red Army: Brandon Schechter, "*Khoziaistvo* and *Khoziaeva:* The Properties and Proprietors of the Red Army, 1941–45," *Kritika* 18, no. 3 (2017): 487–510.

15 Roger D. Markwick and Euridice Charon Cardona, *Soviet Women on the Frontline in the Second World War* (London: Palgrave Macmillan, 2012), 1, 117; S. V. Kudriashov and O. Mozokhin, "Predislovie," in *Partizanskoe dvizhenie v gody Velikoi Otechestvennoi voiny,* ed. S. V. Kudriashov (Moscow: Istoricheskaia literatura, 2015), 20.

16 I. Borisov (commander) and I. P. Mozin (commissar) to D. M. Popov, August 24, 1942, GANISO f. 8, op. 301, d. 43, ll. 22–23.

17 "Demenkov Feoktist Nikolaevich," l. 7, l. 11; I. A. Buleiko, "Smolenskomu Obkomu VKP(b) i Oblispolkomu. Dokladnaia zapiska," undated, NA IRI RAN f. 2, r. II, op. 2, ed. khr. 7g, ll. 1–2.

18 "Demenkov Feoktist Nikolaevich," l. 8.

19 "Demenkov Feoktist Nikolaevich," l. 33.

20 Musial, *Sowjetische Partisanen,* 52–54; see also Slepyan, *Stalin's Guerrillas,* 108.

21 USHMM RG-22.015M, reel 1, frames 1151, 1152; Slepyan, *Stalin's Guerrillas,* 176–84.

22 "Amirov, Gaian Sufiianovich," autobiography, Moscow, June 15, 1942, GANISO f. 8, op. 1, d. 208, ll. 1–4.

23 "Amirov, Gaian Sufiianovich," ll. 6, 7, 14; "Beseda s komissarom otdel′nogo partizanskogo polka imeni XXIV godovshchiny Krasnoi Armii batal′onym komissarom t. Amirovym Gaianom Sufiianovichem," December 31, 1942, RGASPI f. 69, op. 1, d. 283, l. 170b; G. S. Amirov, autobiographical statements from February 13, 1948, GANISO f. 8, op. 1, d. 208, ll. 27–32; February 14, 1948, GANISO f. 8, op. 1, d. 208, ll. 33–38; February 28, 1948, GANISO f. 8, op. 1, d. 208, ll. 39–42.

24 "Amirov, Gaian Sufiianovich," ll. 11–12; RGASPI f. 1M, op. 53, d. 263, l. 143, "Zapiska D. M. Popova A. A. Andreevu i G. M. Malenkovu ob obstanovke v Smolenskoi oblasti," in *Partizanskoe dvizhenie v gody Velikoi Otechestvennoi voiny,* ed. S. V. Kudriashov (Moscow: Istoricheskaia literatura, 2015), 132–34.

25 Mark Edele and Michael Geyer, "States of Exception: The Nazi-Soviet War as a System of Violence, 1939–1945," in *Beyond Totalitarianism: Stalinism and Nazism Compared,* ed. Michael Geyer and Sheila Fitzpatrick (New York: Cambridge University Press, 2009), 365. Edele and Geyer use the phrase "cadres of totalitarian violence."

26 "Stenogramma besedy s komandirom partizanskogo otriada t. Gnezdilovym F. D. ot 31 maia 1942 g.," NA IRI RAN f. 2, r. II, op. 2, ed. khr. 26a, ll. 1–14.

27 "Stenogramma besed s . . . Gnezdilovym," ll. 2–4, quotation l. 2.

28 "Stenogramma besed s . . . Gnezdilovym," l. 4.

29 "Stenogramma besed s . . . Gnezdilovym," ll. 6–11; "Stenogramma besedy t. Briukhanova s t. Amirovym G. S.—komissarom partizanskogo otriada im 24 godovshchiny RKKA i t. Gnezdilovym F. D.—komandir partizanskogo otriada m. 24 godovshchiny Krasnoi armii," August 3, 1942, RGASPI f. 69, op. 1, d. 283, ll. 7–9.

30 "Voronchenko, Vasilii Isaevich," undated biography, probably June 1942, NA IRI RAN f. 2, r. II, op. 2, ed. khr. 7a, l. 18.

31 I. P. Shcherov, *Partizany: Organizatsiia, metody i posledstviia bor′by (1941–1945)* (Smolensk: Universum, 2006), 348; "M. Sarychev. TsK VKP(b) tov. Malinu. Dokladnaia zapiska," February 6, 1942, RGASPI f. 69, op. 1, d. 285, ll. 25–27.

32 Shcherov, *Partizany,* 356, 358; RGASPI f. 625, op. 1, d. 39, ll. 122–42; Cerovic, *Les enfants,* 84; Alexander Gogun, *Stalin's Commandos: Ukrainian Partisan Forces on the Eastern Front* (London: I. B. Taurus, 2016), 160.

33 "Zapiski t. Voronchenko ('Dedushka'). Materialy ot 3 fevralia 1944 g.," NA IRI RAN f. 2, r. II, op. 2, ed. khr. 7z, ll. 19–20; Leonid Smilovitskii, "Antisemitism in the Soviet Partisan Movement, 1941–1944: The Case of Belorussia," *Holocaust and Genocide Studies* 20, no. 2 (2006): 207–34; Anika Walke, *Pioneers and Partisans: An Oral History of Nazi Genocide in Belorussia* (New York: Oxford University Press, 2015), 20, 132.

34 "Instruktor TsK VLKSM Kaverzneva. Dokladnaia zapiska," March 19, 1943, RGASPI f. 1M, op. 53, d. 263, l. 52; Juliane Fürst, "Heroes, Lovers, Victims: Partisan Girls during the Great Fatherland War," *Minerva: Quarterly Report on Women and the Military* 18, no. 3–4 (Fall–Winter 2000): 71.

35 "Pobeda za nami," *Boevoi listok 3-go vzvoda otriada Smert' nemetskim okkupantam,* no. 4, October 4, 1942, BA MA 137 / 15; Walke, *Pioneers and Partisans,* 20.

36 Quoted in Fürst, "Heroes," 53; Markwick and Cardona, *Soviet Women,* chap. 5; RGASPI f. 1M, op. 53, d. 252, l. 19.

37 Slepyan, *Stalin's Guerrillas,* 196; Markwick and Cardona, *Soviet Women,* 31, 117–18, 137; Juliane Fürst, *Stalin's Last Generation: Soviet Post-War Youth and the Emergence of Mature Socialism* (New York: Oxford University Press, 2010), quotation 178.

38 Cerovic, *Les enfants,* 109.

39 For example, GANISO f. 6, op. 1, d. 936, ll. 43–44; Kudriashov, *Partizanskoe dvizhenie;* Michael David-Fox, "Syncretic Subcultures or Stalinism without Stalin? Soviet Partisans as Communities of Violence," *Russian Review* 78, no. 3 (July 2019): 486–501.

40 For example, RGASPI f. 1M, op. 53, d. 263, ll. 20–24; RGASPI f. 1M, op. 53, d. 263, ll. 40–57.

41 Slepyan, *Stalin's Guerrillas,* 3; "Amirov, Gaian Sufiianovich," l. 22.

42 "Amirov, Gaian Sufiianovich," l. 18. See also Amirov, autobiographical statement, February 13, 1948; "Kliatva partizana," USHMM RG-22.015M, reel 1, frame 774; "Moskva, Predsedatel'iu Gosudarstvennogo komiteta oborony, vozhdiu trudiashchikhsia—tovarishchu Stalinu. Ot kolkhoznikov, kolkhoznits, partizan i partizanok enskogo raiona Smolenskoi oblasti," *Pravda,* May 10, 1942, 1.

43 Amirov, autobiographical statement, February 13, 1948, ll. 27–28.

44 "Ravniaites' po peredovym," *Boevoi listok,* October 4, 1942, BA MA MSG 137 / 15.

45 "Stenogramma vstrechi redaktsii 'Komsomol'skaia Pravda' s komandirom partizanskikh otriadov t. Batia," July 8, 1942, RGASPI f. 1M, op. 53, d. 252, ll. 1–28, quotation l. 6; "Biograficheskie dannye i boevye podvigi komsomol'tsa-partizana GRISHINA Sergeia Vladimirovicha," undated, 1943, RGASPI f. 1M, op. 53, d. 247, l. 43–46; "Politdonesenie. O partiino-politicheskoi rabote otdeleniia v partizanskikh otriadakh i sredi naseleniia okkupirovannykh raionov za period s 15 marta po 5 aprelia 1942," RGASPI f. 69, op. 1, d. 1070, ll. 1–8; RGASPI f. 69, op. 1, d. 1069, l. 59, ll. 76–77, ll. 78–81; RGASPI f. 69, op. 1, d. 300, ll. 95–96; RGASPI f. 69, op. 1, d. 285, ll. 25–27; RGASPI f. 69, op. 1, d. 285, l. 76; "Spetssoobshchenie o sostoianii partizanskikh otriadov 'Bati' po sostoianiiu 11.V.42 g.," GANISO f. 6, op. 1, d. 936, ll. 101–3; I. P. Mozin to

D. M. Popov, July 15, 1942, GANISO f. 8, op. 301, d. 43, ll. 7–13. See also Slepyan, *Stalin's Guerrillas,* 232; Shcherov, *Partizany,* 374.

46   I. P. Mozin to D. M. Popov, July 15, 1942, GANISO f. 8, op. 301, d. 43, l. 120b; Slepyan, *Stalin's Guerrillas,* 240; Cerovic, *Les enfants,* 92.

47   "Zapiski t. Voronchenko," l. 17; Dmitrii Komarov, *Smolenskaia oblast' v ogne Velikoi Otechestvennoi: Voina, narod, pobeda* (Smolensk: Svitok, 2015), 123–24.

48   "Zapiski t. Voronchenko," l. 17.

49   Karov, "Nemetskaia kontrrazvedka," 62; Markwick and Cardona, *Soviet Women,* 145.

50   Alexis Peri, *The War Within: Diaries from the Siege of Leningrad* (Cambridge, MA: Harvard University Press, 2017), 93–102.

51   Cited in Slepyan, *Stalin's Guerrillas,* 272.

52   "Stenogramma besedy s. t. Kazubskim V. V. Shtab partizanskogo dvizheniia, d. Ratkevshchina Smolenskogo raiona Smolenskoi oblasti," December 9, 1943, NA IRI RAN f. 2, r. II, op. 2, ed. khr. 31b, l. 80b; Slepyan, *Stalin's Guerrillas,* 67–84; Masha Cerovic, "'Au chien, une mort de chien': Les partisans face aux 'traîtres à la Patrie,'" *Cahiers du monde russe* 49, no. 2–3 (2008): 239–62; Cerovic, *Les enfants,* 139.

53   Alexander Statiev, "Soviet Partisan Violence against Soviet Civilians: Targeting Their Own," *Europe-Asia Studies* 69, no. 9 (2014): 1525–51, quotation 1531; "Stenogramma besedy s t. Shmatkovym P. K., komandirom partizanskogo otriada Znamenskogo raiona Smolenskoi oblasti," May 22, 1942, NA IRI RAN f. 2, r. II, op. 2, ed. khr. 11a, l. 12; GASO f. R-2590, op. 1, d. 1, l. 4; GASO f. 2573, op. 1, d. 235, l. 2.

54   "Romanov, Konstantin Ivanovich (Duminichskii raion). Nekotorye dannye, izvestnye mne o zverstvakh fashistov," July 9, 1942, NA IRI RAN f. 2, r. VI, op. 2, d. 4, l. 509.

55   Karov, "Nemetskaia kontrrazvedka," 36, 62; RGASPI f. 69, op. 1, d. 285, l. 76; Cerovic, "'Au chien,'" 247.

56   "Stenogramma vstrechi redaktsii," ll. 6–8.

57   Slepyan, *Stalin's Guerrillas,* 80; Cerovic, *Les enfants,* 166–69; Security Division 221. Abt. Ic, "Monatsbericht für die Zeit vom 1.–31. Juli 1942," BA MA RH 26-221/38; Abt. Ic report, "Banditenerkundung durch ein V-Mann," September 13, 1942, BA MA RH 26-221/75.

58   Daniel Stotland, *Purity and Compromise in the Soviet Party-State: The Struggle for the Soul of the Party, 1941–1952* (Lanham, MD: Lexington Books, 2018), 74, 86; Mark Edele, "'What Are We Fighting For?' Loyalty in the Soviet War Effort, 1941–1945," *International Labor and Working-Class History* 84 (Fall 2013): 254–55.

59 Shcherov, *Partizany,* 129–36; Komarov, *Smolenskaia oblast',* 155–73; Leonid D. Grenkevich, *The Soviet Partisan Movement, 1941–1944* (London: Frank Cass, 1999), 187–92.

60 BA MA RH 26-221 / 40; RGASPI f. 69, op. 1, d. 285, l. 76; Gerhard L. Weinberg, "The Yelnya-Dorogobuzh Area of Smolensk Oblast," in *Soviet Partisans in World War II,* ed. John A. Armstrong (Madison: University of Wisconsin Press, 1964), 390–457; N. M. Veberinkova and V. A. Prokhorov, "Vspominaia voinu," in *Smolenskaia zemlia. Dorogobuzhskii raion. Ocherki proshlogo i nastoiashchego* (Moscow: Institut Naslediia, 2011), 351–86; statistics from Boris Kovalev, *Posednevnaia zhizn' naseleniia Rossii v period natsistskoi okkupatsii* (Moscow: Molodaia gvardiia, 2011), 50.

61 "Stenogramma besedy s t. Kozubskim," l. 80b; Amirov, autobiographical statement, February 28, 1948, l. 41; "Sekretar' RK VKP(b) Valuev. Smolenskomu Obkomu VKP(b) i Oblispolkomu ot El'ninskogo RK i raiispolkom. Dokladnaia zapiska," no earlier than April 29, 1942, USHMM RG-22.015M, reel 13, frame 866; "Smolenskomu Obkomu VKP(b). Ot sekretaria El'ninskogo RK VKP(b) Valueva Ia. P. [Iakov Petrovich] Otchet o rabote v tylu vraga za period 1.VI-po 25.X-1942g.," USHMM RG-22.015M, reel 13, frame 889; GANISO f. 6, op. 1, d. 936, ll. 62–66; Grenkevich, *Soviet Partisan Movement,* 130. NKVD instructions: Shcherov, *Partizany,* 135, citing GANISO f. 8, op. 2, d. 109, l. 33.

62 "Amirov Gaian Sufiianovich," February 26, 1943, NA IRI RAN f. 2, r. II, op. 2, ed. khr. 2, l. 50.

63 "Obiazatel'noe postanovlenie No. 1 ot 20 marta 1942 g.," USHMM RG-22.015M, reel 13, frame 808; "Smolenskomu Obkomu VKP(b) ot vtorogo sekretaria El'ninskogo RK VKP(b) GUSEVA Ivana Pavlovicha," June 14, 1942, USHMM RG-22.015M, reel 13, frame 849; USHMM RG-22.015M, reel 13, frames 863–69.

64 "Dmitrii Popov. Sekretar' Smolenskogo Obkoma VKP(b). Orginstruktorskii otdel TsK VKP(b) tov. Shamberg," from Riazan, November 1941 (no exact day), USHMM RG-22.015M, reel 1, frames 1145, 1162. On padding lists of partisans recommended for medals: "Nachal'nik Duminichskogo RO NKVD leitenant gosbezopasnosti—Chekmarev," March 3, 1942, GANISO f. 6, op. 1, d. 936, l. 43.

65 "Stenogramma besedy s t. Shmatkovym," ll. 12, 14; "Smolenskomu Obkomu VKP(b). Ot zav. voennym otdelom Znamenskogo raikoma VKP(b) Kolom'eva A. G. (komandira partizanskogo otriada)," NA IRI RAN f. 2, r. II, op. 2, ed. khr. 11b, ll. 1–6, here ll. 2–3; "Otchet o rabote v tylu vraga za period s 1.IV—po 25.X-1942 g. Ot sekretaria El'ninskogo RK VKP(b) Valueva Ia. L.," USHMM RG-22-15M, reel 2, frame 889; Amirov, autobiographical statement, February 28, 1948, l. 410b; USHMM RG-22.015M, reel 13, frame 795; RGASPI f. 69, op. 1, d. 283, l. 70b.

66 Amirov, autobiographical statement, February 28, 1948, l. 41; "Otchet o rabote v tylu vraga za period s 1.IV—po 25.X-1942 g. Ot sekretaria El'ninskogo RK

VKP(b) Valueva Ia. L.," USHMM RG-22.015M, reel 2, frames 887–98; "Steno-gramma besedy, provedennoi s tov. Voronchenko V. I.," June 27, 1942, NA IRI RAN f. 2, r. II, op. 2, ed. khr. 7a, l. 11; "Stenogramma besedy s t. Kozubskim," l. 10; "Zam. Nachal'nika Otdeleniia 4-go otdela UNKVD po Smolenskoi oblasti ml. leitenant gosbezopasnosti (Khantil'). Dokladnaia zapiska na 31 marta 1942," GANISO f. 6, op. 1, d. 936, ll. 54–55.

67 Alexander Dallin, *German Rule in Russia 1941–1945: A Study of Occupation Policies,* 2nd ed. (Basingstoke: Palgrave Macmillan, 1981), 321–35; see Chapter 9.

68 "Sekretariu Obkoma VKP(b) t. Popov. Predsedatel'iu Oblispolkoma t. Mel'nikovu. Ot sekretaria El'ninskogo raikira i pred. raiispolkoma. Dokladnaia zapiska," April 8, 1942, USHMM RG-22.015M, reel 13, frame 795; "Postanovlenie No. 7 Ispolnitel'nogo komiteta El'ninskogo raisoveta deputatov trudiashchikhsia," April 21, 1942, USHMM RG-22.015M, reel 13, frame 788; USHMM RG-22.015M, reel 13, frames 819, 849, 850; GASO f. R-2576, op. 1, d. 5. Cf. Johannes Due Enstad, *Soviet Russians under Nazi Occupation: Fragile Loyalties in World War II* (Cambridge: Cambridge University Press, 2018), 186–89; Kovalev, *Posednevnaia zhizn',* 64–66.

69 USHMM RG-22.015M, reel 13, frame 901; Buleiko, "Smolenskomu Obkomu," l. 1; "Smolenskomu Obkomu VKP(b). Ot sekretaria El'ninskogo RK VKP(b) Valueva Ia. P. [Iakov Petrovich] Otchet o rabote v tylu vraga za period 1.VI-po 25.X-1942g.," USHMM RG-22.015M, reel 13, frames 888–89; "Sekretar' RK VKP(b) Valuev, Pred RIK Anis'kov. Smolenskii Obkom VKP(b) i Oblispolkom ot El'ninskogo RK i Raiispolkom. Dokladnaia zapiska," USHMM RG-22.015M, reel 13, frames 863–69; Karel C. Berkhoff, *Harvest of Despair: Life and Death in Ukraine under Nazi Rule* (Cambridge, MA: Belknap Press of Harvard University Press, 2004), chap. 8.

70 BA MA RH 26-221/72; Ben Shepherd, *War in the Wild East: The German Army and Soviet Partisans* (Cambridge, MA: Harvard University Press, 2004), chap. 5, quotations 132, 194; Dieter Pohl, *Die Herrschaft der Wehrmacht: Deutsche Militärbe-satzung und einheimische Bevölkerung in der Sowjetunion 1941–1944* (Munich: R. Oldenbourg, 2008), 285–86; Weinberg, "Yelnya-Dorogobuzh Area."

71 Security Division 221, 1c report for period December 15 to March 21, 1942, BA MA 26-221/71; 1c report from April 10, 1942, BA MA RH 26-221/34; BA MA RH 26-221/76, Anlage 10; Shepherd, *War,* 133, 134, 194; Pohl, *Herrschaft,* quotation 286; Alexander Hill, *The War behind the Eastern Front: The Soviet Partisan Movement in North-West Russia 1941–1944* (London: Frank Cass, 2005), chap. 8.

72 Security Division 221, Abt. 1c, instruction of September 12, 1942, BA MA 26-221/40; Shepherd, *War,* 125, 151, chap. 6; Christian Hartmann, *Wehrmacht im Ostkrieg: Front und militärisches Hinterland 1941/42* (Munich: R. Oldenbourg, 2009), 662–63, 676–95.

73 "Protokol doprosa obviniaemogo VAIS Villi," January 11, 1944, USHMM RG-06.025, reel 40; Ben H. Shepherd, *Hitler's Soldiers: The German Army in the Third Reich* (New Haven, CT: Yale University Press, 2016), 283–84; Kühne, *Comradeship*, 169; Neitzel and Welzer, *Soldiers*, 74–89.

74 Numerous reports are in BA MA 26-221/40; Shepherd, *War*, 116, 687–88; Pohl, *Herrschaft*, 285; Theo J. Schulte, *The German Army and Nazi Policies in Occupied Russia* (Oxford, UK: Berg, 1989), 130.

75 Komarov, *Smolenskaia oblast'*, 171–72.

7. COLLABORATION AND THE RUSSIAN QUESTION

1   Vasilii Maslennikov, *Bez tsenzury. Smolenshchina. Voina. Plen. Avtobiografiia* (Mozhaisk: Mozhaiskii poligraficheskii kombinat, 2014), 250.

2   Maslennikov, *Bez tsenzury*, 206–7, 246.

3   D. Karov (Dmitrii Petrovich Kandaurov), "Russkaia politsiia v okkupirovannykh nemtsami oblastiakh SSSR v voinu 1941–1945," 57–58, 114, box 20, Research Program on the USSR, Bakhmeteff Archive, Columbia University Rare Book and Manuscript Library; "Bericht über den russischen Ordnungsdienst in rückwärtigen Armeegebiet," Kdt. R. A. 559. Abt. 1c/A.O. Stu.Qu., April 30, 1942, NARA T-501, serial 72, frame 1014; GASO f. R-2573, op. 1, d. 3, l. 24, l. 50; GASO f. 2740, op. 1, d. 15, l. 312; Igor' Ermolov, *Tri goda bez Stalina. Okkupatsiia: Sovetskie grazhdane mezhdu natsistami i bol'shevikami, 1941–1944* (Moscow: Tsentrpoligraf, 2010), 52–53; Igor' Ermolov, *Pod znamenami Gitlera: Sovetskie grazhdane v soiuze s natsistami na okkupirovannykh territoriiakh RSFSR v 1941–1944 gg.* (Moscow: Veche, 2013), 47; A. A. Kostiuchenkov, "Organizatsiia i struktura vspomogatel'noi politsii (strazhi) na okkupatsionnoi territorii Smolenskoi oblasti 1941–1943 godov," *Izvestiia Smolenskogo gosudarstvennogo universiteta*, no. 2 (2012): 215–17.

4   Maslennikov, *Bez tsenzury*, 216–17.

5   Maslennikov, *Bez tsenzury*, 250–53.

6   Korück 559 reports: BA MA RH23/155, 8–13; NARA T-501, serial 72, frames 741–42 (February 1, 1942); T-501, serial 72, frames 806–10 (February 25, 1942); T-501, serial 66, frames 33–34 (no earlier than August 10, 1942); T-501, serial 66, frame 254 (January 10, 1942); T-501, serial 90, frame 1121 (July–August 1943); serial 90, frame 1067 (August 19, 1943).

7   Maslennikov, *Bez tsenzury*, 278.

8   Maslennikov, *Bez tsenzury*, 274–75, 278, 279–310.

9   Stanley Hoffman, "Collaborationism in France during World War II," *Journal of Modern History* 40, no. 3 (1968): 376, 379, 381.

10 Aviel Roshwald, *Occupied: European and Asian Responses to Axis Conquest, 1937–1945* (Cambridge: Cambridge University Press, 2023), 6; Philip Morgan, *Hitler's Collaborators: Choosing between Bad and Worse in Nazi-Occupied Western Europe* (Oxford: Oxford University Press, 2018).

11 Alexander Dallin, *German Rule in Russia 1941–1945: A Study of Occupation Policies,* 2nd ed. (Basingstoke: Palgrave Macmillan, 1981), 46–53, 200; Jürgen Matthäus and Frank Bajohr, eds., *The Political Diary of Alfred Rosenberg and the Onset of the Holocaust* (Lanham, MD: Rowman and Littlefield, 2015).

12 Ian Kershaw, *Hitler: A Biography* (New York: W. W. Norton, 2008), 634; Ian Kershaw, *Hitler* (Edinburgh Gate, UK: Pearson, 1991), 188–89.

13 Dieter Pohl, *Die Herrschaft der Wehrmacht: Deutsche Militärbesatzung und einheimische Bevölkerung in der Sowjetunion 1941–1944* (Munich: R. Oldenbourg, 2008), 297–99.

14 "Ehrfarungen in der Verwaltung des Landes und politische Zielsetzung," no exact date, December 1942, BA MA RH22-235, 224–27; "Besprechung im Ostministerium am 18.12.42," BA MA RH22-235, 212; Timothy Patrick Mulligan, *The Politics of Illusion and Empire: German Occupation Policy in the Soviet Union, 1942–1943* (New York: Praeger, 1988), 126.

15 BA MA RH22-235, 212; Matthäus and Bajohr, *Political Diary of Alfred Rosenberg,* 304–5.

16 Dallin, *German Rule;* Mulligan, *Politics of Illusion,* 50–51.

17 Mark Edele, *Stalin's Defectors: How Red Army Soldiers Became Hitler's Collaborators, 1941–1945* (Oxford: Oxford University Press, 2017), 132–35; Dmitrii Komarov, *Smolenskaia oblast' v ogne Velikoi Otechestvennoi: Voina, narod, pobeda* (Smolensk: Svitok, 2015), 176–79; cf. S. I. Drobiazko, *Pod znamenami vraga: Antisovetskie formirovaniia v sostave germanskikh vooruzhennykh sil 1941–1945* (Moscow: EKSMO, 2004), 41–47, 339–41.

18 Rolf-Dieter Müller, *An der Seite der Wehrmacht: Hitlers ausländische Helfer beim "Kreuzzug gegen den Bolschewismus" 1941–1945* (Berlin: Christoph Links, 2010), 226, 242; Mark Edele, "'What Are We Fighting For?' Loyalty in the Soviet War Effort, 1941–1945," *International Labor and Working-Class History* 84 (Fall 2013): 248–68, 259 (table).

19 Peter Black, "Who Were the Trawniki-Men? Preliminary Data and Conclusions about the Foot Soldiers of 'Operation Reinhard,'" in *Mittäterschaft in Osteuropa im Zweiten Weltkrieg und im Holocaust in Osteuropa,* ed. Peter Black et al. (Vienna: New Academic Press, 2019), 22–24, 35–36, 47–49.

20 "Politsiia iz mestnogo naseleniia," no earlier than July 8, 1943, RGASPI f. 625, op. 1, d. 44, l. 237; Drobiazko, *Pod znamenami vraga,* 269.

21 Drobiazko, *Pod znamenami vraga,* 338; Edele, *Stalin's Defectors,* viii.

22 D. Karov (Dmitrii Kandaurov), "Russkie na sluzhbe v nemetskoi razvedke i kontrrazvedke," no earlier than July 6, 1950, 14–18, 21–22, 53–59, box 280, Boris I. Nicolaevsky Collection, Hoover Institution Library and Archives, Stanford University; D. Karov, "Nemetskaia kontrrazvedka v okkupirovannykh oblastiakh SSSR v voinu 1941–1945 gg.," December 12, 1952, 16–22, box 20, Research Program on the USSR, Bakhmeteff Archive, Columbia University Rare Book and Manuscript Library. See also Harvard Project on the Soviet Social System. Schedule B, vol. 12, case 140, Widener Library, Harvard University, http://nrs .harvard.edu/urn-3:FHCL:965182.

23 Karov, "Russkaia politsiia"; Karov, "Russkie na sluzhbe," 90; Karov, "Nemetskaia kontrrazvedka," 3; Drobiazko, *Pod znamenami vraga,* 39, 123–48; David Thomas, "Foreign Armies East and German Military Intelligence in Russia 1941–45," *Journal of Contemporary History* 22, no. 2 (1987): 261–301.

24 E. V. Kodin, *Miunkhenskii institut po izucheniiu SSSR, 1950–1972 gg.: Evropeiskii tsentr sovetologii?* (Smolensk: SmolGU, 2016); D. Karov, *Partizanskoe dvizhenie v SSSR v 1941–1945 gg.* (Munich: Institut po izucheniiu istorii i kul'tury SSSR, 1954).

25 Karov, "Russkie na sluzhbe," 25, 95, 98, 140; Karov, "Nemetskaia kontrrazvedka," 11, 16.

26 Karov, "Russkie na sluzhbe," 166–67.

27 Karov, "Russkaia politsiia," 57.

28 Karov, "Russkaia politsiia," 12–16.

29 Zam. Nachal'nika 4 otdela UNKVD S/O Leitenant Gos. Besopasnosti Maklashin to Dmitrii Popov, October 1, 1941, GANISO f. 6, op. 1, d. 742, ll. 1–26; GANISO f. 6, op. 1, d. 936, ll. 131–36; BA MA RH 20-2/1176, 159; Karov, "Russkaia politsiia," 13; *Boris Men'shagin: Vospominaniia. Pis'ma. Dokumenty,* ed. Pavel Polian et al. (St. Petersburg: Nestor-Istoriia, 2019), 363–66; Jeffrey Burds, "'Turncoats, Traitors, and Provocateurs': Communist Collaborators, the German Occupation, and Stalin's NKVD, 1941–1943," *East European Politics and Societies and Cultures* 32, no. 3 (2018): 606–38.

30 Komarov, *Smolenskaia oblast',* 117; Jan Gross, *Neighbors: The Destruction of the Jewish Community in Jedwabne, Poland* (Princeton, NJ: Princeton University Press, 2001), 114–18.

31 "Allgemeine Richtlinien für den Aufbau und die Aufgaben der Stadt- und Gemeindewerwaltung," no exact date, NARA T-501, serial 72, frames 1055–62; Karov, "Russkaia politsiia," 18; BA MA MSG 149/3, 103–6.

32 NARA T-501, serial 48, frame 882; Karov, "Russkaia politsiia," 15, 18; "Sekretariu Smolenskogo Obkoma VKP(b) tovarishchu Popovu. Dokladnaia zapiska o rabote Upravleniia NKVD po Smolenskoi oblasti," March 24, 1942, GANISO f. 6, op. 1, d. 742, ll. 49–50; GANISO f. 6, op. 1, d. 936, l. 235.

33 Kostiuchenkov, "Organizatsiia i struktura," 213; Men'shagin, *Vospominaniia,* 204–9, 452.

34 BA MA RH22-235, 44; BA MA RH24-35/98; "Bericht über den russischen Ordnungsdienst," frame 1014. See also, e.g., BA MA RH22-235, 44; GANISO f. 6, op. 1, d. 742, l. 8; Karov, "Russkaia politsiia," 56.

35 "RNNA—Russkaia narodnaia natsional'naia armiia," undated, BA MA MSG 149/3, 81; BA MA RH 22-235, 44; "Bericht über den russischen Ordnungsdienst," frame 1014; Karov, "Russkaia politsiia," 35, 56, 93, 136; Ermolov, *Tri goda,* 302; Johannes Due Enstad, *Soviet Russians under Nazi Occupation: Fragile Loyalties in World War II* (Cambridge: Cambridge University Press, 2018), 173–75.

36 "Protokol doprosa arestovannogo Klishina Kirilla Timofeevich," May 8, 1943," GARF f. 7021, op. 44, d. 24, l. 5.

37 "Protokol doprosa," April 23, 1943, GARF f. 7021, op. 44, d. 24, ll. 1–3.

38 "Wi Kdo Smolensk. Monatsübersicht April 1942 für das Kriegstagebuch," BA MA RW 31/787, 15; "Wi Kdo in Bereich der Kommandatur Smolensk. Monatsbericht. Smolensk," May 16, 1942, BA MA RW 31/787, 21; see also BA MA RW 31/789; BA MA RH 26-221/40; BA MA MSG 149/3, 107; Karov, "Russkaia politsiia," 20–22, 27.

39 Karov, "Russkaia politsiia," 97.

40 Müller, *An der Seite,* 215.

41 "Kak formirovali nemtsami dobrovol'cheskie chasti iz inostrantsev," undated, BA MA MSG 149/3, 106; Inspekteur für Erziehung und Ausbildung der russischen Verbände des Heeres, "Grundsätzliche Leitsätze über Erziehung russischer Freiwilligenverbände," no exact date, 1943, BA MA MSG 137/15; Müller, *An der Seite;* "Pamiatnyi listok dlia nemetskikh voennykh," undated, 1943, RGASPI f. 625, op. 1, d. 49, ll. 332–33; similar brochure, May 1943, RGASPI f. 625, op. 1, d. 49, ll. 356–62.

42 "Kak formirovali," BA MA MSG 149/3, 110–11.

43 Men'shagin, *Vospominaniia,* 43–44, 388–90, 429; NA IRI RAN f. 2, r. II, op. 2, ed. khr. 54, ll. 18–19.

44 Men'shagin, *Vospominaniia,* 73, 388, 414; Sebiast'ian Shtopper [Stopper] and Andrei Kukatov, *Nelegal'nyi Briansk 1941–1943: Nelegal'naia deiatel'nost' razlichnykh sil v okkupirovannykh Brianske i Ordzhonikidzegrade s 6 oktiabria 1941 po 17 sentiabria 1943 goda* (Briansk: Bukvitsa, 2014), 90–91, 240.

45 "Spravka No. 13/3-5757-58 o pokazaniiakh B. G. Men'shagina o D. D. Kosmoviche, M. Vitushko, N. G. Sverchkove i N. F. Alferchike," January 24, 1968, reprinted in *Boris Men'shagin: Vospominaniia. Pis'ma. Dokumenty,* ed. Pavel Polian et al. (St. Petersburg: Nestor-Istoriia, 2019), 72–73, 791–94.

46 Wojciech Roszkowski and Jan Kofman, eds., *Biographical Dictionary of Central and Eastern Europe in the Twentieth Century* (London: Routledge, 2008), s.v. "Radaslau Astrouski," 39–40; Shtopper and Kukatov, *Nelegal'nyi Briansk,* 241.

47 Per Anders Rudling, *The Rise and Fall of Belarusian Nationalism, 1906–1931* (Pittsburgh: University of Pittsburgh Press, 2015), quotation 306–7, 115, 197, 258, 267; Shtopper and Kukatov, *Nelegal'nyi Briansk,* 92; V. Kalush, *In the Service of the People for a Free Byelorussia: Biographical Notes on Professor Radoslav Ostrowski* (London: Abjednannie, 1964), 45.

48 Kalush, *In the Service,* 46; Alfred J. Rieber, *Stalin and the Struggle for Supremacy in Eurasia* (Cambridge: Cambridge University Press, 2015), 261n51.

49 Men'shagin, *Vospominaniia,* 451–52, 454; Shtopper and Kukatov, *Nelegal'nyi Briansk,* 261.

50 Michael David-Fox, "Nachal'nik goroda: B. G. Men'shagin v istoricheskom kontekste," in *Boris Men'shagin: Vospominaniia. Pis'ma. Dokumenty,* ed. Pavel Polian et al. (St. Petersburg: Nestor-Istoriia, 2019), 204–9.

51 "Stenogramma besedy s prepodavatelem Smolenskogo ped. instituta t. Khatskevich S. B.," December 5, 1944, NA IRI RAN f. 2, r. VI, op. 2, d. 16, ll. 1, 10b; Kalush, *In the Service,* 46–47; Leonid Rein, "Local Collaboration in the Execution of the 'Final Solution' in Nazi-Occupied Belorussia," *Holocaust and Genocide Studies,* 20, no. 3 (Winter 2006): 392.

52 Laurie R. Cohen, *Smolensk under the Nazis: Everyday Life in Occupied Russia* (Rochester, NY: University of Rochester Press, 2013), 157–69.

53 Writings by Boris Menshagin published in *Novyi put':* "Slavnaia godovshchina," July 16, 1942, 3; "Opravdannye nadezhdy," October 15, 1942, 2; "Dva goda," July 15, 1943, 5; "My stroim zhiz' po nashemu svobodnomu zhelaniiu," July 18, 1943, 1–2; "Pis'mo v redaktsiiu," August 26, 1943, 4.

54 Stenogramma besedy . . . Khatskevich," l. 4. Astroŭski's successor made extraordinary demands for better treatment of Russians: "Upravliaiushchii Smolenskim okrugom N. N. Nikitin," July 20, 1943, NARA T-501, serial 90, frames 1085–90.

55 Men'shagin, *Vospominaniia,* 73–75, 489–90; Catherine Andreyev, *Vlasov and the Russian Liberation Movement: Soviet Reality and Émigré Theories* (Cambridge: Cambridge University Press, 1987), 24–29, 43–46; Ermolov, *Pod znamenami,* 223–33.

56 Mulligan, *Politics of Illusion,* 165–76; the Smolensk Declaration is translated in Andreyev, *Vlasov,* 206–9.

57 K. M. Aleksandrov, *Ofitserskii korpus Armii general-leitenanta A. A. Vlasova 1944–1945* (St. Petersburg: BLITS, 2001), 34–45; Andreyev, *Vlasov,* 47–48, 51; Men'shagin, *Vospominaniia,* 74; Andrey Artizov et al., eds. *The Vlasov Case: History of a Betrayal,* vol. 1, *1942–1945* (Stuttgart: Ibidem Verlag, 2020), 176–80,

189–96; Alexander Dallin and Ralph S. Mavrogordato, "The Soviet Reaction to Vlasov," *World Politics* 8, no. 3 (1956): 307–22.

58 Drobiazko, *Pod znamenami vraga*, 112, 122; Benjamin Tromly, "Beyond Betrayal: Recent Russian Scholarship on Vlasov and Russian Collaboration," *Russian Review* 80 (April 2021): 294–301; Benjamin Tromly, *Cold War Exiles and the CIA: Plotting to Free Russia* (New York: Oxford University Press, 2019).

59 A. A. Vlasov, "Pochemu ia stal na put' bor'by s bol'shevizmom (Otkrytoe pis'mo general-leitenanta A. A. Vlasova)," August 1943, RGASPI f. 69, op. 1, d. 1152, ll. 1–3.

60 Drobiazko, *Pod znamenami vraga*, 106–21; Andreyev, *Vlasov*, 19–22, 41–42, 55, 59.

61 Tromly, "Beyond Betrayal," 298; Müller, *An der Seite,* 216; Peter C. Hoffmann, "The Attempt to Assassinate Hitler on 13 March 1943," *Canadian Journal of History* 2, no. 1 (1967): 67–83.

62 "Stenogramma besedy . . . Khatskevich," l. 40b; A. V. Okorokov, *Osobyi front: Nemetskaia propaganda na vostochnom fronte v gody Vtoroi mirovoi voiny* (Moscow: Russkii put', 2007), 15–18; Artizov et al., *Vlasov Case,* 1:144, 167; Enstad, *Soviet Russians,* 206.

63 "Poezdka A. A. Vlasova v severo-zapadnye raiony okkupirovannoi chasti SSSR" (by hand: "rabota Dellingskhauzen"), BA MA MSG 149 / 3, 21–25.

64 Artizov et al., *Vlasov Case,* 1:155–58, 180–81. The translated trophy document: "Soveshchanie fiurera s general-fel'dmarshalom Keitel' i generalom Tsietler 8.6.1943 goda v gornoi rezidentsii," RGASPI f. 625, op. 1, d. 48, ll. 82–95.

65 Peter Longerich, *Heinrich Himmler: A Life,* trans. Jeremy Noakes and Lesley Sharpe (New York: Oxford University Press, 2012), 660–61; Mark Mazower, *Hitler's Empire: How the Nazis Ruled Europe* (New York: Penguin, 2008), 464.

66 "Sudite sami!" (signed "Komandovanie Russkoi Osvoboditel'noi Armii"), undated, GASO f. R-2596, op. 1, d. 9, ll. 7–9; Tromly, "Beyond Betrayal," 299–300.

67 Igor' Ermolov, *Russkoe gosudarstvo v nemetskom tylu: Istoriia Lokotskogo samo-upravleniia, 1941–1943* (Moscow: ZAO Tsentrpoligraf, 2009); Alan Donohue, "The 'Lokot' Republic' and the RONA in German-Occupied Russia, 1941–1943," *Journal of Slavic Military Studies* 31, no. 1 (2018): 80–102.

68 Ermolov, *Russkoe gosudarstvo,* 37–38; K. L. Taratukhin, "Livny pri nemtsakh," in *Pod okkupatsiei v 1941–1944 gg. Stat'i i vospominaniia,* ed. Aleksandr Gogun et al. (Moscow: Posev, 2004), 54–75; Shtopper and Kukatov, *Nelegal'nyi Briansk,* 100.

69 Donohue, "'Lokot' Republic,'" 81–82; Ermolov, *Russkoe gosudarstvo,* 24–28; I. V. Gribkov, "Lokotskaia 'Respublika' 1941–1943," in *Pod okkupatsiei v 1941–1944 gg. Stat'i i vospominaniia,* ed. Aleksandr Gogun et al. (Moscow: Posev, 2004), 76–83.

70 "Manifest Narodnoi sotsialisticheskoi partii Rossii," in *Pod okkupatsiei v 1941–1944 gg. Stat'i i vospominaniia,* ed. Aleksandr Gogun et al. (Moscow: Posev, 2004), 84–85; *Golos naroda: Organ Lokotskogo okruzhnogo samoupravleniia,* September 5, 1942, BA MA MSG 137 / 15; BA MA MSG 149 / 3, 125–33, 191; Sebastian Stopper, "Das Brjansker Gebiet unter der Besatzungsherrschaft der Wehrmacht 1941 bis 1943" (PhD diss., Humboldt University, 2012), 123–35; Donohue, "'Lokot' Republic,'" 85, 94–98; Ermolov, *Pod znamenami,* 219–20; "Bericht des Armeeoberkommandos 2—Abt. 1c / A.O (V.A.A.) über die national-sozialistische russische Kampfgruppe Kaminski," undated, NARA T-175, serial 66, frames 582842–52, quotation frame 582850.

71 Stopper, "Brjansker Gebiet," 104–22, quotations 106, 121; Donohue, "'Lokot' Republic,'" 94–98; Ermolov, *Russkoe gosudarstvo,* 140, 145–49.

72 Donohue, "'Lokot' Republic,'" 83–84, 87, 101.

73 Boris Bashilov, "Pravda o brigade Kaminskogo," no exact date, 1952, BA MA MSG 149 / 3, 68–71; Ermolov, *Pod znamenami,* 221; Ermolov, *Tri goda,* 231–32.

74 Ermolov, *Russkoe gosudarstvo,* 125–45, 149–50, 199.

75 Mazower, *Hitler's Empire,* 465; Mark Levene, *The Crisis of Genocide,* vol. 2, *Annihilation: The European Rimlands, 1939–1953* (Oxford: Oxford University Press, 2013), 255–56.

76 Ton'ka-*pulemechitsa* concealed her identity until she was caught by the KGB in 1979 and sentenced to death. She has been the subject of four documentary films, including *Vozmezdie: Dve zhizni Ton'ki Pulemetchitsy* (2010).

77 Levene, *Crisis of Genocide,* 2:255; Donohue, "'Lokot' Republic,'" 98; Mazower, *Hitler's Empire,* 466; Stopper, "Brjansker Gebiet," 133; Timothy Snyder, *Bloodlands: Europe between Hitler and Stalin* (New York: Basic Books, 2010), 248, 302–3.

78 Babette Quinkert, *Propaganda und Terror in Weissrussland 1941–1944: Die deutsche "geistige" Kriegführung gegen Zivilbevölkerung und Partisanen* (Paderborn: Ferdinand Schöningh, 2009); Okorokov, *Osobyi front,* 8.

79 "Rayonkommandatur—O.K.I / 292. Lagebericht für Monat August 1943 (7.16–15.8.1943)," NARA T-501, serial 90, frame 1131; "Abt. 1c. Anlage zum Tätigkeitsbericht der Sicherungs-Division 286," January–March 1942, BA MA RH 26-286 / 6; "Doklad nachal'nika 9 otdela Politupravleniia Zapfront," September 9, 1942, USHMM RG-22, serial 2, frame 502; Okorokov, *Osobyi front,* 198–219.

80 Peter Kenez, *The Birth of the Propaganda State: Soviet Methods of Mass Mobiliza-tion, 1917–1929* (Cambridge: Cambridge University Press, 1985), 8, 10; Philip M. Taylor, *Munitions of the Mind: A History of Propaganda,* 3rd ed. (Manchester: University of Manchester Press, 2013); Thomas Rid, *Active Measures: The Secret History of Disinformation and Political Warfare* (New York: Farrar, Straus and Giroux, 2020), 6–32; Helmut Heiber, ed., *The Early Goebbels Diaries, 1925–1926,* trans. Oliver Watson (New York: Praeger, 1963); Peter Longerich, *Goebbels:*

A Biography, trans. Alan Bance et al. (New York: Random House, 2015), xvii, 62–63, 216. Karel C. Berkhoff argues that Stalinist propaganda could impede its ostensible goal of mass mobilization. Berkhoff, *Motherland in Danger: Soviet Propaganda during World War II* (Cambridge, MA: Harvard University Press, 2012), 4, 12, 34.

81 Okorokov, *Osobyi front*, 6–14. Smolensk examples: BA MA RH 26-221 / 40, document 91; BA MA MSG 17 / 15; NARA T-501, serial 72, frame 742; NARA T-501, serial 51, frame 748.

82 Longerich, *Goebbels*, 537; Okorokov, *Osobyi front*, 37–45.

83 Harvard Project on the Soviet Social System. Schedule B, vol. 11, case 391 (interviewer A.D. [Alexander Dallin]), interview conducted January 21, 1951, Widener Library, Harvard University, https://iiif.lib.harvard.edu/manifests/view/drs:5481333$1i; Artizov et al., *Vlasov Case*, 1:27, 309–10, 310n62; Okorokov, *Osobyi front*, 53, 109–19, 139–45.

84 Viktoria Silwanowitsch, "Intellektuelle Kollaboration und antisemitische Propaganda. Am Beispiel der NS-Besatzungszeitung *Novyj put'*—*Der Neue Weg*, 1941–1943," in *Mittäterschaft in Osteuropa im Zweiten Weltkrieg und im Holocaust in Osteuropa*, ed. Peter Black et al. (Vienna: New Academic Press, 2019), 281–93.

85 A. A. Kostiuchenkov, "Periodicheskaia pechat' na okkupirovannoi territorii Smolenshchiny: Osveshchenie katynskikh sobytii v gazete 'Novyi put'' v 1943 g.," *Vestnik Katynskogo memoriala*, no. 10 (2010): 25–29; "Gorodskoe naselenie pered novym zadachami," *Novyi put'*, December 15, 1941, 1; S. Georgievskii, "Putesh-estvie v drugoi mir (S rabochei delegatsii po Germanii), *Novyi put'*, December 20, 1942, 3; "Govorit smolenskii radiouzel," *Novyi put'*, February 15, 1942, 4; Enstad, *Soviet Russians*, 180–81; Benjamin Tromly, "The Stalinist Political Culture of the Second Wave of the Russian Diaspora: A Case Study," *Quaestio Rossica* 10, no. 2 (2022): 515–30; Okorokov, *Osobyi front*, 69.

86 Berkhoff, *Motherland*, 204; quotations from propaganda brochures: GASO f. 2573, op. 1, d. 173, l. 3; GASO f. R-2596, op. 1, d. 11, l. 5; V. L. Amel'chenkov, *Russkaia pravoslavnaia tserkov' i obshchestvo v period Velikoi Otechestvennoi voiny 1941–1945 godov (na materialakh Smolenskoi oblasti)* (Smolensk: Svitok, 2012), 46–131; Ermolov, *Pod znamenami*, 218–19, 246–73. Cf. the Orthodox revival in Army Group North territories: Enstad, *Soviet Russians*, 137–61.

87 Konstantin Dolgonenkov, "Pravda o bol'shevistskom rae," *Novosti za nedeliu* (Smolensk: Izdatel'stvo *Novyi put'*), July 1, 1943, GANISO f. 8, op. 2, d. 119, l. 15; "Nash put'," *Novyi put'*, April 26, 1942, 1; RGASPI f. 17, op. 43, ed. khr. 1717, l. 211; Il'ia Korneev, "Antisemitizm kak mirovozzrenie," *Novyi put'*, May 3, 1942, 3.

88 "Politicheskaia rabota po razlozheniiu nemetskikh voisk," probably mid-1942, RGASPI f. 625, op. 1, d. 30, ll. 117–22.

89 "Politicheskaia rabota," ll. 117–22; Berkhoff, *Motherland*, 269.

90 Karov, "Russkaia politsiia," 137, 148.

91 Karov, "Russkaia politsiia," 148–57; Rid, *Active Measures.*

92 "Obrashchenie," February 10, 1943, leaflet, RGASPI f. 625, op. 1, d. 44, l. 238; RGASPI f. 625, op. 1, d. 41, l. 72.

93 "Pokazanie Breitman-Petrenko Mikhaila Iosifovicha," April 13, 1943, RGASPI f. 625, op. 1, d. 44, ll. 109–14; Bogdan Musial, *Sowjetische Partisanen 1941–1944: Mythos und Wirklichkeit* (Paderborn: Ferdinand Schöningh, 2009), 242–43; Martin Dean, *Collaboration in the Holocaust: Crimes of the Local Police in Belorussia and Ukraine, 1941–44* (New York: St. Martin's, 2000), chaps. 3–4.

94 "Moi pokazaniia za vremia prebyvaniia v shkole Gestapo No. 12. Breitman-Petrenko Mikhail Iosifovich," April 13, 1943, RGASPI f. 625, op. 1, d. 44, ll. 109–14; interrogation protocols in RGASPI f. 69, op. 1 d. 749.

95 RGASPI f. 69, op. 1 d. 749; see also op. 1, d. 854; f. 69, op. 9, d. 2. Two other Jewish Communists serving as German anti-partisan spies: USHMM RG-68.116M, reel 1, M-37/160. Friedman: Vadim Makhno, *Spravochnik: Polnyi perechen' ob"edinenii i soedinenii 3-go Reikha iz grazhdan SSSR i emigrantov,* 2nd ed. (Lutsk: Volyns'ka oblasna drukarnia, 2010), 11. See also Jared McBride, "The Many Lives and Afterlives of Khaim Sygal: Borderland Identities and Violence in Wartime Ukraine," *Journal of Genocide Research* 23, no. 4 (2021): 547–67.

96 Evgeny Finkel, *Ordinary Jews: Choice and Survival during the Holocaust* (Princeton, NJ: Princeton University Press, 2017); Diana Dumitru, "The Gordian Knot of Justice: Prosecuting Jewish Holocaust Survivors in Stalinist Courts for 'Collaboration' with the Enemy," *Kritika* 22, 4 (2021): 729–56.

97 "Pokazanie Breitman-Petrenko," l. 104; Musial, *Sowjetische Partisanen,* 242–43.

98 Breitman, "Moi pokazaniia," l. 114.

99 "Pokazanie Breitman-Petrenko," l. 108.

100 Jeffrey K. Hass, *Wartime Suffering and Survival: The Human Condition under Siege in the Blockade of Leningrad, 1941–1944* (New York: Oxford University Press, 2021), 31, 117.

8. SEX CRIMES AND A CLASH OVER CIVILIZATION

1 Elsi Eichenberger, *Als Rotkreuzschwester in Lazaretten der Ostfront,* ed. Reinhold Busch (Berlin: Frank Wünsche, 2004), 17.

2 Eichenberger, *Rotkreuzschwester,* 29, 43; Reinhold Busch, *Die Schweiz, die Nazis und die erste Ärztemission an die Ostfront* (Berlin: Frank Wünsche, 2002).

3 Ernst Gerber, *Im Dienst des Roten Kreuzes. Ein Tagebuch 1941/1942,* ed. Reinhold Busch (Berlin: Frank Wünsche, 2002), 6; Peter Fritzsche, *An Iron Wind: Europe under Hitler* (New York: Basic Books, 2016), 137; Eichenberger, *Rotkreuzschwester,* 78, 276–77.

4   Editor's commentary, in Eichenberger, *Rotkreuzschwester*, 5, quotation 8; Fritzsche, *Iron Wind*, 140; Ernst Baumann and Hubert de Reynier, *Leiden und Sterben im Kriegslazaretten*, ed. Reinhold Busch (Berlin: Frank Wünsche, 2009).

5   Eichenberger, *Rotkreuzschwester*, 23, 76, 269.

6   Eichenberger, *Rotkreuzschwester*, 97–99, 114.

7   Elisa Mailänder, "Making Sense of a Rape Photograph: Sexual Violence as Social Performance on the Eastern Front, 1939–1944," *Journal of the History of Sexuality* 26, no. 3 (2017): 489–520; Eichenberger, *Rotkreuzschwester*, 116, 125–26.

8   Sönke Neitzel and Harald Welzer, *Soldiers: German POWs on Fighting, Killing, and Dying*, trans. Jefferson Chase (New York: Vintage Books, 2013), 78–79, 92.

9   Eichenberger, *Rotkreuzschwester*, 133; "Svidetel'skie pokazaniia o zverstvakh, istiazaniiakh i istreblenii sovetskikh grazhdan za stenkami nemetskoi tainoi politsii 'Gestapo' v gorode Smolenske," October 1, 1943, NA IRI RAN f. 2, r. VI, op. 2, ll. 27–29; Laurie R. Cohen, *Smolensk under the Nazis: Everyday Life in Occupied Russia* (Rochester, NY: University of Rochester Press, 2013), 128–31.

10 Eichenberger, *Rotkreuzschwester*, 116, 221.

11 Eichenberger, *Rotkreuzschwester*, 67, 86.

12 Eichenberger, *Rotkreuzschwester*, 32, 116, 131, 281, 299.

13 Busch, quoting physicians' memoirs, in Eichenberger, *Rotkreuzschwester*, 177, 180, 189–90, 193, 198–202; Baumann and Reynier, *Leiden und Sterben*, 95, 131; Andrej Angrick et al., eds., *Deutsche Besatzungsherrschaft in der UdSSR 1941–1945. Dokumente der Einsatzgruppen in der Sowjetunion* (Darmstadt: WBG, 2013), 2:129; NARA T-501, serial 48, Korück 582, frame 885.

14 Cited in Doris L. Bergen, "Sexual Violence in the Holocaust: Unique and Typical?," in *Lessons and Legacies*, vol. 7, *The Holocaust in International Perspective*, ed. Dagmar Herzog (Evanston, IL: Northwestern University Press, 2006), 184.

15 Eichenberger, *Rotkreuzschwester*, 118, 75; Bergen, "Sexual Violence," 193.

16 Willy Peter Reese, *A Stranger to Myself: The Inhumanity of War: Russia, 1941–1944*, trans. Michael Hofmann, ed. Stefan Schmitz (New York: Farrar, Straus and Giroux, 2005), 79, 98; Thomas Kühne, *The Rise and Fall of Comradeship: Hitler's Soldiers, Male Bonding, and Mass Violence in the Twentieth Century* (Cambridge: Cambridge University Press, 2017).

17 Reese, *Stranger*, 194, 75.

18 Kühne, *Comradeship*, 113; Wolfram Wette, *The Wehrmacht: History, Myth, Reality*, trans. Deborah Lucas Schneider (Cambridge, MA: Harvard University Press, 2006); Omer Bartov, *Hitler's Army: Soldiers, Nazis, and War in the Third Reich* (New York: Oxford University Press, 1992).

19 Michael Billig, *Banal Nationalism* (London: Sage, 1995); Neitzel and Welzer, *Soldiers*, 4–6.

20 Marta Havryshko, "Rape on Trial: Criminal Justice Actors in 1940s Soviet Ukraine and Sexual Violence during the Holocaust," in *No Neighbors' Lands in Postwar Europe: Vanishing Others,* ed. Anna Wylegała et al. (London: Palgrave Macmillan, 2023), 205–27; Sonja M. Hedgepeth and Rochelle G. Saidel, eds., *Sexual Violence against Jewish Women during the Holocaust* (Waltham, MA: Brandeis University Press, 2010). Cf. Atina Grossmann, "A Question of Silence: The Rape of German Women by Occupation Soldiers," *October* 72 (Spring 1995): 42–63.

21 Bergen, "Sexual Violence," 193; Neitzel and Welzer, *Soldiers,* 86.

22 George L. Mosse, *Nationalism and Sexuality: Respectability and Abnormal Sexuality in Modern Europe* (New York: Howard Fertig, 1985), 154, 160, 163; Regina Mühlhäuser, *Eroberungen: Sexuelle Gewalttaten und intime Beziehungen deutscher Soldaten in der Sowjetunion, 1941–1945* (Hamburg: Hamburger Edition, 2010), 7, 34, 39; Annette F. Timm, "Sex with a Purpose: Prostitution, Venereal Disease, and Militarized Masculinity in the Third Reich," *Journal of the History of Sexuality* 11, no. 1–2 (2002): 225.

23 Timm, "Sex with a Purpose," 254.

24 Elizabeth Jean Wood, "Sexual Violence during War: Toward an Understanding of Variation," in *Order, Conflict, and Violence,* ed. Stathis N. Kaluyvas et al. (Cambridge: Cambridge University Press, 2008), 321–51; Mailänder, "Making Sense," 494, 497. A comparison with Red Army mass rapes at the end of the war has yet to be written. But see, inter alia, Miriam Gebhardt, *Als die Soldaten kamen: Die Vergewaltigung deutscher Frauen am Ende des Zweiten Weltkriegs* (Munich: Deutsche-Verlags Anstalt, 2015); Vojin Majstorović, "The Red Army in Yugoslavia, 1944–1945," *Slavic Review* 75, no. 2 (2016): 396–421.

25 Mosse, *Nationalism,* 165, 170; Regina Mühlhäuser, "Between 'Racial Awareness' and Fantasies of Potency: Nazi Sexual Policies in the Occupied Territories of the Soviet Union, 1942–1945," in *Brutality and Desire: War and Sexuality in Europe's Twentieth Century,* ed. Dagmar Herzog (Basingstoke: Palgrave Macmillan, 2009), 198; Mühlhäuser, *Eroberungen,* 39–41; Eichenberger, *Rotkreuzschwester,* 67.

26 Regina Mühlhäuser, "Reframing Sexual Violence as a Weapon and Strategy of War: The Case of the German Wehrmacht during the War and Genocide in the Soviet Union, 1941–1944," *Journal of the History of Sexuality* 26, no. 3 (2017): 366–401; David Raub Snyder, *Sex Crimes under the Wehrmacht* (Lincoln: University of Nebraska Press, 2007), xii; Birgit Beck, *Wehrmacht und sexuelle Gewalt: Sexualverbrechen vor deutschen Militärgerichten 1939–1945* (Paderborn: Ferdinand Schöningh, 2004), 229; Mühlhäuser, "'Racial Awareness,'" 211.

27 Wood, "Sexual Violence"; Christian Gerlach, *Kalkulierte Morde: Die deutsche Wirtschafts- und Vernichtungspolitik in Weissrussland 1941 bis 1944* (Hamburg: Hamburger Edition, 1999), 873, 954, 1108.

28 Paula Chan, "Eyes on the Ground: Soviet Investigations of the Nazi Occupation" (PhD diss., Georgetown University, 2023); Havryshko, "Rape on Trial"; Beck, *Wehrmacht;* Snyder, *Sex Crimes.*

29 "Smolenskomu Obkomu VKP(b) i Oblispolkomu ot Dzerzhinskogo RK VKP(b) i raiispolkoma. Dokladnaia zapiska. K materialam o nemetskikh zverstvakh," no earlier than January 31, 1942, GANISO f. 6, op. 1, d. 941, l. 6; "Posledstviia nemetskoi okkupatsii v Dzerzhinskom raione," July 13, 1942, NA IRI RAN f. 2, r. VI, op. 2, d. 2, ll. 12–13; Vasilii Iakovlevich Smirnov, "Zaiavlenie" and "Pis'mo v redaktsiiu," RGASPI f. 5, op. 6, d. 51, ll. 7–9, 12–13.

30 P. I. Kesarev to N. N. Burdenko, October 4, 1943, NA IRI RAN f. 2, r. VI, op. 2, ll. 12, 13.

31 Kühne, *Comradeship,* 173, 293; Beck, *Wehrmacht,* 229; Snyder, *Sex Crimes,* chap. 8; Mühlhäuser, *Eroberungen,* 10, 200–202; Nikolaus Wachsmann, *KL: A History of the Nazi Concentration Camps* (New York: Farrar, Straus and Giroux, 2015), 272; Wood, "Sexual Violence," 342.

32 Kühne, *Comradeship,* 9.

33 Mosse, *Nationalism,* 163; Wachsmann, *KL,* quotation 272; Mailänder, "Making Sense," 502–3.

34 Pauls quoted in Mühlhäuser, *Eroberungen,* 7; L. V. Dudin, "V okkupatsii," in *Pod nemtsami: Vospominaniia, svidetel'stva, dokumenty* (St. Petersburg: Scriptorium, 2011), 269.

35 I. P. Shcherov, *Kollaboratsionizm v Sovetskom Soiuze (1941–1944): Tipy i proiavleniia v gody okkupatsii* (Smolensk: Universum, 2005), 254–55, 258–59; "Erfassung unehelischer Kinder von Reichsdeutschen," NARA T-501, serial 90, frame 1096; Boris Kovalev, *Posednevnaia zhizn' naseleniia Rossii v period natsistskoi okkupatsii* (Moscow: Molodaia gvardiia, 2011), 588–90; Mühlhäuser, *Eroberungen,* 63, 208–23, 248–49, 372.

36 Kesarev to Burdenko, October 4, 1943, l. 3.

37 Mühlhäuser, *Eroberungen,* 32; "Men'shagin—v garizonnuiu komandaturu," February 12, 1942, cited in Leonid Kotov, "V Smolenske okkupirovannom," *Krai Smolenskii,* no. 7–8 (1994): 65.

38 "Stenogramma besedy s t. Egorovoi M. D.," December 2, 1943, NA IRI RAN f. 2, r. VI, op. 2, d. 18, l. 10b.

39 Anna Hájková, "Sexual Barter in Times of Genocide: Negotiating the Sexual Economy of the Theresienstadt Ghetto," *Signs* 38, no. 3 (2013): 503–33.

40 Cohen, *Smolensk,* 224.

41 "Stenogramma besedy s t. Madziuk L. Ia.," December 14, 1943, NA IRI RAN f. 2, r. VI, op. 2, d. 15, ll. 1–3, l. 10b; L. Madziuk, "Dokladnaia," October 22, 1943, RGASPI f. 1M, op. 53, d. 263, ll. 41–43.

42 "Stenogramma besedy s t. Namatevs Z. I.," December 13, 1943, NA IRI RAN f. 2, r. VI, op. 2, d. 14, l. 1; "Sekretariam TsK VLKSM tov. Mikhailovu N. A., tov. Shelepinu A. N. Dokladnaia o rabote podpol'nykh organizatsii v gor. Smolenske," October 27, 1943, RGASPI f. 1M, op. 53, d. 247, ll. 57–62; "Agil'iarova Vasilisa Pavlovna," December 14, 1943, NA IRI RAN f. 2, r. VI, op. 2, d. 17, ll. 1, 7; Madziuk, "Dokladnaia," l. 44.

43 "Stenogramma besedy s t. Madziuk," l. 10b; Madziuk, "Dokladnaia," l. 43.

44 B. N. Polevoi, *Samye pamiatnye: Istorii moikh reportazhei* (Moscow: Molodaia gvardiia, 1980), 148–57.

45 "Stenogramma besedy s t. Madziuk," l. 2.

46 Anna Krylova, "Identity, Agency, and the 'First Soviet Generation,'" chap. 6 of *Generations in Twentieth-Century Europe,* ed. Stephen Lovell (New York: Palgrave Macmillan, 2007), 101–21; Brandon Schechter, "'Girls' and 'Women': Love, Sex, Duty and Sexual Harassment in the Ranks of the Red Army 1941–1945," *Journal of Power Institutions in Post-Soviet Societies,* no. 17 (2016); Roger D. Markwick and Euridice Charon Cardona, *Soviet Women on the Frontline in the Second World War* (London: Palgrave Macmillan, 2012), chap. 1 and 117–19, 127–29. Altogether, the Komsomol Central Committee sent 648 young women behind enemy lines during the war. Markwick and Cardona, *Soviet Women,* 127.

47 Anna Krylova, "Bolshevik Feminism and Gender Agendas of Communism," in *The Cambridge History of Communism,* vol. 1, *World Revolution and Socialism in One Country, 1917–1941,* ed. Silvio Pons and Stephen A. Smith (Cambridge: Cambridge University Press, 2017), 424–48; Anna Krylova, *Soviet Women in Combat: A History of Violence on the Eastern Front* (Cambridge: Cambridge University Press, 2010), 35–83; Seth Bernstein, *Raised under Stalin: Young Communists and the Defense of Socialism* (Ithaca, NY: Cornell University Press, 2017), 41–45, 59–68.

48 "Stenogramma besedy s t. Madziuk," l. 3.

49 "Agil'iarova Vasilisa Pavlovna," l. 4.

50 "Stenogramma besedy s t. Bazykinoi L. K. Smolensk," December 17, 1943, NA IRI RAN f. 2, r. VI, op. 2, d. 26, l. 2.

51 *Boris Men'shagin: Vospominaniia. Pis'ma. Dokumenty,* ed. Pavel Polian et al. (St. Petersburg: Nestor-Istoriia, 2019), 373–75; Shcherov, *Kollaboratsionizm,* 259.

52 "Sekretariu TsK VLKSM. Ot instruktora otdela kadrov TsK tov. Boldinoi V. P. Dokladnaia zapiska," May 9, 1942, RGASPI f. 1M, op. 53, d. 263, l. 17; Kovalev, *Posednevnaia zhizn',* 590–93; Neitzel and Welzer, *Soldiers,* 168–69; Bergen, "Sexual Violence," 186–87; Wood, "Sexual Violence," 325.

53 RGASPI f. 1M, op. 53, d. 263, l. 17.

54 "Stenogramma besedy s t. Namatevs," l. 70b.

55 Vadim Volkov, "The Concept of *Kul'turnost'*: Notes on the Stalinist Civilizing Process," in *Stalinism: New Directions,* ed. Sheila Fitzpatrick (New York: Routledge, 2000), 210–30; Sheila Fitzpatrick, "Becoming Cultured: Socialist Realism and the Representation of Privilege and Taste," in *The Cultural Front: Power and Culture in Revolutionary Russia* (Ithaca, NY: Cornell University Press, 1992), 216–37; Eleonory Gilburd, *To See Paris and Die: The Soviet Lives of Western Culture* (Cambridge, MA: Belknap Press of Harvard University Press, 2018), 31–32; Michael David-Fox, "What Is Cultural Revolution? Key Concepts and the Arc of Soviet Cultural Transformation, 1910s–1930s," in *Crossing Borders: Modernity, Ideology, and Culture in Russia and the Soviet Union* (Pittsburgh: University of Pittsburgh Press, 2015), 104–32; Michael David-Fox, *Showcasing the Great Experiment: Cultural Diplomacy and Western Visitors to the Soviet Union, 1921–1941* (New York: Oxford University Press, 2012), chap. 8, Ehrenburg quoted 286.

56 Jeffrey Brooks, *Thank You, Comrade Stalin! Soviet Public Culture from Revolution to Cold War* (Princeton, NJ: Princeton University Press, 2000), 150–52, 163, 179.

57 "Stenogramma besedy s t. Madziuk," ll. 3, 30b.

58 "Stenogramma besedy s t. Madziuk," ll. 3–30b.

59 "Stenogramma besedy s t. Madziuk," ll. 3, 30b.

60 "Stenogramma besedy s Semenovoi A. A.," December 13, 1943, NA IRI RAN f. 2, r. VI, op. 2, d. 28, ll. 1–4, quotation 10b; "Akt ot 16 marta 1943 goda," GARF f. 7021, op. 44, d. 43, l. 2.

61 "Stenogramma besedy s Semenovoi," l. 10b.

62 Asya Shneiderman, "Okkupirovannyi Smolensk. Sov. Sekretno," September 14, 1942, RGASPI f. 1M, op. 53, d. 246, ll. 74–79.

63 Shneiderman, "Okkupirovannyi Smolensk," l. 740b, l. 770b, l. 76.

64 Shneiderman, "Okkupirovannyi Smolensk," l. 770b.

65 Shneiderman, "Okkupirovannyi Smolensk," l. 74, l. 75, l. 79.

66 Shneiderman, "Okkupirovannyi Smolensk," l. 76.

67 Shneiderman, "Okkupirovannyi Smolensk," ll. 750b, 76; Schechter, "'Girls' and 'Women'"; Oleg Budnitskii, "Muzhchiny i zhenshchiny v Krasnoi Armii, 1941–1945," *Cahiers du monde russe* 52, no. 2–3 (April–September 2011): 405–22; Mie Nakachi, "A Postwar Sexual Liberation? The Gendered Experience of the Soviet Union's Great Patriotic War," *Cahiers du monde russe* 52, no. 2–3 (April–September 2011): 423–40; Masha Cerovic, *Les enfants de Staline: La guerre des partisans soviétiques (1941–1944)* (Paris: Seuil, 2018), 102–9.

68 "Stenogramma besedy s chlenom Komsomol'skoi podpol'noi organizatsii v Smolenske Mironovoi E. S.," December 4, 1943, NA IRI RAN f. 2, r. VI,

op. 20, l. 2; Shneiderman, "Okkupirovannyi Smolensk," l. 79; Markwick and Cardona, *Soviet Women,* 131.

69 "Zhenshchina i ee prava," *Novyi put',* February 15, 1942, 1; "Vozrozhdenie russkoi zhenshchiny," *Novyi put',* May 10, 1942, 1.

70 "Rol' zhenshchiny v obshchestve," *Novoe vremia/Die neue Zeit,* April 8, 1942, 4, NARA T-501, serial 66, frames 177–80; "Zhenshchina i ee prava."

71 "Rol' zhenshchiny v obshchestve"; "Nash put'," *Novyi put',* April 26, 1942, 1; "O novoi nravstvennosti," *Novyi put',* February 22, 1942, 1.

72 Fabrice Virgili, *Shorn Women: Gender and Punishment in Liberation France,* trans. John Flower (Oxford, UK: Berg, 2002), 1–4, 11, 18, 27; Sergey Kudryashov and Vanessa Voisin, "The Early Stages of 'Legal Purges' in Soviet Russia (1941–1945), *Cahiers du monde russe* 49, no. 2–3 (2008): 263–95.

73 Vanessa Voisin, "Spécificités soviétiques d'une épuration de guerre européenne: La répression policière de l'intimité avec l'ennemi et de la parenté avec le traître," *Jahrbücher Geschichte Osteuropas* 61, no. 2 (2013): 196–222; Jeffrey W. Jones, "'Every Family Has Its Freak': Perceptions of Collaboration in Occupied Soviet Russia, 1943–1948," *Slavic Review* 64, no. 4 (Winter 2005): 762–63; Liudmila Novikova, "Criminalized Liaisons: Soviet Women and Allied Sailors in Wartime Arkhangel'sk," *Journal of Contemporary History* 55, no. 4 (2020): 745–63; Serhii Plokhy, "Pilots, Spies, and Girls: Dating at the US Air Bases at Poltava" (paper presented at the Association for Slavic, East European, and Eurasian Studies [ASEEES] annual convention, Boston, December 2018).

74 Kovalev, *Posednevnaia zhizn',* 593–94; Jones, "Every Family."

75 Alexander Solzhenitsyn, *The Gulag Archipelago: An Experiment in Literary Investigation, 1918–1956* (New York: HarperCollins, 2007), 3:10–13. On Red Army mass rape, see Gebhardt, *Als die Soldaten kamen;* Norman M. Naimark, *The Russians in Germany: A History of the Soviet Zone of Occupation, 1945–1949* (Cambridge, MA: Belknap Press of Harvard University Press, 1997), chap. 2; Oleg Budnitskii, "The Intelligentsia Meets the Enemy: Educated Soviet Officers in Defeated Germany, 1945," *Kritika* 10, no. 3 (2009): 633–46, 661–67; and, most famously, Anonymous, *A Woman in Berlin: Diary 20 April 1945 to 22 June 1945,* trans. Philip Boehm (London: Virago Modern Classics, 2011); for interpretive context, see Clarissa Schnabel, *Mehr als Anonyma: Marta Dietschy-Hillers und ihr Kreis* (Noderstadt: BoD, 2015).

76 Nikolai Mitrokhin, *Russkaia partiia: Dvizhenie russkikh natsionalistov v SSSR, 1953–1985* (Moscow: NLO, 2003).

9. SOVIET POWER RETURNS

1 "Stenogramma Sobraniia aktiva Smolenskoi oblastnoi partiinoi organizatsii," June 24–25, 1944, RGASPI f. 17, op. 44, d. 1270, l. 29, ll. 47–50, ll. 135–36;

Nachal'nik Upravlenie NKVD MO Komissar gozbezopasnosti 3 ranga Zhuravlev, "Spetssoobshchenie," August 21, 1944, GANISO f. 6, op. 1, d. 1480, ll. 217–19.

2   "Spetssoobshchenie," ll. 217–19.

3   "Spetssoobshchenie," ll. 217–19.

4   "Spetssoobshchenie," ll. 217–19. On Golovachev, see Geroi strany, "Golovachev, Pavel Iakovlevich," https://warheroes.ru/hero/hero.asp?Hero_id=495, accessed November 3, 2022.

5   Oleg Khlevniuk, *Korporatsiia samozvantsev: Tenevaia ekonomika i korruptsiia v stalinskom SSSR* (Moscow: NLO, 2022).

6   Sheila Fitzpatrick, *Tear Off the Masks! Identity and Imposture in Twentieth-Century Russia* (Princeton, NJ: Princeton University Press, 2005), 283–86; Dmitrii Komarov, *Smolenskaia oblast' v ogne Velikoi Otechestvennoi: Voina, narod, pobeda* (Smolensk: Svitok, 2015), 495; "Protokol No. 2 Sobraniia aktiva partorganizatsii g. Smolenska," November 29, 1944, RGASPI f. 17, op. 44, d. 1285, l. 10; "Protokol Zasedaniia IV oblastnoi partiinoi konferentsii Smolenskoi oblasti," February 7–9, 1945, RGASPI f. 17, op. 45, d. 1570, ll. 78–79; RGASPI f. 17, op. 44, d. 1270, l. 19; Golfo Alexopoulos, "Portrait of a Con Artist as a Soviet Man," *Slavic Review* 57, no. 4 (1998): 776.

7   R. V. Anoshkin and A. P. Katrovskii, *Dinamika naseleniia Smolenshchiny* (Smolensk: Universum, 2009), 22; "Stenogramma Zasedaniia XIII-go Plenuma Smolenskogo oblastnogo komiteta VKP(b)," December 23–25, 1943, RGASPI f. 17, op. 43, ed. khr. 1717, l. 26; RGASPI f. 17, op. 44, d. 1268, l. 24; RGASPI f. 17, op. 44, d. 1270, l. 29; GANISO f. 1844, op. 1, d. 1844, ll. 1–16.

8   "Protokol i stenogramma Zasedaniia XII-go Plenuma Smolenskogo Obkoma VKP(b)," August 21, 1943, RGASPI f. 17, op. 43, ed. khr. 1717, l. 149; RGASPI f. 17, op. 45, d. 1570, l. 282; RGASPI f. 17, op. 44, d. 1285, ll. 2–43; RGASPI f. 17, op. 44, d. 1285, ll. 7, 26; RGASPI f. 17, op. 43, d. 1723, l. 81. Cf. Jeffrey W. Jones, *Everyday Life and the "Reconstruction" of Soviet Russia during and after the Great Patriotic War, 1943–1948* (Bloomington, IN: Slavica, 2008), chaps. 2 and 6.

9   James W. Heinzen, *The Art of the Bribe: Corruption under Stalin, 1943–1953* (New Haven, CT: Yale University Press, 2016), 1, 3, 14, 16; Yoram Gorlizki, "Governing the Interior: Extraordinary Forms of Rule and the Regional Party Apparatus in the Second World War," *Cahiers du monde russe* 52, no. 2–3 (2011): 329, 333.

10 "Dmitrii Mikhailovich Popov," in *Rukovoditeli Smolenskoi oblasti (1917–1991 gody): Biograficheskii spravochnik,* ed. N. G. Emel'ianova et al. (Smolensk: GASO, 2008), 152–53; Yoram Gorlizki and Oleg Khlevniuk, *Substate Dictatorship: Networks, Loyalty, and Institutional Change in the Soviet Union* (New Haven, CT: Yale University Press, 2020), 36.

11 Mark Edele and Michael Geyer, "States of Exception: The Nazi-Soviet War as a System of Violence, 1939–1945," in *Beyond Totalitarianism: Stalinism and Nazism*

Compared, ed. Michael Geyer and Sheila Fitzpatrick (New York: Cambridge University Press, 2009), 365; "Dmitrii Mikhailovich Popov," 153–55; Gorlizki and Khlevniuk, *Substate Dictatorship,* 52.

12 Gorlizki, "Governing," 321–39; RGASPI f. 17, op. 43, ed. khr. 1717, l. 120; RGASPI f. 17, op. 44, d. 1270, l. 43; RGASPI f. 17, op. 45, d. 1570, l. 94.

13 RGASPI f. 17, op. 45, d. 1570, l. 99.

14 "Stenogramma gorodskogo partiinogo aktiva goroda Smolenska," November 28, 1943, RGASPI f. 17, op. 43, d. 1730, ll. 50–52, 58, 66; RGASPI f. 17, op. 43, d. 1723, ll. 44, 51; RGASPI f. 17, op. 43, ed. khr. 1717, l. 110, l. 121; Julie Hessler, "A Postwar Perestroika? Toward a History of Private Enterprise in the USSR," *Slavic Review* 57, no. 3 (1998): 538.

15 Gorlizki and Khlevniuk, *Substate Dictatorship,* 10; Sheila Fitzpatrick, "Stalin and the Making of a New Elite," in *The Cultural Front: Power and Culture in Revolutionary Russia* (Ithaca, NY: Cornell University Press, 1992), 149–82; Jerry F. Hough, *The Soviet Prefects: The Local Party Organs in Industrial Decision-Making* (Cambridge, MA: Harvard University Press, 1969).

16 Franziska Exeler, *Ghosts of War: Nazi Occupation and Its Aftermath in Soviet Belarus* (Ithaca, NY: Cornell University Press, 2022), 120–21; Dmitrii Popov to Georgii Malenkov, December 26, 1941, GANISO f. 6, op. 1, d. 741, l. 18.

17 "Dokladnaia zapiska sek. Medynskogo RK VKP(b) tov. Gamburg," no earlier than February 1942, GANISO f. 6, op. 1, d. 741 l. 59. Oleg Budnitskii has researched a forthcoming work on Red Army violence against the Soviet population.

18 GANISO f. 6, op. 1, d. 742, l. 206.

19 GANISO f. 6, op. 1, d. 941, ll. 6–10; RGASPI f. 17, op. 43, d. 1720, l. 29; "Stenogramma Zasedaniia IX-go Plenuma Smolenskogo Obkoma VKP(b)," April 16–17, 1942, RGASPI f. 17, op. 43, d. 1716, l. 100; "Dokladnaia zapiska o rabote Upravleniia NKVD po Smolenskoi oblasti," March 24, 1942, GANISO f. 6, op. 1, d. 742, ll. 39–51.

20 RGASPI f. 17, op. 43, d. 1716, l. 76; "Zadachi partorganizatsii v osvobozhdennykh raionakh," undated, February 1942, GANISO f. 6, op. 939, d. 143, l. 58.

21 "Dokladnaia zapiska o rabote Upravleniia NKVD po Smolenskoi oblasti," March 24, 1942, GANISO f. 6, op. 1, d. 742, ll. 39–51. Cf. Exeler, *Ghosts of War,* 136–40.

22 RGASPI f. 17, op. 43, d. 1716, ll. 101–2. See also Kondakov's 1942 and 1943 reports declassified from Tsentral'nyi arkhiv FSB Rossii, f. K-72, op. 1, d. 25, https://victims.rusarchives.ru/kondakov-petr-pavlovich, accessed November 15, 2022.

23 Popov to Malenkov, December 26, 1941, l. 18; GANISO f. 6, op. 939, d. 143, ll. 23–93.

24 GANISO f. 8, op. 2, d. 83, l. 32. Reconstruction priorities: GANISO f. 6, op. 1, dd. 741, 742, 937, 939, 941, 1041.

25 See esp. Norman M. Naimark, *The Russians in Germany: A History of the Soviet Zone of Occupation, 1945–1949* (Cambridge, MA: Belknap Press of Harvard University Press, 1997).

26 "Stenogramma Zasedaniia XIV-go Plenuma Smolenskogo oblastnogo komiteta VKP(b)," March 21–22, 1944, RGASPI f. 17, op. 44, d. 1268, l. 44; RGASPI f. 17, op. 43, d. 1716, l. 125.

27 RGASPI f. 17, op. 43, d. 1716, l. 124; RGASPI f. 17, op. 43, ed. khr. 1717, ll. 123–24.

28 "Stenogramma besedy s. t. Kazubskim V. V. Shtab partizanskogo dvizheniia, d. Ratkevshchina Smolenskogo raiona Smolenskoi oblasti," December 9, 1943, NA IRI RAN f. 2, r. II, op. 2, ed. khr. 31b, ll. 1–10, quotations l. 40b, l. 5.

29 "Trudiashchiesia! Rabochie! Krest'iane!," propaganda poster, undated, probably August 1941, NARA T-501, serial 42, frame 1112.

30 Lynne Viola, *Peasant Rebels under Stalin: Collectivization and the Culture of Peasant Resistance* (New York: Oxford University Press, 1996), 12, 220, 232; Alexander Dallin, *German Rule in Russia 1941–1945: A Study of Occupation Policies,* 2nd ed. (Basingstoke: Palgrave Macmillan, 1981), 353; "Stenogramma besedy s. t. Kozubskim," l. 5.

31 "Stenogramma besedy s. t. Kozubskim," l. 5.

32 Decrees: GASO f. 2572, op. 1, d. 235. Implementation, e.g.: GASO f. r-2573 op. 1, d. 3; military deliveries, e.g.: GASO f. 2740, op. 1, d. 15, l. 15; agrarian economists: Hans-Joachim Riecke to Gerhard Klopfer, July 19, 1943, NARA T-175, serial 128, frame 2653693–97. See also Igor' Ermolov, *Tri goda bez Stalina. Okkupatsiia: Sovetskie grazhdane mezhdu natsistami i bol'shevikami, 1941–1944* (Moscow: Tsentrpoligraf, 2010), 167–78; Dallin, *German Rule,* chaps. 15–16.

33 Komarov, *Smolenskaia oblast',* 132; Johannes Due Enstad, *Soviet Russians under Nazi Occupation: Fragile Loyalties in World War II* (Cambridge: Cambridge University Press, 2018), chap. 5; Margot Lyautey and Marc Elie, "German Agricultural Occupation of France and Ukraine, 1940–1944," *Comparativ: Zeitschrift für Globalgeschichte und vergleichende Gesellschaftsforschung* 29, no. 3 (2019), 103–6.

34 "Informatsionno-razvedyvatel'naia svodka No. 4. Zapadnyi front partizanskogo dvizheniia. Zemel'naia reforma provodimaia nemtsami na okkupirovannoi territorii SSSR," October 11, 1942 g., GANISO f. 6, op. 1, d. 741, ll. 1–3.

35 A. S. Kazantsev, *Tret'ia sila: Rossiia mezhdu natsizmom i kommunizmom, 1941–1945,* 4th ed. (Moscow: Posev, 2011), 177.

36 "Stenogramma besedy s t. Zhavoronkovym I. T.," December 12, 1943, NA IRI RAN f. 2, r. VI, op. 2, d. 30, l. 10b, l. 30b, l. 4; other agronomists interviewed in NA IRI RAN f. 2, r. VI, op. 2, dd. 29, 30.

37 "Sicherungs-Division 221. Abt. VII/Kr.-Verw. Div. St. Qu. Lagesbericht für die Zeit vom 1.7 bis 29.7.42"; "WiKdo Smolensk. Monatsübersicht April 1942," BA MA RW 31/787; Enstad, *Soviet Russians,* 128–29; Komarov, *Smolenskaia oblast',* 132–33.

38 Ermolov, *Tri goda,* 246–73; Dallin, *German Rule,* 476–93; GASO f. 2740, op. 1, d. 88, l. 17, l 22; "Stenogramma besedy s t. Tyshko A. V.," December 17, 1943, NA IRI RAN f. 2, r. VI, op. 2, d. 25, ll. 3, 30b, 4. Cf. Enstad, *Soviet Russians,* chap. 6.

39 Dmitrii Popov, "Tsentral'nomu Komitetu VKP(b). Otchet o rabote Smolenskogo Obkoma VKP(b)," around January 1, 1944, GANISO f. 6, op. 1, d. 1473a, ll. 1–37; "Voprosy vostanovleniia sel'skogo khoziastva osvobozhdennykh raionov (po materialov Smolenskoi oblasti)," July 20, 1944, RGASPI f. 17, op. 88, d. 337, ll. 34–36; RGASPI f. 17, op. 88, d. 43, ll. 18–22.

40 RGASPI f. 17, op. 43, ed. khr. 1717, l. 245; "Zam. Nach. UNKVD Smol. Obl. Nazarov. Sekretariu Smolenskogo Obkoma VKP(b) tov. Popovu. Spetssoob-shchenie," March 6, 1944, RGASPI f. 17, op. 122, d. 79, ll. 70–71; "Sekretariu TsK VKP(b) tov. Malenkovu G. M. O rezul'tatakh proverki raboty Smolenskogo Obkoma VKP(b)," probably August 1944, RGASPI f. 17, op. 88, d. 623, ll. 1–13; Dmitrii Popov to Georgii Malenkov, March 15, 1944, RGASPI f. 17, op. 122, d. 79, ll. 66–67; "Prokuror Smolenskoi oblasti Bakharov. Sekretariu Smolenskogo Obkoma VKP(b) tov. Popovu D. M.," February 29, 1944, RGASPI f. 17, op. 122, d. 79, l. 79.

41 Popov to Malenkov, March 15, 1944, ll. 66–67; RGASPI f. 17, op. 88, d. 623, l. 13.

42 RGASPI f. 17, op. 44, d. 1268, l. 258, l. 262.

43 RGASPI f. 17, op. 88, d. 623, l. 6, l. 7; RGASPI f. 17, op. 44, d. 1268, l. 270.

44 "Zam. Zav. Organizatsionno-Instruktorskim otdelom TsK VKP(b) tov. Slepovu," 1944, no exact date, RGASPI f. 17, op. 88, d. 638, ll. 1–8.

45 GANISO f. 6, op. 1, d. 1939, ll. 9–10.

46 L. N. Denisova, *Sud'ba russkoi krest'ianki v XX veke: Brak, sem'ia, byt* (Moscow: ROSSPEN, 2007), 157; Liubov Denisova, *Rural Women in the Soviet Union and Post-Soviet Russia,* ed. and trans. Irina Mukhina (London: Routledge, 2010), 13–23; GANISO f. 6, op. 1, d. 1939, ll. 9–10; Iu. V. Arutiunian, *Sovetskoe krest'ianstvo v gody Velikoi Otechestvennoi voiny,* 2nd ed. (Moscow: Nauka, 1970), 295; Norton T. Dodge and Murray Feshbach, "The Role of Women in Soviet Agriculture," in *Soviet and East European Agriculture,* ed. Jerzy F. Karcz (Berkeley: University of California Press, 1967), 282.

47 RGASPI f. 17, op. 44, d. 1270, ll. 43–44. *V-Leute*: BA MA RH 23/247; RGASPI f. 17, op. 88, d. 623, l. 13.

48 The literal meaning is "apply the methods of *partizanshchina*," a difficult-to-translate label connoting negative features of the partisan phenomenon. RGASPI f. 17, op. 44, d. 1268, l. 272; "O sostoianii zakonnosti v Smolenskoi oblasti," August 29, 1944, RGASPI f. 17, op. 88, d. 623, l. 50.

49 "K. Romanov, sekretar' Smolenskogo Obkoma VKP(b). TsK VKP(b)—Upravlenie Kadrov to. Shatalinu," 1944, no exact date, GANISO f. 6, op. 1, d. 1474, l. 84; GANISO f. 6, op. 1, d. 1473a, l. 30;"TsK VKP(b)—Upravlenie kadrov. Otchet o rabote otdela kadrov Smolenskoi Obkoma VKP(b) za 1945 god," February 2, 1946, GANISO f. 6, op. 1, d. 1939, ll. 1–45; RGASPI f. 17, op. 3, ed. khr. 1717, l. 17; RGASPI f. 17, op. 88, d. 222, l. 5; GANISO f. 6, op. 1, d. 1473a, l. 32.

50 RGASPI f. 17, op. 44, d. 1270, l. 45; GANISO f. 6, op. 1, d. 1473a, ll. 24–25; Exeler, *Ghosts of War,* 147.

51 Interviews with teachers from December 1943, NA IRI RAN f. 2, r. VI, op. 2, d. 26, ll. 1–3; NA IRI RAN f. 2, r. VI, op. 2, d. 25, ll. 1–4; NA IRI RAN f. 2, r. VI, op. 2, d. 22, ll. 1, 10b; NA IRI RAN f. 2, r. VI, op. 2, d. 27, ll. 1–3.

52 "O merakh ulushcheniia politiko-vospitatel'noi raboty v shkolakh," January 1944 (no exact date), GANISO f. 6, op. 1, d. 1656, ll. 1–38; "Stenogramma Utrennogo soveshchaniia po narodnomu obrazovaniiu," January 21, 1944, GANISO f. 6, op. 1, d. 1656, ll. 45–75.

53 Artem Latyshev, "Almost Soviet: Integration of the Liberated Territories of the USSR, 1942–1944," *Jahrbücher für Geschichte Osteuropas* 68, no. 3–4 (2020): 378–402.

54 RGASPI f. 17, op. 43, d. 1730, l. 2; RGASPI f. 17, op. 88, d. 623, l. 13; "Protokol Zasedaniia XI-go Plenuma Smolenskogo oblastnogo komiteta VKP(b)," April 15–16, 1943, RGASPI f. 17, op. 43, ed. khr. 1717, ll. 62–63; RGASPI f. 17, op. 43, ed. khr. 1717, l. 233.

55 Jones, *Everyday Life;* Serhy Yekelchyk, *Stalin's Citizens: Everyday Politics in the Wake of Total War* (New York: Oxford University Press, 2014).

56 USHMM RG-06.025, reel 40.

57 But see Vanessa Voisin, *L'URSS contre ses traîtres: L'épuration soviétique (1941–1955)* (Paris: Publications de la Sorbonne, 2015), esp. 263–74, 371–409.

58 Of 939 "party cases" considered individually by the District Party Committees and the Regional Party Committee on recapturing those districts, 479 were excluded from the Party. Relatively few, 89, were convicted of "direct treason" and actively betraying the Motherland, and 27 more for "anti-party behavior" such as profiteering. "Dokladnaia zapiska ob itogakh rassmotreniia partdel za 1942 g. po Smolenskoi oblasti," no exact date, early 1943, GANISO f. 6, op. 1, d.1195, ll. 1–2.

59 Komarov, *Smolenskaia oblast'*, 10–11, 17.

60 RGASPI f. 17, op. 43, ed. khr. 1717, ll. 310–11; GANISO f. 6, op. 1, d. 1473a, l. 30; RGASPI f. 17, op. 88, d. 222, ll. 2–11.

61 RGASPI f. 17, op. 88, d. 222, l. 22; GANISO f. 6, op. 1, d. 1195, l. 20b.

62 "Sekretariu Smolenskogo Obkoma VKP(b) tov. Popovu. Dokladnaia zapiska. O kommunistakh nakhodivshikhsia na okkupirovannoi territorii. Ekimovichskii RK," GANISO f. 6, op. 1, d. 1202, l. 89; e.g., "Partdelo Roshchinoi Tat'iana Dmitrievny," August 26, 1942, RGASPI f. 17, op. 43, d. 1721, l. 96.

63 "Partdelo Burovtseva Fedorova Il'icha," August 26, 1942, RGASPI f. 17, op. 43, d. 1721, ll. 93–94; "Partdelo Fomicheva Petra Antonovicha," August 26, 1942, RGASPI f. 17, op. 43, d. 1721, l. 102; Exeler, *Ghosts of War*, 151–52. See also RGASPI f. 17, op. 43, d. 1726, ll. 21–22, l. 28, l. 31, l. 41; Other "party cases": RGASPI f. 17, op. 43, d. 1720; d. 1721; d. 1726, d. 1731; GANISO f. 6, op. 1, d. 1202.

64 Exeler, *Ghosts of War*, 162–63; Laurie R. Cohen, *Smolensk under the Nazis: Everyday Life in Occupied Russia* (Rochester, NY: University of Rochester Press, 2013), 15–16.

65 "O sostoianii marksistsko-leninskogo obrazovaniia kommunistov, rukovodia-shchikh kadrov i intelligentsii v Dzerzhinskom raione," no exact date, RGASPI f. 17, op. 43, d. 1721, ll. 241–42; RGASPI f. 17, op. 43, d. 1716, l. 62.

66 Juliette Cadiot and Tanja Penter, "Law and Justice in Wartime and Postwar Stalinism," *Jahrbücher für Geschichte Osteuropas* 61, no. 2 (2013): 166–67; "O sostoianii marksistsko-leninskogo obrazovaniia kommunistov."

67 Steven Levitsky and Lucan Way, *Revolution and Dictatorship: The Violent Origins of Durable Authoritarianism* (Princeton, NJ: Princeton University Press, 2022); Gorlizki and Khlevniuk, *Substate Dictatorship*, 14.

68 Anna Cienciala, Natalia Lebedeva, and Wojciech Materski, eds., *Katyn: A Crime without Punishment* (New Haven, CT: Yale University Press, 2007); Allen Paul, *Katyn: Stalin's Massacre and the Triumph of Truth* (DeKalb: Northern Illinois University Press, 2010); Pavel Polian, "Fenomen Men'shagina: Biograficheskii ocherk," in *Boris Men'shagin: Vospominaniia. Pis'ma. Dokumenty,* ed. Pavel Polian et al. (St. Petersburg: Nestor-Istoriia, 2019), 77.

69 *Boris Men'shagin: Vospominaniia. Pis'ma. Dokumenty,* ed. Pavel Polian et al. (St. Petersburg: Nestor-Istoriia, 2019), 503.

70 Claudia Weber, *Krieg der Täter: Die Massenerschiessungen von Katyn* (Hamburg: Hamburger Edition, 2015).

71 Witold Wasilewski, "The Katyn Issue: International Aspects during World War II," in *The Katyn Massacre: Current Research,* ed. Damian Bebnowski and Filip Musial, trans. Jan Czerniecki (Warsaw: Instytut Pamieci Narodowej, 2020), 64–83. Beria memorandum: Cienciala et al., *Katyn,* 118–20.

72 S. V. Aleksandrov, "Kozel'skii i Iunkhovskii lageria NKVD dlia pol'skikh voennoplennykh v 1939–1941 gg.," *Vestnik Katynskogo memoriala*, no. 6 (2007): 55–63; G. A. Andreenkova, "B. M. Zarubin i Katynskoe delo," *Vestnik Katynskogo memoriala*, no. 14 (2014): 67–80; Weber, *Krieg der Täter*, 57–75; Cienciala et al., *Katyn*, 142, 147 (quotation).

73 "Vospominaniia mestnykh zhitelei—ochevidtsev tragicheskikh sobytii 1940 goda, sviazannykh s rassrelom pol'skikh voennykh ofitserov," in *Dorogami pamiati* (Smolensk: Memorial Katyn', 2006), 4:61–62; Cienciala et al., *Katyn*, 215.

74 Polian, "Fenomen Men'shagina," 77; A. A. Kostiuchenkov, "Periodicheskaia pechat' na okkupirovannoi territorii Smolenshchiny: Osveshchenie katynskikh sobytii v gazete 'Novyi put'' v 1943 g.," *Vestnik Katynskogo memoriala*, no. 10 (2010): 25–36.

75 Cienciala et al., *Katyn*, 226–29; Polian, "Fenomen Men'shagina," 94–96; Marina Sorokina, "Between Power and Experts: Soviet Doctors Examine Katyn," in *Soviet Medicine: Culture, Practice, and Science*, ed. Frances L. Bernstein et al. (DeKalb: Northern Illinois University Press, 2010), 166–67.

76 Paula Chan, "Eyes on the Ground: Soviet Investigations of the Nazi Occupation" (PhD diss., Georgetown University, 2023).

77 Polian, "Fenomen Men'shagina," 89–93; Men'shagin, *Vospominaniia*, 431, 475–76, 504–5; Weber, *Krieg der Täter* 281; Francine Hirsch, *Soviet Judgment at Nuremberg: A New History of the International Military Tribunal after World War II* (New York: Oxford University Press, 2020), 320–26.

78 Polian, "Fenomen Men'shagina," 97–101; Men'shagin, *Vospominaniia*, 365, 704–11.

79 Hirsch, *Soviet Judgment*, 14, 320–35; Weber, *Krieg der Täter*, 290–354; Cienciala et al., *Katyn*, 229–335.

80 Polian, "Fenomen Men'shagina," 80–84.

81 Men'shagin, *Vospominaniia*, 328.

82 Men'shagin, *Vospominaniia*, 504.

83 Men'shagin, *Vospominaniia*, 239, 540–46.

EPILOGUE

1 "Stenogramma besed s komissarom polka im. Lazo tov. Iudenkovym," May 22, 1943, NA IRI RAN f. 2, r. II, op. 2, d. 31a, l. 9; "Stenogramma besedy s. t. Kazubskim V. V. Shtab partizanskogo dvizheniia, d. Ratkevshchina Smolenskogo raiona Smolenskoi oblasti," December 9, 1943, NA IRI RAN f. 2, r. II, op. 2, ed. khr. 31b, ll. 1–10; RGASPI f. 17, op. 41, d. 160, l. 33; Mariia Viatchina

and Anna Iudkina, "Memorializatsiia Kholokosta v Smolenskoi oblasti (1943–1990)," in *Evrei pogranich'ia: Smolenshchina* (Moscow: Sefer, 2018), 237–50.

2 Yoram Gorlizki and Oleg Khlevniuk, *Substate Dictatorship: Networks, Loyalty, and Institutional Change in the Soviet Union* (New Haven, CT: Yale University Press, 2020), 52, citing RGASPI f. 17, op. 127, d. 1352.

3 Seth Bernstein, *Return to the Motherland: Displaced Persons in World War II and the Cold War* (Ithaca, NY: Cornell University Press, 2023), introduction and table 1; Gerard Daniel Cohen, *In War's Wake: Europe's Displaced Persons in the Postwar Order* (New York: Oxford University Press, 2011), 4–5, 19–33.

4 Igor' Balakhanovich, "'Chernyi Kot i ego predvoditeli," *Belaruskaia dumka,* no. 12 (2015): 94–97.

5 Christian Gerlach, *Kalkulierte Morde: Die deutsche Wirtschafts- und Vernichtungspolitik in Weissrussland 1941 bis 1944* (Hamburg: Hamburger Edition, 1999), 211, 211n502; *Boris Men'shagin: Vospominaniia. Pis'ma. Dokumenty,* ed. Pavel Polian et al. (St. Petersburg: Nestor-Istoriia, 2019), 452.

6 Wojciech Roszkowski and Jan Kofman, eds., *Biographical Dictionary of Central and Eastern Europe in the Twentieth Century* (London: Routledge, 2008), s.v. "Radaslau Astrouski," 39–40; Dzmitryj Kasmovič, *Za vol'nuiu i suverenuiu Belarus'* (Vilnius: Gudas, 2006).

7 "Spravka No. 13/3-5757-58 o pokazaniiakh B. G. Men'shagina o D. D. Kosmoviche, M. Vitushko, N. G. Sverchkove i N. F. Alferchike," January 24, 1968, reprinted in *Boris Men'shagin: Vospominaniia. Pis'ma. Dokumenty,* ed. Pavel Polian et al. (St. Petersburg: Nestor-Istoriia, 2019), 72–73, 791–94.

8 Benjamin Tromly, *Cold War Exiles and the CIA: Plotting to Free Russia* (New York: Oxford University Press, 2019), 40, 169–81; Mark Aarons, *War Criminals Welcome: Australia, a Sanctuary for Fugitive War Criminals since 1945* (Melbourne: Black Inc., 2001), 133–53.

9 Aarons, *War Criminals,* 146, 148, 152; Attorneys-General Department, *Report of the Investigations of War Criminals in Australia* (Canberra: Australian Government Publishing Service, 1994), 14; Men'shagin, *Vospominaniia,* 44; Cohen, *In War's Wake,* 49.

10 Aarons, *War Criminals,* 141, 151–52.

11 A. V. Okorokov, *Osobyi front: Nemetskaia propaganda na vostochnom fronte v gody Vtoroi mirovoi voiny* (Moscow: Russkii put', 2007), 69–70; "Istoriia Smolenskoi oblastnoi organizatsii Smolenskoi Soiuza pisatelei Rossii," Soiuz pisatelei Rossii: Smolenskaia oblastnaia organizatsiia, http://sprsmolensk.ru/history, accessed January 29, 2023.

12 A prominent example of a figure who similarly served three regimes and ideologies is Abdurakhman Avtorkhanov, the Chechen Regional Party Committee secretary

from the collectivization era, collaborationist publisher and propagandist in the Dabendorf training camp, and postwar co-founder of Radio Free Europe / Radio Liberty. See Okorokov, *Osobyi front*, 138; Michael David-Fox, "Memory, Archives, Politics: The Rise of Stalin in Avtorkhanov's *Technology of Power*," *Slavic Review* 54, no. 4 (Winter 1995): 988–1003.

13 Elena Zubkova, *Russia after the War: Hopes, Illusions, and Disappointments, 1945–1957* trans. and ed. Hugh Ragsdale (Armonk, NY: M. E. Sharpe, 1998), 16–18; Elena Seniavskaia, *Frontovoe pokolenie, 1941–1945: Istoriko-psikhologicheskoe issledovanie* (Moscow: Institut rossiiskoi istorii RAN, 1995); Stephen Lovell, *The Shadow of War: Russia and the USSR, 1941 to Present* (Malden, MA: Wiley-Blackwell, 2010), 2–6.

14 See photographs and commentaries from "Fotoal'bom: Nashi liudi," https:// uhta24.ru/foto/foto.php?id=20241, accessed March 30, 2024.

15 Vasilii Maslennikov, *Bez tsenzury. Smolenshchina. Voina. Plen. Avtobiografiia* (Mozhaisk: Mozhaiskii poligraficheskii kombinat, 2014), 122.

16 Maslennikov, *Bez tsenzury*, 307–10.

17 Lovell, *Shadow of War*, 294; Zubkova, *Russia after the War*, 25; Vladislav Zubok and Constantine Pleshakov, *Inside the Kremlin's Cold War: From Stalin to Khrushchev* (Cambridge, MA: Harvard University Press, 1996), 36, 51; Michael David-Fox, "The Iron Curtain as Semipermeable Membrane: Origins and Demise of the Stalinist Superiority Complex," in *Cold War Crossings: International Travel and Exchange across the Soviet Bloc, 1940s–1960s*, ed. Patryk Babiracki and Kenyon Zimmer (College Station: Texas A&M University Press, 2014), 14–39.

18 Nick Baron, "Remaking Soviet Society: The Filtration of Returnees from Nazi Germany, 1944–49," in *Warlands: Population Resettlement and State Reconstruction in the Soviet–East European Borderlands, 1945–50*, ed. Peter Gatrell and Nick Baron (Basingstoke: Palgrave Macmillan, 2009), 89–116; Maslennikov, *Bez tsenzury*, 320.

19 Maslennikov, *Bez tsenzury*, 321–27.

20 Maslennikov, *Bez tsenzury*, 328–56, quotation 346.

21 Maslennikov, *Bez tsenzury*, 357–66.

22 Men'shagin, *Vospominaniia*, 547–54.

23 Men'shagin, *Vospominaniia*, 570–71.

24 "Gabriel Superfin," in Men'shagin, *Vospominaniia*, 261; see also 92, 504, 547–54.

25 "K 105-oi godovshchine so dnia rozhdeniia Andreia Fedrorovicha Iudenkova," http://elnya.museum67.ru/, accessed March 30, 2024.

26 Andrei Iudenkov, *Partizanskii polk imeni Sergei Lazo* (Smolensk: Smolenskoe knizhnoe izdatel'stvo, 1960), 10.

27 Iudenkov, *Partizanskii polk,* 16.

28 Vladimir Dobrenko, "Conspiracy of Peace: The Cold War, the International Peace Movement, and the Soviet Peace Campaign, 1946–1956" (PhD diss., London School of Economics and Political Science, 2016), 46; Iudenkov, *Partizanskii polk,* 10, 16.

29 A. F. Iudenkov, ed., *Protiv fal'sifikatsii istorii KPSS* (Moscow: Mysl', 1964), 29; Aleksei Belkov, *"Za rodinu! Protiv Stalina!" Periodicheskaia pechat' russkikh antisovetskikh vooruzhennykh formirovanii v gody Velikoi Otechestvennoi voiny 1941–1945 gg.* (Moscow: Seiatel', 2019), 7.

30 Jonathan Brunstedt, *The Soviet Myth of World War II: Patriotic Memory and the Russian Question in the USSR* (Cambridge: Cambridge University Press, 2021); David Brandenberger, *National Bolshevism: Stalinist Mass Culture and the Formation of Modern Russian National Identity, 1931–1956* (Cambridge, MA: Harvard University Press, 2002); Yitzhak M. Brudny, *Reinventing Russia: Russian Nationalism and the Soviet State, 1953–1991* (Cambridge, MA: Harvard University Press, 2000); Nikolai Mitrokhin, *Russkaia partiia: Dvizhenie russkikh natsional- istov v SSSR, 1953–1985* (Moscow: NLO, 2003).

31 A. F. Iudenkov, ed., *Voina narodnaia: Ocherki istorii vsenarodnoi bor'by na okkupirovannoi territorii Smolenshchiny 1941–1943 gg.* (Smolensk: Moskovskii rabochii, 1985), 3.

32 Nina Tumarkin, *The Living and the Dead: The Rise and Fall of the Cult of World War II in Russia* (New York: Basic Books, 1994), 137–43; Ivo Mijnssen, *Russia's Hero Cities: From Postwar Ruins to Soviet Heroarchy* (Bloomington: Indiana University Press, 2021), quotation 7.

33 Iudenkov, *Voina narodnaia,* 93–101, 115.

34 Tumarkin, *Living and the Dead,* 155, 156–92.

35 Andrei Iudenkov, *Schast'e trudnykh dorog (K biografii moego pokoleniia)* (Volgograd: Izdatel'stvo Volgogradskogo gos. universiteta, 1998), 2:502–3; Alexander Etkind et al., *Remembering Katyn* (Cambridge, UK: Polity Press, 2012), 5–10, 99–113.

36 Tromly, *Cold War Exiles,* 297–98; Tumarkin, *Living and the Dead,* 189–92.

37 Okorokov, *Osobyi front,* 136–37; "Chelovek bez grazhdanstva: Razgovor s Romanom Redlikhom," *Smena,* March 17, 1993, http://krotov.info/spravki/1 _history_bio/20_bio/2005redlih.htm, accessed February 6, 2023; Tromly, *Cold War Exiles,* 297.

38 "Chelovek bez grazhdanstva."

39 Leonid Kotov, "V Smolenske okkupirovannom," *Krai Smolenskii,* no. 7–8 (1994): 54–55; Leonid Kotov, "Relikty voiny. 3: Katyn'," *Krai Smolenskii,* no. 1 (January 1991): 43–51. Kotov died in 1999, and his papers (*lichnyi fond*) are in GASO f. R-292, op. 1.

40 See, for example, Paula Chan, "Documents Accuse: The Post-Soviet Memory Politics of Genocide," *Journal of Illiberalism Studies* 1, no. 2 (2021): 39–57.

41 Kotov, "V Smolenske okkupirovannom," 53–54.

42 Brunstedt, *Soviet Myth;* Anton Weiss-Wendt, *Putin's Russia and the Falsification of History: Reasserting Control over the Past* (London: Bloomsbury Academic, 2020); Anton Weiss-Wendt and Nanci Adler, eds., *The Future of the Soviet Past: The Politics of History in Putin's Russia* (Bloomington: Indiana University Press, 2021); see Michael David-Fox, "Review Essay," *Slavic Review* 81, no. 4 (2022): 1037–45.

43 Hal Brands, "The Ukraine War and Global Order," in *War in Ukraine: Conflict, Strategy, and the Return of a Fractured World,* ed. Hal Brands (Baltimore: Johns Hopkins University Press, 2024), 11; Stephen Kotkin, "Ukraine, Russia, China, and the World," in Brands, *War in Ukraine,* 17–33.

44 See TASS, "Duma Adopts in First Reading Ban on Putting Soviet Union, Nazi Germany on Same Footing," https://tass.com/society/1293829, accessed February 6, 2023.

ACKNOWLEDGMENTS

This book would not have been possible without generous fellowship support from the Mandel Center for Advanced Holocaust Studies of the United States Holocaust Memorial Museum, the Woodrow Wilson International Center for Scholars, the American Council of Learned Societies, and the John Simon Guggenheim Foundation.

Since I arrived at Georgetown in 2011, the university not only provided me sabbatical support and research grants, but it became my cherished academic and intellectual home. I am privileged to have as colleagues a remarkable and unfailingly collegial group of historians in the Department of History and to work with such an accomplished, multidisciplinary cohort of scholars and students at the Edmund A. Walsh School of Foreign Service and its Center for Eurasian, Russian and East European Studies. My Georgetown PhD students—Zhanara Almazbekova, Simon Belokowsky, Paula Chan, Carol Dockham, Elisha Henry, Abby Holekamp, Isabelle Kaplan, Phil Kiffer, Anita Kondoyanidi, Thom Loyd, Erina Megowan, Enrico Osvaldi, Volodymyr Ryzhkovskii, Jonathan Sicotte, Anna Smelova, Stanislav Tarasov, Yuliya Ten, and Perry Young—have helped me and this book more than they may know.

My work from 2014 to 2022 as scholarly advisor at the International Centre for the History and Sociology of World War II and Its Consequences, later the Institute for Advanced Soviet and Post-Soviet Studies of the Higher School of Economics in Moscow, shaped the ideas and research behind this project. It was the privilege of a lifetime to collaborate with Oleg Budnitskii, Oleg Khlevniuk, Ilya Kukulin, Liudmila Novikova, Galina Orlova, and an exceptional group of international colleagues, postdocs, and students to help build what was until its closure one of the most productive research centers in the world on Soviet history and World War II.

I am grateful to all those discussants and critics who took part when I presented chapters and honed arguments at the Russian History Seminar of Washington, DC; the Transnational Approaches to Modern Europe Workshop at the University of Chicago; the History Workshop at the University of California, Berkeley; the Forschungsstelle Osteuropa in Bremen; the Lehrstuhl Geschichte Osteuropas at the Humboldt University; and the Leibniz Centre for Contemporary History in Potsdam.

For help with sources and archives, I am grateful to Michael Gelb, who gifted me his microfilm copies of the Smolensk Archive, to Vadim Altskan of USHMM, and to Igor Caşu in Moldova. Paul Mercandetti and Victoria Kuznetsov were marvelously resourceful research assistants. Benjamin Haas shared his great expertise in navigating the German military archive in Freiburg. At an early stage, Dmitrii Komarov from Viazma generously shared documents and archival expertise, and in Smolensk Oksana Kornilova helped me on numerous occasions with archival materials and sources. I am indebted to Evgenii Kodin and Maksim Kail' for facilitating so many aspects of my research in Smolensk over many years.

Don Fehr of Trident Media Group saw potential in this book at its very outset. It was a joy to work with Kate Blackmer, historical cartographer par excellence. I feel fortunate to have had Kathleen McDermott as my editor at Harvard University Press.

At crucial moments, Evgeny Finkel, Masha Kirasirova, Jürgen Matthäus, and Benjamin Tromly gave me valuable advice and corrected my mistakes. Above all, the book conference organized by my colleague John McNeill at Georgetown in 2022 provided me with a detailed road map for revising the entire manuscript. For their participation and all their questions and commentaries, I am deeply thankful to Greg Afinogenov, Mustafa Aksakal, David Brandenberger, Paula Chan, Diana Dumitru, Charles King, Eric Lohr, Chandra Manning, Aviel Roshwald, and Kathleen Smith. Even afterward, Diana Dumitru, Evgeny Finkel, and Charles King went beyond the call of duty to provide incisive additional comments on the final revision. I am grateful to the reviewers from Harvard University Press for helping me through the last overhaul.

A special message to Katja David-Fox for all her understanding and support. This book is dedicated to our sons, Jacob and Nico.

INDEX

Page numbers in italics refer to illustrations.

purges: 1929, 57–58; of collaborators
with Germans, 335–338; Great Terror
(1937), 99–101
Putin, Vladimir, 8, 370–371; myth of
Great Patriotic War, 11
Puzanov, Lieutenant, 149

Rabinovitch, Samuil, 277
racial classifications/hierarchy: in
German POW camps, 185–186;
German racial community (*Volksgemeinschaft*), 291; and mixed
marriages, 289; Russians/Slavs, 235,
248, 252–253
Raikhman, Leonid, 344, 345, 348
Raikoms (District party Committees), 38
Rakitov, Grigorii, 64–65, 105
rape, 287, 288–289, 291, 311–312. *See also*
sexual violence
Ratibor, Silesia, 3
Red Army: demobilization, 333; mass
violence against civilians, 321–322;
Menshagin's service, 112; military
decision-making, 207–208; "mobile
field wives," 307; motivation of
soldiers/officers, 133; and partisan
movement, 24, 207–208, 210, 231,
292; as POWs, 178, 179, 185, 188;
winter offensive (1941–1942), 149
Redlikh, Roman, 368–369
Redlikh-Kotov debate, 369
Red Star (newspaper), 303
Reese, Willy Peter, 285–286
Regional Military-Revolutionary
Committees (Gubrevkoms), 43
Regional Party Committee
(Gubkom/Obkom), 40–41, 47, 54,
56, 76–77, 104, 117, 124, 142, 208
Reventlow, Ernst zu, 87
Revolution Betrayed (Trotsky), 53
Riecke, Hans-Joachim, 326
Romanov, Konstantin, 227
Romanov, Mikhail, 268

Rosenberg, Alfred: and Hitler, 127, 203;
Lokot', status of, 270; as Nazi ideologist, 84, 86, 121; New Agrarian
Order, 326; as Reich minister,
245–247; Task Force, 2–3, 293
Roslavl (city), 56, 138, 141, 165–166, *178,
178*–179
Roslavl concentration camp, 243, 257
Rückert, Wolfgang, 285
Rudenko, Roman, 13
Rumiantsev, Ivan, 22, 59, 63, 65, 99, 319;
collectivization process and power
structures, 67–69; "military-fascist"
conspiracy rumors, 115; "naked deku-
lakization," 71; on prosperous
peasants, 77; removal as party leader,
104–105; on threat of European war,
116; and Tvardovskii, 80; 25,000ers,
conference with, 75–76; Western
Region party secretary, 101–102
Russia: authoritarianism, contemporary
era, 11; Rus', legacy of, 26; Russian
nationalism, 268–271; war in
Ukraine, 8
Russian Civil War, 42, 220
Russian Liberation Army (ROA), 28,
245, 341; training courses, 273
Russian Liberation People's Army
(RONA), 269
Russian Thought (journal), 355
Rykov, Aleksei, 40

Salazar, Antonio, 27
Schenckendorff, Max von: anti-partisan
operations, 235–237; counterinsurgency, reaction to, 170, 200–201;
death camps, 172; Mogilev Conference, 23–24, 204; recruitment of
collaborators, 246–247; and rural
violence, 25, 158
Scheubner-Richter, Max Erwin von, 84
Schmidt, Rudolf, 268, 269–270
Schmitt, Carl, 207